The History of Medieval Canon Law in the Classical Period, 1140–1234

HISTORY OF MEDIEVAL CANON LAW
Edited by Wilfried Hartmann and Kenneth Pennington

---

*Canonical Collections of the Early Middle Ages (ca. 400–1140):
A Bibliographical Guide to theManuscripts and Literature*

Papal Letters in the Early Middle Ages

The History of Western Canon Law to 1000

The History of Byzantine and Eastern Canon Law to 1500

The History of Canon Law in the Age of Reform, 1000–1140

*The History of Medieval Canon Law in the
Classical Period, 1140–1234*

The History of Medieval Canon Law, 1234–1300

The History of Medieval Canon Law in the Late Middle Ages

The History of Courts and Procedure in Medieval Canon Law

*A Guide to Medieval Canon Law Jurists and Collections, 1140–1500
(http://faculty.cua.edu/pennington/biobibl.htm)*

The History of Medieval Canon Law in the Classical Period, 1140–1234

From Gratian to the Decretals of Pope Gregory IX

Edited by Wilfried Hartmann and Kenneth Pennington

The Catholic University of America Press
Washington, D.C.

Copyright © 2008
The Catholic University of America Press
All rights reserved

The paper used in this publication meets the minimum requirements
of American National Standards for Information Science—Permanence
of Paper for Printed Library Materials, ANSI Z39.48-1984.
∞

LIBRARY OF CONGRESS CATALOGING-IN-PUBLICATION DATA
The history of medieval canon law in the classical period, 1140–1234 :
from Gratian to the decretals of Pope Gregory IX / edited by Wilfried
Hartmann and Kenneth Pennington.
    p. cm. — (History of medieval canon law)
  Includes bibliographical references and index.
    ISBN 978-0-8132-1491-7 (cloth : alk. paper)   1. Canon law—History—
To 1500.   I. Hartmann, Wilfried, 1942–   II. Pennington, Kenneth.
III. Title.   IV. Series.
    KBR160.H57 2008
    262.9′2—dc22   2008009471

Contents

Acknowledgments vii

Abbreviations ix

1. The Establishment of Normative Legal Texts:
   The Beginnings of the *Ius commune* 1
   Michael H. Hoeflich and Jasonne M. Grabher

2. Gratian and the *Decretum Gratiani* 22
   Peter Landau

3. The Development of the *Glossa ordinaria* to
   Gratian's *Decretum* 55
   Rudolf Weigand

4. The Teaching and Study of Canon Law in the
   Law Schools 98
   James A. Brundage

5. The Decretists: The Italian School 121
   Kenneth Pennington and Wolfgang P. Müller

6. The Transmontane Decretists 174
   Rudolf Weigand

7. The Decretalists 1190–1234 211
   Kenneth Pennington

8. Decretal Collections from Gratian's *Decretum*
   to the *Compilationes antiquae*: The Making of the
   New Case Law 246
   Charles Duggan

9. Decretal Collections 1190–1234 293
   Kenneth Pennington

10. Conciliar Law 1123–1215: The Legislation of the Four
    Lateran Councils 318
    Anne J. Duggan

11. The Fourth Lateran Council and the Canonists 367
    A. García y García

12. The Internal Forum and the Literature of Penance
    and Confession 379
    Joseph Goering

    Indices
    General Index 429
    Index of Citations 435
    Index of Manuscripts 437

Acknowledgments

The period covered by this volume has been the most intensely researched in the history of canon law. It covers the years from the birth of canonical jurisprudence in Bologna during the first half of the twelfth century to the promulgation of the *Decretals of Gregory IX* in 1234. In the early twelfth century, Gratian began to teach canon law in Bologna, and, in part because of his revolutionary methodology for teaching canon law, the discipline quickly became a part of the law school's curriculum. By the beginning of the thirteenth century, professors of Roman and canon law had created a common jurisprudence that they called the *Ius commune*. Perhaps the most important point for the reader to remember while reading the following pages is that canon law was not taught, learned, or used in isolation. This volume is devoted to the history of canon law, but Roman law was a constant companion of the canonists. Gratian incorporated Roman law into his Decretum, and the canonists could not have established themselves or their discipline without having integrated the concepts, doctrines, and norms of Roman law into their work. The authors of the following essays concentrate on one side of the *utriusque ius*, but the other side is a constant counterpoint.

This volume owes a great debt to the work of older scholars. The nineteenth century was a significant period for the study of the history of canon law. Scholars turned their attention to Gratian and his immediate predecessors and successors and produced the editions that we still rely on today. The footnotes of this volume will demonstrate that German scholars of the second half of the nineteenth century—Friedberg, Schulte, and others—laid the foundations for modern research. In the second half of the twentieth century the study of canon law became internationalized.

Stephan Kuttner immigrated from Germany to the United States (via Italy) and founded a vigorous "school" of canonical legal studies in North America, first in Washington, D.C. at the Catholic University of America, then at Yale University in New Haven, and finally in Berkeley, California at the University of California's School of Law. European scholars were also important: Gabriel Le Bras and Jean Gaudemet in France, Rudolf Weigand, Walter Holtzmann, Peter Landau, and Knut Wolfgang Nörr in Germany, Domenico Maffei, Ennio Cortese, and Manlio Bellomo in Italy, Antonio García y García in Spain, Walter Ullmann (another emigré) and Christopher Cheney in England, and Adam Vetulani in Poland lent an international luster to the field (this list is partial and arbitrary). When the practice of holding international congresses of medieval canon law began in 1959 the "international" part of the title was entirely justified.

This book, also, is an international effort; it has had international support and a significant history. Many of the essays were first drafted in the early 1990s when the Werner Reimers Stiftung in Bad Homburg, Germany provided support to convene two meetings to discuss the shape and content of a history of canon law. The National Endowment for the Humanities, the Gerda Henkel Stiftung, and the Alexander von Humboldt Stiftung supported the project at different times but in crucial and fundamental ways. The universities of Tübingen and Syracuse and the Catholic University of America also provided necessary assistance for the project and to the editors.

In the time during which this volume was in gestation, two of our authors have died: Charles Duggan and Rudolf Weigand. Both were scholars of great discernment and accomplishments. Their essays in this volume are a fitting tribute to the depth, rigor, and importance of their work and their contributions to scholarship. They are greatly missed.

Wilfried Hartmann and Kenneth Pennington
Tübingen and Washington, D.C.

Abbreviations

ACO	*Acta conciliorum oecumenicorum*
AHC	*Annuarium historiae conciliorum*
AHP	*Archivum historiae pontificiae*
AKKR	*Archiv für katholisches Kirchenrecht*
BDHI	*Bibliothek des Deutschen Historischen Instituts in Rom*
BEC	*Bibliothèque de l'École des Chartes*
BISM	*Bullettino dell'Istituto Storico Italiano per il Medio Evo e Archivio Muratoriano*
B.L.	British Library, London
BMCL	*Bulletin of Medieval Canon Law, New Series*
B.N.	Bibliothèque nationale de France / Biblioteca nazionale / Biblioteca nacional
CCL	*Corpus Christianorum, Series latina*
CCCM	*Corpus Christianorum, Continuatio Mediaevalis*
CHR	*Catholic Historical Review*
CLIA	*Collectio librorum iuris anteiustiniani in usum scholarum* (3 vols. Berlin 1878–1923)
Clm	Codices latini monacenses

COD	*Conciliorum oecumenicorum decreta* ed. Giuseppe. Alberigo et al. (3d edition; Bologna 1973)
Coing, *Handbuch*	*Handbuch der Quellen und Literatur der neueren europäischen Privatrechtsgeschichte: 1. Mittelalter (1100–1500): Die gelehrten Rechte und Die Gesetzgebung* (München 1973)
CSEL	*Corpus scriptorum ecclesiasticorum latinorum*
DA	*Deutsches Archiv für Erforschung des Mittelalters*
DBI	*Dizionario biografico degli Italiani*
DDC	*Dictionnaire de droit canonique*
DHGE	*Dictionnaire d'histoire et de géographie ecclésiastiques*
DMA	*Dictionary of the Middle Ages*
DThC	*Dictionnaire de théologie catholique*
EHR	*English Historical Review*
Friedberg, *Decretum* & Friedberg, *Decretales*	*Corpus iuris canonici*, ed. E. Friedberg (2 vols. Leipzig 1879–81; reprinted Graz 1955)
Gratian, *Decretum* & Gregory IX, *Decretales*	*Corpus iuris canonici*, ed. E. Friedberg (2 vols. Leipzig 1879–81; reprinted Graz 1955)
Holtzmann-Cheney, *Collections*	Christopher R. Cheney and Mary G. Cheney, from the papers of W. Holtzmann, *Studies in the Collections of Twelfth-Century Decretals* (MIC 3; Vatican City 1979)
HRG	*Handwörterbuch der deutschen Rechtsgeschichte*
HUC	D.R. Leader, *The University to 1546* (A History of the University of Cambridge 1; Cambridge 1988)
HUEA	*History of the University in Europe*, 1: *Universities in the Middle Ages*, edited by H. De Ridder-Symoens (Cambridge 1992)

HUO	*The Early Oxford Schools*, ed. J.I. Catto (The History of the University of Oxford 1; Oxford 1984)
IRMAe	*Ius romanum medii aevi*
JE, JK, JL	Philipp Jaffé, *Regesta pontificum romanorum*, ed. secundam curaverunt S. Loewenfeld (JL: an.882–1198), F. Kaltenbrunner (JK: an.?–590), P. Ewald (JE: an.590–882)
JEH	*Journal of Ecclesiastical History*
JTS	*Journal of Theological Studies*
Kuttner, Repertorium	*Repertorium der Kanonistik: Prodromus corporis glossarum* (ST 71; Rome 1937)
Liber extra	*Decretales Gregorii noni*
LMA	*Lexikon des Mittelalters*
LThK	*Lexikon für Theologie und Kirche*
Mansi	*Sacrorum conciliorum nova et amplissima collectio*, ed. J.D. Mansi
MGH	*Monumenta Germaniae Historica*
MIC	*Monumenta iuris canonici*
MIÖG	*Mitteilungen des Instituts für österreichische Geschichtsforschung*
NA	*Neues Archiv der Gesellschaft für ältere deutsche Geschichtskunde*
NCE	*The New Catholic Encyclopedia*
N.S.	New Series
ÖAKR	*Österreichisches Archiv für Kirchenrecht*
Ö.N.B.	*Österreichische Nationalbibliothek*, Vienna
PL	Migne, *Patrologia latina*

Proceedings: Boston, Toronto, Salamanca, Strasbourg, Berkeley, Cambridge, San Diego, Munich, Syracuse, Catania	Proceedings of the International Congresses of Medieval Canon Law published in the *Monumenta iuris canonici*, Series C (Città del Vaticano 1965–2006)
Po. or Potthast	August Potthast, *Regesta pontificum romanorum inde ab anno post Christum natum MCXCVIII ad annum MCCCIV* (2 vols. Berlin 1873–1875)
QF	*Quellen und Forschungen aus italienischen Archiven und Bibliotheken*
RB	*Revue bénédictine*
RDC	*Revue de droit canonique*
RHD	*Revue historique de droit français et étranger*
RHE	*Revue d'histoire ecclésiastique*
RIDC	*Rivista internazionale di diritto comune*
RTAM	*Recherches de théologie ancienne et médiévale*
Savigny, Geschichte	Friedrich Karl von Savigny, *Geschichte des römischen Rechts im Mittelalter* (2d edition; 7 volumes; Heidelberg, J. C. B. Mohr, 1834–51, reprinted Darmstadt: Wissenschaftliche Buchgesellschaft, 1956 and Aalen: Scientia Verlag, 1986 and Goldbach: Keip Verlag, 1998).
SB	*Sitzungsberichte*
SCH	*Studies in Church History*
Schulte, QL	Johann Friedrich von Schulte, *Die Geschichte der Quellen und Literatur des canonischen Rechts von Gratian bis auf die Gegenwart*, 1: *Von Gratian bis auf Papst Gregor IX* (2 volumes; Leipzig 1875–1880, reprinted Graz 1956).

SDHI	*Studia et documenta historiae iuris*
SG	*Studia Gratiana*
ST	Studi e testi
TRE	*Theologische Realenzyklopädie*
TRG	*Tijdschrift voor Rechtsgeschiedenis*
WH 123	Enumeration of twelfth-century papal decretals established by Walther Holzmann; see Walther Holtzmann, *Studies in the Collections of Twelfth-Century Decretals*, ed. and revised by C.R. Cheney and Mary Cheney (MIC, Series B 3; Città del Vaticano 1979)
X	*Decretales Gregorii noni*
ZKG	*Zeitschrift für Kirchengeschichte*
ZRG Kan. Abt. ZRG Röm. Abt. ZRG Ger. Abt.	*Zeitschrift der Savigny-Stiftung für Rechtsgeschichte, Kanonistische, Romanistische, Germanistische Abteilungen*

I

The Establishment of Normative Legal Texts
The Beginnings of the *Ius commune*

Michael H. Hoeflich and Jasonne M. Grabher

The 'rediscovery' of Roman law and the concomitant development of canon law in twelfth-century Europe have intrigued historians since the sixteenth century. The rediscovery and renewal of what the Germans have called 'scientific jurisprudence' played a key role in the development of Charles Homer Haskins' vision of the 'Renaissance of the Twelfth Century' and of R.W. Southern's concept of the scholastic unification of medieval Europe.[1] Central to this notion of rediscovery and renewal is the growth in importance of legal studies at universities during this period and the growing production of university graduates trained in law who could hold important offices in both religious and secular worlds. Equally important to this Renaissance was the growth in two ideas: the law was a discipline worthy of recognition as distinct from theology, and those who worked with the law and with law-related problems formed a distinct group, what we today would call a profession.

The idea of profession and professionalism has fascinated sociologists

---

1. Charles H. Haskins, *The Renaissance of the Twelfth Century* (Cambridge 1927); R.W. Southern, *Scholastic Humanism and the Unification of Europe* (Oxford and Cambridge, Mass. 1995) volume 1.

and historians for decades.² In a 1995 article James Brundage summed up the various definitions of profession that have been proposed by scholars: 'In ordinary usage . . . a profession means a full-time occupation that not only enjoys high social esteem, but also confers privileges and prestige upon its practitioners. Professional prestige, in turn, rests upon mastery of esoteric knowledge and skills unknown and unavailable to non-professionals'.³ The focus of this essay is the history and significance of the last issue raised by Brundage. Namely, we will address his notion that a profession, in order to be a profession, must be founded upon a 'body of esoteric knowledge', the mastery of which is the essential qualification for membership in that profession, and from which professional prestige is derived. Before we proceed with this topic, however, we must first explain how the medieval body of esoteric legal knowledge came into being. An understanding of the texts that people of the twelfth century considered normative 'law' is crucial for any discussion about the establishment of canon law as a discipline.

The texts that constituted the body of esoteric knowledge in Roman law had been in existence for hundreds of years prior to the twelfth century. The Byzantine emperor Justinian's compilation of Roman law in the sixth century was introduced into the West after his successful reconquest of large sections of Italy.⁴ This, and the slow recovery of these lands by Germanic rulers, allowed Roman law to survive in the West.⁵ The texts in

---

2. See, for example, A.M. Carr-Saunders and P.A. Wilson, *The Professions* (Oxford 1933, reprinted London 1964); E. Friedson, 'The Theory of Professions: State of the Art', *The Sociology of the Professions: Lawyers, Doctors, and Others*, ed. R. Dingwall and P. Lewis (London 1983, reprinted London 1987); W.J. Goode, 'Community within a Community: The Professions', *American Sociological Review* 22 (1957) 194–200; T.J. Johnson, *Professions and Power* (London 1972); J. Kultgen, *Ethics and Professionalism* (Philadelphia 1988); R. Pound, 'What Is a Profession? The Rise of the Legal Profession in Antiquity', *Notre Dame Lawyer* 19 (1944) 203–228.

3. James A. Brundage, 'The Rise of Professional Canonists and the Development of the Ius Commune', ZRG Kan. Abt. 81 (1995) 27.

4. Justinian's compilation, later known as the *Corpus iuris civilis*, comprised the *Digest* (533), the *Institutes* (533), the *Codex* or *Code* (revised 534), and the *Novels* (covering Justinian's enactments from 535 to 565). The standard modern edition of the *Corpus* is by T. Mommsen, P. Krüger, R. Schöll, and W. Kroll (Berlin 1872–1895). It has been reprinted many times, both in its entirety and as separate volumes. The most recent version of the entire work appeared in three volumes in 1954 where volume 1 contains the *Institutes* (ed. Krüger) and *Digest* (ed. Mommsen), volume 2 the *Code* (ed. Krüger), and volume 3 the *Novels* (ed. Schöll). A very useful edition of the *Digest* has been published with an English translation: T. Mommsen, P. Krüger, and A. Watson, *The Digest of Justinian*, 4 vols. (Philadelphia 1985). See also the two-volume edition that contains only the revised English translation by Watson (Philadelphia 1998). Samuel Parsons Scott translated the *Corpus iuris civilis* and much more ancient Roman law in *The Civil law, including the Twelve tables, the Institutes of Gaius, the Rules of Ulpian, the Opinions of Paulus, the Enactments of Justinian, and the Constitutions of Leo* (17 vols. in 7; Cincinnati 1932, reprinted New York 1973). The translation is faulty in many ways but is the only translation of the entire *Code* into English.

5. For Roman law in the West prior to the twelfth century, see Ennio Cortese, *Il diritto*

use, however, contained omissions and errors, and the *Digest* was altogether unknown.⁶ Scholars reshaped the *Code* sometime between the end of the seventh century and the beginning of the eighth, keeping the first nine books, but dropping the last three (*Tres libri*),⁷ while the *Novels* survived in an edited form known as the *Epitome Iuliani*.⁸ The *Institutes* were the only part of Justinian's compilation known in their entirety during the early Middle Ages, and they are the only part of the work for which we have numerous early manuscripts complete with glosses.⁹

One source for the survival of Roman law in the early Middle Ages is the canonical textual tradition in the period prior to the legal revival of the twelfth century.¹⁰ Focusing exclusively on the texts of Justinian, the canonists knew and made use of Roman law. The *Digest* played little if any role in their work, but various early canonical collections do include references to the other parts of the *Corpus*. Sections of the *Code* and *Institutes* appear, for example, in the mid-ninth century *Lex Romana canonice compta*, and the later *Collectio Anselmo dedicata*, while the *Novels* in the form of the *Iuliani Epitome* are cited by ninth-century church councils, the *Collectio in IX libris*, the *Collectio Veronensis*, the *Collectio XII partium*, Anselm of Lucca, and Ivo of Chartres, to name only a few.¹¹ Unfortunately, given the low survival rate of early medieval manuscripts, it is very difficult to trace accurately just how and by what means the reception of Roman law in the canonical collections occurred.

Roman law, then, with the notable exception of the *Digest*, was known in parts of early medieval Europe. But it was not until the late eleventh and twelfth centuries that Roman law began to take shape as a 'body of esoteric knowledge' essential to the development of a legal profession. Key to this development was, of course, the reappearance of the *Digest*, the first men-

---

nella storia medievale, 1: *L'alto medioevo* (Rome 1995) with extensive bibliographical information. The classic study is F.C. von Savigny, *Geschichte des römischen Rechts im Mittelalter*, 2d edition, 7 vols. (Heidelberg 1834–1851, reprinted Bad Homburg 1961).

6. The last known citation to the *Digest* prior to the mid-eleventh century is in a letter written by Pope Gregory the Great in A.D. 603; see W.P. Müller, 'The Recovery of Justinian's Digest in the Middle Ages', BMCL 20 (1990) 1–29 at 1 n. 1 for a possible reference of A.D. 679.

7. M. Conrat (Cohn), *Geschichte der Quellen und Literatur des römischen Rechts im frühen Mittelalter* (Leipzig 1891; reprinted Aalen 1963) 53–57, 187–191, 354–355; Savigny, *Geschichte* 3.486–489, 527–533.

8. Conrat, *Geschichte* 132–137; Savigny, *Geschichte* 3.490–504.

9. Conrat, *Geschichte* 57; Savigny, *Geschichte* 3.489–490; For a survey of early glosses on the *Code*, see G. Dolezalek, with L. Mayali, *Repertorium manuscriptorum veterum Codicis Iustiniani* (Ius commune, Sonderhefte 23; Frankfurt am Main 1985).

10. See H. Siems, 'Roman Law in Early Canon Law', in *The History of Western Canon Law to 1000*, ed. W. Hartmann and K. Pennington (Washington D.C., forthcoming).

11. Ibid.

tion of which is found in a document from Tuscany dated to 1076.[12] Shortly thereafter, two canonistic works were completed which made use of the *Digestum vetus* (Books 1–24): the anonymous *Collectio Britannica*, completed c.1090–1093, and the *Decretum* of Ivo of Chartres which appeared slightly later.[13] Early in the next century, Cardinal Gregory of Grisogono included three citations to the *Digestum novum* in his *Polycarpus*.[14] Once again, important clues for developments in Roman law are to be found in canon law collections, while non-canonical manuscript sources are rare. One exception, the *Expositio ad Librum Papiensem*, does contain citations to the texts of Justinian including the *Digest*.[15] At the same time, noticeable improvements in legal practice took place, particularly in the technical precision of notarial acts,[16] and portions of Justinian's compilation began to be more frequently cited in court cases.[17] By the early decades of the twelfth century, then, an interest in and use of Roman law had been gradually expanding for several decades. It was at Bologna, however, that these first tentative steps were expanded into a full-fledged reception of the texts of Justinian into the body of medieval legal scholarship.

The revival of Roman law at Bologna began with a school that tradition says was founded by Irnerius, who was active there c.1112–25.[18] Very little is known about this legendary figure, but it seems clear that he, together with an ever-growing circle of students, began the arduous task of reconstructing Justinian's texts. It took a long time. Wolfgang P. Müller has shown that the emerging school at Bologna and the work of its

12. Ed. J. Ficker, *Forschungen zur Reichs- und Rechtsgeschichte Italiens* (Innsbruck 1874) 4.73; ed. C. Manaresi, I *placiti del 'Regnum Italiae'* (Fonti per la storia d'Italia 97.iii.1; Rome 1960); Antonio Padoa Schioppa, 'Il ruolo della cultura giuridica in alcuni atti giudiziari italiani dei secoli XI e XII', *Nuova rivista storica* 64 (1980) 270–273.

13. See Paul Fournier and Gabriel LeBras, *Histoire des collections canoniques en Occident depuis les fausses décrétales jusqu'au Decret de Gratien* (2 vols. Paris 1931–1932, reprinted Aalen 1971) 2.55–99, 155–163, and most recently, Robert Somerville, *Pope Urban II, the Collectio Britannica, and the Council of Melfi (1089)*, with the collaboration of Stephan Kuttner (Oxford 1996) 3–5, 12; Peter Landau, 'Das Dekret des Ivo von Chartres', ZRG Kan. Abt. 70 (1984) 1–44.

14. P. Fournier, 'Le deux recensions de la collection romaine dite le Polycarpus', *Mélanges d'archéologie et d'histoire* 37 (1918/19) 55–101, also in T. Kölzer, ed., *Mélanges de droit canonique* 2.703-749; J. Gilchrist, 'The Polycarpus', ZRG Kan. Abt. 68 (1982) 441–452.

15. The work was written after 1070 and contains annotations to Lombard and Frankish law compiled in Pavia by jurists who may have had a school there. Manlio Bellomo, *The Common Legal Past of Europe, 1000–1800*, translated from the 2d edition by L.G. Cochrane (Studies in Medieval and Early Modern Canon Law 4; Washington D.C. 1995) 52–53.

16. Ibid. 53–54.

17. See L. Schmugge, 'Codicis Iustiniani et Institutionum baiulus: Eine neue Quelle zu Magister Pepo von Bologna', *Ius Commune* 6 (1977) 1–9.

18. It is not altogether clear whether Irnerius actually taught Roman law at Bologna, although we know he was an advocate there. P. Fiorelli, 'Clarum bononiensium lumen', *Per Francesco Calasso: Studi degli allievi*, ed. Francesco Calasso (Rome 1978) 415–459; Schmugge, 'Codicis Iustiniani et Institutionum baiulus', 1–9; Southern, *Scholastic Humanism* 274–282.

earliest scholars did not rely on a single complete text of the *Digest* prior to the time of Irnerius.[19] Rather, he argues, a Bolognese version of the work gradually emerged in the decades between 1076 and the death of Irnerius (after 1125).[20] Further, he convincingly shows that there is no evidence that the incorporation of the missing parts of the *Infortiatum* (Dig. 24.3–Dig. 25), all of the *Tres partes* (Dig. 35.2.82–Dig. 38), and the *Digestum novum* (Dig. 39–Dig. 50) was based on the now-famous *Codex Florentinus*, a sixth-century manuscript containing the entire text.[21] Irnerius and his pupils were, it seems, responsible for the organization of Justinian's texts. The process began when the *Digestum vetus* and the known sections of the *Infortiatum* were added to the *Institutes* and the first nine books of the *Code*. Next, the missing sections of the *Infortiatum*, the *Tres partes*, and the *Digestum novum* were added. And finally, the missing sections of the *Code* (the *Tres libri*) and the *Novels* were included to complete the reorganization.[22] The final version of Justinian's codification, standard throughout the Middle Ages and beyond, filled five folio volumes in the early modern printed editions. Volume one includes books 1–24.2 of the *Digest*; volume two holds books 24.3–38.17, and volume three, books 39.1–50.17. The fourth volume contains the first nine books of the *Code*, while the final volume is made up of the four books of the *Institutes*, the last three books of the *Code* (the *Tres libri*), and the *Novels* in the expanded version known as the *Authenticum*.[23] This arrangement of Justinian's compilation is known as the *Corpus iuris civilis*. With its completion, medieval Roman law scholars had recovered a 'body of esoteric knowledge'. We shall see subsequently how they were able to master this knowledge and become professionals.

Canon law, unlike Roman law, flourished in late antiquity and the early Middle Ages.[24] In its earliest form the law of the Church was designed to regulate relations between the faithful and to define the rights and obligations of various groups. It also set liturgical norms and provided for

19. Müller, 'The Recovery of Justinian's Digest' 1–29.
20. Ibid. 25. He posits that only the Digestum vetus (Dig. 1–Dig. 24.3.2) and a section of the Infortiatum (Dig. 26–Dig. 35.2.82) were known at Bologna prior to 1112.
21. Ibid. 3–8, 12–14, 22–25. In the Middle Ages, the Florentinus was known as the *Littera Pisana* after the city in which it was located. The text was captured and transferred to its present-day resting place, Florence, in 1411. See Enrico Spagnesi, *Le Pandette di Giustiniano: Storia e fortuna della 'littera Florentina': Mostra di codici e documenti, 24 giugno–31 augusto, 1983* (Florence 1983).
22. Müller, 'The Recovery of Justinian's Digest' 26–27; Bellomo, *Common Legal Past* 62.
23. The fifth volume also includes several medieval works including the *Libri feudorum*, a number of enactments of the Holy Roman emperors, and the Treaty of Constance.
24. The history of canon law in the early Middle Ages is essentially the history of canonical collections, see Lotte Kéry, *Canonical Collections of the Early Middle Ages (ca. 400–1140): A Bibliographical Guide to the Manuscripts and Literature* (Washington, D.C. 1999).

the governance of the Church. Canon law entered a new phase when the emperor Constantine (311–37) embraced Christianity. Under him and his successors, the Church became an integral part of Roman government, growing and adapting to its new role both in structure and in organization. Church councils met to answer questions of doctrine and practice, and also to settle disputes arising within the Christian community. The decisions of these large councils, together with those of smaller regional assemblies known as synods, became important sources of canon law. An additional source of new law came in the form of decisions by bishops, who were authorized by the emperors to address spiritual and moral issues. They set up courts, *audientia episcopalis*, to hear matters that fell under their jurisdiction, although in most cases bishops acted more as mediators than as judges. By the fifth century, the bishops of Rome were beginning to stake out their claim to primacy over the other leaders of the Church. As this claim was strengthened and ultimately accepted in the West, the decisions of the Roman bishops took on a growing importance in the collections of canon law.[25]

The end of Rome's political dominance in the West did not mean the end of canon law. Councils and synods continued to meet, and the church continued to adapt to the changing political and social circumstances of Western Europe. Canon law in this period was far more localized, however, and the *audientia episcopalis* was limited to deciding disputes between clerics. The penitentials, written in the seventh through the ninth centuries, did provide one new source of law, although they rarely were promulgated formally. Designed to help clerics who heard confessions, the penitentials catalogued sins and suggested various kinds of penance depending on the type of sin committed. The penitentials reflect a move away from public penance and contain useful information about what constituted unacceptable behavior.[26]

Conciliar canons, papal letters (*decretals*), and other sources of canon law were compiled from the earliest times, but it was not until the early decades of the eleventh century that canonical compilations of later significance were produced.[27] The most influential of these was the *Decretum*

---

25. Pope Siricius' decretal of 385 is illustrative. See Robert Somerville and Bruce C. Brasington, *Prefaces to Canon Law Books in Latin Christianity: Selected Translations, 500–1245* (New Haven–London 1998) 20–21; 36–46, for an introduction to the text and translation.

26. Ludger Körntgen, *Studien zu den Quellen der frühmittelalterlichen Bussbücher* (Sigmaringen 1993) and C. Vogel, *Les 'Libri paenitentiales'* (Typologie des sources du moyen âge occidental, 27; Turnhout 1978).

27. For information on the earliest collections see Kéry, *Canonical Collections*; on the development of papal decretals, see D. Jasper and H. Fuhrmann, *Papal Letters in the Early Middle Ages* (Washington, D.C. 2001).

of Burchard of Worms (1000–1025).[28] Burchard and his staff of compilers attempted to cover the entirety of canon law in this work. It contains 1,785 canons organized into twenty books, and covers topics from the organization of the church and the jurisdiction and powers of its component parts, to theological topics such as predestination and the resurrection of the dead. Burchard's *Decretum* was the first attempt to organize canon law systematically, and although it is far from easy to understand his organizational schema, the work was enormously popular for several generations after its completion in 1012.[29] Additional eleventh-century compilations emerged out of a movement calling for church reform. Led by Pope Gregory VII, the reformers were determined to use canon law to advance their program for the reorganization of the church.[30] Before they could go any further, however, new compilations of law were needed and, thus, many canonical collections were compiled in the second half of the eleventh century and the first years of the twelfth.

The most important development in canon law, however, occurred between 1125 and 1145, when a Bolognese scholar named Gratian completed a textbook called the *Concordia discordantium canonum*, or *Decretum* for short. As recently as 1997 it was common to date the completion of the *Decretum* to 1140, but such accuracy is no longer possible. Thanks to the groundbreaking work of Anders Winroth, we now know that Gratian's work appeared in several recensions.[31] The first recensions were shorter, clearly argued, had a limited circulation, and were compiled between ca. 1130 and 1139. The vulgate recension, which was destined to become the standard edition, was considerably longer, and had achieved wide circulation by 1150. These texts, more than any others, elevated the study of canon law to a science.[32] Gratian wrote within the same general context as the great civilians of the early twelfth century, and he was part of the same revolution in law associated with the law schools of Bologna.[33] Where Irnerius

---

28. See H. Hoffmann and R. Pokorny, *Das Dekret des Bischofs Burchard von Worms: Textstufen—Frühe Verbrietung—Vorlagen* (MGH Hilfsmittel 12; Munich 1991).
29. See Southern, *Scholastic Humanism* 244–246, 248–250.
30. There have been three recent surveys of the eleventh-century reform movement: Uta-Renate Blumenthal, *The Investiture Controversy: Church and Monarchy from the Ninth to the Twelfth Century* (Philadelphia 1988); Wilfried Hartmann, *Der Investiturstreit* (Enzyklopädie deutscher Geschichte 21; Munich 1993); Johannes Laudage, *Gregorianische Reform und Investiturstreit* (Beiträge der Forschung 282; Darmstadt 1993).
31. Anders Winroth, *The Making of Gratian's Decretum* (Cambridge Studies in Medieval Life and Thought, 4th Series, 49; Cambridge 2000). Peter Landau discusses Winroth's groundbreaking discovery in his chapter on Gratian below.
32. Stephan Kuttner, 'The Father of the Science of Canon Law', *The Jurist* 1 (1941) 2–19.
33. Bellomo, *Common Legal Past* 65–77; Knut Wolfgang Nörr, 'Institutional Foundations of the New Jurisprudence', *Renaissance and Renewal in the Twelfth Century*, ed. Robert L.

and his followers worked to reconstitute the texts of Justinian's compilation, Gratian sought to produce a comprehensive collection of canon law organized in a way that would facilitate study. He did not, however, stop there. Gratian's goal was also to reconcile the numerous contradictions that had developed during eleven centuries of canonical development. His success in accomplishing these goals is clear: medieval canon law teachers adopted the *Decretum* as their fundamental textbook within two decades of its completion.

The structure of Gratian's *Decretum* and his methodology are what make the work revolutionary. He did not simply list legislative enactments or detail general norms. Instead, he grouped his source material to bring out discrepancies of opinion and then used dialectical reasoning to harmonize the contradictions. The complexities produced by Gratian's methodology, both in his use of sources and in his dicta, are what made the *Decretum* so useful both in the classroom and for practitioners who had to apply legal principles to real world situations; the sheer scope of the work ensured its success.[34] While the *Decretum* was never officially promulgated by Church authorities, its importance was recognized within a few years of its first appearance. Teachers used it as the standard textbook on canon law, and officials in the papal chancery assumed knowledge of it by people with whom they corresponded. The canonists, by the end of the 1140s, found in the *Decretum* their own 'body of esoteric knowledge'.

Speaking of Roman and canon law generally once more, the renewal of legal studies in the twelfth century may be seen as a rediscovery or a recreation, depending on whether one is speaking of civil or canon law. In the case of civil law, we should speak of the renewal of interest in Roman jurisprudence deriving in large part from the 'rediscovery' of Justinian's *Digest*. In the case of canon law, we should speak of the recreation of a body of canonical rules through Gratian's compilation and publication of his *Decretum*.

It is important in both cases, however, not to be caught in the myth of fortuity. The renewal of legal studies in the twelfth century was not sparked by chance occurrence, nor can one discount the importance of socio-economic factors in setting the stage for these developments. Indeed, we must recognize that a substantial amount of Roman law was in use before the 'rediscovery', and that there was a considerable body of can-

---

Benson and Giles Constable (Cambridge, Mass. 1982) 324–338; Stephan Kuttner, 'The Revival of Jurisprudence', *Renaissance and Renewal* 299–323.

34. See Southern, *Scholastic Humanism* 288–292.

on law available throughout Christendom prior to Gratian's monumental compilation. Had conditions been right, these earlier sources might well have been enough to form the basis for the required body of esoteric knowledge necessary as a precondition to the formation of a legal profession. But conditions in pre–twelfth-century Europe were not right for the formation of such a profession. Furthermore, the lawyers' rediscovery of the *Digest* and Gratian's compilation of the *Decretum* helped this process in a very important manner.

Although Brundage has defined profession so as to require a body of esoteric knowledge, it is our contention that in the case of theology and law during the Middle Ages, such a body of knowledge had to come in the form of a central text or texts. One crucial aspect of the twelfth-century renaissance in both theology and law is that it was text based. The theologians had the Bible; the lawyers had the *Digest* and the *Decretum*. The whole nature of the medieval approach to knowledge in these two areas bespeaks the overwhelming importance of one or more central, authoritative texts. The very means of expanding knowledge, through glosses and other textual apparatus, required that central and authoritative texts exist. We see this, too, in the way in which both the *Digest* and the *Decretum* were read during this period. Although both books are compilations of earlier material for which the authors are often identified in the text (i.e. the various classical jurists in the *Digest* and Church Fathers and earlier canonists in the *Decretum*), medieval students of these texts were not interested in direct study of the earlier sources. A passage did not gain its importance because of its author; it gained importance because it was included in the *Digest* or *Decretum*. In short, the authoritativeness of the texts came primarily from inclusion in the canonical compilation, not because of the individual author or source. Thus, law was put on the same footing as theology, each with its own central, authoritative, and canonical texts. And, as a matter of course, the essence of being a professional lawyer became the mastery of these texts that were called the *libri legales*.

Let us begin our analysis of the medieval concept of mastery of the texts of the law, both civil and canon, by pointing out a few of the most salient characteristics of both the *Digest* and the *Decretum*. What, perhaps, is most notable about these two foundational texts is precisely how difficult and ungainly they are. Both are compilations of material written by generations of lawyers, officials, and theorists. While both possess an organizational structure, in both cases this structure is maddeningly complex, and there is little to guide the reader. To make a generalization, law books, to be most usable and 'user-friendly', need to be arranged so as to group materials by broad subject areas and then by increasingly narrower subject areas within the broad classifications. Thus, to be most useful, a law book should have a category such as obligations, and within that category, subheadings such as stipulation, mandate, etc. In fact, this broad categorical ordering is found in both Gaius' and Justinian's *Institutes*, books designed for students.[35] The *Digest*, however, is not so easily organized. Each book of the *Digest* has a broad topic, but often, significant amounts of material on that topic will be found in other books. Further, many books seem to have more than one topic, and these topics are often only marginally related to each other, if at all. An example will be illustrative of this problem.

Book 14 of the *Digest* begins with a discussion of the liability of shipowners.[36] It also contains material on the Rhodian Law and the rules for the jettison of cargo.[37] These two topics are broadly related in that each deals with maritime matters, although from a different perspective; one has to do with vicarious liability and the other with specific rules of charter contracts. The third part of the book deals with the liability of principals for acts of their business managers, a subject related to the first rather than to the second topic, while the fourth part deals with principal and agent matters, as does the fifth.[38] The sixth and final part of the book deals with the *Senatus Consultum Macedonianum*, which prohibits creditors from encumbering fathers' estates to satisfy the debts of a son. The law was passed in order to eliminate the incentive for parricide.[39] It is, at least indirectly, related to agency law. But in fact, these sections are not so closely related as to be obviously grouped together, particularly the second on the Rhodian Law. Further, the actual passages that make up each part are even less connected. There are other books of the *Digest* that contain passages also relevant to the topic of agency.[40] Our point is simple; the *Digest* is not an easy book to use if one is trying to find all of the relevant legal rules on a particular subject. In fact, it is decidedly difficult to use for this purpose, and yet that was precisely what practicing lawyers needed to do.

The *Decretum* presents a different but by no means easier organizational structure.[41] It is organized in three main sections. The first part, *Pars pri-*

---

35. For the work of Gaius see the Latin/English edition by W.M. Gordon and O.F. Robinson, *The Institutes of Gaius* (Texts in Roman Law Series; Ithaca 1988).
36. Dig. 14.1.1–7.
37. Dig. 14.2.1–10.
38. Dig. 14.3.1–20; Dig. 14.4.1–12; Dig. 14.5.1–8.
39. Dig. 14.6.1–20
40. For example Dig. 17.2.1–84, which is a discussion of partnership.
41. We refer here to the vulgate recension of the *Decretum*.

ma, is divided into one hundred and one Distinctions (distinctiones), and each Distinction contains chapters (capitula) and dicta on a single topic or group of related topics. The second part, *Pars secunda*, is made up of thirty-six Cases (causae) that are further divided into questions (quaestiones) and chapters. Here too, Gratian inserts dicta where necessary. One section of *Pars secunda*, Question Three of the thirty-third Case, is known as *De penitentia*, and is subdivided into Distinctions as was done in *Pars prima*. Its tone is decidedly theological.[42] Like the books and paragraphs of the *Digest*, the sections of the *Decretum* are often difficult to relate to one other. Once again, were a reader to approach the volume with a particular problem in mind, i.e. how does one deal with ecclesiastical property, he must of necessity, jump from place to place throughout the entire book to find the relevant rules and arguments. Brundage describes the problem well:[43] '... the overall structure of the book [is] inconsistent and confusing... beyond that the meaning and thrust of the arguments themselves often seem difficult to follow the first time through... [Gratian] marshaled the conflicting authorities that he found into units and subunits. Each group of canons within a unit announced one view of a topic, which the next group contradicted'. The very scholastic method that Gratian embraced in compiling the *Decretum* assured that it would be nightmarish to use to answer practical questions, particularly once the concise early version was replaced by the prolix vulgate recension.[44]

In short, neither the *Digest* nor the *Decretum* were texts that lent themselves to problem-solving. Yet problem-solving and the construction of persuasive arguments to that end are and were then the primary tasks of practicing lawyers. Of course, an easy answer to the problems of organizational complexity immediately comes to the modern mind. What the medieval lawyers needed were ancillary texts, including subject indices. Not surprisingly, beginning with the systematic study of these texts at universities, such ancillary texts began to make their appearance.

In Roman law, Irnerius and those who carried on his tradition did not simply assemble the texts of the *Corpus iuris civilis*, monumental though that work was. The civilians of the Middle Ages thought of Justinian's law as living and immutable. In order to explicate difficult concepts, harmonize apparent contradictions, systematize the whole, and, we would

---

42. K. Wojtyla (Pope John Paul II), 'Le Traité 'De Poenitentia' de Gratien dans l'abrégé de Gdansk Mar. F. 275', SG 7 (1959) 355–390.
43. Brundage, *Medieval Canon Law* (The Medieval World Series; London–New York 1995) 47–48.
44. See Southern, *Scholastic Humanism* 288–291.

argue, make the texts more 'user-friendly', they began to write notes or glosses in the margins and between the lines of the texts. These glosses, from which comes the term *glossator*, began as simple explanatory passages and cross references to other pertinent texts in the *Corpus iuris civilis*. Later, glosses developed into elaborate interpretations of a passage, phrase, or even a single word in the text. Eventually, they wrote glosses on one component of the *Corpus*, such as a single title that followed the order of the text, without including it. This type of work was called an 'apparatus'. Other kinds of literary evidence from the Glossators are numerous. They include 'lecturae' or notes students took of lectures, and 'dissentiones' recording the seemingly irreconcilable opinions of past scholars. In addition they produced 'quaestiones', where the arguments on both sides of a particular question are given and lead up to the author's solution, and 'brocardae', usually maxims or definitions written in a way that would aid in memorization. 'Summae' were comprehensive commentaries on whole titles which gathered together what was said on the topic in question in other parts of the *Corpus* (later this refers to commentaries on the whole law). Eventually, 'treatises', or comments on whole subjects without reference to one particular text, were produced.[45]

The most famous of Irnerius' students, and the ones who immediately followed him in teaching at Bologna, were Bulgarus, Martinus, Hugo, and Jacobus. They are collectively known as the Four Doctors.[46] Most of what they wrote survives in the form of glosses, although we also have lectures, distinctions, apparatus, summulae, and treatises primarily by Bulgarus and Martinus. These men took the first steps toward systemizing the law; they began to study and comment on, not just single laws, but whole categories of them. Writers of the next generation composed larger, more complete works on associated topics and even entire parts of the *Corpus* (summae).

The first known substantial summae date from c.1150, but we do not know who wrote them.[47] Slightly later, one Roger, who studied with Bulgarus at Bologna, wrote several important works.[48] He was followed by

---

45. For a detailed bibliography of all these forms of legal literature see Peter Weimar, 'Die legistische Literatur der Glossatorenzeit', Coing, *Handbuch* 168–260. For a discussion of their development (as well as other later types) see Bellomo, *Common Legal Past* 126–148.

46. Regarding the Four Doctors see H. Kantorowicz and W.W. Buckland, *Studies in the Glossators of the Roman Law: Newly Discovered Writings of the Twelfth Century* (Cambridge 1938) 33, 68–111; Bellomo, *Common Legal Past* 112–113; E. Cortese, *Il diritto nella storia medievale, 2: Il basso medioevo* (Rome 1995) 76–88.

47. The two summae are referred to as the Vienna Summa and the Troyes Summa after the cities where important manuscript copies may be found. Weimar, 'Die legistische Literatur' 134, 184–235 passim.

48. Weimar, 'Die legistische Literatur' 138, 177–277 passim.

Placentinus (d. 1194) and Johannes Bassianus (c.1180).[49] These men produced works that were studied and used throughout medieval Europe. They carried on Irnerius' tradition of teaching and scholarship and helped to create a system of law based on the *Corpus iuris civilis*. Their work was superseded in the early decades of the thirteenth century, however, by the two most important Glossators, Azo and Accursius.

Azo was a student of Johannes Bassianus, and he attempted to complete his teacher's *Summa* on the *Code*. Instead of finishing this task, however, Azo published his own *Summa* sometime between 1208 and 1210.[50] This was the last of the series of summae that began with the Troyes *Summa*, and it was the standard work on the *Code* throughout the remainder of the Middle Ages. Azo also wrote a summa on the *Institutes*, and vast numbers of his glosses on the first twenty-four books of the *Digest* and *Code* survive, as does a lectura recorded by one of his students.[51] He died in Bologna, either in 1220 or shortly after 1230.[52] Azo's contribution to the development of legal scholarship goes beyond his continuation of the glossatorial tradition. His approach was different from those who had preceded him in that he did not use everyday occurrences as examples, nor did he use contemporary events to interpret legal principles.[53] This does not mean that Azo regarded the law as something inapplicable to his own day; rather, the concepts and principles contained in the *Corpus* did not require contemporary exemplars to make them valid. He did apply principles found in the law to thirteenth-century Italian cases, but the absence of certain institutions or practices did not in any way invalidate the laws as they had been compiled. Roman jurisprudence governing the duties of ancient Roman civil servants, for example, was no less valid because such officials had ceased to exist.

The period of the Glossators ended on its highest note with the work of Azo's greatest student, Accursius (d. 1263).[54] By the time that Accursius was actively teaching at Bologna, the sheer number of glosses had become so overwhelming that only the most skilled and patient legal scholar could work his way through them. Luckily, Accursius had both skill

49. André Gouron, 'A la convergence des deux droits: Jean Bassien, Bazianus et maître Jean', TRE 59 (1991) 319–332; Weimar, 'Die legistische Literatur' 138, 148–277 passim.
50. Savigny, *Geschichte* 5.1–44; Weimar, 'Die legistische Literatur' 148–240 passim.
51. Weimar, 'Die legistische Literature' 148–250 passim.
52. For the uncertainties surrounding the date of Azo's death see P. Fiorelli, 'Azzone', DBI 4.774–781.
53. Bellomo, *Common Legal Past* 167–168.
54. P. Fiorelli, 'Accorso', DBI 1.116–121; Savigny, *Geschichte* 5.262–305; Weimar, 'Die legistische Literatur' 139–277 passim.

and patience. Relying heavily on the apparatus of his teacher, Accursius set out to bring order to chaos. He chose what he believed to be the most worthwhile of previous works, transcribed, condensed, and edited them, and added his own comments where he felt it necessary. He did this for the *Digest*, the *Code*, the *Institutes* (twice), the *Tres libri*, and the *Novels*. He is also thought to have added the *Libri Feudorum* with glosses by Jacobus Colunbi as a tenth 'collation' of the *Authenticum*. In short, Accursius compiled an apparatus to the whole of the *Corpus iuris civilis*. The individual glosses range from one or two words to several hundred and total somewhere around two million words. Given its size and scope and the erudition of its author, it is not surprising that the apparatus quickly became the standard gloss to the *Corpus*. No subsequent text of the *Corpus* was produced without the apparatus, including the early modern printed editions up to c.1627.[55]

In the canon law tradition, summaries and commentaries on the *Decretum* appeared very early, and those who produced them are known as 'decretists'. Many early manuscripts contain marginal notes and references by students and teachers. When compiled by a single scholar, these notes or glosses are known as a lectura or gloss apparatus.[56] Eventually scholars made systematic studies of all or part of the *Decretum*; the earliest of these summae was completed c.1148, and many others followed.[57]

Thus, the production of texts ancillary to the *Digest* and *Decretum* became a major task for both civil and canon lawyers in the period after c.1140. One could characterize the legal-literary output of the centuries after the rediscovery of the *Digest* and the compilation of the *Decretum* as focused primarily on making these two texts and their contents more usable for problem-solving. Without doubt, the most important ancillary texts produced in this early period were the glosses produced for both works. Conventional wisdom characterizes these glosses as primarily explanatory. The primary purpose of the gloss, in this view, is to explain difficult terms and to expand upon themes in the primary text. Certainly, the glosses did this. But they did more. Glosses also served as primitive indices to the primary texts as well as cross-references to other related texts. If one looks at the substantive content of the glosses developed during the first two hundred years of the legal revival, one discovers that they overwhelmingly tend to consist of an explanation of a word or phrase and/or

---

55. Bellomo, *Common Legal Past* 169–174.
56. Brundage, *Medieval Canon Law* 49.
57. See the essay by Kenneth Pennington, 'The Decretists: The Italian School', in this volume.

cross-references to other passages on similar or related matters. This was true of both civil and canon law glosses. Indeed, Brundage points out that many canonistic glosses consisted almost entirely of cross-references to parallel or related passages elsewhere in the law books.[58]

To focus again on Roman law, one aspect of the problematic organization of the *Digest* and the development of glosses to other Roman law texts is instructive of the accessibility problem and how it was dealt with by the medieval jurists. As has been pointed out, while the *Digest* is rich in substantive law sources but poorly organized, the *Institutes* are wonderfully well organized but their substantive content is quite unsophisticated. If one looks at the extant glosses to the *Institutes*, however, one discovers something quite fascinating.[59] To a large degree, many of the glosses written to this elementary text are not explanatory; rather they tend to be references to *Digest* passages. What this means, in effect, is that the text of the *Institutes* plus gloss was able to function as a finding aid, a proto-index, to the *Digest*. One sees a parallel to this function in another medieval Roman legal text, the *Liber Pauperum* of Vacarius, written in England in the twelfth century.[60]

The *Liber Pauperum* presents many problems to the medieval legal historian, not the least of which is how it was used. John Barton, in his essay 'The Study of Civil Law [at Oxford] before 1380', argues that it may have been used as a substitute for the *Digest*, as a basis for lectures in the Schools, and certainly as 'a textbook for private reading'.[61] He also notes, as had other historians before him, that one peculiarity of the *Liber Pauperum* is that many of the glosses upon it are, in fact, no more than cross-references to the *Digest*. This is quite significant if one believes, as we do, that one of the reasons why the *Liber Pauperum* retained its popularity in England for so long a period is that it was used as a finding aid to the *Digest*, just as several of the continental glossed *Institutes* were so used. What we are seeing here, then, are creative attempts to make it simpler to find key passages in difficult to access legal texts, and we are driven to conclude that these glossed books of Vacarius functioned as proto-indices and, thus, as crucial tools for the mastery of the legal texts which lawyers then used.

58. Brundage, *Medieval Canon Law* 200.
59. Weimar, 'Die legistische Literatur' 182–252 passim.
60. Vacarius, *The Liber Pauperum of Vacarius*, ed. F. Zulueta (Publications of the Selden Society, 44; London 1972); Leonard E. Boyle, 'The Beginning of Legal Studies at Oxford', *Viator* 14 (1983) 107–131, and his 'Canon Law before 1380', HUO 531–564; F. Zulueta and Peter Stein, *The Teaching of Roman Law in England around 1200* (Selden Society, Supplementary series 8; London 1990) xiii–liii.
61. J.L. Barton, 'The Study of Civil Law before 1380', HUO 1.519–530.

Allow us to make another, perhaps more radical, suggestion about another type of finding aid which was used in the early manuscripts of the *Digest* and *Decretum*. Scholars have long known that many manuscripts of these texts contain miniatures. By and large, the miniatures have been studied by art historians and ignored by the legal historians, who were interested only in the substantive content of the volume. In her provocative book, Mary Carruthers has suggested that miniatures in many medieval manuscripts served far more than a decorative purpose.[62] She has argued that they were *aides-memoires* and made it easier for readers to develop a mnemonic structure by which they could memorize and recall the substantive text accompanying the miniature. Carruthers' theory opens up endless possibilities for conjecture. One must be skeptical, however, that all medieval lawyers memorized the *Digest* or *Decretum* to the point where they could readily recall all of their passages, cross-referenced, in sufficient detail to use them in practice. On the other hand, the miniatures, which tend to represent pictorially what the passages next to them deal with, might well have served not only as *aides-memoires*, but also as marks to highlight the subjects of the substantive texts. In short, they served as finding aids for readers flipping through the folios. Indeed, if these illuminations were solely for mnemonic purposes, then miniatures need not have corresponded to the text at all, they need only be memorable. Since many of the miniatures are fairly complex representations of the laws contained in the accompanying texts, it is very possible that they also served to permit the reader to thumb through the leaves and discover the context visually rather than by textual study.

The process surrounding the development of these finding aids demonstrates that from well before the invention of the alphabetical index in the 1290s, legal scholars were creating a variety of finding aids designed to overcome the difficulties of accessibility caused by the length, complexity, and organizational defects of both the *Digest* and the *Decretum*. This push toward the development of such finding aids is strong evidence of a desire on the part of both civilians and canonists to make their foundational texts more usable in practice. Indeed, it is not at all surprising that the manuscript evidence indicates clearly that within a very short period after the introduction of true indices in the 1290s to be used with biblical texts, indices to both the *Digest* and the *Decretum* began to appear.[63] It is also not without significance that as early as the mid-thirteenth century, attempts

---

62. Mary Carruthers, *The Book of Memory: A Study of Memory in Medieval Culture* (Cambridge 1990).

63. For an excellent discussion of the development of finding aids in general see M.A.

were made to reorganize these foundational texts so as to make them easier to access and use. But at the same time, we must recognize that this drive to make the foundational legal texts more accessible and usable by practicing professionals was not wholly successful. For one thing, if one looks closely at the devices developed, such as glosses, one discovers two pertinent facts. First of all, the cross-references found in many glosses are simply wrong. They lead to the wrong passage on a different topic. This imprecision in the cross-references may stem from the fact that the glossator was writing from memory (as Carruthers would suggest) or it may simply reflect how difficult to access medieval manuscripts were. One can easily imagine a mistake entering into a gloss tradition and then being perpetuated by generations of copyists who did not check the accuracy of their textual references. Second, all of these glosses (and other finding aids) are at best highly imperfect tools, not easy to use and of limited efficacy. Even with all of the devices created to make these texts more usable, it is highly likely that legal research by practicing lawyers attempting to find the answer to a specific problem in the *Digest* or *Decretum* must have been extraordinarily difficult.

The point is this: while there is much evidence to show that jurists were concerned with the accessibility of their foundational texts during the first centuries of legal renewal in the High Middle Ages and in the crucial era of the formation of the medieval legal profession, these efforts were of only limited success. The *libri legales* were available but very difficult to use. Certainly during the period before 1300, any attempt to answer a specific question based on an exhaustive survey of relevant passages in the *Digest* or *Decretum* would have been nightmarish to accomplish. It seems relatively clear that 'mastery' as it must be defined in relation to the concept of professionalization was rarely achieved in a pragmatic, practice-oriented sense during this period. The image of civil and canon lawyers sitting in their chambers answering text-based questions after extensive research is, to our minds, simply anachronistic. Without sophisticated finding aids far beyond those that were developed early on, such a scene cannot have occurred.

The picture of the early years of the revival of jurisprudence, both civil and canon, as essentially text-centered and confounded by the problem of accessibility is confirmed by an examination of the ways in which civil and canon law were taught at the universities. All across Europe the curriculum in law developed along very similar lines. Happily, this paradigmatic

---

Rouse and R.H. Rouse, *Authentic Witnesses: Approaches to Medieval Texts and Manuscripts* (Publications in Medieval Studies, 17; Notre Dame 1991) 221–255.

law course has been amply described in the recent works of Barton, Bellomo, Brundage, Maierù, and Ridder-Symoens.[64] Because of this extensive recent scholarship on the subject, we need give here only a brief summary of their findings. Basically, the law curriculum lasted a minimum of seven years and a maximum of fourteen years. Generally, before 1215, would-be lawyers studied both civil and canon law. After the papal prohibition against clerics studying civil law, aspirants would decide which subject they wanted to study. Even with this papal prohibition, however, the evidence indicates that many clerics had to acquire some knowledge of the civil law in their canonical studies.

For our purposes, what is most significant about the early law courses is not the divide between civil and canon law. Rather, the fundamentals of how these substantive subjects were studied are key. The basic law course was completely and wholly text-centered; the civilians studied the *Digest* and *Code*, the canonists studied the *Decretum* and *Decretales*. Each of these works was studied part by part in a series of ordinary lectures. The subject of each of these lectures was a *punctum* or portion of the text. In fact, early on at Paris and later at other universities, these portions were prepared in the form of manuscript *pecia* and sold to the students. It would appear that the purpose of these lectures was to introduce students to the texts covered, and it was during these lectures that the glosses were, if not created, then expounded.[65] Indeed, Cardinal Hostiensis, in his masterwork the *Summa Aurea*, explained that the purpose of the professor in the lecture was to 'give a summary of the text', 'explain difficulties', 'show parallels' to other texts, dispose of contrary arguments by making distinctions, 'answer questions arising from the texts', and point out special aspects (notabilia) of the texts.[66] In addition to the *lecturae*, law professors from an early date also delivered *repititiones* on the same texts covered by the *lecturae*.[67] The purpose of these seems to have been review and, occasionally, greater study in-depth. Professors also participated in public disputations (*quaestiones disputatae*) on special topics.[68] What is so important about this process is that the organizing principal for both the *lecturae*

---

64. See the chapter by James A. Brundage in the present volume.
65. On the importance of oral presentation and discussion of the texts see Southern, *Scholastic Humanism* 193–195.
66. A. García y García, 'The Faculties of Law', HUE 1.398.
67. J.A. de Benavente, *Ars et doctrina studendi et docendi*, ed. B.A. Rodriguez (Salamanca 1972) 2.93.
68. Gérard Fransen, 'Les questions disputées dans les facultés de Droit', *Les Questions disputées et les questions quodlibétiques dans les facultés de Théologie, de Droit, et de Médecine*, ed. B. Bazàn et al. (Typologie des sources du Moyen Âge occidental 44–45; Turnhout 1985) 223–277.

and the *repititiones* was the organization of the books under study. This type of course was perfectly designed for the academic and textual scholar, but far less well-adapted to the needs of someone determined to practice law. Modern legal education is organized by category of legal activity: e.g. contract, tort, property. This organization is based upon categories ultimately based upon the types of actions heard by the courts and by categories defined by types of actual practice. Modern lawyers do not study set texts *qua* texts, but rather use texts to develop an understanding of the substantive content of these categories. Such a categorical legal scheme was available and known to the medieval jurists from Justinian's *Institutes*, but it was never adopted by the medieval law schools. Notably, Alan Watson has convincingly demonstrated that our modern legal categories, in broad outline, derive from the *Institutes* of Roman law, and scholars such as John Cairns and Klaus Luig have shown an equal dependence on the part of modern European law upon these early texts.[69] So why was it that the medieval juristic curriculum did not generally focus on such practice-oriented categories?

The answer to the question leads again to the importance of fundamental texts to the mind-set of the medieval jurists. Just as it was unthinkable to medieval theologians not to study the Bible book by book, it was unthinkable to the medieval jurist not to study law principally through the medium of the *Digest* or *Decretum*. This was the only possible approach for the text-centered culture of the legal renaissance of the twelfth century. Of course, this has significance. It means that there was an inherent conflict in the educational structure between this text-centeredness with its problems of accessibility and the need to provide means by which the medieval jurists could, in fact, solve problems. One place where this seeming contradiction becomes most visible is in the *quaestiones disputatae*. These disputations, unlike lectures and repetitions, were problem- and category-oriented and would have been directly relevant to problems of practice. Thus, it is important to realize that they became a part of the legal curriculum at an early date.[70] And yet they were not the predominant teaching device. Another example of this tension is the fact that in both the lectures and the repetitions, simple explanation of the studied text was not

---

69. A. Watson, *Roman Law and Comparative Law* (Athens, Ga. and London 1991); J.W. Cairns, 'The Formation of the Scottish Legal Mind in the Eighteenth Century', *The Legal Mind: Essays for Tony Honoré*, ed. N. MacCormick and P. Birks (Oxford 1986), 253–277; K. Luig, 'Die Anfäng der Wissenschaft vom deutschen Privatrecht', *Ius Commune* I (1967).

70. We have records of disputations from the time of the Four Doctors at Bologna. Weimar, 'Die legistische Literatur' 241–250.

enough. Professors were also expected to give parallel citations and related texts. By so doing they made these texts more accessible to the lawyer searching for relevant texts to solve a particular problem, in spite of the poor organization of the underlying volumes.

Thus, it would appear that both the production of texts designed to help make using the *Digest, Decretum,* and other fundamental legal texts easier, and the development of the university curriculum in law illustrate the problem of accessibility to the fundamental texts of medieval law and the valiant attempts by academic jurists to resolve these problems. Why did they bother? Why not simply lecture on these books, chapter by chapter, passage by passage? Why struggle to develop finding aids? Why have disputations on special topics rather than on a particular passage? The answer to these questions is simply that from a very early date after the rediscovery of the *Digest* and the compilation of the *Decretum*, those who held power, spiritual and temporal, recognized that trained lawyers could be of immense utility in government and society. To be useful, however, the lawyers had to be able to give advice, argue in court, and solve problems. The texts as they were discovered or compiled were not well-suited to these purposes. For lawyers to come into their own as members of a trusted and needed profession, it was necessary to make problem-solving possible. To do this, one of two things was necessary. Either lawyers and law students had to develop so intimate a knowledge of their texts that they could recall and cross-index them mentally from memory, or the whole panoply of auxiliary devices, from glosses to disputations to indices, had to be developed. The only realistic possibility was, of course, the latter path.

Let us summarize our conclusions as follows. First, the revival of jurisprudence, both civil and canon, in the twelfth and thirteenth centuries was based upon two principal factors: the discovery and compilation of fundamental texts which provided a legal equivalent to the theologian's Bible, and the growing market for individuals whose training suited them to serve the growing needs of church and state. At the same time, the fundamental legal texts of this revival were sufficiently difficult, disorganized, and inaccessible that in order to be usable a whole 'industry' would need to develop, the purpose of which was to make such texts available for problem-solving in practice. Put differently, for the legal profession to arise, it was essential that there be an identifiable core of knowledge which could be mastered and which would provide practitioners with a unique expertise that would answer market demands. The market existed in both temporal and ecclesiastical spheres. The core of knowledge existed in the fundamental texts of the legal revival. What remained to be done was to bridge these two and make the knowledge usable and able to be mastered by mere mortals. In other words, for the profession to arise and develop, an intermediary that could make the texts accessible had to develop as well. This intermediary, of course, was found in the universities and law schools.

The debate as to why the legal revival of the twelfth and thirteenth centuries happened has usually been framed in terms of either/or. Either the growing need for literate, rule-oriented experts in both secular and ecclesiastical spheres caused this to happen, or the rise of the universities and their law schools resulted in the production of lawyers, both civil and canon, who gradually took over control of church and state. But in fact, there is another explanation for the role of the universities in the revival and the rise of the legal profession during this period. Demand for lawyers alone would not have resulted in the revival of jurisprudence and the development of the legal profession as it occurred, because the lawyers, without the various auxiliary aids created by the universities, would not have been able to use the texts they had. It is highly unlikely that such aids could have been crafted outside the universities, for pure practitioners would have had neither the time nor the expertise to do this. They simply would not have possessed the requisite central core of knowledge and mastery thereof. On the other hand, had the universities begun to teach law without the pressures exerted by the needs of practice to make the texts not only accessible, but useful for practice and problem-solving, then legal science would have developed in a far more abstract, text-centered way. It would have been far closer to systematic theology than to what it became. The nature of the medieval law curriculum as it existed exhibits a tension between the need to prepare students for practice (the *repetitiones*, parts of the *glossa ordinaria*, etc), and the text-centered approach of studying the texts page by page and chapter by chapter in the order in which they were composed. This tension might not have existed and the practice-oriented side of the curriculum might not have developed without the market demands put upon academics. Thus, in effect, both the market and the universities were essential to the rise of the legal profession. It was the unique combination of market demand, text-centered culture, a series of inaccessible texts, and the rise of university law schools able to interpret and provide auxiliary texts that together led to the rise of the legal profession in the twelfth and thirteenth centuries. Like so many historical explanations, it is the confluence of several events and attitudes that made what happened, happen.

2

Gratian and the *Decretum Gratiani*

Peter Landau

The name of Master Gratian has long been associated with a twelfth-century collection of Latin sources of canon law. Not only does this collection, definitive and authoritative for many centuries, have systematically arranged texts dating from the early church to the twelfth century, but the texts are discussed and analyzed through Gratian's *dicta* (comments), in which he interpreted the contradictions within the sources and brought them into concordance. By means of his *dicta*, Gratian demonstrated that the canon law of the church was a harmonically complete unity. His goal is also expressed in the original title for the compilation, the *Concordia discordantium canonum*, not *Concordantia*. This title appears early in the manuscript tradition and might well have been coined by Gratian himself.

The name *Decreta* (changed to *Decretum* by later jurists) for Gratian's work is also very early and dates from around 1144. According to modern juristic categories, Gratian's legal collection is regarded as a 'private work', since it was never formally approved by the pope; its supposed confirmation by Pope Eugenius III in Tolentino is a legend. Despite that, from ca. 1140 Gratian's *Decretum* spread rapidly all across Europe and established itself first in Bologna and soon afterwards in other places as the authoritative textbook for teaching canon law. In this way the *Decretum Gratiani* is both the summary of the development of the law of the Christian Church in the first eleven centuries of its existence and the foundation of canonical jurisprudence until the twentieth century. Gratian has quite appropriately been seen as the father of the discipline of canon law.

As early as the middle of the twelfth century the *Decretum* of Gratian was supplemented by the *ius novum* of contemporary papal decretals, which in their turn were taught at European law schools from about 1180. After papal decretal law had been gathered into authoritative lawbooks during the thirteenth and early fourteenth centuries, the *Decretum Gratiani* was preserved as the first part of the *Corpus iuris canonici* along with the later decretal law. Despite the replacement of the *Corpus iuris canonici* by the *Codex iuris canonici* in 1917 (replaced by a new codex in 1983), many legal rules of current Catholic ecclesiastical law rest fundamentally on texts of the *Decretum Gratiani* (henceforward called the *Decretum* in this essay).

The Biography of Gratian

One is essentially left with suppositions so far as the life of Gratian is concerned, since most of the traditions in his biography come from the thirteenth century or even later. The frequent assertion that he was a Camaldolese monk in the house of Sts. Felix and Nabor in Bologna rests, so far as the Camaldolese part goes, on a tradition originating only in the eighteenth century. The tradition of Gratian's residence in the house of Sts. Felix and Nabor goes back to the period around 1250 and the unreliable glossator Odofredus. His place of birth is doubtful as well, since the tradition for a birth in Chiusi is not confirmed. The connection of Gratian with the house of Sts. Felix and Nabor rests on a notice by the glossator Odofredus (about 1260). Robert of Torigny, abbot of Mont-Saint-Michel, certainly made an error in his *Chronicon*, composed between 1162 and 1184, when he described Gratian as the bishop of Chiusi. In the thirteenth century Orvieto (Boncompagnus, *Rhetorica novissima*) and Chiusi (Martin of Troppau, *Chronicon*) were mentioned as birthplaces; finally, in the fourteenth century the village of Carraria near Ficulle was mentioned (Giovanni Colonna, *De viris illustribus*). Since Carraria lies near both Chiusi and Orvieto, the last notice might indeed give the true place of birth (as Seckel said as early as 1900).

The name 'Gratianus' is the only name given to the compiler of the *Decretum* in the earliest records. This name is given by the first witnesses in decretist commentaries, together with the academic title of 'magister' (master), so that it is possible to conclude that Gratian was continuously active as a teacher. A Bolognese decretist active in the seventies, Simon of Bisignano, often described himself as a disciple of Gratian. The highly developed juristic method in the *Decretum*, as well as its reception of many texts of Roman law in stages, makes it very probable that Gratian did his writing in Bologna and that he was active in this town as a teacher of canon law.

In his *Summa*, the canonist Huguccio states that Gratian's work was composed during a time when the legist Jacobus was teaching Roman law and Rolandus Bandinelli, later Pope Alexander III, was teaching theology in Bologna. This is probably good evidence that Gratian himself was active as a teacher in Bologna. Finally, the *Decretum* has two formularies of appeal (C.2 q.6 d.p.c.31) in which the bishops of Bologna and Reggio, as well as an archbishop of Ravenna, are given by name. The shared episcopal years of the three bishops mentioned here lay between 1130 and 1140, and the reference to Bologna could hardly be accidental.

The tradition that Gratian was a monk was first asserted by the author of the *Summa Parisiensis* on the *Decretum*, around 1168. The same *Summa* also mentions Gratian's Italian origin. The great attention paid to monks in the *Decretum* in C.16–20 is significant evidence for the claim of the *Summa Parisiensis*. Still, it is possible that Gratian was a canon regular, because their rights were also particularly respected in the *Decretum*, especially in Causa 19. According to some earlier glosses to the *Decretum*, Gratian was a bishop. In his *Chronicon* Robert of Torigny alleged his episcopal service.

Canonists after 1150 never wrote as if Gratian still lived. Since his work on the *Decretum* ended about 1140, Gratian probably died between 1140 and 1150. The *Summa* of Rufinus, written around 1164, speaks of Gratian as dead. In connection with a judgment of a papal legate in Venice in 1143, a jurist named Gratian is mentioned as one of the assessors of the court, and he may be identified with the father of canonistic jurisprudence. Gratian left his work uncompleted, since there are no *dicta* in the third part. This fact also is firm evidence for the supposition that Gratian could not have completed the *Decretum* in the form in which it circulated after ca. 1145.[1]

The *Decretum*'s Date of Origin

Scholars have for a long time debated the date when Gratian compiled the *Decretum*. On the one hand Gratian's texts extend through the Second

---

1. For a thorough discussion of the evidence in the chronicles and in the writings of the jurists, see John T. Noonan, Jr., 'Gratian Slept Here: The Changing Identity of the Father of the Systematic Study of Canon Law', *Traditio* 35 (1979) 145–172, with full bibliographical citations. Stephan Kuttner's essay 'Research on Gratian: Acta and Agenda', *Proceedings Cambridge* 3–26.

Lateran Council of 1139, so that 1140 has been set as the year of completion (Fournier, Fransen), while on the other hand the *Decretum* has been connected with the Investiture Controversy, so that the first decades of the twelfth century were conceived as the period of composition (Vetulani, Chodorow).² The period around 1140 has been seen as a probable date for the completion of the work of compilation because the canons of the Second Lateran Council of 1139 constitute the latest group of sources. These texts regularly appear at the end of a quaestio, and summaries of these canons are often lacking in the oldest manuscripts; taken together, these two facts argue for the reception of the canons of the Second Lateran Council at the very end of Gratian's work of editing. Since Anders Winroth has established that Gratian compiled two stages of the *Decretum*, the first of which may contain a reference to the Second Lateran Council and consequently may have been completed ca. 1139, one could infer that the vulgate edition of Gratian's *Decretum* was completed only around 1145.³

Even greater problems arise when one tries to make a more precise pronouncement about the date when Gratian began his work. There has been a partial attempt to connect the work of editing with the conflicts of the Investiture Controversy (Chodorow), but this could not be documented from the text of the *Decretum*. It is better to assume that Gratian's work of editing began only after the Concordat of Worms, perhaps around 1125. The collections of canons used by Gratian all date before 1125. Since the editing of the *Decretum* passed through various stages, a period of perhaps a decade and a half for the work is easily conceivable.

Gratian's Sources: Conciliar Canons

In view of the sparse information about Gratian outside his work, modern research has concentrated on studying his sources, analyzing the immediate provenance of individual texts, and studying the stages of composition for the *Decretum*. The analytical table of sources compiled by Emil Friedberg, the last editor of the *Decretum*, in his Prolegomena is still the best available overview.⁴ Several large categories of sources may be distinguished as having provided Gratian with his materials for the *De-*

---

2. Stanley Chodorow, *Christian Political Theory and Church Politics in the Mid-Twelfth Century: The Ecclesiology of Gratian's Decretum* (Berkeley–Los Angeles–London 1972) 255–259, who thoroughly discusses the various scholarly theories about Gratian's date of composition.
3. See my discussion of the recensions of the *Decretum* below.
4. *Decretum Magistri Gratiani* (Leipzig 1879, reprinted Graz 1959) cols. xix–xli.

cretum: the canons of councils, papal decretals, patristic texts, Roman law, Carolingian capitularies, as well as a large portion of forged legal texts. In addition he cited biblical texts and pseudo-apostolic literature in the form of what is called the Canons of the Apostles.

We may make the following observations about the categories of sources used by Gratian: of the pseudo-apostolic writings only the Canons of the Apostles are used, of which 17 of the 50 canons translated into Latin by Dionysius Exiguus are included. These venerable texts of early ecclesiastical law passed all the way into modern codification of Catholic Church law only through Gratian's *Decretum*.

The role of early conciliar canons in Gratian's *Decretum* is considerable. Gratian used almost two hundred chapters of the Eastern councils from the Council of Nicaea to the Council of Constantinople in 869. To be sure, Gratian did not use all the canons that he could have from the early Latin canonical collections. For example, he took only 8 of the 25 canons attributed to the Council of Ancyra in 314. The texts of the Greek councils are reproduced partially in the form contained in the *Dionysiana* and partially in the form preserved by the so-called *Isidoriana vulgata*, the Latin translation used for the *Collectio Hispana* and later by the compilers of Pseudo-Isidore. The consequence of this tradition is that many conciliar canons appear in Gratian twice.[5] It is surprising that 17 canons of the Synod in Trullo of 691/692, not recognized in the West as an ecumenical assembly, appear in Gratian. He ascribed these canons to the ecumenical Council of Constantinople in 680, so he had no problems in receiving them. The texts of the Trullan synod had already entered the tradition of Western canon collections through the *Collectio tripartita* attributed to Ivo of Chartres, which is a major source for Gratian. Gratian also included the canons of the Second Council of Nicaea in 787 and the Fourth Council of Constantinople in 869.

Among the texts cited continually since Dionysius Exiguus in Western canonical collections were the canons of the African councils in late antiquity. Gratian took about a hundred chapters from this material, and he also incorporated the larger portion of the *Statuta ecclesiae antiqua* of Southern Gaul, which he attributed to the Fourth Council of Carthage, in keeping with the tradition in the *Hispana*.

The Spanish councils and the *Capitula* of Martin of Braga provided

---

5. On the *Dionysiana* and the other early medieval collections mentioned in the following paragraphs, see Lotte Kéry, *Canonical Collections of the Early Middle Ages (ca. 400–1140): A Bibliographical Guide to the Manuscripts and Literature* (History of Medieval Canon Law; Washington, D.C. 1999).

Gratian with more than two hundred chapters. While the proportion of Spanish conciliar texts was still comparatively small in Burchard of Worms, they are of central importance in Gratian's *Decretum*. An example of their role can be found in the section of the *Decretum* that justified limiting traditional proprietary-church rights.[6] In the *Decretum* the sequence of Spanish councils extends from the Council of Elvira in 306 to the Sixteenth Council of Toledo in 693.

The proportion of canons of Gallican councils through the Carolingian era in the *Decretum* is also very considerable. It begins with the Council of Arles in 314 and includes councils up to the late ninth century. Gratian also included Carolingian councils of the eastern Frankish kingdom: the councils of Mainz in 813, of Worms in 868, and of Tribur in 895. He preserved a large part of Merovingian and Carolingian ecclesiastical law with these texts. Many canons of councils that took place in Rome were taken from Carolingian sources.

The councils of the tenth and eleventh centuries, before the Gregorian reform, provided Gratian with only a few texts. In this respect Gratian differed from Burchard of Worms but resembled the tendency of collections in the Reform Era in his reluctance to include the canons of these councils.

On the whole, Gratian incorporated only a small selection of conciliar canons from the period between 1070 and 1140 into his *Decretum*, such as, for example, four canons of the Council of Clermont in 1095. In specific cases Gratian's probable direct sources for these later councils can be established. Hence the sole canon of the Council of Troja in Apulia in 1094 that made it into the *Decretum* (c. 1 Concilium Trosleiense = C.35 q.6 c.4) is obviously excerpted by Gratian from the *Collectio tripartita* (*Tripartita* 3.16.14 = Ivo, *Decretum* 9.53). The canons of the Council of Piacenza of 1095, which were almost all taken up by Gratian, mostly passed into the *Decretum* through the *Collection of Three Books*.[7] Gratian also included the canons of the two Lateran councils of 1123 and 1139 in his *Decretum*. The chapters of the Second Lateran of 1139 were the last texts that he placed in the *Decretum* and consequently establish a terminus post quem for the end of his work. Some canons otherwise usually attributed to the First

---

6. e.g. C.16 q.7 c.30 and c.32.

7. In any case c.15 Concilium Placentinum is not found in any collection before the *Decretum*: F.J. Gossman, *Pope Urban II and Canon Law* (The Catholic University of America, Canon Law Studies 403; Washington, D.C. 1960) 121. It is found inserted in a Polycarpus manuscript, Paris, Bibl. nat. 3881; see Jacqueline Rambaud, *L'Age classique 1140–1378: Sources et théorie du droit* (Histoire du Droit et des Institutions de L'Église en Occident 7; Paris: 1965) 57.

Lateran Council appeared in Gratian with the inscription 'Urbanus papa'. With the current state of research it is impossible to make absolutely secure statements about the immediate provenance of the conciliar texts of the period between 1090 and 1140 in Gratian.

Papal Decretal Letters

The genuine papal decretals in Gratian extend from the earliest surviving decretals of Siricius to a decretal of Pope Innocent II to Bishop Odo of Lucca (C.35 q.6 c.8) that is useful for the dating of the *Decretum*. The letters of Popes Leo I, Gelasius I, Gregory I, and Nicholas I are particularly numerous. It must be stressed that a large portion of the letters of Gelasius I and Nicholas I were received into the canonistic tradition only during the period of the Gregorian reform, and the reform collections provided Gratian with this material.[8]

Gratian placed seven decretals of Pope Paschal II in his *Decretum*. Other than the single decretal of Innocent II already cited, his use of decretal law ends with the pontificate of Paschal II, which permits an inference about the period during which the *Decretum* was composed.

Patristic Texts

Patristic texts are extraordinarily numerous in Gratian. According to the fundamental study of Charles Munier, Gratian attributed 1200 chapters to Fathers of the Church, of which 1022 were authentic.[9] That means that more than a quarter of Gratian's chapters are taken from patristic sources. This proportion roughly corresponds to the weight of patristic texts in the collections of Ivo of Chartres, particularly in the *Panormia*. The lion's share of the patristic texts is provided by the Latin Fathers Ambrose, Augustine, Gregory I, and Jerome, with Augustine much predominant. Among the Greek Fathers, Gratian cited primarily John Chrysostom, Origen, and Basil. In Gratian a special role is played by adoptions from the works of Isidore of Seville, especially his Etymologies, which served as the basis for his doctrine of legal sources in the first twenty distinctions. Patristic texts on the whole are distributed quite unevenly across the *Decretum*. They are particularly numerous in the law of the sacraments and in themes relevant to moral theology. Hence about 80 percent of the chapters in the distinction

---

8. On the history of papal decretal letters in earlier canonical collections see Detlev Jasper and Horst Fuhrmann, *Papal Letters in the Early Middle Ages* (History of Medieval Canon Law; Washington, D.C. 2001).

9. *Les sources patristiques du droit de l'église du VIIIe au XIIIe siècle* (Mulhouse 1957) 125–126.

De penitentia derive from the Church Fathers, and in the causae on oaths and on heresy as well as on the just war (C. 22–23) they provide more than two thirds of the texts. The patristic passages are also numerous in the area of tithes, usury, marriage, and excommunication. In contrast, the Church Fathers have provided only a few chapters on procedural law. Among the writings of the Church Fathers, Gratian particularly cited exegetical writings on the Old and New Testaments. That leads to the question of the extent to which biblical citations were adopted into the *Decretum*. Biblical passages often stood alongside canons of councils and decretals in collections of the Gregorian epoch before Gratian. Gratian broke with this tradition (Le Bras), since he did not adopt a single biblical text among his auctoritates, but rather cited the Bible only in his dicta. He uses or explains about 230 biblical passages, a great many of which come from the letters of Paul. A literal interpretation of commandments from the Old Testament was avoided through the aid of allegorical interpretations. Many prescriptions of the Old Testament were seen as bound to their own time, so that Gratian can actually develop the theme of legal change with the aid of the Bible. In the New Testament, Gratian made particular use of the *auctoritas apostolica*, including the pastoral letters in the context of ordination. The New Testament is also cited to justify papal primacy, which Gratian thought that the Roman Church received from Christ Himself. The function of the Bible as an allegorical model actually compels a supplementary positive law of the church, so that Holy Scripture plays an enlivening function for establishing new law (Le Bras).

Roman Law

The research of Vetulani and Kuttner during the last decades has examined the significance of Roman law in Gratian's *Decretum*, and the process through which Roman law was included in his edition has been extensively clarified.[10] Gratian adopted a small number of texts of Roman law from earlier canon collections (22, according to Vetulani). In contrast, about two hundred texts of Roman law were taken into the *Decretum* without the mediation of earlier collections. They come from all parts of the Digest, from the Codex, and from the *Authenticae* of the Codex. A single text

---

10. Adam Vetulani's articles were reprinted posthumously in *Sur Gratien et les Décrétales*, ed. Wacław Uruszczak (Collected Studies 308, Aldershot 1990) and Stephan Kuttner's were also reprinted in *Gratian and the Schools of Law 1140–1234* (2d ed. Collected Studies 185; Aldershot 1994). See now also José Miguel Viejo-Ximénez, 'La recepción del Derecho romano en el Derecho canonico', *Ius ecclesiae* 14 (2002) 375–414, and idem, 'Gratianus magister y Guarnerius teutonicus', *Ius canonicum* 41 (2001) 35–73.

was from the Authenticum, while the Epitome Iuliani was not an immediate source at all. Texts from the *Breviarium Alaricianum*, the *Codex Theodosianus* and the *Constitutions of Sirmond* also entered Gratian's *Decretum* via earlier canonical collections. Roman law was predominantly cited for questions of procedural law, while in the first part of the *Decretum* only very few passages are drawn from the Roman sources. Vetulani concluded, on the basis of the position of Roman-law texts at the end of a particular *quaestio* by Gratian and from the lack of rubrics, that these flowed into the *Decretum* at a late phase of its composition, perhaps only after Gratian's death. The results of the most recent research, according to which we must distinguish two editions of Gratian, has essentially confirmed the thesis of the late incorporation of Roman-law texts, since they are almost all to be found only in the second edition. Yet some passages of Roman law are found in the first edition, including the only text that Gratian took from the Authenticum.[11] Thus we must conclude that Gratian planned to use Roman law from the very beginning. Further, it can be established that all the texts of Roman law were already in Gratian's second edition, so that the presumption that later jurists inserted Roman law texts after the conclusion of all the rest of the compilation cannot be sustained. Finally the capitularies of the Carolingian period must still be mentioned, which provided many texts along with the forgeries of capitularies by Benedictus Levita. On the whole, Gratian received a heritage more diverse than that contained in the entire previous textual tradition.

The Canonical Collections used by Gratian

Since the sixteenth century, scholars have dealt with the question of Gratian's immediate sources, the analysis and identification of the work from which Gratian took a particular text, *fontes formales*, rather than locating the original work from which the text was excerpted, that is the *fontes materiales*.[12] In his edition of Gratian, Emil Friedberg included an extensive section on 'Quibus canonum collectionibus Gratianus usus sit'(Which collections of canons Gratian used) with tables comparing Gratian and fifteen pre-Gratian canonical collections and collections of sentences.[13] One

---

11. To be specific, C.2, q.6, c.28 (Authenticum); C.15, q.3, c.1–4. Roman law is particularly important here for the establishment of the rules permitting women in some cases to give testimony during a trial.

12. For a discussion of the terms 'fontes materiales et formales', see Robert Somerville and Bruce C. Brasington, *Prefaces to Canon Law Books in Latin Christianity: Selected Translations, 500–1245* (New Haven–London 1998) 3–4.

13. *Decretum Magistri Gratiani*, cols. xlii–lxxv.

of those was, to be sure, Peter Lombard, undoubtedly post-Gratian, who, in fact, borrowed texts from Gratian for his *Sentences*. Friedberg demonstrated clearly that as a rule Gratian did not excerpt his texts from original works but usually took them from earlier canonical collections. In recent years intensive comparisons of Gratian's chapters with pre-Gratian canonical collections have fairly certainly identified the direct sources of individual chapters of Gratian. In this process the standard test was that the texts of Gratian appear in similar range and in the same sequence in a specific earlier collection, that Gratian's chapter inscriptions agree with an earlier collection, and that many chapters can be shown to be in only one pre-Gratian collection. In addition there is the consideration that a collection can be considered as a direct source for Gratian only if at least some of its texts are not found in another collection already shown to be a source for Gratian. Consequently a principle of economy rules in postulating the sources used by Gratian.

On the basis of these considerations, several collections analyzed by Friedberg have to be eliminated: the *Collectio Anselmo dedicata*, *Regino of Prüm*, the *Collectio XII partium*, the *Collectio Caesaraugustana*, and the collection of *Deusdedit*. On the other hand, in agreement with earlier research, the central role of the collections attributed to Ivo of Chartres for Gratian's compilation has been confirmed. It can be said with certainty that Gratian zealously exploited Ivo's *Panormia*, which was in any case the most widespread canonical collection in Europe in the first half of the twelfth century. The second place is the *Collectio tripartita*, also attributed to Ivo, the use of which by Gratian is beyond doubt, especially as a source for many conciliar canons and decretals. This conclusion is surprising, since the collection is preserved in only one manuscript from Italy (Berlin, Staatsbibliothek, Hamilton 345). In contrast, comparisons have shown that what is called the *Decretum* of Ivo of Chartres did not serve Gratian as an immediate source, although this has, until now, nearly universally been asserted in scholarly research. In all cases of agreement between Ivo's *Decretum* and Gratian, the texts are also found in the *Panormia* or the *Collectio tripartita*, whose third part (*Tripartita* B) is in any case an excerpt from Ivo's *Decretum*. In keeping with the principle of economy, then, the use of Ivo's *Decretum* by Gratian cannot be accepted any longer. This result is all the more certain because no manuscripts of Ivo's *Decretum* from Italy have been found among those few that have survived. Of the other two collections of Ivo, the *Panormia* was extensively exploited for the first recension; the *Tripartita*, however, was used intensively only for the second recension. The central position of the chapters adopted by Gratian from the corpus of Ivo's collections leads to the conclusion that it was his knowledge of Ivo's collections that provided the decisive push for Gratian's undertaking.

After Ivo, Anselm of Lucca provided Gratian with many texts. Among the many editions of Anselm's collection, an expanded version of Recension A (A') must have served Gratian as a source. There are also concordances with Anselm's Recension Bb from Lucca in some of Gratian's chapters,[14] which deserves attention because of Gratian's connection with Lucca, discernible from C.35 q.6 c.8. In any case, Anselm was used as a source in both of Gratian's recensions.

Finally, two Italian canon collections of the early twelfth century can be counted among Gratian's direct sources: the *Polycarpus* of Cardinal Gregory of S. Grisogono (circa 1111–1113) and *Collectio 3 librorum (The Collection in Three Books)* from the period 1113–1120. Since the *Collection in Three Books*, which survives in only two manuscripts, borrowed a large portion of its texts from the *Polycarpus*, it is often impossible to decide which of the two collections was Gratian's source. The *Collection in Three Books* has been recognized in the more recent research as a major source for Gratian.[15] It was from there that he took a large part of his Pseudo-Isidorian texts and many patristic excerpts that were noted in Friedberg's edition without provenance. According to Kuttner, Gratian took passages in the *Liber de honore ecclesiae* of Placidus of Nonantula from the *Collection in Three Books*. The same is true of the excerpts that he borrowed from Roman law in the *Epitome Iuliani*. The *Collection in Three Books* was used mainly in Gratian's second edition, even more than the *Tripartita*; he frequently turned to the *Polycarpus* in the first edition. We may assume, I think, that the principal sources used for Gratian's compilation were not all already available to him at the start of his work.

Gratian's Theological and Non-canonical Sources

It has been known for a long time that the *Liber de misericordia et iustitia* of Alger of Liège provided Gratian with texts and also served as a model for his dicta. Gratian's textual adoptions from Alger are, however, restricted to small parts of the *Decretum*, particularly to Causa 1.

Gratian's work contains a considerable body of theological texts, especially in *De penitentia* and *De consecratione*. The collection of theologi-

---

14. D.89 c.5; C.3 q.7 c.7; C.3 q.9 c.7; C.16 q.1 c.1.
15. John H. Erickson, 'The Collection in Three Books and Gratian's Decretum', BMCL 2 (1972) 67–75.

cal *Sentences* of Master A.—probably Ailmerus of Canterbury—was a major source. According to Kuttner and Landau, it is likely that Gratian used the collection in an expanded version known through a Florentine manuscript.[16] The *Sententiae Magistri A.* were sometimes used for Gratian's first edition. Gratian also turned to this collection of sentences in his chapters on marriage law.

Among Gratian's non-canonical sources were the sections on legal theory in the *Etymologiae* of Isidore of Seville. Here it is conceivable that Gratian had a complete text of Isidore at hand, or at least an excerpted Isidore containing Book Five of his work. Among Gratian's innovations was his use of Isidore when he discussed legal theory and the doctrine of legal sources in his *Tractatus de legibus*, Distinctiones 1–20. The last, but not least in importance, among Gratian's non-canonical sources was the *Glossa ordinaria* of the Bible, a source that he often used. Many of these texts are contained in the treatise *De penitentia*.

Some of the sources that Gratian did not use are significant. Textual comparisons between Gratian and collections before Gratian also make it possible to disqualify certain works as principal sources for Gratian, or to assign them only marginal significance in editing the *Decretum*. The most striking example is the *Decretum* of Burchard of Worms, which was broadly distributed in Italy in Gratian's time, yet Gratian appears barely to have used it in gathering his texts. The use of Burchard can be shown only in the case of about ten to fifteen chapters of Gratian. These include the sequence C.27 q.1 c. 11–14, which, due to a mysterious mislabeling, 'ex concilio Triburiensi', points to the trail of a particular group of Italian Burchard manuscripts. My own earlier thesis that Gratian made no use whatsoever of Burchard cannot be maintained.

Gratian preferred to use recent canonical collections for his *Decretum*. While it was asserted in early research (Peitz) that Dionysius Exiguus was a principal source for Gratian, it has since been shown (Landau) that Gratian inserted at best only six chapters from the *Dionysiana (Dionysiana-Hadriana*?) after the plan of the *Decretum* had already been conceived, although the additions were made to the first recension. It is also surprising that Gratian never directly used Pseudo-Isidore for his pseudo-Isidorian

---

16. Florence, Laurenziana, Santa Croce Plut. V Cod. 7. Stephan Kuttner, 'Zur Frage der theologischen Vorlagen Gratians', ZRG Kan. Abt. 23 (1934) 243–268, reprinted in *Gratian and the Schools of Law*. Peter Landau, 'Gratian und die Sententiae Magistri A.', *Aus Archiven und Bibliotheken: Festschrift für Raymund Kottje zum 65. Geburtstag*, ed. H. Mordek (Freiburger Beiträge zur mittelalterlichen Geschichte 3; Frankfurt am Main 1992) 311–326, reprinted in Peter Landau, *Kanones und Dekretalen* (Bibliotheca Eruditorum 2; Goldbach 1997) 161–176.

texts. Horst Fuhrmann's standard work on Pseudo-Isidore cited many chapters in Gratian that he thought were without parallels in pre-Gratian collections. However, when Fuhrmann wrote, the influence on Gratian of the *Collection in Three Books,* which contained many Pseudo-Isidore texts, was not known. It can now be excluded that Gratian made extensive use of Pseudo-Isidore, since we have evidence from only a few passages that he copied texts directly from Pseudo-Isidorian decretal manuscripts.[17]

Since Gratian frequently took fragments of letters from the Register of Gregory I—266 in all—using the inscription 'in registro', older research assumed that he must have used this important source in the form of the *Registrum Hadrianum*. According to more recent research (Landau), even these texts from the Register of Gregory I found in Gratian derive almost without exception from canonical collections predating Gratian;[18] the direct use of the Register is probable in only a single case.[19]

Roman Law in the *Decretum*

Kuttner put forward the thesis that Gratian in C.2 q.1 c.2 used the *Lex Romana Visigothorum* because Gratian gave the chapter the inscription 'Constantinus imperator'.[20] However, Gratian's source in this case was Anselm of Lucca, who also ascribed the same text to 'Constantinus imperator'.[21] Consequently, one need not postulate the use of the *Lex Romana* or an epitome as Gratian's source. Gratian used texts of Roman law exclusively from pre-Gratian canonical collections and from the *Corpus iuris civilis*.

In summary it can be said that Gratian drew his chapters predominantly from seven pre-Gratian collections of canons and sentences: Anselm of Lucca, Ivo's *Panormia,* the *Collectio tripartita,* the *Polycarpus,* the *Collection in Three Books,* the *Liber de misericordia et iustitia* of Alger, and the *Sententiae Magistri A*. At the present state of our knowledge, the origins of some patristic fragments, a total of about a hundred—only ten percent of the corpus of patristic texts in the *Decretum*—are unknown. Even in the case of these chapters whose origins remain unclear, it is probable that Gratian drew most of them from *florilegia* of patristic sentences. Among these

17. C.6 q.1 d.p.c.11; C.12 q.2 c.21.
18. Peter Landau, 'Das Register Papst Gregors I. im Decretum Gratiani', *Mittelalterliche Texte: Überlieferung-Befunde-Deutungen: Kolloquium der Zentraldirektion der Monumenta Germaniae Historica am 28./29. Juni 1996* (MGH Schriften 42; Hannover 1996) 125–140.
19. C.27 q.1 c.19 (JE 1496).
20. Kuttner, 'Research on Gratian' 23.
21. Anselm of Lucca, *Collectio canonum una cum collectione minore,* ed. Friedrich Thaner (Innsbruck 1905–1915, reprint Aalen 1965) 3.89 §§ 25–26 (p. 165–166).

hundred or so patristic fragments are six fragments from the work *De vita contemplativa* of Julianus Pomerius, which Gratian attributes to Prosper. Otherwise the corpus is essentially divided among the four great Latin Fathers of the Church. Surprisingly, most of these texts are already contained in Gratian's first recension; only in the case of the excerpts from the works of Ambrose did Gratian add the majority of texts to the second edition. It is to be presumed that Gratian used at least two hitherto unknown patristic *florilegia* for these texts. In the case of Gratian's chapters from Gregory I's *Moralia in Job*, the unusually precise citations in Gratian's inscriptions lead to the conclusion that he used this work directly (as Munier already argued).[22] Gratian also used the Pseudo-Augustinian work from the eleventh century, *De vera et falsa penitentia*.

The Plan and Divisions of the *Decretum*

Gratian's *Decretum* is divided into three principal parts, each of them in turn entirely differently constructed. The first part of his treatise is divided into 101 distinctions (distinctiones), which, after an introduction on the doctrine of legal sources (D.1–20), primarily treat the ordination and election of clerics. The decretists who followed Gratian (Rufinus, Stephen of Tournai) often designate the first part to be a treatise on ecclesiastical offices, 'de officiis'; the law of offices in this case is, however, always closely tied to the sacrament of ordination. Distinctions 81 to 101 provide additional texts and supplements to the themes already treated, and Gratian himself described it as an 'epilogue' to the first principal part (D.81, pr.). A second part (Pars secunda) follows, in which Gratian invented 36 fictive legal cases (causae), each causa to illustrate a theme. After describing the legal case, Gratian posed a series of questions that the case raised. He then provided the relevant legal texts after each question. In his dicta, Gratian resolved the contradictions in the sources and provided an answer to each question.

The table provides the schema of the *Decretum*'s first two parts with an example of how each part should be cited.

Gratian did not order his causae in the second part according to a strict systematic plan, but we can see overarching subject themes in the sets of causae that are loosely joined together. The content of the second part was summarized by the decretist Rufinus as 'ecclesiastica negotia' (ecclesiastical legal matters). At the beginning of his causae, Gratian dealt with the legal problems of clerics (C.1 to 6) and, at the end, with those of laymen (C.27 to

---

22. There are six chapters taken from the *Moralia*, and Gratian noted the book and chapter of the text in his inscription: D.13 c.2; D.45 c.9 and c.14; D.46 c.1 and c.2; D.47 c.3. Each text is also in the first recension.

Pars prima	Pars secunda
101 Distinctiones	36 Causae
divided into chapters	divided into questions
D.1–20 *Tractatus de legibus*	that are divided into chapters
e.g. D.20 c.2	e.g. C.11 q.1 c.1
	C.33 q.3 contains a *Tractatus de penitentia*
	divided into 7 distinctions
	e.g. De pen. D.1 c.22

36). He began the more extensive part concerning the clergy with a discussion of simony (C.1), a subject that is closely related to the principal theme of the Pars prima, ordination. He then treated heresy and, from C.2 to the end of C.6, questions of ecclesiastical criminal procedure. This section of the *Decretum* offered the decretists a point of departure for developing an ecclesiastical penal law and law of criminal procedure (negotia criminalia).

Causae 7 to 10 are dedicated to questions of ecclesiastical constitutional law and organization and include the following topics: the renunciation of office by bishops, the rights of the metropolitans, and the diocesan power of bishops. In this context, Gratian also deals with questions of diocesan property, including payments to bishops (cathedraticum). This last subject provided Gratian with the opportunity to discuss other major questions of property law in C.11 to 14, including the capacity of clerics to testify (C. 12), the right to tithes (C. 13) and the ecclesiastical ban on usury (C.14). In connection with disputes over property law, Gratian also deals with the 'privilegium fori' (the right of a cleric to have his legal case tried in an ecclesiastical court) (C.11). Causae 16 to 20 are dedicated chiefly to the rights of monks and canons regular, as well as to monastic institutions in general. Here too Gratian does not proceed in a strictly systematic way but shifts to other themes during his discussions, such as the doctrine of prescription (C.16 q.3) and the right of ecclesiastical asylum (C.17 q.4). It is also in this section of the *Decretum* that Gratian's most important comments on proprietary churches can be found (C.16 q.7).

Causae 21 to 26 deal with the general obligations of the clerical hierarchy and discuss highly varied areas of law. Important areas under this rubric are a comprehensive treatment of the oath (C.22), of just war, and with it the nucleus for a medieval law of nations (C.23), excommunication (C.24), privileges (C.25), and finally of the crime of magic (C.26). Gratian developed his treatment of privileges by also outlining his doctrine of papal power in the form of a long dictum (C.25 q.1 d.p.c.16).[23]

---

23. See Chodorow's analysis of this dictum in *Christian Political Thought* 141–148.

Causae 27 to 36 are dedicated to legal matters concerning laymen, and the primary subject of these causae is the law of marriage. Gratian presented a very detailed analysis of impediments to marriage that became the foundation of canonical marriage law. He inserted a treatise on penance into his treatise on marriage law (De penitentia) that he divided into seven distinctions after C.33 q.3. In modern literature this section is commonly cited as, for example, De pen. D.1 c.88.

Finally, the second part of the *Decretum* is followed by a third section, entitled *De consecratione*. It is divided into distinctions. In modern scholarship its citation takes the form De con. D.1 c.57, to distinguish it from the distinctions in the first part of the *Decretum*. *De consecratione* was not, however, a part of Gratian's first recension.[24] The subject matter of the third part is primarily dedicated to the sacraments and sacramental matters and is divided into five distinctions. It begins with the consecration of a church and other consecrations of ecclesiastical objects (D.1) and goes on to deal with the Eucharist (D.2), festival days and times of fasting (D.3), baptism (D.4), and confirmation (D.5). There are no *dicta Gratiani* in *De consecratione*, which gives the impression that this part of the *Decretum* was left unfinished.

In a late work published after his death, Rudolph Sohm argued that the complicated structure of Gratian's *Decretum* conformed to a general plan corresponding to the ecclesiastical sacraments.[25] From the beginning until C. 26 the sacrament of ordination determined the order, then marriage and penance, and finally the other sacraments in *De consecratione*. Sohm used this argument to support his general thesis that Gratian's work was the crowning achievement of an epoch of 'Old Catholic Sacramentary Law', in which canon law did not orient itself to the standards of secular jurisprudence. Sohm's impressive and often-rejected thesis (critics have been Gillmann, Mörsdorf, now Landau) fails on the fact that the structure of Gratian's *Decretum* is not completely predetermined in its content by sacramentary law.[26] The teaching on legal sources in the *Tractatus de legibus* (D.1–20) must be classified as jurisprudence and legal theory. In the same way, the 'negotia clericorum' of the second part can hardly be seen

---

24. As demonstrated by Anders Winroth, 'The Two Recensions of Gratian's Decretum', ZRG 114 Kan. Abt. 83 (1997) 22–31 and Rudolf Weigand, 'Chancen und Probleme einer baldigen kritischen Edition der ersten Redaktion des Dekrets Gratians', BMCL 22 (1998) 53–75, especially 75. Winroth expanded and enlarged his argument in *The Making of Gratian's Decretum* (Cambridge Studies in Medieval Life and Thought, 4th Series, 49; Cambridge 2000).

25. 'Das altkatholische Kirchenrecht und das Dekret Gratians', *Festschrift der Leipziger Juristenfakultät für Dr. Adolf Wach* (München-Leipzig 1918, reprinted Darmstadt 1967).

26. See Peter Landau, 'Sakramentalität und Jurisdiktion', *Das Recht der Kirche, 2: Zur Geschichte des Kirchenrechts*, ed. Gerhard Rau, Hans-Richard Reuter, and Klaus Schlaich (Gütersloh 1995) 58–95.

as sacramentary law. Finally, solely on the basis of the fact that *De consecratione* was not a part of the first recension of the *Decretum*, Sohm's thesis fails.

The peculiarity of the *Decretum*'s structure becomes most obvious when we compare it with other contemporary legal collections. In keeping with the organizational structure of other Gregorian reform collections, Anselm of Lucca, whom Gratian used directly, treated the primacy of the pope at the beginning of the first book. He then dealt with the right of appeal to the apostolic see, followed by the rules of procedure. The issue of clerical ordination is treated much later in the second section of the collection. In contrast to Anselm, it is Gratian's sharper juristic differentiation in his treatment of legal sources and the unity of his presentation of the law of ordination and duties and rights of clerical offices in the first part of the *Decretum* that sets the plan of his collection apart from others.

Ivo of Chartres begins the first book of his *Panormia* with the themes of the Christian faith and the sacraments of baptism, confirmation, and Eucharist. From the sacraments and sacramentalia he turns to the rights of the clergy and the hierarchical constitution of the Church. Like Gratian he treated the law of marriage only near the end (Books VI–VII). The orientation to the sacraments and hence to theology is more marked in Ivo, both in his *Panormia* and in his *Decretum*, than in Gratian.

In the eight books of the *Polycarpus*, as is the case with Anselm, Cardinal Gregory of S. Grisogono treated papal primacy first. Then he discussed the hierarchical constitution of the church and the rights of the clergy. As in Ivo's work, these clerical matters precede the law of laymen. Gratian's discussion of legal sources, definitions of law, and jurisprudence in the *Tractatus de legibus* is, consequently, an important and original accomplishment. His placement of ecclesiastical law before that of the laity corresponds to the chief tendency of the Gregorian reform. An orientation to theology still clearly characteristic of Ivo of Chartres is replaced with a more jurisprudential approach.

The Stages of Composition and the Two Recensions of the *Decretum*

The somewhat bizarre organization of the *Decretum*, particularly the placement of the *Tractatus de penitentia* (C.33 q.3), has often led to the supposition that there must be stages of composition of the *Decretum*. As early as 1660 the German scholar Stephan Bochenthaler ascribed a treatise *De penitentia* to Abbot Ernst von Zwiefalten, from whom Gratian was supposed to have taken this portion of the *Decretum*.[27] However, since Gratian also refers to *De penitentia* in Causa 11, an insertion after the completion of the rest of the work is unlikely.[28] The third part, *De consecratione*, was also seen as a later addition.[29] Finally, intensive analysis of the Roman-law excerpts in the *Decretum* by Adam Vetulani and Stephan Kuttner showed that these texts must have been added later and perhaps not by Gratian.[30] Determination of the immediate sources used by Gratian in his individual chapters also led me to the conclusion that Gratian did not draw on all his collections at the same time, and that conclusion led me to assume that there were stages of composition.[31] A decisive turn in this discussion came recently with the discovery of a first recension of the *Decretum* by Anders Winroth.[32] The first recension is preserved in the following manuscripts: Florence, Bibl. Naz. Conv. Soppr. A. 1. 402; Admont 23 and 43; Barcelona, Archivio de la Corona de Aragon, Ripoll 78; Paris, B. N. nouv. acq. lat. 1761.[33] Gratian's text in these manuscripts was earlier interpreted as an abbreviation; Winroth proved that it is an earlier version of the *Decretum*. His study confirms the use of the *Panormia*, the *Tripartita*, Anselm of Lucca, *Polycarpus,* and the *Collection in Three Books* as Gratian's chief sources. The recensions permit us to see much more clearly Gratian's successive use of sources. Ivo's *Panormia* appears to have been the first excerpted, followed by *Polycarpus* and the *Tripartita*, with the *Collection in Three Books* mainly at the end. Canons from the *Tripartita* and the

---

27. Joseph de Ghellinck, *Le mouvement théologique du XIIe siècle* (2d ed. Bruges 1948) 512–514.

28. C.11 q.3 d.p.c.24, although not in earlier recensions.

29. John H. van Engen, 'Observations on "De consecratione",' *Proceedings Berkeley* 309–320.

30. Vetulani and Kuttner's essays are cited above, n. 10.

31. Peter Landau, 'Gratians Arbeitsplan', *Iuri Canonico Promovendo: Festschrift für Heribert Schmitz zum 65. Geburtstag*, ed. Winfried Aymans and Karl-Theodor Geringer (Regensburg 1994) 691–707.

32. Winroth, *The Making of Gratian's Decretum*.

33. Kenneth Pennington and Carlos Larrainzar have argued that St. Gall, Stiftsbibliothek 673 is an even earlier recension of Gratian's *Decretum*; see 'Gratian, Causa 19, and the Birth of Canonical Jurisprudence', *La cultura giuridico-canonica medioevale: Premesse per un dialogo ecumenico* (Rome 2003) 215–236 and an expanded version in *"Panta rei": Studi dedicati a Manlio Bellomo*, ed. Orazio Condorelli (Roma: Il Cigno, 2004) 4.339–355 and C. Larrainzar, 'El borrador del la "Concordia" de Graziano: Sankt Gallen, Stiftsbibliothek MS 673 (= Sg)', *Ius ecclesiae: Rivista internazionale di diritto comune* 11 (1999) 593–666. Anders Winroth has continued to argue that the St. Gall manuscript is an abbreviation: see "The Teaching of Law in the Twelfth Century," *Law and Learning in the Middle Ages: Proceedings of the Second Carlsberg Academy Conference on Medieval Legal History, 2005* (Copenhagen 2006) 41–61. For the Florentine manuscript see also C. Larrainzar, 'El Decreto de Graciano del códice Fd (=Firenze, Biblioteca Nazionale Centrale Conventi Soppressi A.I.402)', *Ius ecclesiae* 10 (1998) 421–489.

Collection in Three Books are very often missing from the first recension. The relation of the first to the second recension proves to be complicated. Supplements of additional texts have been added to all the manuscripts of the first recension. The second recension could rest on an irregularly expanded exemplar of the first recension, which would perhaps explain differences in the sequence of chapters. The second recension certainly does not derive from an authentic, clearly established, archetype. Instances of incoherence between the *dicta Gratiani* and their texts are to a large extent the result of the second recension. The framework of *dicta* was essentially worked out for the first recension. The *dicta* inserted in the second recension are, in part, long and very thorough. One might say that they correspond to the type of 'summula'.

The discovery of a first recension makes possible new, clear conclusions on the sections *De consecratione* and *De penitentia*. *De consecratione* is completely missing in this recension, while *De penitentia* is to be found in a shortened version but already divided into seven distinctions. The Roman law texts are almost all additions of the second recension; only three texts were already included in the first recension, including Gratian's only citation from the Authenticum (C.2 q.6 c.28). Comparisons of the two versions made since the discovery of the first recension make it possible that the same author was not responsible for both versions; one might conclude that Gratian may be considered the author only of the first recension. The only division for which Gratian was responsible was the division of the thirty-six causae of the *Pars secunda* into questions. The division into distinctiones in *Pars prima* was never mentioned by Gratian in his cross-references; rather Gratian described *Pars prima* as the *Tractatus ordinandorum* (C.1 q.7 d.p.c.6). Paucapalea was probably responsible for the division of *Pars prima* into distinctiones as the two canonists who wrote the twelfth-century *Summa Parisiensis* and the *Summa 'Antiquitate et tempore'* attest.

In the middle of the twelfth century some manuscripts divided the text of the entire *Decretum* into titles with rubrics indicating content. The extent and coverage of the titles correspond in part to the distinctions of *Pars prima* and to the questions of *Pars secunda*, but some questions were also divided into various titles and various questions were united into a single title. In *Pars prima*, the number of titles (33) is substantially less than that of the distinctions—the texts of legal sources in D.1 to 14 are brought into a single title, 'De iure scripto et non scripto'. In connection with the division into titles, there is also a division of the *Decretum* into four parts (Leipzig, Universitätsbibl. Haenel 17, Codex F in Friedberg's edition). These divisions are the result of the post-Gratian canonists' interest in bringing canon law into closer conformity with Roman law. Stephen of Tournai and the French School that he founded were important for this development. In Bologna, by contrast, Rufinus and others stressed the independence of canon law and rejected Roman law's tendency to divide works into titles. The division of the *Decretum* into three different parts became definitive by the end of the twelfth century. In the long run the canonists succumbed to the model of Roman law when they began to compile papal decretals in collections.[34]

Alterations and Falsification of Texts in Gratian

Until now, uncertainty about Gratian's immediate sources has hindered the investigation of how he altered or edited the texts that he incorporated into his *Decretum*. Gratian did, without doubt, occasionally shorten or alter his sources (for example, C.2 q.7 c.10). Since he interpreted his texts so skillfully through his *dicta*, he hardly ever needed to alter texts so extensively that he altered their sense. Although he lived in an era that produced many forged conciliar canons and decretals, so far no one has been able to find a forgery that he intentionally composed. Insofar as Gratian included obvious forgeries in the *Decretum* (for example, D.68 c.3), he probably took them from unknown sources. We may also note that when he borrowed inscriptions, in contrast to Burchard of Worms, for example, Gratian followed his immediate source.

Gratian's *Dicta*

The work of Gratian is distinguished from earlier canonical collections by his extensive *dicta*, which in the second recension became in some cases small treatises. Through these *dicta*, Gratian's work took on characteristics of a textbook that has been provided with a plethora of sources. Behind the *dicta* Gratian's range of ideas is clearly visible. He did not mechanically borrow solutions for contradictory sources but provided clear conclusions in his *dicta*. Cross-references in the *dicta* to other parts of the *Decretum* show that the *Decretum* was, in its first recension, already conceived as a unified work for the classroom.

It is remarkable that in his *dicta* Gratian refers to sources that are not cited in the *Decretum*. Many biblical citations, for example, are found only in the *dicta*. They are often tied to important theological reflections, as,

---

34. See Chapter 9 on systematic decretal collections by Kenneth Pennington, below.

for example, in C. 22 where he explains an oath.[35] In one *dictum* Gratian also makes a singular reference to Plato, whose philosophy he knew from the Chalcidius translation of the *Timaeus* (D.8 d.a.c.1). In another *dictum* Gratian refers to the *Breviatio* of Ferrandus, a systematic canonical collection not otherwise used by him and not widely disseminated in manuscripts (D.63 d.p.c.34). He may have used Ferrandus as a lexicon for locating canons. The alteration and expansion of *dicta* in Gratian's second recension must still be investigated in detail.

Gratian's Method

Gratian's method is already defined in the title that he himself certainly gave his work, *Concordia discordantium canonum* (A Concord of Discordant Canons). He starts with concrete problems of canon law for which contradictory answers were possible on the basis of the sources that he collects. Finally Gratian evaluates the legal force of the sources, often ranking them according to their importance. Methodologically he presumes that the force of canons may be limited by cause, person, place, and time, 'ex causa, ex persona, ex loco, ex tempore' (D.29 c.1—a text probably independently formulated by Gratian borrowing from Isidore of Seville).

In addition, Gratian knew Ivo of Chartres' *Prologue* to his collections and could rely on the principles developed in it.[36] Alger of Liège was the first to comment on and to compare canonical sources in his *Liber de misericordia et iustitia*, from which Gratian took his methodology and also many texts. Further, it is probable that Gratian was also familiar with the scholarly method of early scholasticism, especially Abelard's *Sic et non*.[37] Finally, Gratian's achievement is unthinkable without the influence and jurisprudence of the Bolognese school of glossators. Their treatment of the legal texts that they studied in civil law exercised a strong influence on him. Gratian's notable dependence on the Bible in his *dicta* shows that he was thoroughly shaped by a Christian world view deeply steeped in theology.

---

35. See the interesting study of Titus Lenherr, 'Die "Glossa ordinaria' zur Bibel als Quelle von Gratians Dekret', BMCL 24 (2000) 97–129.

36. Ivo's *Prologue* has recently been translated into English and French: *Prefaces to Canon Law Books in Latin Christianity: Selected Translations, 500–1245*, ed. Robert Somerville and Bruce C. Brasington (New Haven–London 1998)132–158 and Jean Werckmeister, *Yves de Chartres: Prologue* (Sources canoniques 1; Paris 1996). See now Bruce C. Brasington, *Ways of Mercy: The Prologue of Ivo of Chartres: Edition and Analysis* (Münster 2004).

37. On the influence of Abelard's methodology now see Christoph H.F. Meyer. *Die Distinktionstechnik in der Kanonistik des 12. Jahrhunderts: Ein Beitrag zur Wissenschaftsgeschichte des Hochmittelalters* (Mediaevalia Lovaniensia, series 1, studia 29; Leuven 2000).

Basic Charateristics of Gratian's Thought in the *Decretum*

At the beginning of his work, Gratian discussed legal sources and types of law in great detail (D.1–14). He distinguished natural law, positive law, and custom from one another. He identified natural law with moral law found in human nature. Consequently, he thought that natural law and biblical law are largely identical. His doctrine became the most important foundation of the medieval doctrine of natural law until Thomas Aquinas.[38]

Gratian's ecclesiology is based on a strict division of clerics and laity in the church: 'Duo sunt genera Christianorum' (C.1 q.12 c. 7). The clergy encompasses those selected by God for exclusive service in the Church; the laity is defined as the 'populus', the people, to whom marriage and the accumulation of property are permitted. In this position, Gratian was probably influenced by Hugh of St. Victor and his *Summa de sacramentis*. The clergy is hierarchically organized according to its grade of ordination (D.25 c.1—the apocryphal Isidorian *Epistola ad Leudefredum*), with each level of ordination tied to distinct official duties. Gratian did not yet make any legal distinction between the powers and rights of orders and the rights obtained through election for ecclesiastical offices.[39] Consequently he did not recognize any distinction in ecclesiastical power between the 'hierarchia ordinis' (hierarchy of order) and the 'hierarchia iurisdictionis' (hierarchy of jurisdiction). But since Gratian does distinguish between 'potestas' (power) and 'executio potestatis' (exercise of power), he has criteria to hinder the illegitimate exercise of power in the Church. The 'executio potestatis' can be effective only if the ordination of an office holder takes place within the Church. Thus Gratian prepared the ground for a conception and division of ecclesiastical offices that is relatively independent of the rank of a cleric by his ordination. The supremacy of the archdeacon over the archpriest, unknown before Gratian, D.25. c.1, is one example. He also underlined the importance of the authority of the archdeacon to control elections to ecclesiastical offices in D.63 c.20.

According to Gratian, ecclesiastical offices are bestowed by election,

---

38. The first twenty distinctions of Gratian's *Decretum* have been translated into English: *The Treatise on Laws (Decretum DD.1–20) with the Ordinary Gloss*, translated by Augustine Thompson and James Gordley, with an Introduction by Katherine Christensen (Studies in Medieval and Early Modern Canon Law, 2; Washington, D.C. 1993).

39. See most recently L. Villemin, *Pouvoir d'ordre et pouvoir de juridiction: Histoire théologique de leur distinction* (Paris 2003).

with the laity strictly prohibited from participating in them. Election is not yet tied to the principle of majority, and disputed elections are to be decided by superiors. Metropolitans, for example, decide disputed episcopal elections. Although Gratian, unlike Anselm of Lucca, did not place papal primacy first, he stressed the power and authority of the pope, particularly over legislation. For him, conciliar canons and papal decretals are legal sources of equal rank. The statement that the pope possesses the 'ius condendi canones' is made for the first time in a *dictum* that he expanded into a treatise (C.25 q.1 d.p.c.16);[40] the formulation corresponds to that in the *Dictatus papae* of Gregory VII.

Even conciliar canons receive their validity as law through the consent of the Roman Church. The pope is in principle bound to the law he has established, but he may alter it at any time and break it in individual cases by granting privileges to institutions or persons. In addition, on the basis of his power to legislate he has an interpretative monopoly over canon law. In bestowing privileges the principle of equity should be respected; consequently, privileges must always be bestowed with the reservation of possible future suspension, 'salva tamen in omnibus apostolica auctoritate'. The formula used by Gratian had already entered papal documents under Pope Celestine II (1143–44).[41] The comprehensive right of the popes, developed by Gratian, to legislate and interpret the law was the foundation for the explosive expansion of papal decretal law starting with the pontificate of Alexander III (1159–81).

In keeping with the principal tendencies of twelfth-century theology, Augustinian tradition in sacramental law predominates in Gratian. He accepted the view that the efficacy of the sacrament does not depend on the worthiness of the dispenser; reordination and rebaptism are excluded from ecclesiastical practice.

In marriage law, Gratian emphasizes the principle of consent and stresses the consummation of the marriage ('copula carnalis'), through which alone a marriage resting on consent becomes a completely valid bond. Gratian's marriage theory, in which copulation played a role in determining the validity of a marriage, did not persuade future theologians and canonists. Peter Lombard and the Parisian theologians defended a theory based solely on consent. But Gratian thought that the free consent of the partners was also indispensable for the creation of a marriage.

---

40. Chodorow, *Christian Political Theory* 141–147.
41. Friedrich Thaner, 'Über Entstehung und Bedeutung der Formel "Salva sedis apostolicae auctoritate" in den päpstlichen Privilegien', Vienna SB 71 (1872) 807–851.

Hence, by himself and without reference to earlier canonistic sources, he developed a differentiated doctrine of erroneous marital situations (C.29). In keeping with a Christian tradition reaching back to the third century A.D., Gratian represents the principle that free persons could contract valid marriages with unfree persons. The Church should separate relatives who marry within the forbidden degrees of consanguinity. It was incest. The separation has a penal character. The classification of impediments to marriage and the development of a special marital jurisprudence emerge only in the epoch of decretists following Gratian.

Gratian devoted much attention to the law of ecclesiastical property. This is true for his treatment of the benefice, and he applied the concept of an ecclesiastical benefice with juristic precision. He also discussed the law of tithes and ecclesiastical ownership rights in great detail. The Roman law of prescription was central to his analysis of these concepts. He considerably reduced the proprietary right of laymen to the churches built or endowed by them. Through Gratian, the concept of a lay 'dominium' over churches gradually vanished and was replaced, by the decretist Rufinus, with the new concept of patronage. In sum, Gratian created several new rules for a specifically ecclesiastical law of property.

In the law of procedure, Gratian borrowed more texts from the Pseudo-Isidorian Decretals than in other areas. He adopted Pseudo-Isidore's rigid rules about the very high standards that accusers and witnesses had to meet before they could be heard in court. By applying these stringent rules to the procedure of ecclesiastical courts, in which ancient Roman modes of proof were employed ('ordo iudiciarius'), Gratian greatly increased the difficulty of bringing about conviction in ecclesiastical criminal cases. Despite his extensive reception of Pseudo-Isidore in procedural matters, Gratian did not accept all of the ninth-century forger's opinions. Hence in a way somewhat different from Pseudo-Isidore, he presumed that a subordinate may accuse someone superior to him in the hierarchy; to him, accuser and accused are of equal moral value; the accused does not suffer any legal consequences because of his status. Gratian did adopt some of Pseudo-Isidore's legal principles, such as the ban on trials of absent persons. In the law of proof, the *Decretum* has a complicated mixture of Roman law and the oath of purgation common in the early Middle Ages ('purgatio canonica'). Appeal from the court of first instance has a great importance in procedural law, since it may be made at any point in the procedure, even before the final sentence of a lower court. On the basis of the texts received by Gratian, a specialized canonistic literature of procedure originated (*Ordines iudiciarii*), which developed the principles of the Roman-canonical trial that became standard for Europe up to the nineteenth century.⁴²

For Gratian, excommunication was the most important ecclesiastical sanction. Further penalties for clerics were deposition and suspension. Within excommunication itself, Gratian distinguished between the anathema (later called major excommunication), which excludes one from the community of the faithful, and minor excommunication, which has as a result only the exclusion from the Eucharist (C.11 q.3 d.p.c.24 § 1). Gratian expressly rejected the declaration of excommunication without trial—'latae sententiae'—which later became common in the twelfth century when the church dealt with heretics.⁴³

Gratian as the Father of Canonistic Jurisprudence

Rudolf Weigand's research on the composition of the glosses and apparatus to the *Decretum* dates the first glosses on the text of the *Decretum* to ca. 1150.⁴⁴ The *Summa* of Paucapalea, a student of Gratian, with which the decretist summa literature began, was composed as early as 1148. The *Decretum* was also epitomized very early in what were called abbreviationes. Early works of this type were the *Abbreviatio 'Quoniam egestas'* dating to ca. 1150 in Southern France (Provence) and the *Abbreviatio* authored by the theologian and canonist Omnebene around 1156, which also circulated outside Italy.⁴⁵ The 'abbreviationes' of the *Decretum* should be distinguished from what are called 'transformationes', which bring the material of the *Decretum* into a different order and with independent commentaries. Among these latter the *Compilatio decretorum* of Cardinal Laborans is of particular interest. This master, who was promoted to the rank of cardinal in 1173, worked between 1162 and 1182. His *Compilatio* is divided into six books, and it combines the sources with a commentary of its own;

42. Linda Flower-Magerl, *Ordines iudiciarii and Libelli de ordine iudiciorum (from the Middle of the Twelfth to the End of the Fifteenth Century)* (Typologie des sources du moyen âge occidental 63; Turnhout 1994) and Kenneth Pennington, 'Due Process, Community, and the Prince in the Evolution of the Ordo iudiciarius', RIDC 9 (1998) 9–47.

43. Elisabeth Vodola, *Excommunication in the Middle Ages* (Berkeley–Los Angeles–London 1986) 28–30.

44. See Rudolf Weigand, 'The Development of the *Glossa Ordinaria* to Gratian's *Decretum*', Chapter 3 in this volume.

45. On three German abbreviations of the Decretum see Alfred Beyer, *Lokale Abbreviationen des "Decretum Gratiani": Analyse und Vergleich der Dekretabbreviationen "Omnes leges aut divine"* (Bamberg), *"Humanum genus duobus regitur"* (Pommersfelden) und *"De his qui intra claustra monasterii consistunt"* (Lichtenthal, Baden-Baden) (Bamberger theologische Studien 6; Frankfurt am Main 1998).

it is preserved in a single manuscript and obviously had almost no success.[46]

Paleae and Addenda to the *Decretum*

The word, 'paleae' designates additions to the text of the *Decretum* that were inserted into the manuscripts after the completion of the second recension of the *Decretum* around 1145. They augment the *Decretum* with older canons not included by Gratian but also with contemporary ius novum and more recent forgeries. Chapters were and are also designated as paleae that entered the *Decretum* twice due to the *Decretum*'s multifarious sources that often duplicated material. These chapters were repetitious and superfluous. The duplicate chapters were originally paleae and were gradually eliminated from the text of the *Decretum* in the twelfth century. The enigmatic term paleae might derive from the name of the canonist Paucapalea, who was perhaps the first to add supplements to the text of the *Decretum*. A major source of paleae was the *Decretum* of Burchard of Worms, which was widely available in Italy during Gratian's lifetime but which he barely used. The insertion of paleae into the *Decretum* can be dated to the period between 1145 and 1180. There are several particularly well known texts among the paleae, such as the chapter on electoral law of the *Regula Benedicti* (D.61 c.14), parts of what is called the *Decretum Gelasianum* (JK 700 in D.15 c.3), and the Donation of Constantine (D.96 c.13 and 14).

From the fourteenth century on, lists of paleae were made. In modern times, since there have been disputes over which chapters may be confidently called paleae, a definitive number of paleae in the *Decretum* cannot be given. Rambaud counted 149 paleae in 1965 and Weigand 169 in 1998; in each case these numbers can be considered only a starting point.[47] In more recent research the assumption has been made that the supplementing with paleae probably rested on a paleae collection independent of the *Decretum* (Rambaud), but the existence of such a collection has not yet been proved.

In the first decades after 1140 canonists inserted paleae into the text of the *Decretum* and other supplements, called addenda to the *Decretum*.

---

46. Norbert Martin, 'Die "Compilatio Decretorum" des Kardinals Laborans: Eine Umarbeitung des gratianischen Dekrets aus dem 12. Jahrhundert' (Ph.D. dissertation, Universität Heidelberg, 1994).

47. On the problem of the paleae, see now Jürgen Buchner, *Die Paleae im Dekret Gratians: Untersuchung ihrer Echtheit* (Pontificium Athenaeum Antonianum, Facultas Iuris Canonici 127; Rome 2000) counted 152 paleae.

These addenda usually collected decretal letters that were not in Gratian or in collections prior to Gratian. For the most part these decretals dated to the years after the completion of the *Decretum*. Among the decretals predating Gratian in these addenda are particularly the decretals 'Relatum' of Leo IX (JL 5153) and 'Inhaerentes' of Honorius II (JL 7401). Post-Gratian texts were taken from the decretals of Popes Eugenius III, Hadrian IV, and especially Alexander III. Some of the addenda also included the canons of the Council of Tours of 1163 and the *Authentica 'Habita'* of Frederick Barbarossa of 1155. Most of the addenda were inserted into Gratian's text between 1150 and 1170. With the growth of the mass of decretals under Alexander III, the necessity emerged to create autonomous collections of decretals, including the older ones, so that the addenda mentioned are lacking in subsequent manuscripts of the *Decretum*.[48]

Gratian's European Reception: Early Manuscripts

The European reception of Gratian began even before the completion of the second recension. The *Decretum* was certainly known at the papal curia from the pontificate of Celestine II (1143–44); it was used in a decision by the bishop of Siena in 1150 (Nardi).[49] The first recension of the *Decretum*, still preserved today in five manuscripts, including three in Austria, France, and Spain, can document the rapid dissemination of the text beyond Italy. The two Admont manuscripts (Admont, Stiftsbibliothek 23 and 43) that preserve the *Decretum* in this original form divided into two volumes were written in Admont itself between 1160 and 1170. The monks of this religious house must have learned of Gratian around 1160. A further manuscript of this recension (Barcelona, Archivio de la Corona de Aragón, Ripoll 78) comes from the Benedictine house of Ripoll in Catalonia, and hence it documents early knowledge of the *Decretum* in Spain.

If manuscripts of the second recension are added to these first recension texts, a total of about 160 manuscripts of Gratian can be attributed to the twelfth century. The *Decretum Gratiani* reached Germany before 1160. Manuscript Mainz, Stadtbibliothek, II.204 was the model for the Gratian manuscript Bremen, Universitätsbibliothek, a.142, which was given to the Bremen Cathedral Library before 1168 by Archbishop Hartwig. Accord-

---

48. For information about the first independent collections of decretals, see Charles Duggan's 'Decretal Collections from Gratian's *Decretum* to the *Compilationes Antiquae:* The Making of the New Case Law', Chapter 8 in this volume.

49. See Thaner, ' Entstehung und Bedeutung'. For Siena see Paolo Nardi, 'Fonti canoniche in una sentenza senese del 1150', *Life, Law and Letters: Historical Studies in Honour of Antonio García y García*, ed. Peter Linehan (SCG 29, Romae 1998) 661–670.

ing to its library catalogue of 1165, the house of Prüfening near Regensburg possessed a codex of Gratian in two volumes that must have been obtained by Prüfening around 1160. This codex can be identified with a manuscript now in Munich (Munich, Staatsbibliothek, lat. 13004). As early as 1170 a Gratian codex was transcribed by the monk-priest Adalbert in the house of Schäftlarn near Munich (Munich, Staatsbibliothek, lat. 17161). Among the oldest *Decretum* manuscripts are Cologne, Dombibliothek 127 and 128, which were written ca. 1160. These manuscripts slightly predate the flowering of the school for canonistic studies in Cologne, which became a significant place to study canon law ca. 1170–1185. The *Abbreviatio decreti* of Omnebene was also transcribed on the lower Rhine after 1160.

Many French Gratian manuscripts of the twelfth century come from the north of France (such as Arras, St. Omer) or from Burgundy (Troyes, Bibl. mun. 103 from Clairvaux). A manuscript comes from southern France about 1180 that later was located in Cîteaux (Baltimore, Walters Art Gallery 777). What is possibly the oldest French codex of Gratian is a manuscript of Paris (Paris B.N. lat. 3884 I and II) that can perhaps be placed as early as around 1160. In Provence the *Decretum* was already known in 1150, which may be gathered from the evidence of the *Abbreviatio 'Quoniam egestas'*. For England, the flourishing of the Anglo-Norman school of canon law after 1180 proves extensive knowledge of Gratian at that time. What is possibly the oldest English manuscript of Gratian is an unglossed codex in Lincoln (Lincoln, Cathedral Chapter Library 138); among the oldest Gratian codices preserved in England are Cambridge, Pembroke College 162 (certainly from Italy) and Cambridge, Gonville and Caius 6 (from France).

In Italy the *Decretum* became a known text in both the north and the south; a codex in Vercelli dates to ca. 1180 (Vercelli, Archivio capitolare, XXV), and a manuscript of Verona was written around 1185 (Verona, Bibl. cap. CLXXXIV). Another manuscript of Gratian in Sicily can be dated to around 1160 (Beaune, Bibl. mun. 5). The early distribution of the *Decretum* in Spain, besides the manuscript from Ripoll of the first recension already mentioned, is witnessed particularly by a codex in Tortosa (Tortosa, Biblioteca Capitular, 240). The miniatures of this manuscript show a close relationship with those of the manuscript from Ripoll. In summation it may be said that the European distribution of the *Decretum* of Gratian began between 1150 and 1160 and reached its apex about 1180.

Editions of Gratian

The *Decretum* of Gratian has been printed frequently since the fifteenth century. There are 45 incunable editions that were printed before 1501 and more than 150 editions printed after that date. The earliest incunable edition appeared in Strasbourg in 1471. Among the printed editions of the sixteenth century is what can be called the first critical edition, produced by the canonist Antoine de Mouchy (Antonius Monchiacenus Demochares); he divided the text with indications of contents (paratitla).[50] The edition of the canonist Le Conte (Contius), a student of Cujas and a professor in Bourges, incorporated the text of Demochares and first appeared in 1570. Le Conte noted the apocryphal nature of many chapters in Gratian. The edition by the Protestant jurist Charles Dumoulin (Molinaeus) was printed first in 1554. It introduced the numeration of the chapters used in later editions and accompanies the text with Dumoulin's critical apostillae. This edition was placed on the *Index librorum prohibitorum*. Later publishers suppressed Dumoulin's apostillae.

The *Editio Romana* appeared in 1582 as the official edition of the Catholic Church, and it has remained the definitive text of Gratian for the Church on the basis of the letter of promulgation, *Cum pro munere pastorali* of Gregory XIII dated 1580. The edition was edited by a commission, called the *Correctores Romani*, that had been established by Pius V in 1566. The cardinals and academic canonists who belonged to the Commission of *Correctores* included the Cardinals Ugo Buoncampagni (later Pope Gregory XIII) and Felice Perreti (later Pope Sixtus V). The Cardinals Francesco Alciati and Antonio Caraffa played a leading role in the commission. For their edition, the *Correctores* compared previous printed editions with the Gratian manuscripts from the Vatican. In order to check the texts in Gratian critically, they drew on pre-Gratian canonical collections, including Anselm of Lucca, as well as on editions of councils and of the works of the Fathers of the church. The goal of the *Correctores* was not an edition of the original twelfth-century text of Gratian, but rather a restoration of the original texts of the sources cited by Gratian, since these texts could claim validity as law, but the work of Gratian that included them could not. On the basis of this goal, the *Correctores* as a rule also corrected Gratian's erroneous inscriptions. On the other hand, they restricted themselves in reconstructing the original source texts insofar as they generally preserved both the initial words of a chapter in Gratian as well as the words on which an explanation in the Ordinary Gloss depended. Where Gratian's text differed from the original sources, they noted a 'lectio vera'

---

50. *Decretorum collectanea* ([Paris]: Apud Carolum Guillard and Gulielmum Desbois, 1547 and 1552); under the title *Decretorum canonicorum collectanea* (Paris: Apud Iacobum Puteanum 1570 and Antwerp: Ex officina Christophori Plantini, 1570 and 1573).

in the margin. The procedure of the *Correctores* can be justified because they wanted to establish a usable text of Gratian together with the medieval gloss, not a philologically correct text based on twelfth-century manuscripts. Their ultimate goal was to preserve the legal tradition of canon law. Through his letter *Cum pro munere pastorali*, Gregory XIII declared the Roman edition to be the sole authentic version, whose text could not be altered. Yet in this way the *Decretum* of Gratian was not granted legal validity as a code of legislation. After the *Editio Romana,* any edition deviating from its text was excluded from the courts and schools of the Roman Church. After 1586 the *Decretum* was provided with title pages indicating it to be the first volume of the *Corpus iuris canonici*; after 1587 it was ordinarily printed bound together with the *Institutiones Iuris Canonici* of Lancelotti, an introductory textbook.[51]

In the following centuries the editions of the Pithou brothers and Justus Henning Böhmer departed from the *Editio Romana*. The edition prepared by Pierre Pithou (1539–96) and François Pithou (1543–1621) did not appear until 1687, long after their deaths; it is a masterpiece of French humanism. The Pithou edition frequently corrected the text of the *Editio Romana* by noting variants taken from French manuscripts. It also provided an alphabetical index of Gratian's chapters.

The leading Protestant canonist, Justus Henning Böhmer (1674–1749), professor at Halle, published a new edition of Gratian in 1747 that offered a text essentially altered from that of the *Editio Romana*.[52] Böhmer used four Gratian manuscripts, and he relied on the thorough edition of Hardouin as the source of the conciliar canons. His edition became standard for the study of ecclesiastical law at Germany's Protestant universities. The next edition of Gratian was produced in 1836 by the Marburg professor Aemilius Ludwig Richter (1808–64), founder of the historical school of ecclesiastical law.[53] In his text Richter adopted the original Roman edition without its later typographical errors; thus the Roman edition can most easily be used today in Richter's edition. Further, he provided comprehensive references to texts and sources in his extensive apparatus on which later editors, especially Friedberg, could build. Emil Friedberg (1837–1910) produced the latest and most critical edition in Leipzig. It was first pub-

51. Giovanni Paolo Lancelotti (1522–1590), *Institutiones juris canonici quibus jus pontificium singulari methodo libris quatuor comprehenditur* (Rome 1588).
52. *Corpvs ivris canonici Gregorii XIII pontificis maximi avctoritate, post emendationem absolvtam editvm in dvos tomos divisvm et appendice novo avctvm* (Halae Magdebvrgicae: impensis Orphanotrophei 1747), reprinted by J.-P. Migne as volume 187 of his PL.
53. *Corpus juris canonici* (Leipzig 1839).

lished in 1879.[54] Friedberg based his edition on eight manuscripts of Gratian from German libraries, of which six were written in the twelfth century. He noted variations from the *Editio Romana* in a separate apparatus. Friedberg included all earlier research on Gratian in the critical apparatus of his edition. Of all the existing editions, Friedberg's is the only one that reproduces the text of the twelfth-century *Decretum*; hence it could be used as the basis of the five-volume concordance to the *Decretum* published by the Monumenta Germaniae Historica.[55] Friedberg's edition does not meet current critical standards; Kuttner's classic critique of his edition is still pertinent.[56] For the future, our goal should be separate editions of Gratian's recensions.

Two classic works of the sixteenth and eighteenth centuries are still of great importance for the critical use of the *Decretum*: (1) Antonius Augustinus (Agustín, 1517–86), *De emendatione Gratiani Dialogorum Libri duo* (Tarragona, 1587), and (2) Carlo Sebastiano Berardi (1719–68), *Gratiani canones, genuini ab apocryphis discreti* (Taurini, 1752–66).

Gratian and Protestant Ecclesiastical Law

The Protestant reformers did not take a unified stand towards Gratian and the validity of his text. Luther severely criticized positive canon law, including the work of Gratian. In contrast, Melanchthon viewed Gratian more positively; consequently there are many citations of Gratian in the Apology of the Augsburg Confession. In general the Lutherans valued the *Decretum* more than decretal law. Protestant canonists Benedikt Carpzow (1595–1666) and Justus Henning Böhmer often cited the *Decretum* in their work. Unlike Luther, Calvin thought that the *Decretum* was superior to decretal law, and he also drew theological teachings from the *Decretum*. A critical and scholarly concern with the text and gloss of the *Decretum* also began very early among the members of the Reformed Church (e.g. Charles Dumoulin). Eventually, the whole *Corpus Iuris Canonici* was received into the Protestant churches as a subsidiary source of law. This borrowing still governs property law (patronage) in the German Evangelical churches.

---

54. *Corpus iuris canonici* (2 volumes; Leipzig 1879; reprinted Graz 1959).
55. *Wortkonkordanz zum Decretum Gratiani*, ed. Timothy Reuter and Gabriel Silagi (5 volumes; MGH, Hilfsmittel 10; Munich 1990). The Bavarian State Library has put Friedberg's edition on the web at: http://mdz.bib-bvb.de/digbib/gratian/text/
56. 'De Gratiani opere noviter edendo', *Apollinaris* 21 (1948) 118–128.

Gratian and the *Codices Iuris Canonici* of the Twentieth Century

After Pope Benedict XV promulgated the *Codex Iuris Canonici* on 27 May 1917, the contents of the *Decretum* ceased to have legal force within the Roman Catholic Church in 1918. Despite this, the *Codex* established in can. 6, n. 2, that those canons containing old law (ius vetus) are to be interpreted 'ex veteri iuris auctoritate' (from the old authority of the law). That statement leaves open the possibility of making use of the text of Gratian in modern jurisprudence. This ruling recurs almost unchanged in the *Codex Iuris Canonici* of 1983 (can. 6 § 2); the new code of canon law promulgated by Pope John Paul II states that canons incorporating old law 'aestimandi sunt ratione etiam canonicae traditionis habita' (ought to be considered according to the norms of the canonical tradition). There is no doubt that the *Decretum* belongs to the canonical tradition of the Church and that, due to the reception of the canons of the old Church in it and also due to its legal validity in the churches of the Reformation, it also has considerable ecumenical significance.

Final Evaluation of the *Decretum*

The *Decretum* and its importance can be evaluated in three ways: (1) The *Decretum* is a fundamental witness to the medieval intellectual world. It was born in the 'Renaissance of the Twelfth Century', to use Charles Homer Haskins' famous formulation, the most creative period of the Middle Ages. In Gratian's century Europe spawned the institution of the university, the architecture of the Gothic cathedrals, and the first great poetic works in the vernacular languages. As an intellectual achievement it equals the achievements of early-scholastic theology. The old legend that Gratian and Peter Lombard were brothers has a certain core of truth. (2) As the father of the discipline of canon law, Gratian represents the first in a long line of jurists who still teach canon law in ecclesiastical and secular universities throughout the world. Gratian established Western canon law as a legal system that differs significantly from the canon law of the Eastern Christian churches. Canonical jurisprudence after Gratian combined theological principles within a juridical framework that is neither purely theology nor purely jurisprudence. Consequently, Rudolph Sohm's question—whether Gratian was a theologian or a jurist—assumed that he was one or the other. In fact, Gratian was both. Gratian brought theology into law again and law into theology. (3) The *Decretum* forms the bedrock of European legal culture. Its content and its methodology shaped the core of the Western legal tradition. The heritage of the *Decretum* in the Western legal tradition includes the establishment of natural law as an important element of our legal systems, the establishment of structures of public law, the spread of principles of international law, the presentation of a law of procedure stressing the legal protection of the individual, the recognition of the person, and the autonomy of the woman in marriage law. In terms of its methodology, the *Concordia discordantium canonum* is a challenge to the art of hermeneutics. Gratian's dialectical argumentation in his *dicta* makes it possible to speak of a new legal science from the twelfth century on. Through Gratian, the history of European jurisprudence was decisively influenced by canonists as well as by the jurists of Roman law, the legists or civilians. Both groups of jurists created the medieval and early modern *Ius commune*. Insofar as genuine ecclesiastical law is able to survive alongside state law, the legal order is not reducible to the will of the state alone. This historical constant in the legal history of the West, the co-existence of the two laws, led in the end to modern democratic pluralism. Master Gratian can claim some credit for this development.

3

The Development of the *Glossa ordinaria* to Gratian's *Decretum*

Rudolf Weigand

Glosses on the *Decretum* probably formed the earliest field of activity for canonists.[1] Their first glosses were short explanations of words. This type of gloss was very old. It can be found in the margins of pre-Gratian canon collections from the early Middle Ages, for example, as in the Dionysio-Hadriana in Würzburg M. p. th. f. 3 dating from the beginning of the ninth century, which has Latin and Old High German glosses in different ninth-century hands and in a Würzburg Universitätsbibliothek manuscript M. p. th. f. 146 from the same period.[2] These early glossed are often more an attempt to get at the correct grammatical meaning than an

---

1. Johann Friedrich von Schulte offers a first comprehensive account, 'Die Glosse zum Decret Gratians von ihren Anfängen bis auf die jüngsten Ausgaben', *Denkschriften der kaiserlichen Akademie der Wissenschaften* (Philosophische historische Klasse 21; vol. 2, Vienna 1872) 1–97. Kuttner, *Repertorium* 1–122, was an important breakthrough. My *Die Glossen zum Dekret Gratians: Studien zu den frühen Glossen und Glossenkompositionen* (SG 25–26; Rome 1991), offers a summary of my own research. There, in four parts, I give first a cumulative edition of the glosses to selected portions of the *Decretum*, which taken together constitute barely one percent of the text, then an overview of important gloss compositions, followed by further information on the glosses of important authors and, finally, a description of the layers of glosses in all manuscripts containing pre-Johannine glosses. This work is the principal foundation for the remarks made in the first parts of the present essay.

2. These manuscripts from the old Würzburg cathedral library are described by Hans

55

attempt to explain the legal implications of a text. The glosses are usually interlinear and consist of simple definitions of words. This type of gloss is frequent in early manuscripts of the *Decretum*. In those cases where a single word is explained by just another, synonymous term, they display no great learning. This kind of gloss also occurs, however, in later gloss layers and apparatus, all the way up to the *Glossa ordinaria*; many of these simple glosses, for example, occur at D.II c. 5.[3]

Because these explanations of words were usually written between lines (often introduced by 'idest' or 'vel') these glosses were often misunderstood by later copyists and incorporated into the text. A good example is at D.II c.4. Here the words 'idest ius naturale' or a similar phrase entered the text at the word 'rationem' in many early manuscripts, while the word 'scriptam' and occasionally even 'idest ius constitutionis' was inserted at the word 'legem' in almost all manuscripts.[4]

Ornately sketched signs in the margins indicated important points. This occurred often in early canonical collections, whenever the reader's attention needed to be drawn to an important definition. This mark is very common in the manuscript of the *Decretum* of Burchard of Worms in Lambach XVI, which up to now has received little notice; the mark probably testifies to the use of the manuscript in the administrative activities of the bishop or other owner.[5] Often, words or clauses that were important and needed emphasis were simply rewritten in the margin.[6]

From an early date, other texts were occasionally quoted in order to provide an explanation or to give supplementary information. Thus, at the beginning of the *Decretum* in the manuscripts Grenoble , Bibl. Mun. 34 (475, Gg), Heiligenkreuz, Stiftsbibl. 44 (Hk), Montecassino, Bibl. Abbazia 64 (Mv) and Vatican., lat. 3529 (Vd), many texts from Roman law are cited (Dig. 1.1.11 and Inst. 1.2.pr.). Later, theologically relevant texts, in addition to canonistic ones, were added in places as extra material, and it is here that the starting point for the so-called paleae probably lies. The earliest references

---

Thurn, *Die Handschriften der Universitätsbibliothek Würzburg*, 3.1 *Die Pergamenthandschriften der ehemaligen Dombibliothek* (Wiesbaden 1984) 4–6 and 72–74.

3. See Weigand, *Glossen zum Dekret Gratians* part 1, glosses 210, 211, 224, 229, 231, 235, 237, 243, 273, 286, 289, 308, 309, 334.

4. Here see the Friedberg edition, n. 27 and 28, above all in his manuscripts A and B (Cologne 127 and 128). See also Weigand, *Glossen zum Dekret Gratians* part 1, 149, 150, 158, 160, 161 with n. 24 and 25, and the following examples.

5. See Rudolf Weigand, 'Die Lambacher Handschrift XVI des Dekrets Burchards von Worms und Bischof Adalbero von Würzburg', *Würzburger Diözesangeschichtsblätter* 52 (1990) 25–36, especially 33–36.

6. Weigand, *Glossen zum Dekret Gratians* 174 and 193, glosses 838 and 948 present two examples of such glosses from the manuscripts Bremen a 142 and Munich 28161. These hardly originated in a scholarly center, but testify, rather, to individuals' personal use of the text.

to parallel or contrary passages, which at first often included the source of the passages, reveal genuinely scholarly use of the *Decretum*.⁷

I see in these glosses a relic from the earliest period, when the division of the *Decretum* into distinctions by Paucapalea had not yet gained acceptance.⁸ This is particularly the case since, in the usual manuscripts of the first gloss composition, the first of the glosses mentioned above was expanded and provided with the now-abbreviated 'allegatio'.⁹

The different kinds of glosses are closely related to the pedagogical methods of the time.¹⁰ Introductory, summary discussions that prepared the hearer or reader to understand a text (summa) or briskly summarized the essential details in the record of a case (casus), provided a way into a problem or legal text. During the reading of the source text that followed, the teacher added explanations of the most varied sort, frequently consisting of just a synonym, or of explanatory definitions or appositions. Later, the 'discursive' glosses quite often became very extensive, coming to form a relatively independent text. This was particularly the case when previously established decisions were cited in support or when aspects of the question that had not been discussed were taken into account, often by bringing in passages from other sources. Occasionally a short legal rule (argumentum) would be abstracted from the glossed passage and provided with parallel passages. Sometimes such legal principles were introduced with the word 'nota' or 'notandum' and thus received particular emphasis. These were subsequently brought together to form collections and further developed into 'brocarda' or 'generalia', in which pairs of counterposed arguments were set together. Another form was 'distinctiones'. Whether they were written schematically or in continuous text, they brought an overall view or discussion of a problem that went beyond the individual passage. A special kind of discussion on a given problem was found in the 'quaestiones', which from early on were brought together to form collections of 'quaestiones'.¹¹

---

7. E.g. gloss on D.84 c.5: 'Contra Martinus papa supra Lector si uiduam (D.34 c.18). Set illud ubi necessitas, hoc ubi nulla necessitas urget.' In a similar vein, a gloss on D.92 c.3 reads: '. . . supra in vii. sinodo Quoniam multos' (D.69 c.1) Printed in its entirety in my description of the above-named 'abbreviatio' in SG 26, 750, no. 11.

8. Evidence in Franz Gillmann, 'Rührt die Distinktioneneinteilung des ersten und des dritten Dekretteils von Gratian selbst her?', AKKR 112 (1932) 504–533; reprinted in R. Weigand ed., *Gesammelte Schriften zur klassischen Kanonistik von Franz Gillmann* (Forschungen zur Kirchenrechtswissenschaft 5.1; Würzburg 1988). Cf. Landau's chapter above.

9. Weigand, *Glossen zum Dekret Gratians* 750, gloss 9a.

10. On this and the following, see Peter Weimar, 'Die legistische Literatur und die Methode des Rechtsunterrichts in der Glossatorenzeit', *Ius Commune* 2 (1969) 43–83.

11. Summarized by Gérard Fransen, 'Les questions disputées dans les facultés de Droit,

Various Gloss Compositions (up to 1190)

In the following, I define 'gloss compositions' as glosses that are transmitted in several manuscripts, that are relatively uniform, and that only partially or sporadically, explain the text. I contrast 'gloss compositions' with a 'gloss apparatus' that explains the text rather comprehensively and was for the most part handed down as a whole.

The First Gloss Composition

From the mass of early glossed *Decretum* manuscripts one gloss composition, written about 1150, may be singled out as representing the earliest attempt by canonists to gloss Gratian's *Decretum*. The 'First Gloss Composition' shows only a casual relationship to the corresponding texts in the summae of Paucapalea, and so must have been written largely independently of him, even though it takes his arrangement of distinctions as self-evident. The 'allegationes', notations of parallel and contrary passages, became increasingly numerous later on, and were as a rule written in the margins, which were still blank. Thus, they could be placed right next to the correct passage, which was made particularly necessary by the fact that they were long written without reference marks.[12] Solutions were also appended to some contrary passages. Perhaps the most significant solution gloss of this Composition and at the same time one of the most frequently copied glosses of the middle of the twelfth century (I have found it in some seventy manuscripts) is that on D.28 c.13, printed by Schulte.[13] A solution gloss on D.30 c.17 with three possible explanations of the contrary passage cited reads identically to Paucapalea's *Summa*.[14] A distinction gloss on C.1 pr., 'Causarum alia dicitur', was also inspired by Paucapalea.[15] Some glosses of 'notabilia', often repeating only one of the source's important sentences (at the beginning of the *Decretum* they very often are almost identical to the *Summarium*), were mainly composed in

---

'Les questions disputées et les questions quodlibétiques dans les facultés de Théologie, de Droit et de Médecine, ed. B. Bazàn et al. (Typologie des sources du moyen âge occidental 44–45; Turnhout 1985) 223–277 with literature.

12. The 'allegationes', occurring in several manuscripts, and printed on 37–44 of my paper, 'Frühe Glossen zu D. 12 cc. 1–6 des Dekrets Gratians', BMCL 5 (1975), 35–51, are part of the 'First Gloss Composition'.

13. Schulte, *Glosse zum Decret Gratians* 8, lines 3–13. I have shown its occurrence in *Glossen zum Dekret Gratians* 423, gloss 72.

14. Paucapalea, *Summa über das Decretum Gratiani*, ed. J.F. von Schulte (Giessen 1890; reprinted Aalen 1965) 26.

15. Paucapalea, *Summa* 51.

three-point form.[16] The following three 'explanations of words' in D.11 c.5 already form a uniform gloss:[17]

> 'Quibus': scilicet constitutionibus; 'utriusque pietatis': scil. laicalis et clericalis; 'affectus': idest dilectio debetur.'

From the standpoint of historical transmission, priority clearly must to be given to this gloss; only later was it taken into the *Summa Parisiensis*.[18]

This 'First Gloss Composition' is preserved relatively complete, though not consistently so, in Chambéry, Bibl. ville 13, Grenoble, Bibl. ville 11 (474), Heiligenkreuz, Stiftsbibl. 43, and Munich, Staatsbibl. lat. 4505, as well as in Barcelona, Archivo Corona Aragón Ripoll 78 (early recension of Gratian), in Bremen, Universitätsbibl. a 142 (substantially only to part 1), and in the first layers of Admont, Stiftsbibl. 48, Biberach, Spitalarchiv B 3515, Darmstadt, Landesbibl. 907, Ghent, Bibl. der Rijksuniversiteit 55, Heiligenkreuz, Stiftsbibl. 44, Luxemburg, B.N. I.139, Madrid, Fund. Lázaro. Galdiano 440, Paris, B.N. 3890, St. Omer, Bibl. Mun. 454, Tortosa, Bibl. cap. 240, and Vaticana, Chis. E.VIII.206. Its inclusion in the Barcelona manuscript may indicate that the systematic glossing of Gratian's *Decretum* began before his final recension appeared. In many other manuscripts it was erased[19] (though about a third of its glosses are still extant in the first layer of Trier, Stadtbibl. 907) or was combined with other glosses, as in, for example in Vatican, lat. 3529. Glosses of the 'First Composition' were integrated into almost all later gloss compositions. An early draft of this composition appears to be preserved in Grenoble 34 (475) and Montecassino 64.[20]

---

16. Many of the glosses that I documented in 'Paucapalea und die frühe Kanonistik', AKKR 150 (1981) 145–152 as n. 1–3, 9a, 16–28 and 30 belong to this category, as do many of those printed in *Glossen zum Dekret Gratians* part II.1, 403–423. P. Kuhlkamp, 'Die erste Glossenkomposition zu C. 16 des Decretum Gratiani', *Ius et Historia: Festgabe für Rudolf Weigand zu seinem 60. Geburtstag*, ed. N. Höhl (Würzburg 1989) 118, has found hardly any agreement with the *Summa* of Paucapalea. The uniform transmission of these glosses already attracted the notice of J. Rambaud-Buhot in 1958: 'L'Étude des manuscrits du Décret de Gratien', *Congrès de droit canonique médiéval Louvain et Bruxelles, 22–26 Juillet 1958* (Louvain 1959) 30f.

17. References in Weigand, *Glossen zum Dekret Gratians* part 1, no. 209, 45.

18. Terence P. McLaughlin, *The Summa Parisiensis on the Decretum Gratiani* (Toronto 1952) 11.

19. Seven still recognizable initials on fol. 6va of Bamberg Can. 15 (Bd) indicate that the 'First Gloss Composition' probably existed here before being almost totally erased to make room for the *Glossa ordinaria*; see Rudolf Weigand, 'Romanisierungstendenzen im frühen kanonischen Recht', ZRG Kan. Abt. 69 (1983) 246, n. 62.

20. See material below on the fourth and later compositions, also my description of individual manuscripts in *Glossen zum Dekret Gratians* IV.

The Second Gloss Composition

The 'Second Gloss Composition' is clearly visible as a separate gloss layer in the old interlinear glosses of four manuscripts, Bamberg, Staatsbibl. Can. 15, Ghent 55, St. Omer 454, and Trier, Staatbibl. 907. It was once, however, distributed relatively widely. In its original form it cites the *Decretum* not by the number of distinctio and causa, but always by title.[21] The *Decretum* was divided into titles, probably in imitation of the tradition employed in the sources of Roman law, and these titles were written in at the appropriate passages of the manuscript, as can still be seen in about a dozen manuscripts. These titles can be best seen in Leipzig, Universitätsbibl. Haenel 17, a unique manuscript in which practically all the 'allegationes' use this method of citation. In addition, the *Decretum* is here divided into four parts, the second part containing causae 1–11, the third causae 12–26, and the fourth everything (except the 'de poenitentia') from C.27 on.[22] In other manuscripts these titles, beginning with 'De iure scripto et non scripto' were transmitted in summary form either at the beginning (as in Vatican lat. 2494) or at the end of the *Decretum* (as in Biberach 3515). The glosses of this Composition are sometimes simple word explanations, but more often explanations referring to other passages in the *Decretum*, cited with the subject title and incipit, and occasionally with reference to Roman law. This Composition may belong to the circle of Guibert of Bornado. In Paris 3890 and 14605 the first two gloss compositions were combined (in 14605 Guibert of Bornado's is added); Paris 3895, moreover, has the glosses of a certain Petrus in the first layer. The first two gloss compositions are combined with glosses of Bernard of Pavia in the first layer of Baltimore, Walters 777 and Marburg, Universitätsbibl. 33. Particularly deserving of mention are Arras, Bibl. mun. 592 (500), Munich 14024 and 28175, Florence, Bibl. Marucelliana A. 298, Gniezno, Bibl. Kapit. 28, Naples, B.N. XII. A. 5, St. Florian III. 5, and Vatican lat. 2494, where, as in many other manuscripts, these glosses are combined with later ones.

These first two gloss compositions should be dated to the 1150s. During this time another system for citing related and contrary source passages in the Decretum came into being. Greek or Latin letters or other conspicuous symbols, normally written in red ink and placed right next to a given passage, served this end. Some solution glosses that harmonized a group of juxtaposed contrary passages with each other might for that reason simply begin with a 'ϑ contra' or a 'λ contra,' which required this symbol to be

---

21. Further information in Weigand, 'Romanisierungstendenzen' 209–249.
22. Ibid. 220–226.

placed at the other, indicated passage.[23] The use of this system is traceable to at least 1160–80 and is present in the work of Rufinus and Bazianus.

The Third Gloss Composition

The mostly unmarked glosses of Rufinus form the 'Third Gloss Composition', which should be dated to approximately 1160, since his Summa was written ca. 1164.[24] This Composition exists uncorrupted as a first layer in Bamberg, Staatsbibl. Can. 14 (Bb), Berlin, Staatsbibl. Phillips 1742 (Bp, first layer) and (always with the siglum R.) as a second layer in Baltimore 777 (Bl). The majority are solution glosses, and for the most part they record his Summa verbatim, as Josef Juncker has shown.[25] A 'λ contra' (or similar sign)[26] stands at the beginning of some of these solution glosses in early manuscripts, though the same statement of contrary passages that appears nearby tallies with it only partially. Now and then, long glosses on distinctions or summae are found, for example, always at the beginning of D.16 or D.74.[27] Some purely explanatory glosses of Rufinus are also found. His glosses appear in almost all later gloss compositions, though usually without a siglum.

The three compositions described here show no mutual overlap, except perhaps for some 'allegationes', as can be seen from the R.-sigla that were later appended to the 'allegationes' in the first layer of the Baltimore manuscript.

The Fourth Gloss Composition

The 'Fourth Gloss Composition' is today best seen in the first layer of Vatican, lat. 2494 and in the first layer of Kraków 357. It contains the glosses of the preceding three compositions more or less completely and enriches them with some new glosses, as with, for example, a long discursive gloss on D.26 c.3 and one on marriage discussed in C.27 q.2, both of which were later frequently copied and occasionally even attributed (though incorrect-

---

23. For more detail on this point: Gero Dolezalek and Rudolf Weigand, 'Das Geheimnis der roten Zeichen', ZRG Kan. Abt. 69 (1983) 143–99, especially 180–92.

24. André Gouron, 'Sur les sources civilistes et la datation des Sommes de Rufin et d'Ètienne de Tournai', BMCL 16 (1986) 55–70 at 68.

25. Josef Juncker, 'Summen und Glossen', ZRG Kan Abt. 14 (1925) 384–474 at 428–38.

26. Evidence in Weigand, Glossen zum Dekret Gratians part 2.3, glosses 23, 27, 31, 34, 37, 39, 40, 41, 42, 44, 45.

27. Rufinus of Bologna, Summa Decretorum, ed. H. Singer (Paderborn 1902; repr. Aalen 1963) 35–36 and 164, lines 4–17. Later on, other 'continuationes' from his Summa occasionally entered a manuscript of the Decretum, as on parts of D. 20–35 as in Brindisi, Bibl. pub. arcives A.I.

ly) to Bernard of Pavia. In addition, some excerpts from the *Summa* of Paucapalea appear here for the first time, such as his long gloss to D.11 c.5[28] and the gloss on the introduction in '*Ordinaturus Magister*'.[29] This composition was written at the beginning or middle of the 1160s, and yet it contains no Cardinalis glosses of any kind and may also be found in Munich 14024 and Prague, Národní Museum XVII. A. 12. A good example of the bringing together of earlier glosses is the gloss on D.5 c.4 s.v. *bonarum mentium*, where the two different solution glosses on the contrary passage in C.22 q.2 c.9 found in the 'First' and 'Second Gloss Compositions' are linked together. These glosses resurfaced many times in later gloss compositions.

The Fifth Gloss Composition

The 'Fifth Gloss Composition' is contained in the principal layer of glosses in Innsbruck 90, in the Malibu, Getty XIV 2, which previously was in the possession of Professor Ludwig, at Aachen, and in Douai 590. It also can be found in later layers of Berlin, Phillips 1742 and Biberach B 3515. The 'Fifth Composition' borrowed many glosses from the 'First Gloss Composition', none from the Second, and took most of its glosses from the Third and Fourth, though it revises glosses from these last two. The result of this is that only a few glosses can be securely attributed to the 'Fourth' or 'Fifth Gloss Compositions'.[30] Of the fifty-eight glosses of Rufinus printed in my *Glossenstudien* part 2.3, the two best manuscripts of this composition, Innsbruck and Malibu, have forty-seven of them verbatim and six more with different wording, so that only five of the fifty-eight Rufinus glosses are missing. Perhaps glosses were also occasionally taken in an abbreviated form from Rufinus' *Summa*.[31] Of the greatest significance, however, are the very numerous Cardinalis glosses marked with his siglum, which are scattered about from C.13 on, especially in C.16 and the sections on marriage law. Evidently, the compiler relied on the most up-to-date glosses for this section.

This composition should be dated to the second half of the 1160s. I am inclined to think that this work was written in France. Because no Cardi-

---

28. Printed in Weigand, *Glossen zum Dekret Gratians* part 1, no. 278; it corresponds to the last seven lines of his commentary on D.11; Schulte's edition 16.

29. Schulte edition 4, slightly modified. Previously, Schulte had printed them in *Glosse zum Decret Gratians* 20 and 40 from Trier, Stadtbibl. 906 and mistakenly attributed them to Johannes Faventinus.

30. This is true, for example, of the glosses in the discontinuous first layer of Toledo, Bibl. del Cabildo 4.5, at least those on C.27 q.2.

31. The three glosses printed in Weigand, *Glossen zum Dekret Gratians* part 2.5 indicate this.

nalis glosses on the first half of the *Decretum* are found in this Composition, though his glosses on this first part occur very frequently in other later compositions (even if not as plentifully as in the sections on marriage law here), one may surmise either that Cardinalis glossed the abovementioned sections first or that the compiler finished his work before Cardinalis' glosses on the first half of the *Decretum* became available to him.

The Sixth Gloss Composition

A compilation dating probably from the beginning of the 1170s can be regarded as the 'Sixth Gloss Composition'. The first glosses from Johannes Faventinus appear in this composition. Some of these glosses match those in Johannes' Summa and consequently were possibly either taken from it or constitute the beginning of his activity as a glossator (during the time he drafted his Summa).[32] This Composition can be found in the first layer of Douai 586, Munich 28175, and Montecassino 66, and in the second layer of Cambrai 646 as well as (partially) in Paris 14317 and Paris, Ste. Geneviève 341. Many Cardinalis glosses taken from earlier compositions appear in a different form in this Composition.

Compositions with b. Glosses

At the end of the 1170s many other gloss compositions emerge. I do not think that it is possible to assign numbers to them because they do not have enough coherence to give them specific names. They occupy a unique position and are probably better placed on the periphery of the main Bolognese tradition. This tradition can be found in the first gloss layers of Baltimore 777, Marburg 33, and Vercelli, Bibl. capit. XXV (118) (and in some glosses of Lilienfeld, Stiftsbibl. 223 and Paris, B.N. 3888 that otherwise contain different material). The composition represented by these three manuscripts is marked by many glosses of b. (Bernard) that are mostly very short and interlinear. They are combined with glosses of the 'First' and 'Second Gloss Compositions', as well as with the supplementary glosses of the 'Fourth Composition'.[33] The fact that none of the gloss-

---

32. At first, I linked the 'Sixth' and 'Seventh Gloss Composition' under the term 'Sphere of the Apparatus Ordinaturus Magister', which may still be seen at many points in my two-volume *Glossen zum Dekret Gratians*. Now, since the dissertation of my student Norbert Höhl, which appears in expanded form in *Die Glossen des Johannes Faventinus zur Pars I des Decretum Gratiani* (Forschungen zur Kirchenrechtswissenschaft; Würzburg 1987), the two compositions can be clearly differentiated.

33. On the glosses of Bernard see below. Evidence for the other statements in Weigand, *Glossen zum Dekret Gratians* part 2.6.

es of Rufinus, Cardinalis, or Johannes Faventinus was incorporated in this composition has given rise to incorrect interpretations of the b.-sigla.

The unusual tradition found in Cambridge, Sidney Sussex College 101 (first and second layer) and Durham, Cathedral Library C. IV. 1 (taken from the Cambridge manuscript) contains glosses from the first three gloss compositions as well as some by Bernard and others, though none by Cardinalis or Johannes Faventinus.

An Unusual Tradition in Bologna

The interlinear glosses in Arras 809 (472) on marriage law and the second layer in Berlin, Phillips. 1742, and Zwettl, Stiftsbibl. 31 constitute a unique Bolognese tradition that is characterized by the glosses of Simon of Bisignano. Zwettl also has a large number of Johannes Faventinus' glosses. As Juncker has already noted, Simon's glosses were probably written before his *Summa*. The Berlin and Zwettl manuscripts contain different traditions of Simon's glosses.[34]

New York, Morgan Library 446 and Trier, Bishöfliche Seminarbibl. 8 manuscripts share some common features in their gloss tradition, both of them having numerous glosses of Johannes Faventinus and of Stephen of Tournai. They also include the first glosses of Huguccio.[35]

French Gloss Compositions

Both of the gloss traditions discussed in this section should probably be dated somewhat earlier than those I have just dealt with, and they should attributed to the French school. The common stock of glosses in the first layers of Heiligenkreuz 44 and Paris 3895 and 14316 is characterized by p.-glosses and others.[36] Heiligenkreuz 44 and Paris 3895 also share many glosses from the 'First Gloss Composition', while Paris has many glosses from the 'Second Composition'.

A common stock of glosses can be found in London, B.L. Arundel 490, St. Florian III. 5, and Troyes 103. This set of glosses is characterized by glosses of Rufinus and, in particular, Stephen, along with additional anonymous glosses of unknown origin but probably French.[37]

---

34. Josef Juncker, 'Die Summa des Simon von Bisignano und seine Glossen', ZRG Kan. Abt. 15 (1926) 326–500.

35. Proof of this in Weigand, *Glossen zum Dekret Gratians* part 3.7, glosses 1, 2, 5, and, for Huguccio, in 2.9, glosses 20, 21, 24, 25, 53, 55, 56, 56a, 58 and 60.

36. See Weigand, *Glossen zum Dekret Gratians* part 2.11 and 2.4 below.

37. Evidence in Weigand, *Glossen zum Dekret Gratians* part 2.12.

A great many glosses from the Bolognese tradition can be found in London, Stowe 378 and Paris 3888.[38] These manuscripts have similar texts of the *Decretum* and also contain similar glosses of Johannes Faventinus and Cardinalis (especially in Paris on marriage law). These glosses were edited and enriched with new material.[39] Around 1186 in the vicinity of Paris, a gloss composition like that in Paris 3888 was used by the author of the *Summa Lipsiensis*.

The Seventh Gloss Composition

The 'Seventh Gloss Composition' was written around 1180 and is preserved in the first layers of Gniezno 28, Munich 28175, Naples XII. A. 5 (only to C. 19), Perugia, Bibl. com. C. M. 4, Salzburg, Stiftsbibl. St. Peters a. XII. 9, and Trier, Staatbibl. 906. It is in the mainstream of the Bolognese gloss tradition. It contains glosses from all of the preceding numbered compositions except the 'Fifth Gloss Composition', as well as additional, and possibly later, glosses from Johannes Faventinus, Petrus Hispanus, and, particularly, Bazianus, that are characteristic of this Composition.[40] The core material of this Composition antedates the *Apparatus 'Ordinaturus Magister'*, which will be described below. Moreover, *Apparatus 'Ordinaturus Magister'* dropped the sigla of the original text in the 'Seventh Gloss Composition'. In some manuscripts, the text was expanded in the 1180s with citations to decretals and with additional glosses from Bazianus.

Originally, I summarily described the 'Sixth' and 'Seventh Gloss Compositions' mentioned above as being part of the 'milieu' ('Umfeld') of the *Apparatus 'Ordinaturus Magister'*. A closer study of Johannes Faventinus' glosses and those of Bazianus permits the two compositions to be clearly distinguished.

The Gloss Apparatus 'Ordinaturus Magister'

The first recension of the gloss *Apparatus 'Ordinaturus Magister'* was composed around or shortly after 1180. Huguccio participated in its com-

---

38. See Rudolf Weigand, 'Burchardauszüge in Dekrethandschriften und ihre Verwendung bei Rufin und als Paleae im Dekret Gratians', AKKR 158 (1989) 429–451.

39. Evidence in Weigand, *Glossen zum Dekret Gratians* part 2.13, which mentions some relationships with Paris, B.N. 3905B and Lilienfeld, Stiftsbibl. 223; see also Höhl, *Glossen des Johannes Faventinus*.

40. See Weigand, *Glossen zum Dekret Gratians* part 2.8 and 9 and some of the glosses in the excursus; see also Höhl, *Glossen des Johannes Faventinus* and my article, 'Bazianus- und B.-Glossen zum Dekret Gratians', *Melanges Gérard Fransen* (SG 20; Rome 1976) 453–496, at 459–477.

position.⁴¹ The introductory gloss that gave its name to this apparatus was taken from the *Summa* of Paucapalea. This gloss can also be found in some manuscripts of the earlier gloss compositions and does not indicate a particular dependence on Paucapalea.⁴² The author of *Apparatus 'Ordinaturus Magister'* took glosses from all the earlier compositions and from many authors, both with and without sigla. He composed a large number of glosses for it as well.

The second recension of the *Apparatus 'Ordinaturus Magister'* was composed at the end of the 1180s. It cites a decretal of Urban III JL 15729 in a gloss on conditional marriage, without reference to a decretal collection.⁴³ The opinions of Huguccio are noted in numerous short glosses and are cited in the manuscripts with 'u.' or 'n', and once with 'mag. u. et nos omnes dicimus' (Master Huguccio told us).⁴⁴ The second recension of this apparatus seems to be linked particularly closely to Huguccio, although there is a passage on C.7 q.1 p. c.42 in which the students distanced themselves from the opinion of their master.⁴⁵

The following may be said about the relationship of the two recensions to the *Summa* of Huguccio:⁴⁶ Of the some 115 glosses of the first recension of the *Apparatus 'Ordinaturus Magister'* that I have studied, seventy-four are identical in many ways, even verbatim, to remarks in his *Summa*. Moreover, at least seven of these glosses (mainly in manuscripts of the 'Seventh Composition' or in Trier, Bishöfliche Sem. 8) were expressly ascribed to Huguccio. No parallels were found in Huguccio's *Summa* for thirty-six of these ascribed glosses. For a few of these glosses the relationship to Huguccio is uncertain. Of the some 120 supplementary glosses in the second recension, ninety-two of them have a clear relationship to Huguccio. Huguccio's sigla usually indicate that his opinion is reported by others. In twenty-four of these glosses, either no relationship with Huguccio can be detected or Huguccio expressly distances himself from the opinion given in them, while on one occasion the students dissociate themselves from the master's viewpoint. I cannot precisely determine the relationship of four other glosses.

41. See my article, 'Huguccio und der Glossenapparat "Ordinaturus Magister",' AKKR 154 (1985) 490–520, and the long excursus in Weigand, *Glossen zum Dekret Gratians* part 2.9.

42. In Kraków, Bibl. Jag. 357 and Vatican lat. 2494 with the "Fourth Gloss Composition', in Montecassino, Bibl. Abbazia 66 and Munich 28175 with the 'Sixth', and in Naples, B.N. XII. A. 5, Perugia, Bibl. com. C. M. 4, and Trier 906 with the 'Seventh Gloss Composition'.

43. Text in Weigand, *Glossen zum Dekret Gratians* part 2.9.182.

44. On C.27 q.1 c.41; text: ibid., 9.167.

45. On C.7 q.1 p.c.42; text: ibid., 9.107.

46. The following are the conclusions of the excursus in Weigand, *Glossen zum Dekret Gratians* part 2.9.

The result of this investigation is that one can say that the *Apparatus 'Ordinaturus Magister'* comes from the school of Huguccio. Yet we should also bear in mind that in his *Summa* Huguccio examines glosses from Cardinalis, Johannes Faventinus, and other authors that are not contained in *Apparatus 'Ordinaturus Magister'*. He took these glosses primarily from the 'Sixth' and 'Seventh Gloss Compositions'. Moreover, some of Huguccio's original glosses are contained only in the 'Seventh Gloss Composition' or in the *Apparatus 'Ordinaturus Magister'*. These findings illustrate the complexities involved in gloss transmission: we must never suppose that all glosses were entered from one manuscript or work; rather, texts from the most varied sources flowed together into the manuscripts or compositions being done at the time.

Erlangen, Universitätsbibl. 342 should head the list of manuscripts of the first recension of *'Ordinaturus Magister'*, since this apparatus was written by several hands as the principal layer and is without erasures.[47] Next comes Graz III 80, which contains the apparatus in its first main layer of glosses.[48] In addition to our apparatus, some glosses from the 'Sixth' and 'Seventh Compositions' are found in the first layer of Madrid, B.N. 251, because these glosses had been written into the margins of the manuscript before *Apparatus 'Ordinaturus Magister'*. This recension is completely preserved in the first layer of Bratislava, Státny Archív C.14, except for a few erasures, and also in Lilienfeld, Stiftsbibl. 222.[49] The apparatus is partially missing at the beginning and at the end of Vatican Ross. 595. It comprises the first layer of glosses with some erasures in Bamberg, Staatsbibl. Can. 13.[50] Perhaps fifteen percent of the glosses are absent from Prague, Metro. Kap. I.19; and more than half of its glosses were entered as a third layer in Reims, Bibl. mun. 676; our apparatus appears as the second layer in Montecassino 66, although there were extensive erasures to make room for the Ordinary Gloss. It appears as a third layer in Cambrai, Bibl. mun. 646 with, again, large-scale erasures; moreover, some glosses were expanded considerably. The first principal layer of glosses in Hereford, Cathedral Library P.VII.3 also contains the apparatus.[51] It is complete from C.27 on in

---

47. An earlier layer, not found in many folios, has only a few 'allegationes' and short glosses.

48. On fol. 49–56, and occasionally elsewhere, other, odd glosses had previously been entered; later, 'continuationes' of Laurentius from an intermediate layer were entered at certain 'causae', followed by the *Glossa ordinaria* (without erasures of the earlier layers).

49. Almost completely erased up to D.50 and at C.2 and 3 for the *Glossa ordinaria*.

50. Glosses of the 'Seventh Composition' were entered first, particularly at the beginning, followed by some excerpts from the *Glossa Palatina*.

51. At C.23 and 24 one layer precedes; other glosses (from f. C. among others) were entered before the *Glossa ordinaria*.

Naples XII. A. 5, while from D.1 to C.19 some of its glosses (forming a layer of their own) supplement the 'Seventh Gloss Composition'. It is interspersed with other material, especially the 'distinctiones' of Richardus, in Paris, Ste. Geneviève 342 and exists only as a greatly damaged third layer of glosses in Rome, Bibl. Angelica 1270. The first recension of *Apparatus 'Ordinaturus Magister'* probably existed completely in Florence, Laur. Edil. 96, Kremsmünster, Stiftsbibl. 364, and Paris 15393 (each in the first layer of glosses), as well as in London Add. 24658 (second layer) and Vatican Pal. lat. 625 (second layer); in each manuscript the layer was almost completely erased.

The glosses of 'argumenta' (and 'allegationes') in our apparatus are mainly extant in Florence, Laur. S. Croce IV sin 1. (first layer), Kraków, Bibl. Jag. 357 (second layer), and Leipzig, Universitätsbibl. Haenel 18 (first layer), while many additional glosses from our apparatus and other material were supplemented in Leipzig's second layer. Our apparatus was entered quite unevenly into Munich 28174 (first layer) and Paris Mazarine 1287 (first layer), sometimes almost completely, at other times not at all. The 'allegationes' are mainly found in Milan, Arch. San Ambrogio M. 57 and Vendome, Bibl. mun. 88 (first layer). Some glosses from our apparatus were supplemented in the second layer of Gniezno, Bibl. Kapit. 28 (at the beginning). Only a few, not easily found, glosses from our apparatus are in Arras, Bibl. mun. 592 (500, second layer), Graz, Universitätsbibl. III 71 (third layer), and Paris, Arsenal 677 (third layer). The apparatus is in Vatican Pal. 622 until C. 27.[52]

No single manuscript of the second recension of the *Apparatus 'Ordinaturus Magister'* remains complete. In Munich 10244 the apparatus is complete as a single layer as far as *de cons.* D.2 c.2 , but it is not in *De poenitentia*. The apparatus of the second recension was largely erased in Munich 27337 (first layer), but the manuscript also has glosses of the first recension. And in Bernkastel–Kues, Hospital 223 (first layer) about a fourth of the glosses are missing due to erasures. Long glosses, perhaps a fifth of them, which should have been entered in the last stage of copying, are missing from Jena, Universitätsbibl. El. fol. 56. In Wolfenbüttel, Landesbibl. Helmst. 33,

---

52. It cannot now be known whether any glosses of this apparatus were in the third gloss layer of Bamberg, Staatsbibl. Can. 15, since almost everything in it was scratched out. No clear relationship to our apparatus is given by the fragments of the earlier glosses in Melk, Stiftsbibl. 261. A few of this apparatus' glosses were, however, entered in Vatican Chis. E. VII. 206 (second layer) and Vat. lat. 2494 (second layer, only up to D.21). Some glosses are also available in Munich 28175 and Trier, Bishöfliche Seminar 8, though this probably derives from the 'workshop' of the apparatus *Ordinaturus Magister*, as is the case with various glosses of Huguccio's.

the apparatus is complete in the principal layer only from C.27 on; before this point, especially from C.1, the manuscript preserves many of the apparatus' glosses mixed with glosses from the 'Seventh Gloss Composition'. Toledo 4.5 begins with C.15 and has *Apparatus 'Ordinaturus Magister'* in the principal layer of glosses, including some from the first recension. Naples, B.N. XII. A. 9 certainly had it in its entirety in its first layer, though only about a fifth of this is extant. Oxford, Bodl. Libr. Lyell 41 had it in its first layer, but this was almost entirely erased to make way for the *Glossa ordinaria*.[53]

An Anglo-Norman Gloss Composition

An 'Anglo-Norman Gloss Composition', which is complete in Antwerp, Museum Plantin M.13 (first principal layer) and Durham, Cathedral Library C.I.7 and C.II.1, and greatly damaged by trimming of the margins in Oxford, New College 210, first layer, should be dated to approximately 1190.[54] It integrates some glosses of the Bolognese tradition, particularly in Durham C.II.1. Here, incidentally, some glosses are attributed to Johannes Faventinus that do not carry his siglum anywhere else. The glosses of the Anglo-Norman school are richly preserved in Cambridge, Gonville and Caius Coll. 676, where the teaching of contemporary Anglo-Norman schoolmen, especially that of John of Tynemouth and Simon of Southwell, is extensively documented. In Paris 3905 B many glosses from Bologna (partly related to Trier 906 and to the 'Seventh Gloss Composition') were combined with the glosses of a French master with the siglum Tv.

Glosses by Individual Authors: Paucapalea

It has already been said above that some of the glosses of the 'First Gloss Composition' were taken from the *Summa* of Paucapalea and probably came from him. Of seventy-two glosses that I have compared,[55] five have a relationship with his *Summa*, and of these, two are simply citations from Roman law. From the gloss to D.5 c.4 as well as from a gloss to D.17 c.1,[56] one can conclude that the wording of the gloss likely predates the *Summa*, since an additional possible explanation appears only in the latter. Some glosses in other early manuscripts, for example in Bremen, Univer-

---

53. Bamberg, Can. 14 has only a very few glosses from our apparatus in its second layer (at the beginning), and these can only be identified by comparison with other manuscripts.
54. For further information with evidence see Weigand, *Glossen zum Dekret Gratians* part 2.14.
55. Evidence in Weigand, *Glossen zum Dekret Gratians* part 2.1.
56. In Paucapalea, *Summa* 147, n. 9a.

sitätsbibl. a. 142 and Paris 14605,[57] were obviously copied out of his *Summa*. More numerous are the excerpts from his *Summa* in Ivrea, Bibl. Capit. 72 (C) and in Cambridge, Corpus Christi Coll. 10, where in particular his 'continuationes' and 'historiae,' which enjoyed an ever-growing popularity, were taken into the text. The incorporation of some of Paucapalea's texts into the 'Fourth' and 'Fifth Gloss Compositions' has already been pointed out above.

Guibert of Bornado

Guibert of Bornado, who came from Brescia, can be traced from documentary evidence in Brescia and at the imperial court between 1156 and 1180. He probably began his career as a civilian. About thirty of his glosses to the *Decretum* are preserved, principally in Bremen a. 142, Paris 14605, and in Mainz, Stadtbibl. II 204; these glosses have the following form: at a given passage a text from Roman law along with a reference to its source is given; this practice is quite similar to that of the 'Second Gloss Composition'.[58]

Rolandus

Master Rolandus has long been known from his *Summa* of the *Decretum*. He is not, however, the later Pope Alexander III.[59] Although his gloss was not copied often, I was able to establish four different traditions, each of which has almost nothing in common with the others:[60] The manuscript St. Florian III 5 has at least twenty-two glosses in which Master Rolandus is quoted, either with the siglum Ro. or R., or anonymously. The siglum R., however, usually stands for Rufinus in this manuscript. Kuttner had already pointed out the glosses labeled 'r' in the manuscript Vatican, lat. 3529 should probably be assigned to Rolandus,[61] and I have identified at least thirty of his glosses that appear in this manuscript.[62]

Without making any claim to completeness, I have printed two dozen more of Rolandus' glosses, from the manuscripts Heiligenkreuz 44 and

57. Ibid. 147–149.
58. See Weigand, 'Romanisierungstendenzen' 201–209.
59. After J.T. Noonan put forth this thesis in 1977, I was able to prove it: 'Magister Rolandus und Papst Alexander III.', AKKR 149 (1980) 3–44, also in *Diritto, persona e vita sociale: Scritti in memoria di Orio Giacchi* (Milan 1984) 1.178–213.
60. Rudolf Weigand, 'Glossen des Magister Rolandus zum Dekret Gratians', *Miscellanea Rolando Bandinelli Papa Alessandro III: Studi raccolti da Filippo Liotta*, ed. F. Liotta and R. Tofanini (Siena 1986) 389–423.
61. Kuttner, *Repertorium* 55–57
62. Weigand, 'Glossen des Magister Rolandus' n. 38–52, 55–57, 63–75.

Paris 14316. Anonymous entries in Heiligenkreuz 44 occasionally go back to Rolandus as well.[63] In eight manuscripts I have found a gloss to D.16 c.10 that should be assigned to this Rolandus; included among the eight is Luxemburg, B.N. I 139, where at least two anonymous glosses come from Rolandus.[64] Around 1180 a Ro. gloss to D.20 c.1 is mentioned only in the 'Seventh Gloss Composition', and his opinion on 'compaternitas' (C.30 q.4) is mentioned in the *Apparatus 'Ordinaturus Magister'*, which is similar to what occurs in the *Summa Coloniensis* and in the glosses and works of the Anglo-Norman school.

An Early Master P(etrus)

In the manuscripts Heiligenkreuz 44, Paris 3895, and 14316, the siglum p. occurs several times in the same layer as the glosses of R(olandus), occasionally even as an alternative to R. From these manuscripts I have documented around eighty glosses, mainly to D.1–30, that carry the siglum p.;[65] for chronological reasons these cannot be attributed to Paucapalea, nor can they be assigned to the later Petrus Hispanus. Whoever is hiding behind these sigla must for the moment remain unknown. He is probably identical with the P(etrus) who in 1159 appended his signature after Rolandus' and before Gundulphus' to a request sent to the emperor Barbarossa.[66] He could be Petrus Blesensis, who wrote his "Speculum" around 1180. Another canidate might be the 'p.' who is cited four times in the *Summa Parisiensis*, but I could find no gloss that matched his opinions in the manuscripts. However, the glosses marked 'p.' in Pommersfelden, Schlossbibl. Schönborn 142 probably belong to a different author. In any case, I have so far been unable to find any direct link to the other p. glosses.

Rufinus

Rufinus' glosses are some of the most frequently transmitted glosses and are mostly anonymous. As was said above, they are in the main identical with the 'Third Gloss Composition'. Somewhat later, additional texts were probably excerpted from his *Summa* for the 'Fifth Gloss Composition'; even later, excerpts from his *Summa* were occasionally inserted into other manuscripts, for example, in Vercelli XXV (118).

---

63. Weigand, 'Glossen des Magister Rolandus' n. 76–99; gloss 81 even appears in Heiligenkreuz with the siglum 'roll.' (n. 100 is incorrect). Six of these glosses are also in Paris, B.N. 3895.
64. Weigand, 'Magister Rolandus und Pabst Alexander' 30 and 22–25.
65. Weigand, *Glossen zum Dekret Gratians* part 3.4.
66. See Weigand, 'Magister Rolandus und Pabst Alexander' 6 with n. 17.

A singular tradition of Rufinus' glosses (mainly to the first part of the *Decretum*), is found in London, B.L. Arundel 490 and St. Florian III.5, and still needs to be more closely investigated. They may be special lectures given by Rufinus.

So far I have been unable to assign a few R. glosses in Marburg 33 and Oxford, Bodleian Douce 218 to either Rolandus or Rufinus.[67]

Stephen of Tournai

A comparison with Stephen's *Summa* shows that some anonymously transmitted glosses probably come from him. It is an open question for me whether these glosses were taken from his *Summa* or are the result of his activity as a glossator. His early glosses are found in Munich, Staatsbibl. lat. 23551, on the first 'distinctiones' of the *Decretum*, and also in London, B.L. Arundel 490 and St. Florian III.5 . The siglum s., and even ss., are found for him in St. Florian. The same sigla can be found in Vatican lat. 3529 and Vercelli, Bibl. cap. XXV (118).[68]

Stephen may have played a decisive role in the dissemination of the 'Second Gloss Composition' discussed above, because a large part of this Composition's tradition comes to us through French manuscripts, and Stephen must be regarded as the founder of the French school. Moreover, at least four of this Composition's glosses in three different manuscripts are attributed to him by means of the siglum s.[69] Finally, we have a gloss preserved only in Florence, Bibl. Marucelliana A.298, a gloss that provides a solution to the contradiction between the palea C.27 q.2 c.8, added here by the glossator's hand, and C.28 q.1 c.16, cited in the gloss with the notation: 's allegatio'. This gloss has an opinion very close to the one that Stephen had given in his *Summa*.[70] It is possible that Stephen's gloss was written near the end of his career at Bologna, around 1160.

Stephen's glosses that were copied with the siglum St(e). were first written by him in the period 1175–80; in general, they have almost no parallels in his *Summa*, and they also cite papal decretals. The greatest number of these glosses appear in New York, Morgan Library 446 and Trier, Bishöfliche Seminar 6:61.8, as well as in the 'Seventh Gloss Composition'

---

67. See Weigand, *Glossen zum Dekret Gratians* part 3.6. Since glosses of Bernard of Pavia are also found in these manuscripts, one may wonder whether these glosses belong to a master of the 1170s.

68. Some references in my 'Studien zum kanonistischen Werk Stephans v. Tournai', ZRG Kan. Abt. 72 (1986) 353.

69. Weigand, 'Romanizierungstendenzen' 236–265 and 248.

70. See gloss 151 in Weigand, 'Romanizierungstendenzen' 243, with the explanation on p. 247–248.

and the *Apparatus 'Ordinandus Magister'*.⁷¹ One may conclude from this evidence that his relationship to Bologna was always very good.

Cardinalis: Raimundus de Arenis (Raymond des Arènes)

The identity of glosses with the siglum C(ar). has been debated for a long time. André Gouron has proposed a solution that I find convincing: Raimundus de Arenis.⁷² I had made another suggestion in 1973, but now think that Raimundus is more likely.⁷³ His glosses are apparently the first nearly always to be copied with his siglum C(ar.). They were consistently copied with the C(ardinalis) siglum from the time of the 'Fifth Gloss Composition'. He commented most fully on C.16 and on marriage law.⁷⁴

The manuscripts Trier, Seminar 8; Gniezno 28; Innsbruck 90; and Malibu, Getty Ludwig XIV 2 are the best suited for research into his glosses. Paris 3888; Montecassino 66; Biberach B 3515; Douai 586 and 590; Munich 28175; and Vatican lat. 2495 also provide evidence of his work in their margins.

Gandulphus

As I indicated earlier, Gandulphus' glosses and teaching have come down to us in varied forms. They are contained in anonymous glosses in Bologna and the 'Anglo-Norman Gloss Composition'.⁷⁵ The manuscripts in New York 446, Verona CLXXXIV (164), and Brindisi, Bibl. pub. arcives. A.1 also provide evidence of his work. Munich 28175 best transmits his glosses as they were known in Bologna. The manuscripts of the 'Seventh Gloss Composition' and, somewhat less frequently, the *Apparatus 'Ordinaturus Magister'* also contain his glosses. Cambrai, Bibl. mun. 646, which has comparatively fewer of Gandulphus' glosses in its first layer, may be an early recension of his work. A greater part of Gandulphus' glosses probably were notes taken from his lectures, because his siglum is appended to

---

71. References in Weigand, 'Studien zum Kanonistichen Werk' and in my *Glossen zum Dekret Gratians* part 3.7 with thirty-seven more of Stephanus' glosses.

72. André Gouron, 'Le Cardinal Raymond des Arènes: Cardinalis?', RDC 28 (1978) 180–192 and further evidence in 'Sur les gloses siglées d et p dans les manuscrits du XIIe siècle', RIDC 8 (1997) 21–34.

73. Rudolf Weigand, 'Die Glossen des Cardinalis (Magister Hubald?) zum Dekret Gratians, besonders zu C.27 q.2', BMCL 3 (1973) 73–95.

74. Rudolf Weigand, 'Die Glossen des Cardinalis—Raimundus de (H)arenis—zu C. 16', *Recht im Dienste des Menschen: Eine Festgabe für Hugo Schwendenwein zum 60. Geburtstag* (Graz 1986) 267–293, and *Glossen zum Dekret Gratians* part 3.8.

75. Rudolf Weigand, 'Gandulphusglossen zum Dekret Gratians', BMCL 7 (1977) 15–48, compare especially 29–38 with 23–29; also Weigand, *Glossen zum Dekret Gratians* part 3.9.

the end of these glosses less often than his contemporaries have their sigla at the end of their glosses; his glosses in the Bolognese tradition often just summarize his opinion, which is the same methodology that we find with many authors in the Anglo-Norman school.[76]

Johannes Faventinus

The glosses of Johannes Faventinus, later the bishop of Faenza (1177–90),[77] appear frequently in the Bolognese tradition from the 'Sixth Gloss Composition' on. This Compostion contains a large number of his glosses that are identical with those in his *Summa*.[78] Approximately 350 glosses on Part One of the *Decretum* (D.1–101) are attributed to him; Munich 28175 offers 171. Gniezno 28 and Montecassino 66 contain 127; Paris 14317 has 126; Naples XII.A.5 has 113; Trier, Seminar 8 has 111; and Paris 3888 has 101 of his glosses. The *Apparatus 'Ordinaturus Magister'* offers a little over forty glosses with his siglum to Part One of the *Decretum*. There may be a few more of his glosses that entered the text anonymously. Vatican lat. 2495 has by far and away the most Jo. sigla on C.1, forty-three. In contrast there are fifteen in both Munich 28175 and Gniezno 28.[79]

Bernard of Pavia

Bernard's glosses to the *Decretum* are mostly short interlinear glosses, best preserved in Marburg 33.[80] It is likely that they originate in the 1170s. Some long glosses that are attributed to him in several manuscripts actually come from earlier authors, since they are already present in the 'Fourth Gloss Composition'.[81] Many of his genuine glosses were also preserved in Kraków 356, somewhat fewer in Vercelli XXV (118) and Baltimore 777, where they appear together with glosses of the 'First' and 'Second Gloss Compositions'.[82] Around a dozen of his glosses to C.28 q.1 are preserved in Cologne, Dombibl. 129, some with his siglum. In other manuscripts it is

---

76. In Munich 28175 a section from his Sentences is quite uncommonly cited at C.33 q.2, see Johannes von Walter, *Magistri Gandulphi Bononiensis Sententiarum libri quatuor* (Vienna 1924) 307; another section from the same work is given to D.23 c.2 in Munich, Staatsbibl. 27337 cf. Walter, op. cit. 354–356.

77. See Norbert Höhl, 'Neue Erkenntnisse zu Leben und Werk des Glossators Johannes Faventinus', *Proceedings San Diego* and the literature cited there.

78. The following comments are based upon the dissertation of Höhl, *Glossen des Johannes Faventinus*. See also *Weigand, Glossen zum Dekret Gratians* part 3.10.

79. See my article, 'Die Glossen des Johannes Faventinus zur Causa I des Dekrets und ihr Vorkommen in späteren Glossenapparaten', AKKR 157 (1988) 73–107.

80. See my 'Bazianus- und B.-Glossen' 477–490.

81. References, also for what follows, in Weigand, *Glossen zum Dekret Gratians* part 3.11.

82. My statements in 'Bazianus- und B.-Glossen' 495 must be modified by this, as must

not always easy to distinguish his glosses from those of Bazianus as these are also marked with only a 'b'. Bernard of Pavia is referred to by b. in the *Summa Lipsiensis*, even if the author has made a mistake in one or two cases. Yet another, so far unknown, B(ernard) is found in Pommersfelden 142.[83]

Simon of Bisignano

With the aid of Berlin, Staatsbibl. Phillips 1742, Juncker had thoroughly examined Simon's glosses in this manuscipt and their relationship to his *Summa*. In general he dated these glosses earlier than his *Summa*.[84] The additional glosses of Simon preserved in Zwettl 31 often have no parallel in his *Summa*. We cannot know whether these were composed later. Many of his glosses are also preserved in New York 446 and in Trier Sem. 8 (particularly on the last causae); these two manuscripts seem to have been made from different originals. Some of his glosses are also in Bamberg Can. 13 (in the beginning of the manuscript), Trier 906, Laon, Bibl. mun. 476, and Marburg 33 (second layer, up to D. 50). That none of his glosses that I have checked entered the *Apparatus 'Ordinaturus Magister'* points to his having been somewhat of an outsider at Bologna. His glosses to the 'causae haereticorum' are especially numerous in Rome, Angelica 1270. Simon's glosses in Brindisi A.1 consist of excerpts from his *Summa*, which have almost nothing in common with his other glosses.

Petrus Hispanus

Petrus' glosses were preserved mainly in the 'Seventh Gloss Composition'[85] as well as in Vatican lat. 2495 and New York 446, which do not belong directly to this composition. Some of his glosses were also incorporated into the *Apparatus 'Ordinandus Magister'*, where he is cited at least

---

the earlier origin, still unidentified on page 448, of some long glosses carrying his siglum. Could Bernard have based his 'lectures' on a manuscript containing the then recently created glosses of the 'Fourth Gloss Composition' and incorporated them?

83. Weigand, 'Bazianus und B.-Glossen' 490–495, also Weigand, *Glossen zum Dekret Gratians* part 3.12.

84. See Juncker, 'Die Summa des Simon von Bisignano'; see also Weigand, *Glossen zum Dekret Gratians* part 3.13.

85. References in Weigand, *Glossen zum Dekret Gratians* part 3.14. Schulte printed a number of his glosses in *Glosse zum Decret Gratians* 64–65; Franz Gillmann printed many more glosses from Bamberg, Staatsbibl. Can. 13 in 'Die Entstehungszeit der Glossa ordinaria zum Gratianischen Dekret', *Zur Lehre der Scholastik vom Spender der Firmung und des Weihesakraments* (Paderborn 1920) 185–187. On the identity of the decretist with the commentator of the Compilatio I, see Kuttner, *Repertorium* and Alfons M. Stickler, 'Decritisti bolognesi dimenticati', SG 3 (1955) 389–391.

once as 'p. ysp.'[86] This makes it possible to posit that another magister 'p.' was known around 1180 or even earlier.

Bazianus

Contrary to the thesis put forward by A. Belloni,[87] Bazianus should not be identified as the Roman law jurist Johannes Bassianus, because the siglum for the latter is always Jo.b., Jo.cre., or something similar, while our canonist is always cited with Bar., Ba., or just with b., depending upon the manuscript and context.[88] His glosses cover the whole *Decretum*.[89] They are found above all in the 'Seventh Gloss Composition', where they were a distinguishing feature.[90] Several of his glosses came into the *Apparatus 'Ordinaturus Magister'*, sometimes with his full siglum Bar., but other times without any siglum at all.

Albertus (de Mora)

Albertus became Pope Gregory VIII (1187). He was cited in the 1180s and by his papal title in Huguccio and in the second recension of the *Apparatus 'Ordinaturus Magister'*.[91] He is also cited as Al(bert<in>us) in the Anglo-Norman school and elsewhere.[92] Whether the siglum 'al.' in Vercelli XXV (118) refers to him or to the Roman law jurist Albericus, whom it occasionally mentions in an appropriate context, cannot be known for certain.

Melendus

Melendus worked from ca. 1180 to 1210 as a canonist in Italy.[93] From 1210 to 1225 he was bishop of Osma. References to him in Johannes Teu-

---

86. This gloss to C.11 q.3 c.36 occurs in both recensions and is printed in Weigand, *Glossen zum Dekret Gratians* part 2.9.130.
87. Annalisa Belloni, 'Baziano, cioè Giovanni Bassiano, legista e canonista del secolo XII', TRG 57 (1989) 69–85. On the earlier state of research see Filippo Liotta, 'Baziano' DBI 7 (Rome 1965) 313–315. See also Diplovatatius on Bazianus in SG 10 (1968) 56, on Johannes Bassianus ibid. 59.
88. Evidence for this in Weigand, *Glossen zum Dekret Gratians* part 2.9.70, 93, 122, 161, as distinguished from glosses 38, 100, 104, 105, 170, 237.
89. I have documented sixty-one glosses from three sections of the *Decretum* showing different forms of his siglum; see Weigand, 'Bazianus- und B.-Glossen', and the literature cited there.
90. See Weigand, *Glossen zum Dekret Gratians* part 3.15 and 2.8.
91. Evidence in Ibid. part 3.16 with references; also part 2.9.143.
92. See Stephan Kuttner and Eleanor Rathbone, 'Anglo-Norman Canonists of the Twelfth Century', *Traditio* 9 (1949–51) 321, 335, and 351–353.
93. Evidence in Stephan Kuttner, 'Bernardus Compostellanus antiquus', *Traditio* 1 (1943) 277–340 at 301–303.

tonicus' *Glossa ordinaria* to the *Decretum* were taken in part from Laurentius, who cited Melendus' teaching from his acquaintance with him. Melendus wrote glosses at least as early as ca. 1180, since a gloss to D.11 c.2 was copied with the sylgum 'm.' into the first recension of the *Apparatus 'Ordinaturus Magister'*.[94] The most reliable transmission of his glosses to the *Decretum* are in Gniezno 28, first layer, probably in a supplementary hand, where among other things he treats a gloss of Johannes Faventinus to D.82 c.2.[95] Gniezno 28 has at least twenty glosses with his siglum in C.11 q.3. I could not find any glosses in Gniezno 28 that concur with those opinions that Johannes Teutonicus included in his *Glossa ordinaria*. Vincentius referred to him repeatedly in his commentaries to the *Compilationes antiquae*.[96]

Huguccio

Huguccio's glosses with the siglum u(g). or a similar one are found frequently in the 'Seventh Gloss Composition' and in the *Apparatus 'Ordinaturus Magister'*.[97] Since they do not appear earlier, Huguccio's glosses were probably written for the *Apparatus 'Ordinaturus Magister'*. Only half of these glosses that I have examined have a relationship to his comments in his great *Summa*.[98] Glosses from his *Summa*, however, often appear in later gloss layers, with or without his siglum.[99] That happened many times in the fourteenth century with the *Rosarium* of Guido of Baysio,[100] who, being deliberate in his work, wanted to supplement the *Glossa ordinaria* with citations from Huguccio, Laurentius, and other authors. It must, however, be stressed that Huguccio's sigla in the *Glossa ordinaria* are not reliable, since they might derive from Laurentius' mistaken belief that the entire *Apparatus 'Ordinaturus Magister'* came from Huguccio; for this reason (as was shown for Johannes Faventinus) he appended Huguccio's siglum to earlier glosses that had no relation to Huguccio or his *Summa*.

---

94. Printed in Weigand, *Glossen zum Dekret Gratians* part 1, no. 66a.
95. Printed with additional examples in ibid. part 3.17.
96. See Rudolf Weigand, *Die bedingte Eheschließung im kanonischen Recht* 1 (Münchener Theologische Studien 3.16; Munich 1963) 283–286.
97. Documentation in Weigand, *Glossen zum Dekret Gratians* part 2.9.
98. For evidence see ibid. part 3.18.
99. Large parts, for example, in Madrid, B.N. 251 (C. 2), third layer, and Fund. Lázaro Galdiano 440, fourth and fifth layer.
100. So in Prague XVII A 12 according to Kuttner, 'Bernardus Compostellanus' 289, n. 56; in contrast, Franz Gillman, 'Der Prager Codex XVII A 12 (früher I B I) und der Dekretapparat des Laurentius Hispanus', AKKR 126 (1953–1954) 3–43, also in SG 7 (1959) 393–445.

David of London

Some glosses in Cambridge, Sidn. Suss. Coll. 101 marked with the name David surely come from David of London, as do two glosses, one to D. 44 pr. and the other to D.45 c.4, with the siglum ddl. in New York 446, and possibly one other with just the siglum d.[101] It is possible that this siglum, which I have found appended to sixteen more glosses in different manuscripts (Madrid, Fund. Lázaro Galdiano 440 gives five d. sigla in its second layer), refers in each case to the same master. Because, however, he studied in Bologna before 1170 this attribution is not certain. A master Daifer, who is cited in some works of the French school, may also be a possible author for one or another of the glosses marked d.[102]

Other Glossators of This Period

I have found thirty glosses marked with the siglum W., chiefly in Munich 28175, but also in New York 446, Munich 14024, and Autun 80a.[103] They might be to be attributed to a master William. One of the Munich glosses has the siglum G. For chronological reasons he cannot be identified with Willielmus Vasco, attested as a professor at Padua after 1226, since a teaching career of some fifty years can hardly be assumed.

Whoever lurks behind the mysterious siglum '4', found in the glosses in Munich 28175 on marriage law,[104] will perhaps forever remain unknown. Possibly a master Cyprian, perhaps even the Roman law jurist, is behind the siglum 'Cy.' that occurs in a few places in Vatican lat. 2495 and Arras 592 (500), but this cannot at all be clearly determined from the seven glosses bearing this siglum that I have so far found.[105]

Fidantia

The few glosses in the *'Apparatus Ordinaturus Magister'* that carry an f.-siglum[106] probably come from the master Fidantia who was a canon in Ci-

---

101. Printed in Weigand, *Glossen zum Dekret Gratians* part 3.19; see also evidence for the following. On the man, see Kuttner and Rathbone, 'Anglo-Norman Canonists' 286.

102. In Arras 271 fol. 187ra his opinion is juxtaposed with David's.

103. Printed in my article, 'W.-Glossen zum Dekret Gratians', *Ministerium iustitiae: Festschrift für Heribert Heinemann* (Essen 1985) 151–159; also Weigand, *Glossen zum Dekret Gratians* part 3.21.

104. These are glosses 957, 1018, 1110, 1161, 1203, 1210, and 1242 on C.27 q.2 in Weigand, *Glossen zum Dekret Gratians*; none exists on C.30 q.4.

105. Printed in ibid. part 3.20.

106. The instances mentioned by Schulte in *Glosse zum Decret Gratians* 13 are only partially right, and to be sure, erroneously attributed to (Joh.) Faventinus.

vita Castellana and to whom the decretal JL 13854 of 21 December 1176 was addressed.[107] The glosses in the later layers of Hereford P.VII.3 and Reims 676 with the siglum f. probably originate with him as well. It must be noted that there is no direct influence of any of these last-named authors on the *Glossa ordinaria*.

From Gloss Apparatus to the Glossa ordinaria

Slowly individual glosses on individual chapters evolved into concatenations of glosses that treated the legal issues in sections of the *Decretum*.

Alanus

The two recensions of his great gloss apparatus were composed about 1192 and 1202 (or 1205), as Stickler has shown.[108] Stickler had previously investigated whether glosses can be traced to Alanus prior to his apparatus and what the relationship of his apparatus was to the preceding tradition of glosses and to the *Glossa ordinaria*.

In three manuscripts of the second recension of the *Apparatus 'Ordinaturus Magister'*, a reference to Alanus' opinion occurs at C.12 q.2 c.65.[109] A gloss to C.18 q.2 c.26 with the siglum 'a.' that is found in Munich 10244 could originate with Alanus, but I have not found it in any other manuscript.[110] Some early glosses of Alanus (or perhaps excerpts from his apparatus) could be in the so-far-unnoticed first layer of glosses in Vienna, Ö.N.B. 2070, since at least two of these glosses to C.27 q.2 substantially match those in his apparatus.[111] The first of these is also preserved in the

---

107. I have reproduced ten of his glosses in *Glossen zum Dekret Gratians* part 3.23. On Fidantia himself, see Stephan Kuttner, 'Bernardus Compostellanus antiquus' 281, n. 16 with his Retractiones in *Gratian and the Schools of Law* (London 1983) 10.

108. Alfons M. Stickler, 'Alanus Anglicus als Verteidiger des monarchischen Papsttums', *Salesianum* 21 (1959) 346–406. I would not attribute two short glosses to D.93 c.23, mentioned by Stickler on 373, n. 29 and 376 of the above article, that bear the siglum 'sec. la.', to Laurentius. This is because Laurentius could hardly have been a glossator before 1192, but rather began his work after 1200. Indeed, in Laurentius the two glosses to the above passage read as follows:'v. patri: . . . uel potest intelligi mistice de diabolo et concupiscentia carnis et eius motibus ut in glosis hic depictis' (Vat. Pal. lat. 658 fol. 22rb). Laurentius is obviously referring to the *Apparatus 'Ordinaturus Magister'*, which he often used at other times as well, since the glosses there read: v. *patri*: idest diabolo; v. *matri*: carnali concupiscentie; v. *filios suos*: idest motus illicitos: Erlangen, Universitäts bibl. 342 and Madrid, B.N. 251. These glosses offer an allegorical, or as Laurentius puts it, 'mystical', explanation of words that Alanus evidently took from the same source and characterized as allegorical interpretation (sec. allegoriam). By an accidental transposition of the letters 'al.' to a siglum 'la.' these glosses were altered.

109. Evidence for this and the following in Weigand, *Glossen zum Dekret Gratians* part 3.24.

110. Printed by Schulte in *Glosse zum Decret Gratians* 51.

111. These are glosses 780b and 1289 in Weigand, *Glossen zum Dekret Gratians* part 1.

last layer of Madrid, Fund. Lázaro Galdiano 440, where his glosses and Huguccio's were also entered. 'Continuationes' from the second recension of his apparatus were in part (from C.12) entered into Lilienfeld 222 between the *Apparatus 'Ordinaturus Magister'* and the *Glossa ordinaria*.[112] Alanus drew on various sources. Huguccio's *Summa* is almost certainly the point of departure for some passages that are reminiscent of the *Apparatus 'Ordinaturus Magister'*, especially when the author explicitly says so on several occasions (for example at D.11 and 12). Because I have found no texts at C.27 q.2 and C.30 q.4, it is rather doubtful that Alanus took the glosses directly from Huguccio. It is more certain that at C.1 q.3 c.4 he integrated several of the Cardinalis' glosses into his work; these glosses were transmitted in the 'Seventh Gloss Composition' and also, all except one, in the *Apparatus 'Ordinaturus Magister'*. At this same passage I have found a gloss in layer three of Paris 3888 that matches the second recension of Alanus' apparatus. The same holds for a short gloss in Paris 3885 to D.12 c.1. His apparatus was not used for the *Glossa ordinaria*, though perhaps Laurentius drew upon Alanus occasionally.[113]

Bernardus Compostellanus antiquus

This canonist, who was already little known in the fourteenth century, wrote several works in the first decade of the thirteenth century, among them the glosses to Gratian's *Decretum* that Kuttner first brought to light from citations of the *Glossa palatina*.[114] I was able to identify what was probably his complete gloss apparatus to the *Decretum* in the last layer of Gniezno 28.[115] Excerpts from this or later glosses are in Vatican lat. 1367 and Charleville, Bibl. mun. 269 as they exist in the *Glossa ordinaria*.[116] Bernardus was an original and independent thinker who probably exercised only an indirect influence on the *Glossa ordinaria*.[117] His influence on the *Ordinary Gloss* was primarily through Laurentius. For reasons we cannot

112. Alfons M. Stickler has pointed out his 'glosses' in the last layer of Reims 676 in 'Il decretista Laurentius Hispanus', SG 9 (1966) 480–481.
113. Laurent Mayali in 'Note on the Legitimization by Subsequent Marriage from Alexander III to Innocent III', *The Two Laws: Studies in Medieval Legal History Dedicated to Stephan Kuttner*, ed. Mayali et al. (Washington DC 1990) 70, n. 54 cites a text from Alanus that came into the *Glossa ordinaria* in a somewhat altered form through Laurentius.
114. Kuttner, 'Bernardus' 292–310.
115. Weigand, 'Neue Mitteilungen aus Handschriften', *Traditio* 21 (1965) 482–484.
116. Kuttner, 'Bernardus' 292 and 304–306. None of his glosses are in St. Omer 476 second layer (Bernard of Pavia), Munich, Staatsbibl. 28175 (Bazianus), or Pommersfelden, Schlossbibl. Schönborn 142, as I indicate in the description of these manuscripts in *Glossen zum Dekret Gratians* part 4.
117. See Alfons M. Stickler, 'Der Kaiserbegriff des Bernardus Compostellanus antiquus', SG 15 (1972) 103–124, esp. 123–124 with an explanation of his outsider's role.

know, Johannes Teutonicus suppressed any mention of Bernardus in his gloss.[118]

Laurentius Hispanus

Laurentius, from 1218 to 1248 bishop of Orense in Spain, was at the peak of his scholarly activity in Bologna during the years 1210 to 1214. His gloss apparatus is called the *Glossa palatina* after the first manuscript found to contain it, Pal. lat. 658 of the Vatican library. Stickler, basing his work on Kuttner's research,[119] thoroughly analyzed it [120] and provided a detailed description of its manuscripts. I was able to find two additional and nearly complete traditions in Laon, Bibl. com. 476 (principal gloss layer) and Perugia, Bibl. com. C. M. 4 (final principal layer); prior to its total erasure, Melk 259 could also be added to the previous two. Kuttner had noted the very great similarity of this apparatus to the *Glossa ordinaria* and thought at first that it must have been a *Summa* on the *Decretum* of Johannes Teutonicus.[121] As my research has shown, it was principally, perhaps exclusively, Laurentius who brought the glosses of the early period (which had grown up slowly and were then increased and organized into groups in the *Apparatus 'Ordinaturus Magister'*) into the *Glossa ordinaria*.[122]

Laurentius incorporated forty-four, or nearly a third, of the 147 glosses in the *Apparatus 'Ordinaturus Magister'*—about half of which are not found in earlier works and so must first have been composed by him—into his apparatus without changing them. (Almost of these were longer glosses.)[123] An additional eight, however, were altered or shortened. Approximately half of these appear in the *Glossa ordinaria*. Twenty-four were unaltered.

A search of selected passages in Laurentius' commentary for the sources that he used reveals the following: a quarter of his comments on D.11 pr. to D.11 c.6 were taken from the *Apparatus 'Ordinaturus Magister'* and

118. Evidence in Kuttner, 'Bernardus' 306–308.
119. Kuttner, *Repertorium* 79–92.
120. Stickler, 'Il decretista' 461–549. See also Antonio García y García, *Laurentius Hispanus: Datos biográficos y estudio crítico de sus obras* (Rome and Madrid 1956). There are no glosses of Laurentius in the *Apparatus 'Ordinaturus Magister'* although Gillmann, 'Die Entstehungszeit der Glossa ordinaria' had wrongly argued that the siglum 'l.' in Bamberg, Staatsbibl. Can. 13 stood for Laurentius.
121. Stephan Kuttner, 'Eine Dekretsumme des Johannes Teutonicus (Cod. Vat. Pal. lat. 658)', ZRG Kan. Abt. 21 (1932) 141–189.
122. Summary in Weigand, *Glossen zum Dekret Gratians* appendix 2 with detailed data for the following statistics.
123. Laurentius apparently regarded it as a work of Huguccio, for whom he provided some glosses with the siglum h., even though they give no evidence of being in the *Summa* of Huguccio.

slightly under a quarter from Huguccio's *Summa*. Huguccio was probably also the source of additional short glosses that Laurentius altered or shortened. It is likely that Laurentius composed the remaining fourth independently, in particular the glosses on D.11 c.1 and c.4. About half of these glosses entered the *Glossa ordinaria*.

Exactly a fifth of the material to D.12 pr. to D.12 c.6 was drawn from the *Apparatus 'Ordinaturus Magister'*, while two fifths (though partly modified) came from Huguccio's *Summa*. So far I have not discovered the source of the remaining material. Only a few lines of this material went into the *Glossa ordinaria*. Almost half the commentary on C.1 q.3 cc.4, 13–15 comes from the *Apparatus 'Ordinaturus Magister'*, including an 'allegatio' to a decretal not infrequently attributed to the *Compilatio prima*. Only one seventh of the commentary to C.27 q.2 c.11 came from the *Apparatus 'Ordinaturus Magister'*, and more than a third was taken from the *Summa* of Huguccio. Two thirds of this commentary entered the *Glossa ordinaria*. The same general pattern holds for the other sections that I studied, C.30 q.4 and de cons. D.4 c.1.

Laurentius probably relied on the apparatus of Bernardus Compostellanus antiquus for his choice of words, as he sometimes cites him by name, though only once in the sections that I have more thoroughly studied. In contrast, he cites Huguccio five times (three of these times, however, are with reference to the glosses of the *Apparatus 'Ordinaturus Magister'*), Johannes Faventinus three times, Cardinalis, Gandulphus, and Melendus each twice, and Rufinus once.

Glossa ordinaria of Johannes Teutonicus

The close connection of the Johannes Teutonicus' *Glossa ordinaria* with the apparatus of Laurentius has been known since Kuttner's early work on the *Glossa palatina*.[124] Kuttner modified his conclusions somewhat later,[125] but he did not doubt the close relationship between Laurentius and Johannes. I will now present the results of my research into the sources of Johannes' apparatus.

I examined glosses on D.11 and D.12. Twenty, usually very short ones, come from the *Summa* of Huguccio while ten, mostly longer, ones were taken from Laurentius. The long glosses to D.11 c.4 and D.12 c.4 (s.v. *contrario more*), concerning the use of various customary laws in legal proceedings, had contemporary importance, and Johannes formulated these

124. See Kuttner, 'Dekretsumme'. A clear picture emerges from the texts published by Kuttner in parallel columns.
125. Kuttner, *Repertorium* 93–99.

on his own. Bartholomaeus Brixiensis, who revised Johannes' apparatus, wrote two substantive additions to these two glosses. In the remaining sections almost all the glosses come from Laurentius. There are five from Huguccio, and perhaps three from Johannes himself, leaving aside small modifications in the other glosses.

I have checked seventeen passages of Johannes' *Glossa ordinaria* for citations of Bazianus, Gandulphus, and Melendus (from D.19 c.8 to C.11 q.3 c.71), but I have found only a few. The research of Zeliauskas confirmed Johannes' use of Laurentius and Huguccio.[126] Of the ninety-one texts of Johannes Teutonicus that he examined, fifty-one are taken from Laurentius. Johannes took ten from Huguccio. In my own work I found that his teaching on conditional marriage agree more or less with Laurentius.[127] He did not use Huguccio because he thought his teaching on conditional marriage was antiquated, and his glosses on natural law relied heavily on Laurentius.[128]

From Landau's research on the law of patronage it becomes clear that Johannes relied upon Huguccio in some passages and upon Laurentius in others, and then quite frequently composed independently.[129]

In his opinions on the part of the laity in episcopal elections in D.63, Johannes relied very little on Laurentius, since he adopted ideas from French apparatus of glosses.[130] In Lenherr's book, on the other hand, the relevant passages on heretics' power of excommunicating and deposing are shown to be identical with those of Laurentius.[131] Although he altered some texts and left sigla off of others, Johannes Teutonicus incorporated about a third of Laurentius' texts on clerical continence into his *Glossa ordinaria*.[132]

---

126. Josephus Zeliauskas, *De excommunicatione vitiata apud glossatores (1140–1350)* (Studia et textus historia juris canonici 4; Zürich and Rome 1967). In appendix XVI, he gives 131 texts from Huguccio (63–85), in appendix XLII, 100 texts from Laurentius (171–185) and in appendix XLIII, 132 texts from the *Glossa ordinaria*.

127. See my *Bedingte Eheschließung* 379–383 in comparison with 333–334.

128. See my *Die Naturrechtslehre der Legisten und Dekretisten von Irnerius bis Accursius und von Gratian bis Johannes Teutonicus* (Münchener Theologische Studien 3.26; Munich 1967) 255–226 in comparison with 251–254.

129. Peter Landau, *Ius patronatus: Studien zur Entwicklung des Patronats im Dekretalenrecht und der Kanonistik des 12. und 13. Jahrhunderts* (Forschungen zur kirchlichen Rechtsgeschichte und zum Kirchenrecht 12; Cologne-Vienna 1975) printed comparative texts.

130. See H. Müller, *Der Anteil der Laien an der Bischofswahl* (Kanonistische Studien und Texte 29; Amsterdam 1977) 181–186.

131. Titus Lenherr, *Die Excommunications- und Depositionsgewalt der Häretiker bei Gratian und den Dekretisten bis zur Glossa ordinaria des Johannes Teutonicus* (Münchener Theologische Studien 3. 42; St. Ottilien 1987) 328–331 and 318–321.

132. Filippo Liotta, *La continenza dei chierici nel pensiero canonistico classico da Graziano a Gregorio IX* (Milan 1971) 310–26; these texts are collated with pp. 344–352 and editions of the *Glossa ordinaria*.

To sum up: Johannes Teutonicus often simply repeated Laurentius, who, in turn, took many glosses from the *Apparatus 'Ordinaturus Magister'*. The *Summa* of Huguccio is Johannes' second principal source. Whether he consulted other commentaries on the *Decretum,* and if so which ones, seems to me, as before, an open question.

Since we know that Laurentius' *Glossa palatina* was written ca. 1214 and that the apparatus was always Johannes' starting point, we can conclude that Johannes began his work on the *Glossa ordinaria* ca. 1214.[133] I have so far not found any evidence that Johannes was active as a glossator before this period. He made use of the regulations of the Fourth Lateran Council of 1215 at the relevant points in his work. At the same time, he wrote his apparatus to the Fourth Lateran Constitutions. He referred to them many times in his *Glossa ordinaria*. So, his apparatus (in contrast to that of Laurentius) was thoroughly up-to-date. And because he excluded outdated discussions from it, he paved the way for its rapid and general reception. Because he does not, for the most part, cite the Fourth Lateran Constitutions from *Compilatio quarta* (which he wrote in the fall of 1216 or the following winter), he must have finished his work in 1217 at the latest (if not at the end of 1216). He cited *Compilatio quarta* at the end of a few glosses. This evidence may point to his incorporating these citations late in his work; he cited other decretals from the Collection of Alanus even though he put many of them into his *Compilatio quarta*. This evidence also argues for his having finished the *Glossa ordinaria* before he completed his work on *Compilatio quarta*.

On the basis of Bamberg Can. 13, Gillmann argued that Johannes may have revised his gloss. As evidence he listed more than 130 citations that Johannes made to the Constitutions of the Fourth Lateran Council and to *Compilatio quarta* in Johannes' apparatus in Bamberg Can. 13 that were not in his Ordinary Gloss.[134] When I checked half of these citations in seven other manuscripts I found that nearly a fifth of them were not in Johannes' Ordinary Gloss. Consequently I have concluded that Bamberg does have later interpolated additions. Other citations are occasionally missing in one or another manuscript; for this reason I prefer to view this as a problem in transmission rather than as an indication that various versions of the apparatus existed.[135] If, however, the regular absence of some

---

133. I summarize Stephan Kuttner, 'Johannes Teutonicus', *Neue deutsche Biographie* 10 (1974) 571–573.

134. Gillmann, *Zur Lehre* 184–220; reprinted as no. 12 in Weigand, *Gesammelte Schriften*.

135. To give just one example of the problem: the gloss to D.23 c.1 s.v. *disponendi* ends in Admont, Stiftsbibl.35 (Ab), Beaune, Bibl. mun. 5 (Be), Grenoble, Bibl. mun. 62 (Ge), Paris, B.N. 3903 (Pb) and 14317 (Pd) with the 'allegatio' 'in constitutione Innoc(entii) Sepe' (4 Lat. c.

citations or glosses, or parts thereof, in two manuscripts should be even further substantiated, that could indeed point to an earlier recension (or a draft before his final copy).

Thus we cannot determine whether Johannes wrote additional glosses to the *Decretum* after the publication of his apparatus. Some glosses that carry the siglum Jo. in Vatican lat. 1367 and particularly in Bamberg Can. 13, (Ba) do, however, point in this direction.[136] The problem needs to be examined further with a careful comparison of manuscripts.[137] On the basis of 160 passages in the *Glossa ordinaria*, twelve of which have citations from the Fourth Lateran Council (or additions in Vatican lat. 1367), I can now say that Johannes published his apparatus in an early form, or allowed it to be transcribed, ca. 1216.[138] This version can be found in Grenoble 62 (482), Paris, B.N. lat. 3903, and Trier 907 (2182a). The supplements to the *Glossa ordinaria* in Vat. lat. 1367 sometimes go back to this early version or offer material from the *Apparatus 'Ordinaturus Magister'* and Laurentius. Whether individual glosses, especially in Bamberg Can. 13 and Trier 907, come from Johannes or from later authors is made difficult to determine by the lack of sigla.

Of the approximately fifty manuscripts that have the apparatus of Johannes Teutonicus, only those that have become known since Kuttner's *Repertorium* are listed here:[139] Admont 35 (very usable), Avranches, Bibl. ville 148, Brindisi, Bibl. pub. arcives. A.1 (third layer, only a few fragments),

---

39). Instead of 'Sepe' Munich, Staatsbibl. 14024 (Mf) has 'extra iiii. de dolo et cont. Contingit (4 Lat. 40 [4 Comp. 2. 4. 2]) Jo.' written over an erasure; this is also in Ba and was added in Ge and Pb in a similar fashion. The textual tradition is complex. More work must be done to clarify this problem.

136. Of those texts that have later citations from Ba [mentioned below (n. 143)], I have not found thirteen of them in any other manuscript. Four of these carry the contemporary siglum Jo., and in one other text a later hand added this siglum. Because glosses of Philippus of Aquileia, a student of Johannes Teutonicus, occur in this layer of Ba, one ought to think of later, supplementary glosses of Johannes Teutonicus.

137. See Kuttner 'Johannes Teutonicus', 572.

138. Evidence in Rudolf Weigand, 'Hat Johannes Teutonicus seinen Glossenapparat zum Dekret Gratians in mehreren Fassungen publiziert?' *Vom mittelalterlichen Recht zur neuzeitlichen Rechtswissenschaft: Bedingungen, Wege und Probleme der europäischen Rechtsgeschichte*, ed. Norbert Brieskorn, Paul Mikat, Daniela Müller, and Dietmar Willoweit (Rechts- und Staatswissenschaftliche Veröffentlichungen der Görres-Gesellschaft Neue Folge 72; Paderborn 1994) 147–166.

139. Almost all are listed by Kuttner in 'Bernardus Compostellanus' 292, n. 77 with the retractationes appended to the reprinted essay in *Gratian and the Schools of Law 1140–1234* (Collected Studies 185; London 1983). There Grenoble 72 should read 62. Kraków 357 should be deleted. Of the manuscripts mentioned in Kuttner, *Repertorium* 95–99, Frankfurt, Stadtbibliothek 1 (now correctly Barth. 7), Montecassino 68 and Madrid 12790 should be removed, since they contain the later version of Bartholomaeus Brixiensis. In the case of Trier 907, Klostenneuburg 101, and Vienna 2082, Kuttner's suspicions have been confirmed, and his question marks should be removed.

Graz 71 (final layer, incomplete), Graz 80 (second principal layer), Grenoble 62 (482), Ivrea 72 (C, large lacunae), Klosterneuburg, Stiftsbibl. 87, Lublin, Bibl. Uniwer. Katol. 1, Munich 14024 (principal layer), Olomouc, Statní Archiv C. O. 401, St. Mihiel, Bibl. mun. 5, Tarazona, Bibl. Catedral 10 (fragments), Venice, B.N. IV. 117.

By 1220 at the latest, Johannes had ended his academic activity in Bologna and had returned to Halberstadt, where, according to the traditional identification of him with Johannes Zemeke, he became the magister of the cathedral in 1220 and then dean of the cathedral in 1235. At the end of 1241, less than four years before his death in 1245, he was made cathedral provost.

Additions to the Glossa ordinaria by Bartholomaeus Brixiensis and Others

In his *Repertorium*, Kuttner listed seven manuscripts that have glosses from the period between Johannes Teutonicus and Bartholomaeus Brixiensis;[140] two of these, however, do not contain later glosses.[141] If the gloss additions of earlier authors, particularly of Huguccio, Alanus, and Laurentius, in later gloss layers are ignored, then we can conclude that the authors below wrote additional glosses to Johannes' apparatus.

Bernardus Compostellanus antiquus was probably the first to write additional glosses. They can be found in Vatican lat. 1367.[142] It is possible that some of the b. sigla in the *Glossa ordinaria* were his additonal glosses. This is probably the case at D.18 c.10 s.v. *rationem*, which, at the end of Johannes' gloss in Bamberg Can. 13, bears the siglum Jo. after *Ex litteris* and, still in the same hand, the siglum 'b.' after the supplementary sentence (with an 'allegatio').[143]

Philippus of Aquileia, a student of Johannes Teutonicus, wrote some supplementary glosses for his teacher's apparatus; these glosses were part-

140. Kuttner, *Repertorium* 100–102. Durham C. III. 1 should be rejected because the 'extra iiii.' ought to be read as 'supra iiii.'; I have found no evidence of any kind for the use of compilationes II–IV, as my description of glosses makes clear: *Glossen zum Dekret Gratians* part 4. The glosses marked 'F. C.' in Hereford, Cathedral Library P. VII. 3 come from Fidantia in the period before 1200.

141. Independent glosses are probably (for the most part) excerpts from his earlier apparatus as a comparison with Gniezno, Bibl. Kapit. 28 (final layer) shows. There are no additions in Pommersfelden, Schlossbibl. Schönborn 142 from Bernardus, contrary to Müller's statement in *Der Anteil* 149, n. 43; Müller attributed the b. siglum (instead of Bar.) in the *Glossa ordinaria* to Bernardus alone.

142. In the manuscripts of the two recensions that have been checked, I found no other sigla. On the other hand, many of the incunabula that have been consulted have the siglum 'io.' twice, and only a few having an eccentric traditon have the siglum 'b'.

143. Gillman prints twenty-seven of his glosses in 'Die Entstehungszeit' 188–191.

ly incorporated in Johannes' apparatus in Bamberg Can. 13 and were partly supplemented by another hand.[144] In Munich 14024 , some of his glosses were written as additions to the *Glossa ordinaria* and were occasionally incorporated into it.[145]

A certain 'magister Guido', who probably also composed a Casus to *Compilatio tertia*, wrote glosses to the *Decretum* that were incorporated into the apparatus of Johannes in Bamberg Can. 13 and are in an additional layer in Paris 3903.[146]

Saint Raymond of Peñafort also wrote glosses to the *Decretum* around 1220. These have been preserved in at least three manuscripts: Paris, B.N. 3903, Tours, Bibl. mun. 559, and Vatican lat. 1367. These glosses were in a supplementary layer to the *Glossa ordinaria*.[147]

Some glosses that appear in Vatican lat. 1367 are ascribed to authors who are otherwise not known as commentators on the *Decretum*: Damasus, Jacobus of Albenga, Martin of Zamora, Pelagius, and lastly Vincentius, who was widely known as a decretalist.[148]

Willielmus Vasco, who wrote his apparatus to the *Decretum* before 1210, authored additional glosses after the publication of the *Glossa ordinaria*;[149] these too are also preserved in Vatican lat. 1367.[150]

In addition, there are some anonymous, supplemental glosses that were incorporated into various manuscripts and even into the *Glossa ordinaria* later. Examples of these can be found in Bamberg Can. 13.[151] How

---

144. In an investigation of the first part of the *Decretum* I have found seven of his glosses, none of which has a parallel in Bamberg, Staatsbibl. Can. 13. Sometimes these are only short remarks, as at the end of the long gloss v. *Secundum* to D.19 c.8: 'et ei consentit magister phi.' or at the end of the gloss s.v. *metropolitani* to D.64 c.4: 'Quod non credit ma. f.' A whole gloss exists for D.24 c.7: 'Magister filipus intelligit hoc cap. . . . fuit. f.', and in an additional gloss to D.55 (c.11?) he cites 5 Comp. 1.11 c.1. I have found only an anonymous, though characteristic, parallel in Munich 14024 to those five glosses on the first part of the *Decretum* from Bamberg that Gillman printed. While the second (longer) half of Johannes' very long gloss to D.70 c.2 s.v. *in duabus* was replaced by a text of Philippus (Gillmann 191), in Munich, the corresponding first sentence, although with a different 'allegatio', was incorporated without the rest of the text. In the Munich manuscript a gloss refers to 'constitutionem Honorii extra de religi. do. c. ult.' (4 Comp. 3.13.3, but 4 Lat. c.13), in Bamberg the text reads: 'decre. Dudum' (Potth. 7546?).

145. Gillmann, 'Die Entstehungszeit' 191–193; Kuttner, *Repertorium* 95 and 101. I have not investigated how far the transmission is the same.

146. Kuttner, *Repertorium* 101–103 and 449–452.

147. Kuttner, 'Bernardus Compostellanus' 335.

148. Kuttner, 'Bernardus Compostellanus' 336–340.

149. Alfons M. Stickler, 'Der Dekretist Willielmus Vasco', *Études Le Bras* (Paris 1965) 705–728, also in BMCL 1 (1971) 76–78.

150. Gillmann, 'Die Entstehungszeit' 192–193 offers some examples; the false attribution of the siglum '"l.' which the scribe had misread as Laurentius instead of 'legendum'. See also the supplementary text in Trier, Stadtbibl. 907 at D.23 c.1.

151. Kuttner, *Repertorium* 100–103.

far some of these texts were subsequently adopted by Bartholomaeus could be determined only by a laborious study of the manuscripts.

The glosses of Bertrandus, contained in the second layer of Berlin, Staatsbibl. lat. fol. 2 after the revised *Glossa ordinaria* of Bartholomaeus, were written between 1234 and 1241. His opinions were often cited in Guido's *Rosarium*.

The Revised Recension of the Glossa ordinaria by Bartholomaeus Brixiensis

With the publication of the decretals of Gregory IX in 1234, a revision of the *Glossa ordinaria* became indispensable if it was to retain its function. Bartholomaeus Brixiensis carried out this task.[152] During the 1220s in Bologna, Bartholomaeus probably studied canon law with Tancred and Roman law with Hugolinus Presbyteri. He wrote an important set of quaestiones that were widely cited and circulated. Later he revised various other works and died at Bologna in 1258.

Although mainly based on printed sources, Schulte's account remains the starting point for studying Bartholomaeus' work.[153] Kuttner on the other hand, has sifted through and fully examined the manuscript tradition.[154] As Bartholomaeus wrote in his preface ('Quoniam novis supervenientibus causis'), he wanted to improve the apparatus to the *Decretum* by correcting what it was necessary to correct and supplying material which it seemed necessary to supply. His most important editorial work was to change all the citations of papal decretals from Johannes' references to them in the *Compilationes antiquae* to their new arrangement in the Decretals of Pope Gregory IX. He also incorporated new decretals and offered new solutions to old questions.[155] Citations of decretals in Johannes went back to the *Compilationes prima, secunda,* and *tertia,* the Fourth Lateran Council's Constitutions, and occasionally to *Compilatio quarta*. He changed them all to conform to their place and form in the *Decretals of Gregory IX* (also referred to as the *Liber extra* or *Gregoriana*).[156] He also cit-

---

152. About him see Schulte, QL 2.83–88; R. Abbondanza, 'Bartolomeo da Brescia', DBI 6 (Rome 1964) 691–696 has a bibliography.

153. Schulte, *Glosse zum Decret Gratians* 77–82, 86–87; see 26–29 and 92–93. for the printed works from the period 1471–1571 that he used as well as the Roman edition of 1584.

154. Kuttner, *Repertorium* 103–122.

155. Bartholomaeus' Preface has been translated by Robert Somerville and Bruce C. Brasington, *Prefaces to Canon Law Books in Latin Christianity: Selected Translations, 500–1245* (New Haven–London 1998) 236.

156. Schulte, *Glosse zum Decret Gratians* 79–82 with many references that are abridged in Schulte, QL 2.87. Bartholomaeus occasionally forgot to make a correction. Thus, in the

ed other writings, such as his own *Quaestiones* or the opinions of Jacobus and his teachers Tancred and Hugolinus.[157] All these changes have caused some confusion in assigning the sigla found in manuscripts and printed editions. I have found an interesting example of this confusion at D.74 c.8 s.v. *contradices.*, where the siglum Bar. must be read as Bazianus.[158]

Bartholomaeus thoroughly updated the apparatus by including a discussion of those decretals that appeared right after 1217, particularly those decretals of Gregory IX in his *Liber extra*. He often agreed with Johannes' opinions (and disagreed with Huguccio), but at other times he corrected or modified Johannes' positions. He sometimes introduced his remarks with 'hodie vero' (today, however) or some other such phrase. Sometimes he simply endorsed Johannes' view without giving additional reasons or evidence. At times he sharply criticized Johannes. Whenever he qualified or expanded upon a statement made by Johannes, he took pains sufficiently to explain why he did so.[159] Finally, Bartholomaeus added concreteness to some of Johannes' statements by highlighting exceptions, putting forward modifications, and introducing other possible solutions with 'vel'. He added summaries and, above all, solutions wherever Johannes had left a question open.[160]

Bartholomaeus' work on the *Glossa ordinaria* was truly a scholarly achievement for his time, when less importance was given to originality and more to a faithful and accepted passing on of traditional teaching. His work has continued to receive positive appreciation in modern times as well.[161]

A reference to a decretal of Innocent IV at C.23 q.4 c.27 led Schulte to date the revision of the *Glossa ordinaria* to the period somewhere be-

---

gloss to C.11 q.1 c.18 s.v. *mox depositus* found in manuscripts and printed works as c.3 of the Fourth Lateran Council, 'ut in constitutione Innocentii Excommunicamus', instead of X 5.7.13.

157. In the remarks inserted into the gloss to D.74 c.8 s.v. *tot scriptis*, Bartholomaeus quotes these three authors who, he says, had responded together at a public session as reported. In the four manuscripts that were checked a simple 'h.' stands for Hugolinus (each one occurring at the beginning and ending of a text); one manuscript has changed an 'et h.' at the end of a text into a 'b.', perhaps a siglum for Bartholomaeus. In the sentence of Johannes' gloss that directly follows this, however, the 'h.' signifies Huguccio!

158. The gloss from the *Apparatus 'Ordinaturus Magister'* in the *Glossa palatina* and Johannes has the siglum 'bar.', but the manuscripts of Bartholomaeus' version that have been checked have 'baz.'; almost all the printed editions revert to 'Bar.' The gloss with the siglum 'Baz.' at C.35 q.6 c.4 is a later addition, since I have not seen it in Johannes Teutonicus nor in the majority of incunabula.

159. Evidence in Schulte, *Glosse zum Decret Gratians* 81 and n. 6–11.

160. Examples in ibid. 82, n. 1–7. His long summarizing glosses in particular present such modifications.

161. See Gabriel Le Bras, 'Bartholomeus Brixiensis', DDC 2.217.

tween 1238 or 1240 and 1245, an opinion that has so far remained uncontested by scholars.[162] I, however, found this citation in only eight of the twenty-five manuscripts of Bartholomaeus' *Glossa ordinaria* that I have examined.[163] In order to test a supposition that two recensions exist,[164] I have studied some fifty passages. Bartholomaeus inserted three additions into Johannes' long gloss to D.50 c.6 s.v. *De his*: 'Set certe quicquid dicat Jo.—in questionibus.b.', then 'Et hoc expresse dicitur—Inquisitionis.', and finally at the end 'Hodie autem—Inquisitionis.b.' While the first addition exists in all the manuscripts that I examined, part of the second and the whole of the third are absent in ten manuscripts, and among these ten are seven of the eight manuscripts that contain the citation to Pope Innocent IV's decretal. A look at the gloss to D.24 c.3 s.v. *civitatis* presents similarly surprising results. All manuscripts and printed editions have an addition by Bartholomaeus one fourth of the way into the long gloss, 'Carentis—mediis', that Johannes wrote to this 'distinctio': 'et est hodie—prebendarum. b.' Yet, a double addition at the end of the passage was transmitted in a very different manner: 'Vel capitulum ipsum—et confirmare' forms the conclusion of the gloss in most of the later printed editions. It is absent in precisely those manuscripts that omit the addition: 'Hodie autem expressum est quod uacante sede potestas conferendi beneficium non deuoluitur ad capitulum arg. extra ne sede uacante Illa' (X 3.9.2).

In almost the very same manuscripts, a gloss to C.16 q.3 d.p.c.15 v. *utiliter* on statutes of limitations is cited in an abbreviated fashion and without any express mention of Bulgarus, Placentinus, or Johannes Bassianus. The gloss to the palea D.18 c.11 is missing in the manuscripts that mention the novel. On the other hand, an expansion of Johannes' gloss to D.23 c.1 s.v. *disponendi* was transmitted in only nine (or perhaps ten) manuscripts. An expansion of the gloss to D.11 c.4 s.v. *vincat* occurs in only five manuscripts and a few printed editions and so can scarcely belong to the authentic apparatus. Moreover, the last sentence of Bartholomaeus' addition to the gloss to D.1 c.4 s.v. *Mos est longa* is found in only about a third of the manu-

162. Schulte, QL 2.87; Evidence in Schulte, *Glosse zum Decret Gratians* 81, n. 3 and 87.
163. I found the text 'Hodie recurre super hoc ad nouellam' in the following manuscripts unmarked by any siglum: Cambridge, Gonville and Caius Coll. 6, Florence, Biblioteca Laur. S. Croce I sin. 1, Kraków, Bibl. Jag. 356, Rouen, Bibl. mun. E 21 (707); it appears with the siglum B. in Florence, Biblioteca Laur. Edil. 96, Graz, Universitätsbibl. III 69, and Pommersfelden, Schlossbibl. Schönborn 142, and with the siglum Jo. in Boulogne-sur-mer, Bibl. mun. 118. The text is completely lacking in all the other manuscripts that I have examined.
164. Sven Stelling-Michaud, *Catalogue des manuscrits juridiques (droit canon et droit romain) de la fin du XIIe au XIVe siècle conserves en Suisse* (Geneva 1954) 22–24, speaks of two different recensions of the *Glossa ordinaria*, one with the so-callled Laurentius type in Genèva Bibl. pub. univ. lat. 60 that he describes as 'après 1245', and the other found in the other two manuscripts that he calls the 'première révision (antérieure à 1245)'.

scripts and is absent in some printed editions. Almost all the same manuscripts have two small additional glosses to D.1 c.1 s.v. *moribus* that also are found in only a few incunabula.[165]

To me, all of these variations in transmission seem to suggest losses of texts or textual additions over time rather than separate recensions of Johannes' *Glossa ordinaria* in Bartholomaeus' revised version. His revision of the *Glossa* should be placed around 1234-41, since no solid evidence points to the years after 1241, and Bartholomaeus apparently does not cite any texts later than the *Liber extra* of 1234, apart from citations to his *Quaestiones*, the first recension of which he wrote before 1234 and then (presumably quite soon thereafter) revised.[166] His *Casus*, which constitutes a revision of of the *Casus* of Benencasa,[167] occasionally found its way into manuscripts of the *Decretum*[168] as did the latter's, and were included almost without exception in later printed editions (especially from 1501 on).

The so-called 'Laurentius-type' of the *Glossa ordinaria* was common in Bologna during the fourteenth century and presumably goes back to the influence of the *Rosarium* of Guido of Baysio.[169] Many glosses in it carry the siglum of Johannes, though its glosses are otherwise mostly unsigned. Above all, however, many of its glosses are ascribed to Laurentius, who indeed was most often Johannes' model. With respect to its classification of the *Decretum*, it is noteworthy that C.1 is still reckoned as part one, of which tractatus de poen.—C.36 forms part three and de cons. part four. The reference to the novella is probably always found in it.[170]

Incunabula with the Glossa ordinaria

Of the forty-five incunabula listed by Erich Will,[171] I have examined the following seventeen at many points: Strasbourg 1471 (Will 1, 116), Mainz

---

165. E.g. Mainz 1472, Basel 1476, 1481, and 1486, as well as Strasbourg 1489. These have some supplemental texts that I have so far not found in either manuscripts or other printed editions.

166. Abbondanza, 'Bartolomeo da Brescia' 693–695. and Martin Bertram, 'Kanonistische Quästionensammlungen von Bartolomäus Brixiensis bis Johannes Andreae', *Proceedings Cambridge* 265–281, esp. 268 with literature.

167. Kuttner, *Repertorium* 229–230 and Kuttner, 'Bernardus Compostellanus' 284 with Retractationes; Abbondanza, 'Bartolomeo da Brescia' 694.

168. Kuttner identified the *Casus* of Benencasa in conjunction with the apparatus of Alanus in Paris, B.N. 15393; I have found it in the last layer of Madrid, B.N. 251. Bartholomaeus' *Casus* are, among other places, preserved in Boulogne-sur-mer, Bibl. mun. 118 and Burgos, Archivo y Bibl. Cat. 4.

169. Kuttner, *Repertorium* 116–22 is fundamental.

170. Erich Will, *Decreti Gratiani Incvnabvla: Beschreibendes Gesamtverzeichnis der Wiegendrucke des Gratianischen Dekretes* (SG 6; Bologna 1959).

171. Ibid. 1–280, most especially 116–277. This section will give only the following for each

1472 (Will 3, 124), Rome 1476 (Will 6, 137), Basel 1476 (Will 8, 139), Venice 1477 (Will 9, 145), Venice 1479 (Will 14, 154), Basel 1481 (Will 16, 164), Venice 1483 (Will 19, 180), Nuremberg 1483 (Will 20, 184), Basel 1486 (Will 25, 204), Venice 1489 (Will 28, 212), Strasbourg 1489 (Will 29, 216), Basel 1493 (Will 33, 231), Nuremberg 1493 (Will 35, 241), Venice 1496 (Will 37, 250), Venice 1498 (Will 40, 262), Basel 1500 (Will 44, 269).

The first printing, Strasbourg 1471 (presumably also Strasbourg 1472, Will 2. 120), is noteworthy for the following characteristics of its glosses:

The gloss 'Olim licuit' to D.2 c.6 is incorrectly attached to D.2 c.5. in this edition as in the majority of printed editions as well as in many manuscripts. The gloss to D.4 c.3 s.v. *iudicent* is present without its final sentence: 'Dicas quod—quaedam', which is also the case in most incunabula and manuscripts. The gloss D.11 c.4 v. *vincat* has an addition: 'Et pone casum—ut extra de consuetudine c. fin.', which is only rarely found elsewhere. A sentence, marked in later printed editions as an addition to the gloss D.19 c.6 s.v. *Plures* and bearing the siglum Cy., should not be a separate gloss but should be attached to the gloss itself (and without a siglum).

A completely different manuscript, which served as the basis of Mainz 1472, which in all the texts that I examined is identical with Basel 1476, 1481 (and probably also Basel 1482, Will 17, 171), and 1486[172] and Strasbourg 1489 (as well as Strasbourg 1490, Will 30, 221 and perhaps even Strasbourg 1484, Will 22, 194), has different unique features. All of these editions have six small additions to D.1 pr. and c.1 and two glosses that are absent elsewhere. The long gloss to D.1 c.2 s.v. *ius generale* is supplemented in these editions by the addition: 'Est et aliud quod est equum, non tamen iustum, C. de furtis l. Si quis (Cod. 6.2.20), C. de iudic. Placuit' (Cod. 3.1.8). The gloss to D.1 c.12 s.v. *hereditatibus* is entirely missing. The gloss 'Olim' is here, and only here, correctly appended to D.2 c.6. There is an addition at the end of the gloss to D.3 c.3 s.v. *privatorum* that I have not found elsewhere: 'Secus tamen in sententiis et—Quoniam', with reference to X 2.30. 7 and to X 1.29.14.6. The last sentence to the glosses D.4 c.3 s.v. *iudicent* and s.v. *non licebit* is found only in this edition and in the later printed editions; it is absent in the other incunabula. The two additional texts to D.11 c.4 and D.19 c.6 described above as characteristic of Strasbourg 1471 also are found in this edition. A unique addition can be found at the end of the gloss to D.12

---

incunabulum: place and year of publication, the number assigned to it in Will's list with the relevant page number in his article.

172. Perhaps Lyon 1495 also belongs to this group of texts, since the printer Michael Wenssler (Will 36, 249) is evidently the same one who composed Basel printings.

pr. s.v. *Quod*: 'Set male—sensu quia generaret absurditatem legi', which partially corresponds the first half of the addition from Guido's *Rosarium* in later printed editions. The end of the gloss to D.23 c.1 s.v. *funguntur* has the addition: 'Hodie papa facit hoc', which I have not found elsewhere. The additions to the gloss D.24 c.3 s.v. *civitatis* are in these printings, and the 'allegationes' from C.2 q.6 of the later printed editions can be found only in these incunabula. The addition in the gloss to C.1 q.3 c.15 s.v. *consuetudinis* from 'nisi' on in the later printed editions is found only in these incunabula. There is only one gloss by Bazianus to C.35 q.6 c.4 v. *Confessi* in these incunabula; it reappears in later printed editions.

These examples should make clear how much these incunabula differ in their text. The editors of later printed editions had obviously gone back to one of our incunabula for some of these additions. Small variations in other incunabula do not merit attention here. In any case, the absence of particular glosses is very rare, contrary to what Schulte thought.[173] Yet, it is worth mentioning that in Venice 1496 (and probably also in Venice 1499, Will 43, 267, Venice 1500, Will 45, 275 and Venice 1501) a reference to one or more writers was very often inserted into the text of a gloss or appended at its end with the notation 'Adde. . .' This notation is found eight times in D.1. alone

In the incunabulum printed in Basel during the year 1500 and edited by Sebastian Brant, references to the contents of the relevant gloss first appear in the margin (on many occasions at D.1 c.1 and 2 alone), which set a precedent for later editions.[174] These in turn deserve some attention.

Later Printed Editions

Among later printed editions, the Parisan edition of 1501 by Jean Chappuis, which was printed by Rembolt, is of particular importance.[175] In addition to introductory summaries and indices that Chappuis added to Gratian's text he also included numerous additions to the gloss itself.[176] There

---

173. Schulte, *Glosse zum Decret Gratians* 91, n. 5, thought that there was obvious confusion with a gloss of Johannes Faventinus; see my *Glossen zum Dekret Gratians* part 2.9. 126–218.

174. He also edited the edition printed in Basel 1493.

175. Aldo Adversi, 'Saggio di un catalogo delle edizioni del *Decretum* Gratiani posteriori al secolo XV', SG 6 (1959) 281–451, counts 164 printed editions from the period 1501–1959, among them six published at Lyon in 1624 (nos. 119–124). On average, exactly one edition appeared each year prior to 1624. The next 330 years saw only forty editions. They most often did not have *Glossa ordinaria* in their margins, a fact that Adversi does not always make clear.

176. Everything that Schulte, *Glosse zum Decret Gratians* 27–29, 90, 94, and other relevant literature say about the edition of 1505 holds true for the first edition Paris 1501, as a comparison of 290 and 292 in Adversi's study makes clear.

are three main additions. The first was the *Casus* of Bartholomaeus Brixiensis, which Chappius placed at the beginning of each chapter in the *Decretum*. The 'Divisiones domini Archidiaconi' were taken from the *Rosarium* of Guido of Baysio. He put them at the beginning of each distinctio and quaestio in order to indicate into which 'partes' the whole is divided and where each individual part begins.[177] Guido, however, had taken these divisions from John of Phintona and Petrus de Salinis, as he says in the *Rosarium*. The incorrect attribution of John of Phintona, which stemmed from the abbreviation Jo(hannes) de Fan(tutiis), appears in almost all printed editions and goes back to the late fifteenth century.[178] Brant's Basel edition of 1500 was expanded with the 'Tabula praegnans per glossarum medullis in marginibus positis'. The summaries to the gloss were written on the outer margin of the page in alphabetical order.[179] An alphabetical index of subjects (with references to individual columns) was then included in the edition. The index in later editions has ca. 4,000 entries.[180]

In an edition of Lyon in 1515, I have found two other kinds of additions that are absent in the editions from Lyon in 1554 and 1555: A gloss from Guido's *Rosarium* was added to a previously unglossed text, often with the siglum 'Archid.', (D.1 c.3). Furthermore, additiones were appended to some glosses, usually from the *Rosarium* (e.g. D.3 p.c.2 s.v. *legato*, D.6 c.1 s.v. *ad vesperam*, D.11 c.5 s.v. *quae orientem*, D.12 pr. s.v. *Quod*).

Charles Dumoulin (Carolus Molinaeus) included many of these additions in his edition Lyon 1554, in which he wrote a large number of glosses that included much textual criticism (using the siglum C. M.) that provoked anger in Rome. The papal curia ordered them to be eradicated.[181] The attempt of Rome to purge all offensive or ambiguous passages from the text of the gloss led to some removals and intrusions in the 1570s but

---

177. In Friedberg's edition of 1879 and its reprints these 'partes' were still given, three, for instance for the small D.3, each beginning (as do most) with a dictum Gratiani.

178. While normally only jo., jof., or jo. de f. is in the edition of Guido's *Rosarium* in Strasbourg c. 1473 (GW 3744), Venice 1481 (GW 3747) most often has io. de fa. or io. de fan.

179. Schulte, *Glosse zum Decret Gratians* 93–95, calls them 'paratitla' and mistakenly connects them to the text of the *Decretum*. They appeared in Paris 1547, since they first appeared there on the title page and were attributed to A. Demosthenes, a professor at the Sorbonne. Whether and how far these synopses differ from each other can not be determined without a close examination.

180. In the editions examined, Lyon 1515, 1554, 1555, Antwerp 1572, and Turin 1588, for example, about a dozen nearly identical entries are listed under the heading of 'Jews'. There are thirteen such entries in the edition of Turin 1588, and one of them unique to it. At D.1 c.12 the addition in Turin notes in common with the other editions: 'Judaei et gentiles subsunt imperio'.

181. Schulte, *Glosse zum Decret Gratians* 93, gives some examples. In the exemplar held in the university library at Würzburg, which I have used, some of these 'glosses' are covered with a layer of chalk.

was then fortunately discontinued.[182] Instead, explanatory additions were appended to the side of the relevant gloss. In this expanded version the gloss was reproduced almost unchanged in the printed editions that followed.

Appendix: Authors' sigla

This is a list of sigla that are found in the manuscripts. The canonists in this list are those who glossed Gratian's *Decretum* before the revision of the *Glossa ordinaria* made by Bartholomaeus Brixiensis. That means that this list also includes many decretalists and Roman law jurists who are or could be cited in the *Glossa ordinaria*. From the period after Bartholomaeus, only those authors who frequently appear in the supplementary layers of manuscripts and later printed editions or who are often quoted from the *Rosarium* of Guido of Baysio are noted. That one siglum can stand for several authors is not uncommon for the period. More information on the often difficult assignment of the sigla can be found in my *Glossen zum Dekret Gratians*, particularly part 3 on individual authors and part 4 on the description of individual manuscripts. Capital and lowercase vary and usually have no significance. I have expanded the sigla to give the full name of each jurist.

a., al., ala.	Alanus
ac.	Accursius (Roman law jurist)
al., alb.	Albertus de Mora (Gregory VIII)
alb.	Albericus (Roman law jurist)
ald.	Aldricus (Roman law jurist)
ar., Archi.	Archidiaconus (Guido of Baysio)
az.	Azo (Roman law jurist)
B., Bar.	Bartholomaeus Brixiensis
b., Ba., Bar., bas., Baz.	Bazianus
b., b´., ber	Bernardus Compostellanus antiquus
b., b´.	Bernard of Pavia
b., b´.	another master B(ernard)
b., bul., bur.	Bulgarus
ben.	Benencasa
b´t´.	Bertrandus
C., Car., r.d.h., *also just* h.	Cardinalis Raimundus de Arenis
c.p.	Cantor parisiensis

182. See Schulte, *Glosse zum Decret Gratians* 93, n. 1 and 28. In the exemplar of the printed edition Antwerp 1572, in the possession of the university library at Würzburg, the 'Censura in glossas iuris canonici ex archetypo Romano' is appended on four unnumbered pages. At the end of this 'censura' the following sentence appears: 'Vtiliter haec Censura adiungetur Glossis Iuris canonici antehac editis. 6. Maij Anno 73. J. Molanus Regius libr. Censor.' Because of these remarks, the objectionable glosses were struck through with ink, for example the gloss to D.1 c.5 s.v. *religioni conveniat*.

Cy., C.y.	Cyprian? (Roman law jurist)
D., d., ddl.	David of London
d., da.	Damasus
f. *see also* ph.	Fidantia Civitatensis
f., f.C.	
G., g., Gan., g(de)dl´.	Gandulphus
G., Gra.	Gratianus
g., Ge., Ger.	Gerard Pucelle
g. de bornado	Guibert of Bornado
G.	Guido (master)
G., g., gui.	Guido of Baysio, Archidiaconus
G., guil. see also W. Ga., Gua.	Garnerius, Irnerius (Roman law jurist)
h.	*see also* Cardinalis
h., ho.	Hostiensis
h., Hu(g)., n., U., ug., ugucc., V.G., y., yg.	Huguccio
h., hug(ol).	Hugolinus (Roman law jurist)
hon.	Honorius
in., innoc.	Innocent III, Innocent IV
Ja.	Jacobus de Albenga
Ja.	Jacobus
Jo., *also* J., *later* Jof., Jo.fa.	Johannes Faventinus
Jo.	Johannes Teutonicus
jo. an.	Johannes Andreae
Jo.b., Jo.ba., Jo.cre.	Johannes Bassianus (Roman law jurist)
Jo. Cal.	Johannes Calderinus
Jo. de d. Johannes de Deo	Johannes of Phintona
Jo. de f. (fin.), *in printed editions mistakenly as* Jo. (de) Fan., *also* Joan.	
jo.jo. Johannes (de)	Johannis
Jo. t(i).	John of Tynemouth
l., la., lau.	Laurentius (Glossa palatina)
m., mar.	Martinus Gosia (Roman law jurist)
m., mar.	Martinus of Zamora
M., mel., mer.	Melendus
n.	*see* Huguccio
p.	Paucapalea
p. (an earlier master Petrus)	Petrus Blesensis?
p., p. ysp.	Petrus Hispanus
p. de s.	Petrus de Salinis
p.b.	Petrus Brito
pe.	Pelagius Gaitan

per., pri.	Percival or Princivallis of Milan
ph., phi., f., fil.	Philip of Aquileia
pi.	Pillius (Roman law jurist)
pla.	Placentinus (Roman law jurist)
R., Ray.	Raymond of Peñafort
R., Ri.	Richardus Anglicus, Richard de Mores
r., Ro., Rol., R.l.	Rolandus
R., ru.	Rufinus
r.d.h.	*see* Cardinalis
s., sic.	Sicard of Cremona
s., si., sy.	Simon of Bisignano
S., S.d.S.	Simon of Southwell
s., St., Ste., Stef.	Stephen of Tournai
T., ta.	Tancred
th.	Thomas
tu., tv., ty.	a French master
u., ug., V.G.	*see* Huguccio
v., vin.	Vincentius
W.	Willielmus

4

The Teaching and Study of Canon Law in the Law Schools

James A. Brundage

University teaching of canon law is as old as the universities themselves, and every medieval university provided for it.¹ Exactly when this began is impossible to say, as it is not possible to assign a precise date for the appearance of the earliest universities in Europe. Canon law was certainly taught in some systematic fashion in private schools at Bologna before Gratian's book appeared, and teachers at Paris were lecturing on the *Decretum* within a decade of its appearance.² A generation or so later—certainly by the 1190s—canon law was being taught at Oxford.³ By the first

---

1. The fundamental treatment of the history of medieval universities remains H. Rashdall, *The Universities of Europe in the Middle Ages* (2d ed. Oxford 1936), now supplemented by HUE. Peter Classen 'Die hohen Schulen und die Gesellschaft im 12. Jahrhundert', *Studium und Gesellschaft im Mittelalter*, ed. J. Fried (MGH Schriften 29; Stuttgart 1983) 1–26, adds appreciably to our understanding of the educational context from which universities emerged.

2. On university teaching of law in general, and also for basic bibliographical information about legal studies in specific universities, see esp. H. Coing, 'Die juristische Fakultät und ihr Lehrprogramm', in Coing, *Handbuch* 1.39–128.

3. See now HUO, especially the chapter by L.E. Boyle, 'Canon Law before 1380' 531–64. Also fundamental is T.H. Aston, 'Oxford's Medieval Alumni', *Past & Present* 74 (1977) 3–40, which analyzes data from A.B. Emden, *Biographical register of the University of Oxford to A.D. 1500* (Oxford 1957–1959). The earliest surviving Oxford statute collection dates in its present form from 1313 or perhaps slightly before, although it incorporates earlier material; G. Pol-

decade of the thirteenth century the private schools of canon law had become part of the corporate structure of universities in all three places. Cambridge soon followed suit and offered instruction in canon law shortly after the university began to take form there in about 1209.[4] By 1250, when the university framed its earliest surviving statutes, a formally structured faculty of canon law was prominently in evidence.[5]

We know few details about the curriculum in these early stages of the development of canon law faculties, although the canonistic literature, which was largely a by-product of teaching, testifies to its broad outlines.[6] It is safe to say that the *Decretum* of Gratian formed the centerpiece of instruction from the beginning, for the earliest surviving evidence about the content and methods of university instruction in canon law took the form of glosses on passages of Gratian's text. Indeed, the *Decretum* itself seems unmistakably designed for, and may well have been the product of, the classroom. The very structure of Gratian's work—his sequence of topical units (the *tractatus decretalium epistolarum, tractatus ordinandorum, tractatus de simonia, tractatus de matrimonio,* etc.)—as well as his expository tactics throughout the work (especially his use of hypothetical cases in part two of the *Decretum*) evokes the smell of ink, of warm bodies wrapped in damp gowns, the chill of classrooms on winter mornings, the tattoo of dialogue between student and teacher. It is apparent, too, from the Roman law passages added to the *Decretum* early in its history, as well as from the frequent, almost compulsive, references to Roman law in the work of many decretists, that students of canon law needed a substantial grounding in Roman law as a basis for professional study of the canons, and their teachers assumed a basic familiarity with civilian terms and concepts. Ex-

---

lard, 'The Oldest Statute Book of the University', *Bodleian Library Record* 8 (1968) 69–91; but see also M.B. Hackett, 'The University as a Corporate Body' HUO 1.53–54. See in addition R.W. Southern, 'Master Vacarius and the beginning of an English academic tradition', *Medieval Learning and Literature: Essays Presented to Richard William Hunt,* ed. J.J.G. Alexander and M.T. Gibson (Oxford 1976) 257–286, as well as Stein's introduction to F. de Zulueta and P. Stein, *The Teaching of Roman Law in England around 1200* (Selden Society, Supplementary series 8; London 1990).

4. HUC esp. 192–201; J.A. Brundage, 'The Cambridge Faculty of Canon Law and the Ecclesiastical Courts of Ely', *Medieval Cambridge: Essays on the Pre-Reformation University,* ed. P.N.R. Zutshi (Woodbridge, Suffolk 1993) 21–45; and, in addition, T.H. Aston, G.D. Duncan, and T.A.R. Evans, 'The Medieval Alumni of the University of Cambridge', *Past & Present* 86 (1980) 9–86, which not only presents an exhaustive analysis of information from A.B. Emden, *Biographical Register of the University of Cambridge to 1500* (Cambridge 1963), but also draws instructive comparisons between Oxford and Cambridge.

5. M.B. Hackett, *The Original Statutes of Cambridge University: The Text and its History* (Cambridge 1970).

6. On the genres of canonistic literature see A. García y García, 'The Faculties of Law' HUE 394–97.

perienced teachers disagreed, however, about the stage in a law student's career at which he should begin to study civil law, as Cardinal Zabarella noted in a treatise on the study of law that he wrote about 1400. Zabarella himself maintained that prospective canonists ought to begin their legal education with canon law and venture into civilian studies only after they had grasped the rudiments of the canonical system.[7] The Oxford canon law faculty, however, assumed that students would complete their civil law studies before commencing work in canon law.[8] Several brief, elementary handbooks survive that were probably designed, at least in part, to meet this need. These manuals, of which the *Liber pauperum* of Vacarius is probably best-known, introduced students to the main institutions of Roman law.[9] Those students trained in Roman law likewise needed a working knowledge of canon law, and there were similar manuals designed for that purpose.[10]

Universities gradually reduced their customary practices to writing, although few of these early statutes survive. Some Paris statutes from 1215 do survive, to be sure, but they were dictated by a papal legate, Robert Courson, and shed little light on curricular matters;[11] likewise the Montpellier statutes of 1220 are not much help, since they deal only with the medical faculty. The Montpellier law faculty was not established until 1289.[12] Bologna's statutes were systematically organized by Johannes Andreae in 1317, although the law faculty had put some of its regulations into written form as early as the 1250s, when Innocent IV confirmed them.[13]

---

7. See Zabarella's *Tractatus de modo docendi et discendi ius canonicum et civile*, ed. T.E. Morrissey, 'The Art of Teaching and Learning Law: A Late Medieval Tract', *History of Universities* 8 (1989) 59.

8. See Boyle, 'Canon Law before 1380' HUO 1:538–539, 541–543.

9. *The Liber pauperum of Vacarius*, ed. F. de Zulueta (Selden Society publications 44; London 1927), as well as the glosses published in Zulueta and Stein, *The Teaching of Roman Law*. See also Southern, 'Master Vacarius and the Beginning of an English Academic Tradition' 266–273, and Peter Stein, 'Vacarius and the Civil Law', *Church and Government in the Middle Ages: Essays in Honour of C. R. Cheney*, ed. C.N.L. Brooke, D.E. Luscombe, G.H. Martin and D.M. Owen (Cambridge 1976) 119–137 (reprinted Stein, *The Character and Influence of Roman Law*, [London 1988] 167–168), also Zulueta and Stein, *The Teaching of Roman Law* 1.xiii–liii. On other such compendia see also M. Bertram and M. Duynstee, 'Casus legum sive suffragia monachorum: Legistische Hilfsmittel für Kanonisten im späteren Mittelalter', TRG 51 (1983) 317–363; A.B. Palacios, 'La *Concordia utriusque iuris* de Pascipoverus', *Proceedings Berkeley* 139–151.

10. See esp. Ingrid Baumgärtner, 'Was muß ein Legist vom Kirchenrecht wissen? Roffredus Beneventanus und seine *Libelli de iure canonico*', *Proceedings Cambridge* 223–245.

11. *Chartularium universitatis Parisiensis* ed. H. Denifle and É. Chatelain (Paris 1891–1899; reprinted Bruxelles 1964; hereafter CUP) 1:67–68, no. 8 (1208–1209), 1:78–80, no. 20 (1215), 1:136–39, no. 79 (1231); S.C. Ferruolo, 'The Paris Statutes of 1215 Reconsidered', *History of Universities* 5 (1985) 1–14.

12. Fournier, *Statuts* 2.17–18, no. 903.

13. The statutes of the Bologna law faculty in the redaction by Johannes Andreae have

The text of some slightly later university statutes, probably from the 1270s, was recently discovered in a manuscript at Berkeley, California by Domenico Maffei.[14] Oxford had some written constitutions by 1254, but its earliest surviving statutes are certainly no earlier than ca. 1275, roughly a generation later than the Cambridge statute collection of ca. 1250.[15] Thus it is difficult to say just when formal regulations first embodied a requirement that students of canon law show some preparation in Roman law. Still, expressly required or not, a working knowledge of the elements of Roman law was a practical necessity for canonists. Honorius III's 1219 prohibition of the teaching of Roman law in Paris or its vicinity was thus a blow to canonistic studies, and in particular to the standing of the nascent University of Paris as a center for the training of canon lawyers.[16] The prohibition was renewed by Pope Innocent IV in 1254, then later modified by Pope Clement V in 1307.[17] Honorius' decretal, *Super speculum*, in addition forbade both secular priests and regular clerics of all kinds, as well as any who held benefices, to study civil law. The pope apparently intended thereby to discourage the study of law in order to enhance the prestige and attractiveness of theological studies, and of the Parisian theology faculty in particular. Complaints that students were deserting the arts and theology to study the lucrative sciences of law and medicine were already rife before the end of the twelfth century, and Honorius' decretal responded, at least in part, to these criticisms.

The decretal failed, however, to reverse the trend that critics decried. The number of law students, both civilians and canonists, continued to increase, and a considerable fraction of those students were clerics. Would-be canonists at Paris, to be sure, now had to do their civil law studies else-

---

been published by C. Malagola, *Statuti delle università e dei collegi dello studio bolognese* (Bologna 1888; reprinted Torino 1966) 3–46, as well as by H. Denifle, 'Die Statuten der Juristen-Universität Bologna vom J. 1317–1347 und deren Verhältnis zu jenen Paduas, Perugias, Florenz', *Archiv für Literatur- und Kirchengeschichte des Mittelalters* 3 (1887) 196–397 (hereafter SUB).

14. D. Maffei, 'Un trattato di Bonaccorso degli Elisei e i più antichi statuti dello Studio di Bologna nel manoscritto 22 della Robbins Collection', BMCL 5 (1975) 73–101. On the date of this collection see M. Boháček, 'Puncta Codicis v rukopisu XVII.A.10 narodniho musez v Praze', *Studie o rukopisech* (German summary at 19–22).

15. For the English universities see G. Pollard, 'The Oldest Statute Book of the University', *Bodleian Library Record* 8 (1968) 69–91; Hackett, *Original Statutes* 6–7.

16. CUP 1.90–93 no. 32; also X 5.33.28, *Super speculum*: Stephan Kuttner, 'Papst Honorius III. und das Studium des Zivilrechts', *Festschrift für Martin Wolff: Beiträge zum Zivilrecht und internationalen Privatrecht* ed. E. von Caemmerer, F.A. Mann, W. Hallstein, and L. Raiser (Tübingen 1952) 79–101; reprinted with original pagination in Kuttner. *Gratian and the Schools of Law, 1140–1234* (London 1983).

17. M. Fournier and L. Dorez, *La faculté de Décret de l'Université de Paris au XVe siècle* (Paris 1895–1942) 1.6–7 no. 5 and 1.8–9 no. 10.

where—usually at Orléans, which became the principal beneficiary of *Super speculam*. Even outside of Paris, clerics usually found it advisable to complete their civil law preparation before receiving major orders, but the available evidence suggests that no significant decrease in the numbers of clerical law students resulted from Honorius' decretal.[18] At most, *Super speculam* may have succeeded in slowing the rate of increase in the numbers of clerics who studied law.

The content of the canon law curriculum centered on the texts of the current canonistic collections and was gradually enlarged as new texts became available. Thus canonistic studies in the late twelfth century concentrated at first almost entirely on the *Decretum*, but then expanded as new decretal collections, such as the ones that we now call the *Quinque compilationes antiquae*, appeared.[19] The promulgation of the *Liber extra* in 1234 caused a curricular upheaval. This comprehensive text immediately supplanted the older ones, which soon dropped out of use. Similarly during the second half of the thirteenth century, the *Novellae* of Innocent IV and other collections of post-Gregorian *extravagantes* briefly gained a toehold in the curriculum, only to be ousted when the *Liber Sextus* appeared to replace them. The *Constitutiones Clementinae* likewise found an immediate place in the canonistic curriculum, and, for reasons not altogether easy to explain, was the last medieval collection to be added to the curricular structure of the canon law schools.[20]

Since the canon law curriculum was so strongly text-centered, supplies of reliable copies of the basic texts and commentaries were essential to the functioning of the canon law schools.[21] Hence the book trade and

---

18. Hard figures on numbers of law students are difficult to pin down at most universities until the fifteenth century. Prior to that, enrollment figures for Oxford and Cambridge have been more closely studied than those for most Continental universities; see esp. Aston, 'Oxford's Medieval Alumni' and Aston, Duncan, and Evans, 'The Medieval Alumni of the University of Cambridge'. On other universities note also A.M. Campbell, *The Black Death and Men of Learning* (History of Science Society Publications, new series 1; New York 1931) 159–160, 166, as well as R.-C. Schwinges, 'Admission' and A. García y García, 'The Faculties of Law' HUE 1.171–94, 400–401.

19. This is apparent not only from the promulgation decrees that Innocent III attached to 3 Comp. and Honorius III to 5 Comp., but also from the gloss apparatus to the various *Compilationes antiquae*, since these were by-products of the teaching of the *compilationes* in the schools. See also V. Piergiovanni, 'Il primo secolo della scuola canonistica di Bologna: Un ventennio di studi', *Proceedings Berkeley* 252–254.

20. E. Fournier, 'L'enseignement des Décrétales à l'Université de Paris au moyen âge', *Revue d'histoire de l'église de France* 26 (1940) 58–62.

21. Bellomo, *Saggio sull'università nell'età del diritto comune* (Catania 1979, reprinted Rome 1994) 60–61; H. Bresc, 'Egemonia e vita del diritto nello specchio del consumo del libro in Sicilia (1300–1500)', *Scuole diritto e società nel mezzogiorno medievale d'Italia* ed. M. Bellomo (Catania 1985) 1.183–201.

the study of canon law enjoyed an intimate, indeed symbiotic, connection. The schools created a dependable and profitable market for copies of canonical texts and consequently booksellers, suppliers of parchment, binders, and copyists swarmed around them. So, too, did less respectable hawkers of new decretals. Not all the documents offered for sale were genuine, for ateliers of forgers soon appeared to take advantage of the demand for the latest law. Stephen of Tournai in a letter to the pope painted a vivid picture, both of the feverish commercial activities around the law schools at the beginning of the thirteenth century and of the problems that resulted:[22]

> Again, if a case comes up that should be settled under canon law either by your judges-delegate or by the ordinary judges, there is produced from the vendors an inextricable forest of decretal letters presumably under the name of Pope Alexander [III] of blessed memory, and older canons are cast aside, rejected, expunged. When this plunder has been unrolled before us, those things that were wholesomely instituted in councils of holy fathers do not settle the case, nor is conciliar prescription followed, since letters prevail which perchance advocates for hire invented and forged in their shops or cubicles under the name of Roman pontiffs. A new volume composed of these is solemnly read in the schools and offered for sale in the market place to the applause of a horde of notaries, who rejoice that in copying suspect opuscula both their labor is lessened and their pay increased.

The problem did not die out soon; at the end of the fifteenth century one of the deans of the canon law faculty at the University of Paris, Ambroise de Cambrai, had a record as a forger of false papal bulls.[23]

Booksellers and producers found students and practitioners of canon law a steady market, and no doubt a profitable one, which they continued to tap for centuries. The enormous number of surviving manuscripts of law texts attests to their activity. After the invention of printing, fifteenth- and sixteenth-century printers and booksellers quickly discovered that canonistic texts and commentaries provided one of the most profitable and dependable staples of the book trade. The market for canon law

---

22. Adapted from the translation by L. Thorndike in *University Records and Life in the Middle Ages* (Columbia University Records of Civilization, Sources and Studies 38; New York 1944; reprinted New York 1975) 23–24; text in H. Denifle *Die Entstehung der Universitäten des Mittelalters bis 1400* (Berlin 1885; reprinted Graz 1956) 745, n. 1, and in CUP 1:47–48, no. 48. See also C. Duggan, '*Improba pestis falsitatis*: Forgeries and the Problem of Forgery in Twelfth-Century Decretal Collections (with special reference to English cases)', *Fälschungen im Mittelalter: Internationaler Kongreß der Monumenta Germaniae Historica München, 16.–19. September 1986* (Schriften der Monumenta Germaniae Historica 33.1–6; Hannover 1988) 2:319–361.

23. G. Le Bras, 'La faculté de droit au moyen âge', *Aspects de l'Université de Paris* (Paris 1949) 88–89.

books remained reliable for decades, even centuries, because demand was steady and relatively inelastic, while new products (i.e. new laws, collections, and treatises) added to, but did not supplant, old products. Canon law was for publishers a dependable money machine.[24]

References to booksellers and book producers in Bolognese records from the mid-thirteenth century reveal a brisk trade in both new and used copies of all of the principal canon law texts, as well as the major gloss collections and commentaries on them.[25] The prices mentioned in these documents demonstrate how valuable a collection of legal texts and commentaries could be. In 1265, for example, copies of the *Liber extra* sold at Bologna for prices ranging from £25 bolonense to £110 bolonense. By way of comparison, a house in the parish of San Felice changed hands in that year for £30 and another house in the Borgo Pollicino went for £46, while half a vineyard could be had for £25 10s.[26] High prices for portable goods inevitably bred temptation. Theft of books from students presented irresistible opportunities for the unscrupulous and continuing problems for civic authorities.[27] Other, presumably more honest, entrepreneurs were prepared, for a price, to transport law books to distant regions, a service of obvious interest to those who had accumulated a collection of books during their student days and wished to send home the nucleus of a law library when they returned to practice.[28]

The basic structure of a system of academic degrees in canon law had begun to emerge by the beginning of the thirteenth century. It was very likely modeled upon patterns already established in the law schools.

---

24. F.R.P. Soetermeer, *Utrumque ius in peciis: Die Produktion juristischer Bücher an italienischen und französischen Universitäten des 13. und 14. Jahrhunderts* (Ius commune, Sonderhefte 150; Frankfurt, 2002); E. Will, 'Decreti Gratiani incunabula: Beschreibendes Gesamtverzeichnis der Weigendrucke des Gratianischen Dekrets', SG 6 (1959) 1–280; A. Adversi, 'Saggio di un catalogo delle edizioni del *Decretum Gratiani* posteriori al secolo XV', SG 6 (1959) 281–451.

25. SUB (1317) §36, ed. H. Denifle, 298–301; B. Bruggi, 'Il catalogo dei libri degli stationarii negli statuti della Università Bolognese dei giuristi', *Studi e memorie per la storia dell'Università di Bologna* 5 (1920) 3–44.

26. *Chartularium studii Bononiensis* (Bologna 1909–; 15 vols. to date; cited hereafter as CSB) 5:9 (no. 13), 29 (no. 58), 32 (no. 63), 60 (no. 124): sales of decretals; 51 (no. 104), 66 (no. 138): house prices; 84 (no. 179): vineyard. See also A. Perez Martin, 'Büchergeschäfte in Bolognese Regesten aus den Jahren 1265–1350', *Ius commune* 7 (1978) 7–49.

27. A. Palmieri, 'Furti di libri e di vivende a scolari dell'antico studio Bolognese', *Studi e memorie . . . Bologna* 9 (1926) 189–198.

28. E.g., CSB 7:59 (no. 106), 60 (no. 108), 60–61 (no. 109), 67 (no. 122); see esp. S. Stelling-Michaud, *L'université de Bologne et la pénétration des droits romain et canonique en Suisse aux XIIIe et XIVe siècles* (Travaux d'humanisme et renaissance 17; Geneva 1955) 100–114, and 'Le transport international des manuscrits juridiques bolonais entre 1265 et 1320', *Mélanges d'histoire économique et sociale en hommage au Professeur Antony Babel* (Geneva 1963) 1:95–127.

Teachers of Roman law had used the title 'Doctor of Laws' from the second half of the twelfth century onwards. This was at first simply an honorific title, designating anyone learned in the law; it came to designate an academic degree only in the course of the thirteenth century.[29] At first, those who completed the formal course of canonistic training were called, both by themselves and by others, 'master of decrees' ('magister decretorum').[30] Then by about 1220 the title 'doctor of decrees' ('doctor decretorum') began to come into use, and by mid-century this was the usual style and title of fully trained canonists.[31]

Academic preparation for the study of canon law showed no uniform standards or requirements. As a practical matter, some previous schooling was essential, but what that consisted of might vary enormously. No student could hope to learn much in any faculty of a medieval university without a reasonable command of Latin. Some study of civil law was also essential for canon law students, as we have seen, and several universities encouraged prospective canonists to complete a degree in civil law before beginning to study canon law. Some study of the Bible was occasionally required as well of students of canon law, although they were not especially encouraged to take a theology degree preparatory to admission to canon law studies.[32]

At Bologna the course of study for the doctorate in canon law lasted nominally six years. A first-year student, known as a 'rudis auditor', was expected to follow only the most elementary points made in lectures. Second- and third-year students, called 'provecti', were expected to follow lectures at a more sophisticated level.[33] A student who had completed four years of study was eligible to sit for a private examination, and those who passed became licentiates in canon law and were permitted to lecture in the afternoons on a single tractate in the *Decretum* or a single title of the *Liber extra*. After a fifth year of study the student was allowed to lecture on a whole book. Those who completed the sixth year were eligible to pro-

---

29. See generally Peter Weimar, 'Zur Doktorwürde der Bologneser Legisten', *Aspekte europäischer Rechtsgeschichte* (Frankfurt a/M. 1982) 421–443; reprinted in his *Zur Renaissance der Rechtswissenschaft im Mittelalter* (Goldbach 1997) 307*–329*.

30. The style Master of the Decrees appeared early in the thirteenth century and remained in use for several generations, e.g., CSB 3:169, no. 151 (1208) and 3:197–199, no. 181 (1223).

31. The title 'Doctor of Decrees' appears at Bologna in a document of 1218, CSB 3:185–186, no. 169; see also CSB 3:200, no. 182 (1223). A 'doctor decretorum' who appears in Oxford documents of 1217 and 1218 had very likely taken his degree at Bologna; the degree of Doctor of Canon Law seems not to have been granted at Oxford before 1235; Boyle, 'Canon Law before 1380' HUO 1:534, 548.

32. Schwinges, 'Admission' HUE 1:175–176.

33. Bellomo, *Saggio* 226–227.

ceed to the final, public examination, which concluded with a ceremony in which they received the insignia of the doctorate.[34]

Professorial lectures on canon law at Bologna were so arranged that two professors each presented a course of lectures on the *Decretum* every year, one in the mornings and the other in the afternoons. Late-thirteenth-century statutes prescribed in great detail the order of presentation that each professor must follow and a timetable that he was expected to observe. Thus, for example, the morning course began at the beginning of part one and the lecturer was supposed to reach Distinction twenty-three by the end of October and Distinction fifty-one by the end of November. By the end of February he should have reached Distinction 101 and in March he should have begun to treat part two. He was scheduled to reach Case twenty-four by August. Meanwhile the afternoon course concentrated on parts two and three. The lecturer began in October with the first Case and was supposed to reach question four of Case two by the end of the month. He had a series of deadlines to meet in order to complete his treatment of the last three distinctions of the *Tractatus de consecratione* by the close of the academic year in August.[35]

Two other professors likewise offered courses on the *Liber extra* each year, paralleling the two courses on the *Decretum*. The morning *Decretals* course dealt with Books one and two, while the afternoon course commenced with Book three, followed by Books four and five. The statutes also prescribed deadlines for the completion of each portion of each book, similar to those for the *Decretum* courses.[36] To facilitate systematic compliance with the regulations, canonical textbooks were divided into 'points' (*puncta*). Each 'point' was a norm or rule of law that lecturers were required to cover. Some 'points' were designated 'ordinary' and these had to be dealt with in 'ordinary' lectures, while 'extraordinary points' were dealt with by those who gave the 'extraordinary' lectures.[37]

The curriculum of the canon law school at Oxford followed a strikingly different pattern. Oxford cast civil law as a kind of preparatory course for canon law, rather than a distinct field of study in its own right. In contrast to Bologna, for example, which had municipally funded professorships that supported a corps of permanent (or at least long-term) teachers, Oxford relied almost totally on its own newly minted bachelors and

---

34. SUB §§ 53, 55, 57–58, ed. Denifle, 217, 329–330, 332–338; Rashdall, *Universities* 1.221.
35. Maffei, 'Un trattato di Bonaccorso degli Elisei' edits the statutes at 93–101. The relevant lecture regulations occur at lines 256–287 on 101.
36. Ibid. 99–101, lines 200–255.
37. Bellomo, *Saggio* 192–196.

doctors as its teaching staff.³⁸ The canonical texts themselves, the *libri legales*, were the same in Oxford as those that students studied in canon law faculties at Continental universities. It is no great surprise to discover that the Oxford curriculum was evidently modeled on that at Paris, and that the Cambridge curriculum had many features reminiscent of Oxford, while all three of these resembled one another more than they did the canon law curricula at Bologna and other Italian universities.³⁹ First, in the early fourteenth century, Oxford demanded that candidates for degrees in canon law show specific preparation in civil law. Admission to the degree of Bachelor of Canon Law (B.Cn.L.; often called the licentiate elsewhere) required three years of preliminary study in civil law. Students who had already taken the doctorate in civil law (D.C.L.) had already fulfilled this requirement and had to spend only one year hearing lectures on Gratian's *Decretum*, although those who did not have the D.C.L. must spend a second year studying the *Decretum*. All candidates for the B.Cn.L. had to attend a three-year cycle of lectures, both ordinary and extraordinary, on the *Liber extra*, *Sext*, and *Clementines*. Admission to the doctorate in canon law (D.Cn.L.) at Oxford required a further year of civil law (D.C.L.s were of course exempt from this), as well as two years' study of the Bible (from which D.C.L.s were also excused), an additional year's study of the *Decretum*, and two further years of lectures on the decretal collections.⁴⁰ It should be noted, however, that intending graduates routinely secured exemptions from part of the curricular requirements by petitioning for a 'grace', for which they paid a fee to the university treasury at Oxford and Cambridge (and presumably elsewhere).⁴¹

Everywhere candidates for both the baccalaureate and the doctorate in canon law were supposed to participate regularly in disputations as well as to attend the prescribed courses of lectures and 'repetitiones', but uni-

---

38. Boyle, 'Canon Law before 1380' HUO 1:535, 538–40, 563–64.

39. For Cambridge see *Statuta antiqua* §§ 100–101, 122 (1300 X 1390) *Documents relating to the University and colleges of Cambridge... published by direction of the commissioners appointed by the Queen to inquire into the state, discipline, studies, and revenues of the said university and colleges* (London 1852) 1.365–66, 376–77, summarized in Leader, HUC 1.193–94. On Paris see CUP 2.503–504, no. 1040 (1340), 2.691–97, no. 1188 (after 1335); M. Fournier and L. Dorez, *La faculté de Décret de l'Université de Paris au XVe siècle* (Paris 1895–1942) 1.10–11, 15–16, no. 13, 17. For Bologna see above 105–106, as well as SUB (1432) § 55, ed. Denifle 329–30. The summary in A. Sorbelli, *Il medioevo (secc. XI–XV)* (Storia della Università di Bologna 1; Bologna 1940) 89, is misleading.

40. L.E. Boyle, 'The Curriculum of the Faculty of Canon Law at Oxford in the First Half of the Fourteenth Century', *Oxford Studies Presented to Daniel Callus* (Publications of the Oxford Historical Society, 2d ser. 16; Oxford 1964) 135–62, as well as 'Canon Law before 1380' HUO 1.541–48.

41. See A.B. Cobban, *Medieval English Universities: Oxford and Cambridge to c. 1500* (Aldershot 1988) 84–85.

versity authorities sometimes found the disputation requirement difficult to enforce.[42] In order to receive the first degree in canon law (the licentiate or B.Cn.L.), students had to pass a private oral examination at the end of their course and to lecture as inceptors, or beginning teachers, in the afternoons. Candidates for the doctorate in canon law had in addition not only to pass a public examination, but also to lecture as regent masters for two years.[43] Those who took degrees in canon law had to pass formal examinations on their knowledge of the subject and demonstrate their skill in applying its principles to concrete problems.[44] In 1173 Pope Alexander III required that applicants for a teaching license first pass an examination.[45] Some sort of qualifying examination for prospective teachers of canon law was apparently in use at Bologna by 1219, when Honorius III confirmed the practice in a brief letter. This evidence is corroborated by Odofredus (d. 1265), who referred to the examinations given by the *antiqui doctores* during his student days, that is to say before about 1220.[46] Examinations were at first apparently given by the archdeacon of Bologna, but by the fourteenth century seven doctors of law were needed to conduct a degree examination.[47] Guido de Guinis recounts the story of

42. By 1376 the problem had become so acute at Oxford that King Edward III intervened (no doubt at the request of university authorities) to enforce the disputation requirement; *Calendar of the Patent Rolls Preserved in the Public Record Office* . . . 1374–77 (London 1916) 290–93. On the form and content of disputations see Bellomo, *Saggio* 216–22 and F.M. Powicke, 'Some Problems in the History of the Medieval Universities', *Transactions of the Royal Historical Society*, 4th series, 17; London 1934) 1–18 at 13–15.

43. Boyle, 'Curriculum' 153–156; also H. G. Richardson, 'The Oxford Law School under John', *Law Quarterly Review* 57 (1941) 319–38, and, for comparison, Hackett, *Original statutes* 30–33, 131, 136–137; Bologna statutes of 1432 §§ 57–58, ed. Denifle 332–338. See also García y García, 'Faculties of Law' HUE 1.399. For examples of formal examiners' reports, together with specimens of the ceremonial speeches that accompanied the formal conferral of degrees at Bologna see E. Conte, "Un sermo *pro petendis insignis* al tempo di Azzone e Bagarotto," *Rivista di storia del diritto italiano* 60 (1987) 71–86 and C. Piana, *Nuove ricerche su le università di Bologna e di Parma* (Spicilegium Bonaventurianum 2; Florence 1966) 3–108.

44. J.K. Hyde, 'Universities and Cities in Medieval Italy', *The University and the City: From Medieval Origins to the Present* ed. T. Bender (New York 1988) 16, points out that examinations to test achievement were a novelty introduced in this period. For Italian universities in the fifteenth and sixteenth centuries, see Paul F. Grendler, *The Universities of the Italian Renaissance* (Baltimore-London 2002).

45. P. Nardi, 'Relations with Authority' HUE 1.79–80. Earlier monastic schools and palace schools had nothing of the sort and would probably have found the whole notion of examinations either repugnant to their sensibilities or irrelevant to their purposes.

46. Honorius III in Po 6094 (28 June 1219); text in M. Sarti and M. Fattorini, *De claris archigymnasii Bononiensis professoribus* ed. C. Albicino and C. Malagola (Bologna 1888–1896; reprinted Torino 1962) 2:260, no. 17. Odofredus, *Lectura super Codice* (Lyon 1552; reprinted Bologna 1968–1969) to Cod. 4.65.22, vol. 1, fol. 259ra.

47. D. Maffei, 'Dottori e studenti nel pensiero di Simone da Borsano', SG 15 (1972) 229–249 at 237; Weimar, 'Zur Doktorwürde' 424–427. On the examination system at Paris see Powicke, 'Some Problems' 15–18.

his own examination at Bologna, where his examiners included Accursius, who taught at Bologna from about 1215. Guido had the temerity to claim during the examination that Accursius' gloss to Dig. 5.3.31 v. *debebit* was mistaken. Despite that gaffe he passed the examination, although not before receiving a dressing-down from the author of the gloss. In another account, a student of Jacobus Balduini who was examined by a board that again included Accursius did not fare as well. On this occasion Accursius insisted that the candidate must be failed.[48]

Candidates for admission to examinations either had to conform to certain general requirements in the law itself, or else had to receive dispensations from the appropriate authority to exempt them from one or more specific regulations. The law demanded that legal practitioners must be free, male, Catholic, and of legitimate birth. In addition they must not be deaf, dumb, blind, or disreputable ('infamis').[49]

Professional training as a canon lawyer tended to be long and consequently expensive. The Bologna statutes, for example, required a minimum of six years of legal studies for the doctorate in canon law and seven years for the civil law doctorate,[50] while at Oxford the statutes demanded seven years of canon law studies, after three years of preliminary studies in civil law, to become a B.Cn.L., plus an additional three years as an inceptor and (after 1333) a further two years as a regent in order to receive the doctorate in canon law.[51] In practice, substantial numbers of those who took canon law degrees secured waivers from some portion of these requirements. Even so, the degree courses were lengthy and it is not surprising to find that most students who began studies in canon law failed to stay the full course. Many came to university, studied law for one or two years, and then left to use their legal training to secure such preferment and rewards as they could find.[52]

The content of the canon law curriculum was well established, and apparently had been fixed in place for quite some time, by the third quarter

---

48. E.M. Meijers, *Etudes d'histoire du droit* (Leiden 1956–73) 3:33.

49. All of these requirements appeared in classical Roman law (Dig. 3.1.1.3,5; 3.1.4; 3.3.41; 50.17.2) and were adopted wholesale by Gratian at C.3 q.7 c.2, as well as C.15 q.3 d.a.c.1 and c.2. The candidate must be at least seventeen years old by the time he commenced practice, according to Dig. 3.1.1.3; Gratian, C.3 q.7 c.2. On infamia see Francesco Migliorino, *Fama e infamia: Problemi della società medievale nel pensiero giuridico nei secoli XII e XIII* (Catania 1985) and E.M. Peters, 'Wounded Names: The Medieval Doctrine of Infamy', *Law in Mediaeval Life and Thought*, ed. E.B. King and S.J. Ridyard. (Sewanee Mediaeval Studies, No. 8; Sewanee 1990) 43–89.

50. SUB (1432) § 55, ed. Denifle, 329–330.

51. Boyle, 'Canon Law before 1380' HUO 1.543–546.

52. R.C. Schwinges, 'Student Education, Student Life' HUE 1.195–200.

of the thirteenth century, from which time university and faculty statutes that specify the details of curriculum presentation and duration have survived. Degree requirements in canon law, as in other university faculties, were framed primarily in terms of the numbers and kinds of lectures that the candidate must have heard.

University lectures were of two main types: ordinary and extraordinary (sometimes called cursory). Ordinary lectures typically took place in the early morning hours and dealt with the texts deemed central to the work of the faculty. These lectures were usually delivered by senior doctors of the faculty. When teaching personnel were scarce or over-committed, however, some ordinary lectures might even be given by well-qualified holders of the bachelor's degree, as happened in the canon law faculty at Cambridge, for example, in the early fourteenth century.[53] Extraordinary lectures, by contrast, were usually given by more junior teachers (often those who had just received the bachelor's degree) during the afternoons and on feast days when ordinary lectures were not permitted.[54] 'Repetitiones', or review sessions, were also commonly held in the afternoons. Odofredus described the lecture method that he followed, which he had no doubt learned from his own teachers at Bologna:[55]

> First, I shall give you the summaries of each title before I come to the text. Second, I shall put forth well and distinctly and in the best terms I can the purport of each law. Third, I shall read the text in order to correct it. Fourth, I shall briefly restate the meaning. Fifth, I shall solve conflicts, adding general matters (which are commonly called 'brocardica') and subtle and useful distinctions and questions with the solution, so far as divine Providence shall assist me. And if any law is deserving of a review by reason of its fame or difficulty, I shall reserve it for an afternoon review.

The number and prominence of canon law lectures devoted to various texts changed, of course, as the law itself grew and developed over time, for the legal curriculum naturally stressed current law and the most recent decrees. Thus in the late twelfth and early thirteenth centuries, lectures on Gratian's *Decretum* formed the core of the canonistic curriculum, supplemented by lectures on the decretal collections. Once the *Liber extra*

---

53. Cobban, *The Medieval English Universities* 167.

54. This distinction was already in place by 1215 at Paris, for it appears in the decrees of Cardinal Robert Courson; CUP 1.78–80, no. 20, translated in Thorndike, *University Records* 28; Rashdall, *Universities* 1.205–207.

55. Odofredus, in Savigny, 3.541–42, 553; trans. in Thorndike, *University Records* 67. Cf. Hostiensis' description of proper lecturing style in *Summa aurea* 5.9 *De magistris* § 6 (Lyon 1537; reprinted Aalen 1962), fol. 235ra–rb (see summary in Hoeflich and Grabher's essay above), as well as the statutory prescriptions in SUB (1317) §44, ed. Denifle 313–15, and García y García, 'Faculties of law' HUE 1.398–400.

appeared, it quickly became the principal text, and lectures on Gratian became less prominent.[56] By the early fourteenth century the *Liber Sextus* and the *Clementines* began to rival the *Liber extra* in the lecture lists, and the study of Gratian's book became a distinctly secondary subject in the curriculum.

Lengthy courses of study inevitably meant high costs. Those of modest means must have found it impossible to defray the expense of a canon law degree entirely from their personal resources,[57] but some assistance was available for the clever, the ambitious, the industrious, and the lucky. Clerics who were fortunate enough to hold benefices or other revenue-producing church appointments, for example, might obtain leaves of absence for up to five years in order to study at a university without forfeiting the income to which their positions entitled them.[58] Johannes Teutonicus argued that all university students ought to have benefices to support them while they studied, and Innocent III expressly approved the practice in 1207 (X 3.4.12).[59] The right of a student to a benefice was considerably broadened in 1219 by Honorius III's decretal *Super speculam*, although Honorius specified that study leaves should be available only for the study of theology.[60] Papal dispensations for this purpose subsequently became very common.[61] This development was made possible in part by the changes in the kinds of income that members of cathedral chapters received. Prior to the twelfth century their income was usually paid in kind (mainly food) distributed daily to chapter members; this income had to be consumed quickly and on the spot. By the thirteenth century cathedral canons more commonly received cash payments, which were clearly more portable and this in turn made it possible for chapter members to be absent for protracted periods without forfeiting use of their income.[62] The practice of granting beneficed clerics protracted study leaves, however, could and did lead to glaring abuses, as Rashdall has observed, but this practice was notoriously common among pseudo-students nominally en-

---

56. See description of curriculum above.

57. On student costs and finances at Oxford see J.I. Catto, 'Citizens, Scholars and Masters' HUO 1.170–73; for Bologna see Stelling-Michaud, *L'université de Bologne* 88–89.

58. L.E. Boyle, "The Constitution 'Cum ex eo' of Boniface VIII: Education of Parochial Clergy," *Mediaeval Studies* 24 (1962) 263–302, reprinted in his *Pastoral Care, Clerical Education and Canon Law, 1200–1400* (London 1981), no. VIII.

59. Ordinary Gloss to D.37 c.12 v. *neque magistros*.

60. CUP 1.91 (No. 32); X 5.5.5.

61. P. Kibre, *Scholarly Privileges in the Middle Ages: The Rights, Privileges, and Immunities of Scholars and Universities at Bologna, Padua, Paris, and Oxford* (Mediaeval Academy of America Publications 72; Cambridge 1962) 33, 40, 63, 69, and passim; Stelling-Michaud, *L'université de Bologne* 89–90.

62. See J. Barrow, 'German Cathedrals and the Monetary Economy in the Twelfth Century', *Journal of Medieval History* 16 (1990) 13–38.

rolled in the faculty of canon law at Paris.⁶³ Colleges and halls within the universities could supply scholarships and fellowships for some, and a few colleges regularly reserved appointments for men studying canon law.⁶⁴ A few students were lucky enough to find public or private patrons willing to support them during their studies, and of course many students relied upon financial help from their families in order to meet expenses, while others were able to sustain themselves, either wholly or in part, through work as servants, teachers, or copyists.⁶⁵ Beyond that, students regularly sought loans, sometimes from endowed loan-chests held by the universities,⁶⁶ sometimes from collegiate funds,⁶⁷ or, in Italy particularly, from their teachers, some of whom augmented their teaching income by lending money to students—often at exorbitant rates of interest.⁶⁸

The most frequently criticized cost of legal training at universities everywhere was the expense of the ceremonies involved in taking a degree. Degree-taking rituals involved a round of pageantry and gift-giving that culminated in the formal investiture of the candidate with the symbols of his new status, followed by an elaborate and costly banquet, all paid for by the new graduate.⁶⁹ It was common, however, for students to secure a dis-

---

63. Rashdall, *Universities* 1.438–439.

64. Schwinges, 'Student education' HUE 1.235–42; D.E.R. Watt, 'University Clerks and Rolls of Petitions for Benefices', *Speculum* 34 (1959) 213–229; J.R.L. Highfield, 'The Early Colleges' HUO 1.225–63 at 245, 249; T.H. Aston and R. Faith, 'The Endowments of the University and Colleges to *circa* 1348' HUO 1.265–309 at 288–289; Catto, 'Citizens, Scholars and Masters' HUO 1.191–92; *Documents . . . Cambridge* 2.21–22 (Peterhouse Statutes c. 24) 417–18 (Trinity Hall Statutes, 1352, c. 1); A.B. Cobban, *The King's Hall within the University of Cambridge in the later Middle Ages* (Cambridge Studies in Medieval Life and Thought, 3d ser. 1; Cambridge 1969) 77–79; C. Crawley, *Trinity Hall: The History of a Cambridge College, 1350–1975* (Cambridge 1976) 11–12; B. Marti, *The Spanish College at Bologna in the Fourteenth Century* (Philadelphia 1966) 128.

65. F. Pegues, 'Royal Support of Students in the Thirteenth Century', *Speculum* 31 (1956) 454–62; H. Boockmann, 'Die Rechtsstudenten des Deutschen Ordens: Studium, Studienförderung und gelehrter Beruf im späteren Mittelalter', *Festschrift für Hermann Heimpel zum 70. Geburtstag* (Veröffentlichungen des Max-Planck-Instituts für Geschichte 36; Göttingen 1972) 2.313–75; J. Paquet, 'Coût des études, pauvreté et labeur: Fonctions et métiers d'étudiants au moyen âge', *History of universities* 2 (1982) 15–52; P. Trio, 'Financing of University Students in the Middle Ages: A new Orientation', *History of Universities* 4 (1984) 1–24; R.C. Schwinges, 'Student Education, Student Life' HUE 1.241.

66. These are particularly well-documented at Oxford and Cambridge; Rashdall, *Universities* 3.35–36; Catto, HUO 1.172–73; Aston and Faith, HUO 1.275–87; G. Pollard, 'Medieval Loan-Chests at Cambridge', *Bulletin of the Institute of Historical Research* 17 (1939–1940) 113–29.

67. Aston and Faith, HUO 1.288, 301; Boyle, 'Canon Law before 1380' HUO 1.550; Leader, HUC 1.73.

68. J. Fried, 'Vermögensbildung der bologneser Juristen', *Università e società nei secoli XII–XVI* (Pistoia 1982) 48–51; P. Sambin, 'Giuristi padovani nel quattrocento tra attività universitaria et attività publica: I. Paolo d'Arezzo (†1443)', *Università e società* 367–397 at 387; Stelling-Michaud, *L'université de Bologne* 91–98.

69. Rashdall, *Universities* 1.226–31, 284–87, 450, 460–62, 483–89; Catto, HUO 1.190.

pensation from the obligation to furnish a banquet, in return for a payment to the university treasury.[70] The heavy expenses that attended graduation were no doubt one reason why so many law students left the universities without taking their degrees. Contemporaries perceived this situation as dysfunctional, and Pope Clement V sought to alleviate it by placing a cap on the expenses of taking the doctorate. The limit of 3,000 'livres Tournois' that he established, however, was so high that the doctorate still remained far beyond the means of many who might otherwise have qualified.[71]

The study of canon law demanded close application and success required considerable feats of concentration and memory. Students memorized as a matter of course enormous numbers of laws and had to be able to recall them readily, since the lectures they heard bristled with references and citations. A thirteenth-century legist, Martino da Fano, advised law students to make a daily practice of committing references to memory; he added, 'And finally, as you lie in bed or walk about the street, go over what you have learned and say, "Today I have learned so many laws, and these are the opening words of each."'[72] That Martino's advice reflected the realities of student life is amply evident from numerous lectures, 'reportationes', 'quaestiones', and other academic exercises preserved from medieval law schools. The need for abundant memorization and ready recall was reinforced by the practice in the faculty of decrees at Paris of lecturing without notes—and at times without light either.[73]

University instruction in canon law aimed primarily at equipping students with professional qualifications that would enable them to practice, whether as advocates or in the role of canonical judges, such as bishops' officials, commissaries, or auditors.[74] University training in canon law was also a desirable credential for prospective appointees to administrative positions in the church, such as bishops' chancellors, vicars general, or archdeacons.[75] Significant numbers of law graduates, moreover, attained even higher dignities as bishops, archbishops, cardinals, and popes.[76] But cler-

---

70. Cobban, *Medieval English universities* 84–85.
71. Clem. 5.1.2.
72. Quoted from Martino's *De regimine et modo studendi* in Powicke, 'Some problems' 14. See also the advice of Cardinal Zabarella, in his *Tractatus de modo docendi et discendi ius canonicum*, ed. Morrissey, 48, 51, 54–57.
73. CUP 3.425–39, No. 1528–31.
74. Stelling-Michaud, *L'université de Bologne* 203–230, lists many examples of such appointments. The provincial Council of Tours (1236) c.2, 4 demanded that bishops' officials have a minimum of five years of legal training; Mansi 23.412.
75. For examples see Stelling-Michaud, *L'université de Bologne* 156–62.
76. Stelling-Michaud, *L'université de Bologne* 162–63; Aston 'Oxford's Medieval Alumni' 27–32, and Aston, Duncan, and Evans, 'Medieval Alumni of Cambridge' 67–84.

ics without an academic background in canon law were also appointed to these positions and then had to acquire the necessary legal knowledge quickly after appointment. They could rarely afford to spend six or seven years in legal studies, nor in many cases could they readily leave their positions and migrate to some distant city to attend a university for that purpose. Private teaching of canon law, accordingly, continued to be in demand even after university law faculties were well established. Men with academic legal training were often willing to share their learning with those who needed to acquire it and could afford to pay for it. As might be expected there are only occasional traces of this private canonical study present in the records currently available, making it difficult to determine how commonly it occurred.[77]

One well-documented example from the late twelfth century in England involved Abbot Samson of Bury St. Edmunds. Shortly after his election as abbot in 1182 Samson was appointed a papal judge-delegate, 'A task of which he had neither knowledge nor experience, though he was learned in the liberal arts and in the Holy Scriptures, being a literate man, brought up in the schools and once a schoolmaster, well known and approved in his country. He forthwith called to him two clerks skilled in the law and associated them with himself, making use of their counsel in ecclesiastical business, and studying the decrees and decretal letters, whenever he had time, so that within a short time by reading of books and practice in cases he came to be regarded as a wise judge, proceeding in court according to the form of law'.[78]

Abbot Samson was probably not typical, but scattered references to private study and teaching of canon law do indicate that such arrangements were not uncommon. A few examples can illustrate the point. Gerald of Wales boasts in gaudy detail of his own successes both as a student and as a teacher in private schools that had not yet become part of a university.[79] A thirteenth-century General Chapter of the English Benedictines provided explicitly that monks might study canon law, so long as they did so in private schools within their own community.[80] Likewise the Cistercians, who forbade members of their order to study canon law at universities,

---

77. J. Verger, 'Patterns' HUE 1.36–37; A. Maierù, *University Training in Medieval Europe* (Education and Society in the Middle Ages and Renaissance, 3; Leiden 1994) 43.

78. Jocelin of Brakelond, *Cronica*, ed. and trans. H.E. Butler (Medieval Classics Series; New York 1949) 33–34.

79. See *De rebus a se gestis* 2.1–2 and 2.16 in Gerald's *Opera*, ed. J.S. Brewer, J.F. Dimock, and G.F. Warner (Rolls Series 21; London 1861–91) 1.45–48, 72–73.

80. *Documents illustrating the activities of the general and provincial chapters of the English Black Monks, 1215–1540*, ed. W.A. Pantin (Camden Society 3d ser. 45, 47, 54; London 1931–37) 1.27–28.

and even expelled monks who did so, nonetheless permitted the study of canon law and even civil law when it took place within the order's own houses of study.[81]

Non-professional study of canon law also occurred in cathedral and monastic schools. Since the primary function of these schools was to train up clerics and since every cleric with the cure of souls, whether secular or religious, required at least some rudimentary knowledge of the canons, study of canonical texts formed a usual part of their curriculum. Consequently, the Third Lateran Council under Pope Alexander III in 1179 (c.18) required every cathedral to maintain a schoolmaster to instruct clerics and poor scholars in the liberal arts free of charge (X 5.5.1). A canon of the Fourth Lateran Council in 1215 (c.11) went beyond this to require cathedral chapters to provide a teacher of theology as well (X 5.5.4) in order to instruct their students in the skills required to exercise the cure of souls. This certainly included some elementary canonistic learning.[82] Canonical collections, manuals, and treatises appear in nearly every surviving cathedral and monastic library catalog. Glossaries and marginal comments in canonical texts show that some study of canon law often formed part of the course in rhetoric in schools of liberal arts and legal materials were evidently studied in these schools as a matter of routine.[83]

Teaching canon law at a university formed part of the lengthy process of professional qualification. In all universities, not surprisingly, a significant share of canon law teaching was done by inceptors and regent masters. These were advanced students in the later stages of their degree work, and at some universities they comprised virtually the entire active teaching staff of the canon law faculty.[84] Elsewhere, most notably in Italy and Spain, universities also had a corps of more-or-less permanent professors, for whom teaching comprised a major part of their professional ca-

---

81. *Statuta capitulorum generalium ordinis Cisterciensis (1116–1789)* ed. J.M. Canivez (Louvain 1933) 3.359–60, 393, 401, 406.

82. See the comment of Geoffrey of Trani, *Summa super titulis decretalium* to X 5.5 pr. (Lyon 1519; repr. Aalen 1968), fol. 204rb–va; Cf. J.E. Sayers, *Papal Judges Delegate in the Province of Canterbury, 1198–1254: A Study in Ecclesiastical Jurisdiction and Administration* (Oxford historical monographs; London 1971) 130–131 and B. Smalley, *The Study of the Bible in the Middle Ages* (Oxford 1952; reprinted Notre Dame 1964), 51–52, 62–63, 75–77.

83. Thus, e.g., Vat. lat. 1339 includes glosses on the *Collection in Five Books* that point to its use in a rhetoric course; likewise Vat. lat. 1347 contains a glossary of canonical terms that likewise seems intended for non-professional teaching purposes. I am grateful to Bruce C. Brasington for calling these two manuscripts to my attention.

84. 'Inceptor' was the usual term for a student who lectured as part of the requirements for the licentiate or B.Cn.L., while 'Regent' denoted a more advanced student fulfilling the final requirement for the doctorate; Rashdall, *Universities* 1.284–287, 409–410, 530–531; W.J. Courtenay, *Teaching Careers at the University of Paris in the Thirteenth and Fourteenth Centuries* (Texts and Studies in the History of Mediaeval Education 18; Notre Dame 1988).

reers, although many of these men also practiced as legal consultants and some attained high rank in the ecclesiastical hierarchy.[85] Appointments to these well-paid professorships were much sought-after, and competition was correspondingly keen. The positions were often funded by local governments, who regarded the presence of a university law faculty in their town as an important civic asset.[86]

Teachers of canon law were paid in two principal ways: by student fees and (at some universities, mainly in southern Europe) by salaries from public funds.[87] University teachers in the Middle Ages might also hold prebends and other kinds of ecclesiastical benefices; those who did so were, at least in principle, expected to teach without demanding any further reward. This ideal was not strictly observed in practice, however, and in any case primarily affected teachers of theology, not law.[88]

Students were notoriously reluctant to pay the fees they owed, and teachers were sometimes embarrassed to demand them directly. Odofredus observed that it was common practice for professors in his day to appoint two students in each class to collect fees from the rest, but he complained that this did not always produce full payment either.[89] On another occasion, Odofredus exasperatedly declared at the end of a term that in the following term he would give only his course of ordinary lectures (for which he was paid by the city), but that he would not give any extraordinary lectures, 'for students,' he said, 'are not good pay-masters; they want to know, but not to pay up' (quia scholares non sunt boni pagatores; quia volunt scire, sed nolunt solvere).[90] At one point the pope intervened to admonish law students at Bologna that they too must pay their professors the sums they had agreed upon.[91]

Law teachers at Paris, Oxford, and Cambridge received no salaries from the public purse and so relied for their incomes primarily upon student fees. This contrasts to the practice in numerous Italian, French, and Spanish cities, where law professors were salaried from quite an early period. In principle salaried professors were supposed to forego fees from

85. Courtenay, *Teaching Careers* 17–20, 31–33.
86. G. Brucker, 'Renaissance Florence: Who Needs a University?' *The University and the City* 48–50.
87. Both practices, as medieval jurists were well aware, had roots in antiquity; K. Visky, 'Retribuzioni per il lavoro giuridico nelle fonti del diritto romano', *Iura* 15 (1964) 5–8.
88. On compensation for medieval university teachers generally see Gaines Post, 'Masters' Salaries and Student-fees in the Mediaeval Universities', *Speculum* 7 (1932) 181–198.
89. Odofredus, *Lectura* to Dig. 45.1.79 v. *Si procuratori* (Lyon 1552; reprinted Bologna 1968) fol. 127vb.
90. Odofredus, *Lectura* to Dig. 24.2.11, vol. 2, fol. 192rb.
91. Denifle, *Entstehung* 199.

their students, although they could accept spontaneous gifts from them. In practice, however, teachers expected to collect student fees in addition to the salaries attached to their university appointments and regularly did so.[92] Municipal payments to a law professor at Reggio began as early as 1188 and public subventions for teachers of law become common in the thirteenth century, remaining so throughout the later Middle Ages.[93] Professorial salaries were most commonly paid from municipal revenues, but there were exceptions. The counts of Toulouse paid professorial salaries at the University of Toulouse. Frederick II and his Angevin successors in the Two Sicilies supported the professors of Naples University. The kings of Castile paid salaries at Salamanca, while in Portugal professorial salaries at Coimbra and Lisbon were met from general ecclesiastical revenues.[94] Salaries of publicly paid law professors were often set at a handsome level to attract prestigious lawyers; teaching contracts sometimes included guarantees of job security and other benefits, occasionally with schedules of projected salary increments. By the early 1500s cities were bidding furiously against one another for the services of the stars of the academic legal profession and famous law teachers could command lucrative premiums.[95] Bologna took the extreme step of prescribing the death penalty for any professor over the age of fifty who left Bologna without the permission of the city magistrates to take up a teaching appointment elsewhere.[96] The salaries paid to law professors were typically much higher than those available to their colleagues in other faculties, by a ratio as high as 50:1, a situation that understandably provoked envy and resentment among teachers of theology and the liberal arts.[97]

Law professors seldom confined their professional activities entirely

92. Post, 'Masters' Salaries and Student-fees' 198; D. Zanetti, 'À l'université de Pavie au XVe siècle: Les salaires des professeurs', *Annales: Économies, sociétés, civilisations* 17 (1962) 421–433; A.B. Cobban, 'Elective Salaried Lectureships in the Universities of Southern Europe in the Pre-Reformation Era', *Bulletin of the John Rylands Library of Manchester* 67 (1984–85) 662–687; P. Denley, 'Career, Springboard, or Sinecure? University teaching in fifteenth-century Italy', *Medieval Prosopography* 12 (1991) 95–114; and S. da Borsano in Maffei, 'Dottori e studenti' 245–246.

93. E.g., Savigny, *Geschichte* 3.240–242; Denifle, *Entstehung* 197; Sarti-Fattorini, 1:255–256, 481–492, 495; Rashdall, *Universities* 1.209–212 and 2.17, 42–43, 71, 81, 339; C.G. Mor, *Storia dell'Università di Modena* (2d ed. Modena 1963) 46–47; Thorndike, *University Records* 32, 35, 164, 360–361; Johannes Fried, *Die Entstehung des Juristenstandes im 12. Jahrhundert* (Forschungen zur neueren Privatrechtsgeschichte 21; Cologne 1974) 122–123, 206, 209–210; L. Martines, *Lawyers and Statecraft in Renaissance Florence* (Princeton, 1968) 262.

94. Post, 'Masters' Salaries and Student-fees' 187–188, 193, 195.

95. See, e.g., A. Alciato's accounts of the spirited bidding for his services between rival universities in his *Lettere,* ed. G.L. Barni, 2, 100, 118 (Florence 1953) 3–4, 165–166, 186–187; also M.P. Gilmore, *Humanists and Jurists: Six Studies in the Renaissance* (Cambridge 1963) 66–67.

96. Rashdall, *Universities* 1.171.   97. J. Verger, 'Teachers', HUE 1.153.

to teaching and relatively few made it a life-long career.[98] Many, perhaps most, even among the elite group of salaried professors, engaged at least occasionally in practice as legal advisers and advocates, while those who taught for limited periods as inceptors or regent masters often later became ecclesiastical functionaries, judges, or private practitioners.

For the majority, teaching law marked a transitional stage in careers that ultimately carried them out of the academic world altogether; it represented the culmination of their preparation for practice and other responsibilities, rather than a permanent occupational niche. By the thirteenth century, former teachers of canon law—that is, men who had continued their legal training far enough to be qualified to teach the subject for a few years at the university level—became an elite group from whose ranks came disproportionately large numbers of archdeacons, cathedral canons, commissary judges, bishops' officials, auditors of the Rota, bishops, cardinals, and even popes.[99] This pattern of preferment continued for centuries, but more, many more, of those who completed a formal course of training in canon law, which perhaps included a period of teaching, undoubtedly settled for less visible careers as advocates or other legal practitioners in the local ecclesiastical or secular courts that functioned throughout Western Christendom. The vocational histories of these men are obscure, and for the most part the stories of their personal lives are dimmer still.[100] There remain only fleeting marks in the surviving records—we often know these men simply as names that flit from time to time through a court's act book, with perhaps an occasional mention in a charter's witness list, or an entry or two in a guild book. Others did not manage even that, their presence reduced to the merest shadow, as when a clerk might note: 'Among those present, the plaintiff's advocate', or 'The defendant's advocate failed to appear'. We know that they existed and that they were employed in their profession, but we know nothing more, not even their names.

In different periods of the Middle Ages canonists in different geographical regions enjoyed exceptional mobility as a result of the relative uniformity of their training. Canonistic skills were highly portable, which enabled practitioners to find employment, either long-term or short-term,

---

98. Denley, 'Career, Springboard, or Sinecure?' 112–114.

99. D. Girgensohn, 'Wie wird Man Kardinal? Kuriale und ausserkuriale Karrieren an der Wende des 14. und 15. Jahrhundert', QF 57 (1977) 138–162.

100. Recent prosopographical studies of university-trained lawyers have begun to make use of biographical information of this sort; see. e.g., R.C. Schwinges, *Deutsche Universitätsbesucher im 14. und 15. Jahrhundert* (Stuttgart 1986), Robert Gramsch, *Erfurter Juristen im Spätmittelalter: Die Karriermuster und Tätigkeitsfelder einer gelehrten Elite des 14. und 15. Jahrhunderts* (Leiden 2003), and Ad Tervoort, *The Iter italicum and the Northern Netherlands: Dutch Students at Italian Universities and Their Role in the Netherlands' Society (1426–1575)* (Leiden 2005).

almost anywhere.[101] Thus, for example, an analysis of the names of canonists that appear in documents from the crusading states in the Latin East shows that many of them practiced briefly in Jerusalem or elsewhere in the Levant, often just for one or two years, and then presumably returned to Western Europe.[102]

The wide range of possibilities that qualifications in canon law opened up to those who possessed them not only attracted a large number of students to the schools of the canonists, but also alarmed those who taught in other disciplines. Increasingly loud and angry complaints make it clear that from the mid-twelfth century onward theologians and teachers of liberal arts felt threatened by the rapid expansion of the professional study of law and appalled by the allure that legal careers held for students. 'Prelates are more inclined to reward advocates and pleaders with plump prebends than to give the plums of an ecclesiastical career to worthy preachers', lamented Gautier de Coinci (ca. 1177–1236), 'wherefore clever clerks go to Bologna to learn law and duplicity'.[103] Every subsequent generation throughout the Middle Ages voiced similar complaints. 'Gospels and Doctors both are laid aside', deplored Dante in the fourteenth century, 'while mangled margins show the toil laid out on the Decretals',[104] much as Gautier a hundred years before had mourned that law's health meant theology's decline; 'So Bologna grows fat, as Paris shrivels'.[105] Even lawyers complained at times about the uncouth discourse and uncertain morality of those who prematurely deserted divinity and literary studies to acquire a superficial knowledge of the technicalities of the law.[106]

The study of law not only robbed theologians and liberal arts teachers of their audiences, but critics also charged that it led to the moral deterioration of those who prospered from it. 'Legal practitioners', exclaimed Peter of Blois about 1160, 'strive only for lucre, while the honored name

---

101. H. de Ridder-Symoens, 'Mobility' HUE 1.280–304.

102. J.A. Brundage, 'Latin Jurists in the Levant: The Legal Elite of the Crusader States', *Crusaders and Muslims in Twelfth-Century Syria*, ed. M. Shatzmiller (Leiden 1993) 18–42.

103. Gautier de Coinci, 'Vie de Seinte Léocad, qui fu Dame de Tolete et du Saint Arcevesque', lines 1107–1116, 1123–1130 in É. Barbazan, *Fabliaux et contes des poètes françois des XIe, XIIe, XIIIe XIVe et XVe siècles*, 2d ed. by M. Méon (Paris 1808; reprinted Geneva 1976) 1.306–307.

104. Dante, *Paradiso* 9.133–135: 'Per questo l'Evangelio e i dottor magni / son derelitti; e solo ai Decretali / si studia, si che pare al'lor vivagni'.

105. Gautier de Coinci, 'Vie de Seinte Léocad', lines 1135–1136: 'Ainsi Paris pert molt de craisse, et Bologne la crasse encraisse'.

106. R. Niger, *Moralia regum* ed. H. Kantorowicz and B. Smalley, 'An English Theologian's View of Roman Law: Pepo, Irnerius, Ralph Niger', *Medieval and Renaissance Studies* 1 (1941) 237–251, reprinted in Hermann Kantorowicz, *Rechtshistorische Schriften* (Karlsruhe 1970), 243–244; G.B. Flahiff, 'Ralph Niger: An Introduction to His Life and Works', *Mediaeval Studies* 2 (1940) 104–126 at 115–116.

and splendid profession of the advocate is soiled by greed'.[107] St. Bernard of Clairvaux emphatically agreed. 'These men,' he thundered, 'have taught their tongues to speak lies. They are fluent against justice. They are schooled in falsehood'. And he advised Pope Eugene III, 'Cut off their lying tongues and shut their deceitful mouths'.[108] St. Bernard's savage sentiments resonated among innumerable later medieval critics and helped to produce a rich literature of vituperation, which accused lawyers and the courts of almost every conceivable variety of moral turpitude, intellectual insufficiency, and functional inadequacy.[109]

The very ferocity and ubiquity of these denunciations was a measure of both the importance of the lawyers in the society of the high Middle Ages and the degree to which legal culture permeated the intellectual life of the era.[110]

107. Peter of Blois, letter to a friend, CUP 1.33, no. 27: 'Hodie soli avaricie militant patroni causarum: illudque quondam venerabile nomen et gloriosa professio advocati notabili venalitate vilescit, dum miser et perditus linguam vendit, lites emit, matrimonia legitima dissolvit, amicitias rumpit, sopitarum litium cineres resuscitat, pactiones violat, retrectat transactiones, privilegia frangit, et in capturam pecunie pedicas et retiacula tendens, jura omnia intervertit'. In fairness to the lawyers, however, it must be added that Peter's account surely reflects personal disappointments. He himself had studied canon law, but had failed to secure the rewards that he obviously believed his talents merited; see R.W. Southern, *Medieval Humanism and Other Studies* (Oxford 1970) 105–132 at 108–109.

108. Bernard of Clairvaux, *De consideratione ad Eugenium papam tertiam libri quinque* 1.10.13, *Sancti Bernardi Opera*, ed. J. Leclercq, C.H. Talbot, H.M. Rochais, et al. (Rome 1957–1977) 3.408–409; English version from *Five Books on Consideration: Advice to a Pope* trans. J.D. Anderson and E.T. Kennan (Cistercian Fathers Series 37; Kalamazoo 1976) 44. See further J.A. Brundage, 'St. Bernard and the Jurists', *The Second Crusade and the Cistercians*, ed. M. Gervers (New York 1992) 25–33.

109. L. Chiapelli, 'La polemica contro i legisti dei secoli XIV, XV e XVI', *Archivio giuridico* 26 (1881) 295–322; C. Kenny, 'Bonus jurista malus Christa', *Law Quarterly Review* 19 (1903) 326–334; E. Meynial, 'Remarques sur la réaction populaire contre l'invasion du droit romain en France aux XIIe et XIIIe siècles', *Romanische Forschungen* 23 (1907) 554–584; K. Strecker, 'Quid dant artes nisi luctum!', *Studi medievali* n.s. 1 (1928) 380–391; J.A. Yunck, '"The Venal Tongue": Lawyers and the Medieval Satirists', *American Bar Association Journal* 46 (March 1960) 267–270 and *The Lineage of Lady Meed: The Development of Mediaeval Venality Satire* (University of Notre Dame Publications in Mediaeval Studies 17; Notre Dame 1963) 143–159 and *passim*; Stephan Kuttner, 'Dat Galienus opes et sanctio Justiniana', in *Linguistic and Literary Studies in Honor of Helmut A. Hatzfeld*, ed. A.S. Crisafulli (Washington, D.C. 1964) 237–246, also reprinted with original pagination in Kuttner, *History of Ideas and Doctrines* (2d ed. London 1992); J.W. Baldwin, 'Critics of the Legal Profession: Peter the Chanter and His Circle', *Proceedings Boston* 249–229; P. Ourliac, 'Troubadours et juristes', *Cahiers de civilisation médiévale* 8 (1965) 159–177; J.A. Brundage, "Vultures, Whores, and Hypocrites: Images of Lawyers in Medieval Literature," *Roman Legal Tradition* 1 (2002) 56–103.

110. On the cultural role of the learned lawyers see esp. W.J. Bouwsma, 'Lawyers and Early Modern Culture', *American Historical Review* 78 (1973) 303–327; M.P. Gilmore, 'The Lawyers and the Church in the Italian Renaissance', *Studi senesi* 75 (1963) 7–29; B. Guenée, *Tribunaux et gens de justice dans le bailliage de Senlis à la fin du moyen âge (vers 1380–vers 1550* (Paris 1963) 3; Brucker, 'Renaissance Florence: Who Needs a University?' 52–53; D.R. Kelley, 'Jurisconsultus perfectus: The Lawyer as Renaissance Man', *Journal of the Warburg and Courtauld Institute* 51 (1988) 84–102.

5

The Decretists
The Italian School

Kenneth Pennington and Wolfgang P. Müller

Although it was not a highly polished text and its organization made it difficult to use, Gratian's *Decretum* quickly became the standard textbook of medieval canon law in the Italian and transmontane schools. Its flaws were created by its long period of gestation but were minor when compared to its utility. The *Decretum* began as a book for teaching, and it remained a text for the classroom.[1]

In the formative age of canon law, that age following Gratian when the study of canon law became a discipline in the schools, not just at Bologna but at Paris and other many centers, the jurists began to fashion the first tools to construct a legal system that met the needs of twelfth-

---

Wolfgang Müller is the author of Section II of this chapter, entitled 'The *Summa Decretorum* of Huguccio', pages 142–160. Kenneth Pennington has written the other sections of the chapter.

1. See the preceding chapter on Gratian by Peter Landau. Also Terence McLaughlin, *The Summa Parisiensis on the Decretum Gratiani* (Toronto 1952) xvi–xvii summarizes a series of comments on Gratian by a French canonist. See also the numerous comments of canonists quoted by John T. Noonan, 'Gratian Slept Here: The Changing Identity of the Father of the Systematic Study of Canon Law', *Traditio* 35 (1979) 145–172. Stephan Kuttner, 'Research on Gratian: Acta and Agenda' *Proceedings Cambridge* 13–15, discussed the 'untidy seams' in Gratian's text, which were long recognized as signs of the long development of the text.

century society. Gratian's *Decretum* surveyed the entire terrain of law but was only an introduction to the law of the past. It did not answer many contemporary problems directly, although it provided a starting point for providing solutions to contemporary legal disputes. The three most pressing areas in which the jurists created a new jurisprudence with principles and concepts drawn from ancient Roman law were court procedure, marriage law, and the structure of ecclesiastical government. In the first half-century after Gratian, the jurists concentrated on these problems, and their teachings and writings reflect these concerns.

The disciples and successors of Gratian at Bologna and elsewhere continued his work of bringing order to the new discipline of canon law in two ways. Almost immediately they began to write *summae* and glosses on the *Decretum*, and, within several decades, the work of the jurists evolved into standard apparatus, which, along with the *Decretum*, formed the foundation of the teaching of canon law.[2] At the same time, they experimented. They modified Gratian's text and, to a lesser degree, reorganized it.

The textual changes took three forms. The jurists added additional chapters of canon law and excerpts of Roman law to the *Decretum*.[3] They called these new texts 'paleae'. To make Gratian's book more accessible to a wider audience, they composed abbreviations of the entire book, and, rarely, reorganized Gratian's material so completely that the result was a new work.[4] For the most part, anonymous jurists did this work.

The earliest changes may have been the addition of chapters to Gratian. They were inserted into the text itself or added to the margins. Although the canonists of the twelfth century called them paleae, they did not know whence the term came. Huguccio conjectured that the word meant 'chaff' added to the good grain; other authors thought that the term was derived from the name of Paucapalea, one of the first commentators on the *Decretum*. He, they surmised, had been responsible for the paleae added to Gratian's text.[5] Three points can be made about the paleae. First, when the canonists inserted chapters into Gratian's text they followed a practice of earlier canonists,[6] and this method of modifying

---

2. See Rudolf Weigand's chapter on the evolution of the Ordinary Gloss, above, chapter 3.

3. See Peter Landau on Gratian (above, chapter 2) for further comments on this practice.

4. On the 'abbreviationes' see Alfred Beyer, *Lokale Abbreviationen des "Decretum Gratiani": Analyse und Vergleich der Dekretabbreviationen "Omnes leges aut divine" (Bamberg), "Humanum genus duobus regitur" (Pommersfelden) und "De his qui intra claustra monasterii consistunt" (Lichtenthal, Baden-Baden)* (Bamberger theologischer Studien 6; Frankfurt am Main 1998).

5. The most thorough examination of paleae is J. Rambaud, 'Les additions', *L'Age classique 1140–1378*, 100–129. She discusses the origins of the word on p. 100.

6. Uta-Renate Blumenthal discovered a manuscript of the eleventh-century collection

collections of canon law would continue into the thirteenth century.[7] Second, not all chapters that twelfth-century canonists labeled paleae were additions. They may have come from Gratian himself. Third, some paleae that were clearly added to the *Decretum* after it left the atelier of Gratian were not listed in the medieval catalogues of paleae.[8] Although we cannot, as yet, establish the 'recensions' of the *Decretum* that were used in various parts of Europe, Rudolf Weigand has isolated a 'French Recension', dating to the end of the twelfth century, into which French canonists incorporated many additional paleae.[9] With further studies like Weigand's, we should be able to identify the texts of Gratian that circulated around the various schools.

Stephan Kuttner wrote in his *Repertorium* that the 'Epitomizing of legal sources belongs to the oldest form of medieval juristic literature'.[10] The canonists produced many abbreviations of Gratian's text, some of them having been produced shortly after Gratian finished his work.[11] In France, for example, the first sign that Gratian had been received in Northern Europe was an abbreviation of the text *Quoniam egestas*, written ca. 1150. The importance of such abbreviations was not limited to those who had no or little legal training. There are seven manuscripts of *Quoniam egestas*, and four of them are glossed. The glosses are evidence that professional jurists also used abbreviations in their work. As the second word in the title of *Quoniam egestas* suggests, there was an economic motive for producing these works. The twelfth-century canonists named these abbreviations *Excerpta canonum*, *Flores libri decretorum* or *Flores patrum seu canonum*, and *Exceptiones decretorum*. The abbreviators sometimes shortened the texts rather mechanically, but did, at times, add their own 'dicta' that supplemented or replaced Gratian's.[12] These abbreviations were, for the most part, composed in the twelfth century, and the genre almost disappears by the be-

---

of the Seventy-Four Titles with numerous additions; most early collections evolved similarly. See 'Codex Guarnerius 203: A Manuscript of the Collection in 74 Titles in San Daniele del Friuli', BMCL 5 (1975) 11–33; Horst Fuhrmann, 'Reflections on the Principles of Editing Texts: The Pseudo-Isidorian Decretals as an Example', BMCL 11 (1981) 1–7.

7. See my comments in chapter 9 below.

8. Titus Lenherr, 'Fehlende "paleae" als Zeichen eines überlieferungsgeschichtlich jüngeren Datums von Dekret-Handschriften', AKKR 151 (1982) 495–507, discusses paleae in the manuscripts and cites the pertinent bibliography. On the lists of paleae, see Harmut Zapp, 'Paleae-Listen des 14. und 15. Jahrhunderts', ZRG Kan. Abt. 59 (1973) 83–111.

9. 'Zusätzliche "Paleae" in fünf Dekrethandschriften', ZGR Kan. Abt. 78 (1992) 65–120.

10. *Repertorium* 257.

11. Jacqueline Rambaud-Buhot, 'Les divers types d'abrégés du Décret de Gratien: De la table au commentaire', *Recueil des travaux offerts à M. Clovis Brunel* (Paris: 1955) 397–411 and the study of three German abbreviations by Beyer, *Lokale Abbreviationen*.

12. See Schulte's comments in SB Vienna, 57 (1867) 224–262.

ginning of the thirteenth. Some of the abbreviations were the work of local jurists and were probably meant to serve the needs of local bishops.[13]

The compilers of these works were largely anonymous. The only exception is the Abbreviation, or more accurately a reorganization of Gratian ('transformatio' or 'reconcinnatio'), of Omnibonus, who composed his epitome of Gratian 1156–1157.[14] Omnibonus taught law at Bologna during the pontificate of Pope Eugenius III. Later he became bishop of Verona in 1157 and died there in 1185.[15] When he revised the *Decretum*, Omnibonus adopted the tripartite plan of Gratian. He shortened the first part to 26 distinctions, the first eight corresponding to Gratian's *Tractatus de legibus* (D.1–21). In the second part he adhered, for the most part, to Gratian's organization. Although he incorporated about half the chapters of Gratian, he sometimes shortened them radically. Omnibonus copied many of Gratian's 'dicta', but he added a number of his own. His 'dicta' supplement and occasionally replace Gratian's. It is likely that Omnibonus's *Abbreviatio* is a reliable witness to the text of Gratian as it first circulated widely outside of Italy.[16] Rudolf Weigand has presented evidence that Omnibonus' work may have been known and used by Rufinus. If so, it occupied a more important place in the early history of decretist thought than is generally recognized.[17]

Cardinal Laborans worked twenty years on the most original and complete reworking of Gratian's text, finally finishing his task in 1182. Pope Alexander III had elevated Laborans to the cardinalate in 1173, and his curial duties undoubtedly delayed the completion of the work.[18] Laborans had three goals: to improve Gratian's organizational plan, to eliminate repetitions, and to produce a shorter text. He divided his text into six books, and each book was subdivided into 'partes' that were further subdivided into 'capitularia' or 'tituli'. Each capitularium contained chapters. What-

---

13. E.g. *Abbreviatio Bambergensis*, see Alfred Beyer, 'L'Analyse de l'Abbrevatio Bambergensis', BMCL 20 (1990) 71–74, which was expanded in Beyer, *Lokale Abbreviationen*.

14. Kuttner lists seven manuscripts of Omnibonus's *Abbreviatio* in his *Repertorium*. To those may be added: Vatican, Reg. lat. 1039 (Kuttner, 'Additional notes on the Roman law in Gratian', *Seminar: An annual extraordinary number of the Jurist* 12 (1954) 69) and Cologne, Stadtarchiv W folio 248 [Glossed] (Bertram, 'Some additions to the "Repertorium der Kanonistik",' BMCL 4 (1974) 12). See Rudolf Weigand, 'Die frühen kanonistischen Schulen und die Dekretabbreviatio Omnebenes', AKKR 155 (1986) 79–91, in which he discusses the date, format, and organization of Omnibonus' text, correcting Vetulani and Rambaud-Buhot.

15. See Adam Vetulani and Wacław Uruszczak, 'L'oeuvre d'Omnebene dans le MS 602 de la Bibliothèque municipale de Cambrai', *Proceedings Toronto* 11–26 and Jacqueline Rambaud-Buhot, 'L'Abbreviatio Decreti d'Omnebene', *Proceedings Berkeley* 93–107.

16. Stephan Kuttner, 'Research on Gratian: Acta and agenda', *Proceedings Cambridge* 13, discusses the importance of other abbreviations for the shape of Gratian's early text.

17. Weigand, 'Dekretabbreviatio' 82–91.

18. Norbert Martin, 'Die "Compilatio decretorum" des Kardinals laborans', *Proceedings Berkeley* 125–135.

ever the merits of Laborans reorganization were, by 1182 Gratian's *Decretum* was too well established as a school book to be easily displaced. Laborans's work languished unnoticed and unused in a single manuscript.[19] Other reorganizations of the *Decretum* were equally unsuccessful.[20]

I. APPARATUS OF GLOSSES AND SUMMAE ON THE DECRETUM

In spite of its cumbersome and inelegant organization, Gratian's *Decretum* became the centerpiece of canonical jurisprudence in the second half of the twelfth century. Gratian's successors endorsed his choice of Bologna as the center for the teaching of canon law. If one thinks in modern terms Rome might have been a logical and better choice. The papal curia was, ultimately, the source of new legislation. Bologna, however, was perfectly suited to foster the new discipline. Roman law was already a flourishing discipline there. No matter what Gratian's attitude to or knowledge of Roman law was, by the end of the twelfth century no canonist could practice his trade without a thorough mastery of Justinian's codification.[21] Bologna had been an important center for the teaching of law since the 1120s. Popes, kings, and emperors recognized the importance of Bologna and the new disciplines by the middle of the twelfth century.[22] Frederick Barbarossa issued an imperial privilege to the students of Bologna in 1155, the 'Authentica "Habita",' and Pope Alexander III took a significant step in recognizing Bologna's importance when he addressed a letter announcing his election to the bishop, canons, doctors, and masters of Bologna in 1159.[23] Later Pope Lucius III granted the students of Bologna papal protection against rapacious landlords in 1176–1177.[24] The school of law at

---

19. Vatican Archives S. Petri C 110, fol. 1r–243v.

20. Kuttner lists two in his *Repertorium* 269–271 (London, B.L. Royal 9.A.viii and Oxford, Bodleian 291). He also noted a fragment of another 'reconcinnatio' in Vat. lat. 4977, fol. 1r–6v.

21. Gabriel Le Bras, 'Bologne monarchie médiévale des droits savants', *Studi e memorie per la storia dell'Università di Bologna* N.S. 1 (1956) 1–18 and G. De Vergottini, 'Lo studio di Bologna, l'Impero, il Papato', *Studi e memorie per la storia dell'Università di Bologna* N.S. 1 (1956) 19–95. Rudolf Weigand, 'Romanisierungs im frühen kanonischen Recht', ZRG Kan. Abt. 79 (1983) 200–249. See also Hoeflich and Grabher, chapter 1 above.

22. Cf. the suggestion of Anders Winroth, *The Making of Gratian's Decretum* 157–174, that the teaching of law at Bologna did not begin until the 1130s. For evidence of much earlier teaching of Roman law in Bologna see K. Pennington, 'The Birth of the *Ius commune*: King Roger's Legislation', RIDC (2006) 1–40.

23. JL 10587. On the date of the *Habita* see Winfried Stelzer, 'Zum Scholarenprivileg Friedrich Barbarossas (Authentica "Habita")', DA (1978) 123–165.

24. Peter Landau, 'Papst Lucius III. und das Mietrecht in Bologna', *Proceedings Toronto* 511–522.

Bologna was vigorously engaged in teaching and training jurists, and the empire and the papacy slowly began to understand the significance of jurists' work for the governance of their institutions. The papal and imperial privileges were the first glimmer of recognition that the school at Bologna was more than just a quaint place where an ancient legal system was pondered. As Knut Wolfgang Nörr has remarked, 'Windmills, after all, are built only where the wind blows'.[25] The law that was studied in Bologna may have been learned, but it was far from being purely academic.[26]

The papacy took notice of the law school in Bologna for many reasons. The Church had become a much more juridical institution during the course of the twelfth century. St. Bernard's famous lament in his letter to Pope Eugenius III (1153) that the papal palace is filled with those who speak of the law of Justinian confirms what we can also detect in papal decretal letters. The new jurisprudence influenced the *arengae* and the doctrine of decretals—undoubtedly a result of jurists working at the curia. The rush to bring legal disputes to Rome became headlong in the second half of the twelfth century. Litigants pressed the capacity of the curia to handle their numbers. Popes delegated cases to judges-delegate, but the curia was still overburdened.

Procedure presented problems in need of authoritative solutions. As ecclesiastical courts began to render judgments on the basis of written and oral evidence, judges, litigants, and jurists began to worry about correct judicial procedure.[27] The first notice we have that the papal curia asked for guidance from the law school at Bologna was ca. 1130 when Aimeric, the papal chancellor, asked Bulgarus to compose a short treatise on procedure. Bulgarus' tract has been preserved in several versions and had a rather wide circulation.[28] By the 1170s the papal chancery had been mentioned in papal decretals, and the first canonist, Albert of Morra, later Pope Gregory VIII, was appointed chancellor by Pope Alexander III.[29] The Church

---

25. Knut Wolfgang Nörr, 'Institutional Foundations of the New Jurisprudence', *Renaissance and Renewal in the Twelfth Century*, ed. Robert L. Benson and Giles Constable (Cambridge, Mass. 1982) 325.

26. Kenneth Pennington, 'Learned Law, Droit Savant, Gelehrtes Recht: The Tyranny of a Concept', *Rivista internazionale di diritto comune* 5 (1994) 197–209 and *Syracuse Journal of International Law and Commerce* 20 (1994) 205–215.

27. Kenneth Pennington, 'Due Process, Community, and the Prince in the Evolution of the Ordo iudiciarius', *Rivista internazionale di diritto comune* 9 (1998) 9–47.

28. Linda Fowler-Magerl, *Ordo iudiciorum vel ordo iudiciarius: Repertorien zur Frühzeit der gelehrten Rechte* (Ius commune, Sonderhefte 19; Frankfurt 1984) 35–40. On procedural tracts written in France during the 1160s, see André Gouron, 'Canon Law in Parisian Circles before Stephan of Tournai's *Summa*', *Proceedings San Diego* 497–503.

29. JL 14139 = 1 Comp. 2.15.3 and JL 14142 = X 2.22.3; see Nörr, 'Institutional foundations' 330–331; Pope Alexander III (Rolandus Bandinelli) had been chancellor, but Noonan

became a church of law from the papal curia to local courts. And lawyers began to play a visible role in its administration. From the twelfth century on, distinguished jurists were often rewarded with high ecclesiastical offices. Of the twelfth-century canonists, Omnibonus (Verona), Sicardus (Cremona), Stephen (Tournai), Johannes Faventinus (Faenza), Huguccio (Ferrara), and Bernardus Papiensis (Faenza, then Pavia) became bishops. This pattern was not unique to Italy. Canonists were rewarded with episcopal appointments in France and England during this period.[30]

Bernard was not the only churchman who had misgivings about these developments within the church. Local bishops resented the growing centralization of the church and objected to their loss of prerogatives to the papacy.[31] Litigants were quick to seize the advantages that distant courts and far-away judges presented. They used the appeal as an instrument of delay or even fraud. In the late twelfth century, popes Clement III and Celestine III countered these widespread abuses by attempting to restrict appeals to Rome.[32] By this time, however, the system was entrenched. Papal justice may have been imperfect, but its success was due to litigants who voted for it with their feet. The heavier the burden on the papal curia, the quicker the curia expanded to meet the need. In the early thirteenth century Pope Innocent III remarked, partially in jest, that there was always an abundance of lawyers in Rome. His comment reflects the practical side of Bologna's relationship to the papacy. The papal curia provided the forum; Bologna sent her jurists.

Although papal decretal letters surpass the *Decretum* as the basic texts for the study and practice of canon law by the beginning of the thirteenth century, Gratian's *Concordia* reigned without significant rivals from ca. 1140 to 1190. The jurists in Bologna and elsewhere produced commentaries on the *Decretum*, and the jurists made it the central text of their teaching. The earliest works on the *Decretum* fall into two types: 'apparatus' and 'summae'. Stephan Kuttner has observed that both literary types originate as imitations of the works of the Roman lawyers on the

---

and Weigand have proven definitively that he cannot be identified with the canonist Rolandus; see my discussion below.

30. John W. Baldwin, 'Studium et regnum: The Penetration of University Personnel into French and English Adminstration at the Turn of the Twelfth and Thirteenth Centuries', *Revue des études islamiques* 44 (1976) 199–215.

31. Kenneth Pennington, 'Bishops and Their Dioceses', *Folia canonica* 5 (2002) 7–17.

32. See the remarks of Stanley Chodorow, 'Dishonest Litigation in the Church Courts, 1140–98', *Law, church, and society: Essays in honor of Stephan Kuttner*, ed. K. Pennington and R. Somerville (Philadelphia 1977) 189–191. On Alexander III's attitude towards appeals, see Antonio Padoa Schioppa, 'I limiti all'appello nelle decretali di Alessandro III', *Proceedings San Diego* 387–406.

Code and the Digest, but the canonists produced treatises that combined elements of both the apparatus that analyzed individual laws and words within each law and the *summa* that treated each topic of the law book synthetically.³³ The canonistic *summae* often synthesized and paid attention to detail at the same time. To a certain extent, one may distinguish these two literary types by examining the way in which a work was transmitted. Apparatus were most often, but not always, written in the margins of the manuscripts of the law books, while *summae* were most frequently written separately from the book on which they commented.³⁴ *Apparatus glossarum*, 'coherent marginal commentaries which were formally published by individual authors', to use Kuttner's definition, appear only in the first decades of the thirteenth century.³⁵ Twelfth-century *Decretum* manuscripts contain an infinite variety of marginal glosses that are an admixture of coalescing *apparatus* and individual glosses. In many respects, these glosses to the *Decretum* can be considered the most important accomplishment of the Bolognese jurists in the twelfth and early thirteenth centuries. Since Rudolf Weigand has treated these glosses and their evolution into the Ordinary Gloss of the *Decretum* in the previous chapter, I will deal with the other literary works of the Bolognese jurists here.

Bologna became the center of the world of canonical jurisprudence in the second half of the twelfth century. Although canon law was taught at many transmontane centers—primarily at Paris, but also at Tours, Reims, Cologne, Oxford, and other smaller cities—neither the documentary nor the literary sources provide enough information with which we may write the history of a particular school. We can distinguish between cismontane and transmontane works, but we can rarely attribute an anonymous summa produced north of the Alps to a particular center with any certainty. At Bologna, however, we are on much firmer ground. We know the names of jurists who taught there and can catalogue their works. But even at Bologna, we have very little biographical information with which to flesh out their careers. In contrast to the anecdotes that circulated about the Roman law jurists, the canonists do not seem to have participated in public forums that would have given rise to anecdotal stories.³⁶

Paucapalea was one of Gratian's first successors at Bologna and taught

---

33. Christoph H.F. Meyer, *Die Distinktionstechnik in der Kanonistik des 12. Jahrhunderts: Ein Beitrag zur wissenschaftsgeschichte des Hochmittelalters* (Mediaevalia lovaniensia, Series 1, Studia 29; Leuven 2000), discusses the methodology of the twelfth-century jurists..

34. See Kuttner's comments, *Repertorium* 62–66, 123–125.

35. Stephan Kuttner, 'Bernardus Compostellanus Antiquus: A Study in the Glossators of the Canon Law', *Traditio* 1 (1943) 277–340, reprinted with valuable additional notes in *Gratian and the Schools of Law, 1140–1234* (Variorum Collected Studies; London 1983).

36. See Kenneth Pennington, *The Prince and the Law: Sovereignty and Rights in the Western*

in his shadow. Unreliable testimony of some jurists credited him with introducing the distinctions in the first and third parts of the *Decretum* and with adding the paleae to Gratian's text.[37] Almost nothing is known of his relationship to Gratian or of his public career.[38] The only certainty is that he wrote the oldest commentary on Gratian's *Decretum*, probably sometime between 1144 and 1150. His *Summa* was influential. Rufinus, Rolandus, and the anonymous *Summa Parisiensis* cited the work and quoted from it. The author of the *Summa Parisiensis* attributed to Paucapalea the division of parts one and three of the *Decretum* into distinctions.[39] Since Anders Winroth's discovery of earlier stages of Gratian's text we have come to know with certainty that Gratian was responsible for the first 101 distinctiones. John van Engen has raised doubts about whether Gratian was the compiler of *De consecratione*, which was also divided into distinctiones.[40]

Historians have traditionally assigned the commentary on the *Decretum* that begins with the words 'Quoniam in omnibus rebus' to Paucapalea. The basis of this identification is the priority of the text to other Bolognese *summae*, the presence in 'Quoniam in omnibus rebus' of quotations that later canonists attributed to Paucapalea, and a rubric of a Stuttgart manuscript that called extracts from Paucapalea's *Summa*, 'Excerpta ex Summa Pauce palee'.[41] Not everyone has been convinced by this slim evidence. John T. Noonan attempted to prove that 'Quoniam in omnibus rebus' was an early but derivative work.[42] He argued that *Sicut uetus testamentum*, an anonymous *summa* that exists in only one manuscript, was Paucapalea's.[43] Rudolf Weigand has expressed his doubts about assigning this *Summa* to Paucapalea with several different arguments.[44] The most powerful objection to Noonan's conjecture is that only one manuscript

---

Legal Tradition (Berkeley–Los Angeles–London 1993) 15–31, in which the anecdotes of Bulgarus and Martinus are discussed.

37. Kuttner, *Repertorium* 125–127.

38. Rudolf Weigand, 'Frühe Kanonisten und ihre Karriere in der Kirche', ZRG Kan. Abt. 76 (1990) 135–155 at 136. Although the name is unusual, we cannot be sure that his name has been preserved in any Bolognese document. It appears twice in documents from San Vittore of Bologna, *Chartularium studii Bononiensis* 3 (Bologna 1916) 120. There was also a Paucapalea who was bishop in Sardinia, see A. Mocci, 'Documenti inediti sul canonista Paucapalea', *Atti Accademia Torino* 40 (1905) 325.

39. *The Summa Parisiensis on the Decretum Gratiani*, ed. Terence P. McLaughlin (Toronto 1952) x–xi. D.1 c.1 s.v. *fas*: 'Distinctiones apposuit in prima parte et ultima Paucapalea'.

40. John H. van Engen, 'Observations on "De consecratione",' *Proceedings Berkeley* 309–320 and Peter Landau's comments in chapter 2.

41. Stuttgart, Landesbibl. Jur. 62 [earlier H.71].

42. 'The true Paucapalea?' *Proceedings Salamanca* 157–186.

43. Florence, Bibl. naz. Conv. sopp. G.IV.1736. Gérard Fransen discovered the prologue of 'Sicut uetus testamentum' in Madrid, Bibl. nac. 87 (C.1), fol. 3r, cf. 'Manuscrits canoniques (1140–1234) conservés en Espagne', RHE 48 (1953) 230.

44. 'Paucapalea und die frühe Kanonistik', AKKR 150 (1981) 137–157.

exists of the 'true Paucapalea'. It would be remarkable if the first important commentator on Gratian, who was generally acknowledged by later canonists to be a significant figure, would have left such a limited manuscript tradition behind.

As Kuttner and Weigand have demonstrated, a number of early Gratian manuscripts contain Paucapalea's glosses. His work and teachings were well known in Bologna. The later canonists gave Paucapalea pride of place among Gratian's immediate followers. His *Summa* is neither long nor detailed.[45] It consists largely of excerpts from Gratian's own text. Although it is not an impressive work, one would not expect the first commentary on Gratian to dazzle with great sophistication.

The prologue of Paucapalea's *Summa* is a measure of his purpose. Although Gratian began his *Decretum* with a tract on various types of law, Paucapalea focused on the judicial process, which the jurists called 'ordo iudiciarius'. This is not surprising. The jurists of the period were intensely interested in understanding how they could adapt the rules governing the judicial process in Roman law to their own courts. Paucapalea believed that the origins of ecclesiastical procedure could be found in the Old Testament.[46]

> It seems to me that it is useful to show the forms of procedure, the origin of ecclesiastical law and its process to those who do not know. The first form for pleading seems to have been used in paradise. The Lord questioned Adam about the crime of disobedience there, and he tried to justify himself by alleging that his wife should bear the blame by saying: 'The wife that you gave me, gave me <the apple> and I ate it'.

Paucapalea's explanation had a long history, and later jurists returned to the story of Adam and Eve to locate the beginnings of Romano-canonical procedure.[47] They noted that all the basic ingredients of the judicial process were present: God summoned Adam to court, he accused him, and Adam was permitted to reply to the charge.

---

45. Of the manuscripts listed by Kuttner, *Repertorium* 125–126, Alençon, Bibl. mun. 134 and Olso, Historical Institute of the University, are not Paucapalea's *Summa*. Weigand speaks of fifteen manuscripts and four fragments, 'Paucapalea und die frühe Kanonistik', AKKR 150 (1981) 143–144.

46. Paucapalea, *Summa*, ed. Schulte, prologue: '. . . ideoque mihi videtur, agendarum causarum formam ecclesiastici iuris originem eiusque processum non esse inutile ignorantibus reserare . . . Placitandi forma in paradiso primum videtur inventa, dum prothoplastus de inobedientiae crimine ibidem a domino interrogatus criminis relatione sive remotione usus culpam in coniugem removisse autumat dicens: "mulier, quam dedisti, dedit mihi et comedi".'

47. See my discussion of the importance of his Prologue in my *The Prince and the Law* 142–143 and my 'Due Process' 18–20.

Paucapalea covered elements of the judicial process in his commentary on Causa 2 to Causa 7 of Gratian's *Decretum*, and he laid out the most important elements of procedure in ecclesiastical trials. The 'ordo iudiciarius' must be used (C.2 q.1). The judge must hear the evidence presented in court (C.2 q.1 c.12). Because unlearned judges and ordinary men violently dispossess litigants without the 'ordo iudiciarius', the circumstances under which property could be expropriated must be understood (C.3 q.1) In disputes over property, the plaintiff's property must be restored before the trial (C.2.q.2). A judge must be impartial; if not, his sentence may be appealed (C.2 q.6). Plaintiffs cannot be criminals or infamous (infames) (C.3 q.5).[48] Testimony may not be heard if the defendants are absent (C.3 q.9). In certain crimes like heresy and simony, even women, slaves, criminals, and the infamous may present evidence in court (C.6 q.1). Litigants must be judged in their own forum, unless they appeal to Rome (C.3 q.6).

Paucapalea's *Summa* was short, concise, and clear. He summed up Gratian's *Decretum* for students and offered a guide to its contents.

A number of anonymous jurists wrote similar introductions to Gratian after Paucapalea. The *Summa* in Alençon, Bibl. mun. 134, which was first thought to be a work of Paucapalea, is that of another author who based his work on the master's.[49] He is a witness to the work of those jurists who taught at Bologna immediately after Paucapalea. Weigand has shown that he used Paucapalea's *Summa* and also the earliest glosses to Gratian's *Decretum*.[50] The *Summa 'Ius aliud diuinum'* is also an early work that was written soon after Paucapalea's *Summa*. The *Summa 'Sicut uetus testamentum'* is more expansive and later, for, as Rudolf Weigand has shown, it incorporates much of Rufinus' *Summa*.[51]

The two most important teachers of the 1150s in Bologna were Rolandus and Rufinus. Rolandus had long been identified as Pope Alexander III, but Noonan and Weigand have shown that the canonist and the pope cannot be the same person. Noonan addressed the question using only printed materials, but he made a very persuasive case that the canonist Rolandus was probably not Rolandus Bandinelli (Pope Alexander III). He noted that Friedrich Maassen was the first historian to conjecture, in 1859, that

---

48. On the concept of infamia, see the fundamental study of Francesco Migliorino, *Fama e infamia: Problemi della società medievale nel pensiero giuridico nei secoli XII e XIII.* (Catania 1985).

49. *Traditio* 15 (1959) 452.

50. Rudolf Weigand, 'Paucapalea' 144–155.

51. Ibid. 151–153, where Weigand prints texts from Alençon 134. On the *Summa 'Ius aliud diuinum'* in Milan, Ambrosian Library, H.94, sup. fol. 73r, 74r–80v, 81v, see Kuttner, 'Bernardus Compostellanus' 279, n. 1, and Weigand, loc. cit. 156, n. 63.

Rolandus and Alexander were the same person. Later historians accepted Maassen's identification, and the connection between the jurist, theologian, and pope became a commonplace in reference books.[52] A number of historians argued that Rolandus' elevation to the papal throne was evidence for the transformation of the Church into a 'juridical' institution.[53] Noonan showed how slight the evidence was that supported the connection. On the positive side, Noonan did decide that Rolandus wrote the theological tract *Sententiae*.[54]

Weigand confirmed Noonan's conclusions with evidence from manuscripts.[55] When he had written about conditional marriage in canon law, Weigand had detected doctrinal differences between the jurist and the pope.[56] But there was also evidence in the archives that called into question the prevailing opinion. The earliest notice of a Magister Rolandus in Bologna is dated 1154. He witnessed a judgment in which the four doctors of Roman law—Bulgarus, Martinus, Hugo, and Jacobus—were also present.[57] Since Rolandus Bandinelli had become a cardinal deacon in 1150, Rolandus' position in the list of witnesses and the absence of his cardinal's title would indicate that there was a Magister Rolandus teaching at Bologna who was not Bandinelli. Another letter addressed to Frederick Barbarossa in 1159 from a Magister Rolandus confirms his existence. Four masters, including a Rolandus, asked Frederick to reconsider his expulsion of some scholars from Bologna.[58] We do not know the circumstances surrounding this request, but Rolandus and his colleagues must have occupied a public position of importance to have written the letter.

Weigand presented the most conclusive evidence that Rolandus Bandinelli and Magister Rolandus could not have been the same person from a careful examination of the manuscripts of the *Summa*. His analysis revealed that Rolandus had written five recensions of his *Summa*. He dated the earliest ca. 1150, the others to the next decade. Rolandus composed

---

52. John T. Noonan, 'Who was Rolandus?', *Law, Church, and Society: Essays in Honor of Stephan Kuttner*, ed. K. Pennington and R. Somerville (Philadelphia 1977) 21–48. Unfortunately scholars are still making this connection, see *The Papacy: An Encyclopedia* (New York–London 2002) 19, 489.

53. Weigand, 'Frühe Kanonisten' 137.

54. *Die Sentenzen Rolands nachmals Papstes Alexander III.*, ed. A.M. Gietl (Freiburg im Breisgau 1891).

55. Rudolf Weigand, 'Magister Rolandus und Papst Alexander III.', AKKR 149 (1980) 3–44.

56. Rudolf Weigand, *Die bedingte Eheschliessung im kanonischen Recht: Die Entwicklung der bedingten Eheschliessung im kanonischen Recht, ein Beitrag zur Geschichte der Kanonistik von Gratian bis Gregor IX.* (Münchner theologische Studien 3.16; Munich 1963) 116–126.

57. Weigand, 'Magister Rolandus' 5.

58. Weigand, 'Magister Rolandus' 6–7.

his *Sententiae* after the third recension (ca. 1155) and then wrote the final two recensions of the *Summa*.⁵⁹ Weigand concluded that if earlier historians had been aware that Rolandus had revised his *Summa* so extensively, over such a long period of time, they would never have connected Rolandus and Alexander III. Rolandus' *Summa* was sometimes copied into the margins of manuscripts. Rolandus treated the first part of Gratian's *distinctiones* very brusquely, limiting his comments to indications of what the contents of the *distinctiones* were. Weigand discovered that manuscripts contain the same text written into their margins.⁶⁰

Although Friedrich Thaner, the nineteenth-century editor of Rolandus' *Stroma ex Decretorum corpore carptum,* printed his commentaries on C.1–36 as one continuous work, Stephan Kuttner has shown that Rolandus never intended to write a comprehensive commentary on the *Decretum*. ⁶¹ He wrote a *Summa* on C.1–C.26 and a 'much more important' and extensive *Commentum* on C.27 to C.36, 'De coniugio' (Concerning marriage).⁶²

It is not surprising that Rolandus should have focused on the law of marriage in his most significant juridical work. It was a topic of intense interest and importance for the jurists in the second half of the twelfth century.⁶³ Although 'the medieval Christian law of marriage was in large part the creation of Pope Alexander III' in his decretals, the jurists laid the groundwork for the doctrines incorporated into his decretals and interpreted his decretals after they were issued.⁶⁴ They wrote tracts on mar-

---

59. Weigand classified the manuscripts to which he had access. First recension: Bologna, Archiginnasio A.48, fol. 32r–60r; Second: Berlin, Staatsbibl. fol. 462, fol. 131r–146r, 87v–88v (perhaps the fragment on fol. 147r–147v) and Grenoble, Bibl. mun. 627, fol. 131r–145r; Third: Stuttgart, Hauptstaatsarchiv, VI.63 and Worcester, Cathedral Lib. Q.70, fol. 41r–96v; Fourth: Berlin, Staatsbibl. Savigny 14 and London, B.L. Royal 11.B.ii, fol. 57r–91r; Fifth: Stuttgart, HSA, VI.62. Gérard Fransen discovered another manuscript: Liège, Grand Seminaire, 6.N.15, fol. 147r–178r. Stickler has examined Zürich, Zentralbibl. C.97.II in 'Iter helveticum', *Traditio* 14 (1958) 466–468, and concluded that it is not a recension of Rolandus, but a different author's work, even though he was quite dependent upon Rolandus. Stickler's work will have to be checked against Weigand's recensions.

60. Rudolf Weigand, 'Glossen des Magister Rolands zum Dekret Gratians', *Miscellanea Rolando Bandinelli Papa Alessandro III,* ed. Filippo Liotta (Siena 1986) 389–423 at 419–423: Darmstadt, Landesbibl. 907, Pommersfelden, Bibl des Grafen Schönborn 142, Baltimore, Waters Art Gallery 777, Montecassino, Bibl. Abbaziale 66, Rouen, Bibl. mun. 707.

61. (Innsbruck 1874, repr. Aalen: 1973).

62. Stephan Kuttner, 'Did Rolandus of Bologna write a "Stroma ex Decretorum corpore carptum"?' BMCL 20 (1990) 69–70.

63. See Charles J. Reid, Jr. *Power over the Body, Equality in the Family: Rights and Domestic Relations in Medieval Canon Law* (Emory University Studies in Law and Religion; Grand Rapids, Michigan–Cambridge 2004) 25–68.

64. Quoted from James A. Brundage, 'Marriage and Sexuality in the Decretals of Pope Alexander III', *Miscellanea Rolando Bandinelli: Papa Alessandro III,* ed. Filippo Liotta (Accademia senese degli intronati; Siena 1986) 57–83 at 59. On the dating and importance of Alex-

riage laws and collected papal decretals that reported matrimonial decisions at Rome.[65]

Weigand has pointed out that the tracts on marriage were, along with the treatises on procedure, the first topics of canon law to which the canonists devoted monographs.[66] The first of these were strongly theological in character; in the second half of the century they took on a much more juristic flavor. The questions that confronted the canonists were theological, legal, and difficult. Charles Donahue has neatly summarized the results of the twelfth-century transformation of marriage law:[67]

> <Alexander's> principle rules for the formation of marriage, rules which he makes explicit in others of his later decretals <are that> present consent freely given between parties who are capable of matrimony makes a valid marriage, which, except in the most unusual circumstances, bars all other marriages while the parties are living <and that> future consent freely given between parties who are capable of matrimony makes an indissoluable marriage if that consent is followed by intercourse between the parties.

Papal legislation and canonistic jurisprudence overturned fundamental principles of customary marriage law that held sway in Europe before the mid-twelfth century. Pope Alexander's decretal legislation weakened the authority of the family and lords to control marriages. Gratian seemed to maintain that parental consent, a solemn ceremony, dower or dowry are all required for a valid marriage. Alexander and the canonists swept these rules away.[68]

Rolandus produced a large number of glosses, scattered in the margins of twelfth-century manuscripts of the *Decretum*, and they attest to his teaching at Bologna. Weigand has printed glosses from St. Florian, Stiftsbibl. III.5, Vat. lat. 3529, and Heiligenkreuz, Stiftsbibl. 44 that are signed with Ro. or R. He demonstrated convincingly that Rolandus wrote them.[69] Rolandus's opinions are also reported in the glosses of other canonists and in

---

ander's marriage decretals, see Charles Donahue, Jr. 'The Dating of Alexander the Third's Marriage Decretals: Dauvillier Revisited after Fifty Years', ZRG Kan. Abt. 68 (1982) 70–124.

65. Rudolf Weigand, 'Kanonistische Ehetraktate aus dem 12. Jahrhundert', *Proceedings Strasbourg* 59–79. The second part of the *Collectio Cantabrigensis* contains decretals of Alexander III treating marriage and may have circulated as a separate work. See Pennington, '*Epistolae Alexandrinae*: A Collection of Pope Alexander III's Letters', *Miscellanea Rolando Bandinelli, papa Alessandro III*, ed. Filippo Liotta (Accademia senese degli Intronati; Siena 1986) 337–353 at 341–342.

66. Weigand, 'Ehetraktate' 59. These anonymous tracts may be found under 'Marriage tracts' at http://faculty.cua.edu/pennington/1140i-p.htm.

67. 'Policy of Alexander the Third' 251–252.

68. Ibid. 270–279. With the discovery of earlier recensions of Gratian's *Decretum*, it remains to be examined whether Gratian's opinion changed as he enlarged his text.

69. Weigand, 'Glossen des Magister Rolandus' 393–419.

quaestiones of the period. Thaner printed 36 *quaestiones* in which Rolandus is often cited. Weigand concluded his studies of Rolandus with the observation that he probably taught at Bologna in the 1160s and that his opinions were commonly cited by the canonists until the 1180s.

Although Rolandus has attracted more attention from modern historians because they had identified him with Pope Alexander III, Rufinus was the major figure at Bologna in the 1150s. He was born in central Italy. He may have been a disciple of Gratian, but he never linked himself directly to the Magister. The exact dates when he taught canon law at Bologna are very uncertain. It was long thought that he became bishop of Assisi, but the evidence for that is very tenuous.[70] He finished his *Summa* sometime around 1164.[71] We do not know when he died.[72]

At the end of Rufinus's *Summa*, an anonymous scribe dubbed him 'the first elegant commentator or interpreter of that golden book, the *Decretum*'.[73] Modern historians have concurred. Robert Benson described Rufinus' constitutional thought as embodying 'imagination, originality, and high juridical precision'.[74] His personality was forceful, education broad, and opinions mordant. Kuttner called his *Summa* the first large-scale work of the Bolognese school that combined the two literary genres of the *summa* and the *apparatus glossarum*.[75] In length and detail, his *Summa* surpassed the *summae* of all his predecessors. Rufinus also wrote a large number of glosses that are preserved in the margins of early manuscripts of the *Decretum*.[76]

Rufinus knew and used the *summae* of Paucapalea and Rolandus, and he had a solid foundation in Roman law. He also cited the *Lombarda*, vari-

---

70. Roman Deutinger, 'The Decretist Rufinus—A Well-Known Person?' BMCL 23 (1999) 10–15. See also Adele Simonetti, 'Rufino di Assisi e il cod. C.30 Sup. del Ambrosiana', Studi medievali 31 (1990) 125–142.

71. See André Gouron, 'Sur les sources civilistes et la datation des Sommes de Rufin et d'Etienne de Tournai', BMCL 16 (1986) 55–70. Weigand, 'Frühe Kanonisten' 138–140.

72. Robert Benson, 'Rufin', DDC 7 (1961) 779–84. On the Rufinus' career see Weigand, 'Frühe Kanonisten' 138–140.

73. Quoted by Robert Benson, *The Bishop-Elect: A Study in Medieval Ecclesiastical Office* (Princeton 1968) 57, from Heinrich Singer, *Summa decretorum* (Paderborn 1902; reprinted Aalen 1963) xviii, Moulins, Bibl. mun. 22, fol. 166v: 'Rufinus aurei uoluminis decretorum elegans apparator siue expositor primus'. One should not use the Johann F. von Schulte edition of Rufinus' *Summa* (Giessen 1892); it is based on a corrupted manuscript tradition.

74. *Bishop-Elect* 57. For an analysis of Rufinus' importance for jurisprudential thought, see Brian Tierney, '*Ius* and Metonymy in Rufinus', *Studia in honorem eminentissimi cardinalis Alphonsi M. Stickler*, ed. Rosalio Iosepho card. Castillo Lara (Studia et textus historiae iuris canonici 7; Roma 1992) 549–558.

75. *Repertorium* 132.

76. Weigand, 'Paucapalea' 154, lists manuscripts that contain 'Rufinusgut' in their margins. See chapter 3, pp. 71–72.

ous theologians, including Hugh of St. Victor, possibly Peter Lombard, and the grammarian Papias.[77]

Rufinus' *Summa* became the most influential commentary on Gratian in Bologna during the 1160s and 1170s. Stephen of Tournai was Rufinus' student and chose his *Summa* as the model for his own. Johannes Faventinus used Rufinus' *Summa* extensively. Later decretists such as Huguccio and Johannes Teutonicus still cited Rufinus at the end of the twelfth and the beginning of the thirteenth centuries. Rufinus also influenced commentators on Gratian's *Decretum* outside Italy. A number of transmontane *summae* were very dependent upon Rufinus. The following anonymous *summae* borrowed directly from him: *Distinctiones Monacenses*, Summa *'Inperatorie maiestati'*, Summa *'Permissio quedam'*, Abbreviatio *'Exceptiones euangelicarum'*, Summa *'Elegantius in iure diuino'*, Summa *'Antiquitate et tempore'* (Pseudo-Rufinus), Summa *'Prima primi uxor Ade'*, and Summa *'Conditio ecclesiastice religionis'* (Pseudo-Rufinus). The Summa *'Conditio ecclesiastice religionis'* was in large part plagiarized from Rufinus.[78]

After Rufinus, Stephen of Tournai wrote the most influential *Summa* of the next Bolognese generation of jurists.[79] His biography and literary acitivity present several complex problems. As his name indicates, Stephen was French, born in Orléans ca. 1128, and lived until the beginning of the thirteenth century (died 1203). He studied at Bologna in the 1150s, became a regular canon in Orléans in 1155, studied in Chartres, and was elected abbot of St. Euverte in Orléans in 1167, abbot of St. Geneviève in Paris, 1176, and in 1191, bishop of Tournai.[80] Herbert Kalb has dated his *Summa* to ca. 1166,[81] and Rudolf Weigand has demonstrated that the numerous glosses found in the margins of early *Decretum* manuscripts signed 'St' or 'Ste' are Stephen's, were written after his *Summa*, and circulated with other Bolognese glosses in the 1170s.[82] Weigand has also suggested that Stephen's *Summa* may have gone through two recensions and was written ca. 1165–1167.[83] However, the

---

77. *Summa Decretorum*, ed. Singer, cx–cxxvi, gives a detailed analysis of the non-canon law sources of Rufinus. Herbert Kalb, 'Bemerkungen zum Verhältnis von Theologie und Kanonistik am Beispeil Rufins und Stephans von Tournai', ZRG, Kan. Abt. 72 (1986) 338–348.

78. Benson, 'Rufin' 781–782.

79. *Repertorium* 133–35, 'Interim checklists', *Traditio* 11 (1955) 440–441, 12 (1956) 563, and 13 (1957) 469. For two more fragments from Dublin and Leningrad, see 'Retractationes' p. 9 by Kuttner, *Gratian and the Schools*.

80. P. Delhaye, 'Etienne de Tournai', DHGE 15 (1963) 1274–78. Weigand, 'Frühe Kanonisten' 140.

81. *Studien zur Summa Stephans von Tournai: Ein Beitrag zur kanonistischen Wissenschaftsgeschichte des späten 12. Jahrhunderts* (Innsbruck 1983) 108–112.

82. 'Studien zum kanonistischen Werk Stephans von Tournai', ZRG Kan. Abt. 72 (1986) 352–361. See also Kuttner, 'Bernardus Compostellanus' 282–283, n. 20.

83. On the dating see André Gouron, 'Sur les sources civilistes' 69. The formula at the

textual problems of the *Summa* will be solved only after Schulte's inadequate, partial edition is replaced with a critical edition.[84] In addition to his *Summa*, he wrote a large number of letters, sermons, and poems.[85] One of his poems was written while he was in Bologna.[86]

As Kuttner has demonstrated, the anonymous *summae* 'Quoniam status ecclesiarum', 'Cum in tres partes', 'De iure naturali', and 'De multiplici iuris diuisione' drew heavily upon Stephen's work.[87] He was well-informed about Anglo-Norman politics, and he reacted to the issues of the Thomas Becket dispute with King Henry II in his *Summa*.[88]

Stephen developed several ideas in his prologue to the *Summa* that reflect developments in the evolution of canonistic jurisprudence after Gratian.[89] He introduced his *Summa* with an invitation to a jurist and a theologian to share a meal, one in which both could partake.[90] And, he continued, just as they had two different approaches to law, the world was governed by dualities: there are two people in God's world, clerics and laymen, two *principatus*, the *sacerdotium* and *regnum*, and two orders of juris-

---

end of C.2 in Stephen's *Summa* 188, does not help with the dating, because only one manuscript gives 1165 as a date, while the others all give the date as 1145, which must be correct, since the pope's name is given as Eugenius. Stephen must have worked for a long time on his *Summa*. An earlier recension of his *Summa* seems to occur in Munich, Staatsbibl. lat. 17162. Most manuscripts do not have all three parts of the *Summa* traditionally attributed to him. Stephan Kuttner showed that part three treating *De consecratione* was not Stephen's, but the work of a French canonist who was familiar with the masters of theology at Paris; see 'The Third Part of Stephen of Tournai's *Summa*', Traditio 14 (1958) 502–505.

84. Stephen of Tournai, *Die Summa über das Decretum Gratiani*, ed. Johann Friedrich von Schulte (Giessen 1890, reprint Aalen 1965). Schulte decided that the material that Stephen borrowed from Paucapalea, Rolandus, and Rufinus did not have to be edited, and he left it out of his edition.

85. *Lettres d'Etienne de Tournai*, ed. J. Desilve (Valenciennes-Paris 1893). Migne published the sermons, PL 211.

86. Lucien Auvray, 'Un poème rythmique et une lettre d'Etienne de Tournai', *Mélanges Paul Fabre: Études d'histoire du moyen âge* (Paris 1902) 279–291 at 284–290 found in Paris, B. N. lat 11867, fol. 104v and Vatican, Queen Christine 157, front flyleaf. One verse of 46 discussed law: "Quia de civilibus et humano iure / In celesti curia non habentur cure, / Nec apertum separat ab occulto fure / Nec vult ut in mutuo veniant usure." This evidence is not conclusive that Stephen wrote it or that he wrote it in Bologna.

87. *Repertorium* 136–141 and 'Anglo-Norman canonists' 293, *Gratian and the Schools of Law*, Retractationes 28. K.W. Nörr, 'Die Summen "De iure naturali" und "De multiplici iuris diuisione",' ZRG Kan. Abt. 48 (1962) 138–163.

88. Kalb, *Studien* 110–112.

89. Kalb, *Studien* 113–120, edits the prologue on the basis of fourteen manuscripts. See Weigand's remarks and corrections in 'Studien' 350.

90. Herbert Kalb has explored the connections between law, legal sources, and theology in Stephan's thought: 'Bermerkungen zum Verhältnis von Theologie und Kanonistik an Beispiel Rufins und Stephans von Tournai', ZRG Kan. Abt. 72 (1986) 338–348; 'Non adversi sed diversi: Konfligierende Rechtsquellen und die Dekretistik am Beispiel Stephans von Tournai', MIÖG 105 (1997) 346–360.

diction, divine law and human law. Like Paucapalea, he traced the origins of divine law, by which he meant canon law, to paradise or the Old Testament, when the rules governing the judicial process were first established by God's handling of Adam's defense or Moyses' rule of evidence. Stephen is typical of the early decretist tradition in equating the *ordo iudiciarius*, judicial procedure, with the legal system. Later, the canonists would begin to perceive that the origins of the legal system was better understood by considering the source of law as the will of the legislator.[91]

Sometime after 1171, Johannes Faventinus wrote a *Summa* that borrowed much material from Rufinus and Stephen of Tournai.[92] Although large portions of the work are derivative and were copied word for word from the sources, it enjoyed great popularity as is evident by the wide dispersal of the surviving manuscripts.[93] Johannes was born in Faenza, studied and later taught at Bologna, and, if he was identical to the Johannes who became bishop of Faenza, may have supported the Emperor Frederick Barbarossa against Pope Alexander III. He left Bologna in the late 1170s.[94] He became a canon of the cathedral in Faenza by 1174; later, between 1174 and 1177, he was elected bishop of the city. He died during the siege of Acre (1189–1191) while participating in the Third Crusade.[95]

After he became bishop of Faenza, Johannes was a judge-delegate in a number of cases. He also advised Pope Urban III on an important point of marriage law at the papal curia. The *Summa Reginensis* reports that when Urban wished to protect a man from being forced to consummate a marriage in which he had stipulated that his father must consent, Johannes supported the pope's interpretation of the law against the opinion of the cardinals.[96]

Johannes' *Summa* was a mixed apparatus, combining the characteristics of an apparatus of glosses and a treatise on the *Decretum*. Since much of it

---

91. See Pennington, *The Prince and the Law*, passim.
92. Norbert Höhl, 'Wer war Johannes Faventinus? Neue Erkenntnisse zu Leben und Werk eines bedeutendsten Dekretisten des 12. Jahrhunderts', *Proceedings San Diego* 189–203 and Karl Borchardt, 'Archbishop Gerard of Ravenna and Bishop John of Faenza', *Proceedings San Diego* 573–592.
93. Höhl counts 53 manuscripts, 'Wer war Johannes Faventinus?' 189, n. 2. See the listing in Kuttner, *Repertorium* 143–145, with two more noted by Kuttner in 'Bernardus Compostellanus' 281 n.11, and eleven others in 'Retractiones' of *Gratian and the Schools of Law* 9. Norbert Höhl has studied his glosses in *Die Glossen des Johannes Faventinus zur Pars I des Decretum Gratiani* (Forschungen zur Kirchenrechtswissenschaft; Würzburg 1987).
94. Alfons Stickler, 'Jean de Faenza ou Joannes Faventinus', DDC 6 (1957) 99–102. Weigand, 'Frühe Kanonisten' 143. Herbert Kalb, 'Das Recht der Herrscherabsetzung bei Johannes Faventinus: Ein Beitrag zum Verhältnis von regnum—imperium—sacerdotium in der frühen Dekretistik', ZRG Kan. Abt. 78 (1992) 159–182.
95. See the articles of Höhl and Borchardt cited in notes 93 and 94 above.
96. Borchardt, 'Archbishop Gerard and Bishop John' 591. The decretal that decided this case was 1 Comp. 4.5.4 (X 2.5.5).

is borrowed literally from Rufinus and Stephen, one may say, with Stickler, that we have an implicit edition of his *Summa* in the editions of their works, although this generalization is misleading at times.[97] Johannes also wrote a large number of glosses to the *Decretum* after he finished *Summa*. Whether these glosses may be said to constitute an apparatus or not, they are present in many manuscripts. Weigand has found marginal glosses of Johannes in 56 manuscripts.[98] Faventinus was most important, perhaps, for summing up the Bolognese tradition on the *Decretum* before the 1170s.

Other canonists of this period whose work was known outside of Bologna remain shadowy figures with only cryptic references in the works of others or scattered glosses in the margins of *Decretum* manuscripts to resurrect them from oblivion. Simon of Bisignano referred to a 'Magister Gandulphus, whose authority was great in the Church of God'.[99] A Gandulphus may have written an abridgement of Peter Lombard's *Sentences* between 1160 and 1170, and another Gandulphus, glosses to the *Decretum* sometime after 1170.[100] Whether these two Gandulphuses are the same is not certain. We can also not be confident about the identity of the glosses that might be attributed to him in the margins of *Decretum* manuscripts. Many are signed with a single 'g.', which is not sufficiently strong evidence to distinguish his glosses from other jurists whose names begin with G.[101] Nevertheless Bolognese and transmontane canonists cited Magister Gandulphus frequently in their works. He was an independent thinker whose doctrines attracted wide attention. Weigand points out that Honorius, the author of the Anglo-Norman *Summa 'De iure canonico tractaturus'*, referred to 'g.' more often than to any other canonists.[102] In early Gratian manuscripts, Weigand has discovered another contemporary canonist, Guibert de Bornado, who may have been trained in Roman law and whose glosses reflect this jurist's unusual, for his time, application of Roman jurisprudence to the problems of canon law.[103] He was a judge in the court of

97. Ibid. 102.
98. Kuttner first noted the glosses in *Repertorium* 11. Rudolf Weigand, 'Die Glossen des Johannes Faventinus zur Causa I des Dekrets und ihr Vorkommen in späteren Glossenapparaten', AKKR 157 (1988) 73–107. Höhl has edited Johannes glosses to the *Distinctiones* of Gratian in *Die glossen des Johannes Faventinus zur Pars I des Decretum Gratiani: Eine literargeschichtliche Untersuchung* (2 vols., Dissertation, University of Würzburg 1987).
99. Schulte, QL 132 n.8, to C.23 q.5 c.12: 'Magister uero Gandulphus, cuius magna est in ecclesia Dei, dicit . . .'
100. The commentary on the Sentences is edited by J. von Wolter, *Magistri Gandulphi Bononiensis Sententiarum libri quatuor* (Vienna 1924); see Charles Lefebvre, 'Gandulphe', DDC 5 (1953) 933–935.
101. Rudolf Weigand, 'Gandulphusglossen zum Dekret Gratians', BMCL 7 (1977) 15–48.
102. Ibid. 15.
103. Ibid. 44–46. Rudolf Weigand, 'Romanisierungstendenzen im frühen kanonischen

Frederick Barbarossa, active between 1159 and 1178. He had his origins in Brescia, where he was named a consul and a judge in documents. He also appeared in ecclesiastical courts. In 1174 he represented an abbess before the archbishop of Milan. Perhaps he provided an intellectual and worldly model for later jurists like Johannes Bassianus.

One of the last canonists whom we may place in the first generation of jurists after Gratian was Simon of Bisignano. Kuttner observed that he is the first canonist since Rufinus to write a thoroughly original commentary on the *Decretum* with very little borrowing from early canonists, effectively abandoning the 'plagiarizing' methodology of Stephen of Tournai and Johannes Faventinus.[104] He finished his *Summa* between 1177 and 1179 and cited decretals fairly frequently in his commentary.[105] Simon also left a number of glosses to the *Decretum* but did not write an apparatus. Juncker published a large number of his glosses with parallel passages in his *Summa*.[106] He demonstrated that if one carefully examines the mode of transmission and the content of glosses, we may isolate the work of a glossator and, in the case of Simon, distinguish between the contents of his *Summa* and glosses to the *Decretum*.[107] Juncker also has shown that some of Simon's opinions reported by other canonists can be found only in his glosses and not in his *Summa*. By this time the character of canonistic commentaries was changing. The outpouring of papal decretals and the systematic incorporation of Roman law into canonical jurisprudence was well underway. Simon's works reflects both trends, and he cited decretals and Roman law fairly frequently. His work directly influenced the French decretist, Sicardus of Cremona, and the anonymous *Summa 'Dubitatur a quibusdam'*.[108]

In his studies of early Gratian manuscripts, Stephan Kuttner noted that the sigla of many different jurists were appended to marginal glosses.[109] Only careful studies of the manuscripts and their transmission has enabled us to know which of these glosses were products of Bologna. Rudolf Weigand has explored the marginal glosses of those jurists who

---

Recht', ZRG Kan. Abt. 69 (1983) 201–209, continued the story of Guibert. See also his chapter on the Ordinary Gloss in this volume (above, chapter 3, p. 73).

104. Kuttner, *Repertorium* 148–49. *Traditio* 11 (1955) 441.

105. Josef Juncker, 'Die Summa des Simon von Bisignano und seine Glossen', ZRG Kan. Abt. 15 (1926) 326–500. Walther Holtzmann, 'Zu den Dekretalen bei Simon von Bisignano', *Traditio* 18 (1962) 450–459. Weigand, 'Frühe Kanonisten' 145. An edition in PDF format of Simon's *Summa* by Pier Aimone can be found on the web at http://www.unifr.ch/cdc/summa_simonis_de.php

106. Juncker, 'Simon von Bisignano' 362–389, 397–436.

107. Juncker, 'Simon von Bisignano' 445–463, where he discusses the issue of whether a witness can be forced to render testimony.

108. Kuttner, *Repertorium* 151, 154.

109. *Repertorium* 3–12. Also Juncker, 'Simon von Bisignano' 350–359.

are known by only their initials.¹¹⁰ A certain 'W.', whom Weigand thinks may have been a Master Willielmus, wrote glosses in the 1170s that are preserved the margins of two manuscripts in New York and Munich, although not much more can be said about him.¹¹¹ The signed glosses of many other canonists remain to be explored.

The attribution of some glosses can be intriguing but difficult. The early manuscripts of the *Decretum* contain many glosses signed 'c.' that scholars have connected with a canonist, 'Cardinalis'. His glosses are difficult to date, contain no references to decretals or Roman law, and are, for the most part, only brief comments on the texts. They were probably written ca. 1160. Weigand located many of these glosses in manuscripts of Malibu and Innsbruck.¹¹² Maassen and Schulte proposed Cardinal Gratian. Stickler conjectured that Johannes Sutrinus might be Cardinalis, while Weigand has changed his mind. First he put forward Hubaldus and then Hermannus.¹¹³ André Gouron and Rudolf Weigand now think that Raymond des Arènes, a French cardinal and jurist, might be the elusive canonist.¹¹⁴ In any case, Cardinalis was occasionally quite critical of Gratian, and later Bolognese canonists referred to him quite frequently.

A major figure at Bologna in the 1180s was Bazianus (or Basianus), whose opinions were cited in many apparatus of glosses and in *summae*. He has been often confused with Johannes Bassianus, a jurist of Roman law. Recently, Annalisa Belloni has argued that the legist known as Johannes Bassianus and the canonist known as Bazianus are the same person, and Domenico Maffei has seen some reason to agree with her hypothesis.¹¹⁵ Rudolf Weigand, however, has put forward convincing arguments that the two jurists' identities were separate.¹¹⁶ In any case, the canonist

110. For a discussion of these manuscripts and glosses and their importance for the development of canon law, see his chapter 3, above, on the development of the Ordinary Gloss.

111. 'W.-Glossen zum Dekret Gratians', *Ministerium iustitiae: Festschrift Heribert Heinemann zur Vollendung des 60. Lebensjahres*, ed. André Gabriels and Heinrich J.F. Reinhardt (Essen 1985) 151–159.

112. Rudolf Weigand, 'Die Glossen des Cardinalis (Magister Hubald?) zum Dekret Gratians, besonders zu C.27 q.2', BMCL 3 (1973) 73–95. The Malibu manuscript was formerly owned by Peter Ludwig of Aachen and is now in the J. Paul Getty Museum, Malibu, California (without signature) and Innsbruck, Univ. Bibl. 90.

113. Weigand, 'Glossen des Cardinalis' 73–74. Also Weigand, 'Magister Rolandus' 5, n. 14.

114. 'Le cardinal Raymond des Arènes: *Cardinalis*?' RDC 28 (1978) 180–192, reprinted in *La science du droit dans le Midi de la France au Moyen Age* (London 1984). Weigand, 'Frühe Kanonisten' 141. See Weigand's remarks on the identity of Cardinalis in his chapter on the Ordinary Gloss above, p. 73.

115. 'Baziano, cioè Giovanni Bassiano, legista e canonista del secolo XII', TRG 57 (1989) 69–85 and *Le questioni civilistiche del secolo XII: Da Bulgaro a Pillio da Medicina e Azzone* (Ius commune, Sonderheft 43; Frankfurt 1989) 15–20, 25–29 Domenico Maffei, 'Fra Bologna, Montpellier et Palencia: Studi su Ugolino de Sesso', RIDC 1 (1990) 16, n. 32.

116. See Weigand's comments in his chapter on the Ordinary Gloss, p. 76.

Bazianus was the first to be doctor of both laws (doctor utriusque iuris) and can be seen as a benchmark for Romanization of canon law in the 1180s and the Romanization of the canonists.[117] As Wolfgang Müller has demonstrated in the following section, Bazianus had great influence in the 1180s, particularly on a work that supplemented Huguccio's *Summa*, the so-called *Continuatio prima*.

One of the last of the decretist twelfth-century *summae* is the *Summa Reginensis*.[118] First discovered and attributed to the school of Bologna by Kuttner, and later studied in detail by Stickler, this anonymous *summa* was finished ca. 1191.[119] Stickler attributed it to Petrus Beneventanus, but the evidence of his authorship is too slender for certainty. Its author taught in Bologna, was quite likely from Southern Italy, cited Huguccio's *Summa* and *Compilatio prima*, and acknowledged Huguccio as his master. Kuttner and Stickler noted an independence of thought in spite of his dependence on Huguccio. Kuttner speculated that the author of the *Summa Reginensis* may have left his commentary on Gratian incomplete when Huguccio's *Summa* was published because he was daunted by Huguccio's enormous success.[120] Whatever the case, its author remained unknown and its influence was slight.

II. THE SUMMA DECRETORUM OF HUGUCCIO

With the publication of *Compilatio prima*, the first commonly accepted decretal collection, in 1191, the schools of canon law received a new intellectual focus. Scholarly attention gradually shifted from Gratian's *Decretum* to more recent compilations of authoritative texts, which took into account the steadily growing flow of papal legislation. Simultaneously, older decretist doctrine also reached a turning point. Fifty years of learning since Gratian found their most elaborate and refined expression in the *Summa decretorum* (ca.1188–1190) of the Bolognese canonist Huguccio.[121]

Wolfgang Müller is the author of Section II of this chapter.

117. See Michael Hoeflich's and Jasonne Grabher's chapter above (chapter 1). Also Rudolf Weigand, 'Romanisierungstendenzen im frühen kanonischen Recht', ZRG Kan. Abt. 69 (1983) 200–49 and 'Frühe Kanonisten' 145 and 155, n. 97.

118. Vat. Reg. lat. 1061, fol. 1r–48v, Knut W. Nörr, *Zur Stellung des Richters im gelehrten Prozeß der Frühzeit* (Munich 1967) 42, n.27, discovered that C.30 was actually the *Summa* of Honorius. See Weigand on the northern decretalists in this volume (chapter 6).

119. Kuttner, *Repertorium* 160–166. Alfons M. Stickler, 'Decretisti bolognesi dimenticati', SG 3 (1955) 375–410.

120. Kuttner, *Repertorium* 165.

121. Cf. W.P. Müller, *Huguccio. The Life, Works, and Thought of a Twelfth-Century Jurist*

Modern historians agree on Huguccio's excellence as a jurist. He combined analytical depth with an encyclopedic grasp of contemporary legal (and theological) literature. His intellectual achievement has been examined in numerous monographs and articles that present him as 'the greatest of all decretists', if not the 'greatest canonist of the Middle Ages'.[122]

Prior to completing his *Summa*, Huguccio had already contributed to the composition of a gloss apparatus on the *Decretum* known as *Ordinaturus Magister*. Successive generations of canonists did not hesitate to ascribe to his pen the whole work, transmitted in two recensions of 1180 and 1190 respectively.[123] But it was the *Summa* that eventually eclipsed all earlier canonistic commentaries and began to exert a strong influence on papal decision-making. Especially during the pontificate of Innocent III (1198–1216), Huguccio's doctrinal views helped shape the contents of many important decretals.[124] The contribution of the *Summa* to the literary development of the discipline was lasting as well. Before long, the *Summa* came to serve as a major source for Johannes Teutonicus' Ordinary Gloss on Gratian's *Decretum*.[125]

Life and Works

During the Middle Ages, Huguccio's biography circulated in two distinct versions. Each remained confined to the literary genre which had created it, so that scholars did not put both traditions together until modern times.[126] The oldest biographical tradition of his life developed at the school in Bologna. Its origins can be traced back to shortly after the promulgation of the *Decretales* by Pope Gregory IX (1234). The new compilation

---

(Washington, DC 1994); G. Catalano, 'Luci ed ombre sulla figura scientifica di Uguccione da Pisa', *Il diritto ecclesiastico* 114 (2003) 3–27.

122. 'Huguccio, der hervorragendste unter den ältesten Dekretglossatoren, ja der größte Kanonist des Mittelalters': F. Gillmann, 'Romanus pontifex iura omnia in scrinio pectoris sui censetur habere', AKKR 92 (1912) 4, who cites J. F. v. Schulte, *Die Stellung der Konzilien, Päpste und Bischöfe vom historischen und kanonistischen Standpunkte und die päpstliche Konstitution vom 18. Juli 1870* (Prague 1871; reprint Aalen 1976) 264; see also A.M. Stickler, '(Hugh) Huguccio', NCE 7 (1967) 200–201.

123. R. Weigand, *Die Glossen zum Dekret Gratians. Studien zu den frühen Glossen und Glossenkompositionen* (SG 25–26; Rome 1991) 451–563.

124. For example, C. Egger, 'Papst Innocenz III. als Theologe. Beiträge zur Kenntnis seines Denkens im Rahmen der Frühscholastik', AHP 30 (1992) 55–123; P. Diehl, 'Heresy as Grounds for Divorce', *Proceedings Munich* 975–996.

125. Among later canonists who made extensive use of Huguccio's work were Bartholomaeus Brixiensis, the final redactor of the *Glossa ordinaria* (ca. 1236), and Guido de Baysio, the author of the *Rosarium* (1300).

126. Müller, *Huguccio* 21–66; G. Catalano, 'Contributo alla biografia di Uguccione da Pisa', *Il diritto ecclesiastico* 65 (1954) 3–67; C. Leonardi, 'La vita e l'opera di Uguccione da Pisa decretista', SG 5–6 (1956/57) 37–120.

included several letters which Pope Innocent III had sent to the bishop of Ferrara. Canonists who commented on the Gregorian *Decretales* still knew that during Innocent's pontificate (1198–1216), the Ferrarese episcopate had been under the rule of a certain Huguccio (1190–1210).[127] From the introductory flourish of two of the decretals they learnt about Bishop Huguccio's former career as someone who had 'taught canon law' through his 'lectures and writings'.[128] Confronted with these hints, commentators like Goffredus of Trani (1243) and Bernardus of Parma (1234–1263) first spoke of the Ferrarese prelate as 'Master Huguccio', which implied his identification with the author of the *Summa decretorum*.[129] They were understood in this way by Johannes de Deo (1243), who introduced 'Huguccio, bishop of Ferrara' once explicitly as 'Master'.[130] Later on, this link was handed down as a historical fact by the gloss apparatus of Hostiensis (1265–1271) and Johannes Andreae.[131] Hostiensis's contribution was to add precision to the laconic statements of his fellow teachers by addressing Bishop Huguccio as 'our master'. Equally important, he not only employed this formula in the context of Innocent's two decretals, but also let it spill over into the rest of his work. Wherever an argument dealt with Huguccio of Ferrara, Hostiensis supplied the title 'magister noster'.[132] Johannes Andre-

127. Leonardi, 'La vita' 62–77, has discussed the papal correspondence with Ferrara; Bishop Huguccio's administrative activities are treated by Catalano, 'Contributo' 11–43, and A. Samaritani, *Cronotassi dei vescovi di Voghenza (secc. V–X) e di Ferrara (dal sec. VIII al pontificato di Innocenzo III, a. 1198)* (Ferrara 1988) 51–60.

128. 'Quanto te magis' (1 May 1199) = Po. 684 = 3 Comp. 4.14.1 = X 4.19.7, addresses Bishop Huguccio with the words: 'Quanto te magis novimus in canonico iure peritum'; 'In quadam nostra' (5 March 1209) = Po. 3684 = 3 Comp. 3.33.7 = X 3.41.8.

129. Goffredus Tranensis, Apparatus on X 3.41.8 s.v. *epistola decretali*: 'Magister Huguccio episcopus Ferrariensis respexit decretalem illam "Cum Marthe".' The full gloss is cited by K. Pennington, ZRG Kan. Abt. 72 (1986) 420 n.13 = 'Further Thoughts on Pope Innocent III's Knowledge of Law', in: idem, *Popes, Canonists and Texts, 1150–1550* (Aldershot 1993) no. II; Bernardus Parmensis, *Glossa ordinaria* on X 3.41.8 *Respondemus* (Syracuse N.Y., University Library, Arents Collection 1, fol. 186rb): 'Ad questionem magistri Huguccionis episcopi Ferrariensis, qui opinionem predictam secutus <est>'.

130. *Summa super iv causis decretorum*: 'Magister Huguccio summus in peritia decretorum olim Ferrariarum episcopus . . . composuit quandam summam super corpore decretorum, sed . . . morte preventus non potuit omnino perficere - deficit enim in xxiii Ca. q. iiii c. Est iniusta (c.33)' (Vatican, Bibl. Apost. lat. 2280, fol. 371ra). The full text of Johannes's prologue has been printed by F. Gillmann, 'Die Abfassungszeit der Dekretsumme Huguccios', AKKR 94 (1914) 243 n.1, reprinted in *Gesammelte Schriften zur klassischen Kanonistik von Franz Gillmann*, ed. R. Weigand (3 vols; Forschungen zur Kirchenrechtswissenschaft; Würzburg 1988–1993) vol. 1, no. 8.

131. First observed by K. Pennington, 'The Legal Education of Pope Innocent III', BMCL 4 (1974) 70–77 = idem, *Popes, Canonists and Texts* no. I.

132. Besides the comment on X 3.41.8, ed. Strasbourg 1512, vol. 2, fol. 176vb, which Hostiensis copied from Goffredus of Trani (n.129 above), his attitude emerges most clearly from a gloss on X 4.19.7 s.v. *per tuas*: 'O magister Huguccio episcope Ferrariensis qui hanc movisti questionem! Unde et dicit [sc. Innocentius]: "Quanto te novimus", quasi dicens:

ae (before 1317) misunderstood Hostiensis and turned the same formula into 'his master' (i.e. the teacher of Innocent III). Canonists and historians after him considered Johannes Andreae as their principal source for evidence of a pupil-teacher relationship between Pope Innocent III and Huguccio.[133] Johannes perpetuated this 'legend', along with the identification of the bishop and the canonist, in a short piece especially devoted to biographical matters (ca.1348).[134] One hundred and fifty years later (1511), Thomas Diplovatatius still presented Johannes's account as the best biography available from canonistic sources.[135]

Meanwhile, a rather different picture of Huguccio's life was drawn by a number of medieval chroniclers, who treated Huguccio as an important figure of Ferrarese history. The first to do so was Friar Salimbene of Parma in 1283, who departed strikingly from the data gathered by the medieval canon lawyers.[136] Besides showing himself well-informed about the exact length of Huguccio's pontificate (1 May 1190 to 30 April 1210), he claimed for him the authorship of the *Derivationes*, a massive Latin etymological dictionary of even greater renown among contemporaries than the canonist's *Summa*.[137] In addition, Salimbene asserted that Bishop Huguccio was a Pisan by origin, another detail unfamiliar to the jurists.[138] Later chroniclers repeated this information. Riccobaldus of Ferrara (1312)

"Tu forsan melius scires solvere quam nos nisi quia quicquid diceremus ius est . . . et ad nos talia pertinent" (Vienna, N.B. lat. 2114, fol. IIIrb; ed. Strasbourg 1512, vol. 2, fol. 239va)'.

133. On such grounds rejected as legend by K. Pennington, 'Legal Education' 70–73; contra: W. Imkamp, *Das Kirchenbild Innozenz' III*. (Stuttgart 1983) 38–45. Pennington has responded to Imkamp's objections in: ZRG Kan. Abt. 72 (1986) 417–423 = idem, *Pope, Canonists and Texts* no. II.

134. *Adnotationes super speculum Durantis, Praefatio*: 'Hugo: Certum est quod vidit primam et secundam compilationem. In sua tamen summa rarissime decretales allegat, et si allegat . . . non tamen allegat sub compilatione vel sub rubrica, motus ut puto quia non fuerint papales. Quod illas viderit patet, quia decretalis In quadam, De celebr. miss. (X 3.33.8), et decretalis Quanto, De divor. (X 4.19.7), directe fuerint ad ipsum tunc Ferrariensem episcopum, ut ibi dixi' (ed. Lyon 1521, fol. 2va).

135. T. Diplovatatius, *De claris iurisconsultis* 2, ed. H. Kantorowicz, F. Schulz, and G. Rabotti (SG 10; Bologna 1968) 60–62.

136. 'Ugutio natione Tuscus, civis Pisanus, episcopus Ferrariensis fuit; librum Derivationum composuit; viriliter et digne episcopatum rexit et laudabiliter vitam suam finivit. Et alia quedam opuscula composuit que sunt utilia et habentur a pluribus: que etiam vidi et legi non semel neque bis. Anno Domini mccx ultimo die Aprilis migravit ad Christum. Et stetit in episcopatu xx annis minus uno die', *Chronica*, ed. O. Holder-Egger (MGH SS 32; Hannover 1905–1913) 27 n.5; ed. F. Bernini (Bari 1942) 36; ed. G. Scalia, (Bari 1966) 38.

137. *Uguccione da Pisa: Derivationes*, ed. E. Cecchini and G.Arbizzoni (Florence 2004); cf. Müller, *Huguccio* 43–48.

138. No canonist seems to have associated Pisa with the *Summa*'s author before Egidius Spiritalis de Perusio in his *Libellus contra infideles et inobedientes et rebelles Sancte Romane Ecclesie ac summo pontifici* (ca. 1323–1328), ed. R. Scholz, *Unbekannte kirchenpolitische Streitschriften* (Rome 1914), which includes a reference to 'Huguccio Pysanus' (III).

added that the bishop had composed the *Derivationes* in the 1190s. Neither he nor anyone else knew about the possible link between the bishop and the *Summa decretorum*.[139]

It was left to modern times and to the efforts of the Camaldulese antiquarian Mauro Sarti (1769) to coordinate these non-contradictory, but oddly unrelated biographical pieces of evidence. Sarti concluded that Huguccio had been the eminent Bolognese decretist and author of the *Summa decretorum*. He was elevated in 1190 to the episcopal see of Ferrara. While bishop, he published the *Derivationes* and carried out numerous charges as a papal delegate. He died in 1210.[140]

For a long time, scholarship accepted Sarti's reconstruction without serious challenge. Closer analysis of the evidence, however, seems to indicate that the connection between the canonist and the grammarian rests on little more than the recurrence of Huguccio's name. As a matter of fact, the tendency to conflate the two Huguccios is much older than the above-cited literary testimonies would suggest. In the minds of certain medieval scribes, the identity of the canonist and the grammarian was equally taken for granted. In a famous passage of the *Summa*, the canonist Huguccio had referred to the *Agiographia*, a minor etymological work of his. One of the two manuscripts known to Giuseppe Cremascoli, the modern editor of the *Agiographia* (1978), contains a reference to 'the reason we have diligently noted in the *Derivationes*'. For Cremascoli, this remark tied the *Summa* and the *Derivationes* by way of the *Agiographia* definitively to one and the same author.[141] A third copy of the *Agiographia* discovered in 1995 by Martin Bertram, on the other hand, has confirmed previous suspicions that Huguccio's purported words, 'the reason we have noted in the *Derivationes*', represented a mere interpolation. The newly found manuscript omitted the questionable cross-reference but also incorporated similar ones into other sections of the *Agiographia*, where they could not be found in the two copies known to Cremascoli.[142]

---

139. *Compilatio chronologica* (ca.1312): '[A.D.1191?] Hugutio natione Pisanus episcopus Ferrariensis agnoscitur, qui datus adiutor a Sede Apostolica abbati Nonantulano homini prodigo et indigno ex libro Papiae qui illic est librum derivationum composuit (ed. Muratori, RIS 9.245–246)'.

140. M. Sarti and M. Fattorini, *De claris archigymnasii Bononiensis professoribus* (1769), ed. C. Albicinius and C. Malagola (2d edition, Bologna 1888) 1.370–376.

141. 'Et quare in Libro Derivationum assignavimus', ed. G. Cremascoli, *Uguccione da Pisa. Liber de dubio accentu. Agiographia: Expositio de symbolo apostolorum* (Spoleto 1978) 156 lines 494–496.

142. M. Bertram, 'Zu Huguccio', QF 75 (1995) 596–600; full analysis of the new manuscript in W. Müller, 'Eine neue Handschrift von Huguccio's Agiographia', ibid. 545–552; also Müller, *Huguccio* 48–60.

Although anonymous copyists of the thirteenth and fourteenth centuries were prepared to attribute all works by someone named Huguccio to a single author, research in the *Derivationes* and twelfth-century grammatical writings has begun to produce evidence that renders the presence in Bologna of a second Huguccio, teacher of grammar at Bologna since the 1160s, more than likely. Apart from the *Derivationes*, composed at Bologna and including, once, the specific date of '1161', there is also the *Summa artis grammatice* of a certain 'Oguicio', written at Bologna during the 1160s and preserved today in a single Munich manuscript (Clm 18908). The text, based on the grammatical work of a Parisian master, Robert Blund, shows that this 'Oguicio' had studied for an extended period in France.[143] A strong French background is also suggested by the overall dependency of Huguccio's *Derivationes* on Osbern of Gloucester's *Panormia* or *Liber Derivationum* (ca. 1148–1160), whose work was completely unknown outside of the Anglo-French orbit at the time, and numerous references in the *Derivationes* to philosophical and grammatical writings from teachers of the so-called 'School of Chartres'.[144] Huguccio of Pisa, a grammarian trained in France and teaching at Bologna during the 1160s, would be, in sum, a far better candidate for the 'Magister Ugicio Pisanus' who later appears as well in a Bolognese charter of 1199.[145] At that date, his namesake, the canonist of unknown origin, had already left Bologna for the episcopal see of Ferrara.

While the *Summa decretorum* nowhere produces compelling proof of an identification with Huguccio, the grammarian, it provides very good indirect evidence attesting to the canonist's subsequent career as bishop of Ferrara. For example, the drafting of the *Summa* ended abruptly, sometime between 1188 and 1191, which coincides remarkably well with Huguccio's election to the see of Ferrara in May 1190.[146] In similar fashion, Pope Inno-

---

143. H. Kneepkens, *Het "Iudicium constructionis". Het leerstuck van de constructio in de 2de helft van de 12de eeuw* (2 vols; Nimjegen 1987) 1.139–143; E. Pérez Rodriguez, 'La Summa artis grammaticae de Hugutio y la gramatica del siglo xii', in: *Gli umanesimi medievali*, ed. C. Leonardi (Florence 1998) 479–490.

144. Among them commentaries by Petrus Helias and William of Conches, cf. R. Hunt, 'Hugutio and Petrus Helias', *Medieval and Renaissance Studies* 2 (1950) 174–178 = *The History of Grammar in the Middle Ages*, ed. G.L. Bursill-Hall (Amsterdam 1980) 145–149; E. Jeauneau, 'Deux redactions des gloses de Guillaume de Conches sur Priscien', *Recherches de théologie ancienne et médiévale* 27 (1960) 223–225. Huguccio's most important single source was Osbern of Gloucester, *Liber Derivationum*, ed. P. Busdraghi et al. (Spoleto 1996).

145. Printed by Sarti and Fattorini, *De claris* 2.165–166; from Bologna, Archivio Comunale Demaniale 1/829 (a fourteenth-century notarial copy).

146. First noted by Sarti and Fattorini, *De claris* 1.370; further Gillmann, 'Die Abfassungszeit' 238–242; F. Heyer, 'Namen und Titel des gratianischen Dekrets', AKKR 94 (1914) 513 n. 57.

cent III's letters to Huguccio discuss doctrinal views of Bishop Huguccio, which reveal strong parallels to pertinent comments in the *Summa*.[147]

Consequently, we have no reason to question that the renowned decretist and Huguccio, bishop of Ferrara, were one and the same person. On the other hand, his identity with the Bolognese grammarian of the 1160s, author of the *Derivationes* and Pisan by birth, rests on little more than the identity of names and a handful of interpolated manuscript references.

The Summa Decretorum

Although the Glossa ordinaria of Johannes Teutonicus (1215/18) soon superseded the Summa as the standard commentary on Gratian's *Decretum,* scholarly interest in Huguccio's work continued throughout the later Middle Ages. Before the invention of the printing press, the *Summa* was copied and circulated widely in numerous manuscripts. More than forty of them still exist today.[148] It was not until the end of the fifteenth century that jurists ceased to turn to the *Summa*. Perhaps due to its enormous size, the work never appeared in print and quickly faded from view. Four centuries of silence followed, interrupted only by the occasional biographical remarks of antiquarians.[149]

Friedrich Maassen (1857) and Johann Friedrich v. Schulte (1875) were the first modern legal historians who again studied the *Summa* in detail. During the 1950s, and under the guidance of Alfons Stickler, an international project was established to examine the manuscripts of the *Summa*. Thirty manuscripts were collated for an edition, and the first of 16 planned volumes, covering Huguccio's comment on Gratian's Distinctions 1–20, has been published by Oldrich Přerovský.[150]

Date and stages of composition

Franz Gillmann has convincingly shown that Huguccio completed his *Summa* between 1188 and 1190.[151] Indirect clues, scattered all over the

---

147. Compare the papal rescripts of 1199 and 1209 (n. 128 above) to the passages of the *Summa* discussed by Egger, 'Papst Innocenz III.'; and Diehl, 'Heresy'.

148. See the list of manuscripts in the Přerovský edition, *Summa decretorum* xii–xxiii (n. 150, below).

149. G. Cremascoli, 'Uguccione da Pisa: Saggio bibliografico', *Aevum* 42 (1968) 123–168, has surveyed references to Huguccio in publications prior to Sarti and Fattorini, *De claris* (1769).

150. Huguccio Pisanus, *Summa decretorum*, 1: *Distinctiones I–XX*, ed. Oldrich Přerovský (MIC, Series A, 6; Città del Vaticano 2006). F. Maassen, 'Beiträge zur Geschichte der juristischen Literatur des Mittelalters, insbesondere der Decretisten-Literatur des 12. Jahrhunderts', SB Vienna 24 (1857) 35–46; Schulte, QL 1.156–170.

151. Gillmann, 'Die Abfassungszeit' 233–251; see also his remarks in, *Die Notwendigkeit der Intention auf Seiten des Spenders und des Empfängers der Sakramente nach der Anschauung der*

work, suggest that Huguccio wrote after the death of Pope Gregory VIII (December 1187) and during the pontificate of his successor, Clement III (1187–1191). This fully confirms the only concrete date of 1188 that Huguccio attached to a fictitious charter formula.[152] Gillmann further established that the canonist never quoted *decretales extravagantes* by title, as a canonist writing after the introduction of the *Compilatio prima* into the canonistic curriculum (1191–1192) would have done. Gillmann finally pointed to the fragmentary state of the *Summa*, which does not comment on the *Cause hereticorum* (C.23–26) beyond C.23 q.4 c.33. Why did Huguccio abandon his task at such an odd point? Gillmann's answer was that the break occurred when the canonist received word of his election to the episcopal see of Ferrara (1190). He must have left Bologna in a hurry.

Although later research has not added new material to Gillmann's findings, several scholars, emphasizing a single piece of contradictory evidence, have questioned his chronology. In Huguccio's comment on C.23 q.1 c.4, Gillmann himself had discovered a mention of the decretal *Litteras tuas*, issued by Pope Innocent III as late as 1201.[153] Gillmann declared this passage an interpolation, but other scholars have been more hesitant to do away with it. Significantly, the manuscripts seem unanimous in attesting to the authenticity of the passage.[154] Among the hundreds of papal letters Huguccio cites, however, there is no other text issued after 1190 or quoted from a later decretal collection. Huguccio certainly would have referred to *Compilatio prima*, if he had written his work in, say, 1201. Otherwise, it would have been outdated and unsuitable for the practical purposes of canonistic literature. It seems therefore hardly likely that the reference to Innocent III constitutes proof that Huguccio was drafting the final portions of the *Summa* after he had become bishop.

Frühscholastik (Mainz 1916) 33 n.1; idem, *Zur Lehre der Scholastik vom Spender der Firmung und des Weihesakraments* (Paderborn 1920) 4 n.2.

152. *Summa*, C.2 q.8 p.c.5 s.v. *Libellorum*: Sarti and Fattorini, *De claris* 1.371, had misread the date as '1178'. The mistake was corrected by Gillmann, 'Die Abfassungszeit' 241 n.2, yet again perpetuated by Leonardi, 'La vita' 54, 87 n.174.

153. *Summa*, C.23 q.1 c.4 s.v. *quod sibi iubetur*: 'Ar. quod pendente causa matrimonii propter dubium licite videtur posse reddi utrumque debitum ... Quod tamen non est usquequaque observandum, ut in extra Innocentii iii "Litteras tuas" (= Po.1560, from 1201)', cf. Gillmann, 'Die Abfassungszeit' 244 n.; Huguccio's authorship of the fragmentary section on *Cause hereticorum* is confirmed by a gloss on C.23 q.4 c.24 § 7 s.v. *sunt in illa clerici*. It refers ('sicut ibi exposuimus') to a passage at *Summa*, D.12 c.8, which in fact includes the appropriate explanation.

154. According to S. Kuttner, 'Retractationes vii', in: *Gratian* 12, the reference is transmitted in at least six of ten MSS (Vatican, Bibl. Apost. lat. 2280, fol. 244ra–b; Florence, Laur. S. Croce Plut. I sin. 4, fol. 278va; Florence, Laur. Fesul. 126, fol. 101ra; Admont 7, fol. 318ra; Lons-Le-Saunier, Arch. 12 F.16, fol. 306va; Paris, B.N. lat. 3892, fol. 267ra). The other four are: Madrid, B.N. lat. 11962; Rouen, B.M. 749; Tarazona, Cat. 151 (3); Verona, Cap. cxciv.

Another consideration is that Huguccio did not compose his *Summa* by strictly following the order of Gratian's *Decretum*. Prior to commenting on the *Cause hereticorum*, Huguccio had already covered Causa 27 and those *cause* that followed. This is a clear indication that Huguccio wrote his *Summa* in various stages. His commentary on Gratian may well reflect patterns of lecturing at canon law schools, which reserved certain parts of the *Decretum* for extraordinary treatment.[155]

Other evidence allows us to establish a relative chronology for various portions of Huguccio's *Summa*. His work includes many cross-references, which call the reader's attention to relevant comments elsewhere in the text. Huguccio included those hints in succinct formulations, which regularly employ a verb in past or future tense. By using terms such as 'invenies', or 'sicut dictum est', Huguccio of course meant little more than 'as said below' or, 'see above'. The situation is different, however, where the canonist speaks in the first person. 'Dicemus' and the like, often combined with the formula 'Deo volente', refer to a gloss yet unwritten, while 'ut dixi' directs the reader to a part of the work finished earlier. By tracking down these formulations, we can discern that Huguccio wrote his *Summa* in five stages:

1. Prologue; D.1–101; C.2–22; C.27–33 q.2; C.33 q.4–C.36.[156]
2. Causa 1.[157]
3. *De consecratione*.
4. *De penitentia*.[158]
5. C.23–C.23 q.4 c.33 (*Cause hereticorum*).[159]

---

155. L. Prosdocimi, 'La "Summa decretorum" di Uguccione da Pisa. Studi preliminari per una edizione critica', SG 3 (1955) 349–374, concluded (359–360) that 'proprio la C.1 e il De cons. siano le ultime parti composte . . . dopo di che non sarebbe rimasto ad Uguccione che accingersi al commento delle Causae Haereticorum'.

156. A remark at D.54 c.15 points to C.17 q.4 c.34 ('sicut ibi dicemus'); another one advises the reader to consult C.7 q.1 c.3 in connection with C.11 q.1 c.25 ('ibidem melius assignabimus'); C.12 q.2 c.15 refers back to D.23 c.6 ('ut dixi'), C.32 q.4 c.11 to the prologue ('ut in principio huius operis diximus'). The formula 'Deo volente' is employed to call the reader's attention from C.2 q.2 a.c.1 to C.3 q.1; C.3 q.4 c.12 to C.11 q.3; C.13 q.1 a.c.1 to C.16 q.1 c.42; and from C.22 q.4 c.20 to C.32 q.2 p.c.10.

157. There seems to be no cross-reference that would establish the relative position of Causa 1 after stage 1. At any rate, Huguccio completed it prior to *De consecratione* (stage 3), cf. De cons. D.2 c.73: 'Sed hoc plenius distinximus i q.i Si fuerit (c.30) (Admont, Stiftsbibliothek 7, fol. 436ra)'; also De cons. D.4 c.140; while writing these lines, he had not yet completed De pen. and the fragment on C.23, see next note.

158. As is evident from De pen. D.3 c.21: 'Hoc capitulum invenitur infra, de con.v. di. Nichil (c.23), et ibi est diligenter a nobis expositum' (Vat. lat. 2280, fol. 304vb); and De pen. D.3 c.7: 'Assignavimus iam et alias causas quare huiusmodi pene . . . remaneant post baptismum, . . . ut infra de con. di.iiii Sine penitentia (c.99) (Admont 7, fol. 491va)'.

159. That the fragment on Causa 23 belongs to the latest parts of Huguccio's work is

Closer examination of the manuscript tradition of the *Summa* likewise illustrates that the work was produced in non-linear fashion. Scholars have identified numerous irregularities in the textual tradition, which arose from the five stages of composition. Many copies omit some of Huguccio's comments on Causa 1, *De consecratione*, *De penitentia*, and the *Cause hereticorum*, or have them appended to the end of the main text.[160]

Supplements to Huguccio's *Summa*

The composition of the *Summa* in various stages had yet another important ramification. Confronted with a text that did not comment on all parts of Gratian's *Decretum*, scribes were anxious to supply the missing sections from elsewhere. Borrowing from the works of other decretists, they included foreign material without distinguishing it clearly from Huguccio's own. This has complicated the consultation of the *Summa* for scholars. Non-authentic interpolations have prompted numerous misattributions, and it remains uncertain if all of the non-Huguccionian passages have been identified. According to our present knowledge, the *scriptoria* supplied the textual gaps of the *Summa* in the following fashion:[161]

1. Supplements on Causa 1 (stage 2)
   1.1 *Summa* Paris 15397 (Paris, B.N. lat. 15397*)
   1.2 *Continuatio prima* (*Summa Casinensis*) (Paris, B.N. lat. 15396–15397)
   1.3 *Summa Lipsiensis* (Luxembourg, B.M. 144)
   1.4 *Ecce vicit leo* (Bamberg, Bayerische Staatsbibl. Can. 41; St. Petersburg, Publ. Lib. Fol. II vel. 10*)
2. Supplements on *De consecratione* (stage 3)
   2.1 *Summa Lipsiensis* (Luxembourg, B.M. 144)
   2.2 *Ius naturale* (Tarazona, Cat. 151 [3])
3. Supplements on *De penitentia* (stage 4)
   3.1 Alanus ab Insulis, *De penitentia* (Fulda, Landesbibl. D.22*)[162]
   3.2 *Summa Transitum ponit* (Verona, Bibl. Capit. CXCIV*)

---

proved by a passage at C.23 q.4 c.24 § 6 s.v. *Est enim et tale*: 'Hic ponit alium modum inferendi. Hoc multo melius intelliges si que diximus de istis duobus modis inferendi infra, de con. di.v. Numquam (c.33), respexeris' (Lons–Le-Saunier 12 F. 16, fol. 311rb). Accordingly, the question of priority concerns De pen. only.

160. The most comprehensive survey of the manuscripts is in Müller, *Huguccio*, 76–80; cf. *Summa*, ed. Přerovský.

161. In the following survey, an asterisk [*] indicates supplements which are appended to the main text of Huguccio's *Summa*.

162. Fulda, D.22, fol. 291r–294r (ed. PL 210.111–198): Prosdocimi, 'I manoscritti' 261.

4. Supplements on the *Cause hereticorum* (stage 5)
   4.1 *Summa Quid culpatur* (Fulda, Landesbibl. D.22*)
   4.2 *Summa* Paris 15397 (Paris, B.N. lat. 15397)
   4.3 *Continuatio prima (Summa Casinensis)* (Paris, B.N. lat. 3891; Luxembourg, B.M. 144; Bamberg, Bayer. Staatsbibl. Can.41; St. Petersburg, Publ. Lib. Fol. II vel. 10; Paris, B.N. lat. 15397; Cambrai, B.M. 612; Rouen, B.M. 749; Admont, Stiftsbibl. 7; Leipzig, Univ.bibl. 985; Florence, Laur. Plut. I sin.4; Vatican, Bibl. Apost. lat. 2280; Paris, B.N. lat. 3892; Lons–Le-Saunier, Arch. Dép. 12 F.16; Salamanca, Univ. 1930; Florence, Laur. Fes. 126)
   4.4 *Summa Lipsiensis* (Luxembourg, B.M. 144)
   4.5 *Ius naturale* (Tarazona, Cat. 97 [9]; Tarazona, Cat. 151 [3]*)
   4.6 *Ecce vicit Leo* (Vatican, Bibl. Apost. Borgh. 272)
   4.7 *Summa Ostenditur hic* (Verona, Bibl. Capit. CXCIV)
   4.8 Johannes de Deo, *Summa super quatuor causis decretorum* (Madrid, B.N. lat. 11962; Vat. Bibl. Apost. lat. 2280*; Paris, B.N. lat. 3892*; St. Petersburg, Publ. Lib. Fol. II vel. 10*)

Due to the *horror vacui* of the medieval scribes, the manuscript tradition of the *Summa* incorporated many texts of other decretist writings. Some of them have also survived outside of it, but five texts are uniquely preserved in connection with Huguccio's work. Besides the half-page fragment replacing the treatise on *De penitentia* in the copy from Verona, there is another incomplete excerpt in the Fulda manuscript. Verona CXCIV and Paris 15396–15397 contain full commentaries on sections not covered by Huguccio in his *Summa*. The fifth case, finally, is peculiar, because the transmission of the text of Johannes de Deo together with Huguccio's work cannot be attributed to mere chance. Johannes's *Summa super iv causis decretorum* (ca. 1243) was designed from the beginning as a continuation of Huguccio's unfinished efforts. To convey this purpose to the reader, Johannes not only wrote an appropriate foreword and a versified epilogue but also began his text at the very point where Huguccio had stopped, C.23 q.4 c.33.[163]

Continuatio prima (Summa Casinensis)

Not surprisingly, the bulk of foreign supplements concentrate on the *Cause hereticorum*, which Huguccio had never completed. The so-called *Continuatio prima* was the most important and extensive supplement. It

---

163. Foreword and Epilogue printed by Gillmann, 'Die Abfassungszeit' 243–244 n.

circulated separately in only one manuscript (Montecassino 396) but was incorporated into fifteen copies of Huguccio's work.[164] Its frequent recurrence in association with the *Summa* has led many scholars to assume that there was a particular connection between Huguccio's *Summa* and the *Continuatio*. By using, for example, the title of *Continuatio prima*, they have suggested that the circumstances of its composition were somehow related to the fragmentary state of the *Summa*. Similarly, the anonymous 'Continuator' has often been considered as a 'pupil' of Huguccio, whose principal purpose was to take down what he had heard in the master's lectures.[165] Closer analysis reveals, however, the self-standing character of the work.

That the anonymous author actually never intended to 'continue' Huguccio's commentary on the *Cause hereticorum* is proved by the date of composition. Franz Gillmann established long ago that the *Continuatio* was written around 1185–1186, several years before Huguccio finished his *Summa*.[166] Similarly, a look at the format of the *Continuatio* renders doubtful any assumption that its original function was supplementary. After all, a full inventory of the surviving parts comprises not only the text on the *Cause hereticorum*, but also two other texts, on Causa 1 and on *De consecratione*. The three parts of the text occur in the manuscript Montecassino 396 (hence the title of *Summa Casinensis*), whereas Paris 15396–15397 contains the two sections on C.23–C.26 and Causa 1.

Concerning the general character of the work, the *Continuatio* shows strong doctrinal preferences. Rather than to Huguccio, the work is indebted to the teachings of his contemporary Bazianus, whose name is quoted on almost every page. Compared to his, Huguccio's influence, though undeniable, was clearly secondary.[167] Moreover, even after completion the

---

164. The text was first described by Schulte, QL 157–161, who erroneously saw in it the work of Johannes de Deo; corrected by L. Tanon, 'Rufin et Hugutio', *Nouvelle revue historique de droit français et étranger* 13 (1889) 694; cf. also Kuttner, *Repertorium* 158, 66 (where the unidentified text in Montecassino 396 is called *Summa Casinensis*); idem, 'Bernardus Compostellanus' 283 n. 23 = idem, with 'Retractationes vii', in: *Gratian*.

165. See Kuttner, 'Bernardus Compostellanus' 283 n. 23, where the Continuator is characterized as Huguccio's 'pupil'. Prosdocimi, 'La "Summa decretorum"' 368, asked if the 'Continuatio': 'non potrebbe essere, nella sua sostanza almeno, di Uguccione stesso?'

166. Gillmann, AKKR 92 (1912) 367. The Continuator wrote after the death of Pope Lucius III (25 Nov. 1185; cf. 'Continuatio', C.1 q.1 c.38 *quolibet horum* [Montecassino 396, p. 117a]), whose memory, however, was still fresh. Pope Lucius is cited five times, his successor Urban III (1185–1187) only once.

167. I have counted more than thirty quotes of 'Basianus' (including interpolations, see next note); the *Continuatio* further refers to Johannes Faventinus on 14, to Huguccio (cf. Schulte, QL 1.158 n. 9) on 13 occasions. Cardinalis (7), Gandulphus (6), Rolandus (1), and Petrus Manducator (1) are also mentioned.

text remained curiously susceptible to the interpolation of gloss material signed by 'bar.' Some of these intruded materials repeat remarks already present in the original.[168] There are also striking parallels between opinions which decretist tradition commonly ascribed to Bazianus and certain views expressed by the 'Continuator'.[169] While this seems to provide good evidence for an identification of the author with Bazianus, other passages of the 'Continuatio' speak against it. The anonymous writer actually criticized 'bar.' on several occasions, which in the last analysis excludes the possibility that Bazianus could have written the work.[170] Still, the literal correspondences as well as the constant references to Bazianus indicate that the *Continuatio* must represent some kind of annotated account (*reportatio*) of Bazianus's lectures.[171]

The *Continuatio* (or rather: *Summa Casinensis*) cannot be reduced, as often done, to the exercise of an unknown 'pupil' of Huguccio. While it was a supplement to Huguccio's *Summa* in the manuscripts, its author did not intend it to be. Historically, the text stands out as an important indirect witness to the canonistic doctrines of Bazianus. Nowhere else, it seems, are his lectures recorded in such a comprehensive fashion.[172]

---

168. E.g. *Continuatio*, C.1 q.3 c.14 s.v. *altare decimas* (Montecassino 396, p. 130a; Paris 15396, fol. 105va); C.24 q.1 c.39 s.v. *a clericatu* (Montecassino 396, p. 162a; Paris 15397, fol. 54rb), cf. C.24 q.1 p.c.39 s.v. *in detestatione* (ibid.); De cons. D.1 c.48 s.v. *eadem hora cruci.* (Montecassino 396, p. 181b); De cons. D.2 c.23 s.v. *commiscere* (Montecassino 396, p. 188a). Four other glosses, ascribed to 'bar.' and repeating statements made by the Continuator, do not appear in all of the MSS: C.1 q.1 c.108 s.v. *Si quis potuerit probare se nescire* (Montecassino 396, p. 124b; *om.* Paris 15396, fol. 103va); C.1 q.1 c.111 s.v. *Si statim* (Montecassino 396, p. 125a; *om.* Paris 15396, fol. 103vb); C.1 q.7 c.2 § 3 s.v. *Si lapsus post baptismum* (Montecassino 396, p. 133a; *om.* Paris 15396, fol. 106va); C.23 q.3 c.11 s.v. *pre multitudine* (Montecassino 396, p. 139a; *om.* Paris 15397, fol. 47vb).

169. *Continuatio*, C.1 q.7 c.9 s.v. *et per te*: 'Arg. quod per alium alii potest fieri promissio. Quod verum est si fit mandatarius cui promittitur'. The later decretist tradition, from *Ius naturale* onwards, attributed this gloss to Bazianus: A. Padoa Schioppa, 'Sul principio della rappresentanza diretta nel diritto canonico classico', *Proceedings Toronto* 114–115; another instance, *Continuatio*, C.1 q.3 c.4 s.v. *simoniace pravitatis usus* (Paris, 15396, fol. 104vb; Montecassino 396, p. 128a–b), gives an opinion, which in Huguccio's *Summa*, C.1 q.3 c.4 s.v. *sub cuius redemptione*, ed. R. Weigand, 'Huguccio und der Glossenapparat "Ordinaturus Magister",' AKKR 154 (1985) 490–520 at 511, is recorded as 'notula bar.'

170. Continuatio', C.26 q.2 c.10 s.v. *Si de area* (Montecassino 396, p. 173b; Paris 15397, fol. 57vb); De cons. D.1 c.35 s.v. *Si quis* (Montecassino 396, p. 180b); De cons. D.2 c.28 s.v. *pars in altari* (Montecassino 396, p. 187b). C.1 q.7. c.23 s.v. *Nec ulla necessitas* is omitted from one of the manuscripts (Montecasscino 396, p. 135a; *om.* Paris 15396, fol. 47vb).

171. Cf. T. Lehnherr, *Die Exkommunikationsgewalt der Haeretiker bei Gratian und den Dekretisten bis zur Glossa Ordinaria des Johannes Teutonicus* (St. Ottilien 1987) 226–228. *Reportationes* of lectures held at the medieval law schools have been surveyed by F. Soetermeer, 'Un catégorie de commentaires peu connue: Les "commenta" ou "lecturae" inédites des précurseurs d'Odofrède', RIDC 2 (1991) 47–67.

172. An exception may be *Summa* Paris 15397, cf. Müller, *Huguccio* 84 n. 84, which appears closely tied to Bazianus' teachings. His glosses are preserved in many manuscripts. Inciden-

Huguccio's Doctrinal Views: 'A Moment of Synthesis'

Legal historians have examined the teachings of the *Summa* and noted its author's unusual intellectual qualities. On every folio, the work attests not only to Huguccio's comprehensive grasp of older decretist doctrine but also to his great ability to transform complex and disputed issues into coherent and clear-cut doctrine. These were the chief characteristics of Huguccio's accomplishment, in which modern scholarship has recognized 'a moment of synthesis'.[173]

Due to the lack of a printed text and other editorial tools, an exhaustive analysis of the *Summa* remains impossible. There are, on the other hand, numerous detailed monographs on certain aspects of decretist doctrine, which illustrate Huguccio's extraordinary gift to distill substance from the overwhelming mass of older canonistic discourse. Studies have also illustrated recurrent themes and fundamental notions that appear again and again in his work. These underlying principles served Huguccio as a guide helping him to forge intricate juridical problems into a powerful 'synthesis.' At the same time, his conclusions gave his opinions an air of austerity that did not escape the attention of his contemporaries. Since the days of Johannes Teutonicus (fl. 1215), the 'rigor Huguccionis', Huguccio's rigor, has been invoked in almost proverbial fashion.[174]

One of the best-studied areas of Huguccionian thought is his theory of ecclesiastical government. Students have examined the remarks of the *Summa* on the relationship between the secular and spiritual powers and the proper functioning of church hierarchy. They have established that Huguccio viewed the two realms, clerical and lay, from an essentially 'dualist' standpoint, treating them as autonomous, divinely instituted entities.[175] Huguccio exalted the authority of the emperor and subordinated kings, princes, and lesser rulers to him. They merely held an inferior status of delegated imperial authority. Huguccio further expounded the independence of secular jurisdiction. The right to confer imperial power,

---

tally, Bazianus' identification with the civilian Johannes Bazianus seems unfounded, considering that his contemporary Huguccio was always careful to distinguish 'bar.' from 'Iob.' For a summary of this much-debated question, see Charles Donahue, 'Bassianus, that is to say, Bazianus? Bazianus and Johannes Bassianus on Marriage', RIDC 14 (2003) 41–82.

173. 'Un momento di sintesi': S. Mochi Onory, *Fonti canonistiche dell'idea moderna dello stato* (Milan 1951) 141; for a more detailed discussion of what follows, Müller, *Huguccio* 5–19, 139–151.

174. Particularly telling is the formulation of Johannes *Teutonicus, Glossa ordinaria*, D.50 c.6: 'Huguccio . . . cum rigore suo'.

175. Full analysis by G. Catalano, *Impero, regni e sacerdozio nel pensiero di Uguccio da Pisa* (Milan 1959).

for example, rested solely with the electoral body of the princes, so that subsequent papal coronation added nothing of substance. Similarly, the pope could not depose the emperor unless he was called upon to do so by the princely electorate.[176] On the other hand, Huguccio made sure, too, that his dualist position secured ecclesiastical independence. On numerous occcasions, he forcefully stated that the church enjoyed full legislative and jurisdictional sovereignty.[177]

An account of Huguccio's dualist approach remains, however, inaccurate without a mention of the hierocratic tendencies in his thought. In particular, he and his fellow canonists employed excommunication as a powerful tool of control by spiritual authorities. Huguccio, for example, did not hesitate to overstep the ordinary jurisdictional borderlines 'ratione peccati', in order to correct sinful behavior. The *Summa* granted ecclesiastical judges the authority to suspend, at least in part, the feudal obligations of a vassal to his excommunicated lord and even to maintain the applicability of unjust and illicit sentences.[178] To save the presumed sinner from eternal damnation was more important for Huguccio than to avoid possible abuses of temporal jurisdiction. The same concern for the sake of the individual's soul accounts for yet another hierocratic element in his teaching, his adherence and application of canonical equity, *equitas canonica*, to legal problems. Huguccio frequently employed this concept in order to reserve certain legal cases to church jurisdiction, or to promote the application of canonical rules in the secular courts as well.[179]

---

176. Cf. ibid.; also F. Kempf, *Papsttum und Kaisertum bei Innocenz III.: Die geistigen und rechtlichen Grundlagen seiner Thronstreitpolitik* (Rome 1954) 213–218; E. Peters, *The Shadow King. Rex inutilis in Medieval Law and Literature, 754–1327* (New Haven and London 1970) 120–131.

177. Müller, *Huguccio* 121–137, discusses Huguccio's views regarding the legislative autonomy of the church. The procedural privileges of the clergy are treated at *Summa*, C.11 q.1 a.c.1 s.v. *Quod clericus*.

178. An ordinary appeal was the only remedy admitted by Huguccio: J. Zeliauskas, *De excommunicatione vitiata apud glossatores (1140–1234)* (Zurich 1967) 270, 276, 63*–85*. The effects of the sanction on feudal obligations has been treated by Catalano, *Impero* 35–44, 79–80; T. Lehnherr, 'Der Begriff "executio" in der Summa Decretorum des Huguccio', AKKR 150 (1981) 15–20, 34–36. Concerning ecclesiastical competence over laymen 'ratione peccati', A. Stickler, 'Der Schwerterbegriff bei Huguccio', *Ephemerides iuris canonici* 3 (1947) 211–215.

179. L. Scavo Lombardo, *Il concetto di buona fede nel diritto canonico* (Rome 1944) 65–70, has analyzed Huguccio's understanding of *equitas canonica*. Huguccio used the concept to promote ecclesiastical competence in cases involving usury: T.P. Mc Laughlin, 'The Teachings of the Canonists on Usury (xii, xiii, and xiv Centuries)', *Mediaeval Studies* 1 (1939) 84; 2 (1940) 18; to criticize the Roman laws of marriage: G. Minnucci, *La capacità della donna nel processo canonistico classico: Da Graziano a Uguccione da Pisa* (Milan 1989) 107–120; and, most notably, to require good faith in prescription and usucaption: Scavo Lombardo, *Il concetto* 65–66; N. Vilain, 'Préscription et bonne foi du Decret de Gratien (1140) à Jean d'André (†1348)', *Tradi-

In dealing with the internal structure of the church, Huguccio built his argument around the fundamental tenet of papal monarchy. It was common decretist doctrine that the pope had received his prerogatives directly from God. God's chief goal in granting the pope this authority was to ensure the unity of the church. Huguccio spelled out every aspect of this position in his *Summa*. The pope could summon to his court every case within the church's ecclesiastical jurisdiction and review every administrative act. The pope alone issued legislation that would affect the church as a whole.[180] Constitutional safeguards and limitations against the papal abuse of these powers remained rather undeveloped. Papal initiative was to be controlled neither by a conciliar body nor by the college of cardinals. Huguccio restricted their influence to advisory functions in papal government, following the general maxim that 'the pope is to be judged by no one'. With the acumen of a systematic thinker, he also felt the need to reconcile this principle of papal immunity from judgment with the famous case of Pope Anastasius (D.40 c.6), who had fallen into heresy and was condemned for it. The *Summa* argued that Anastasius had acted as his own accuser when he openly refused to abandon his heretical views. Huguccio's extensive discussion demonstrates that he was seriously concerned about possible papal transgressions against the 'articles of faith' and the 'general status of the church'. He concluded that the pope could render himself liable not only as a persistent heretic, but also as a notorious criminal.[181]

From a modern viewpoint, the treatment of Anastasius may appear to be academic, since it failed to confront the absolutist implications of decretist ecclesiology. In reality, popes would rarely go so far as to insist publicly on unorthodox teachings, or commit crimes 'on the altar', as the *Summa* once put it.[182] Huguccio and the other jurists never elaborated a

---

tio 14 (1958) 121–189, at 139 n. 8. In general see P. Landau, '*Aequitas* in the 'Corpus iuris canonici', *Syracuse Journal of International Law and Commerce* (1994) 95–104.

180. M. Ríos Fernández, 'El primado del romano pontifice en el pensamiento de Huguccio de Pisa decretista', *Compostellanum* 6 (1961) 47–97; 7 (1962) 97–149; 8 (1963) 65–99; 11 (1966) 29–67; K. Pennington, *Pope and Bishops: The Theory of Papal Monarchy in the Twelfth and Thirteenth Centuries* (Philadelphia 1984) 81–110.

181. B. Tierney, *Foundations of the Conciliar Theory: The Contribution of the Medieval Canonists from Gratian to the Great Schism* (Cambridge 1955; reprinted Leiden, New York, and Cologne 1998) 58–63, 248–250; Ríos Fernández, 'El primado' 7.135–144, 11.61–67.

182. Cf. *Summa*, D.40 c.6 s.v. *a fide devius*: 'Ego autem credo quod idem sit de quolibet crimine notorio quod papa possit accusari et condempnari si admonitus non vult cessare. Quid enim? Ecce, publice furatur, publice fornicatur, publice committit simoniam, publice habet concubinam, publice eam cognoscit in ecclesia, iuxta vel super altare.... Numquid sic scandalizare ecclesiam non est quasi heresim committere?' (ed. Tierney, *Foundations* 249). The passage illustrates that Huguccio was never afraid to use strong language in order to make his point.

system of formal checks and balances, or a set of constitutional parameters. Still, they had at their disposal moral and theological principles, which sufficiently reassured them of the essential stability of the canonical order. After all, the endurance of the ecclesiastical structure had been guaranteed by God himself, who had promised that the Church of Peter 'shall not fail'. Although heretical acts and laws might occasionally upset the community of the faithful, injustice would not prevail in the end.[183] Relying on this 'serene assurance', Huguccio also put strong emphasis on the intrinsic quality of normative provisions. To command obedience, he argued, authoritative pronouncements had to conform to justice and reason. In dubious cases, the focus must be on substantive content rather than its formal source. This is particularly highlighted in Huguccio's treatment of possible conflicts between conciliar and papal legislation:[184]

> But behold! A council has been summoned from all over Christendom. A doubt emerges. One opinion is proposed by the pope, another one by everybody else. Whose is to be preferred? The argument here says, the pope's. I distinguish and say: If either one contains an iniquity, it is overruled; if none seems to contain any iniquity and there is doubt as to which states the truth, both are equal and to be upheld. . . . However, if the pope demands that his opinion be held and not that of the council, one ought to obey him.

It is clear from these words that the authority of the papacy did not provide the highest standard of legitimacy for canonical rules. Although the supreme head of the church had the formal right to overrule conciliar decisions, it was left to the informal criterion of equity to pass the ultimate judgment on any type of legislation. There is no doubt about Huguccio's resolve to enforce this principle. The *Summa* often surprises modern students with its sharp and rather irreverent criticism of papal decretals.[185]

---

183. Lc 22.32, 'I have prayed for you, Peter, that your faith shall not fail', is quoted by Gratian at D.21 a.c.1; Huguccio's interpretation has been discussed by B. Tierney, *The Origins of Papal Infallibility 1150–1350* (Leiden and London 1972; reprint 1988) 50–51. The medieval canonistic understanding of the passage is aptly summarized in his '"Only the Truth has Authority": The Problem of "Reception" in the Decretists and in Johannes de Turrecremata', in: *Law, Church, and Society. Essays in Honor of Stephan Kuttner*, ed. K. Pennington and R. Somerville (Philadelphia 1977) 69–96, at 89 (reprinted in: Tierney, *Church Law, and Constitutional Thought in the Middle Ages* [London 1979]): '[The canonists] were expressing a serene assurance that in actual fact, in the ongoing life of the church, the truth always would come to be accepted by the church as a whole (whatever its immediate source) and would eventually be proclaimed through the church's institutions'.

184. *Summa*, C.9 q.3 c.17 s.v. *semper valebit*; the Latin text has been printed by Ríos Fernández, 'El primado' 11.48 n. 14; see also Tierney, 'Only the Truth' 75–76; Pennington, *Pope and Bishops* 21–22.

185. Noted since Schulte, QL 1.164–65 n. 25–26. Particularly striking is *Summa*, C.27 q.2 p.c.45 § 3 s.v. *Sed concedatur*. It refers to JL 15176, a letter by Pope Lucius III, as 'pessima opinio'.

As if that were not enough, Huguccio's text quoted above continues by posing yet another obstacle to the unrestricted exercise of papal power in the church:

> I consider this to be true if articles of faith are involved, or something not depending on the will of others. But if it is something that does depend on it, it has no validity without their willing consent, no matter whether the council agrees or not. So if, for example, the pope wanted to impose continence on exorcists and acolytes, he could not. If he passed such a law, it would be invalid without their consent, as is argued in D.31 c.1.

Contrary to the invocations of 'equity' and 'truth', which draw upon categories other than tangible norms, this passage introduced a directly enforceable limit on papal action. It states in uncompromising language that the pope, with or without the council, cannot legislate against the 'will of others', in what adds another key element to Huguccio's ecclesiological vision. Speaking of the 'will', Huguccio, of course, did not intend to promote individualism without limitations. As the reference to Gratian's Distinction 31 shows, he confined the concept to the specific case of clergy in the lower orders, who cannot be forced by the pope to take a vow of chastity.[186]

Twelfth-century canonists denied that the pope had the right to modify certain precepts of divine and natural law. Although they did not specify them in great detail, the vows attached to the clerical orders or the monastic habit were undoubtedly included.[187] Still, Huguccio's insistence on the binding effects of individual promises went much farther than usual. Medieval and modern students have noted the 'rigor' of his reasoning. It was the expression of his attempt to integrate an extremely voluntaristic understanding of guilt into canon law doctrine. None of the other jurists developed a concept of liability that came as close to being applicable indiscriminately in both the penitential forum and the judicial courts of the church.

It is important to note, in conclusion, that Huguccio's teachings reflect the full range of doctrinal positions taken by twelfth-century canonists. Gratian's *Decretum* had provided them with an array of excerpts from older canonical collections and contained many contradictory statements. Like Huguccio, his predecessors had noted the coexistence of constitution-

---

186. The rubric to Gratian's D.31 c.1 reads: 'Qui castitatem non promisit ab uxore sua separari non cogatur'.

187. The dispensability of natural law in decretist literature has been treated by R. Weigand, *Die Naturrechtslehre der Legisten und Dekretisten von Irnerius bis Accursius und von Gratian bis Johannes Teutonicus* (Munich 1967).

al and absolutist elements in the traditional ecclesiastical structure, of intention and circumstance in the evaluation of guilt and sin, and of penitential and disciplinary objectives in the various forms of punishment. To resolve these tensions, they also had to formulate their dogmatic preferences. Research has suggested, for example, that Sicardus of Cremona (fl. 1181) and, particularly, Rufinus (fl. 1164) anticipated Huguccio's voluntaristic analysis of guilt, whereas Stephen of Tournai put emphasis on procedural questions and distinguished sharply between sin and guilt.[188] Canonists after Huguccio continued to develop their own conceptual hierarchies and gradually moved away from his rigid voluntarism. They soon came to admit that circumstance could modify intention in the form of the Roman concept of *metus* (fear), allowed numerous dispensations from vows and contracts, left the enforcement of simple promises to the discretion of the damaged party, and undermined the validity of marriage by pure consent. In this way, they hoped to adjust Huguccio's fundamentalist approach to a more realistic appreciation of changing situations. By abandoning the austere simplicity of his extreme voluntarism, however, they also lost sight of Huguccio's accomplishment as a systematic thinker. Before long, it became clear that his *Summa* represented only 'a moment' of synthesis.

III. MINOR LITERARY GENRES BEFORE 1190

Law and other fields of study in the twelfth and thirteenth centuries developed a methodology to harmonize discordant doctrines. At Bologna the jurists used the 'Solutio contrariorum' as a principle to reconcile conflicting texts, and they created several different literary genres from it. The first literary texts of canon law to incorporate 'Solutio contrariorum' were series of citations from canon law and Roman law that first make their appearance in the margins of manuscripts of legal texts.[189] From these humble beginnings 'distinctiones', 'notablilia', 'brocardica', also called 'genera-

---

188. H. Kalb, *Studien zur Summa Stephans von Tournai* (Innsbruck 1983) 31–64; and his 'Bemerkungen zum Verhältnis von Theologie und Kanonistik am Beispiel Rufins und Stephans von Tournai', ZRG Kan. Abt. 72 (1986) 338–348; and Ronald Knox, 'The Problem of Academic Language in Rufinus and Stephan', *Proceedings Berkeley* 109–123, have argued that Rufinus and Stephan were diametrically opposed in their ecclesiological approaches.

Kenneth Pennington is the author of this section and the final section of this chapter.

189. See the remarks of Stephan Kuttner, 'Revival of Jurisprudence', *Renaissance and Renewal in the Twelfth Century*, ed. R.L. Benson and G. Constable (Cambridge, Mass. 1982) 313–314. See now Christoph H.F. Meyer, *Die Distinktionstechnik in der Kanonistik des 12. Jahrhunderts: Ein Beitrag zur Wissenschaftsgeschichte des Hochmittelalters* (Mediaevalia Lovaniensia, Series 1, Studia 29; Leuven 2000).

lia', and 'quaestiones' evolved. One must, however, remember that these literary forms were not rigid categories. The jurists sometimes freely incorporated elements of one type into another.

1. Distinctiones

Stephan Kuttner first emphasized the importance of *distinctiones* for canonical jurisprudence.[190] Kuttner defined the genre as 'the analysis of a term through the citation of contrary texts. The subject of the analysis can be facts, ideas and concepts from the sources, rules of law, and legal relationships'.[191] Peter Weimar has noted that '"to distinguish" is an elementary method of logic' that was fundmental to scholastic approaches to knowledge in the schools.[192] The legists first developed *distinctiones*, and the canonists adopted them. The purpose of the early canonical *distinctiones* was to present solutions to the contrarieties of the texts, and in this way canonical *distinctiones* were different from the Roman law *distinctiones*, which did not emphasize the solution of a particular problem. The early legists distinguished between *distinctiones* and *solutiones contrariorum*. In canon law, as Kuttner has observed, the very emphasis that Gratian's followers gave to the concept of *concordia* influenced the development of the genre. The canonists systematized their *distinctiones* very often by following the organization of the *Decretum*.

In spite of Kuttner's first attempt to categorize the *distinctiones* more than forty years ago, little work has been done on them. It is difficult to determine their time of composition and place of origin. Most are written by jurists who have remained anonymous. With few exceptions, the remaining manuscripts speak for limited use and influence. The canonists did employ the methodology, but rather than writing self-standing works they incorporated *distinctiones* into their glosses and commentaries. The French *Summa 'Inperatorie maiestati'* is an early example of mixing the genre of the *summa* and *distinctiones*.[193]

---

190. Kuttner, *Repertorium* 208–227. The first extended study of the genre was by Emil Seckel, 'Distinctiones Glossatorum', *Festschrift der Berliner Juristischen Fakultät für Ferdinand von Martitz* (Berlin 1911) 277–436.

191. Kuttner, *Repertorium* 209: '"Distinctio" ist die Zerlegung eines Oberbegriffs durch Heranziehung entgegengesetzter Sondermerkmale. Gegenstand der Zerlegung können Tatbestände, quellenmässige Begriffe und Ausdrücke, Rechtsregeln und Rechtsbeziehungen sein'.

192. 'Die legistische Literatur als gelehrte Literatur', Coing, *Handbuch* 142–143.

193. Kuttner, *Repertorium* 179–180. Another example of this 'mixed genre' has been recently published, *Distinctiones 'Si mulier eadem hora' seu Monacenses*, ed. A.J. de Groot (Rechtshistorische reeks van het Gerard Noodt Instituut, 36; Nijmegen 1996), whose work has

The most notable exception to the generalization that *distinctiones* were not an important literary genre is the work of Richardus Anglicus (Richard de Mores).[194] His work is preserved in 17 complete or fragmentary manuscripts and are this English canonist's most significant work. They were written ca. 1196–1198. Giulio Silano, who edited his *distinctiones*, has noted that Richardus wished to offer to his students an instrument with which they could study Gratian's *Decretum*. The work was organized after Gratian's plan and reflected Richardus's Parisian theological background.[195] Richardus organized his work as an introduction to Gratian and as a guide to juridical concepts. On D.2 c.4, in which Gratian excerpted a passage from Isidore of Seville defining constitutions and edicts as those acts that a king or emperor 'constituit uel edidit', he explained:[196]

> D.ii. Constitutio uel edictum est: principis, unde 'exiit edictum a Cesare Augusto'. Pretoris, ut ff. de edicto edil. cur. per totum titulum. Iudicis, xxiv. q.iii. De illicita.

Richardus' aphoristic formulation noted that a constitution or edict orginated in a command of the prince but could be promulgated by lesser magistrates such as the praetor, or a judge. This exact and precise wording is typical of this genre. If we may judge by the number of manuscripts, Richardus' work had a significant popularity in the early thirteenth century but not many imitators.

2. Notabilia

Kuttner defined *notabilia* or *argumenta* as 'all observations that, in a wider sense, direct the reader's attention to a particular place in a legal text ... In a narrower sense, all the comments of the jurists that begin with phrases as "Nota quod" or "Notandum", "Arg. quod", "Hinc collige", are *notablilia*'.[197] Most of the collections are anonymous, often very short, but Ricardus Anglicus claimed in the prologue to his *distinctiones* that he had written a collection of *argumenta* to the *Decretum*.[198] Paulus Hunga-

---

now been replaced by *Distinctiones 'Si mulier eadem hora' seu Monacenses*, ed. Rosalba Sorice (MIC, Series A, Corpus Glossatorum, 4, Città del Vaticano 2002).

194. The best biography of Richardus is Stephan Kuttner, 'Ricardus Anglicus (Ricardus de Mores ou de Morins)', DDC 7 (1965 [1960]) 676–681.

195. Silano, 'The "Distinctiones Decretorum" of Richardus Anglicus' (Ph.D. Dissertation, University of Toronto, 1981).

196. Ibid. 93.

197. Kuttner, *Repertorium* 232–233 and 'Réflexions sur les Brocards des Glossateurs', *Mélanges Joseph de Ghellinck, S.J.* (Gembloux 1951) 2.770–771 (reprinted in *Gratian and the Schools of Law*).

198. Kuttner, 'Anglo-Norman Canonists' 337: "singula argumenta per ordinem decre-

rus was the author of two influential collections of *notabilia* on *Compilationes secunda et tertia*. If one may judge from the present geographical locations of the manuscript of these works, northern jurists, judges, and clergy found them more useful than southerners.[199] The canonists wrote *notabilia* on the *Decretum* and on the *Decretals*, often in connection with *casus* of a work. Later manuscripts of the Decretals of Gregory IX and subsequent printed editions often added *notabilia* from many sources.[200]

3. Brocarda or Generalia

The medieval jurists called another early literary genre 'brocardica', 'brocarda', or 'burchardica'.[201] The origins and precise meaning of the term have vexed scholars. The most commonly accepted explanation of the term is that it derives from the Latin word, 'broccus', 'sharp teeth'. The teeth represent the arguments for and against a particular legal rule or principle.[202] No one still accepts the older guesses that the term meant 'pro et contra' or was derived from Burchard of Worms' name. Defining 'brocarda' has been difficult because the texts mix what seem to be (at least to the modern scholars) several different types of writing. In the twelfth century Johannes Bassianus defined the genre as 'Argumenta ad causas de facto annotamus, que loci generales uel generalia uel uulgariter brocarda appellantur'.[203] As Johannes pointed out, the brocarda are 'arguments' for specific cases. They were called 'generalia', but commonly 'brocarda'. The jurists constructed lists of brocarda by beginning with a legal concept or rule and then listing allegations that either supported or contradicted the generalization. The lists of allegations are sometimes constructed much like notabilia, with no contrary arguments, or they have 'pro' and 'contra' allegations. At times, contradictory rules follow one another. The civilians began writing brocarda, and the canonists quickly followed their lead.[204]

---

torum'. A fragment of the work may be contained in Zwettl, Stiftsbibl. 162, but Kuttner and Fransen have expressed doubts that this is the work to which Richardus referred; cf. Kuttner, *Gratian and the Schools of Law*, Retractationes, p. 36.

199. A convenient list may be found at http://faculty.cua.edu/pennington//1140i-p.htm under "Notabilia."

200. Stephan Kuttner, 'Notes on the Glossa ordinaria of Bernard of Parma', BMCL 11 (1981) 88–89.

201. See Peter Weimar, 'Argumenta brocardica', SG 14 (1967) 89–123 and 'Brocarda, Brocardica', LMA 2 (1982) 707–708; Kuttner, 'Réflexions sur les brocards des glossateurs'.

202. Weimar, 'Argumenta' 106–109.

203. Quoted by Weimar, 'Argumenta' 95.

204. For a survey of the literature on the brocarda, see Matthias Schwaibold, *Brocardica 'Dolum per subsequentia purgari': Eine englische Sammlung von Argumenten römischen Rechts aus dem 12. Jahrhundert* (Ius commune, Sonderhefte, Texte und Monographien 25; Frankfurt am Main 1985) 96–123.

4. Quaestiones

The collections of *quaestiones* constitute the most fertile, important, and difficult minor genre of canon and Roman law scholarship.[205] As André Gouron has put it: 'The *quaestiones disputatae* appear to us to be one of the most remarkable genres created by medieval jurisprudence'.[206] Although a minor genre in the twelfth century, *quaestiones* and their practical equivalents, *consilia*, emerged as the most important literary genres of the later Middle Ages.

To a certain extent, the *quaestiones* are annotated, expanded brocarda and are always organized according to a 'pro et contra' schema. They treat legal problems that have no obvious solution in the sources or that resolve contradictions of the texts themselves. Twelfth-century theologians wrote *quaestiones de sacra pagina* in which they solved problems pertaining to the interpretation of the Bible, and the civilians wrote *quaestiones legitimae* dealt with the interpretation of the *leges*. Most importantly, Gratian constructed the original core of his *Decretum* as a long series of 'cases' for which he formulated series of questions.

André Gouron has pointed to a striking parallel between Roman law and canonical *quaestiones*.[207] The literary genre was invented at Bologna by the Roman lawyers. Bulgarus was particularly important for its development. The canonists followed in their footsteps, and the two earliest canonical collections of *quaestiones* produced in Bologna may be reflected in the *Quaestiones Stuttgardienses* and *Barchinonenses breves*.[208] From ca. 1160 to 1190, however, the diffusion of the *quaestiones* seems to have taken place north of the Alps. As Gouron observes, the *quaestio* was the Bolognese product of export par excellence.

The earliest *quaestiones* are difficult to date and place. Place names and

---

205. The most up-to-date survey of the Roman and canonical 'quaestiones', with full bibliography, is Gérard Fransen, 'Les questions disputées dans les facultés de Droit', *Les questions disputées et les questions quodlibétiques dan les facultés de Théologie, de Droit et de Médecine*, ed. B. Bazàn et al. (Typologie des sources du Moyen Âge occidental 44–45; Turnhout 1985) 223–277. Fransen spent his life exploring the *quaestiones*. Articles that he published after 1985 are: 'Questiones Barcinonenses breues', BMCL 15 (1985) 31–49; 'Questiones Aschaffenburgenses', BMCL 16 (1986) 71–86; 'Questionum fragmentum Sedunense', BMCL 17 (1987) 65–75; 'Questiones Vindobonenses', *Studia in honorem eminentissimi cardinalis Alphonsi M. Stickler*, ed. Rosalio Iosepho card. Castillo Lara (Studia et textus historiae iuris canonici, 7; Roma 1992) 115–136. See also André Gouron's important article in the same volume: 'La diffusion des premiers recueils de questions disputées: Des civilistes aux canonistes' 157–169.
206. 'La diffusion' 157.
207. 'La diffusion des premiers recueils de questions disputées' 167.
208. See Fransen's articles in note 205 above.

the names of canonists can suggest the general place of origin, and the inclusion or exclusion of decretals and their dates can help to pinpoint their time of composition.[209] Northern redactors shaped and edited collections of *quaestiones* that often had Bolognese models as their core material. The same ur-*quaestio* may be redacted several different times and attributed to several different jurists. For example, Fransen and Gouron have discovered anomalies in passages of the collections of Northern *quaestiones* that clearly betray the cismontane origins of the original texts.[210] Fransen has pointed out a striking example in which a *quaestio* containing references to Milan, Parma, and Reggio and preserved in a Stuttgart manuscript was edited by an anonymous jurist whose text we have in a Bamberg manuscript. The Northern jurist referred to Cologne, Metz, and Toul, cities with which he was familiar, instead of the Italian cities.[211]

Historians have traditionally named collections of *quaestiones* after the library in which the manuscript is housed, but, as should now be clear, this practice is deceiving. Often a manuscript's origins and contents were far removed from the geographical area where it currently resides. As we explore the contents of these collections, we should assign more descriptive and accurate names to them.

In the second half of the twelfth century, the canonists began to write *quaestiones decretales*, that is, *quaestiones* interpreting the *decreta* of canon law. The origin of this genre lies in the work of the canonists when they commented on their texts (during their 'lectio'). They would often precede their comments on a particular problem with the words 'queritur', 'dubitatur', or 'solet queri'. They would then solve the formulated question. In general the *quaestiones decretales* were concerned with doctrinal interpretation, 'enodatio', and the solution of contrarieties.

The *quaestiones decretales* and *quaestiones legitimae* are a subspecies of the *quaestiones disputatae*.[212] The masters in the schools held disputations outside their regularly scheduled lectures, quite often on Friday or Sunday (*quaestiones veneriales et dominicales*). A concrete case would be posed,

---

209. An example of the difficulties can be seen in the canonistic 'quaestiones' in the Collectio Gratianopolitana. Gouron identifies Grenoble, Bibl. mun. 391 as reflecting the opinions of French jurists Gui Francesc and a certain Johannes who was a student of Placentinus. Annalisa Belloni has attributed the collection to Bazianus and Johannes Bassianus, *Le questioni civilistiche del secolo XII* 15–20.

210. 'La diffusion des premiers recueils de questions disputées' 163 and n. 19.

211. Fransen, 'Questions disputées' 237.

212. Fransen calls them 'genres voisins', and he discusses the difficulty of constructing a topology that is too rigid; see 'Questions disputées' 237–239. The best introduction to the genre and its importance is now Manlio Bellomo, *I fatti e il diritto tra le certezze e i dubbi dei giuristi medievali (secoli XIII–XIV)* (I libri di Erice, 27; Roma 2000).

and the master would solve it. By the beginning of the thirteenth century some of these questions had become standard fare in the schools, taken up by different masters year after year, and the canonists would refer to these questions of law under the generic title *quaestiones dominicales*. Another title given to questions that had become standard was *quaestiones quaternales*, that is, sets of *quaestiones* that the stationiers sold as a 'quaternio', a quire of parchment consisting of four double pages.[213] The *quaestiones disputatae* dealt with a particular situation and set of facts, either fictive or real, and differed from the *quaestione decretales* that presented 'cases' to be discussed. But, as Stephan Kuttner has noted, 'to define the genus of *quaestiones decretales* by more specific characteristics would do violence to the elasticity of the literary type in its actual use . . . cases are found in the *quaestiones decretales*, so also the *quaestiones disputatae* often include theoretical problems'.[214] Somewhat surprisingly the collections of *quaestiones* are not organized according to topics. The jurists seem to have repressed their passion for organization when they put their *quaestiones* together and circulated them. Some collections may contain *quaestiones* on only one theme, like marriage, but even this is relatively rare.[215]

Exceptions to this generalization are the *quaestiones* contained in *summae*. The canonists incorporated the *quaestio* into their *summae* and created a hybrid literary form, the *summa quaestionum*. The French canonist Sicardus of Cremona may have been the first to divide his *Summa Decretorum* into *quaestiones principales* and *incidentes*. Sicardus may very well have been influenced by French theological writings that included *quaestiones*. Evrard of Ypres, who was a monk at Clairvaux, was one of the first to write a *Summula decretalium quaestionum*, and the transmontane canonists produced a number of similar *summae*, the most important being the *Summa decretalium questionum* of Magister Honorius.[216] The Bolognese also adopted this literary form. In the early thirteenth century, Richardus Anglicus and Damasus wrote popular *summae quaestionum*.[217]

---

213. A standard of book production since late antique times, see Bernhard Bischoff, *Paläographie des römischen Altertums und des abendländischen Mittelalters* (Grundlagen der Germanistik, 24; Berlin 1979) 34–35, translated into English by Dáibhí Ó Cróinín and David Ganz as *Latin Paleography: Antiquity and the Middle Ages* (Cambridge 1990).

214. Together with Eleanor Rathbone, 'Anglo-Norman Canonists of the Twelfth Century', *Traditio* 7 (1949–1951) 313, reprinted in Kuttner's *Gratian and the Schools of Law*.

215. Fransen, 'Questions disputées' 238–239.

216. See Kuttner and Rathbone, 'Anglo-Norman Canonists' 315–316 and Retractationes in *Gratian and the Schools of Law*. Benno Grimm, *Die Ehelehre des Magister Honorius: Ein Beitrag zur Ehelehre der anglo-normannischen Schule* (SG 24; Roma 1989). Grimm prints excerpts from the *Summa* 231–387. For further information see Rudolf Weigand's chapter (chapter 6, below) on the transmontane canonists.

217. *Traditio* 11 (1955) 448 and 12 (1956) 566 for lists of manuscripts.

Gérard Fransen (†1995) worked on the collections of *quaestiones* in the manuscripts for more than twenty-five years and published the preliminary results of his studies in a series of articles. The goal of his research was to classify the *quaestiones* by type and index them according to subject matter and themes—to create a *Corpus quaestionum*. Following the schema first proposed by Kuttner, one could classify *quaestiones* chronologically according to the following criteria: (I) *Quaestiones* that do not cite decretals or only rarely cite them. (II) *Quaestiones* that were written at the time of the primitive decretal collections and *Compilatio prima*. (III) *Quaestiones* of the French and English Schools. (IV) Collections of *quaestiones* composed in the early thirteenth century.[218] Early *quaestiones* were often not written by the master himself but by students who recorded or 'reported' the proceedings, hence the term *quaestiones reportatae*. This type of reporting gradually gave way to the master's own formulation of the form of the *quaestio* as the genre became more sophisticated. Some of the early *quaestiones* do not have solutions, some do not set out the facts of the case, and some present only one side of the argument. Again, as the genre evolved, the jurists systematically conformed to the same pattern: Case, pro and contra arguments, solution. Fransen classified early *quaestiones* according to their form and content: (I) those written by a *reportator* and corrected (*quaestiones reportatae*); (II) those 'in search of a theme', that is, those in which the scribe or redactor has left out the case and has given only the pro and contra allegations;[219] (III) a more sophisticated category of *quaestiones* containing the case, pro and contra allegations for each subdivision of the argument, a discussion of the arguments, and a solution with an explanation, rather than a simple assertion of the pro or the contra.[220] This last became the standard format of the *quaestio*.[221]

The disputations became a regular academic exercise. In the second half of the twelfth century the jurists gradually began to treat problems regularly outside their ordinary lectures. And the recitation of academic problems became less pertinent and interesting. Roffredus Beneventanus wrote ca. 1215:[222]

---

218. Kuttner, *Repertorium* 244–245. See also Kuttner, 'Bernardus Compostellanus' 320–327 (with Retractationes) and 'Anglo-Norman canonists' 311–316.

219. 'Les "questiones" des canonistes: Essai de dépouillement et de classement (I)', *Traditio* 12 (1956) 566–569.

220. 'Les "questiones" des canonistes (II)', *Traditio* 13 (1957) 481.

221. Fransen, 'Questions disputées' 232–234.

222. *Quaestiones* (Rome 1511), quoted by Fransen, 'Questiones disputées' 264: 'Cum essem Aretii . . . et cogitarem quid utile et fructuosum possem sociis de legum scientia demonstrare, considerans quod in scolis dominorum Bononiensium sabbatine questiones

> When I was in Arezzo... I thought that it would be useful and fruitful to show my companions something about the scientific knowledge of law. I reflected that the *Quaestiones sabbatinae* of Pilius are discussed in the lecture halls of the Bolognese masters, but I thought it more useful to present cases of fact than to recite the writings of Pilius.

The *quaestiones* of Pilius were well-established school texts,[223] and Roffredus thought their recitation a sterile exercise. Instead he offered 'quaestiones de facto emergentes', a relatively new term that meant a case, either real or fictive, to which the jurist would pose a question of law.[224] *Quaestiones* became 'de facto emergentes' as a matter of course during the thirteenth century. By making this change the jurists seem to have exchanged academic nitpicking for practical challenges.

Like the *distinctiones*, the majority of twelfth- and early thirteenth-century *quaestiones* are anonymous. Only in the thirteenth century do *quaestiones* regularly contain a rubric or colophon identifying the author. The complicated textual transmissions of *quaestiones* can be illustrated by examining the manuscript tradition of Johannes Teutonicus' *Quaestiones*.[225] One manuscript, Klosterneuburg, Stiftsbibl. 656, contains 36 *quaestiones*. A rubric identifies Johannes as the author of these *Quaestiones disputatae*.[226] Since the collection survives in only one manuscript, we cannot be sure whether the Klosterneuburg manuscript reflects Johannes' intention to redact his *quaestiones* or an editor's work. In any case, this single manuscript indicates that Johannes' *quaestiones* did not enjoy the same popularity as Damasus' collection, which survives in a score of manuscripts.

Johannes wrote the *quaestiones* at Bologna over an extended period of time. Nine of the *quaestiones* refer only to the *Decretum* and *Compilatio prima*, indicating that they were finished before 1210.[227] He cited *Compilationes secunda* and *tertia* in the remaining questions and referred to Fourth Lateran canons in two.[228] The *quaestiones* have the flavor of school exercises, and this impression is confirmed by Johannes' reference to the subject of one of them as a *quaestio dominicalis* in his commentary to *Compilatio tertia*:[229]

---

domini Pylei tractarentur, et quia erat utilius questiones de facto emergentes tractare in sabbatis quam illas scriptas domini Pylei recitare...'.

223. *Quaestiones aureae* (Rome 1560; reprinted Turin 1967).
224. Fransen, 'Questions disputées' 241.
225. Gérard Fransen, 'A propos des Questions de Jean le Teutonique', BMCL 13 (1983) 39–47.
226. Klosterneuburg, Stiftsbibl. 656, fol. 35r: 'Incipiunt questiones disputate et determinate per magistrum Johannem Theutonicum'.
227. *Quaestiones* 17, 18, 19, 21, 22, 23, 25, 27, 30.
228. *Quaestiones* 4, 35.
229. Johannes Teutonicus, 3 Comp. 1.6.9 v. *in minori*, ed. Pennington, 63–64: 'Arg. ad

This is an argument of a *quaestio dominicalis* that if a judge from whom a litigant appeals is appointed the appellate judge to whom one has appealed, nevertheless the judge may hear the appeal.

The question was, in other words, a standard topic that a jurist might choose to dispute as a school exercise. *Quaestio* 22 of the Klosterneuburg collection, written long before his commentary on *Compilatio tertia*, treated the same subject. Johannes had very likely discussed the question as a class disputation in Bologna and then published it, since it has the character of one that he wrote rather than that of a 'reportatio'. In the intervening years between the writing of the question and his commentary on *Compilatio tertia* (ca. 1218), his opinion had not changed. His solution in each was exactly the same.[230]

Johannes's *quaestiones* also circulated independently. Gérard Fransen has discovered eight of them in a Paris and four more in a Graz manuscript.[231] Question 22, dealing with the problem of an appellate judge and mentioned above, is found in the Paris manuscript. The same subject is treated in collections of questions in Fulda and Zwettl.[232] But the texts of Johannes' *quaestiones* have intriguing differences. Thus, the conclusion of question 34 in the Klosterneuburg collection is the opposite of the solution proposed in the Parisian text.[233] Which opinion may we attribute to Johannes? On the present manuscript evidence, it is impossible to determine whether Johannes changed his mind or whether a redactor changed his opinion for him.

The *quaestiones* were utilitarian texts intended to aid students' understanding of legal problems. They treated commonly asked questions and introduced students to the methodology of the jurists. Since the same themes seem to have been repeated in the classroom by different jurists,

---

questionem domincalem quod si iudex a quo appellatur efficitur eiusdem iurisdictionis, cuius est iudex ad quem est appelatum, quod nichilominus possit cognosncere de causa'. In a gloss to 3 Comp. 1.6.1 v. *in minori*, ed. Pennington, 44, Johannes qualified his remarks: 'Ad questionem quod si iudex a quo appellatur eligitur ad dignitatem illius ad quem appellatur, quod non possit recusari tamquam suspectus, infra eodem, Querelam (c.6), tamen tenetur alii delegare'.

230. Question 22, Klosterneuburg, Stiftsbibl. 656, fol. 40r: 'Cognita est causa coram episcopo. Appellatum est ab eo ad archiepiscopum. Interim moritur archiepiscopus; Ille episcopus substituitur a quo fuit appellatum. Queritur utrum de causa illa possit cognoscere? . . . Solutio. Dicimus quod delegare debet hanc causam, ut ff. de iurisdic. om. iud. l. Pretor, nec credo habere locum distinctionem que inuenitur extra. de offic. et pot. iud. del. Quoniam abbas'.

231. Paris, B.N. nouv. acq. lat. 2443, fol. 134r–135v (qq. 14, 15, 19, 22, 25, 26, 34, 35, 36, 26) and Graz, Universitätbibl. 138, fol. 268v (qq. 13, 32, 33, 35). Fransen, 'Questions de Jean le Teutonique' 43–46.

232. Ibid. 45.   233. Ibid. 44.

they must not have had the same 'authorial voice' or authority in the courts that other forms of literature had. To some extent, the repetition of themes and standard questions must account for Roffredus' irritation with the disputations of questions as school exercises. He wanted a livlier genre that reflected the practice of the courts. Consilia would soon answer his need and concerns.

5. Consilia

The lack of any systematic study of early canonistic consilia remains a lamentable lacuna of historical scholarship. Fransen defines *consilia* as 'the advice given by jurists for an actual case that has already begun or for which justice should be rendered'.[234] They are written for the litigants or for the judge(s). It can be very difficult, if not impossible, to separate a *consilium* treating a concrete case from a theoretical *quaestio*. And it is almost certain that *quaestiones* sometimes took their *casus* from *consilia*, substituting abstract names and places for the actual, and thereby adapting them to the practices of the schools.[235]

Very early on, the canonists and the civilians were called upon to give authoritative answers to legal problems. The well-known story of the encounter between Frederick Barbarossa and his jurists, Martinus and Bulgarus, is an example of the relationship between those who were learned in law and those who were not. Frederick was riding on horseback with Bulgarus and Martinus. He asked them whether, according to law, he was the lord of the world. Bulgarus replied that he was not lord over private property. Martinus said that he was the lord of the world. Frederick got off his horse and presented it to Martinus. He gave nothing to Bulgarus. Bulgarus lamented 'I lost an equine because I upheld equity, which is not equitable'. Frederick wanted reassurance that his imperial power was universal, and he turned to his jurists for support.[236] Although the emperor did not ask them for a written opinion, the same preoccupation with wanting to know their rights led merchants, clerics, women, and judges, who were very often not learned in the law, to ask the jurists (iurisperiti) for help; their needs for counsel produced primitive consilia. All levels of

---

234. 'Questions disputées' 239–240. For general considerations on the genre, see Mario Ascheri, *I consilia dei giuristi medievali: Per un repertorio-incipitario computerizzato* (Siena 1982). For some discussion, if disappointing, of consilia found in the Tuscan archives, see Chris Wickham, *Courts and Conflict in Twelfth-Century Tuscany* (Oxford 2003) 210–211.

235. See Manlio Bellomo, *Aspetti dell'insegnamento giuridico nelle università medievali: Le "quaestiones disputatae"* (Cultura giuridica dell'Eta medievale e moderna, 1; Reggio Calabria 1974) 78–81.

236. The literary tradition of this story is discussed in my *The Prince and the Law* 14–34.

society turned to the jurists and their newly established 'scientia', while the jurists solidified their status with the maxim 'ignorantia iuris non excusatur' (ignorance of the law is no excuse). Knowledge of law became a necessity of life. Before the rebirth of legal learning—in the 'Age without Jurists' to use Manlio Bellomo's memorable phrase—law was not a highly technical discipline, and legal procedure was not based on complicated rules of evidence.[237] All that changed with the introduction of the 'ordo iudiciarius'. By the end of the twelfth century, jurists rendered opinions on a wide variety of issues. The consilium had been born.

The rich archives of Italy contain much unexplored material that could shed much light on the development of the *consilium* as a literary genre. We have, for example, a very early example of a written response to a question of law in a Florentine document. Ranuccinus, a judge in Pistoia, asked two jurists and the archbishop of Pisa for opinions in a dispute between Rainaldus and Nicholas being heard in his court. The archbishop, Lotharius of Cremona, had been a professor of Roman law at Bologna. Sometime after 1209, but before 1211, Ranuccinus asked him for a *consilium* ('petuisset consilium'). He sent him the testimony of the litigants and witnesses ('uisis et auditis confessionibus et allegationibus utriusque partis et dictis testium intellectis'). Lotharius wrote a very short response that barely gives us the facts of the case.[238] He advised Ranuccinus that Nicholas should be condemned to pay thirty denarii every year and should be ordered to restore Rainaldus' detained goods. Two other 'iurisperiti' endorsed Lotharius' *consilium*, Bandinus de Gaetano, a noted Bolognese jurist, and 'Sexmundus, ciuis Lucanus iurisperitus'. Another early example of a consilium comes from Germany. Between 1223 and 1228 Johannes Teutonicus wrote a consilium addressing a certain 'prepositus', who had asked Johannes a question touching the rules of monastic life. Could women who had professed the Benedictine rule in a monastery that had been founded by a mother house permitting the eating of flesh and the use of linens and beds continue to practice the same lax rule at the new foundation?[239] Johannes concluded that although he would not consider them true Benedictines—but Benedictines only insofar as they were accustomed to wear a black habit—he did think that they could continue to observe the mother house's rule.

237. Manlio Bellomo, *L'Europa del diritto comune* (Roma 1989; translated into English as *The Common Legal Past of Europe*, Washington, D.C. 1995), title of chapter two, p. 34.
238. Archivio di Stato di Firenze, Diplomatico di Pistoia 12. . . n. 8, edited in 'Lotharius of Cremona', BMCL 20 (1990) 48.
239. Kenneth Pennington, 'A "Consilium" of Johannes Teutonicus', *Traditio* 26 (1970) 435–440.

Johannes did not cite any legal texts to support his opinion and referred only to another case of another German monastery as an argument for his position. The prepositus for whom he wrote was very likely not learned in law and did not want the issues of the problem confused by learned allegations to canon and Roman law. Although we have only a copy of the original, the last line of the text informs us that Johannes had appended his seal to the consilium in order to give authority and authenticity to it.[240] Attaching a seal to a *consilium* became standard practice of the jurists in later centuries.

Consilia like these mark the beginning of a literary genre that dominates the jurisprudence of the late Middle Ages. We know little about how these documents evolved into a practical and academic literary genre. Much digging must be done in the Italian archives before we can fully understand the development of consilia as a genre of legal literature and their use in the courts of Europe.

6. Casus

The decretists and the decretalists wrote 'casus' for the *Decretum* and the 'collectiones decretalium'. They defined a *casus* of a chapter in the *Decretum* or a decretal in a collection as, in the words of Boncompagno in his *Rhetorica novissima*, 'Casus est specificatio intellectus legis vel decreti seu decretalis vel constitutionis' (A 'casus' is the specific contents of a law, decree, decretal, or constitution).[241] The genre developed relatively late, and the Benencasa wrote the first *casus* for Gratian that Bartholomeus Brixiensis later revised. He finished his *casus* in the 1190s.[242] The *casus* was then employed for decretal collections. Richardus Anglicus (de Mores) composed a *Casus decretalium* for *Compilatio prima*; the *casus* became a standard part of canonistic commentaries.[243]

---

240. Pennington, 'Consilium' 437: 'Et ut nulla super hoc hesitatio habeatur, presentem paginam sigillo proprio consignauj'.

241. Quoted by Kuttner, *Repertorium* 228.

242. See additional manuscripts and corrections to biographical details in Kuttner, 'Bernardus Compostellanus' 284, n. 26.

243. See Robert C. Figuiera, 'Ricardus de Mores and his Casus decretalium: The Birth of a Canonistic Genre', *Proceedings San Diego* 169–187.

IV. SCHOOL OF BOLOGNA AT THE END OF THE TWELFTH CENTURY

Stephan Kuttner wrote that 'about 1190, the intense activity of interpreting the *Decreta* came to a standstill'.[244] The main reason for this cessation, argued Kuttner, was the transformation of canon law from a discipline based on the explication of Gratian's *Decretum* to one based on papal decretals. We shall turn to the decretalists (jurists who commented on the decretals) in subsequent chapters. For now we can only note that the intense preoccupation with the systematic organization of papal decretals into collections and the jurists' use of these collections in the classroom injected much life and vigor into the study of canon law. A few canonists still produced works treating Gratian, but, again as Kuttner has written, they 'were intended for other purposes than that of adding to the exegetic discussion'.[245] Richardus Anglicus wrote his *distinctiones* on the *Decretum* during this period,[246] and Benencasa of Arezzo composed his *Casus decretorum*.[247] Benencasa's summaries of the chapters of the *Decretum* were designed to aid the student's remembrance and to outline the contents of each chapter.

Huguccio's monumental *Summa* on Gratian's *Decretum*, which he finished just before 1192, also seems to have given the jurists at Bologna pause. Although the canonists continued to write apparatus for the *Decretum*—Alanus Anglicus composed the first recension of his apparatus ca. 1192[248]—the intense work of the previous forty years abated. On the eve of Pope Innocent III's pontificate (1198–1216), the canonists had fashioned a sophisticated canonical jurisprudence, Bologna had become a great international center for the study of canon law, and these jurists were well-prepared to face the flood of decisions and legislation that would pour forth from the young, energetic pope's curia. The formative age of canon law had passed. An age in which law would dominate the institutions of Europe had begun.

244. Kuttner, 'Bernardus Compostellanus' 283.
245. Ibid. 284.
246. Manuscripts listed in *Traditio* 11 (1955) 444.
247. Kuttner, *Repertorium* 228–230.
248. Kuttner, 'Retractationes', *Gratian and the Schools of Law* 13, notes on the basis of information from Peter Landau that Alanus' second recension dates ca. 1205. In older scholarly literature, Alanus' apparatus was referred to as *Apparatus 'Ius naturale'*.

6

The Transmontane Decretists

Rudolf Weigand

The title of this chapter has been chosen to underline both the Northern canonists' connections with, and their differences from, Italian decretists. The title also underlines the author's conviction that the Bolognese school set the standard for the academic study of canon law. To take one example, it was the Bolognese-educated decretist Stephen of Tournai who founded or helped to found the French school of decretists. However, for various reasons this simple assertion is laden with ambiguity. Did there exist in France during the first half of the twelfth century a center of studies that continued to transmit and teach a tradition of canon law going back to Ivo of Chartres? There is clear evidence for Reims, where there was a school for the study of Roman law between 1118 and 1136 under Master Alberic.[1] However, there is no certain evidence for the study of canon law. The situation at Paris seems not to have been very different. Bartholomew, later bishop of Exeter, studied and taught there; according

---

1. André Gouron, 'Une école ou des écoles? Sur les canonistes francais (vers 1150–vers 1210)', *Proceedings Berkeley* 235, his 'Les "Quaestiones de juris subtilitatibus": Une œuvre du maître parisien Albéric', *Revue historique* 303 (2001) 343–362, his 'Canon law in Parisian circles before Stephan of Tournai's Summa', *Proceedings San Diego* 497–503, and his 'Le manuscrit de Prague, Metr. Knih. J. 74: Á la recherche du plus ancien décrétiste à l'Ouest des Alpes', ZRG Kan. Abt. 83 (1997) 223–248.

to Gerald of Wales, he was better educated in Roman than in canon law.[2] Although Bartholomew wrote (probably ca. 1160) a penitential manual for confessors that circulated widely, it was not the product of teaching. He used the works of Ivo of Chartres, Burchard of Worms, Peter Lombard, and Gratian, and possibly also, on occasion, Rufinus' *Summa*.[3]

Thanks to the wide-ranging research of André Gouron, our knowledge of the early law school or the teaching of law (or, alternatively, the knowledge of law) in southern France is more precise and stretches further back into the past.[4] He has demonstrated that the *Summa Institutionum Iustiniani* in Pierpont Morgan Library 903 was probably compiled around 1127 in or near Die, near Valence in Southern France.[5] The 'fratres et consorcii, participes et coheredes Romanorum legum Pontius Toranensis' and 'Ugo Avinionensis', to whom the readers of the *Summa* are referred for further information, are named as witnesses to a grant in a charter issued by the bishop of Die. Other evidence indicates that the *Summa* is very early and has relatively archaic contents (for example, a reference to Pepo). Since Valence is referred to in a legal case, this reference supports the conclusion that Southern France was where it was composed. Consequently it would seem that in this early period jurists were teaching Roman law in Provence. It is possible that these teachers had studied Roman law in Bologna under Martinus. This supposition is confirmed by a letter of a monk of St. Victor, Marseilles, written to the newly elected abbot of his monastery between 1124 and 1127, from which we learn that, at the time he was writing, the monk was staying in Italy to study Roman law, as many others from Southern France were also doing.[6]

From Southern France, with its intellectual receptiveness to the study

---

2. Stephan Kuttner and Eleanor Rathbone, 'Anglo-Norman Canonists of the Twelfth Century', *Traditio* 7 (1949–51) 295 refers only to his studying in Paris. Kuttner and Rathbone also stressed his activity as a teacher there. See also A. Morey, *Bartholomew of Exeter, Bishop and Canonist: A Study in the Twelfth Century* (Cambridge 1937) 4–5.

3. Morey, *Bartholomew of Exeter* 175–300, with provisional details of sources, and see Kuttner and Rathbone, 'Anglo-Norman Canonists' 295 n.23. Morey edits the text from only one manuscript, leaving the question of different recensions unresolved, though there are obvious clues in the brief descriptions of the other 17 manuscripts. Morey, *Bartholomew of Exeter* 164–166.

4. André Gouron, 'Die Entstehung der französischen Rechtsschule', ZRG Rom. Abt. 93 (1976) 138–160, reprinted as no. IX in his collected essays, *La science du droit dans le Midi de la France au Moyen Age* (London 1984) with addenda printed as an appendix (page 6).

5. Edited by P. Legendre, *La Summa institutionum 'Iustiniani est in hoc opere'* (Ius commune Sonderheft 2; Frankfurt 1973).

6. Jean Dufour, G. Giordanengo, and A. Gouron, 'L'attrait des "leges:" Notes sur la lettre d'un moine victorin (vers 1124/1127)', *Studia et documenta historiae et iuris* 45 (1979) 504–529; the letter is also printed in PL 151. 639–42. Anders Winroth prefers to date this letter to the 1180s, 'The Teaching of Law in the Twelfth Century', *Law and Learning in the Middle Ages:*

of Roman law, comes the earliest datable literary evidence for the study of the *Decretum* in France: the abbreviation of the *Decretum*, '*Quoniam egestas*' and its glosses, which were first examined by Johann Friedrich von Schulte.[7] The work was most likely composed in 1150, since that year is cited at C.2 q.6 d.p.c.31 in a formula for making an appeal. The date appears in four out of five manuscripts that I have consulted; only the Paris manuscript omits the year, which suggests (as does other evidence) that it is a later copy. As revealed by its links with the *Exceptiones Petri*, the '*Quoniam egestas*' was written in Southern France, which is also the place of origin of the latter work.[8] The *Exceptiones Petri* follow the *Abbreviatio* '*Quoniam egestas*' in the recently discovered Prague manuscript. Furthermore, there are numerous references in the *Abbreviatio* to the *Exceptiones*. These glosses are also to be found in several other manuscripts. According to the preface, the author was hindered by his 'egestas' from making a complete copy of Gratian's *Decretum*, and therefore he made extracts from this great work.[9] In addition to this, the glosses in each of the manuscripts are clearly the work of the author himself, for he writes: 'Contrarietates cum earum determinationibus quas in libro cognovi hic annotavi'. Indeed, a large number of the glosses are *solutiones contrariorum*, often in a somewhat roundabout formulation.

First of all, the compiler of the *Abbreviatio* '*Quoniam egestas*' assembled a table of contents of the *Decretum*, which is to be found in the three oldest of the five manuscripts that I have consulted. He followed, more or less, Paucapalea's division of Gratian's *Decretum* into distinctions, which he must have had available to him shortly before 1150.[10] He listed 100 distinctions, occasionally omitting some (e.g. D.73 Palea, D.97), while giving

---

Proceedings of the Second Carlsberg Academy Conference on Medieval Legal History, 2005, ed. Helle Vogt and Mia Münster-Swendsen (Copenhagen 2006) 41–62 at 48–49.

7. Rudolf Weigand, 'Die Dekretabbreviatio Quoniam egestas und ihre Glossen', *Fides et Ius: Festschrift für Georg May zum 65. Geburtstag*, ed. W. Aymans, A. Egler, and J. Listl (Regensburg 1991) 249–265; Johann Friedrich von Schulte, 'Über drei in Prager Handschriften enthaltene Canones-Sammlungen', SB Vienna Phil.-Classe 42 (1867) 222–229; Kuttner, *Repertorium* 263–264, lists seven manuscripts, of which I have used five. J. Rambaud-Buhot incomprehensibly dates this work as late as the first half of the thirteenth century: 'Les diverses types d'abrégés du Décret de Gratien: De la table au commentaire', *Recueil de travaux offert à M. Clovis Brunel* (Paris 1955) 403–406, 411.

8. André Gouron, 'La science juridique française aux XIe et XIIe siècles: Diffusions du droit de Justinien et influences canoniques jusqu'à Gratien', *Études sur la diffusion des doctrines juridiques médiévales* (London 1987) 42–44, especially 76–77. On the *Exceptiones Petri*, see Peter Weimar, 'Zur Entstehung des sogenannten Tübinger Rechtsbuchs und der Exceptiones legum Romanarum des Petrus', *Studien zur europäischen Rechtsgeschichte*, ed. W. Wilhelm (Frankfurt am Main 1972) 1–24.

9. Printed by Schulte 'Über drei in Prager Handschriften' 222–223.

10. On this and the following see Weigand 'Die Dekretabbreviatio Quoniam egestas'.

multiple entries for others (e.g. D.71, D.75). The actual contents of the *Abbreviatio 'Quoniam egestas'* does not completely agree with his table, since several of the distinctions cited in the latter are lacking completely in the main text (e. g. D.72–74, 76–78, 80 are missing out of D.70–80). However, the summary of Part One of the *Decretum* in the later manuscript Paris, B.N. lat. 15001 agrees with the contents that follow, although it omits the *Causae* and the *De cons*. The author makes excerpts from the *Dicta Gratiani* in the same way that he does from the 'auctoritates', often providing only a single sentence with an abbreviated inscription, and quite often only the 'summarium'. Some texts that he did not think were important he put in the margins (as Vacarius was doing at the same time in England). In later manuscripts these are sometimes inserted into the text. Since he formulated his solutions of contradictory passages as glosses, we may conclude that he judged the whole *Decretum* to be a unitary authority, including the *Dicta Gratiani*. He was also well-acquainted with the Bolognese methodology of commenting on texts.

One may now make a case for including Master Rolandus in the French school, since his identification with the later Pope Alexander III has definitively been disproved.[11] His main work, the commentary on matrimonial law and the *Summa* to C.1–C.26,[12] probably really belongs to the Bolognese school, but his connections with France are obvious in his other writings.[13] We know that he was in Montpellier around 1162. While he was there he witnessed a decision of Alexander III in a marriage case, as is clear from a *quaestio*.[14] Grabmann assumed that his *Sentences*, in which Rolandus incorporated a distinction on betrothal that was similar to that of the theological school of Abelard, were products of Northern France.[15] Furthermore, according to Rolandus, a 'consensus de praesenti' alone was not enough to effectuate a marriage, but only in association with a confirmatory act such as giving a ring, swearing a vow, or consummating the union.[16] This view corresponds with a gloss in the *Abbreviatio* and is also contained in Rolandus' *Quaestiones*.[17]

11. Cf. Rudolf Weigand, 'Magister Rolandus und Papst Alexander III', AKKR 149 (1980) 3–44, with discussion of earlier secondary works.

12. Stephan Kuttner, 'Did Rolandus of Bologna write a "Stroma ex Decretorum corpore carptum"?', BMCL 20 (1990) 69–70.

13. In 1980 I wrote that he showed clear French links: Weigand, 'Magister Rolandus' 43.

14. Ibid. 33.

15. Martin Grabmann, *Die Geschichte der scholastischen Methode* (Freiburg 1911) 2.224–227. He even remarked that Rolandus was Abelard's pupil in more than one respect (p. 227).

16. See the *Fragmentum Cantabrigiense* on C.27 q.2 in principio that is printed in Weigand, *Die bedingte Eheschließung im kanonistischen Recht* (Münchener theologische Studien, 3: Kanonistische Abteilung, 16; Munich 1963) 120, no. 41.

17. Weigand, 'Die Dekretabbreviatio Quoniam egestas' 262, no. 18. On Rolandus' mar-

Rolandus' connection with France is probably the reason why his glosses had very limited transmission, something that I have been able to show from three different families of manuscripts.[18] The manuscript St Florian, Stiftsbibl. III 5 contains traditional French (as well as other) material; much more so do Heiligenkreuz, Stiftsbibl. 44, Paris, B.N. lat. 3895 and 14316. These manuscripts preserve in the same layer of glosses the work of Rolandus and of a French Magister P.;[19] these glosses probably originated in the period after the completion of his commentary on the *Decretum*, because they echo it only rarely. A gloss that I published, no. 97 to C.32 q.1 d.p.c.10, does correspond to the commentary on C.32 q.1 c.3,[20] but only in later recensions. Thaner did not find it in his manuscript. Since this text is, furthermore, not preserved in Bologna, Archiginnasio A 48 nor in Grenoble, Bibl mun. 627, this gloss corresponds only to the fourth recension of his commentary.[21] It is unfortunately impossible to identify the figure hidden behind the fairly common siglum R. in Marburg, Universitätsbibl. 33 and Oxford, Bodleian Library Douce 218.[22] A master in a Northern European school, active between 1150 and 1170, is likely, especially in the case of the Oxford manuscript.

It is not possible to determine who is meant by the siglum p. a contemporary of Rolandus. According to the manuscript transmission it must refer to a French author, who would probably have been active in the 1150s or, at the latest, the 1160s. It may refer to Peter of Blois, who later (ca. 1180) wrote a so-called *Speculum*, but this conjecture is not certain.[23]

The glossator Cardinalis, whose identity was for so long a puzzle, can now be definitely assigned to the Southern French school, since, as André

---

riage thought, see Charles J. Reid, Jr., *Power over the Body, Equality in the Family: Rights and Domestic Relations in Medieval Canon Law* (Emory University Studies in Law and Religion; Grand Rapids, Michigan and Cambridge 2004) 78–79, 110, 144. The *quaestio* is edited by Friedrich Thaner, *Summa magistri Rolandi* (Innsbruck 1874, reprinted Aalen 1962) 278.

18. Rudolf Weigand, 'Glossen des Magister Rolandus zum Dekret Gratians', *Miscellanea Rolando Bandinelli Papa Alessandro III*, ed. F. Liotta and R. Tofanini (Siena 1986) 389–423.

19. On the glosses to both, see Weigand, *Die Glossen zum Dekret Gratians: Studien zu den frühen Glossen und Glossenkompositionen* (SG 25–26; Rome 1991) 570–583.

20. Thaner, *Summa magistri Rolandi* 160, lines 8–10.

21. In any case, Rolandus seems to have written the commentary on the law of marriage first, since Bologna, Archiginnasio A 48, Berlin, Staatsbibl. lat. 462, and Grenoble, Bibl. de la ville 627, each of which contains either the first or the second recension, have only this commentary and not that on C.1–26 immediately before. Is it possible that he wrote the commentary on C.16 first, since this is more detailed than that on the other *causae*? In print it runs from p. 36 to p. 58, while the other *causae* run from p. 13 to p. 36 and from p. 58 to p. 112. London, B.L. Royal MS 11 B ii contains, besides the commentary on marriage law, only the commentary to C.16.

22. Weigand, *Glossen zum Dekret Gratians* 585–586.

23. Cf. my considerations in ibid. 582–583. Or might Peter of Louveciennes be meant?

Gouron was the first to propose, he is to be identified with Raimundus de Arenis (Raymond des Arènes) from Nimes, later cardinal.[24] I have now been able to confirm Gouron's identification through a reevaluation of a passage in the *Summa Coloniensis* of an opinion of Raimundus de Arenis and by comparing it with the glosses of Cardinalis to C.30 q.4 and to C.16 (earlier I had proposed other suggestions for the occasionally occurring siglum 'h.' or 'r. d. h.').[25] Raimundus' earliest glosses to the *Decretum*, probably in the 1150s, are preserved under the siglum 'h.' or 'r. d. h.' in Vatican lat. 3529, which also transmits many of Rolandus' glosses. My explanation for the unusual form of the siglum is that the letter 'r.' was reserved for Rolandus and Rufinus. If I am right this would also explain why the siglum C. or Car. won such early acceptance to describe him after his elevation to the cardinalate in 1158 (Pope Hadrian IV obviously knew him from his time in Southern France). He was one of the cardinals who voted for the anti-pope Victor, and on account of this rebellious gesture he is said to have been temporarily imprisoned in Pisa on his way to Victor's 'council' in Pavia.[26] Might he also have been known at this time in Bologna as a former master? In any case, Raimundus' glosses occur later quite often in Bolognese gloss compositions, including in Huguccio's *Summa*. Huguccio cited him and occasionally disagreed with him.

Raimundus' glosses were transmitted for the first time on a large scale only in the 'Fifth Gloss Composition', above all in the two manuscripts Innsbruck, Universitätsbibl. 90 and Malibu, Getty Ludwig XIV.2. His glosses first appear in the second part of the *Decretum*, chiefly in C.16 and on matrimonial law. One could almost refer to both of these sections as an apparatus by Cardinalis, using the term in its widest sense. Moreover, these are the same sections to which Rolandus devoted particular attention. For this reason, I am now on the whole inclined to attribute the 'Fifth Gloss Composition' to the French school. One must not forget, however, that there was always a lively exchange between the jurists of

---

24. André Gouron, 'Le Cardinal Raymond des Arènes: Cardinalis?', RDC 28 (1978) 180–192, printed with corrections in Gouron, 'La Science' 12.

25. Rudolf Weigand, 'Die Glossen des Cardinalis (Magister Hubald?) zum Dekret Gratians, besonders zu C. 27 q. 2', BCML 3 (1973) 73–95; idem, 'Die Glossen des Cardinalis—Raimundus de (H)arenis—zu C.16', *Recht im Dienste des Menschen: eine Festgabe für Hugo Schwendenwein zum 60. Geburtstag*, ed. K. Lüdicke, et. al (Graz 1986) 267–283; idem, *Glossen zum Dekret Gratians* 600–605. A further argument for this ascription is the use of the Collectio Hispana in glosses of Cardinalis, as has been recently pointed out by Peter Landau, 'Vorgratianische Kanonessammlungen bei Dekretisten und in frühen Dekretalensammlungen', *Proceedings San Diego* 114–115.

26. References and secondary literature in Weigand, *Glossen zum Dekret Gratians* 603–604.

Bologna and those of Southern France. Aside from the glosses of Cardinalis on C.16 and on marriage, the largest share is made up of the glosses of the 'First Gloss Composition' (fairly sporadic), the 'Third' (Rufinus) and the 'Fourth', though quite often with some characteristic alterations that occur only in this work.[27] The exemplar of both these manuscripts was written in France; this is proved, as far as I am concerned, by the fact that occasionally the text of the *Decretum* is changed in ways that are characteristic of French texts. For example, in C.11 q.1 p.c.26, the penultimate sentence with Gratian's reference to D.8 c.1 is missing, and instead a normal reference 'supra di.viii c.i.' is written as a gloss in the margin.

The next datable canonistic work, even though it is in fact only a treatise on procedure, is the *Rhetorica ecclesiastica*. It was written in the diocese of Hildesheim around the year 1160. Linda Fowler-Magerl proposed this date and provenance on the basis of a thorough analysis of all the different formulae in the eight known manuscripts of this work.[28] Later, ca. 1175, it was taken to Cambrai or Reims, where Ludwig Wahrmund thought it was written, on the basis of the Vienna manuscript that he used for his edition.[29] In addition the treatise surfaced in Würzburg (before 1186), Windberg (before 1191), Mainz, and Schaffhausen and thus circulated widely in Germany. With this treatise jurisprudence reached Germany, and a German jurist(s) produced the first legal work of more than local influence. In addition to Gratian's *Decretum* the author used some works by French authors, a usage not at all unusual for this period. At any rate the author of the treatise may be 'Bertoldus magister scolarum', who was called a *scholasticus* in 1149 and was active in Hildesheim at this time.[30]

Stephen of Tournai published his *Summa Decreti* in about 1165–1167 and gave a powerful impetus to the study of canon law in France, especially in Paris.[31] Two small treatises on procedure, which we do not need to look at more closely here, were composed there almost simultaneously.[32] Fur-

---

27. Ibid. 443–446, with the relevant references. See my discussion of these 'Compositions' in Chapter 3 of this volume.

28. Linda Fowler-Magerl, *Ordo iudiciorum vel ordo iudiciarius: Repertorien zur Frühzeit der gelehrten Rechte* (Ius commune, Sonderhefte 19; Frankfurt 1984) 45–56.

29. Ludwig Wahrmund, *Quellen zur Geschichte des römisch-kanonischen Prozesses im Mittelalter* (Innsbruck 1906) Volume 1, part 5.

30. Fowler-Magerl, *Ordo iudiciorum* 50–51. On this work see also Peter Landau, 'Die Anfänge der Verbreitung des klassischen kanonischen Rechts in Deutschland im 12. Jahrhundert und im ersten Drittel des 13. Jahrhunderts', *Chiesa, diritto e ordinamento della 'Societas christiana' nei secoli XI e XII: Atti della nona settimana internazionale di studi medioevali, Mendola, 28 agosto–2 settembre 1983* (Milan 1986) 278.

31. See the chapter in this volume by Pennington on the Italian school.

32. André Gouron, 'Canon Law in Parisian Circles before Stephen of Tournai's *Summa*', *Proceedings San Diego* 497–503.

thermore, as a spinoff from Stephen's *Summa*, two *summae* on Part Two of the *Decretum* were probably written there; these were, however, at first attributed to the Bolognese school.[33] These are the *Summae 'Quoniam status ecclesiarum'* (Paris, B.N. lat. 16538) and *'Cum in tres partes'* (Paris, B.N. lat. 16540), which are identical in many long passages.[34] A characteristic of both these *summae* is that they link texts from the *Decretum* (including numerous citations) with a brief commentary that is mostly taken from Stephen's *Summa*, although with occasional deviations.[35] This type of commentary, which was also used in the more or less contemporary *Summa Coloniensis* (though at a more sophisticated level), and the transmission of this text solely in Paris manuscripts, appear to provide sufficient proof to show that both these works can be attributed to the French school.

An important work of the early Paris school is the *Summa 'Magister Gratianus in hoc opere'* preserved only in Bamberg, Staatsbibliothek Can. 36.[36] This work is also known as *Summa Parisiensis*, a name that its editor retained to show to which school it belonged.[37] The author is well-acquainted with the earlier Bolognese tradition, since he uses the 'First Gloss Composition' in addition to the *summae* of Paucapalea, Rolandus, and Rufinus.[38] In particular, he discusses many details about the structure of the *Decretum* and the work of Paucapalea, who he says was the first to undertake the division of Parts One and Three into distinctions (Gillmann and others have confirmed his statement). Furthermore, he tells us about the 'paleae',[39] about which he says more than once that they were added by Paucapalea, as in the case of the palea with the beginning word 'Constantinus' at D.96 c.13–14.[40]

---

33. This is the view of Kuttner, *Repertorium* 136–139; he briefly analyzed both *summae*, but he also thought French origin was a possibility for them.

34. As, for example, at C.24 q.1, as shown by Titus Lenherr, *Die Exkommunikations- und Depositionsgewalt der Häretiker bei Gratian und den Dekretisten bis zur Glossa ordinaria des Johannes Teutonicus* (Münchner Theologische Studien 42; St Ottilien 1987) 273–276. It is no longer possible to establish whether this was also the case at C.32 q.8 on conditional marriage, since C.32 q.2–C.33 q.2 are lacking in Paris, B.N. lat.16540 because of missing folia.

35. Josephus Zeliauskas, *De excommunicatione vitiata apud Glossatores (1140–1350)* (Zürich and Rome 1967) provides examples of dependence and occasional differences by printing in parallel corresponding passages from the three *summae* in Appendices VIII–X, 10*–51*.

36. Kuttner, *Repertorium* 177–178, with comments on earlier studies.

37. Terence P. McLaughlin, *The Summa Parisiensis on the Decretum Gratiani* (Toronto 1952).

38. The author made use of the gloss to D.11 c.5, in Weigand, *Glossen zum Dekret Gratians* no. 209 (McLaughlin, *Summa Parisiensis* 11), gloss no. 602b to C.1 q.3 c.4 (McLaughlin 93) and also the gloss to D.9 c.9, which Stephen also incorporated into his *Summa* (McLaughlin xxix). Therefore, this text cannot be used as evidence for the author's dependence on Stephen.

39. References in McLaughlin, *Summa Parisiensis* x–xv.

40. J.F. von Schulte wrongly interpreted his actual meaning, that this palea should be enlarged from c.12, as we can also see from Friedberg's edition at note 212.

The author of this *Summa* already demonstrated a characteristic of the French school of inserting unusual additional texts into Gratian's *Decretum*: for example, the decretal *Relatum* attached to C.13 q.2 d.p.c.7, on which he also comments. He also added the quotation from the Codex 1.3.30 at the end of C.1 q.7, which he cites verbatim and comments on, since, as he explains, the text can be found in only a few manuscripts of the *Decretum*.[41] Although the French school tended to be rather theologically inclined, this author commented on C.33 q.3 in only a few sentences and probably not at all on the *De consecratione*, since no commentary is to be found in the Bamberg manuscript. However, his commentary on C.27–C.29, which is not in the only extant manuscript, is supposed to have been missing only from the exemplar from which this manuscript was copied. Although the editor reckoned that the date of composition of this *Summa* was about 1160,[42] the late 1160s seem more probable, since, according to Kuttner, only a later date makes it possible to reconcile, on the one hand, a mention of Placentinus and the use of Stephen of Tournai's *Summa*, and, on the other, the fact that the author of the *Summa Coloniensis* used this work.[43]

To the same school and period (1160–1170) also belongs the *Summa Elnonensis* discovered by Gérard Fransen. The only fragment of this work so far discovered, in Valenciennes, Bibl. mun. 193, fol. 111rb–115rb, contains a commentary on C.2–C.26.[44] This *Summa* fragment could come from the school of Gerard Pucelle, who is cited ten times in this short commentary, as M. Ge. Some anonymous quotations cited in other passages should also be attributed to him. In any case, this work allows us to recognize that its author had some talent.

Gerard Pucelle, later bishop of Coventry (1183–1184), was at home in academics and ecclesiastical politics; he commuted, so to speak, back and forth between England, France and Germany.[45] First he studied and

---

41. McLaughlin *Summa Parisiensis* 100. Jacqueline Rambaud-Buhot found this passage from the Codex at the end of C.1 in nine French manuscripts of the *Decretum*, including the oldest one known to her, Paris, B.N. lat.3884, 'Le "Corpus juris civilis" dans le Décret de Gratien d'après le manuscrit lat. nouv. acq. 1761 de la Bibliothèque nationale', BFC III (1954) 54–64 at 63.

42. McLaughlin, *Summa Parisiensis* xxxii.

43. Stephan Kuttner, *Gratian and the Schools of Law 1140–1234* (London 1983) 30 (correcting no. VIII, 300). Gouron agrees with him: 'Une école' 233.

44. Gérard Fransen, 'Colligite fragmenta: La *Summa Elnonensis*', SG 13 (1967) 85–108.

45. For a summary of his life, see Kuttner and Rathbone, 'Anglo-Norman Canonists' 296–303, and in addition Johannes Fried, 'Gerard Pucelle und Köln', ZRG Kan. Abt. 68 (1982) 125–315. Gerard must also be the author of the M.G. glosses in Stephen's *Summa* in Berlin lat. q.193, partly published by Friedrich Thaner, 'Zwei anonyme Glossen zur Summa Stephani Tornacensis', SB Vienna 79 (1875) 211–233, here 223, 225f., 231. On 221, however, he misdates the layer of glosses completely, since he takes 'sanctus Thomas' to be Thomas Aquinas, and not correctly as Thomas Becket, canonized in 1173.

taught theology and Roman and canon law in Paris (ca. 1155–1165). At the peak of the Becket dispute, Pucelle travelled on a mission to the Emperor Frederick Barbarossa, although he belonged to Becket's 'familia'. In these years (1165–1168) he also taught in Cologne, where he held a prebend. After this he returned to England. He had one more brief stay in Cologne ca. 1180, where he taught with a papal dispensation. The short-lived Cologne school is supposed to have received essential inspiration from him. During his first stay there he wrote a *Summa* on Part Two of the *Decretum* (ca. 1167) preserved as *Quoniam omissis centum distinctionibus* in Verdun, Bibl. mun. 35 and Ghent, Bibl. Rijksuniv. 1429, as can be seen from the evidence of a few of the formulae for accusations, appeals, and so on.[46] Through his travels and teaching, Pucelle drew together, in a sense, the French, Rhenish, and early Anglo-Norman schools into a single entity.

The main work of the Cologne school is the *Summa Elegantius in iure divino*, usually simply known as *Coloniensis*. It has survived in three manuscripts, which in part display different recensions: Bamberg, Staatsbibl. Can. 39 represents the earliest version, Vienna, Ö.N.B. 2125 and Paris, B.N. lat. 14997 a later revision.[47] This *Summa* has been edited in an exemplary fashion by Gérard Fransen with help from Stephan Kuttner, in the *Monumenta iuris canonici*, although the prolegomena and the glosses have never appeared.[48] The material is presented in an original way, well-organized for teaching purposes, with its own distinction-divisions, which, however, follow the general pattern of the *Decretum*. Passages from the latter are not cited but are referred to, often very summarily. No commentary is given for Part Three of the *Decretum*. The author certainly used (as shown in the edition's *apparatus fontium*) Rufinus' and Stephen's *summae*, the *Summa Parisiensis* and, in addition, a few works of Roman law (Bulgarus and Rogerius) and the *Rhetorica ecclesiastica*. Furthermore, the author used the then extant addenda at the end of individual codices and several glosses from the Bolognese school. It has not yet been possible to identify the author conclusively. The 'Frater Godefridus' who is said to have compiled the work according to an entry in the Paris manuscript might be, or rather

---

46. Kuttner and Rathbone, 'Anglo-Norman Canonists' 299 and n. 20; Kuttner, 'Gratian' 30, which also gives references to 'exercises' from the Cologne school. The better manuscript of this *Summa*, in Ghent 1429, fol. 43va–72rb, was discovered by Dirk Van den Auweele, 'Le codex Gandauensis 1429: Un Parcensis précieux', *Recherches de théologie ancienne et médiévale* 49 (1982) 205–221, here 217–219.

47. Kuttner, *Repertorium* 170–172, with a discussion of the earlier literature.

48. Gérard Fransen and Stephan Kuttner, eds., *Summa 'Elegantius in iure divino' seu Coloniensis*, as vol. 1 of Series A in four parts: Part I (1969) (Sections 1–3); Part II (1978) (Sections 4–7); Part III (1986) (Sections 8–12 iterum) and Part IV (1990) (sections 13–15, on marriage). Both Fransen and Kuttner have died.

might have become, the Augustinian canon at Cologne described by Caesarius of Heisterbach as having been a teacher in Reims in about 1153.[49] On the basis of several formularies containing the siglum *B*, another possibility might be Master Bertram or Berthold of Saxony or of Metz, who was renowned for his great knowledge of Roman and canon law.[50] He wrote a commentary with the title *De regulis iuris*,[51] and was a canon of St. Gereon in Cologne (ca. 1170) and later bishop of Metz, 1180–1212.[52] Furthermore, I consider it possible, indeed likely, that the mostly unique glosses on the *Decretum* in Cologne, Dombibliothek 127 were also written ca. 1170 by a master of the Cologne school.[53]

The *Summa 'Antiquitate et tempore'*, preserved in Göttingen, Universitätsbibl. iur. 159 to D.89 c.2, may also be from a jurist in the group surrounding Gerard Pucelle. It may have covered only Part One of the *Decretum* (it might even be a supplement to other *summae* that cover only Part Two). It was written by a master of the liberal arts who made use of Rufinus' *Summa*.[54] This work is found in three other manuscripts, but only to D.10; in this version of the work the remaining distinctions contain an abbreviated working text of Rufinus' *Summa* and the *Summa 'Antiquitate et tempore'*. The prologue *'Videndum que materia'* belongs to this group as well; it can probably be attributed to Gerard Pucelle on the basis of a marginal siglum G.[55] In addition, the commentary on the *De consecratione* beginning *'Fecit Moyses tabernaculum'*, which is preserved in three manuscripts with Stephen's *Summa*, including Mainz, Stadtbibl. 477 (including a part of the *Summa 'Antiquitate et tempore'*) seems to belong to the periph-

---

49. Kuttner and Rathbone, 'Anglo-Norman Canonists' 299–300.

50. Stephan Kuttner, 'Bertram of Metz', *Traditio* 13 (157) 501–505.

51. Bertrandus Metensis, *De regulis iuris*, ed. Severino Caprioli (Pubblicazioni della Facoltà di Giurisprudenza, Università di Perugia, 27; Perugia 1981). Bertram also composed a *Summula de probationibus*, see Fowler-Magerl, *Ordo iudiciorum* 219–220.

52. P. Gerbenzon, 'Bertram of Metz the author of *Elegantius in iure divino (Summa Coloniensis)?*', *Traditio* 21 (1965) 510–511. Fowler-Magerl indirectly raises the question whether the Berthold who occurs in Hildesheim ca. 1160 might be a possible identification: *Ordo iudiciorum* 51.

53. Description and some characteristic glosses in Weigand, *Glossen zum Dekret Gratians* 782–785.

54. Kuttner, *Repertorium* 178–179, and Kuttner, *Traditio* 11 (1955) 446, and see also idem, 'Gratian and Plato', *Church and Government in the Middle Ages*, ed. C.N.L. Brooke, D.E. Luscombe, G.H. Martin, and D.M. Owen (Cambridge 1976) 93–118, reprinted in *The History of Ideas and Doctrines of Canon Law in the Middle Ages* (London 1980). Composition in Cologne has been supported by the findings of Peter Landau that the author used Cresconius' collection in the form in which it was earlier available in Cologne: 'Vorgratianische Kanonessammlungen bei Dekretisten und in frühen Dekretalensammlungen', *Proceedings San Diego* 93–116.

55. Kuttner, *Repertorium* 184 and his 'The Third Part of Stephen of Tournai's *Summa*', *Traditio* 14 (1958) 505, n. 16.

ery of this school. Its author taught in the French school but was for a time a pupil and great admirer of Rufinus in Bologna.[56]

A work of rather inferior value, from an intellectual point of view, is the text known as *Distinctiones Monacenses*, or more accurately, *Distinctiones 'Si mulier eadem hora'*. One of its editors, however, wished to assign it to the genre of *Quaestiones*.[57] This simple work consists almost exclusively of extracts from other works, especially the *Summa Parisiensis*.[58] Hence, it may quite easily have been written in Westphalia, perhaps in the abbey of Liesborn, because the abbot of that house and a provost of Cappenberg are mentioned in the text. Since there is evidence from both monasteries for literary activity at an elementary level at the time in question, we can assume that this work was written at one of these two houses. It survives in three manuscripts.

Probably the earliest offshoot of Gratian's *Decretum* from the Anglo-Norman area is the rather brief *Summa 'De multiplici iuris divisione'* of ca. 1170, which has come down to us in three English manuscripts.[59] Its text is based extensively on Stephen of Tournai's *Summa*, which is reproduced in a very summarized form.

Odo of Dover demonstrates much more independent thought in his *Summa*.[60] Although his work sometimes looks like a simple abbreviation of Gratian's *Decretum* over long passages, and in other places borrows much from Stephen's *Summa*, he added a number of summaries that are more or less the author's own work. Perhaps his most creative teaching was his commentary on natural law.[61] Here too the date of writing should probably be placed around 1170.

According to the most recent findings, the fragment *'Tria sunt per que*

---

56. Kuttner, 'The Third Part' 502–505; partial edition in von Schulte's edition of Stephen of Tournai's *Summa* 259–280.

57. A.J. de Groot, 'Probleme bei der Ausgabe der sogenannten Distinctiones Monacenses', *Proceedings Salamanca* 187–194. The work takes its name from the first manuscript to be discovered, Munich, Staatsbibl. 16084, fol. 38v–62. Now printed in two editions: *Distinctiones 'Si mulier eadem hora' seu Monacenses*, ed. A.J. de Groot (Rechtshistorische reeks van het Gerard Noodt Instituut, 36; Nijmegen 1996) and *Distinctiones 'Si mulier eadem hora' seu Monacenses*, ed. Rosalba Sorice (MIC, Series A: Corpus Glossatorum, 4; Città del Vaticano, 2002).

58. de Groot, 'Probleme bei der Ausgabe'; Kuttner, *Repertorium*, 215, also mentions the *summae* of Rufinus and Stephen as works drawn on. However, the commentary on conditional marriage vows was certainly taken from Rolandus' *Summa*. See Weigand, *Bedingte Eheschließung* 150–151, 106–107.

59. Kuttner, *Repertorium* 139–141; Kuttner and Rathbone, 'Anglo-Norman Canonists' 293.

60. Kuttner, *Repertorium* 172–177; Kuttner and Rathbone, 'Anglo-Norman Canonists' 293. The work survives only partially in London, B.L. Cotton Vit. A.iii, fol. 111–218v.

61. Rudolf Weigand, *Die Naturrechtslehre der Legisten und Dekretisten von Irnerius bis Accursius und von Gratian bis Johannes Teutonicus* (Münchner Theologische Studien 26; Munich 1967) 160–163.

religionis' in Munich, Staatsbibl. 16084, fol. 34r–35r can be attributed to the French or the Anglo-Norman school of the period after 1170. Although the views of Rufinus loom large in the work, the author cited a decretal of Alexander III to the archbishop of Rouen that confirms its Northern French origins.[62]

In the area around Salzburg and Admont, the use of the new texts of canon law seems to have left its earliest traces ca. 1170. Earlier, however, the archbishop of Salzburg, Eberhard I (1147–1164), had addressed a query to Pope Hadrian IV (1154–1159) about the marriage of slaves, and Hadrian replied in the important decretal *Dignum est* that slaves should be allowed to marry even without the consent of their lords.[63] This decretal was shortly afterwards included in the treatise on marriage '*Cum alia sacramenta*',[64] which was, for the most part, an extract from Peter Lombard's *Sentences*.[65] In, or near, Salzburg a very fine manuscript of Gratian's *Decretum* (now Munich, Staatsbibl. 13004) was copied around 1170.[66] It contains several idiosyncrasies: the famous introduction '*In prima parte*' is here called '*Claves titulorum*' as it appears in Admont, Stiftsbibl. 23, which is an earlier recension of Gratian's *Decretum*.[67] The manuscript also contains an otherwise unknown introduction to the *Decretum* '*Hoc opus inscribitur*' that refers to 37 books of the *Decretum*, Part One and the 36 Causae, but not Part Three. At the end of the manuscript comes the treatise '*De sacrilegiis*,' which also occurs in Admont 43, at the close of Part Two.[68]

The *Collectio Admontensis* is appended to Admont 43. It has been analyzed and named by Stelzer.[69] This work consists of the treatise '*De sacrilegiis*', 286 chapters taken from Ivo's *Panormia*, and finally 54 Roman law

---

62. Kuttner, *Repertorium* 133; Lenherr, *Exkommunikationsgewalt* 207–211 and n. 57.

63. On this see Peter Landau, 'Hadrians IV. Dekretale *Dignum est* (X 4.9.1) und die Eheschließung Unfreier', *Collectanea Stephan Kuttner* (SG 12; Rome1968) 511–553.

64. Rudolf Weigand, 'Kanonistische Ehetraktate aus dem 12. Jahrhundert', *Proceedings Strasbourg*, 63.

65. Winfried Stelzer, *Gelehrtes Recht in Österreich: von den Anfängen bis zum frühen 14. Jahrhundert* (Vienna-Cologne-Graz 1982) 17–21, with reference to further decretals for this recipient, 20, n. 12.

66. See Weigand, *Glossen zum Dekret Gratians* 848–850, with further references to secondary literature.

67. See Anders Winroth, *The Making of Gratian's Decretum* (Cambridge Studies in Medieval Life and Thought, 4th Series, 49; Cambridge 2000) 23–26 for a description of Admont 23 and 43.

68. Hubert Mordek, 'Auf der Suche nach einem verschollenen Manuskript', *Aus Kirche und Reich: Festschrift für Friedrich Kempf zu seinem 57. Geburtstag und 15. Doktorjubiläum F. Kempf*, ed. H. Mordek, et al (Sigmaringen 1983) 187–200, with a color reproduction.

69. Stelzer, *Gelehrtes Recht* 22–44, under the chapter-heading 'Ausstrahlung der südfranzösischen Schulen von Valence und Die' (some of the copies used originally came from these).

texts, which partly were derived from known Southern French sources. The texts at the end are, however, taken from the *Edictum Theoderici*. These texts are similar, though in a different order, to those in the opening quires of Admont 48, a manuscript of the *Decretum* of Italian provenance, though the passages with which we are concerned were copied at Admont, where the textual compilation probably took place.

The only thing that can be definitely stated about the place of origin of the *Abbreviatio 'Exceptiones ecclesiasticarum regularum'* is that it was not Italy. At any rate, nine out of the ten manuscripts identified to date are preserved in German and Austrian libraries, while the tenth, now Vat. Pal. lat. 228, was written in Paris.[70] Apart from Paris, possible places of composition might be Mainz, or perhaps Salzburg or Admont. In addition to Gratian's *Decretum*, the compiler used Rufinus' *Summa* (chiefly at the start of the section on marriage, but also elsewhere for the glosses), and, as an introduction, Ivo's famous prologue that is missing in only two of the ten manuscripts. The basic complement of glosses is similar in most of the manuscripts and was conceived simultaneously with the text, since occasionally passages from Gratian are divided between the main text and the glosses. Certainly Ivo's *Panormia*, *Decretum*, and his Prologue, were known and valued at Admont, as the two texts we have just mentioned prove; a possible argument in favor of Mainz is the fact that one of the manuscripts is of Mainz provenance.[71]

The famous *Summa Monacensis* is from the Northern French school, more particularly from the area around Paris.[72] It can be dated to the early years of the 1170s, since the only surviving manuscript contains a letter formulary datable to 1175–1178. The formulary refers to the circle around Conrad von Albeck who later became provost of Neustift near Bremen.[73] This evidence does not, however, fix the date of the *Summa* itself. It is probably earlier, though not before 1170, since the son of Henry II of England is mentioned as an example of co-rulership in a father's lifetime. The

---

70. Listed in Rudolf Weigand, 'Die Dekretabbreviatio *Exceptiones ecclesiasticarum regularum* und ihre Glossen', *Cristianità ed Europa: Miscellanea di studi in onore di Luigi Prosdocimi*, ed. C. Alzati (Rome-Freiburg-Vienna 1992) 133–151, for which eight manuscripts were used. Seven manuscripts are listed by Kuttner, *Repertorium* 260, but of these the Basel manuscript should be omitted. According to Schulte the two 'extracts' have nothing to do with this *abbreviatio*. In addition Bernkastel-Kues, Hospital 229, fol. 1ra–55ra should be added to the list; it lacks the prologue and begins at D.4 d.p.c.3 owing to loss of folios.

71. Now Darmstadt, Landesbibliothek 542; it may have belonged to Archbishop Christian of Mainz (1167–1183), Weigand, 'Die Dekretabbreviatio *Exceptiones*' 134. Sicardus of Cremona stayed at Mainz in the late 1170s.

72. Munich, Staatsbibl. lat. 16084, fol. 1–9, 11–16, 18–27; Kuttner, *Repertorium* 179–180.

73. Stelzer, *Gelehrtes Recht* 44–52, 58–59, 191.

young Henry was crowned king on 14 June 1170.[74] This *Summa* was written in a very condensed form and divided the material into numerous distinctions to present it tersely and precisely. Certain problems, however, are dealt with relatively fully and in an original way. For example the author spent an inordinate amount of time on the question of conditional marriage vows, which takes up about 10 percent of the explanation of law on marriage.[75] It is possible that, in contrast to fragments of other juristic works, this *Summa* may not be the polished work of a single author but preserves the best record of the *summulae*, distinctions, and other statements of an unknown author of the French school.[76]

The following works, several of which are contained in the same manuscript, should be viewed as fragments and miscellaneous writings associated with the *Summa Monacensis*, probably going back to the same Parisian master through other students or other traditions. They are: The *Summa* fragments 'Iuditiorum instrumenta',[77] 'Questio si iure naturali'[78] and 'Boni a Deo patre',[79] as well as the prologue of Peter of Louveciennes.[80] The *Summa* 'Inter cetera que ecclesiastice dignitati', of which a presumably 'complete' copy was found in Leiden, Bibl. Rijksuniv. Vulc. 48, fol. 9–24, likewise belongs to the same group as the *summae* named above but is markedly more dependent on Odo of Dover in its treatment of natural law.[81] A small fragment with the same incipit as the text in Munich Clm 16084, fol. 64v–65 deviates from it at several points, even though it goes only as far as D.1 c.4.[82] The *Distinctiones* opening 'Consuetudo,' which are preserved in somewhat differing forms in three manuscripts, should clearly also be counted among the texts surrounding the circle of the *Summa Monacensis* since they agree with its text in many long passages.[83] To this group probably also belongs

---

74. Ibid. 51, n. 49. This is also a clear sign that the work was composed in northern France.

75. Weigand, *Bedingte Eheschließung* 160–168. The siglum 'R' occurring there refers to Magister Rolandus, not Rodoicus (as I then thought, owing to a lack of alternatives). Stelzer *Gelehrtes Recht* 44, n. 5, lists the modern scholars who have referred to this *Summa* in their work.

76. Stephan Kuttner, 'A Forgotten Definition of Justice', SG 20 (1976) 73–110.

77. Munich, Staatsbibl. lat. 16084, fol. 28–29; Kuttner, *Repertorium* 181.

78. Kuttner, *Repertorium* 181; in Arras 271 this work ends at fol. 181vb, as noted by Kuttner in *Traditio* 15 (1959) 499, where he also referred to a third manuscript, Oxford, University College 117, fol. 149ra–151vb, which breaks off in D.96.

79. Ibid. 183; Munich, Staatsbibl. lat. 16084 fol. 74–77 to D.18.

80. Ibid. lists three editions. This same Peter is the author of glosses on the *Summa* of Stephen of Tournai in Berlin, Staatsbibl. lat.q.193, which have been partly published by Thaner 'Zwei anonyme Glossen' 227–229.

81. Weigand, *Naturrechtslehre* 166–172 and 464–466.

82. Ibid. and Kuttner, *Repertorium* 182.

83. Kuttner, *Repertorium* 219; Kuttner, *Traditio* 11 (1955) 447, 15 (1959) 499. According to

the prologue 'Omnia poma vetera', which comes at the end of the *Distinctio* 'Consuetudo' in the Arras manuscript.⁸⁴ The precise relationship of these fragments and works to each other will become clear only once they are edited, which is not likely to happen in the foreseeable future.⁸⁵

A few gloss compositions from various periods that should probably be viewed as French have been discussed briefly above.⁸⁶ Because the basic stock of Bolognese material in these and other works is often large, it is not always possible to determine a transmontane provenance for them. This is especially true of the collections of *Quaestiones* that have been extensively analyzed and partly edited by Gerard Fransen.⁸⁷ However, the *Quaestiones Aschaffenburgenses*, discovered only two decades ago and thoroughly analyzed by Fransen, probably belong to the French school in their present form.⁸⁸ This compilation of *Quaestiones* preserved in Aschaffenburg, Stiftsbibl. 26, fol. 197r–207v, may have been produced between 1174 and 1179. It cites the *Summa* of Rufinus once; Master Gido, Ga., Gaid., Ie., G., and M.D. are also cited and have not yet been properly identified. I think it is not impossible that the sigla G. and Ga. might refer to Gandulphus. It is not yet possible to decide whether M.D. refers to David of London, Daifer, or another master.

Around the year 1180 in Chartres, Peter of Blois the Younger had dealt with fifty legal problems, without following any particular literary genre. His work can, I think, be considered a form of *Distinctiones*.⁸⁹ The first chapter deals with methodological questions concerning the origins of

---

Kuttner, the text is also contained in Arras 271 (1064) fol. 182r–188, though with missing folios after fol. 185 and 187.

84. Ibid. 154. Probably also on the flyleaf of Angers, Bibl. mun. 64 (57) noted by H. van de Wouw, *Notae Atrebatenses in Decretum Gratiani* (University of Leiden Dissertation, 1969) 13, n. 15.

85. Kuttner, *Traditio* 17 (1961) 499 announced a forthcoming 'study on the very complex manuscript tradition of . . . the writings from the circle of the *Summa Inperatorie maiestati*', which will not appear. In connection with this, it would be useful to find out if the *Distinctiones* 'Tria consideranda sunt in electione' that are entered into the margin of Oxford, Bodl. Barlow 37, from fol. iv onwards, belong to the same group: Stephan Kuttner, 'The Decretal *Presbiterum*' (JL 13912)—A Letter of Leo IX', BMCL 5 (1975) 134, n. 8.

86. See my chapter on the Ordinary Gloss to the *Decretum* in this volume.

87. Gérard Fransen, 'Les questions disputées dans les facultés de Droit', *Les questions disputées et les questions quodlibétiques dans les Facultés de Théologie, de Droit et de Médicine*, ed. B. Bazàn (Typologie des sources du Moyen Âge occidental 44–45; Turnhout 1985) 223–277, esp. 228–230.

88. H. van de Wouw, 'Notes on the Aschaffenburg Manuscript Perg. 26', BMCL 3 (1973) 97–107, esp. 98–99, 102–103 and Gérard Fransen, 'Questiones Aschaffenburgenses', BMCL 16 (1986) 71–86.

89. Kuttner, *Repertorium* 220, lists ten manuscripts from the edition of T.E. Reimarus, *Petri Blesensis opusculum de distinctionibus in canonum interpretatione adhibendis, sive ut auctor voluit Speculum Iuris Canonici* (Berlin 1837).

canon law and the contradictions that are found in canonical sources. Other chapter rubrics are formulated as rules of law. There are distinctions in the margins containing parallel and contrary passages. The work is partly dependent on the *Summa Monacensis*. Peter may have written a short *Ordo iudiciarius* in addition to this work.[90] We cannot now know whether the p.-glosses preserved in some French manuscripts should be attributed to him.

In spite of his Italian origins, Sicardus of Cremona, who also composed a well-known chronicle and a widely used liturgical work, the *Mitrale*, can be considered a transmontane canonist, because he studied and wrote north of the Alps.[91] After studying in Paris he taught from about 1179 to 1183 in Mainz. After becoming a canon in the cathedral chapter in Paris he composed his *Summa* on the *Decretum*. It survives in numerous copies.[92] It has characteristics typical of the French school.[93] The *Summa* is original, systematically didactic, and deals with individual problems tersely, often with *distinctiones*. Sicardus was an important literary link between the transmontane and Italian schools: twelve out of twenty-eight manuscripts are to be found in the German-speaking regions. On several occasions Sicardus' *Summa* was copied together with the almost-contemporary *Summa* of Simon of Bisignano,[94] whose importance for the textual history of several canonistic problems is becoming clear in numerous studies.[95] The unusual *Quaestio* collection in Pommersfelden, Schloss Bibl. Schönborn 41 (2918), fol. 1–69v, was probably inspired by Sicardus's activity as a teacher in Mainz.[96] Its arguments are presented as legal proceedings in which the legal texts are not explicitly cited but are cited without indications of

90. Fowler-Magerl, *Ordo iudiciorum* 94–96, questions Peter's authorship, in spite of the marginal note Berlin, Staatsbibl. qu. 193 that asserts his authorship.

91. His Chronicle is edited by O. Holder-Egger in MGH Scriptores 31 (1903), though Holder-Egger thought the chronicler and the canonist were different people; Stephan Kuttner, 'Zur Biographie des Sicardus', ZRG Kan. Abt. 25 (1936) 476–478. The *Mitrale* is printed in PL 213.13–436.

92. Kuttner, *Repertorium* 150–153 still ascribed it to the Bolognese school. There is a list of 27 manuscripts in *Traditio* 12 (1956) 562, to which Oxford, University College 117, fol. 129v–140rb should be added: see *Traditio* 16 (1960) 533. Unfortunately, P.J. Kessler was unable to complete his edition of this *Summa*.

93. The first person to make this ascription was Stephan Kuttner, 'Réflexions sur les Brocards des Glossateurs', *Mélanges Joseph de Ghellinck, S.J.* (Gembloux 1951, reprinted in *Gratian and the Schools of Law*) 767–792, especially 783–788.

94. Kuttner, *Repertorium* 153: Augsburg, Staatsbibl. 1, Bamberg, Staatsbibl. Can. 38 and Rouen, Bibl. mun. 710.

95. See Weigand, *Bedingte Eheschließung* 171–176 and my *Naturrechtslehre* 184–186 passim; Lenherr, *Exkommunikationsgewalt* 216–218 and 287; Hubert Müller, *Der Anteil der Laien an der Bischofswahl* (Kanonistischen Studien und Texte 29; Amsterdam 1977) 66–69, who shows that there were two recensions of this *Summa*.

96. Alfons M. Stickler, 'Decretistica Germanica adaucta', *Traditio* 12 (1956) 603, and Landau, 'Die Anfänge' 281.

where they can be found, as in the *Summa Coloniensis*. A connection with Mainz is proven by the form for appeals (fol. 8v: '. . . subdiaconus, servus Moguntine ecclesie'), as well as by the rest of the manuscript's contents.[97]

Everard of Ypres, later monk of Clairvaux, studied arts and probably also theology and canon law in Paris and compiled there his *Breviarium Decreti* or *Summula quaestionum decretalium*.[98] It is a *Summa* in the form of *Quaestiones* and almost exclusively (though sometimes misleadingly) an excerpt from the *Summa Monacensis*, and therefore, a very unsophisticated work.[99]

The French *Summa 'Tractaturus magister'*, preserved only in Paris, B.N. lat. 15994, joined together the elements of commentary and summaries and therefore, according to Kuttner, belongs to the category of a 'mixed' *Summa*.[100] Its anonymous author borrowed from the *Summa Monacensis* and from the most recent *summae* of the Bolognese and transmontane schools. He based his ideas on the doctrine of natural law from the *summae* both of Simon and of Sicardus of Cremona.[101] Therefore, the period of composition must be around 1182–1185.

The *Summa 'Et est sciendum'*, written more or less at the same time (1182–1185) was analyzed by Franz Gillmann in 1927 on the basis of Stuttgart, Landesbibl. hist. fol. 419, fol. 34–49.[102] Gillmann published about a third of it.[103] The author came from the ecclesiastical province of Sens, had already written another work (another *Summa*) on the *Decretum*, used Burchard's *Decretum* repeatedly and often cites decretals of Alexander III.[104] This work was one of the models frequently used by the *Summa Lipsiensis*, especially for

---

97. The edition by Fransen that was announced by Stickler (see note 96 just above) will not appear. The reference to the transcription of Pommersfelden, Schloss Bibl. Schönborn 41, fol. 1–69v in *Traditio* 19 (1963) 511 as an 'Exceptum decretorum' leaves the authorship of this work open.

98. The only known manuscript is Reims, Bibl. mun. 689, fol. 1–74, discovered and analyzed by Kuttner, *Repertorium* 187–190, with extracts from the prologue and the afterward. The last-mentioned is probably not the work of the author, since, unlike the prologue, it refers to him in the third person, and it describes the work as *Decretalium summulam questionum*.

99. Kuttner, *Repertorium* 190; Kuttner and Rathbone, 'Anglo-Norman Canonists' 314; Müller, *Anteil der Laien* 69–70; my point is most clearly seen in Zeliauskas, *De excommunicatione* Appendices XXV and XXVI, where the relevant texts are printed from both works and are cross-referenced with arabic numerals.

100. First discovered by Kuttner, *Repertorium* 184–187. Unfortunately, the edition prepared by J. Hanenburg has never been published.

101. Weigand, *Naturrechtslehre* 186–188.

102. Kuttner, *Repertorium* 195–196.

103. Franz Gillmann, 'Die Dekretglossen des Codex Stuttgart. Hist. f.419', AKKR 107 (1927) 192–250. Reprinted with additions *Gesammelte Schriften zur klassischen Kanonistik von Franz Gillmann*, 1: *Schriften zum Dekret Gratians und zu den Dekretisten,* ed. R. Weigand (Forschungen zur Kirchenrechtswissenschaft 5.1; Würzburg 1988) no. 14.

104. Kuttner, *Repertorium* 196; Gillmann, 'Die Dekretglossen', 201–207.

Part One of the *Decretum*; it was also used by Huguccio in the school of Bologna.[105]

The *Summa 'Permissio quedam'* is extant in three manuscripts and dealt only selectively with Gratian's *Decretum*. Its author borrowed extensively from the *Summa Monacensis* and knew important works of the Bolognese school such as Johannes Faventinus and Simon of Bisignano, as well as a Magister d. (possibly David of London). In spite of this, the author was not just a compiler of texts. For example, while discussing marriage vows he invented a phrase that has been retained in educated speech to this day: 'condicio sine qua non'.[106] This expression was adopted by Honorius and Huguccio, which suggests that this *Summa* was known in Bologna soon after it was written, ca. 1185. (The *Summa Lipsiensis* either did not know or did not use this particular formula).

The *Summa 'Reverentia sacrorum canonum'* is preserved only in Erfurt, Stadtbibl. Amploniana quart. 117, fol. 116r–140v, where it breaks off in C.1 q.7 c.2.[107] Scholars have generally recognized that it belongs to the French school. There are many quotations from philosophical and theological writings in the text. Since the decretals are still cited without titles and thus before the first systematic decretal collections, it must have been written in about 1185 or soon after. The author was skilled and sophisticated and could present material systematically, as we see by comparing his own independently worked out doctrine of natural law with that of other jurists.[108]

The *Principium 'Deus omnipotens'* that is a kind of inaugural lecture about general legal questions treating the division of the *Decretum* can be dated to the 1180s.[109] The author's style was unusual. He laced his text with allegories, proverbs, and metaphors and demonstrates that he had training in rhetoric. He should, therefore, be regarded as Northern French with, most likely, Parisian origins.

I shall deal with the *Notae Atrebatenses* here, since, unlike Kuttner and their editor, H. van de Wouw, I do not attribute them to the Bolognese school but to a school in Northern France.[110] The term *Notae* is appro-

---

105. Gillmann, 'Die Dekretglossen' 215–220, 232–237. Also J. Hanenburg, 'Decretals and Decretal Collections in the Second Half of the Twelfth Century', TRG 34 (1966) 577–582. On Huguccio's use of the *Summa*, see Kuttner, *Repertorium* 192–194 and *Traditio* 17 (1961) 533.

106. Weigand, *Bedingte Eheschließung* 183–186. The unidentified letters in n. 15 must be read as 'et cum qua'.

107. Kuttner, *Repertorium* 194–195.

108. Weigand, *Naturrechtslehre* 188–192.

109. Kuttner, *Repertorium* 191; ed. F. Kunstmann, AKKR 10 (1863) 345–352, who ascribed it, on insufficient evidence, to Sicardus.

110. Kuttner, *Repertorium* 146f.; known as the *Commentum Atrebatense* from the only manuscript discovered by Kuttner, Arras, Bibl. mun. 271 (1064) fol. 149–160v and see now van de Wouw *Notae Atrebatenses*.

priate, since the work is really more a collection of materials than a completed work intended for publication.[111] The author cited Bolognese jurists frequently: Rufinus twice, Johannes Faventinus four times, Albertus twice, Gandulphus three times, and Simon twice. He appropriated Bolognese materials without acknowledging his sources.[112] References to a few cases from Northern Italy could also have been taken from these sources. Much more significant to my mind, however, are the borrowings from the *Summa Monacensis* and the quotation from, or sometimes exact copying of, the *Summa 'Permissio quedam'* in several passages. I have also shown that there are parallel passages in works of the Anglo-Norman school.[113] Since we cannot date these works precisely, and the most convincing evidence for the provenance of any work is the origin of the sources used by the author, I am convinced that, given the preponderance of evidence, these *Notae* were written in Northern France ca. 1185.

The sigla ty, tu, and tv in the frequently very long glosses of Paris, B.N. lat.3905B represent an important Northern French magister, who was active in the 1180s, perhaps in Paris, and who had a strong interest in theology.[114] He may be the author of other anonymous glosses in this manuscript that are not found in other manuscripts.[115] The core of the glosses is Bolognese, but this fact does not argue against composition in Northern France. One of ty's students might have been involved in the compilation.[116]

Anglo-Norman glosses before ca. 1180 are difficult to identify, since the Bolognese glosses dominate so completely until then.[117] Nonetheless, the Anglo-Norman school may be responsible for the glosses that are relat-

111. van de Wouw, *Notae Atrebatenses*, xvi points especially to two fragmentary references to D.88 c.7 and D.92 c.6, both ending 'etc. ut in libro', by which the author was referring to glosses in his copy of the *Decretum*, which only he could use.

112. The sentences on D.11 c.2 commented on in detail in van de Wouw, *Notae Atrebatenses*, xxvii–xxviii, come from the Seventh Gloss Composition; see Weigand, *Glossen zum Dekret Gratians* 23 as gloss 65a from seven manuscripts; it is identical to Trier, Stadtbibl. 907 and Durham, Cathedral Library C.I.7.

113. van de Wouw, *Notae Atrebatenses*, xxxiv–xlii.

114. Kuttner, *Repertorium* 40; Kuttner and Rathbone, 'Anglo-Norman Canonists' 320, n. 47; Alfons M. Stickler, 'Zur Kirchengewalt in den Glossen der Hs. lat.3905 B der Bibl. Nat. Paris', *Miscellanea André Combes* (Rome 1967) 2.63–73; also in *Divinitas* 11 (1967) 459–470.

115. This is true of e.g. the eight glosses on *De consecratione* D.4 c.1–5, in Weigand, *Glossen zum Dekret Gratians* nos. 1751, 1792, 1836, 1838, 1886, 1905, 1915 and 1916, of which only the last bears ty's siglum.

116. Weigand, *Glossen zum Dekret Gratians* 893f.; the gloss to D.10 pr. cited by Stickler 'Zur Kirchengewalt' 67, contains the words 'Ma(gister) meus sentit in contrarium . . .'.

117. Cf. the attempt by Rudolf Weigand, 'Die anglo-normannische Kanonistik in den letzten Jahrzehnten des 12. Jahrhunderts', *Proceedings Cambridge* 250–257, which, together with Weigand, *Glossen zum Dekret Gratians* forms the basis for what follows; see also my chapter in this volume on the *Glossa ordinaria*.

ed to each other in the first layer of glosses in Cambridge, Corpus Christi College 10 and Cambridge, Pembroke College 162. These glosses partly belong to the 'First Gloss Composition' and are partly *continuationes* of Paucapalea's *Summa* or *Definitiones*. Ascription to the Anglo-Norman school is possible, because the second layer of glosses in Pembroke 162 contains the Gloss Composition that I shall treat next. We may suspect an origin north of the Alps for the glosses in Cambridge, Fitzwilliam Museum Maclean 135. Transmontane authorship may be attributed to the glosses in Cambridge, Gonville and Caius College 6 on the basis of a few archaic *notabilia* glosses. Cambridge, Sidney Sussex College 101 might, however, have been written in Northern Italy ca. 1180, since it contains some glosses of Bernard of Pavia in its first two layers, as well as glosses from the 'First' and 'Third Gloss Compositions'. Perhaps this manuscript came to England, where the *Notabilia* 'Clericus apud civilem iudicem', which were relevant to the Becket dispute, were added at the end.[118] The third layer of glosses in Sidney Sussex College 101 contains, amongst other things, glosses of Master David (of London). He wrote unusual glosses that are also preserved in New York, Pierpont Morgan Library 446 with the siglum ddl.[119] At present it is not possible to state with certainty whether all glosses marked with the siglum d should be attributed to this Master David.[120] The glosses in Durham, Cathedral Library C.III.1 also point to Bolognese origins, but new, original material by various authors suggests origins in the Anglo-Norman world. The clearest example of this is a long gloss to the *De consecratione* D.4 c.1 that occurs only in Durham C.II.1 and Gdansk, Bibl. Nauk. Mar. fol. 77.

A gloss composition of the 1180s typical of this school occurs as the main layer of glosses in the manuscripts of Antwerp, Museum Plantin-Moretus M.13, Durham C.I.7, and C.II.1, as well as fragmentarily in Oxford, New College 210 and Cambridge, Pembroke College 162 (in the second layer of glosses).[121] Each of these manuscripts has, in addition to a common stock of glosses, a relatively large proportion of individual glosses, so that it is not safe to assume authorship by one single master. I think the large number of philosophical and theological questions is typical of this school. Also typical are their frequent references to the viewpoints of earlier authors from Bologna: Rufinus, Rolandus, Albertus, Gandulphus,

---

118. Kuttner, *Repertorium*, 234; Kuttner and Rathbone, 'Anglo-Norman Canonists' 294.
119. Weigand, *Glossen zum Dekret Gratians* 625–631, glosses 14–16 and 18–20.
120. Most probably glosses no. 1, 2, 4, 8–11 in Weigand, *Glossen zum Dekret Gratians*.
121. Weigand, *Glossen zum Dekret Gratians*, 566–568, with references to the previously published glosses; see also the glosses in ibid. 668–669, 718, 730–372, 875–876, and Weigand, 'Die anglo-normannische Kanonistik' 253–257.

John Faventinus, and Cardinalis. The decretals of Alexander III are cited sometimes without a title, but sometimes according to the titles used in the *Appendix Concilii Lateranensis*; there is at least one example of that in each of the manuscripts. Apparently Johannes Faventinus was held in high favor, since occasionally glosses that elsewhere do not bear his siglum are attributed to him in these manuscripts. I would date the first layer of glosses in Arras, Bibl. mun. 27 (32) and 599 (507) rather earlier and would ascribe them to Northern France. Although the earlier Bolognese glosses predominate and glosses typical of the Gloss Compositions described immediately above can be found in one or both Arras manuscripts, these apparatus do not yet cite decretals.[122]

Although these manuscripts have not been closely examined, some adaptations of other *summae* that were probably written in Northern France or in England should be mentioned at this point. Durham V.III.3 contains on fol. 30–77 a *Summa* with the incipit 'De iure naturali', which is partly a paraphrase of Rufinus' *Summa*, although it contains glosses not in Rufinus and often refers to decretals of Alexander III—mostly, however, in the marginal glosses.[123] In the same manuscript, on fol. 78–93, there is an abbreviated version of Simon of Bisignano's *Summa*, with the incipit 'Lex erit omne quod ratione constiterit', which also has a few marginal glosses.[124] The *Summa 'Dubitatur a quibusdam'*, which likewise is an extract from Simon's *Summa*, could possibly have been written in a Northern French school, especially since it is preserved in Arras 271 (1064) on fol. 162r–177v, following the *Notae Atrebatenses* (see above).[125] It is difficult to fit the *Summa* fragment in London, B.L. Add. 34391, fol. 97,[126] into the French school, although it does show similarities in form to the *Summa Coloniensis*.

The *Summa 'Omnis qui iuste iudicat'* was discovered by Schulte in Leipzig, Universitätsbibl. 986 and named the *Summa Lipsiensis*. It was written by an Anglo-Norman author in Paris, not in Oxford.[127] It survives not only in that manuscript that bestows its name, but also in three partial copies, which are currently being used as the basis for the edition just re-

---

122. Weigand, *Glossen zum Dekret Gratians* 670–671, 677.
123. P. Legendre, 'Miscellanea Britannica', *Traditio* 25 (1959) 494, 496.
124. Ibid. 494.
125. Kuttner, *Repertorium* 154; Kuttner and Rathbone, 'Anglo-Norman Canonists', 314, n. 66.
126. Legendre, 'Miscellanea Britannica' 495.
127. Kuttner, *Repertorium* 196–198, 201–204; J.F. von Schulte, 'Die Summa Decreti Lipsiensis des Codex 986 der Leipziger Universitätsbibliothek', SB Vienna 68 (1871) 37–54. See now Landau, 'Rodoicus Modicipassus'. Now printed, *Summa 'Omnis qui juste iudicat' sive Lipsiensis*, ed. R. Weigand, P. Landau, and W. Kozur, adlaborantibus S. Häring, K. Kiethaner, and M. Petzolt. MIC, Series A: Corpus Glossatorum 7; Città del Vaticano 2007).

cently published.[128] The author took John Faventinus' *Summa* as his starting point, and that work is the source of nearly a third of the text. In addition, many of John's glosses are incorporated into the work as they appear in Paris, B.N. lat. 3888. The *Summa* of Simon of Bisignano furnished another Bolognese source for the *Summa*. From the French school only the *Summa 'Et est sciendum'* seems to have been used extensively. A list of jurists cited in the text can give a different impression of the *Summa*: John Faventinus tops the list with 85 citations, followed by Gandulphus with 71 and Cardinalis with 40, 13 of these in C.30 q.4 alone. Bernard of Pavia is cited 14 times in the text under the siglum 'b.', although this siglum is used in the glosses to the Leipzig manuscript to refer to another, probably Anglo-Norman, master. Rufinus is cited six times, Albertus and Stephen twice each, and Rolandus, Simon of Bisignano, Daifer, Gerard Pucelle (as Mag. G. Conventr. eps.) and the English Simon of Apulia once each.[129] Hugh of St. Victor, a theologian, is cited twice, while from among the Roman lawyers Bulgarus is named twice and Irnerius and Martinus once each. Several passages reveal a school relationship with the Anglo-Norman glosses cited above.[130]

Occasionally the author comments on added texts (paleae) in Gratian's *Decretum*, as for example when he cites the Codex *Si quemquam* (Cod. 1.3.30) from C.1 q.7, which, in fact, is actually to be found in the text of the *Decretum* after C.1 q.7 c.26 in Paris, B.N. lat. 3888, and also in a few other French manuscripts.[131] The decretals are still cited without a title, probably from the *Appendix Concilii Lateranensis*.[132] The date of composition is to be placed around 1186.

The *Summa 'In nomine'*, which is preserved in only a very fragmentary form in Oxford, Oriel College 53, fol. 356r–363v, is very closely related at the beginning of the work to the *Summa Lipsiensis*.[133] Only a more thorough analysis than has yet been carried out will establish whether this re-

---

128. Rouen, Bibl. mun. 743 (E.74) lacks C.3 q.7 pr.–C.6 q.3 c.4; Luxembourg, B.N. 144 provides commentary to C. 1, C.23–26 and *De consecratione* within a manuscript of Huguccio; Laon, Bibl. mun. 371bis contains C.12, C.23–26 and *De consecratione* instead of Honorius' *Summa*.

129. Simon of Apulia, chancellor of York from 1190 and later bishop of Exeter (1214–1223) probably wrote a *Summa* himself, as noted by Kuttner and Rathbone, 'Anglo-Norman Canonists' 306 and n. 14.

130. Weigand, 'Gandulphusglossen' 15–48 compares 16 passages from this *Summa* with other passages that mention this author.

131. Rambaud , 'Le "Corpus juris civilis",' 63, cites eight further French manuscripts in her index, among them the very old manuscript Paris, B.N. lat. 3884.

132. For this collection see Charles Duggan's essay in this volume.

133. Kuttner, *Repertorium* 199–204, with different foliation.

lationship to the *Lipsiensis* continues or whether its reliance on a Bolognese exemplar becomes even stronger later on in the text. The date of composition, as in the case of the *Summa Lipsiensis*, is about 1186–1187.[134]

The *Summa quaestionum* of Honorius was the most successful work of the Anglo-Norman school, and its style and organization had significant influence on later works.[135] Honorius came from Kent and in the years ca. 1185–1195 taught canon law, first in Northern France (perhaps Paris) and later on in Oxford. He was made archdeacon of Richmond but struggled for years in the courtroom to obtain the office. He won a decision in his favor in 1202, but in 1208 he was imprisoned because he was deeply in debt. He died between 1210 and 1213.[136]

Honorius divided the *Summa quaestionum* into three sections, which he calls *Distinctiones*. He deals first with questions of procedural law and related issues in a section entitled *De rescriptis*. In the next section, *De simonia*, he covers the law on consecration and ecclesiastical offices. The final section treats marriage and is called 'On natural law and on prohibitions'.[137] Honorius called his work *Quaestiones decretales*, and in it he deals with basic, practical questions, demonstrating independence of mind and exhibiting a talent for interpreting sources. He was capable of making very subtle points that he may well have adopted from French theologians and from Sicardus of Cremona. However, Bolognese canon lawyers are by far the most frequently named authorities: Gandulphus occurs 22 times, John Faventinus 11 times and Simon (of Bisignano) 8 times.[138] Honorius cited 106 different *Extravagantes*, mostly from Alexander III (there are eight references to JL 14110) as well as four to decretals of Pope Lucius III. Almost all of them are cited with titles from the *Appendix Concilii Lateranensis*, a work to which the *Summa Lipsiensis* had not referred. The date of compo-

---

134. The *Summa 'In nomine'* has additional material on natural law and more than the *Summa Lipsiensis* (Kuttner, *Repertorium* 203), suggesting a slightly later date of composition.

135. Kuttner, *Repertorium* 424; Kuttner and Rathbone, 'Anglo-Norman Canonists' 304–316, on Honorius' life.

136. *Magisteri Honorii Summa 'De iure canonico tractaturus'*, ed. Rudolf Weigand, Peter Landau, Waltraud Kozur, et al. (MIC, Series A, 5.1; Vatican City 2004) xiv–xxi. See also Waltraud Kozur and Karin Miethaner-Vent, 'Titel in der Quaestionen- und Dekretsumme des Magister Honorius: Neues zu Aufbau und abfassung der beiden Summen', *Proceedings Catania* 153–168.

137. For a detailed study of Honorius' teaching on marriage see Benno Grimm, 'Die Ehelehre des Magister Honorius', SG 24 (1989) 231–386, who offers an edition of the ten titles on marriage law from 5 manuscripts: Bamberg, Staatsbibl. Can.45, Douai, Bibl. mun. 640, Leipzig, Universitätsbibl. 984, Paris, B.N. lat. 14591 and Zwettl, Stiftsbibl. 162. Königsberg, Universitätsbibl. 21 has been lost since World War II; Laon 371bis contains only Part II, and on Munich, Staatsbibl. 16083 see below.

138. Information provided from the edition in preparation by W. Kozur, Würzburg, on whose work the following is based.

sition for the *Summa quaestionum* is ca. 1186, since Honorius repeated the same material on natural law that occurs in the *Summa Lipsiensis*.[139]

An idiosyncratic combination of twelve of the forty titles in Honorius' *Summa quaestionum* (some reworked), with 25 separate questions on excommunication and sacrilege taken from another master, are to be found in Munich, Staatsbibl. lat. 16083, fol. 52va–73va. These twelve titles are at the end of a group of single questions, following the order of the *Decretum*, on D.1–50 and *De consecratione* D.4.[140] The composition of this collection can have occurred only after 1190, since passages from the *Summa* of Huguccio are incorporated into the introductory question on natural law and since, in the subsequent section, *Compilatio prima* provides the basis for quotation from decretals.[141]

Honorius may be connected with the questions on marriage law written in Paris in the 1180s and preserved in Paris, B.N. lat.3934, fol. 102r–v and 103vb, but this has not yet been ascertained. Nor is it certain who is intended by the siglum Magister G. in these questions.[142] *Compilatio prima* forms a base for other *Summae quaestionum* in Avranches, Bibl. mun. 149, fol. 129–130v and in Vienna, Ö.N.B. 2163, fol. 52–74v, the latter perhaps written in about 1205–1206 in Bologna.

In this same period the *Summulae quaestionum* were written, preserved in Douai 649, the longest one of which is concerned principally with conditional marriage ceremonies and is certainly of French origin.[143]

Honorius wrote a *Summa* to the *Decretum* on a large scale, previously known as the *Summa 'De iure canonico tractaturus'*.[144] Since it bears what looks, especially at the beginning, like a very close relationship to the *Summa Lipsiensis*, scholars have undervalued its independence, which is in fact very great.[145] The text, as preserved in the only manuscript, Laon, Bibl. mun. 371 bis, fol. 83ra–170v, has several lacunae. The commentary recorded there for C.12, C.23–C.26, and *De consecratione* is taken over from the *Summa Lipsiensis*, even though Honorius commented on C.12 at least,

---

139. Weigand, *Naturrechtslehre* 196–203.
140. A thorough analysis by W. Kozur, 'Die Quaestionensumme des Honorius und die Summen im Clm 16083', *Proceedings Munich* 467–501.
141. Weigand, *Naturrechtslehre* 221–223.
142. Kuttner and Rathbone, 'Anglo-Norman Canonists' 315 and also for what follows.
143. Weigand, *Bedingte Eheschließung* 320–324.
144. Kuttner, *Repertorium* 198–199; identified partly through reference to his *Summa Quaestionum* by Rudolf Weigand, 'Bemerkungen über die Schriften und Lehren des Magister Honorius', *Proceedings Salamanca* 195–212, with references to earlier secondary literature. Now printed: *Magisteri Honorii Summa 'De iure canonico tractaturus'*.
145. Kuttner, *Repertorium* 201–203; Weigand, *Naturrechtslehre* 196–201.

and probably also on the other sections. Furthermore, the commentary to C.32 q.4 c.5–C.36 q.2 c.10 is lost, because some folios are missing.

Occasionally in his *Summa Decreti*, Honorius compressed the same argument, which can be found in his *Summa quaestionum* so tersely that the meaning emerges clearly only when both works are read together. Among the authorities cited, Gandulphus (cited 92 times), and Johannes Faventinus (75 times) are followed by Cardinalis with 40 references and Rolandus with 13, the latter exclusively at C.30 q.4. Albertus is cited four times and a certain B, not yet identified, twice. Among the theologians he refers to Cantor Parisiensis seven times and Magister Hugo 'in sententiis suis' once. The Roman lawyer cited most often is John Bassianus (mostly as Jo. Cre), from whom he probably also took over the 'regula Garnerii' on the subject of judicial confession.[146]

The decretals are cited from the *Appendix Concilii Lateranensis*, although a few of them might have been cited from a preliminary version of the Tanner *Collectio*.[147] The latest decretal cited is JL 16036 of Gregory VIII, dated 18 November 1187; at one point Honorius remarked that Gregory VIII and Clement III had permitted the pawning of ecclesiastical property.[148] This points to a date of composition of about 1188–1190. As in the case of the *Summa quaestionum*, the place of composition was probably Northern France, since examples are taken from the Paris area.[149] Honorius' *Summa* was known early on at Bologna too, as evidenced by a few glosses 'sec. hon.' in Munich, Staatsbibl. lat. 27337, and by the *Summa Reginensis* in Vat. Regin. lat. 1061, in which the text of this Bolognese *Summa* is completely replaced by Honorius' *Summa* at C.30.[150]

Richardus Anglicus, or Richardus de Mores, of Lincoln (1161–1242), is better known as a decretalist who wrote a number of works in Bologna during the last decade of the twelfth century.[151] However, he completed his study of canon law in Paris and probably began teaching there in the circle surrounding Honorius. At the age of 25, in 1186–1187, he wrote a *Summa quaestionum* with the incipit 'Circa ius naturale'. He divided the work into 37 titles and followed the topical organization of the *Decretum*.

---

146. K.W. Nörr, 'Zur Herkunft des Irnerius', ZRG Rom. Abt. 82 (1965) 327–329; in Munich, Staatsbibl. lat. 16083 also from Honorius, but with the unusual, and later, addition 'teotonici os aureum'.
147. See Charles Duggan's essay in this volume on the Tanner collection..
148. Weigand, 'Bemerkungen' 198–199.
149. *Magisteri Honorii Summa 'De iure canonico tractaturus'* xiv.
150. Honorius' text in the *Summa reginensis* was discovered by Knut W. Nörr, *Zum Stellung des Richters im gelehrten Prozeß der Frühzeit* (Munich 1967) 42, n. 27.
151. See Pennington's chapter 7 on the decretalists in this volume.

Richardus imitated Honorious in the way in which he handled the sources, although his style of argumentation is more often closer to the *Summa Lipsiensis* than to Honorius' *Summa quaestionum*.[152] He made intensive use of the questions in the *Summa* of Simon of Bisignano. In the years that followed, he was probably in Oxford participating in Vacarius' school before he wrote a larger number of works at Bologna during the years 1194–1198. Among these was a very short *Summa* on the *Decretum*,[153] in which he referred frequently to his *Distinctiones*, which were written at the same time and which circulated widely.[154]

Traces of English masters can be found in many apparatus of glosses preserved in the margins of manuscripts. This is particularly true of Master Ascelinus, who is cited in the third apparatus-like layer of glosses in London, B.L. Add. 34391, fol. 39–40, a *Decretum*-like fragment with several layers of glosses.[155] Like Magister Galt, cited in the same text, Ascelinus had probably been trained primarily in Roman law, as had Gui Francesc, whose glosses are found in London, B.L. Royal MS 11.B.xiv appended by the letter 'g.'. Gouron has demonstrated that 'g.' was a lawyer in Provence during the second half of the twelfth century.[156]

We can observe the teaching activity of various canonists in Oxford in the 1190s from the rich glosses of Cambridge, Gonville and Caius College MS 676.[157] John of Tynemouth seems to have been the leading scholar in this circle of jurists. Putting aside his teaching career, John became archdeacon of Oxford, a post that he held until his death in 1221. His lectures survive in the form of a *Reportatio*; in them he interpreted the sources confidently, discussed favorable and hostile views of other masters, cited masters from Bologna, and used contemporary case law to bring them up to date. In his writings (and those of his colleagues), John was sensitive to the opinions of earlier canonists and the historical evolution of canonistic

---

152. Kuttner and Rathbone, 'Anglo-Norman Canonists' 329–339 and 355–358; the work survives in Montecassino 396, 191–247 and Zwettl 162, fol. 145r–173ra.

153. Contained in London, B.L. Royal 11.A.ii, Reims, Bibl. mun. 86, fol. 1–5v and Olomouc, Statní Archiv C.O. 209.

154. Kuttner, *Repertorium*, 222–227; *Traditio* 11 (1955) 444; *Traditio* 12 (1956) 564. See also Stephan Kuttner, 'Ricardus Anglicus (Ricardus de Mores ou de Morins)', DDC 7 (1965 [1960]) 676–681.

155. Legendre, 'Miscellaneanea Britannica' 493, 495; he was a pupil of Vacarius' school, see Kuttner and Rathbone, 'Anglo-Norman Canonists' 333.

156. André Gouron, 'Qui était l'énigmatique maitre G.?' *Journal des savants* (Paris 1990) 269–289.

157. Kuttner and Rathbone, 'Anglo-Norman Canonists' 317–327 and 340f. is fundamental for this section and also on the teaching process; further discussion by Charles Duggan, 'The Reception of Canon Law in England in the Later Twelfth Century', *Proceedings Boston* 371–377, 388–390.

thought. For example, he cited John Faventinus and Gandulphus frequently on the problem of the validity of sacraments performed by simoniacs when he discussed the problem in C.1 q.1.[158] He cited Huguccio often, but his references to the opinions of Rolandus, Rufinus, Albertus, and Bazianus are less frequent.[159] Occasionally he referred to the views of Cardinalis. He included Cardinalis' glosses in his apparatus, with or without a siglum, though in the latter case, John never attributed the glosses to himself.[160] He mentioned contemporary French theologians several times. The Anglo-Norman canonists cited him as Jo. in their glosses to Anglo-Norman collections of canons. Examples can be found in the margins of the Leipzig manuscript of the *Appendix Concilii Lateranensis*.[161]

Simon of Southwell was the other important canonist of this group. He could pride himself on having previously taught in Bologna and Paris, where he had been able to convince Petrus of his point of view.[162] Simon was canon of Lincoln and later of Lichfield; the last mention of his name in the sources was in 1209. As yet it cannot be established whether he is the magister intended by the siglum S. in the glosses in Durham, Cathedral Library C.II.1.[163]

Nicholas de Aquila is mentioned only seldom. In later life he was dean of Chichester (ca. 1197–1217), elected bishop of Chichester in 1209, but not consecrated.[164] He is probably to be identified with the Magister Nicholaus frequently named in the *Quaestiones disputatae Londinenses* (written after 1196).[165]

John of Kent is named in both Durham C.II.1 and the *Quaestiones disputatae Londinenses*. He later became canon and chancellor of St Paul's

---

158. Weigand, 'Gandulphusglossen' 24–28, glosses 11, 13. 15–23, 26, 28, 30, 34, 44, 46, 50, 51, 53. Gandulphus can hardly have been responsible for all these utterances, since far fewer glosses are transmitted in Bolognese compositions, ibid., 30–31, nos. 9–19. Rather, the passages in question are often explained through his teachings ('sec. Gan.').

159. Listing of the various folios by Duggan, 'Reception' 374–375.

160. Weigand, *Glossen zum Dekret Gratians* compared only the Cardinalis text against the passages on marriage law being examined and discovered two mentions of Cardinalis (gloss 997, with the siglum Jo. ti., and gloss 1069) as well as ten out of forty of his glosses, including six with the siglum C.

161. Peter Landau, 'Studien zur Appendix und den Glossen in frühen systematischen Dekretalensammlungen', BMCL 9 (1979) 1–21, and 'Die Glossen zum Collectio Cheltenhamensis', BMCL 11 (1981) 9–27, especially 23–24.

162. Kuttner and Rathbone, 'Anglo-Norman Canonists' 326–327.

163. Weigand, *Glossen zum Dekret Gratians* 657–658 prints ten glosses to C.2, without finding clear criteria for attributing them.

164. Kuttner and Rathbone, 'Anglo-Norman Canonists' 317, 320, 327–328 for the following.

165. London, B.L. Royal 9 E vii, fol. 191–199; James A. Brundage, 'The Treatment of Marriage in the Quaestiones Londinenses', *Manuscripta* 19 (1975) 86–97.

Cathedral, London. He wrote a *Summa de penitentia* between 1212 and 1220.[166]

A Gregory (of London) is also mentioned in these glosses and in the *Quaestiones Londinenses*. He is possibly the author of the *Mirabilia Romae*.[167]

The *Summa* fragment *Quamvis leges seculares* in Paris, Ste-Geneviève 342, fol. 185r–187v treats only a few distinctions from Part One of the *Decretum*.[168] Tierney's analysis showed that although the prologue is based on the *Summa Lipsiensis*, the commentary was almost exclusively an extract from Huguccio's *Summa*. As a convenient summary of Huguccio's big work, it would have made it easier for jurists in England and Northern France to make their first acquaintance with the great decretist.[169]

The gloss composition in this same Paris *Decretum* manuscript (Ste-Geneviève 342) may come from the same circle or, more generally, from Northern France. Whatever its origins, its author based his work on the gloss *Apparatus 'Ordinaturus Magister'*, which in many places he cited almost verbatim. At other passages, however, for example at C.1, he incorporated only a few of its glosses. At the same time, it contains a substantial amount of material that is not derivative, and in this material the decretals are cited according to *Compilatio prima*.[170] In other passages, especially on the subject of marriage, several of Richardus Anglicus' *Distinctiones* are incorporated into the text, but some of these are substantially enlarged.[171] This evidence establishes that this composition can have been written no earlier than ca. 1200.

The *Summa 'Induent sancti'*, was first examined by Brian Tierney. It is sometimes known as the *Summa Duacensis* after the earliest manuscript to be discovered (Douai, Bibl. mun. 649, fol. 96r–140v).[172] Richard M. Fraher has an edition in press that is based on three manuscripts. According to Fraher, the date of composition falls between 1193 and 1195, since the author uses Alanus' gloss apparatus, published ca. 1192, in its first recension.

---

166. Joseph Goering, 'The Summa de penitentia of John of Kent', BMCL 18 (1988) 13–31. See also Chapter 12 in this volume.

167. Kuttner and Rathbone, 'Anglo-Norman Canonists' 320, 327–328.

168. Kuttner, *Repertorium*, 204–205; Brian Tierney, 'Two Anglo-Norman Summae', *Traditio* 15 (1959) 483–491.

169. Perhaps excerpts were made from Huguccio's *Summa* in an early stage when C.1, C.23–26, *de pen.* and *de cons.* were still lacking.

170. Of the 15 glosses to C.1 documented in Weigand, *Glossen zum Dekret Gratians*, nine are unique to this manuscript; of these glosses, 586 clearly is based on *Compilatio prima* and not on an Anglo-Norman collection, while five are identical with Comp. I and one (685b) shows a link to the Anglo-Norman Gloss Composition.

171. Weigand, *Glossen zum Dekret Gratians*, glosses 769 1337.

172. Tierney, 'Two Anglo-Norman *Summae*'; Kuttner found the manuscript in 1938: *Traditio* 13 (1957) 466.

Given the geographical range of the places mentioned in the text, the author must be from Northern France.[173]

The Hague manuscript of this work has additions that would suggest a theological orientation, e. g. the mention of Gilbert de la Porée and references to glosses on the Bible. In this manuscript work is ascribed to John of Noyon: 'Summa magistri Johannis Noviomensis'.[174] This John is certainly to be regarded as the author of both recensions of this *Summa*, and therefore the work of revision and expansion must have occurred between 1193 and 1198. At the beginning of the Luxembourg manuscript, in the margin, are twelve distinctions that have their origins in different Bolognese exemplars, e.g. the eighth distinction, concerning custom (also found in the Douai manuscript) is taken from the second recension of the *Apparatus 'Ordinaturus Magister'*. John of Noyon, while he was a canon of Saint Quentin and a papal judge-delegate, decided, with two others judges, a lawsuit between the deacon and the canons of Saint Quentin. He also defended Queen Ingeborg before the Synod of Soissons in 1201. After 1200, he appears repeatedly in the circle of Baldwin of Flanders, and accompanied him on the Fourth Crusade. While on crusade, John died in 1204 as the bishop-elect of Acre.

The *Summa 'Prima primi'* was copied after the text of the *Decretum* in London, B.L. Royal 11.D.ii, fol. 321ra–332ra.[175] This Anglo-Norman *Summa* is very much dependent on the extract from Huguccio, but the *Summa 'Quamvis leges'* and the *Summa 'Induent sancti'(Duacensis)* also provided much material to the author. These borrowings did not preclude the author from putting forward original and independent ideas, especially on natural law. In particular, the author rejected the multiple divisions of natural law favored by the Anglo-Norman school; he saw natural law as representing the original order of things before the Fall, an interpretation not found elsewhere.[176] This *Summa* was written after 1203, since its author cited two decretals of Innocent III from that year.

---

173. R.M. Fraher, 'Alanus Anglicus and the Summa *Induent sancti*', BMCL 8 (1976) 47–54; at 48, n. 6 refers to Luxembourg 135, fol. 174–206 and The Hague, Museum Meermanno-Westreenianum 10 B 33. This edition was announced as forthcoming in 1984 (though the number of pages was not stated) on the dust-jacket of *Proceedings Berkeley* and also in the *Proceedings San Diego*. Unfortunately, the edition remains in page proofs

174. P.C. Boeren, 'Un traité eucharistique inédit du XIIe siècle', *Archives d'histoire doctrinale et littéraire du moyen âge* 53 (1978) 181–204, sketches the contents of the manuscript at 182–184: it contains the theological *Summa* of Prepositinus (fol. 1–98v) our *Summa* is contained on fol. 99–159v and on fol. 160–197, the *Abbreviatio* of the Sentences of Peter of Poitiers, attributed to the same Master John.

175. Kuttner, *Repertorium*, 205–206; Tierney, 'Two Anglo-Norman *Summae*' 483–491.

176. Weigand, *Naturrechtslehre* 214–215. The author makes consistent use of this theory in his commentary to D.8 c.1 (fol.321rb) and even portrays canon law with respect to private

Around the year 1200 the study of canon law attained some importance in the diocese of Passau. Eilbert of Bremen wrote an effusive dedication in his *Ordo Iudiciarius* to Bishop Wolfger of Passau (1191–1204). In this work, which survives only in Vienna, Ö.N.B. 2221, fol. 39r–45r, he converts most of the Hildesheim *Rhetorica ecclesiastica* into verse, presumably for his teaching of canon law at the Passau cathedral school.[177] There is no way of telling whether Eilbert had glossed the *Decretum* during his time in Bremen. However, there is some likelihood that he was responsible for the sporadic second layer of glosses in Bremen, Universitätsbibl. a.142.[178]

Bishop Wolfger's attempts to expand the jurisdiction of church courts and to establish the study of law in Passau can also be seen in a decretal that he requested, *Ad nostram audientiam*, that declared that elements of customary procedure were not to be employed when rendering a sentence in ecclesiastical courts.[179] Wolfger's efforts become especially clear in the above-mentioned manuscript Vienna 2221, which was probably intended as an endowment copy for the school that his brother Sigehard, provost of the collegiate church of St. Pölten, established at St. Pölten. This manuscript also contains, in addition to Eilbert's *Ordo*, the oldest *Ordo iudiciarius*, an abbreviation of the *Decretum*, and also the *Medulla matrimonii* of Altmann of St. Florian, who is supposed to have taught at Passau or St. Florian in the first decades of the thirteenth century.[180]

Altmann received his education in the cathedral school at Freising under Rahewin (†1170–1177). He learned the skill of writing verses at Freising, a genre in which he composed several of his writings on the *Decretum*. These, like his other poetic works, can be recognized by the acrostic 'Altman' in the initial letters of the first six lines. He composed three works of canon law in verse. The first was the *Medulla matrimonii* (ca. 1200) in 686 hexameters, found at the end of a copy of Huguccio's *Summa*. In 1204

---

property as an offshoot of imperial law: 'et sublato iure imperatorum sublatum est ius canonicum'.

177. On Eilbert, Winfried Stelzer, 'Eilbert von Passau: Ein sächsischer Kanonist im Umkreis Bischof Wolfgers von Passau', AKKR 27 (1976) 60–69; the verse *Ordo* was edited by Ludwig Wahrmund, *Quellen zur Geschichte des römisch-kanonischen Prozesses im Mittelalter* (Innsbruck 1906) 1.5.

178. On this manuscript see Weigand, *Glossen zum Dekret Gratians* 695–698, which prints the glosses from this layer up to D.13.

179. Po. 604, 3 Comp. 1.3.2 (X 1.4.3); see Othmar Hageneder, *Die geistliche Gerichtsbarkeit in Ober- und Niederösterreich* (Graz-Vienna-Cologne 1967) 15–16, notes 45–48 and K. Pennington, 'Due Process, Community, and the Prince in the Evolution of the Ordo iudiciarius', RDIC 9 (1998) 16–17.

180. Described by Winfried Stelzer, 'Zur Pflege des gelehrten Rechts in der Diözese Passau um 1200', *Codices Manuscripti* 1 (1975) 77–83; on what follows, Stelzer, *Gelehrtes Recht* 70–120.

he wrote an *Ordo iudiciarius* and finally a *Ysagoge iuris* between 1210 and 1220, a work of more than 5,000 hexameters that incorporated material from his previous works and in which he paid constant attention to new law, for example the Constitutions of the Fourth Lateran Council. The manuscript presently known as St. Florian XI.720 is supposed to have been his own personal copy. He undoubtedly owned the *Decretum* manuscript St. Florian, Stiftsbibl. III.5, from which he borrowed several glosses for his exemplar of the *Ysagoge*. The glosses in the second layer of glosses in this manuscript, with quotations from *Compilatio prima*, could have been his own, since a few titles occur in his *Ysagoge* that seem to derive from this source.[181] Altmann died in 1222 or 1223.

The gloss apparatus *Ecce vicit leo*, from the French school and written in the period soon after 1200, was first analyzed and made known by Kuttner in 1937, on the basis of seven manuscripts, some of which were incomplete.[182] Since then, seven or possibly eight additional manuscripts, again some incomplete, have been discovered.[183] This diffusion of manuscripts establishes this apparatus as among the most successful works of the French school.

The manuscripts most often used by scholars, St. Florian XI.605 and Paris, B.N. nouv. acq. lat. 1576, probably represent two different recensions, since in the Paris manuscript additional decretals are occasionally cited or an additional explanation is given.[184] The first recension was probably written as early as ca. 1200, since no decretals dated 1200 or later are cited.[185]

---

181. Stelzer, *Gelehrtes Recht*, especially 117–118.

182. Kuttner, *Repertorium* 59–66.

183. Płock, Diocesan Seminary 64 (Vetulani, SG 1.264–266, the manuscript was lost in World War II); Florence, Bibl. Med. Laurenziana Gadd. reliq. 2 (Kuttner, 'Bernardus Compostellanus' 288, n. 50); Salamanca, Bibl. univ. 2491 (formerly Madrid, Palacio II.15, Gérard Fransen, 'Manuscrits canoniques (1140–1234) conservés en Espagne', RHE 48 (1953) 226–227); Madrid, Universidad Central, Bibl. de la Facultad de Derecho, vo. 1137, Obra 449 Est. 16 Tabla 1 Classif. 348.17, second layer of glosses and erasures (Weigand, *Glossen zum Dekret Gratians* 831–832, with references to Garcia); Hamburg, Staats- und Universitätsbibliothek, cod. jur. 2231 (M. Bertram, 'Some Additions to the Repertorium der Kanonistik', BMCL 4 [1974] 11–12); Leningrad, Pub. Bibl. II mbr.10 (C.1); Vatican, Borgh. lat. 272 (C.23–26); Liège, Univ. 127 E contains parts of the work, *Traditio* 11 (1955) 444, 447 and 12 (1956) 563.

184. References in Müller *Anteil der Laien* 157, n.8; also Weigand, *Naturrechtslehre* 418 and n. 35; the two Spanish manuscripts that I collated for this passage on the whole agree with the Paris manuscript.

185. According to Müller's findings, the decretal *Dilecti* of February 7, 1200, which determined the law on episcopal elections, is not in St. Florian, Stiftsbibl. XI 605, but only in Paris, B.N. lat. 1576 (Müller, *Anteil der Laien* 157, n. 8 and 161, n. 26). Zeliauskas, *De excommunicatione* prints in his Appendix XL, pp. 157*–164* four different decretals of Innocent III from St. Florian and Laon, Bibl. mun. 371bis, the latest of which is Potthast 700, dated 16 May 1199 (later X 5.39.29).

Since Kuttner found a decretal from 1202 in Paris, B.N. nouv. acq. lat. 1576 cited in an allegation, the second recension was perhaps written soon after that year. As Kuttner pointed out, French provenance for this work is clear from references to French theologians and place names.[186]

The gloss apparatus *Animal est substantia*, originally known as the *Summa Bambergensis*, is incomplete in all four manuscripts in which it occurs.[187] In Bamberg, Staatsbibl. Can. 42, fol. 29–119 it ends at C.24 q.3 c.6, and has other lacunae.[188] In Liège, Bibl. univer. 127.E, where the apparatus occurs as the only layer of glosses to the *Decretum*, certain leaves and quires are missing.[189] Another commentary (Alanus) is provided to *De consecratione* in this manuscript. In Luxembourg, B.N. 139 the texts of the commentary occur sporadically as the fourth layer of glosses, though occasionally another commentary is given instead, for example, from D.4 c.3 to D.16 c.1.[190] In Bernkastel Kues, Hospital 223 this apparatus occurs in sections as the second layer of glosses. Another commentary that shows some kinship with our apparatus and that which Stickler named the *Glossa Cusana* is added to *Animal est substantia*.[191] At several points the *Glossa Cusana* is more closely related to the apparatus *Ecce vicit leo* than to *Animal est substantia*.[192] It will only be possible to disentangle the network of relationships between these apparatus from the French school once they have been critically edited. *Animal est substantia* can be dated to between 1206 and 1210, since the last datable decretal cited is from the year 1206, and *Compilationes secunda* and *tertia* were not used. At first glance, it seems that several intermediate collections were used (Gilbert, Alanus, *Compila-*

186. This is proved also by the use of the decretal *Ad aures* of Alexander III to the archbishop of Canterbury, JL 14316 (Zeliauskas, *De excommunicatione* app. XL, no. 22, who was however, unable to verify it), which was not incorporated into Comp. I nor into the *Liber extra*, but which occurs in *Collectio Lipsiensis* 11.28, *Brugensis* 12.9, and Tanner 2.9.2.

187. Kuttner, *Repertorium* 206–205; Weigand, *Bedingte Eheschließung* 297, n. 34 lists the three other manuscripts and establishes the identity of the work as an apparatus from its transmission predominantly in gloss form.

188. In addition, C.1 also is lacking; on the other omissions (especially in C.2) and changes, see E.M. de Groot, *Doctrina de iure naturali et positivo humano in Summa Bambergensi (DD. 1–20)* (Druten 1970) 2, with the text of the first 20 distinctions printed pp. 1*–111*.

189. Described by Gérard Fransen, SG 1.298–300; the longest omission is from C.33 q.2 to de pen. D.2 c.45.

190. de Groot, *Doctrina de iure naturali* 4; also my description in Weigand, *Glossen zum Dekret Gratians* 820–822; C.15 q.3 p.c.4–C.18 q.1 c.1 are missing because of the loss of a quire.

191. For a precise summary of the apparatus *Animal est substantia*, see BMCL 1 (1971) 73–75. The treatment of marriage law, for example, is taken from this apparatus up to C.33 q.2. The *Glossa Cusana* is printed by de Groot, *Doctrina de iure naturali* 112*–119*. Weigand, *Naturrechtslehre* 249, 302–304, prints both texts in parallel.

192. According to Lenherr, *Exkommunikationsgewalt* 245, n. 115, the *Glossa Cusana* at C.24 q.1 c.35 is identical with the apparatus *Ecce vicit leo*. I found several important agreements with *Ecce vicit leo* at C.35 q.6 c.4 that were simply added on with repetitions of material.

tio Romana). The connections with France cannot be overlooked, nor can the author's sometimes excessive use of Roman law sources.

The gloss apparatus in the first layer of glosses in Douai, Bibl. mun. 592 is occasionally referred to as the *Glossa Duacensis*;[193] in its material and its handling of sources it shows kinship with the apparatus *Animal est substantia*. Unfortunately, part of this text (which was copied into the manuscript in the thirteenth century) was erased to make room for the *Glossa ordinaria*. This apparatus, like the preceding one, was composed between 1205 (or 1208) and 1210, since it contains decretals from the collection of Gilbert with *Compilatio secunda*, together with others possibly from the collection of Bernardus Compostellus' *Collectio Romana*.[194]

A fragment of a gloss apparatus from the same period (before 1201) to C.13–C.15 is contained in Evreux 106, fol. 126–135v, in the same layer of glosses. Here Aristotle's Nicomachean Ethics is cited several times, suggesting, as do other pieces of evidence, a French provenance.[195]

Three further French masters of this period ought to be mentioned, if only superficially. The unknown magister whose students collected examples of his teachings in the *Quaestiones* in Douai, Bibl. mun. 649 possessed great pedagogic abilities and independence of mind; he gives lengthy and subtle discussions of the most varied legal problems with sophisticated legal argumentation.[196] From the decretals cited, these questions can be dated to the period between 1205 and 1210.

A Master Peter Peverellus, or Penerchus, whose name occurs as a canon in Paris from 1207 to 1213, composed the *Ordo iudiciarius 'Sapientium affectant omnes'* around this time.[197] He had studied civil law with Johannes Bassianus in Bologna and Placentinus in Montpellier. He died probably in 1214 as bishop-elect of Agde (he had been elected in 1213). His experience

---

193. Kuttner, *Repertorium* 37; Alfons M. Stickler, 'Die Glossa Duacensis zum Dekret Gratians', *Speculum iuris et ecclesiarum: Festschrift für Willibald M. Plöchl zum 60. Geburtstag* (Vienna 1967) 385–392.

194. The dating is based on the finding of Kuttner, *Repertorium* 36, that a quotation from the decretal *Pastoralis* (19.12.1204) was used; if, however, the collection of Bernard of Compostellanus was also used, then the work would have to be later than 1208, when this collection was compiled.

195. Ibid. 36–37; that date has not been noticed elsewhere, to the best of my knowledge.

196. Kuttner and Rathbone, 'Anglo-Norman Canonists' 315; Weigand, *Bedingte Eheschließung* 320–324.

197. This work occurs *inter alia* in Douai, Bibl. mun. 649, fol. 1–6v; on it see J.M. Carbasse, 'L'ordo iudiciorum "Sapientiam affectant omnes",' *Confluence des droits savants et de pratiques juridiques* (Actes du Colloque de Montpellier, 12–14 Dec. 1977; Milan 1979) 13–36, esp. 23–24. See also Fowler-Magerl *Ordo iudiciorum* 130–133 and Gero Dolezalek, *Repertorium manuscriptorum veterum Codicis Iustiniani* (Ius commune, Sonderhefte 23; Frankfurt 1985) 498, n. 43a.

in canon law was confirmed by his having been appointed papal judge-delegate twice by Innocent III. Furthermore, he was cited twice as 'Magister PP' at C.16 q.7 c.29 on the law of advowson, in the apparatus *Animal est substantia*.[198]

Around 1214 or just before, Benedict of Sawston, bishop of Rochester 1215–1226, gave lectures on law in Paris.[199] His views were also mentioned in the *Quaestiones* of Stephen Langton.

At the end of this chapter I think it is necessary to summarize the most important criteria used to assign the works and authors discussed above to the transmontane schools. The findings of earlier scholars, especially Johann Friedrich von Schulte, Franz Gillmann, and Stephan Kuttner, have provided a guide to establish the following characteristics:[200]

1. Although the weight of the evidence must be considered in each case, style, contents, and references all provide powerful arguments for attribution to a particular school. Thus, a frequent use of rhetorical elements, in particular theological questions (not dictated by the source being commented on), and summary treatments of particular questions, point on the whole to France, possibly to Paris, though the last point is also characteristic of the *Summa* of Simon of Bisignano from Bologna. It is pointless to measure citations quantitatively by author, since so many tend to come from the Bolognese school. If one relied on citations to transmontane jurists for identifying place of origin, the main works of the Anglo-Norman school would have to be re-attributed to Bologna. Rather, what we are seeing here is the 'historicizing' tendency of the Anglo-Norman school at its prime, applying large numbers of opinions from the authoritative jurists to disputed questions. The Bolognese John Faventinus and Gandulphus were in fact *the* authorities by whom the transmontane canonists measured themselves and their thought. By contrast, it is much more significant if a magister who can be attributed to a particular area or school in France or England (or the Rhineland) is cited, even if only occasionally. Also significant are references to Parisian theologians. A characteristic of the French school in the early thirteenth century is an almost excessive

---

198. Carbasse, 'L'ordo iudiciorum' 24, n. 38 and 27, n. 47. Peter Landau, *Ius patronatus* (Cologne and Vienna 1975) 166, n. 586, prints this quotation from Bamberg Can.42. It is missing from Liège 127 E through homoeoteleuton; C.16–C.17 are missing from the Luxembourg, B.N. manuscript because of loss of leaves, and in Bernkastel the other apparatus is given at this point.

199. Kuttner and Rathbone, 'Anglo-Norman Canonists' 289.

200. The listing of the three groups of arguments proceeds as in van de Wouw, *Notae Atrebatenses*, though I come to a different conclusion on the subject of these *Notae* through a qualitatively different weighting of the arguments.

use of Roman law in argumentation. Might this have been the reason why Honorius III forbade the study of civil law in Paris? Moreover, the way in which writers disagree with the opinions of the Bolognese, or the *Francigenae,* or others, can be a clear index, except where two opinions are simply being opposed to each other objectively. It can be very illuminating to consider the particular sources cited, for example, the use of Cresconius in the *Summa 'Antiquitate et tempore'*. Also, the presence of particular additions in Gratian's *Decretum* can be evidence of the French school.[201]

2. References to places are useful when they are not dependent on the source being interpreted. For example, a reference to France in C.1 q.3 c.4 is of no consequence, because the phrase used in the text is 'usus in Galliarum partibus'. When, however, there is mention of Paris or of Chartres or of a monastery near Paris, occuring in examples of legal cases or problems, this evidence is very significant, especially if Italian towns are referred to in similar cases in other *Summae*. Personal and place names in formularies can be important clues, though one must bear in mind that the names might easily have been altered by a copyist. The reporting of facts from certain geographical areas is equally significant. The personal circumstances of the author—for example, his place of study and the geographical area of his activity, as revealed in his works or in other sources, where they can be clearly allocated—can be very informative, as in the case of Gerard Pucelle. Furthermore, the area within which the manuscripts of a work circulated can be decisive. For example, the *Abbreviatio* '*Exceptiones ecclesiasticarum regularum*', although partly based on Rufinus' *Summa*, circulated in the German-speaking area.

3. The relationship to other works of a particular school is significant only if the texts in question are roughly contemporary with each other. For example, the enormous quantity of tacit appropriations from John Faventinus' *Summa* (Bologna) is not decisive for the provenance of the *Summa Lipsiensis*, whereas the similar texts on natural law among its six or seven different versions, with the other (almost) contemporary works of the Anglo-Norman schools, are crucial. Primarily, it is not a question of the quantity but of the type of connections and similarities. All these elements can only be evaluated as a whole at any one time, although a clear chronological order is not always possible. For this reason, and since the transmontane decretists cannot always be assigned to a single school (Gerard Pucelle taught in Paris, Cologne, and Oxford), this chapter has not been subdivided according to the schools but has adopted a chronological

---

[201]. Cf. Rudolf Weigand, 'Zusätzliche *Paleae* in fünf Dekrethandschriften', ZRG Kan. Abt. 78 (1992) 65–120.

approach through the description of individual authors and anonymous works.

When did transmontane writings on the *Decretum* end and why? As yet, this question can be answered only with hypotheses. However, it is an unquestionable fact that after 1210 no important decretistic work appeared north of the Alps for a long time. Possibly the great apparatus of Laurentius and Johannes Teutonicus in Bologna around 1215 were a cause. When Johannes Teutonicus' work was recognized as the *Glossa ordinaria*, Bologna finally achieved a monopoly that paralyzed other centers, at any rate as far as the academic study of canon law was concerned, although not, or not always, where it was a matter of lecturing or practical application. Furthermore, the study of decretals became ever more dominant, and after 1210 and especially after 1234, dominated academic activity. However, after 1210 not much more can be reported about the study of decretals north of the Alps either. The Bolognese or Northern Italian monopoly over canon law was to be an established fact for a long time to come.

7

The Decretalists 1190 to 1234

Kenneth Pennington

I. The Decretalists 1190–1210

Bernard of Pavia, also known as Bernardus Balbi, inaugurated the age of the decretalists, the name given by scholars to those jurists who concentrated on papal decretals in their teaching and writing. He had glossed Gratian's *Decretum* during the 1170s, beginning his career at Bologna in the age of the decretists. Like his teacher, Huguccio, Bernard followed a 'cursus honorum' that became a common pattern for jurists in the thirteenth century.[1] He studied and taught at Bologna, became provost of Pavia in 1187 and bishop of Faenza in 1191, where he succeeded Johannes Faventinus to the episcopal seat; then, in 1198, the canons of Pavia sent his name to Innocent III as their choice for the next bishop of Pavia (the technical term, as Innocent had elegantly explained to the canons, is 'they postulated him'). Innocent gave his permission to translate Bernard from Faenza to Pavia.[2] The pope continued a trend of canonists becoming bishops that

---

1. On whether Bernard studied with Huguccio, see Rudolf Weigand, *Die bedingte Eheschliessung im kanonischen Recht* (Munich 1963) 241, n. 2 and F. Cantelar, who believes that 'doctor meus Vg.' may refer to Hugh of St. Victor instead of Huguccio, 'Doctor meus Hugo: Huguccio de Pisa o Hugo de San Victor?' ZRG Kan. Abt. 55 (1969) 448–457.
2. K. Pennington, *Pope and Bishops: The Papal Monarchy in the Twelfth and Thirteenth Centuries* (The Middle Ages; Philadelphia 1984) 96–98.

had begun in the twelfth century. Bishops, cardinals, and popes who had been jurists became a commonplace in the thirteenth century.

Bernardus' glosses were preserved in the twelfth-century apparatus on the *Decretum*, the *Ordinaturus magister*, and Rudolf Weigand has demonstrated that his glosses form a significant part of the foundation of the *Ordinaturus*.[3] Through his glosses, and perhaps his school, he influenced the writing of Johannes Teutonicus' Ordinary Gloss in the early thirteenth century. But his importance for the development of canon law at the end of the thirteenth century is far greater than just his glosses on the *Decretum*.[4] He gave form and organizational principles to the study and teaching of papal decretals that remained standard in the schools for the rest of the Middle Ages. He compiled a collection of decretals and other texts that Gratian had excluded and called it a *Breviarium extravagantium*. Every later collection of papal decretals adopted the organizational pattern that Bernard had created for this collection. After the compilation of *Compilationes secunda* and *tertia* after ca. 1210, Bernard's *Breviarium* was cited as *Compilatio prima* by the canonists.

Bernard's *Breviarium* was a turning point for canonistic scholarship. Papal decretals had begun to occupy an ever more important position in canon law since the 1160s, but the canonists had not yet devised a way to deal with them. At first the canonists compiled small, unsystematic collections and often attached them as appendices to Gratian's *Decretum*. Gradually they made larger collections, but since they did not arrange them systematically, these collections were difficult to use or to consult, and impossible to teach.[5]

Bernard compiled his *Breviarium* between 1189 and 1190, while he was provost of Pavia. The new collection took the school at Bologna by storm. Although, like Gratian's *Decretum*, it was a private collection, the canonists immediately used it in their classes and wrote glosses on it. After Bernard became bishop of Faenza, he wrote a *Summa*, which he called a *Summula*, on the titles of the *Breviarium*.[6] His models were the 'summae' that the ci-

---

3. 'Frühe Glossen zu D.12 cc.1–6 des Dekrets Gratians', BMCL 5 (1975) 35–51 at 49. Weigand, 'Zur Handschriftenliste des Glossenapparats "Ordinaturus Magister",' BMCL 8 (1978) 41–47 at 45 and 'Bazianus und b.-Glossen zum Dekret Gratians', SG 20 (1976) 453–496 at 477ff. On the importance of the *Ordinaturus Magister* see Weigand's chapter 'The Development of the *Glossa ordinaria* to the *Decretum*', Chapter 3 above.

4. Gabriel Le Bras, 'Bernard de Pavie', DDC 2 (1937) 782–789.

5. See Duggan's chapter in this volume on unsystematic collections and my chapter on the systematic collections and, in particular, on *Compilatio prima*.

6. Bernardus Papiensis, *Summa decretalium*, ed. E.A.T. Laspeyres (Regensburg 1860; reprint Graz 1956) 1: 'Ego B., qui decretales et extravagantia compilavi, tunc praepositus Papiensis, nunc Faventinus episcopus licet indignus, super eodem opusculo summulam Christo duce aggredior elimare'.

vilians wrote on the *Codex* of Justinian, and with it he began a new literary genre, the 'summae titulorum'. His purpose was to write a textbook for beginning students, in which the terms, definitions, and categories of each title were discussed. Like his *Breviarium*, his *Summa* was an immediate success, as attested by the large number of manuscripts that have survived.[7]

The first title of his *Summa* was 'De constitutionibus' (Of constitutions). Bernardus began his commentary by defining a 'constitutio':[8]

> First we must see what a constitution is, who can promulgate it, for which reasons it may be established, what is the <legislator's> office, what may a <new> constitution prejudice . . . A constitution is a human law (ius) redacted in writing . . . The emperor may promulgate a constitution in temporal affairs, and a city may establish a municipal law. In ecclesiastical matters the pope, a general synod, a patriarchal synod, and a metropolitan synod may promulgate a constitution. Constitutions are promulgated to coerce wrongdoers and to define new questions of law.

Bernard introduced students to canon law in his *Summa* and fully incorporated Roman law into his text. It was preeminently useful. Later jurists excerpted and summarized it.[9]

His *Summa* served as an introduction to Bernard's blueprint for a new system of canon law. He also wrote a set of glosses to his *Breviarium* that might have been a coherent apparatus. We cannot determine exactly whether Bernard's glosses ever circulated as a self-standing apparatus. All the manuscripts in which his glosses are preserved have 'mixed glosses', that is, his glosses are mixed with those of other canonists. A number of manuscripts preserve all or a part of his apparatus.[10] As one would expect of an early apparatus to a new collection, Bernard's glosses contained 'concordances to individual titles, cross-references, "notabilia" and "argumenta", occasionally also "solutiones contrariorum" and "solutiones generalium".'[11] We do not yet know exactly when he wrote these glosses; we

---

7. Kuttner, *Repertorium* 387–389, with corrections in *Gratian and the Schools*, 'Retractationes' 16. Martin Bertram added another manuscript, Alba Iulia, Bibl. Batthyanyana 166 ('Some Additions to the "Repertorium der Kanonistik",' BMCL 4 (1974) 10.

8. *Summa*, ed. Laspeyres, 2–3.

9. E.g. Lilienfeld, Stiftsbibl. 220 (Rudolf Weigand, 'Neue Mitteilungen aus Handschriften', BMCL 21 [1965] 490–91), the *Summa 'Vtilitati sociorum meorum'* in Gniezno, Bibl. Kapit. 50, fol. 75r–108v and Trier, Stadtbibl. 922/909, fol. 61r–90v, *Summa Bruxellensis*, Brussels, Bibl. Royal 1407–1409, fol. 1r–90r (Kuttner, *Repertorium* 390–391).

10. Kuttner lists manuscripts in his *Repertorium* 323, and added additional manuscripts in 'Bernardus Compostellanus' 312, n. 19 and 'Retractationes' 17. Stickler thinks that a manuscript (uncatalogued) of the Sitten (Sion), Archiv des Domkapitels, may be the full apparatus of Bernard.

11. Kuttner, 'Bernardus Compostellanus' 312.

may assume that Bishop Bernard remained an active and productive jurist.

Bernard also wrote short monographic treatments of marriage and elections in the canonical tradition. Marriage law continued to preoccupy the canonists of the late twelfth century. Bernard wrote a *Summa de matrimonio* that Laspeyres edited along with Bernard's *Summa decretalium*; later Kunstmann improved upon Laspeyres' edition.[12] Bernard adopted an epistolary form and addressed the work to a certain 'noble and dear lord, G.' whom Kunstmann identified as William, the bishop of Ravenna (1190–1201). His identification must be wrong because, as Kuttner has shown, Bernard wrote the work between 1173 and 1179.[13] The text is divided into rubrics, and Bernard carefully treated the impediments to marriage and confirmed the consensual nature of marriage that had just recently been adopted during the pontificate of Pope Alexander III.[14]

Although marriage was a central concern of canon law, election and the electoral process also preoccupied the canonists during the course of the twelfth century. Electoral theory governing papal, episcopal, and capitular elections rapidly became more complicated and sophisticated. Bernard was the first to write a monographic treatment of the subject.[15] He finished his tract between July 1177 and March 1179, just before the Third Lateran Council (1179).[16] There he set forth the general principles governing an ecclesiastical election and then, in the manner of a 'summa quaestionum', posed a series of questions that he answered. At the end he wrote a short *Ordo electionis*, that is, general procedures to be followed when holding an election.

Bernard wrote 'notabilia' or, as he called them, 'argumenta', that Kuttner discovered in a Melk manuscript[17] and a *Casus decretalium* that Laspeyres has partially edited.[18] The rubric of the Frankfurt manuscript

12. *Summa decretalium*, ed. Laspeyres 287–306. Kunstmann, AKKR 6 (1861) 217–262.

13. Additional manuscripts are listed by Kuttner, 'Bernardus Compostellanus' 295, n. 25 and 'Retractationes' 15.

14. See in particular, Charles J. Reid, Jr. *Power over the Body, Equality in the Family: Rights and Domestic Relations in Medieval Canon Law* (Emory University Studies in Law and Religion; Grand Rapids, Michigan–Cambridge 2004) with a detailed bibliography of earlier work. Charles Donahue, Jr. 'The Policy of Alexander the Third's Consent Theory of Marriage', *Proceedings Toronto* 251–281 is still a good introduction.

15. Robert L. Benson, *The Bishop-Elect: A Study in Medieval Ecclesiastical Office* (Princeton: 1968) 99–101.

16. Edited by Laspeyres, *Summa decretalium* 307–323. On the date see Peter Landau, 'Zum Ursprung des "ius ad rem" in der Kanonistik', *Proceedings Strasbourg* 89, n. 35. Kuttner noted two additional manuscripts, 'Retractiones' 15, *Gratian and the Schools*.

17. Melk, Stiftsbibl. 333 (190), fol. 252v–254v.

18. Laspeyres, *Summa decretalium* 327–352. Kuttner notes three new manuscripts: 'Bernardus Compostellanus' 299, n. 41 (also cancelling the Novara manuscript reported in the *Repertorium*) and 'Retractationes' 16, in *Gratian and the Schools*.

informs us that he finished this last work after he had become the bishop of the town of his birth, Pavia, in 1198.[19] Bernard worked on all aspects of canon law. He glossed Gratian, organized papal decretals into a coherent body of material, wrote on the central institutions of the Church, elections and marriage, and composed a *Casus decretalium*, a summary of the contents of each decretal, that helped to guide students, judges, and jurists through the thickets of the new papal jurisprudence. Almost single-handedly, Bernard transformed the discipline.

Pope Celestine III (1191–1198) had the reputation in Bolognese circles of not being learned in law, but during his pontificate the Bolognese jurists intensively cultivated their fields.[20] Bernard's *Breviarium* (*Compilatio prima*, the 'First Compilation') became a centerpiece of their writing and teaching. Richardus Anglicus, an English canonist (de Mores), wrote an important commentary on the *Breviarium* ca. 1198.[21] His apparatus is complete, although the manuscripts mix his apparatus with the glosses of others.[22] Richardus included many glosses of Bernard of Pavia in his apparatus, although exact attribution can be very difficult to prove.[23] He also copied passages from Bernard's *Summa decretalium*. The other canonists whom he cites are difficult to identify. They are signaled by one- or two-letter abbreviations (sigla) that do not provide many clues. Richardus copied a number of glosses of 'Si.' into his apparatus; we do not know for certain who this master is, although historians have proposed various jurists.[24] Lefebvre has noted that Richardus cited Roman law much more frequently than either Huguccio or Bernard of Pavia did, but he has also indicated that Richardus' use of Roman law was uneven in his other works.[25] His attitude toward Roman law may have been influenced by the Roman law jurist Johannes Bassianus.

Richardus must have been one of the first canonists to use Bernard's

---

19. Noted by Laspeyres, *Summa decretalium* 327: 'Casus decretalium a B'ernardo Pap. epi.'

20. Pennington, *Pope and Bishops* 11.

21. Franz Gillmann, 'Richardus Anglikus als Glossator der Compilatio Ier.' AKKR 107 (1927) 575–655. Stephan Kuttner, 'Richardus Anglicus (Richard de Mores ou de Morins)', DDC 7 (1960 [1965]) 680–681. Kuttner and Eleanor Rathbone, 'Anglo-Norman Canonists of the Twelfth Century: An Introductory Study', *Traditio* 7 (1949–1951) 279–358 at 327–339; printed texts 353–355, reprinted in *Gratian and the Schools*.

22. Richardus's manuscripts are listed in Kuttner, *Repertorium* 324–325; *Traditio* 12 (1956) 560–561; Kuttner, *Gratian and the Schools*, 'Retractationes' 17.

23. Charles Lefebvre, 'Les gloses à la "Compilatio prima" et les problèmes qu'elles soulèvent', *Proceedings Boston* 63–70 at 66–67 and 'Les gloses à la "Compilatio prima" du ms. Pal. lat. 652 de la Bibl. Vaticane', SG 20 (1976) 135–156.

24. Lefebvre, 'Les gloses à "Compilatio prima",' *Proceedings Boston* 68–69.

25. Ibid. 69.

Breviarium in the classroom at Bologna. Certainly his apparatus was one of the earliest. He is also one of the first signs of the 'internationalization' of Bologna. In the five decades on both sides of the year 1200, the canonists at Bologna were transformed into a group with pan-European origins. The canonists of the mid-twelfth century had been almost entirely Italian. Now, Englishmen, Germans, Hungarians, Frenchmen, and Spaniards studied and taught at the 'Alma mater studiorum'. Richardus taught at Bologna from ca. 1191 to ca. 1202. He returned to England, becoming a canon in the Priory of Merton and soon afterwards prior of Dunstable.[26] During that relatively short period of time he produced a remarkable variety of work besides his apparatus to *Compilatio prima*. He gave valuable bibliographical information in the Prologue of his *Distinctiones:*[27]

> Lest anyone places not much worth on the present work, let him know that I have compiled 'argumenta per ordinem decretalium' to the very last chapter, 'solutiones generalium' in a 'Commentum' of the decretals, have written an useful, necessary 'Summa de ordine iudiciario' and brought together 'Continentia distinctionum et Continuationes causarum et Solutiones questionum et Series paragraforum'.

As Kuttner has observed, the exact meaning of each item in this catalogue of works is not absolutely certain.[28] In addition to his apparatus to Bernard's *Breviarium*, Richardus wrote (1) *Ordo iudiciarius*, (2) *Summa quaestionum*, (3) *Summa brevis* on the *Decretum*, (4) *Distinctiones*, (5) *Argumenta* or *Notabilia decretorum*, (6) *Casus decretalium*, (7) *Generalia* or *Brocarda*.

Fowler-Magerl believes that Richardus wrote his *Ordo iudiciarius* before he arrived in Bologna, probably in England or Paris. He cited decretals from an unknown collection that was divided into books and not titles, probably from a collection that was similar to the 'Bamberg Group', an Anglo-Norman collection. Although the manuscripts of his *Ordo iudiciarius* have not been thoroughly studied, it seems that Richardus revised it after he arrived in Bologna and changed his allegations to the decretals by attempting to bring them into conformity with the *Breviarium*.[29] He arranged it as an 'Ordo of titles' after the pattern established by Johannes Bassianus. Later Tancred noted that Richardus had cited both Roman and canon laws in his *Ordo*. Richardus was also aware that his use of Roman law was unusual and mentioned that no one should calumny his

---

26. Kuttner, 'Ricardus Anglicus' 677 and the dissertation of Giulio Silano, 'The "Distinctiones Decretorum" of Richardus Anglicus: An Edition' (Ph.D. Dissertation, Toronto 1981) 4–5.
27. Printed by Kuttner, *Repertorium* 224 and Silano, 'Distinctiones' 88–89.
28. Kuttner, *Repertorium* 224–225.
29. E.g. Vercelli, Bibl. cap. 176, 1r–13r.

text because he used it.³⁰ He must have been a man of affairs as well as an academic. Later in his career, after his return to England and while he was Prior of Dunstable, the pope and the king of England appointed him judge-delegate in a number of important cases.³¹ Jane Sayers has found forty-eight cases in which he was an officer of the court.³² His early interest in procedure seems to have stood him in good stead during a long career that ended only with his death in 1242.

Richardus did not mention another work of his pre-Bolognese period in the introduction to his *Distinctiones*: the *Summa quaestionum*. It is preserved in two manuscripts.³³ The structure of the *Summa* roughly follows that of the *Decretum*. The work is a systematic discussion of canonical doctrine.³⁴ Richardus wrote it ca. 1186, probably in Paris. The *Summa* is closely related to the Anglo-Norman school, especially the *Summa Omni qui iuste iudicat*, also called *Summa Lipsiensis*, and the *Summa quaestionum* of Honorius. Kuttner thinks that Richardus consciously suppressed the *Summa* in the *Prologus distinctionum*.³⁵

The *Summa brevis* was a summary of the *Decretum* that Richardus wrote between 1196 and 1198. Kuttner and Rathbone studied the text and edited a small part of it.³⁶ Richardus used verse as a mnemonic and heuristic device. He referred frequently to his *Distinctiones*. Kuttner has pointed out that although the *Summa* was a work of modest proportions, its author's pride in it was not insubstantial.³⁷

Richardus' *Distinctiones decretorum* was his most significant work. It was well received; there are nineteen manuscripts.³⁸ It is, as nearly as we can tell, almost contemporary with the *Summa brevis*. However, Kuttner noted that although Richardus mentioned the *Summa brevis*, the *Generalia*, and the *Apparatus decretorum* in the *Prologus Distinctionum*, Richardus referred to the *Distinctiones* in all three works. Consequently, the chronology of Richardus' writings presents us with difficulties. Four of the manuscripts

---

30. Linda Fowler-Magerl, *Ordo iudiciorum vel ordo iudiciarius: Begriff und Literaturgattung* (Ius commune, Sonderhefte 19; Frankfurt am Main 1984) 114–119, with a list of manuscripts.

31. Kuttner, 'Ricardus Anglicus' 677. Jane Sayers has discussed his judicial acitivity and printed a calendar of his cases in *Papal Judges Delegate in the Province of Canterbury 1198–1254: A Study in Ecclesiastical Jurisdiction and Administration* (Oxford Historical Monographs; Oxford 1971) 114–118 and 296–301.

32. Sayers, *Papal Judges Delegate* 114.

33. Monte Cassino, Bibl. del'Abbazia 396 and Zwettl, Stiftsbibl. 162. The Zwettl manuscript has interpolations that may or may not be Richardus's revisions.

34. Kuttner and Rathbone printed excerpts of it in 'Anglo-Norman canonists' 355–358.

35. Kuttner, 'Ricardus Anglicus' 678.   36. 'Anglo-Norman canonists' 353–355.

37. 'Ricardus Anglicus' 678–679.

38. *Traditio* 11 (1955) 445; 12 (1956) 564; 13 (1957) 469; 15 (1959) 499. Giulio Silano edited the *Distinctiones* in his Toronto dissertation (note 26 above).

do not have the *Prologus*, and Richardus may have published this version of the *Distinctiones* first.[39] They were very influential on the *Glossa Palatina*.

Richardus mentioned a work in the *Prologus distinctionum* called 'argumenta per ordinem decretalium'. This work has never been found, but Kuttner thinks that at least part of it may be preserved in a Zwettl manuscript.[40]

Bernard of Pavia's *Breviarium* was undoubtedly the most significant contribution to canon law in the late twelfth century, and Richardus wrote a *Casus decretalium* for it in which he provided each decretal with a resumé.[41] It is the first 'casus' written for a collection of decretals. The purpose of the work was to offer students and practicing lawyers a guide to his collection. Laspeyres published excerpts of it in his edition of his *Summa decretalium*, comparing it to Bernard of Pavia's *Casus decretalium*.[42] Bernard himself used Richardus' *Casus* when he composed his own *Casus decretalium*.

Richardus also wrote an important apparatus on Bernard's *Breviarium*. He seems to have composed it over the long period of time that he was teaching at Bologna. It was one of the most important early commentaries on Bernard's collection, and Richardus' glosses are found in all later commentaries. He combined his works by incorporating his collection of *Generalia* or *Brocarda* into his *Apparatus decretalium* to the *Breviarium*, which he also published separately. One manuscript contains both versions of the text.[43] The order of the *Brocarda* followed the *Breviarium*.[44] His work had lasting fame; Johannes Andreae still thought Richardus' *Generalia* deserved mention in the fourteenth century.[45]

Petrus Hispanus first arrived in Bologna during the pontificate of Pope Alexander III. Like so many other canonists he spent some time at the Roman curia.[46] He wrote glosses to Gratian's *Decretum* and later glossed Ber-

---

39. Douai, Bibl. mun. 649, London, B.L. 10.C.iii, Oxford. Bodl. Selden supr. 87, Trier, Stadtbibl. 922.

40. 'Ricardus Anglicus' 679, Zwettl, Stiftsbibl. 70r–72v.

41. Three manuscripts of the work exist, see Kuttner, *Repertorium* 398. The Munich manuscript has the rubric in a contemporary hand: 'Casus magistri Ricardi'.

42. *Summa decretalium* 327–352.

43. Bruges, Bibl. publ. de la Ville 366, fol. 27va–40vc, 49ra–50va (first version), fol. 51ra–54vb (second version); see Kuttner, 'Retractationes' in *Gratian and the Schools* 41. Other manuscripts are listed in 'Retractiones', loc. cit., *Traditio* 11 (1955) 444, 13 (1957) 470, 16 (1960) 533 and 562–563.

44. Kuttner, 'Réflexions sur les brocards' 778–782.

45. Johannes Andreae to *Speculum* of Guilielmus Durandus, 2.2. De presumpt. § Presumptio est arg., cited by Kuttner, 'Réflexions dur les brocards' 779, n. 48.

46. Gero Dolezalek, 'Another fragment of the Apparatus "Militant siquidem patro-

nard of Pavia's *Breviarium*.⁴⁷ His apparatus, detached from the text of the decretals, is found in one manuscript, while other glosses are scattered in the layers of glosses covering the margins of many manuscripts.⁴⁸

Another Englishman, Alanus Anglicus, followed Richardus Anglicus to Bologna and began teaching there during the pontificate of Celestine III. His first work was a commentary on the *Decretum* that he completed about 1192, in the shadow of Huguccio's great *Summa*.⁴⁹ Although he referred to Bernard's *Breviarium,* he often cited decretals with just their beginning words and did not attribute them to any collection. We may conclude from this piece of evidence that he probably began working on his apparatus in the late 1180s. As was common in juristic texts, a dating clause that Alanus included, May 5, 1192, permits us to know for certain at what time he wrote his commentary on C.2 q.8.⁵⁰ He continued to work on the text and published a second edition of his commentary. He cited Pope Innocent III's important decretal *Pastoralis*, which was issued in 1205. This is the last datable reference in his apparatus.⁵¹ He referred to the opinions of Melendus, Johannes Bassianus, Laurentius Hispanus—in the first recension—and Huguccio in his text. It is not yet clear whether he commented on the entire *Decretum*. The apparatus to *De consecratione* that circulated with four other works in the manuscripts is also found attached to Huguccio's *Summa*, the 'Ordinaturus Magister', and other gloss compositions. Consequently it is very doubtful whether we may assign this part of the text to Alanus.⁵²

---

ni",' BMCL 5 (1975) 131, Troyes, Bibl. mun. 385, fol. 72ra: 'Magister P. Hyspanus dicit quod numquam fuit decretalis, et dicebat se audisse dominum papam eam reprobantem'. See also Anne Lefebvre-Teillard, '"D'oltralpe": Observations sur l'apparat *Militant siquidem patroni*', *Amicitiae pignus: Studi in ricordo di Adriano Cavanna*, ed. Antonio Padoa Schioppa, Gigliola di Renzo Villata, and Gian Paolo Massetto (Milan: Giuffrè Editore, 2003) 2.1311–1335.

47. Antonio García y García, 'La canonística ibérica (1150–1250) en la investigación reciente', BMCL 11 (1971) 66, 'La canonística ibérica medieval posterior al Decreto de Graciano', *Repertorio de historia de las ciencias eclesiásticas en España* (Salamanca 1967) 1.408, n. 29.

48. Kuttner, *Repertorium* 324, Würzburg, Univ.-Bibl. Mp.th. fol. 122, fol. 17r–26v. For a list of manuscripts containing 'P.' glosses, *Repertorium* 12.

49. Kuttner, 'Bernardus Compostellanus' 289 first attributed the anonymous apparatus 'Ius naturale' to Alanus. Stickler dated the first recension to ca. 1192; see Alfons M. Stickler, 'Alanus Anglicus als Verteidiger des monarchischen Papsttums', *Salesianum* 21 (1959) 371–72. Peter Landau dated Alanus's second recension to ca. 1205; see Kuttner, 'Retractationes' in *Gratian and the Schools* 13. Manuscripts are listed in Stickler's article, 348–349. Also SG 12 (1967) 129, n. 56.

50. Kuttner, *Repertorium* 68–69.

51. Kuttner, *Traditio* 22 (1966) 476.

52. Gérard Fransen, 'Un commentaire au "De consecratione",' *Traditio* 13 (1957) 508–509; Kuttner, 'Retractationes' in *Gratian and the Schools* 13. Consequently, three of the manuscripts listed by Stickler, 'Alanus Anglicus' 348–349, contain only the commentary on 'De consecratione' and should not be included: Seo de Urgel, Bibl. capit. 8, Tarazona, Bibl. de

Having two recensions of Alanus' apparatus on the *Decretum*, scholars have been able to distinguish, as they rarely can, between earlier and later stages of his thought. Stickler has described the first recension of his gloss as a modest work of Alanus' youth in which he presented the arguments of others, only rarely offering an authoritative opinion of his own: it was a 'compendium of current opinion'.[53] In his second recension, he put forward his own views without hesitation. Stickler has given us a concrete example of the development of Alanus' thought in his study of Alanus' theories of church and state. In his first recension, Alanus recorded the 'dualistic' views of Rufinus, Simon of Bisignano, and Huguccio and was content to repeat their ideas without adding much of his own. As Stickler puts it: 'Alanus seems to support uncompromising dualism in the first recension of his apparatus on the *Decretum*.'[54] In the second recension he changed his stripes from dualist to hierocrat.

Sometime before 1210, but after 1201, Alanus finished an apparatus to Bernard of Pavia's *Breviarium*.[55] He incorporated the glosses of Richardus Anglicus and others. His apparatus exercised considerable influence on later glossators. The text of his apparatus is, however, often mixed with other apparatus in the manuscripts, and his glosses can be difficult to disentangle from other layers of glosses. Alanus compiled a *Collectio decretalium* and wrote an apparatus of glosses to his second recension of the compilation.[56] These glosses circulated widely in the schools.[57] Two of Alanus' students, Albertus and Johannes Galensis, borrowed from Alanus' glosses on his own collection for their apparatus on *Compilatio secunda* and *Compilatio tertia* respectively.

We cannot always assign authorship to the apparatus of glossators who worked in the schools before the appearance of *Compilationes secun-*

---

la Catedral 151, and Madrid, Bibl. nac. 251. Alanus' prologue to his apparatus on the *Decretum* circulated as an independent work, Kuttner, loc. cit. For further information about the manuscripts of 'Expleto', see Elisabeth Vodola, 'Legal Precision in the Decretist Period: A Note on the Development of the Glosses on "De consecratione" with Reference to the Meaning of "cautio sufficiens",' BMCL 6 (1976) 60–61, n. 19.

53. Stickler, 'Alanus Anglicus' 375.

54. 'Alanus Anglicus' 389.

55. Kuttner, *Repertorium* 325–326. Erlangen, Univ.-Bibl. 349, that contains Alanus' apparatus in its first layer of glosses, is discussed by Rudolf Weigand, 'Mitteilungen aus Handschriften', *Traditio* 16 (1960) 558–560. A manuscript in Salzburg, Stiftsbibl. St. Peter, a.ix.18, fol. 2r–117v (also mixed with material of Richardus) can also now be included; see Stephan Kuttner, 'The Collection of Alanus: A Concordance of its Two Recensions', *Rivista di storia del diritto* 26 (1953) 38.

56. On Alanus' collection see Chapter 9 on the systematic decretal collections in this volume.

57. Kuttner, 'Collection of Alanus' 51–52, prints a selection of texts from Vercelli, Bibl. capit. LXXXIX.

da et tertia ca. 1210–1211. An apparatus to the *Breviarium* that begins 'Militant siquidem patroni' provides an example of the difficulties.[58] There is some evidence from the manuscripts that the apparatus is from a transmontane canonist. Two other anonymous works, 'In quibusdam libris' and 'Quia breuitas est amica audientie', are from the 'school' of Petrus Brito, an English canonist, whose glosses and opinions are cited frequently in Northern European texts.[59] Weigand and Kuttner have identified a number of anonymous apparatus in which Brito is mentioned, and one may refer to them as a group.[60] The Northern decretalists who are known to us primarily from scattered glosses and quaestiones adapted the text of *Compilatio prima* to their needs and glossed at least some of the texts that they added to Bernard's *Breviarium*.[61] Another English canonist, Gilbertus Anglicus, compiled a collection of decretals in the early years of the thirteenth century. Like Alanus, he also composed an apparatus for his own canonical collection.[62] Albertus and Tancred borrowed from his apparatus when they wrote on *Compilatio secunda*.

The last major figure who taught canon law at Bologna during the first decade of the thirteenth century was Bernardus Compostellanus, sometimes referred to as 'antiquus' to distinguish him from his later namesake of the mid-thirteenth century. Stephan Kuttner devoted a magisterial ar-

58. Gero Dolezalek, 'Another fragment of the Apparatus 'Militant siquidem patroni', BMCL 5 (1975) 130–132; Dolezalek lists all known manuscripts p. 131, n. 3. See also Lefebvre-Teillard, 'D'Oltrape' 1311–1319.

59. Rudolf Weigand, 'Neue Mitteilungen aus Handschriften', *Traditio* 21 (1965) 480–491 and 'Glossenapparat zur Compilatio prima aus der Schule des Petrus Brito in St. Omer 107', *Traditio* 449–457; Franz Gillmann, 'Petrus Brito und Martinus Zamorensis Glossatoren der Compilatio I', AKKR 120 (1940) 60–64. See also Anne Lefebvre-Teillard, 'Petrus Brito... Sur quelques aspects de l'enseignement du droit canonique à Paris au début du XIII siècle', RHD 79 (2001) 153–177 and 'Un curieux temoin de l'école de Petrus Brito: Le manuscrit Paris, Bibliothèque Nationale latin 9632', BMCL 26 (2004–2006) 125–152.

60. Weigand, 'Schule des Petrus Brito' 456, Kuttner, 'Bernardus Compostellanus' 317. The manuscripts are Lilienfeld, Stiftsbibl. 220, 'Quia breuitas'; Paris, B.N. 15398, 'In quibusdam libris'; Paris, B.N. 9632; Brussels, Bibl. royale 1407–1409; London, Lambeth Palace 105, Erlangen, Univ.-Bibl. 349, and St. Omer, Bibl. mun. 107. Weigand prints the prologue and extensive extracts from 'Quia breuitas' in 'Neue Mitteilungen' 485–491.

61. These additions have been studied by Gérard Fransen (see Chapter 9, below, on the systematic decretal collections). Weigand prints a long gloss from St. Omer 107 to one of the additional decretals, 1 Comp. 1.27.4 bis: 'Schule des Petrus Brito' 452. Fransen also mentioned that some of the additional decretals were glossed, 'La tradition manuscrite de la "Compilatio prima",' *Proceedings Boston* 58–59; Kuttner and Rathbone, 'Anglo-Norman canonists' remains the best introduction to the world of the northern European canonists. For further information about Petrus Brito, see Kuttner's 'Retractationes' in *Gratian and the Schools* 18–19.

62. On Gilbertus' collection see Chapter 9 on the systematic decretal collections. On his glosses, Kuttner, *Repertorium* 313, 'Collection of Alanus' 37–38, and Rudolf von Heckel, 'Die Dekretalensammlungen des Gilbertus und Alanus nach den Weingartner Handschriften', ZRG Kan. Abt. 29 (1940) 116–357.

ticle to Bernardus in 1943 in which he thoroughly described Bernardus' literary activity.[63] The reputation of this Spanish canonist was rapidly eclipsed in the Middle Ages, and, until Kuttner resurrected him, modern historians knew very little about him. In large part, his fate was not due to his lack of talent or merit, but to the situation in Bologna during the years that he taught. The teaching of canon law must have been difficult in the years between ca. 1200 and 1210. The schools had accepted, if in the North with some modifications, Bernard of Pavia's *Breviarium* as a text that they taught and glossed with regularity. Together with Gratian's *Decretum*, Bernard's *Breviarium* became a standard school text. Bernard had included the decretals of Popes Alexander III, Lucius III, Urban III, Gregory VIII, and Clement III in his collection, but the massive flow of decretals from Rome had increased rather than abated since 1191. To a certain extent, the Northern canonists ameliorated the problem by modifying Bernard's *Breviarium* when they added decretals to the collection under appropriate titles.[64]

This practice created several problems. Adding decretals to an existing collection was cumbersome. Further, if the texts of the collections were to change constantly, the apparatus of the canonists would face almost immediate obsolescence. Gilbertus, Alanus, and Bernardus Compostellanus compiled collections that updated papal decretal legislation, but their fellow canonists did not accept their collections as they had Bernard of Pavia's. Each of the three canonists had glossed his own collection. However, other canonists did not give them the same attention. One may presume that all three introduced their collections into the classroom. The manuscripts indicate that the collections did circulate, and we have evidence that contemporary and even later canonists cited decretals from their collections.[65] In the early thirteenth century, teachers and students alike must have wondered which books they should teach, study, and gloss.

Bernardus Compostellanus' works illustrate these difficulties. He compiled his collection of decretals in 1208, but the schools did not accept it. He emulated Gilbertus and Alanus by writing an apparatus of glosses on his canonical collection but had no greater success than they in winning the acceptance of his colleagues in the schools. He wrote glosses on the *Decretum* and *Compilatio prima*, and Kuttner discovered a series of thirty-two 'quaes-

---

63. Kuttner updated the article in 1983 by reprinting it and adding 'Retractationes' in *Gratian and the Schools*.

64. Fransen, 'Tradition manuscrite' 59, notes that the last datable decretal that he had found in the northern manuscripts dated to 1193. He wondered why, since these manuscripts were still glossed in the first decade of the thirteenth century, the canonists did not continue to add decretals.

65. Kuttner, 'Bernardus Compostellanus' 318–319. In the first two books of his apparatus to *Compilatio tertia*, Johannes Teutonicus referred to Gilbertus's collection once.

tiones' that were preserved in Vienna and Zwettl manuscripts.⁶⁶ Since a number of the 'quaestiones' mentioned problems at Vicenza, Kuttner speculated that Bernardus might have moved to Vicenza when a school of law was established there between 1204 and 1209.⁶⁷ But, as he notes, this is only an attractive conjecture.⁶⁸

Rudolf Weigand discovered the complete apparatus of Bernardus on the *Decretum* in a Gniezno manuscript.⁶⁹ His glosses in the manuscripts have been confused with those of Bernard of Pavia, and his gloss is mixed with those of others in the Gniezno manuscript. Bernardus wrote this apparatus ca. 1205. At about the same time, he finished an apparatus on *Compilatio prima*. Johannes Andreae, who was deeply interested in the history of his discipline, mentioned glosses of Bernardus on *Compilatio prima* and *secunda*, but we have evidence for only the first.⁷⁰ As with his glosses on the *Decretum*, his apparatus on *Compilatio prima* is mixed with those of other canonists, and the various strata must be examined very carefully to distinguish one from the other.⁷¹ As the selection of glosses published by Kuttner demonstrate, Bernardus studied Roman law with Azo.⁷² He cited a range of canonistic opinions in his glosses, including some decretalists, like his Spanish countryman, Pelagius, whose works we have only in fragments. Pelagius had an adventurous career. He became cardinal bishop of Albano, and was appointed by Pope Honorius III as one of the leaders of the Fifth Crusade.⁷³ Kuttner has noted that the two leading canonists of the next generation, Johannes Teutonicus and Tancred, did not cite Bernardus as frequently as they did other canonists of his generation. This may be due to Bernardus' having been an outsider, but, if he did move to

---

66. Kuttner, 'Bernardus Compostellanus' 324–325: Vienna, Ö.N.B. 2163 and Zwettl, Stiftsbibl. 162. Gérard Fransen, 'Deux collections de questiones', *Traditio* 21 (1965) 492–501, partially edited the questions from the two manuscripts. See also García y García, 'La canonística ibérica' 55.

67. Savigny, *Geschichte* 3.307. Vicenza attracted scholars from England, Provence, and Germany.

68. Kuttner, 'Bernardus Compostellanus' 326–327.

69. Weigand, 'Neue Mitteilungen' 482–485: Gniezno (Gnesen), Bibl. Kapit. 28. Weigand prints several excerpts from Bernardus's apparatus, pp. 483–484.

70. Kuttner, 'Bernardus Compostellanus' 310–320 and 'Retractationes' to the same pages. Kuttner lists manuscripts that contain Bernardus's glosses, including Freiburg im Br., Univ. 361a, discovered by Gérard Fransen, which includes some glosses of Bernardus.

71. Modena, Bibl. Estense a.R.4.16, for example, contains four strata of glosses, of which the first contains Bernard of Pavia and the third Bernardus Compostellanus.

72. Kuttner, 'Bernardus Compostellanus' 314–319.

73. D. Mansilla, 'El cardenal hispano Pelayo Gaitán (1206–1230)', *Anthologica annua* 9 (1961) 417–473; García y García, 'Canonística iberica' 54–55; Kuttner, 'Bernardus Compostellanus' in 'Retractationes' 17. Some glosses to the *Decretum* are found in Vat. lat. 1367 and to *Compilatio prima* in Modena, Bibl. Estense a.R.4.16 (but note that Stickler has shown that the glosses signed just 'p.' are not Pelagius', but those of Petrus Hispanus).

Vicenza from ca. 1205 to 1210, his stay might have broken the continuity of his influence on the Bolognese canonists.

Kuttner has noted Bernardus' independence of thought, his affinity for his countrymen Melendus Hispanus and Pelagius, and the respect that other canonists had for his opinions.[74] Stickler has explored Bernardus' conception of the imperial office in his glosses to the *Decretum* and offered several examples of his sharp wit and unusual, almost eccentric, ideas.[75] Bernardus seems to have been the only Bolognese canonist who maintained that the Greek emperor, not the Western, was the true holder of imperial power. Bernardus' opinion may have been part of a 'Spanish' attitude toward the German emperor.

French canonists also taught at Bologna in the early thirteenth century. Willielmus Vasco or William of Gascony had a long career. His earliest glosses date to the period before 1210. Adam Vetulani discovered a manuscript of Vasco's apparatus to the *Decretum* in the library of the cathedral chapter at Poznan (Posen), but could not identify the author.[76] His work on the *Decretum* had been known only from the fragments preserved in two French manuscripts.[77] On the basis of this slender evidence Alfons Stickler wrote about Willielmus' political theory.[78] Later Stickler studied the Polish manuscript and recognized the correspondence between the French and Polish texts.[79] The manuscript contains Willielmus' apparatus from D.50 to the end of the *Decretum*. Another Polish *Decretum* manuscript also contains glosses that are probably those of Vasco. An introductory prologue to the *Decretum*, 'Missurus in mundum', has now been definitively attributed to Vasco.[80] In this work on the *Decretum*, he cited *Compilatio prima* but not 'tertia'. He may have glossed *Compilatio prima*. A Parisian manuscript contains a large number of glosses signed 'w.' to

---

74. 'Bernardus Compostellanus' 300–303 and 316–317.

75. Alfons M. Stickler, 'Der Kaiserbegriff des Bernardus Compostellanus Antiquus', SG 15 (1972) 103–124. See also Gaines Post, *Studies in Medieval Legal Thought: Public Law and the State 1100–1322* (Princeton: 1964) 482–493, for the opinions of another Spanish canonist who opposed German imperial pretentions.

76. 'Les manuscrits du Décret de Gratien et des oeuvres des Décrétistes dans les bibliothéques polonaises', SG 1 (1953) 217–288. Poznań (Posen), Archiwum Archidiecesjalne 28. Knut Wolfgang Nörr studied the manuscript in 'Summa Posnaniensis', *Traditio* 17 (1961) 543–544.

77. Grenoble, Bibl. mun. 62 and Beaune, Bibl. mun. 5. Kuttner described the Beaune manuscript in *Repertorium* 32–33. See also Kuttner, 'Another copy of Willielmus Vasco's Apparatus on Gratian', *Traditio* 22 (1966) 476–478.

78. 'Der Dekretist Willielmus Vasco und seine Anschauungen über das Verhältnis der beiden Gewalten', *Études Gabriel Le Bras* (Paris 1965) I 705–728.

79. 'Zum Apparat des Willielmus Vasco', BMCL 1 (1971) 76–78.

80. Pier Virginio Aimone Braida, 'Il proemio "Missurus in mundum",' BMCL 13 (1983) 27–38.

the first compilation.⁸¹ However, the attribution of authorship to certain canonists is very difficult. There may have been other 'w.'s active at Bologna during this time. Willielmus continued to teach at Bologna until 1222, when he transferred to Padua.⁸² Historians have assigned *Additiones* to Johannes Teutonicus' Ordinary Gloss to the *Decretum*⁸³ and glosses on Honorius III's *Super speculam* to him, but the evidence is speculative.⁸⁴ There is other manuscript evidence of Vasco's activity after 1210. An interesting gloss added to *Compilatio tertia* in the margin of a Graz manuscript reported that 'W. Gas.' stated Pope Innocent III had been asked to distinguish between a decretal letter in *Compilatio secunda* and one in *tertia*.⁸⁵ Other manuscripts in Admont, Graz, Cordoba, Modena, and Paris have additional layers of glosses signed by a certain 'w.' to *Compilatio prima, secunda, tertia*, and *quarta*.⁸⁶ If all of these glosses refer to Vasco, they bear evidence of a long, if not distinguished, career.

Another Iberian canonist who taught in Italy during the period prior to 1210 was Silvester (Silvestre Godinho).⁸⁷ One more 'episcopal canonist', Silvester came from Braga, later became an archdeacon, then dean, and finally archbishop of his native city. He probably left Italy ca. 1215. After studying at Bologna, he taught canon law there. We do not know if he wrote a full apparatus of glosses on any major work, but historians have discovered scattered glosses to the *Decretum*, *Compilationes prima* and *tertia*, and to Alanus' decretal collection. The only complete work of Silvester that we have is a small apparatus of glosses that he wrote to Pope Innocent III's decretal *Pastoralis*.⁸⁸ The pope had responded with lengthy

81. Paris, B.N. lat. 3932, see Kuttner, *Repertorium* 327.
82. Charles Lefebvre, 'Guillaume Guacus', DDC 5 (1953) 1075–1076.
83. Stephan Kuttner, 'Willielmus Vasco and the glosses on Gratian of MS Vatic. lat. 1367', in an appendix to 'Bernardus Compostellanus' 333–340. Rudolf Weigand informs me that Pommersfelden, Bibl. Schönborn 142 does not contain glosses of Vasco.
84. Kuttner drew attention to a charter of 1219 in which a certain 'magister Guillielmus de Guasconia' is a witness, *Repertorium* 453; The apparatus of glosses to *Super speculam* in Florence, Laur. Santa Croce V sin. 4 and Lisbon, Bibl. nat. Alcob. 381, fol. 224r–224v is not identical. The Santa Croce manuscript has a dozen glosses signed 'g.' or 'guill.'; the same glosses in the Lisbon manuscript are not signed. There are glosses in the Lisbon manuscript that are not in the Florentine.
85. Graz, Univ. Bibl. 374, fol. 263v.
86. Admont, Stiftsbibl. 22 and Cordoba, Bibl. del Cabildo, 10. On the Cordoba manuscript see García y García, 'Canonistica hispanica', *Traditio* 23 (1967) 505–506. Kuttner, 'Willielmus Vasco' 337, n. 42 for references to the other manuscripts.
87. A.D. Sousa Costa, *Mestre Silvestre e Mestre Vicente* (Braga 1963). García y García, 'Canonística ibérica' 56–57 and *Estudios sobre la canonística portuguesa medieval* (Fundación Universitaria Española, Monografías 29; Madrid 1976) 106–108 with the bibliography cited.
88. Stephan Kuttner, 'Glosses of Silvester on the decretal "Pastoralis",' *Traditio* 22 (1966) 474–476 and 'Bernardus Compostellanus' with 'Retractationes' 310. Kuttner notes that the

answers to a number of questions that the bishop of Ely had posed and sent his replies to Ely in 1204. The canonists immediately recognized *Pastoralis* as a rescript of exceptional importance. The entire letter circulated in Bologna, sometimes as an appendix to canonical collections. Alanus distributed it, section by section, among the various titles of his collection. Bernardus Compostellanus included it in his collection as well.[89] In spite of its inclusion into the two major collections of the period 1205–1210, Silvester glossed it as a separate work. This might have been because he recognized its importance, or because he was reluctant or unwilling to gloss the collections of Alanus and Bernardus, or, simply, because he glossed the decretal before Alanus had compiled his collection. In any case his glosses and their transmission provide an example of how important papal texts were received and circulated in the first decade of the thirteenth century.[90]

The Modena, Salzburg, and Vercelli manuscripts to which I have been referring are probably typical of the texts that the canonists used for establishing papal decretal law in the early thirteenth century.[91] Each contains a copy of *Compilatio prima* with mixed strata of glosses, each contains several collections of decretals that date to the period 1200 to ca. 1210, some of which are glossed.[92] From the supplementary, small collections of decretals that were added to these manuscripts from other collections to supplement Gilbertus, Alanus, and Bernardus, one may conclude that these collections were used for some time after they had been superseded by new collections.

The appearance of *Compilatio tertia*, quickly followed by *Compilatio secunda*, dramatically changed the 'ad hoc' situation of collecting and teaching decretals. Pope Innocent III authenticated Petrus Beneventanus' collection, *Compilatio tertia*, and a papal imprimatur help to assure its success. Johannes Galensis (John of Wales) compiled *Compilatio secunda* a short time later, and, although unaided by papal approval, his collection became, within a very short time, a 'received text' in the law schools. The success of these collections was probably due as much to timing as to the

---

manuscripts of the apparatus in Modena, Bibl. Estense a.R.4.16 and Zwettl, 162 contain slightly different versions of Silvester's text and may represent two recensions.

89. See Kenneth Pennington, 'The making of a decretal collection: The genesis of Compilatio tertia', *Proceedings Salamanca* 90–92.

90. *Pastoralis* was not a singular example. *Super speculam* also was glossed as a separate text before it was included in *Compilatio quinta*; see Stephan Kuttner, 'Papst Honorius III. und das Studium des Zivilrechts', *Festschrift für Martin Wolff*, ed. E. von Caemmerer et al. (Tübingen 1952) 80–81 and his comments in 'Glosses of Silvester' 476.

91. Modena, Bibl. Estense a.R.4.16, Vercelli, Bibl. capit. LXXXIX, and Salzburg, St. Peter's, a.ix.18.

92. Kuttner described all three manuscripts: Modena: 'Bernardus Compostellanus' 310–312; Vercelli: 'Collectio of Alanus' 37; Salzburg: 'Collectio of Alanus' 37–38.

canonists' editorial skills. The schools needed certainty and these collections provided it.[93]

II. The Decretalists from 1210 to 1234

The law school of Bologna reached a high point in its history from ca. 1210 to 1225. Although it would remain Europe's premier law school until the sixteenth century, every important canonist taught there in the early thirteenth century. There were no competitors. During this period the school was remarkably international. The teachers in Bologna at this time came from the four corners of Latin Christian Europe. During this period the canonists of the north almost completely cease writing commentaries, and the indications of their acitivities are scant.[94] They no longer commented on Gratian, they did not gloss the new compilations of papal decretals. The Bolognese canonists glossed the two new compilations, as well as Bernard's *Breviarium*. Their world was self-contained and their horizons limited. They referred only to their own works and the works of others who taught at Bologna. A new style of writing glosses also developed. The canonist would copy the gloss of another canonist and include it in his own apparatus, appending a siglum identifying the canonist who had written it. Canonists sometimes 'edited' these glosses, but by and large they faithfully repeated their comments. Consequently their apparatus pullulate with the sigla of other jurists. Tancred brought this methodology to maturity when he composed the Ordinary Glosses for the first three compilations. In his apparatus, his own comments seem to be submerged in the tide of glosses from other canonists.

A new group of canonists who had been students during the first decade of the century reached maturity and during the second decade produced a remarkable body of work. They witnessed a transformation of canon law. In their student days most had studied Roman law intensively and almost all sat at the feet of the greatest Romanist of the time, Azo. The 'romanization' had been underway for almost fifty years, but they applied Roman jurisprudences more completely and comprehensively than earlier generations had done. They continued to gloss and teach Gratian's *Decretum*, but papal decretal legislation was now firmly established by the *Compilationes antiquae*, as they would be later called: the first, second, and third compilations. The great and the not so great threw themselves into

---

93. On these collections, see Chapter 9, below, on systematic decretal collections.
94. They did re-edit *Compilatio tertia*, see K. Pennington, 'The French recension of Compilatio tertia', BMCL 5 (1975) 53–71, reprinted with additional information in *Popes, Canonists, and Texts 1150–1550* (Collected Studies Series 412; Aldershot 1993).

writing apparatus on this collections: The great were Laurentius Hispanus, Vincentius Hispanus, Johannes Teutonicus, and Tancred; the not so great, Albertus, Johannes Galensis, Damasus Hungarus, Jacobus de Albenga, Zoën, and Raymond of Peñafort. Many lesser figures are also known from very fragmentary sources and scattered glosses in the margins of manuscripts: Johannes Garsias Hispanus, Martinus Zamorensis, Phillip of Aquileia, Marcoaldus, Petrus Hispanus Portugalensis, and Ambrosius.

Laurentius Hispanus was one of the earliest and most creative of this group. His thought is marked by intellectual vigor and leavened with humor. He studied at Bologna in the first decade of the thirteenth century, heard Azo's lectures on Roman law, and taught from ca. 1205 to 1214. After leaving Bologna, he became 'magister scholarum' of Orense in 1214. The cathedral chapter elected him bishop in 1218.[95] He remained bishop of Orense until his death in 1248.

Laurentius wrote glosses on Gratian's *Decretum* and the first three *Compilationes antiquae*. His siglum (l., lau., laur. his.) appears in the margins of many manuscripts and in the commentaries of later canonists, especially Johannes Teutonicus, Tancred, and Bernardus Parmensis. Until recently it was thought that he had never written a complete apparatus to the *Decretum*, or, if he had, that no copies of it still existed. Alfons Stickler has argued that a widely disseminated and influential commentary, known as the *Glossa Palatina* after the Vatican manuscript containing the text, was Laurentius'.[96] The *Glossa Palatina* does, without a doubt, contains much Laurentian material and may have been written and arranged by him.

Three French manuscripts contain a layer of glosses that are 'reportationes' of Laurentius' lectures on the *Decretum*.[97] But all three manuscripts, together with the *Glossa Palatina*, do not give a uniform textual basis of what Laurentius may or may not have said in his lectures or written in his apparatus. The readings in these manuscripts and in the *Palatina* rarely report exactly the same glosses. Consequently, the *Glossa Palatina* is probably the best guide to his thought, assuming that he did write a formal apparatus. The glosses attributed to Laurentius in *De poenitentia* of Gratian's *Decretum* present even greater textual problems. They are exasperatingly divergent.[98]

---

95. Antonio García y García, *Laurentius Hispanus: Datos biográficos y estudio crítico de sus obras* (Cuadernos del Instituto Jurídico Español, Delegación de Roma 6; Roma-Madrid 1956) and 'Canonística ibérica' 55–56.

96. Alfons M. Stickler, 'Il decretista Laurentius Hispanus', SG 9 (1966) 461–549. The manuscript was first discovered by Stephan Kuttner, who attributed it to Johannes Teutonicus.

97. Kuttner, 'Bernardus Compostellanus' 289 n. 56: Paris, B.N. lat. 15393, Paris, Bibl. Mazarine 1287, and Charleville, Bibl. mun. 269.

98. Kuttner, 'Bernardus Compostellanus' 289–290.

At least a part of the reason why the textual traditions of the early decretalists' glosses and apparatus present such intricate textual problems may be that the 'scriptoria' producing or 'publishing' these works were only beginning to establish formal procedures for copying them. A canonist's work may have circulated in several different forms, and the buyer may have wanted several different apparatus in the margins of his manuscript. The canonists themselves abetted this process by writing, relatively speaking, short apparatus.

Petrus Beneventanus' *Compilatio tertia*, a collection that contained only the decisions of Pope Innocent III, sparked intense interest among the canonists, and all the major figures in Bologna wrote apparatus on it. Johannes Galensis had composed individual glosses on *Compilationes secunda* (his own collection) but did not write an entire apparatus. We know his glosses to the *Secunda* primarily from their inclusion into the Ordinary Gloss of Tancred. Johannes was one of the earliest canonists, however, to gloss *Compilatio tertia*, and his apparatus on the *Tertia* is preserved in two manuscripts.[99]

Laurentius also wrote glosses on the first two compilations, but, like those of Johannes Galensis, his glosses are preserved only in the apparatus of others. Since no manuscript of apparatus to *Compilatio prima* and *secunda* has been found, he may not have written a formal apparatus of glosses to the collections. Students may have taken notes from his lectures and circulated them independently of an apparatus. He wrote one of the first apparatus on *Compilatio tertia*, and his work is charaterized by subtlety, wit, and insight. A small example of this can be seen from the opening gloss of his apparatus to *Compilatio tertia*. Quoting Paul's letter to the Romans (12:5), Pope Innocent III had written in the arenga of the decretal that we are one body with Christ and each person shares the limbs of another—a platitude.[100] Laurentius noted dryly on Innocent's metaphor: 'I cannot perceive how one man may be the limb of another'.[101]

Laurentius had a gift of placing old problems in new settings—or seeing paradoxes or difficulties in the proverbial. Perhaps prodded by the out-

---

99. Munich, Staatsbibl. 3879, fol. 150r–266v, originally contained only Johannes' gloss; later a scribe added Johannes Teutonicus' apparatus and erased much of Galensis to make way for the new text. At one point, the scribe replaced an entire quire, fol. 174r–181v, with the text of *Compilatio tertia* and Johannes Teutonicus' apparatus, thereby eliminating any traces of Galensis for that section.

100. 3 Comp. 1.1.1 (X 1.2.6): 'Cum omnes unum corpus simus in Christo, singuli autem alter alterius membra . . .'

101. Laurentius to loc. cit., Admont 55, fol. 101r: 'Hoc non aduerto quomodo unus homo sit membrum alterius'. Laurentius' apparatus was edited by Brendan McManus for his Syracuse University dissertation (1991).

pouring of judicial decisions and decretal legislation from Rome, he broke sharply with the traditional definitions of legislative power that the jurists held when he described the prince's authority to change law. In a gloss to Innocent III's decretal *Quanto personam* he adopted a truly revolutionary idea: the prince may make iniquitous law, for the prince's will is held to be reason. Germanic and earlier learned conceptions of law confused the content of law—that law must be just and reasonable—with the source of the law, the will of the prince. Before Laurentius, the jurists had accepted and propounded the idea that a law could not be valid unless it embodied reason. By separating the prince's will from reason, Laurentius located the source of legislative authority in the will of the prince and laid the intellectual groundwork for a new conception of authority in which the prince or the state might exercise power unreasonably, but legally. He can be said to have begun the voluntarist tradition in political thought.[102]

Although we can identify the authors of most of the apparatus on the *Compilationes antiquae*, one anonymous treatise, named by the first words of the text, *Servus appellatur*, has defied all attempts to link a jurist with it. Franz Gillmann concluded that it was Laurentius' apparatus.[103] Although some historians are still misled by Gillmann's thesis, it was definitively disproved when Knut Wolfgang Nörr identified Laurentius' apparatus to *Compilatio tertia* in Admont and Karlsruhe manuscripts.[104]

The most prolific of the canonists from this period was Vincentius Hispanus. He was born in what today is Portugal, studied law in the first decade of the thirteenth century, heard Roman law from Azo. He was appointed dean of the cathedral chapter at Lisbon in 1212, quite probably in absentia, and administrator of the diocese of Lisbon in 1217. A few years later in 1224 he became chancellor to Sancho II. In 1228 he was bishop-elect of Idanha-Guarda. He was finally confirmed bishop in 1235. He died while holding this office in 1248. Javier Ochoa Sanz has staunchly maintained that Vincentius was bishop of Saragossa and died in 1244.[105] Stephan Kuttner

---

102. On Laurentius' thought see Kenneth Pennington, *Pope and bishops* 17–19 and 'Law, Legislative Authority, and Theories of Government, 1150–1300', *The Cambridge History of Medieval Political Thought c. 350–c. 1450*, ed. J.H. Burns (Cambridge 1988) 427–429.

103. Gillmann, *Des Laurentius Hispanus Apparat zur Compilatio III.* (Mainz 1935 and reprinted in his *Gesammelte Schriften zur klassischen Kanonistik von Franz Gillmann*, 2–3: *Schriften zu den Dekretalisten*, ed. Rudolf Weigand, Forschungen zur Kirchenrechtswissenschaft, 5; Würzburg: 1993). Gillmann's claim was rebutted by Gaines Post, 'The so-called Laurentius-Apparatus to the decretals of Innocent III in Compilatio III', *The Jurist* 2 (1942) 5–31. Kuttner lists the manuscripts of *Servus appellatur* in 'Bernardus Compostellanus' 287–288, n. 46.

104. Nörr, 'Der Apparat des Laurentius zur Compilatio III.' *Traditio* 542–543.

105. Javier Ochoa Sanz, *Vincentius Hispanus: Canonista boloñés del siglo XIII* (Cuadernos del Instituto Jurídico Español 13; Roma-Madrid).

has pointed out, however, that a Bishop Vincentius, 'rector iuris canonici et glossator', was appointed to a commission at the Council of Lyons in 1245.[106] If this man was our canonist, Ochoa's contention that Bishop Vincentius of Saragossa was the Bolognese canonist cannot be right.[107]

Vincentius was a man of many parts. He served Iberian interests at the curia, lectured and wrote on canon law, and spent the second half of his life in the service of the church. While a bishop he wrote a major commentary on the Decretals of Gregory IX that circulated widely and was well known. He was the only canonist who bridged the *Compilationes antiquae* and the Gregorian Decretals by glossing both. During his stay in Bologna he composed an apparatus to *Compilatio prima* and *tertia* and a commentary, in two recensions, on the constitutions of the Fourth Lateran Council.[108] After Vincentius became bishop, he wrote a massive commentary on the *Gregoriana* that he rewrote at least once, and into which he incorporated much from his earlier apparatus. In the prologue of the work, he referred to himself as 'Vincentius episcoporum Hispanie minimus'.[109] Glosses on the *Decretum* and to *Compilatio secunda* are also to be found in the apparatus of other canonists.[110] He also wrote a partial casus for *Compilatio tertia* and a complete one for the *Gregoriana*.[111] García y García has recently edited a small commentary that he wrote on the *Arbor consanguinitatis et affinitatis*.[112] A Roman manuscript contains a short tract at-

---

106. Stephan Kuttner, 'Vincentius Hispanus', *Traditio* 17 (1961) 537–541 and 'Wo war Vincentius Hispanus Bischof?', *Traditio* 22 (1966) 471–474.

107. Ochoa turned his attention once again to the question in 'El glosador Vincentius Hispanus y titulos comunes "de foro competenti" canonico', *Miscellanea in onore dei Professori Anastasio Gutierrez e Pietro Tocanel* (Rome 1982) 429–488 at 444–466.

108. His commentary on *Compilatio prima* exists in only one manuscript: Leipzig, Univ.-Bibl. 983, with some individual glosses in Vendôme, Bibl. mun. 89, *Repertorium* 326–327. Manuscripts on *Compilatio tertia* are listed in *Repertorium* 356–357, with the list in *Traditio* 13 (1957) 467–468. Another manuscript was discovered by Martin Bertram in Paris, B.N. lat. 11714, fol. 54r–105v ('Some additions to the "Repertorium der Kanonistik",' BMCL 4 [1974] 14–15). Antonio García y García has edited Vincentius' apparatus to the Fourth Lateran constitutions and a casus to the constitutions that may be his: *Constitutiones Concilii quarti Lateranensis una cum Commentariis glossatorum* (MIC, Corpus Glossatorum 2; Città del Vaticano 1981) 273–284 and 461–475.

109. *Repertorium* 374, n. 2, Ochoa, *Vincentius Hispanus* 140–147 discusses the manuscripts, but denies the existence of two recensions. Kuttner, *Traditio* 17 (1961) 539–540.

110. Glosses to *Compilatio secunda* are found in the second stratum of Erlangen, Univ.-Bibl. 394 and the third stratum of Melk, Stiftsbibl.518; see Kuttner, *Traditio* 17 (1961) 538–539.

111. Bertram, 'Some additions' 11, adds one manuscript, Bruges, Bibl. pub. de la ville 366, fol. 9r–18v, to those of his casus to 3 Comp., and Kuttner lists manuscripts in *Traditio* 17 (1961) 539. See Kuttner, *Repertorium* 374, n. 2, for information about his casus on the Decretals of Gregory IX.

112. García y García, 'Glosas de Juan Teutónico, Vicente Hispano y Dámaso Húngaro a los Arbores Consanguinitatis et Affinitatis', ZRG Kan. Abt. 68 (1982) 153–185 at 175–183.

tributed to Vincentius on *De interdicto uti possidetis*.[113] The text is not preserved in another manuscript. García has also noted that the attribution is not certain.[114]

In a Vatican manuscript Vincentius' glosses are appended by the words 'bonus' and 'hilaris'.[115] This indication of his irenic character notwithstanding, he sometimes made sharp comments about his fellow jurists. He made particularly unseemly remarks about Johannes Teutonicus and Tancred.[116] In spite of his antipathy for them, Johannes and Tancred included a large number of his glosses into their works. He does not seem, for the most part, to have been a particularly innovative jurist. Studies of his work have not uncovered any significant contributions that he made to medieval jurisprudence.

Vincentius was a committed nationalist. Gaines Post has studied his comments on nationalities and nations.[117] He loved his 'noble Spain' and praised Spaniards because they acted with deeds, not like Frenchmen, who relied on words. He made his most extended comments on Spain when he glossed Innocent III's *Venerabilem*. 'In France, England, Germany and Constantinople, the Spanish are renowned because they rule over the Blessed Lady Spain'.[118] Post may have exaggerated the extent of Vincentius' nationalism, but the canonist did have a keen sense of his Spanish origins that is unusual for the early thirteenth century.

Damasus Hungarus was an important figure in Bologna during the pontificate of Innocent III and was already a 'magister Decreti' at the beginning of that pontificate. He wrote a variety of works, composing an apparatus for each of the first three *Compilationes* (although his apparatus to *Compilatio tertia* has never been found), an apparatus for the Fourth Lateran Constitutions, Brocarda on the *Decretum*, an apparatus on the *Arbor consanguinitatis*, and two summae on the decretals, one a short overview of the five books of the decretals, the other a summa on the titles.[119] His *Quaestiones* circulated widely.[120] Damasus seems to have left Bologna ca. 1217.

---

113. Richard M. Fraher, 'Tancred's "Summula de criminibus": A New Text and a Key to the Ordo iudiciarius', BMCL 9 (1979) 24; first noted by Kuttner, *Traditio* 17 (1961) 541.
114. García y García, 'Canonística Ibérica' 57–58 and *Estudios sobre la canonística portuguesa* 108–112.
115. Vatican, Borgh. lat. 264, fol. 5r, cited by Ochoa, *Vincentius Hispanus* 66.
116. Ochoa, *Vincentius Hispanus* 68–69.
117. Post, *Studies in Medieval Legal Thought* 482–493.
118. To use Post's rather free translation, ibid. 489.
119. On Damasus, see García y García's chapter below.
120. For more information about this work and their manuscripts, see Chapter 5 above, on the decretists.

Only one German made his mark in Bologna during the city's 'international phase'. Johannes Teutonicus rivaled Laurentius as a creative jurist, produced prolifically while he pursued his short teaching career (ca. 1210–1218), and wrote the most successful work of this period: the Ordinary Gloss to Gratian's *Decretum*. He was, nevertheless, much less successful than Laurentius, Vincentius, and other major jurists at gaining high ecclesiastical office. His personality may not have sparkled. His glosses have a sarcastic bite at times. In his original, introductory gloss to his commentary on *Compilatio tertia* he spoke scornfully of papal titles.[121] He also limited the authority of papal legates and generally opposed the centralization of authority within the church.[122] Not surprisingly, perhaps, Pope Innocent III did not approve his request to authenticate his new collection of decretals. A contemporary document recorded that he left the papal curia in anger because of his disappointment.[123]

Angry or not, Johannes, and the other Bolognese canonists, often took the road to Rome. Innocent III remarked to an English litigant that there was no shortage of lawyers in Rome; Johannes and his colleagues ensured that the curia was well served. Occasionally the canonists record a snippet from a curial case. Johannes wrote that he had heard Innocent III say, 'If I say that "I elect him if it will please the pope", it would be quite the same as saying "I will sleep with this man's wife if it will please him".'[124] One is left wondering whether Innocent's sharp tongue was directed at an argument that Johannes had proferred. If so, it is another piece of evidence that Johannes never did establish cordial relations with the pope. Nor did he ingratiate himself in other ecclesiastical circles. He died in 1245, after having been elected provost of the cathedral chapter of Halberstadt in 1241—a lowly post in the colonies. In one of his epitaphs he is called Semeca. However, on a plaque in Halberstadt, where he was probably born and was buried, he was not given that name but called only the 'lux decretorum'.[125]

---

121. Stephan Kuttner, 'Universal pope or servant of God's servants: The Canonists, Papal Titles, and Innocent III', *Revue de droit canonique* 32 (1981) 109–149.

122. K. Pennington, 'Johannes Teutonicus and Papal Legates', AHP 21 (1983) 183–194; see also my remarks about Johannes' ecclesiology in "Representation in Medieval Canon Law," *The Jurist* 64 (2004) 361–383.

123. Kuttner, 'Johannes Teutonicus' 633. Pennington, 'Genesis of Compilatio tertia' 76.

124. For the context of this remark see Pennington, 'Further Thoughts on Innocent III's Knowledge of Law', *Popes, Canonists and Texts, 1150–1550* (Collected Studies 412; Aldershot 1993) II p. 9.

125. Winfried Stelzer has written the best short account of his life: 'Johannes Teutonicus', *Die deutsche Literatur des Mittelalters: Verfasserlexikon* 4 (1982) 777–783. Photos of his tomb and epitaph can be viewed at http://faculty.cua.edu/pennington/JohTeuTomb3.htm

Johannes established his place in legal history with his gloss to the *Decretum*. In the revised version by Bartholomaeus Brixiensis, Johannes' Ordinary Gloss has made him one of the most important glossators of the early thirteenth century. Nonetheless, as a piece of legal writing, it is not as original or as coherent as his commentaries on the decretals. This may seem somewhat paradoxical since his gloss to the *Decretum* was read for centuries, while Tancred's commentaries on the decretals replaced his apparatus on *Compilatio tertia* in the early 1220s. The paradox is easily resolved. Writing a gloss on Gratian imposed limitations on Johannes. He had to explicate Gratian by pulling together the many strands of decretist thought and weaving them together to create a complete tapestry of church law. To achieve the brevity that an introduction demanded, Johannes surveyed and summarized earlier canonistic thought on a chapter, sometimes presenting a series of 'sic et non' allegations. When Bartholomaeus edited Johannes' gloss he wrote in his preface that 'sometimes I have given solutions that Johannes omitted'. All the printed editions of the Ordinary Gloss contain Bartholomaeus' revision, and it cannot be relied upon for an accurate report of Johannes' thought. The printed text does not distinguish clearly between Johannes' gloss and Bartholomaeus' additions, and it sometimes leaves out parts of Johannes' apparatus.[126]

The end of Pope Innocent III's pontificate was a time of intense activity for Johannes. He wrote a commentary on the canons of the Fourth Lateran Council (1215) very soon after the Council ended.[127] A short time later, he compiled a new collection of Innocent's decretals into which he incorporated the new conciliar canons. Innocent refused to authenticate the collection, but Johannes immediately provided his collection with an apparatus.[128] Slowly, *Compilatio quarta* was accepted by the schools.[129] Johannes also wrote an apparatus on *Compilatio tertia* that was his most important sophisticated work.[130] He leaned heavily upon the earlier glossators of the collection—Johannes Galensis, Laurentius, and Vincentius—and included

126. Kuttner, *Repertorium* 93–99, *Traditio* 1 (1943) 292, n. 77, lists manuscripts; also see his 'Retractationes' in *Gratian and the Schools* 291, n. 77.

127. Edited by García y García, *Constitutiones Concilii quarti Laternaensis* 175–270.

128. The great sixteenth-century canonist, Antonio Agustín, edited and published Johannes' apparatus in 1576, *Antiquae collectiones decretalium* (Ilerdae 1576), reprinted Paris 1609 and 1621. The edition was reprinted in Agustín's *Opera omnia* (Lucca 1769) 4.610–692.

129. For the genesis of *Compilatio quarta*, see Chapter 9 on systematic decretal collections.

130. Edited by K. Pennington, *Johannis Teutonici Apparatus glossarum in Compilationem tertiam* (MIC, Series A, 3.1; Città del Vaticano 1981), books one and two. The last three books are transcribed from Admont, Stiftsbibl. 22, in Pennington's Cornell University Ph.D. dissertation, 1972, and a revised version can be found on the web at http://faculty.cua.edu/pennington

many of their glosses in his work. In comparison to his Ordinary Gloss, his apparatus to *Compilatio tertia* was a less far-ranging work, for the contents of a decretal collection did not inspire speculative or discursive thought as readily as the heterogeneous chapters of the *Decretum*. The decretals forced the canonists to concentrate on the cases. They had to explain the case and place the decision in a larger context. From the internal evidence of his commentaries, Johannes finished his apparatus on *Compilatio tertia* and *Compilatio quarta* at almost the same time as his gloss on the *Decretum*. But his work on the *Decretum* probably had a much longer period of gestation. He referred to his gloss on Gratian many times in his apparatus on *Compilatio tertia* but cited his apparatus on the *Compilationes* only twice in his gloss on the *Decretum*.[131] Johannes never cited decretals of Innocent's successor, Honorius III, in any of his works. Since a 'Magister Johannes' of Halberstadt appears in the *Regesta* of the archbishop of Magdeburg in 1218, Johannes must have left Bologna ca. 1217–1218.[132] He wrote a consilium while in Halberstadt, but unlike many of his contemporaries he did not continue writing after he left Bologna.

Johannes wrote a short commentary on the *Arbor consanguinitatis* that García y García has edited.[133] Two works have been attributed to him for which conclusive evidence of his authorship is lacking. The first is a series of glosses on Honorius III's constitution, *Super speculam*, which are preserved in manuscripts of Florence and Lisbon.[134] The glosses are signed 'jo.' but contain nothing in them that would permit us to connect them to Teutonicus. There was another 'jo.' who was writing and perhaps teaching in Bologna during the 1220s, and this canonist may have been the commentator whose glosses on *Super speculam* are preserved in the manuscripts.[135] There is a post-1234 work, contained in two complete manuscripts, on the titles of the decretals (*Tituli decretalium*) that is attributed to a certain Johannes Teutonicus in a colophon.[136] It is unlikely that this work was written by the Halberstadt Johannes.

In his Ordinary Gloss to the *Decretum* Johannes called his *Quaestiones*

---

131. C.9 q.1 c.7 s.v. *ordinandum* and C.15 q.3 c.3 s.v. *pupillis*.
132. Stelzer, 'Johannes Teutonicus' 777.
133. García y García, 'Glosas de Juan Teutónico, Vicente Hispano y Dánaso Húngaro a los Arbores Consanguinitatis et Affinitatis' 161–175.
134. Florence, Laur. Santa Croce V sin. 4 and Lisbon, Bibl. nat. Alcob. 381, fol. 224r–224v.
135. Stelzer, 'Johannes Teutonicus' 781. The glosses of this second Johannes can be found in several manuscripts: Padua, Bibl. Ant. II.35, fol. 113v; Cordoba, Bibl. del Cabildo, 10, fol. 197v; Graz, Bibl.-Univ. 106, fol. 264v, 268r; Admont, Stiftsbibl. 22, fol. 205r, fol. 256r, fol. 260v; Graz, Univ.-Bibl. 374, fol. 235r.
136. García y García, 'Canonistica hispanica' 460–461. The colophon is in Seo de Urgel, Bibl. del Cabildo 2019. Stelzer, 'Johannes Teutonicus' 782.

that he had disputed while teaching 'dominicales'.[137] Thirty-six have been preserved in a Klosterneuburg manuscript and other questions can be found in other manuscripts.[138] Johannes cited the first three compilations of decretals and the Fourth Lateran canons in them. He did not refer to his own *Compilatio quarta*. They all treat theoretical problems that do not seem to have been connected with real court cases.

Historians have noted what appears to be the reluctance of the schools to accept Johannes' *Compilatio quarta*. They have conjectured that, since none of the other canonists wrote an apparatus for it, they must have been reluctant to use it in the classroom.[139] There may have been other reasons for the limited reception of Johannes' collection. A significant factor may have been that the Bolognese studium was frequently disrupted after 1215, and these disruptions may account for the departures of Laurentius, Vincentius, and Johannes Teutonicus. The turbulence may also be responsible for the falling off of works that can be dated after 1217. In contrast to the outpouring of works between 1210 and 1217, much of it by non-Italians, the only major works produced there from 1217 to ca. 1230 were by Italians: Tancred's Ordinary Glosses on the *Compilationes antiquae*, and Jacobus of Albenga's and Zoën's apparatus on *Compilatio quinta* discussed below.

Clashes between town and gown had rocked Bologna much earlier. The year 1204 was marked by a secession of students and professors to Vicenza. We are not, unfortunately, well-informed about these squabbles. However, we do know that a quarrel between Tuscans and Lombards in 1215 resulted in a secession to Arezzo in which Roffredus Beneventanus took part. Bologna responded by promulgating a statute requiring every scholar to swear allegiance to the city. In 1217 Pope Honorius III urged the revocation of the statute. The city ignored the pope, who then placed the scholars of the university under a ban. Rashdall thought that the Bolognese studium may have closed down entirely between 1217 and 1220. In 1222, a major secession of the students led to the foundation of the studium at Padua.[140] In 1225 Frederick II attempted suppress the studium by withdrawing imperial privileges.[141]

---

137. Johannes Teutonicus to C.18 q.2 c.16 s.v. *acquisierit*.

138. For further information see Chapter 5 on the decretists.

139. Stephan Kuttner, 'Johannes Teutonicus, das vierte Laterankonzil un die Compilatio quarta' *Miscellanea Giovanni Mercati* (6 vols. ST 121–126; VaticanCity 1946) 5.608–634, reprinted in *Medieval Councils, Decretals, and Collections of Canon Law* (London 1980).

140. Hastings Rashdall, *The Universities of Europe in the Middle Ages*, ed. F.M. Powicke and A.B. Emden (Oxford 1936) 1.169–171.

141. Rashdall, *Universities of Europe* 2.11.

If scholarship declined in Bologna after ca. 1217, it almost disappeared in northern centers. In 1219 Pope Honorius III issued a constitution, *Super speculam*, in which he forebade monks to study medicine and Roman law at the University of Paris.[142] Honorius' reasons for promulgating the decree have been much debated. Although he may have had several objectives, Honorius probably wanted to protect the school of theology at Paris from being damaged by the popularity of law. In any case, Roman law ceased to be taught at Paris. *Super speculam* must have created difficulties for people who wished to study canon law at Paris. By 1219, a knowledge of Roman law was essential for a student of canon law, and Honorius may have unwittingly contributed to the decline of canonistic scholarship north of the Alps. Although canon law was taught at Paris and elsewhere, the vigorous transmontane canonistic scholarship of the twelfth century collapsed in the thirteenth. In contrast to the numerous summae on the *Decretum*, quaestiones, brocarda, and collections of decretals that northern canonists produced before ca. 1215, they left far less to mark their teaching in the thirteenth century. They reshaped and edited Bolognese works like *Compilatio tertia* and Tancred's *Ordo iudiciarius*, but wrote little. There were distinguished teachers at Paris, but their teaching did not lead to writing.[143] Consequently, Bologna and other Italian schools dominated canonistic scholarship of the thirteenth century.

III. Decretalists 1217–1234

We cannot be certain that the turbulence at Bologna in the 1210s and 1220s brought an end to the 'international' era of the studium and was responsible for the slacking pace of juristic writing on canon law between 1217 and 1225. We can say, however, that after 1217 the studium was dominated by one figure, Tancred of Lombardy, often referred to as Tancred of Bologna.[144] He studied at Bologna, heard the lectures of Azo on Roman law, and sat at the feet of 'his master' Laurentius in canon law. He became a canon and then, in 1226, archdeacon of the cathedral chapter of Bologna. Pope Honorius III selected him to compile a collection of his decretals sometime before 1226. By this time Tancred's stature was so great, and

---

142. The best survey of *Super speculam* is Stephan Kuttner, 'Papst Honorius III. und das Studium des Zivilrechts', with Kuttner's analysis of other historians' views in 'Retractationes' in *Gratian and the Schools of Law*. See also Chris Coppens, 'The Teaching of Law in the University of Paris in the First Quarter of the 13th Century', RIDC 10 (1999) 139–173, especially 157–168.

143. Anne Lefebvre-Teillard, 'Petrus Brito legit . . . Sur quelques aspects de l'enseignement du droit canonique à Paris au début du XIII siècle', RHD 79 (2001) 153–177.

144. L. Chevailler, 'Tancredus', DDC 7 (1962) 1146–1165.

his rivals so few, that it is difficult to imagine whom Honorius might have chosen other than the archdeacon.[145]

The 1220s were the years of Tancred at Bologna. The most significant jurists of the early thirteenth century had departed for their homelands; Tancred remained. He wrote prolifically on the entire 'corpus decretalium'. His commentaries on the first three *Compilationes* became the Ordinary Glosses that were copied into most manuscripts after ca. 1220. He wrote first recensions of his apparatus to *Compilatio prima* and *secunda* ca. 1210–1215, revising both works after 1220. He finished his apparatus to *Compilatio tertia* between 1220 and 1225. Curiously, unlike all his predecessors who compiled new decretal collections, he wrote no glosses or apparatus for *Compilatio quinta*. He also ignored the Fourth Lateran Constitutions and *Compilatio quarta*.

Tancred changed the style of writing apparatus to the decretals. His predecessors, Laurentius, Vincentius, and Johannes Teutonicus, took the glosses of other canonists, reshaped and edited them, and placed them in their own commentaries without often attributing the source of their text.[146] Tancred changed that practice in his apparatus. He incorporated the glosses of other canonists with very little change and appended the sigla of their authors. His own comments to each decretal were often short. Consequently, his apparatus take on the character of a survey of opinion on a particular text and are blander commentaries than those of his predecessors. He does not seem to have been a man of strong opinions.

Continuing the tradition of the twelfth-century decretists, Tancred composed major tracts on procedure and marriage. He began by writing three 'summulae' on procedure between 1210 and 1215.[147] He composed a major tract on matrimony at the same time.[148] His matrimonial tract was widely disseminated because it was often appended to the first three books of Raymond de Peñafort's *Summa de casibus*. Sometime after 1234 Raymond revised Tancred's text, and the stationers often placed the revision after the third book of Raymond's *Summa*.[149]

After 1216 he finished an extensive *Ordo iudiciarius* that later jurists in

145. On Tancred's work in compiling *Compilatio quinta*, see my 'Systematic decretal collections' and Leonard E. Boyle, 'The Compilatio quinta and the registers of Honorius III', BMCL 8 (1978) 9–19.

146. In Books 3–5 of Johannes Teutonicus' commentary on *Compilatio tertia*, he seems to have anticipated Tancred's methodology. See the Prolegomena of Pennington, *Johannis Teutonici Apparatus glossarum*.

147. Richard Fraher, 'Tancred's 'Summula de criminibus': A New Text and a Key to the Ordo iudiciarius', BMCL 9 (1979) 23–35.

148. *Tancredi Summa de matrimonio*, ed. A. Wunderlich (Göttingen 1841).

149. *Repertorium*, 445.

Italy and France revised and adapted during the next two decades.[150] Finally, in the 1230s, Bartholomaeus Brixiensis edited the *Ordo* once again. In its various forms, Tancred's *Ordo* enjoyed great popularity and influence on subsequent procedural tracts; it circulated in numerous manuscripts during the thirteenth and fourteenth centuries.[151] Tancred introduced his *Ordo* by invoking his 'carissimi socii' who had pressed him to write a text explaining the judicial process. Noting that Richardus Anglicus had written on ecclesiastical procedure and the Roman lawyer Pillius on Roman law procedure, he promised to accept the rules of Roman law when not contradicted by the canons; otherwise the norms of the sacred canons would be preferred to the 'leges'.[152]

The other canonists who were Tancred's contemporaries in the 1220s and 1230s were not as prolific. Marcoaldus of Padua was a German canonist who taught at Padua ca. 1226–1236. Honorius III addressed a copy of *Compilatio quinta* to Marcoaldus of Padua, a certain sign of his importance at the time. But he wrote very little from which we might measure his importance. All we have are a few scattered glosses to *Compilatio quarta* in two manuscripts.

Surviving works are not necessarily a good guide to a jurist's works, for we know that some were lost. But any work from the thirteenth century that has not survived probably was not widely read or copied. Another canonist who taught at Padua at this time was Philippus of Aquilea, who also wrote glosses on the *Decretum* and the *Compilationes antiquae;* his opinions are occasionally cited by later canonists.[153]

Honorius III's new decretal collection did not provoke a flurry of commentaries or an outpouring of new work. Only two canonists, Jacobus of Albenga and Zoën Tencararius, wrote apparatus of glosses for it. Neither their apparatus nor the collection itself seem to have been widely read and used.[154] Jacobus of Albenga taught at Bologna and later became bishop of the city of his birth. He wrote glosses on the *Decretum, Compilationes prima* and *quarta*.[155] Zoën was also a Bolognese master, a canon in the Cathedral at Bologna, and he became bishop of Avignon in 1240. He fostered ties to Bologna while he was in Southern France. In 1257 he founded a college for Southern French students at Bologna.

---

150. Fowler-Magerl, *Ordo iudiciorum* 129–130. Edited by Friedrich C. Bergmann, *Libri de iudiciorum ordine* (Göttingen 1842, repr. Aalen 1965).
151. Fowler-Magerl, *Ordo iudiciorum* 128.
152. Bergmann, *Libri* 89.
153. Pennington, 'Making of a Decretal Collection' 77, n. 27.
154. Kuttner, *Repertorium* 382–385. Pennington, 'French Recension' 67–69.
155. N. Brieskorn, 'Jabobus de Albenga', LMA 5 (1990) 255.

The last major figure in the period before 1234 was the Catalan Dominican, Raymond of Peñafort. He studied at Bologna and then taught law between 1218 and 1221. After his return to Barcelona, he entered the Dominican order in 1222. Pope Gregory IX summoned him to Rome in 1230 and asked him to compile a new codification that would reduce all earlier collections of decretals to one volume. Raymond wrote glosses on the *Decretum* and on *Compilatio antiquae* but completed only one work of any length while at Bologna, a *Summa iuris canonici,* in which he planned to treat the 'profound depths of canon law' in seven 'particles'.[156] The work is partially preserved in two manuscript fragments, and we do not know if Raymond finished the entire work.[157] In the prologue to the *Summa* Raymond confessed that he undertook the work with reluctance. Even though 'socii' encouraged him to leave a memorial of his work for posterity, he felt as if he would be 'a dwarf leaping over the shoulders of giants'.[158] We may discount his rhetoric as a humble commonplace, but we should also note that, although canon law had been taught for only seventy-five years at Bologna, the jurists of the school of canon law ca. 1217 looked upon their predecessors as giants.

As Stephan Kuttner has pointed out, Raymond departed from their format of writing 'summae' in several respects in this work of his youth in spite of his proclaimed reverence for his illustrious predecessors. He does not follow the organization of Gratian or of the *Compilationes antiquae.* The main divisions of his work were: (1) Variae species et differentiae iuris; (2) De ministris canonum, differentiis et officiis eorundem; (3) De ordine iudiciario; (4) De contractibus et rebus tam ecclesiarum quam clericorum; (5) De criminibus et poenis (6) De sacramentis; (7) De processione Spiritus sancti. Raymond, though, discussed the 'materia' of each title, solved doubtful questions under each, and then formulated 'notabilia' for each. Later, he followed the same organizational principles in his *Summa de casibus,* which he began after his return to Barcelona in 1222 and finished the first recension ca. 1225.[159]

---

156. *Summa de iure canonico,* ed. Xaverio Ochoa and Aloisio Diez (Universa biblioteca iuris, I.A; Roma 1975) 4: 'Ego Raimundus, catalanus, professor iuris canonici, opus supra vires aggredior, per quod in profundo pelago iuris canonici agnus cum agnis peditare, et natare valeant elephantes. Distinguitur ergo hoc opus per septem particulas propter sancti Spiritus gratiam septiformem'. This inadequate edition replaces one by José Rius y Serra, *Sancti Raymundi de Penyafort Opera omnia,* 1: *San Raimundo de Penyafort, Summa iuris* (Barcelona 1945). On the defects of both editions see Stephan Kuttner in *Seminar* 8 (1950) 52–67 (reprinted in *Studies in the History of Medieval Canon Law*) and *The Jurist* 37 (1977) 385–386.

157. Vat. Borgh. 261, fol. 91r–102v and a small fragment discovered by Gérard Fransen in Bamberg, Staatsbibl. can. 19, fol. 258ra–vb.

158. *Summa* ed. Ochoa, 4: 'nanus humeros vis transilire gigantum'.

159. See Kuttner, 'The Barcelona Edition of St. Raymond's First Treatise on Canon Law',

His *Summa de casibus*, not the *Summa iuris canonici*, became his major 'memoriale' for the future. He incorporated much of the material from the *Summa iuris canonici* into the *Summa de casibus* with only minor re-editing of the material. Raymond wrote the *Summa de casibus* as a guide for priests in the confessional. It was a smashing success. Hundreds of manuscript copies exist; it was glossed, abbreviated, and versified over the next three hundred years.[160] Since it had been composed for the 'forum internum' it did not have much influence on academic law.[161]

IV. Minor Literary Works of the Decretalists

We have already touched upon the genres of minor literary works in our chapter on the Italian decretists in this volume. The decretalists continued to produce 'abbreviationes', 'notabilia', 'brocarda', 'distinctiones', 'casus', 'quaestiones', and 'consilia'.[162] As the Compilationes antiquae were incorporated into the school curriculum, the canonists composed 'abbreviationes', 'casus', and 'notabilia' for each. Most of these works are anonymous, but a few canonists acknowledged their authorship. Richardus Anglicus and Bernardus Papiensis wrote 'casus' for Compilatio prima.[163] Paulus Ungarus, who like Raymond of Peñafort became a Dominican in 1221, composed two influential collections of 'notabilia' on *Compilationes secunda* and *tertia*, which circulated widely, and Petrus Hispanus Portugalensis, who taught at Bologna in the 1220s and then moved to Padua ca. 1229, wrote 'notabilia' for *Compilatio quarta*. We have already mentioned the popular Brocarda of Richardus and Damasus in our chapter on the decretists. The 'quaestiones' of the decretalists become an increasingly important literary genre during the thirteenth century. By ca. 1250, the only minor genres that survive are 'quaestiones' and 'casus'.

Seminar 8 (1950) 52–67 and 'Zur Entstehungsgeschichte der Summa de casibus des hl. Raymund von Penyafort', ZRG Kan. Abt. 39 (1953) 419–434; both articles are reprinted in *Studies in the History of Medieval Canon Law* (London 1990) with 'Retractationes'.

160. Pennington, "Summae on Raymond de Pennafort's *Summa de casibus* in the Bayerische Staatsbibliothek, Munich," *Traditio* 27 (1971) 471–480; for a fuller analysis of the *Summa de casibus* see Joseph Goering's 'The Internal Forum', Chapter 12 below.

161. See my remarks on Raymond in 'The Church from Pope Innocent III to Pope Gregory IX', *Domenico di Caleruega e la nascita dell'ordine dei frati predicatori, Todi, 10–12 ottobre 2004* (Spoleto 2005).

162. The best summary of the decretalists' works is still Kuttner's *Repertorium* 397–433.

163. Kuttner, *Repertorium* 398–399; 'Bernardus Compostellanus Antiquus' 299; On Richardus Anglicus and his *Casus decretalium*, see Robert C. Figueira, 'Ricardus de Mores and his *Casus decretalium*: The Birth of a Canonistic Genre', *Proceedings San Diego* (Vatican City 1992) 169–188.

V. The Law Schools ca. 1234

We are not well informed about the state of the law schools in the 1220s and 1230s. Much of our evidence must be garnered from literary works, and we cannot readily tell where a work was written. Even more difficult to determine is where students studied law and in what numbers. André Gouron has written about Southern France that 'we know nothing about the audiences attracted by those professors <who migrated to France, and> nothing about the number of their students'.[164] What Gouron observed about Southern France can be extended to every area of Europe in the early thirteenth century. In Italy, law schools had been established at Modena ca. 1182, Reggio by 1210, Vicenza for a short time (ca. 1204–1209), and Arezzo ca. 1215.[165] As can be deduced from one of Honorius III's bulls of promulgation for *Compilatio quinta* that was addressed to Marcoaldus of Padua, a number of canonists had migrated to Padua, and a flourishing center of legal studies was established there after a translation of masters and students to Padua in 1222.[166] In 1226, Buoncompagno read his *Rhetorica Antiqua* to the assembled professors of canon and civil law in the cathedral.[167] Vercelli made a contract with some students in Padua to transfer to Vercelli, and a school was established in 1228. The terms of the contract also dictated that three doctors of Roman law, two decretists and two decretalists, would also transfer. The bishop of Vercelli was a doctor of canon law, Hugo of Sesso, and he may have been instrumental in bringing the students and teachers to his city. He had already played a role in the first law school on the Iberian peninsula at Palencia while he was a canon of the cathedral chapter there.[168]

Cities began to compete for the privilege of having a legal studium. Emperor Frederick II chartered a new university at Naples in 1224. Frederick probably wished to strengthen the study of law in the *Regno* and protect the interests of the city and the professors who had been teaching there for some time. He forbade his subjects to attend any other school and appointed, according to some sources, Roffredus Beneventanus and Petrus of Isernia, his faithful servants, to teach there.[169] At Lyon in 1245,

---

164. Gouron, 'The Training of Southern French Lawyers during the Thirteenth and Fourteenth Centuries', *Post Scripta* (SG 15; Rome 1972) 219–227 at 219.
165. Rashdall, *Universities of Europe* 2.2–9.
166. Ibid. 10.
167. Ibid. 11.
168. Ibid. 11–12, 26–28. Vito Piergiovanni, 'Tracce della cultura canonistica a Vercelli', *L'Università di Vercelli nel medio evo: Il Congresso storico Vercellese, Vercelli 23–25 ottobre 1992* (Vercelli 1994) 243–254. Domenico Maffei, 'Fra Cremona, Montpellier e Palencia nel secolo XII: Ricerche su Ugolino da Sesso', RIDC 1 (1990) 9–30.
169. Ibid. 22–23. Manlio Bellomo has examined the problems of understanding Freder-

Pope Innocent IV decreed that a *Studium generale* be established at the Roman curia. Canon and Roman law would be studied at the curia, and the school would teach procurators, advocates, notaries, and curialists.[170] By the middle of the thirteenth century, secular and ecclesiastical princes fostered the study of law in their territories. They were motivated by an awareness of the importance of law for good government.[171]

Bologna still enjoyed primacy of place, and with the promulgation of the *Decretales Gregorii noni*, the Bolognese studium produced a massive amount of literature in response to the new codification. Other centers of legal studies would not rival Bologna until the fourteenth century.

Even though northern canonists no longer produced the mass of literary work that they had in the twelfth century, the teaching and study of canon law continued to flourish outside of Italy as well. The school at Paris continued as a center in spite of Honorius III's prohibiting the study of Roman law, which certainly must have damaged the school of canon law. Students at Paris who studied canon law had to study Roman law elsewhere or be content with an incomplete understanding of canonical principles. A mastery of canon law was no longer possible without a firm grasp of Roman law. In spite of this handicap, Paris still attracted first-rate teachers. Hostiensis taught there in the 1230s.[172] The bishop of Montpellier claimed license to confer degrees in both laws during the 1230s.[173] Roman law had to be taught somewhere, and the absence of Roman law instruction in Paris encouraged other centers to establish schools. In 1235 Pope Gregory IX clarified several points of dispute that had emerged over interpretations of *Super speculam*. He stated that Honorius' decretal had prohibited the study of Roman law only at Paris, not at Orléans.[174] It is likely that canon law was studied at Angers during the same period.[175]

---

ick's foundation in 'Federico II, lo "Studium" a Napoli e il diritto comune nel "Regnum",' RIDC 2 (1991) 135–151.

170. Agostino Paravicini Bagliani, 'L'Église romaine d'Innocent III à Grégoire X (1198–1274)', *Histoire du Christianisme des origines à nos jours*, 5: *Apogée de la papauté et expansion del la Chrétienté (1054–1274)*, ed. André Vauchez et al. (N.p. 1993) 569–570.

171. See Pennington, 'Politics in Western Jurisprudence', *The Jurists' Philosophy of Law from Rome to the Seventeenth Century*, ed. Andrea Padovani and Peter Stein (Dordrecht 2005).

172. Pennington, 'Enrico da Susa, detto l'Ostiense (Hostiensis, Henricus de Segusio o Segusia)', DBI 42 (Roma 1993) 758–763 and in English, "Henricus de Segusio (Hostiensis)," *Popes, Canonists, and Texts 1150–1550* (Collected Studies Series 412; Aldershot 1993).

173. Ibid. 128–129; Johannes Bassianus, the Roman law jurist, taught somewhere in southern France, not necessarily, as Rashdall states, in Montpellier. Gouron dates the beginning of canon law at Montpellier to the second half of the century; see 'Les premiers canonistes de l'école montpelliéraine', *Mélanges offerts à Jean Dauvillier* (Centre d'histoire juridique méridionale; Toulouse 1979) 361–368.

174. Ibid. 143.

175. Ibid. 153.

A treaty of 1229 between King Louis IX of France and Raymond of Toulouse stipulated that the count should pay the salaries of two decretists at Toulouse.[176] There is evidence of canonists teaching at Béziers and Narbonne by mid-century.[177]

In Spain, canon law was taught at Palencia in 1208–1209 at a school established by King Alfonso VIII.[178] García y García has proposed that the *Collectio Salmanticense* was compiled and edited in central Spain sometime between 1212 and 1217.[179] If he is correct, this collection may be evidence of teaching activity there at an early date.

We are fairly well informed about the teaching of canon law at Oxford.[180] A student, a nobleman named Emo, came from Friesland to Oxford to study Roman and canon law. According to his autobiography, he studied Vacarius' *Liber pauperum*, *Decreta*, and *Decretales* ca. 1196–1200. Afterwards he returned to Freisland and put his legal knowledge to good use.[181] Thomas of Marlborough studied canon law at Oxford in the 1190s, and in his chronicle he named three masters with whom he studied: John of Tynemouth, Simon of Sywell, and Honorius.[182] The monk who continued the chronicle of Thomas of Marlborough noted that Thomas had brought books of canon and civil law to Evesham with which he had taught both subjects at Oxford and Exeter (ca. 1200).[183] Like the Italian schools, Oxford had its turmoil in the early thirteenth century. A student killed his mistress and fled in 1209. The town hanged two of his companions for the crime. This violation of the school's clerical immunity led to the dispersal of the students and masters until 1214.[184] After this hiatus, teaching of canon law began again ca. 1214. A Mr William Scott and Mr Henry Bishopstone taught canon law at Oxford ca. 1220. Scott was addressed as 'Doctor Decretorum' in a papal mandate. A note in a Salisbury record of 1220 mentioned that Bishopstone lectured on canon law at Ox-

---

176. Ibid. 163.
177. André Gouron, 'Canonistes et civilistes des écoles de Narbonne et de Béziers', *Proceedings Toronto* (Vatican City 1976) 523–536.
178. Ibid. 67.
179. 'Una coleccion de decretales en Salamanca', *Proceedings Boston* (Vatican City 1965) 71–92 and 'Un antecedente ibérico de la actividad compilatoria de San Rámon de Peñafort', *Escritos del Vedat* 7 (1977) 199–207.
180. The chapters of R.W. Southern, 'From Schools to University' and Leonard E. Boyle, 'Canon Law before 1380', in *The History of the University of Oxford*, 1: *The Early Oxford Schools*, ed. J.I. Catto (Oxford 1984) 1–36 and 531–564.
181. Southern, 'Schools to University' 17–19; see Jason Taliadoros, *Law and Theology in Twelfth-Century England: The Works of Master Vacarius: 1115/20–c. 1200)* (Disputatio 10; Turnhout 2006) 1–23.
182. Ibid. 19.
183. Rashdall, *Universities of Europe* 3.32. Boyle, 'Canon Law before 1380' 532.
184. Southern, 'Schools to University' 26.

ford.[185] Leonard Boyle believes that canon law did not become a higher faculty granting a doctor of canon law until the promulgation of Gregory IX's Decretals in 1234. The school of Roman law became a separate faculty at about the same time.[186] By 1239, the most distinguished canonist and Romanist to teach in England during the Middle Ages, William of Drogheda, was 'regens in legibus'.[187] By the third decade of the thirteenth century, the study of canon law was impossible without a thorough knowledge of Roman law, and the two disciplines were found in all university centers except Paris.[188]

The study of canon law had been established in many centers outside of Italy by 1234. There were undoubtedly many more centers than those for which we have evidence. When Pope Gregory IX sent his Decretals to Bologna and Paris in 1234, he tacitly acknowledged the long tradition of canon law at Paris by addressing his bull to the two oldest centers of canonistic studies. However, without Roman law, Paris declined as a center for legal studies. Bologna reigned without a serious rival for the next century. The study of canon law and Roman law had become an integral part of legal studies throughout Europe, and its jurisprudence became the *Ius commune* of Europe. Ignorance of its doctrines and principles was no longer possible in the episcopal courts of Christendom. While papal letters rebuking the legal ignorance of episcopal recipients are common in the twelfth and early thirteenth centuries, they become rare after 1234. The *Ius commune* had become a key element of ecclesiastical learning and government.[189]

185. Boyle, 'Canon Law' 535.
186. Ibid. 537–539.
187. Ibid. 536. On Drogheda see Jane E. Sayers, 'William of Drogheda and the English Canonists', *Proceedings Cambridge* 205–222.
188. J.L. Barton's observations, 'The Study of Civil Law before 1380', *The History of Oxford Unviversity, 1: The Early Oxford Schools*, 522, about Roman law not being useful for the graduate of ca. 1330 ignores the primary use to which knowledge of civil law was probably put: canon law.
189. See my 'Learned Law, Droit Savant, Gelehrtes Recht: The Tyranny of a Concept', RIDC 5 (1994) 197–209 and *Syracuse Journal of International Law and Commerce* 20 (1994) 205–215, and 'Politics in Western Jurisprudence' *passim* for the importance of the *Ius commune* in medieval society.

8

Decretal Collections from Gratian's *Decretum* to the *Compilationes antiquae*
The Making of the New Case Law

Charles Duggan

The history of canonical collections from Gratian's *Decretum* (1125–1139) to the *Compilationes antiquae* (1189–1191 to 1226) presents a pattern of almost impenetrable complexity.[1] Their earliest origins lie in the *paleae* (additional material inserted at appropriate points in Gratian manuscripts and gradually absorbed into the text) and in the groups of such items, identified as 'appendices to the *Decretum*', which were devised as supplements to Gratian's text and began to include post-Gratian decretals. Contemporaneously, however, wholly independent collections began to be made of the latest decretal letters, in a continuing effort to keep up-to-date with the latest rulings on matters of law and procedure.

Two factors explain the rapid evolution of this new style of canonical collection from the mid-twelfth century onwards. The first was the general reception of the *Decretum* (*ex* 1139), both in ecclesiastical courts and in the schools of higher learning; the second was the consolidation of the

---

1. Cf. Chapter 2, above, on the *Decretum* by Peter Landau, and Chapter 9, 'Decretal Collections 1190–1234', by Kenneth Pennington.

twin concepts of the pope as Universal Ordinary and of the Roman curia as a court of appeal for all Christians. These both had ancient origins, and both were restated in the *Decretum*,[2] which proclaimed the juridical authority of papal judicial letters in unambiguous terms: 'Decretal letters, therefore, have the same legal force as conciliar canons'.[3] The academic success of Gratian's compendium of what canonists came to call the 'old law' ('ius antiquum') and its resulting wide dissemination across the Latin West, created the conditions for, and encouraged the emergence of, the so-called 'new law' ('ius novum'), based on current papal decisions and conciliar decrees.

The old law was not abandoned, however, for the *Decretum* remained the first book of the corpus of canon law until the early twentieth century; but the greater sophistication of professional teachers of law in Bologna and elsewhere, and the rapidly changing world of the twelfth century created problems; and, increasingly, such problems were referred to the pope for decisions. The essentially centripetal element in this development is something insufficiently recognized, but every decretal was a response from the centre to a consultation or appeal. There was no compulsion on unknown Norwegian settlers in a distant island,[4] or parishioners of an isolated Yorkshire village,[5] to submit their local problems for papal rulings. But they did so; and so did many others; and the resulting decretal letters became the major source of new law. Thus occurred one of the most intensely creative phases in the history of canonical codification in the Middle Ages. Beginning as individual additions to manuscripts of the *Decretum*, this impulse to collect contemporary decretals and conciliar canons produced increasingly large compilations, which ultimately culminated in the formal promulgation by Gregory IX of the *Liber extra* (1234), popularly known as the Gregorian *Decretals*.

The study of the decretal collections has been complicated by the scholarly tradition, established in the nineteenth century and continued to the

---

2. C.9, q.3, c.17.

3. Gratian, D.20 *Dictum ante* §1: 'Decretales itaque epistolae canonibus conciliorum pari iure exequantur'. On papal decretals from their origins to th eleventh century, see Detlev Jasper and Horst Fuhrmann, *Papal Decretals in the Early Middle Ages* (History of Medieval Canon Law; Washington, D.C. 2001).

4. *Decretales ineditae saeculi XII*, ed. and rev. S. Chodorow and C. Duggan, MIC *Series B: Corpus Collectionum* 4 (Vatican City 1982) 149–151 no. 86, Alexander III to Archbishop Øystein of Trondheim, concerning people on an island (Greenland?) twelve days' journey from Norway.

5. Charles Duggan, 'Decretals of Alexander III to England', *Miscellanea Rolando Bandinelli, Papa Alessandro III*, ed. F. Liotta (Accademia Senesi degli Intronati; Siena 1986) 116 no. 25: Alexander III (or possibly Lucius III) to Archbishop Roger of York, authorizing a chapel of ease.

present day, of identifying each collection as it was found by the then current location, irrespective of the manuscript's provenance or the origin of its texts; and where such a collection was found to be a family archetype, the same misleading name was conferred on its descendants as a group, whatever their ancestry or lineage. Since provenance and modern location rarely coincide, this practice not only entails great confusion but obscures the historical context in which the collections were made and circulated. The extant primitive[6] collections compiled before *Compilatio prima* (1189–91) are classified in five groups—the English, Bridlington, Tortosa, French, and Italian families.[7] The systematic collections comprise a 'Paris' collection *(Parisiensis secunda)*, three groups or families (Worcester, Appendix, and Bamberg), and a further six collections *(Tanner, Bruges, Frankfurt, Rouen, St-Germain, and Avranches)*.

With some exceptions,[8] however, this conventional nomenclature of the family groups and their individual members is misleading. The *collectio Alcobacensis prima*, for instance, in the Catalan 'Tortosa' family, is a manuscript of Portuguese provenance, once owned by the Cistercian abbey of Alcobaça, but its contents were derived almost entirely from Exeter, Worcester, and Canterbury sources, recording commissions respectively to Bishops Bartholomew of Exeter and Roger of Worcester as judges-delegate, and responses and rulings to Archbishop Richard of Canterbury. Again, the primitive 'Berlin' collection *(Berolinensis prima)* is named from its archival location, but it is a member of the Italian family of collections, and was quite probably an early work of the influential canonist Bernard of Pavia, author of an early version of the *Collectio Lipsiensis*, now in Leipzig, and of *Compilatio prima* itself (both compiled in Bologna).[9]

Even the apparently appropriate title *Appendix concilii Lateranensis* is not an accurate description of all the members of its family (although it is applicable to other entirely unrelated collections), and it says nothing about the provenance of the work. The collection acquired its name from the fact that its *editio princeps,* published by Petrus Crabbe in the sixteenth century, was based by Bartolomaeus Laurens on a manuscript now lost,[10]

---

6. For the distinction between 'primitive' and 'systematic' collections, see below at n. 14.
7. Walther Holtzmann originally included the Worcester family in his list of 'primitive' compilations, but there are good reasons to regard it as systematic: see below, at nn. 14–19.
8. For example, the Worcester family and the Canterbury collection.
9. The construction of a new and more historically fitting nomenclature has been considered, but the project was abandoned since most of the references in the learned literature would be rendered obsolete.
10. P. Crabbe, *Concilia omnia tam generalia quam particularia...* (2d ed. Cologne 1551) 2.820–944; reprinted in Mansi 22.248–453.

in which the decretal collection followed the canons of the Third Lateran Council (1179)—as indeed it does in the related Leipzig and Vienna manuscripts discovered later, and also in the St. John's fragment in Cambridge. But in an important member of the family, now at Lincoln, the probable place of origin for the archetype, the elements appear in reverse order, the conciliar canons themselves being an appendix to the decretals.

Likewise, the influential 'Bamberg' group of twelve collections or fragments descends from a lost archetype, which Deeters named the *Urbambergensis*. Its earliest surviving member is now in the Staatsbibliothek in Bamberg (previously in the cathedral library), but it is almost certainly of French provenance, and very probably was made at Tours post-1185. Related manuscript survivors are now in Amiens, Paris, Tortosa (two copies), Oxford, and Paris (a collation from a lost manuscript); but, excluding the Tortosa copies, the manuscripts belonged originally to the Premonstratensians of Selincourt, the Benedictines of St. Cornelius in Compiègne, the Cluniac monks of St. Andrew in Northampton, and the Benedictines of Marmoutiers, respectively. There is therefore no validity in ascribing the name of 'Bamberg' either to the original collection or to its descendants. But the usage is too broadly established for replacement now. Again, the 'Frankfurt' collection was first discovered in the State University Library in Frankfurt, but three related manuscripts were later identified in Paris, Troyes, and London, belonging originally to Rouen, the Cistercian abbey at Clairvaux, and the Benedictine abbey of St. Maximin in Trier. The original 'Frankfurt' collection was made in France, probably at Sens or Troyes, and the St. Maximin codex was completed in England, perhaps at Lincoln. Meanwhile, the 'Leipzig' collection was completed by Bernard of Pavia in Bologna, as a transitional stage between his early systematic collection *Parisiensis secunda* (1177 x 1179) and his epoch-making *Breviarium extravagantium*, later known as *Compilatio prima* (1189 x 1191). The so-called 'Bamberg', 'Frankfurt,' and 'Leipzig' collections have therefore no German basis in their origins or completion. They are works of French, English, and Italian ancestry.[11] There are, indeed, no extant collections of German authorship and extremely few decretals of German provenance.

The regional statistics published by Holtzmann record a total of 1055 decretals in the corpus of decretal collections for the period from Eugenius III (1145–1153) to Celestine III (1191–1198). Of this total, 434 were addressed to recipients in England, and a further 75 to recipients in the English king's

---

11. Inspection of the Bamberg codex in the Staatsbibliothek, Can. 17 (P.I.II), fol. 1–47, from the cathedral library, especially its colored ornamentation, suggests a non-English provenance.

continental lands, making a total of 509. No other region received a remotely comparable number of commissions so recorded. Next in total in the collections are the Italian decretals, with 199, and those to recipients in the French king's lands, to the total of 133. In contrast, the number to German recipients is merely thirteen, this negligible number reflecting to some extent the course of papal-imperial relations, and most notably the schism of 1159–1177, when the emperor Frederick I supported a sequence of three anti-popes against Alexander III, until the papal-imperial reconciliation at Venice in 1177.[12] The total of Irish decretals found in the collections is merely two, both from Clement III, despite the fact, for example, that more Irish prelates than English attended the crucially important Third Lateran Council of 1179, a high point in Alexander III's pontificate. With the loss of the papal registers from the years in question, this statistical evidence has been much discussed, but it cannot be accepted as a faithful reflection of the reality of relations between the curia and the various regions. From the broader historical viewpoint, it must be evaluated in conjunction with the exceedingly rich records in regional archives of all kinds. The volume of papal letters preserved in the archives and published in the Göttingen *Papsturkunden* volumes, notably for France, and also for the Low Countries, Spain, and Portugal, provides a contrasting picture with that of the decretal collections.

The disproportionately large number of English decretals in the twelfth-century collections and the English provenance of most of the extant early post-Gratian collections have been known for some time, but there has been some hesitation in accepting the conclusion, suggested by such evidence, that the early formative collections were of English authorship, or derived substantially from the records of English judges-delegate (expanded to a lesser extent from similar continental sources, notably from Italy and France). In fact, some of the earliest collections were manifestly compiled in England and composed very largely of English decretals; and they can be identified as the works of canonists in the circles of English bishops, some of them famous judges-delegate. At intermediate stages, the collections passed through the hands of professional canonists in the schools, notably at Oxford/Lincoln, Rouen, Reims, Tours, Sens, and Bologna, where they were dismantled, reorganized, and combined with materials from other sources, but their impact is discernible in the mature and highly professional collections made at Bologna at the end

---

12. W. Holtzmann, 'Über eine Ausgabe der päpstlichen Dekretalen des 12. Jahrhunderts', *Nachrichten von der Akademie der Wissenschaften in Göttingen*, Philologisch-historische Klasse (1945) 15–36 at 34.

of the century. In fact, much of the official law of the *Gregorian Decretales* (1234) was indirectly derived from such earlier collections: the corpus of decretals and their sequence on numerous topics in the 1234 collection can be retraced through Bernard of Pavia's *Compilatio prima* to systematic collections from the mid-1180s, and thence back to English collections from the closing years of Alexander III's pontificate.[13]

'Primitive' and 'Systematic' Collections

In announcing his projected edition of all twelfth-century decretals in post-Gratian collections, Holtzmann published details of all known relevant collections, arranged under the headings 'before *Compilatio prima*' and 'before *Compilatio secunda*'.[14] The two groups were subdivided into 'primitive' and 'systematic' collections, and further subdivided into groups. The essential basis of this distinction was that a collection is properly systematic only if fully and professionally organized according to subject-matter, its individual letters being dismembered, if they deal with more than a single topic, and the resulting component parts distributed under precisely phrased headings or titles. To cite a typical example—Alexander III's decretal *Quamvis simus*, in response to several questions submitted to him by bishop Richard of Winchester, appears as a single entity in the 'primitive' Bridlington collection (ca. 1181), though subdivided into eight component parts and furnished with individual rubrics.[15] But in transmission through the later 'systematic' collections, the letter was dismembered and its constituent chapters detached and distributed under precisely focused titles— in eight distinct chapters in the *Appendix* and Bamberg collections, from which four chapters survived into the official *Decretales* of 1234.[16]

---

13. For the systematic working-out of the origins and transmission of the early decretal collections, and the resulting impact on the general corpus of decretal law, see Charles Duggan, *Twelfth-Century Decretal Collections and Their Importance in English History* (University of London Historical Studies 12; London 1963); idem, 'Papal Judges Delegate and the Making of the "New Law" in the Twelfth Century', *Cultures of Power: Lordship, Status, and Process in Twelfth-Century Europe*, ed. T.N. Bisson (Philadelphia 1995) 172–199.

14. Holtzmann, 'Über eine Ausgabe' 21–24; cf. Stephan Kuttner, 'Notes on a Projected Corpus of Twelfth-century Decretal Letters', *Traditio* 6 (1948) 345–351.

15. Oxford, Bodleian Library, MS 357, fol. 85v (Bridlington 23). Cf. Duggan, 'Papal Judges Delegate', 178–180.

16. Hans-Eberhard Lohmann, 'Die Collectio Wigorniensis (Collectio Londinensis Regia): Ein Beitrag zur Quellengeschichte des kanonischen Rechts im 12. Jahrhundert', *ZRG Kan. Abt.* 22 (1933) 35–187 at 180–181 (*Wigorniensis* 6.2a-I). One misleading consequence of the dismemberment of decretals and the distribution of their component parts is that the parts sometimes appear as individual letters in Jaffé-Loewenfeld, *Regesta pontificum romanorum*. For example, *Quamvis simus* appears as three separate letters in Jaffé: cf. JL 14156 (parts a, b, d–f, h), 14152 (part c), 14154 (part g).

Although Holtzmann's classification had the advantage of simplicity, it was not entirely satisfactory, since it resulted in the classification of the 'Worcester' group of English collections (from 1181) as primitive, because the individual decretals were left intact in them, whereas the earlier *Parisiensis secunda* collection (ca. 1177 x 1179), made by the Bolognese canonist Bernard of Pavia, was listed as systematic, despite its exploitation of pre-Gratian material and its inclusion of many undissected decretals, which were dismembered and redistributed in later collections. In an attempt to clarify the distinction between primitive and systematic collections, Jacoba Hanenberg proposed that a collection should be considered systematic only if it covered the whole field of legislation and if its structure followed an overall plan of composition, to which Peter Landau added that a collection in books and titles should be considered systematic independently of its dissection of individual decretals.[17] In the light of these considerations, it seems appropriate now to assign the 'Worcester' family to the systematic tradition, which, in any case, indirectly derived much of its material from it. The 'Worcester' collections were thoroughly professional in concept and in presentation. They were based primarily on the records of English judges-delegate, notably at Exeter and Worcester, and were explicitly designed for the guidance of judges-delegate. The final and largest book in the 'Worcester' collection itself (*Wigorniensis*), for example, is entitled 'Ad informandum iudices in diversis casibus quandoque emergentibus'; and numerous decretals throughout the collection are furnished with rubrics. Indeed, Peter Landau has described the collections of the 'Worcester' group as practical manuals of the new law, without any admixture of pre-Gratian material.[18] Both the Bolognese *Parisiensis secunda* and the English 'Worcester' collection may be deemed systematic, and springs from which the later main lines of transmission descended.

The basic distinction between the two categories thus becomes a distinction between 'primitive' collections, which have no discernible pattern of subject-matter organization, and 'systematic' collections, which arrange their material into subject categories. But within this latter category, one can distinguish between an early stage in the process of systematization and its mature and fully developed form. Following the reclassification

17. Jacoba Hanenburg, 'Decretals and Decretal Collections in the Second Half of the XIIth Century', TRG 34 (1966), 522–599, especially 591–592; cf. Peter Landau, 'Die Entstehung der systematischen Dekretalensammlungen und die europäische Kanonistik des 12. Jahrhunderts', ZRG Kan. Abt. 65 (1979) 124.

18. Landau, 'Entstehung' 128, 'Wir haben also in den Sammlungen der Wigorniensis-Gruppe die für den praktischen Gebrauch bestimmten Manuale des ius novum vor uns—in ihnen konnte daher für vorgratianische Texte überhaupt kein Platz sein'.

of the 'Worcester' family as systematic, Holtzmann's original designation of six families of 'primitive' collections must be modified from six to five. They comprise thirty-two collections, pre-dating *Compilatio prima* in technical transmission. They range in date of compilation from the mid-1170s to post-1195, and they fall into five groups, mostly on the basis of their original provenance. The 'Tortosa' (*Dertusensis*) group has three members, the 'French' group has four, and the 'Italian' group has five. The remaining ten collections are clearly English in provenance—the 'English' group comprises seven members and the 'Bridlington' group has two.[19] The preponderance of English collections at this crucially important formative phase of evolution is self-evident. But it is even greater in reality than the group and individual names suggest, since it is readily apparent, on collation, that the absorption of English decretals into the continental collections was far greater than the reverse process.

The First Phase: Appendices to Gratian

The earliest supplements to Gratian's *Decretum* were the numerous additional texts, the so-called *paleae*, inserted where appropriate in Gratian manuscripts. They are aptly treated in conjunction with Gratian's work and have long been the subject of scholarly evaluation. But their source is to be found primarily in the early post-Gratian canonical collections identified as 'appendices' to the *Decretum*, which literally follow the *Decretum* in some manuscripts but survive independently in others. They vary in size from a very few to almost a hundred items, and record a remarkably creative stage of transition from the *Decretum* to the decretal collections, properly so-called, based primarily on recent decretal letters and conciliar canons, and dating from the mid-1170s.[20] The *Decretum* appendices and the decretal collections are fundamentally different in character, however, since the latter are essentially books of new law—*ius novum*—and lead through a dynamic and complex transition to the *Compilationes antiquae* (from 1189), and thence to the *Decretales* of 1234.

The Decretal appendices still lack a coordinated and comprehensive study, though Holtzmann had advanced preparations for such a work, and analysis of individual collections or clusters of collections have been pub-

---

19. Listed in Walther Holtzmann, *Studies in the Collections of Twelfth-Century Decretals*, ed. and revised by C.R. Cheney and Mary Cheney (MIC, Series B 3; Vatican City 1979) xxxi–xxxii; note that the Worcester (*Wigorniensis*) group has been reclassified, and is now considered the second of the systematic collections.

20. Kuttner, *Repertorium* 286, 'Die Collectio Oenipontana (Innsbruck)'—'Sammlung von 89 Grössenteils vorgratianischen Stücken, darunter 5 Dekretalen Alexanders III.'.

lished by Kuttner, Weigand, and others. They have been identified in the following libraries, from which they take their names—Biberach, Darmstadt, Graz, Heiligenkreuz, Innsbruck, Munich, Pommersfeld, Troyes, and Harvard.[21] It has long been recognized that a network of interconnections can be traced, in varying degrees, between these 'appendices.' They are works of canonical expertise and learning, which are drawn primarily from the records of commissions to papal judges-delegate and the canons of recent councils, of Tours (1163) and of the Third Lateran Council (1179). It is not surprising that the 'appendices' were, in turn, appropriate sources from which the *Decretum* itself was supplemented with the paleae, simultaneously providing a source for early decretal collections.[22]

It is not possible here to provide a full or satisfactory survey of this intensely creative phase in the history of canonical codification, but the scope and nature of the decretal appendices and their interrelationships are nowhere more amply exemplified than in Weigand's analysis (1983) of four such works, respectively at Heiligenkreuz (44 items), Pommersfeld (29+1 and 51 items) and Munich (21 items), together with the Munich fragment of a decretal collection.[23] For each of the five collections, the identification of *paleae* is noted, together with other appropriate reference, and for the Pommersfeld *Anhang*, the corresponding location of items in the Heiligenkreuz and Darmstadt manuscripts are recorded, revealing very strikingly their affiliation. In a comparable and complementary way, Kuttner's examination of a Gratian manuscript at Biberach-an-der-Riss sheds light on the various ways whereby canonists might build on Gratian's work.

The Biberach 'appendix' is not a single and integrated collection, but comprises a series of texts distributed through the *Decretum*. At nine sepa-

21. (1) Biberach-an-der-Riss, Spitalarchiv MS B 3515; cf. Stephan Kuttner, 'The "Extravagantes" of the Decretum in Biberach', BMCL 3 (1973) 61–71. (2) Darmstadt, Landesbibl MS 907, fol. 255r–256v (from Benedictine Abbey of Weingarten); see Kuttner, *Repertorium* 16, 274. (3) Graz, Univ.-Bibl, MS III.69, fol. 283v–284v. (4) Heiligenkreutz MS 44, fol. 298ra–300vb. (5) Innsbruck, Univ.-Bibl, MS 90, fol. 273–277; cf. F. Maassen SB Vienna 24 (1857) 64–66; Kuttner, *Repertorium* 286. (6) Munich, Staatsbiblio. lat. 28175, fol. 2ra–vc: not to be confused either with the *Fragmentum Monacense* (which occurs in the same manuscript, fol. 318ra–320rb) or the *Collectio Monacensis*, discussed below. (7) Pommersfeld MS 142 (2744), fol. 238vb–240ra; Kuttner, *Repertorium* 19–20. (8) Troyes, Bibliothèque de la Ville MS 103, fol. 2, 265v–66; cf. Kuttner, *Repertorium* 287–288. (9) Cambridge, Mass., Harvard Law Library MS 64, final two folios; Holtzmann-Cheney, *Collections*) xxviii. On these collections, see Weigand, n. 23 below.

22. Cf. J. Rambaud-Buhot, 'Les paleae dans le Décret de Gratien', *Proceedings Boston* 23–31, which concludes, 'Ces collections n'ont pas seulement servi à compléter le Décret, elles ont encore été la source des grandes collections de Décrétales de la fin du XIIe et du début du XIIIe siècle'.

23. Rudolf Weigand, 'Die Dekretanhänge in den Handschriften Heiligenkreuz 44, Pommersfelden 142 und München 28175', BMCL 13 (1983) 1–25; cf. idem, 'Zusätzliche Paleae im Dekrethandschriften', ZRG Kan. Abt. 88 (1992) 65–120.

rate points additional texts, including decretals, were entered by various hands in blank spaces or in the margins, as single items or in groups. In his report on these supplements, Kuttner discussed the possible sources in an earlier collection. Among the possibilities, he considered a Paris fragment and appendices to Gratian in the Innsbruck, Darmstadt, and Harvard manuscripts.[24] He also noted a 'parallelism' between the Biberach supplements and the Italian primitive collection Cusana (at Bernkastel-Kues).[25] The complex web of possible interrelationships is seen in his study of the nine insertions. Some point to Cusana as the most closely related, others to the Paris fragment.[26] This evidence led him to the conclusion that the Biberach manuscript offers 'an interesting example for the way in which extravagantes were collected from various sources and appended to individual copies of the *Decretum*'.[27] Similarly, the Troyes fragment, *Fragmentum Trecense*, records a stage in canonical codification between the *Decretum* and the early decretal collections.[28] It survives in three folios at the beginning and end of a Clairvaux volume, now in the Bibliothèque de la Ville in Troyes. The first folio in the volume (fol. 2r) preserves three decretals of Alexander III, to archbishops Henry of Reims and William of Sens, respectively (22 March 1171/72[29] and 2 June 1173/74), and an otherwise unknown letter of advice on procedural questions to archdeacon Robert of Châlons-sur-Marne, undated, but probably also 1171 or 1172.[30] The group is of evident importance in suggesting the provenance of the volume. The second component (fol. 265v and 266r), at the end of the volume, has the character of an appendix to Gratian, including both earlier and recent decretals, conciliar canons, and civilian texts. At least seven of these items (nos. 4, 6, 7, 10, 12, 14, 21) occur as *paleae* in Gratian manuscripts, and several others are canons of Alexander III's council at Tours in 1163 (nos. 5, 17–20). The group opens with Leo IX's much-discussed decretal *Relatum est auribus*,[31] followed by two items of unusual interest. The first of these,

24. Fragmentum B: Paris, B.N. lat. 15001, fol. 121vb–122r; cf. Kuttner, *Repertorium* 286–287.
25. Stephan Kuttner, 'Extravagantes' 61–71; cf. Rudolf Weigand, 'Die Dekrethandschrift B 3515 des Spitalarchivs Biberach an der Riss' BMCL 2 (1972) 76–81.
26. Kuttner, 'Extravagantes' 64.
27. Ibid. 71.
28. Troyes, Bibliothèque de la Ville 103, fol. 2, 265v–266; cf. Kuttner, *Repertorium* 287–288 (*Collectio Trecensis*); J. Rambaud-Buhot, 'L'Étude des manuscrits du Décret de Gratien conservées en France', SG 1, 133–139, especially 136 no. 23.
29. WH 299, JL 12020, 1171–1172, Ludwig Falkenstein, 'Pontificalis maturitas vel modestia sacerdotalis? Alexander III. und Heinrich von Frankreich in den Jahren 1170–72', AHP 22 (1984) 80 and n. 177: probably 1172.
30. Chodorow-Duggan, *Decretales ineditae* 21–22 no. 12, 1171–1172.
31. JL 4269: 20 April 1052.

Si qui clerici. . .immunis, is assigned to Alexander III, without identification of the addressee, and dated 31 January (1172). It is in fact an excerpt from Alexander's *Sicut dignum*, to Bishop Bartholomew of Exeter, on the appropriate penances for those involved in Becket's murder, but the selected segment contains important exceptions to the application of the Second Lateran Council's decree *Si quis suadente*, on the penalties for laying violent hands on a clerk.[32] The second item, *Si diversa pars. . . accepisse constiterit*, is a garbled conflation, in which excerpts from decretals to Roger of Worcester[33] and William of Sens[34] appear as a single entity.

The Second Phase: The 'Primitive' Collections

Although they had some features in common with the independent decretal collections, the essential characteristic of the *paleae* and the decretal appendices was their relationship with the *Decretum*, to which they were supplementary. The primitive decretal collections, in contrast, were compiled essentially from the new law as progressively defined in recent decretal letters and conciliar legislation. The earliest collections were unofficial in character, assembled and disseminated without papal initiative or authority, though the latter was explicit in almost every text that they contained, whether decretal or conciliar canon. They were also essentially private compilations, records of current law as it evolved through the workings of ecclesiastical jurisdiction. The canons of recent councils, notably of Tours (1163) and the Third Lateran Council (1179), lent an air of authority to many early collections, which sometimes opened with them, but it was the recent decretals that gave them their defining character. In their first creative stages, the collections recorded the professional interests and functions of the collectors, notably in the circles of papal judges-delegate. Thus they were composed primarily of decretals relating to litigation and jurisdiction, general principles and specific cases, the commissioning of judges-delegate, appeals, confirmation of judgments, and similar aspects of the judicial process.

The English Group

Although the whole of Western Europe shared to a greater or lesser degree in the expansion of the papal-appellate system that produced the

---

32. Cf. X 5.39.1–3 (wrongly addressed to the archbishop of Sens).
33. M. Cheney, 'JL 13162, Meminimus nos ex: One Letter or Two?' BMCL N.S. 4 (1974) 66–70.
34. *Sicut Romana*, JL 12293. The full text of the letter occurred as the third item on the opening fly-leaves (fol. 2rb) of the manuscript.

case law from which the collections were assembled, it was English canonists who took the lead in compiling and collating the materials as they were issued; and in any event, almost every extant primitive collection, of whatever provenance and family, reveals evidence of the formative influence of English sources. Seven early collections of English provenance have been identified: *Wigorniensis altera*, in a manuscript from Worcester cathedral priory, now in the British Library; *Belverensis*, from the Benedictine priory of Belvoir in Leicestershire, a dependency of St. Albans, now in the Oxford Bodleian Library; *1, 2, 3 Cantuariensis*, in the British Library; *Roffensis*, from Rochester cathedral priory, now in the British Library; *Regalis*, now in the British Library; *Dunelmensis prima*, in the Durham cathedral library; and *Fontanensis*, from the Cistercian abbey of Fountains, now in the Oxford Bodleian Library.[35]

Wigorniensis altera is the earliest English survivor, and it predates any of the known continental collections. Its ten decretals are all addressed to English or French recipients,[36] though the inscriptions are omitted from all but two of the letters.[37] Although there are only four dating clauses in the manuscript, nothing in the collection can be certainly dated later than 1175.[38] Apart from the two letters that retain their inscriptions (to Exeter and Norwich respectively), one each was sent to archdeacon Geoffrey of Lincoln, Henry of Reims, Roger of York, and William of Sens, and four (perhaps five) to Roger of Worcester. The manuscript is clearly of Worcester provenance, and was housed in the priory library in the Middle Ages. It was presumably assembled at Worcester by canonists in the circle of Bishop Roger (1164–1179), whose commissions are extensively recorded in the collections generally. Nevertheless, in some details, the collection is less accurate than a related sequence in the Belvoir collection, a product of the circle of Gilbert Foliot, bishop of London. This

---

35. *Wig. alt.*: London, Brit. Libr. Royal 11 B.ii, fol. 97r–102; *Belv.*: Oxford, Bodleian e Mus. 249 (S.C. 27835), fol. 121ra–135rb; *1–3 Cant.*: London, Brit. Lib. Royal 10 B iv, fol. 42v–61v; *Roff.*: London, Brit. Libr. Royal 10.C.iv, fol. 137v–154r; *Reg.*: London, Brit. Lib. Royal. 15 B.iv, fol. 107v–118v; *1 Dun.*: Durham, Cathed. C.III.1, fol. 5v–18r; *Font.*: Oxford, Bodleian Laud Misc. 527 (S.C. 814), fol. 24r–45v. Duggan, *Decretal Collections* 68–84. For analyses of *Wig. Alt.*, *Belv.*, 1,2,3 Cant., and *Roff.* see ibid. 152–187, cf. pll. I–III. For analyses of *1 Dun.* and *Font.* see Holtzmann-Cheney, *Collections* 75–115; cf. C. Duggan, 'A Durham Canonical Manuscript of the Late Twelfth Century', SCH 2 (1965) 179–185.

36. The collection is set out in 12 chapters, but chapters 2–3 and 4–5 belong respectively to single letters.

37. Chapters 1 and 7, addressed respectively to Bartholomew of Exeter and William of Norwich.

38. Chapter 1, to Bartholomew of Exeter, 31 January 1172; 3, to Roger of Worcester, 26 Nov. 1164; 11, to Henry of Reims, 22 March 1171–1172; 12, to Roger of York, 2 June 1173–1174.

small Worcester collection is a perfect example of a compilation made in the household of a notable English judge-delegate. It may be significant that four of the decretals in *Wigorniensis altera* are found also in the Troyes fragment, which has a comparable date, suggesting the existence of an even earlier Worcester fragment. The Belvoir collection survives in a volume of materials relating to Gilbert Foliot's career as bishop of London (1163–1187). It is a composite work in four parts, written in stages by different hands. It opens with the canons of the Council of Tours (1163) and a group of decretals (9–18) related to *Wigorniensis altera*, but in a different order and possibly closer to their common source in textual details. Nothing can be positively dated later than 1175 in this collection and the structure reveals both the chronological evolution and the successive stages of its compilation. Moreover, it shows the drawing together of materials from at least two English dioceses and their association with the latest promulgated law (Tours and Westminster). Even more significantly, the Worcester material can be traced through a succession of English and Continental collections. In Holtzmann's judgment, the closely parallel arrangement of the group in the Belvoir and St. Florian collections attested the presence of an Italian influence, or of an Italian collection, in England.[39] This argument is almost certainly the reverse of the truth. Date, contents, and circulation in early English collections all point to an English source in the entourage of Bishop Roger of Worcester and the circulation of that material in England.

The Canterbury collection is appropriately so named, in respect of contents and provenance.[40] No later pope than Alexander III is named in it, and the canons of the 1179 Lateran Council form its fourth and final part. Its three component groups of decretals record the familiar predominance of commissions to English judges-delegate and prelates. The collection is primitive, having no apparent pattern of organization or dismemberment of individual decretals, but a practical and professional interest is seen in marginal rubrics, relating to the office of judge-delegate, citation, recusal, and many other aspects of the judicial office.[41] Its opening sequence of thirteen decretals includes nine letters addressed to the archbishop of Canterbury, several jointly with his suffragans, while others relate to religious in the Canterbury province or to England generally. This element establishes the provenance of the collection and records one

---

39. Holtzmann-Cheney, *Collections* 43–47, especially p. 47.
40. Duggan, *Decretal Collections* 73–76; analysis, 162–171; comparative table, 171–173.
41. A judge-delegate can sub-delegate a case; how long the delegate's jurisdiction lasts; recusal of a judge is not admissible where appeal is forbidden; etc.

of two sequences of Canterbury decretals that were transmitted through later collections and finally into *Compilatio prima* and the *Decretales* of 1234, where they are distributed through the appropriate titles.

The related Rochester collection is a handsomely presented work in 151 items. It opens with the canons of the Third Lateran Council, followed by a sequence of decretals (27–69) corresponding with the Canterbury collection, but in a different order. The second part in the collection is of the same mixed character of primitive collections in general, intermingling English and continental decretals, with the former predominating. Its date of completion is later than that of the Canterbury collection, since five decretals of Lucius III (1181–1185) have been incorporated: decretal 119, to the bishop of Worcester, decretals 121, 145, and 146 to Bishop John of Norwich, and decretal 150 to Bishop Walter of Lincoln. The collection is followed by a later addition of Celestine III's decretal *Prudentiam tuam* (17 June 1193) to Dean John of Rouen. John, in fact, was the nephew of Archbishop Walter of Rouen, to whom the last letter in the base collection had been addressed (in his capacity as bishop of Lincoln).

At first sight, the Royal collection is less imposing than the Canterbury and Rochester collections,[42] its cursive script giving the impression of careless haste. But the appearance belies its technical advance. Although there is no formal division into books and titles and no system of numeration,[43] the work is furnished with a substantial corpus of 'rubrics' which summarize the key elements of many individual letters or chapters. These rubrics not only reflect the professional interests of the collector(s), but also demonstrate the expert character of the finished work. Some sequences focus on specific canonical questions, like the canon law of marriage, for example;[44] and many deal with highly technical points of juridical process: that an appeal can be made on an 'incidental' question; that sentence is not to be deferred through an appeal based on falsehood; that an appeal is to be accepted on minor matters; that a case may not be prolonged beyond the appointed day; that an appeal is to stand, unless prohibited; and many similar, succinctly stated, canonical principles. The presence in the volume of the judge-delegate formulary *A.B.C. iudices*, a widely used manual on judge-delegate procedures, further emphasizes the professional-

---

42. Duggan, *Decretal Collections* 81–84.
43. The work comprises 126 decretals and conciliar canons arranged in 162 un-numbered *capitula*: Charles Duggan, 'Twelfth Century Decretal Collections and Their Importance in English History' unpublished Ph.D. thesis, University of Cambridge (2 vols. 1954), 2, Appendix II.5a.
44. Rubrics 58–64 could be placed under the heading 'De statu st iure coniugii sive contracti sive contrahendi': cf. 76–82, 82–83.

ism of the work.⁴⁵ Since the collection contains no material later than the death of Alexander III, a date of compilation of ca. 1181 can be proposed; and its possession by Worcester cathedral in the Middle Ages may indicate it provenance.⁴⁶ Wherever it was compiled, however, its compilers were certainly expert canon lawyers.

In contrast, the first 'Durham' collection is an assemblage of three distinct parts, respectively of 50, 59, and 71 chapters,⁴⁷ two of which are otherwise unknown, and of these one is a forgery and the other is part of a papal privilege.⁴⁸ The first component in the collection is a gathering of decretals, conciliar canons, patristic texts and papal letters, with a final letter addressed to Bishop Udalric of Treviso (d. 1179). The letter is otherwise known only in the Italian primitive *Ambrosiana*, without identification of recipient. Holtzmann identified the opening five folios of this part as extracts from Burchard of Worms, in an altered sequence. Another sequence of decretals in this part, including early texts, the conciliar canons of Tours, items from Pseudo-Isidore, and letters of Eugenius III, occurs in the same order in the Innsbruck (*Oenipontana*) appendix to Gratian, and establishes the 'Durham' collection's affiliation with that first formative phase of post-Gratian works. In Holtzmann's judgment, this part of the 'Durham' collection was derived from a pre-1177 Italian source. The second part of the collection, apparently in the same hand, is composed predominantly of Alexander III's decretals, with an *arbor consanguinitatis* and the canons of the Third Lateran Council. The letters in this part of the collection, and their component chapters, are furnished with rubrics and were all sent by Alexander III, except for a sequence of three sent respectively by popes Eugenius III, Celestine III, and Innocent III. In contrast with the early Italian links in the previous part, the 'Durham' collection at this stage has demonstrable links with English primitive collections, notably with the 'Canterbury' collection, in both parts one and two.

The third and final part of the collection opens with the canons of the Council of Tours (1163). These are followed by a collection of decretals, mostly of Alexander III, including two texts from Gregory VII's register and one of Deusdedit (cc.26–28), and a forged text addressed to the

---

45. F. Donald Logan, 'An Early Thirteenth-Century Formulary', *Studia Gratiana*, 14 (1967): *Collectanea Stephan Kuttner*, 4, 75–87; Duggan, *Decretal Collections* 82; cf. idem, 'Papal Judges Delegate' above, at n. 13.

46. Mary G. Cheney, *Roger, Bishop of Worcester, 1164–1179* (Oxford 1980) 198.

47. Duggan, *Decretal Collections* 69, 78–79; Holtzmann-Cheney, *Collections* 75–99.

48. The letters are addressed respectively to the monks of Lenton priory in Nottinghamshire and to Master R. of York.

monks of Lenton. The whole work ends with four decretals of Lucius III, but these are manifest additions in later hands.

The 'Bridlington' Family

Although in one sense belonging to the 'English' group, the 'Bridlington' family is discussed as a separate entity because of the striking relationship between its two collections. The Bridlington and Claudian collections are named from the medieval location of the former in the Augustinian priory of Bridlington in Yorkshire and the present location of the latter in a Cotton Claudius manuscript in the British Library.[49] Neither collection is at present available in printed analysis, but they are discussed in unpublished analyses in the Cambridge University Library, and in the Holtzmann papers. The collections differ markedly in their physical appearance; the Bridlington collection is handsomely written in double columns on large folios, with little marginal addition, and the Claudian collection is transcribed in double columns, in a small neat hand, with an elaborate marginal apparatus. The collections are closely related for part of their contents and evolved independently from a common archetype. Despite their neat and professional appearance, there is no outward indication of subject-matter organization, and many of their longer decretals are left undissected. The collections comprise 193 items in *Bridlingtonensis* and 216 in *Claudiana*, numbered in sequence in both collections, except where *Bridlingtonensis* breaks off the numeration at 174 (recte 173). In addition to the decretals, which form the bulk of their contents, the canons of the Council of Tours (1163) appear as the concluding items in *Bridlingtonensis* (186–193); and the canons of Tours and of the Third Lateran Council (1179), and a series of thirty-seven propositions under the heading 'Concilium Ricardi Cantuariensis Archiepiscopi' (1175)[50] are found in *Claudiana* (23, 84, and 24, respectively). The collections clearly share a common ancestor, or family archetype, which is preserved as an entity in *Claudiana* (1–107), and as two disjointed parts in *Bridlingtonensis* (1–40 and 68–119).

The date of completion of the Bridlington collection has been placed at ca. 1181, since its inscriptions name no pope later than Alexander III (1159–1181), but the name of his successor, Lucius III, appears in rubric in the outer margin of fol. 118rb, beside a letter that was certainly sent by Al-

---

49. Bridlington = *Collectio Bridlingtonensis*: Oxford, Bodleian Library, MS Bodley 357 (S.C. 2452), fol. 80r–133v; Claudian = *Collectio Claudiana* London, British Library, Cotton Claudius A. iv, fol. 189–216. For both, see Duggan, *Decretal Collections* 84–95 and pl. iv; idem, 'Decretal Collections', (thesis) Appendix III; Holtzmann-Cheney, *Collections* 132–134.

50. Propositions for debate at the Westminster Council of 1175: see Mary Cheney, 'The Council of Westminster 1175: New light on an old source', SCH 11 (1975) 61–68.

exander. It is entirely probable that the rubric insert was intended for the inner margin, where the otherwise unknown decretal *Grave gerimus* appears without its sender's name, since the possibility that Lucius III was the author of *Grave gerimus* was independently conjectured, when the decretal was first printed in 1982.[51] It was also then suspected that a further decretal, *Quia nos duxit*, to Bishop John of St. Andrews, was issued by Lucius.[52] This evidence suggests a date of completion of 1182. In contrast, the additions to the common stock in *Claudiana* include letters as late as Urban III's pontificate (1185–1187), ending with an excerpt from Urban's *Cum venisset ad apostolicam*, to the abbots of Rufford and Croxton and the prior of Thurgarton, *post* 26 June 1186–1187.[53]

An analysis of the 'Bridlington' collections reveals the familiar characteristics of English collections, in recording primarily the judicial activities of English judges-delegate, above all the prelates of Worcester, Exeter, and Canterbury. The Claudian collection has in addition the highly significant insertion of the 'propositions' for archbishop Richard's 1175 Council of Westminster. In technical presentation, the 'Bridlington' collections are remarkable for their full and well-developed system of rubrics, and especially for the imposing marginal apparatus in *Claudiana*, including numerous *supra* and *infra* references, both for individual letters and for their constituent parts. It was left to the posthumous publication of Holtzmann's materials in 1979 to reveal his discovery that a substantial sequence of decretals in the non-archetypal element in *Claudiana* is related to a late recension of the seminal *Appendix Concilii Lateranensis*. Holtzmann realized that the collection is a subsidiary branch of that tradition, passing beyond previous collections in its subject-matter rubrics and marginal references. The compiler had a good knowledge of Roman law, and the texts he included were almost always better than those in Bridlington. The *Claudiana* collection is, therefore, in Holtzmann's apt summation, 'particularly valuable for the literary history of the genre'.[54]

The 'Tortosa' Group

The Tortosa (*Dertusensis*) group of collections comprises Tortosa I (*Dertusensis prima*), Eberbach (*Eberbacensis*), and Alcobaça I (*Alcobacensis prima*). Tortosa I is now in the library in Tortosa;[55] Eberbach and Al-

---

51. Bridlington 131: Chodorow-Duggan, *Decretales ineditae* 66–67 no. 39.
52. Bridlington 146: Chodorow-Duggan, *Decretales ineditae* 143–144 no. 83.
53. Claudiana 216: WH 527, JL 15731, 26 June 1186–1187.
54. Holtzmann-Cheney, *Collections* 134.
55. Tortosa Bibl. Capitular, MS 144, fol. 1–29; analyzed by Holtzmann, 'Beiträge zu den Dekretalensammlungen des zwölften Jahrhunderts', ZRG Kan. Abt.16 (1927).

cobaça I belonged to the Cistercian abbeys of Eberbach and Alcobaça in the Middle Ages, but are now in the British Library and the National Library of Lisbon, respectively.[56] The collections have a common stock, but the Tortosa and Alcobaça manuscripts have substantial supplements, independently of each other. Through the loss of a quire from the Alcobaça codex, a sequence of conciliar canons and decretals is missing, but it can be inferred that the lost decretals almost certainly corresponded with the opening sequence in the Tortosa collection. The Tortosa and Alcobaça manuscripts were certainly written in the Spanish peninsula—the script of the Tortosa collection is Spanish, and it has uniquely surviving Spanish decretals among its closing items. The Alcobaça collection has notes in Portuguese and Spanish, written by a later hand on its opening folio recto, and an otherwise unknown letter of Alexander III to the king of Portugal within the decretal collection. No Spanish or Portuguese connections appear in the Eberbach collection. Although bearing an early 'ex libris' of the monastery, the manuscript was written in northern France and was one of the books imported into the monastery to augment its library. Derivation from Clairvaux, Eberbach's mother house, has been proposed, but that remains a supposition.[57] Early possession by a monastic community, however, seems confirmed by its sole marginal comment, on the exemption of monks from tithe payment—'hic probatur quod monachi non tenentur solvere decimis'.

Holtzmann named the family 'the Tortosa (*Dertusensis*) group', and proposed the period following the Third Lateran Council (March 1179) as its *terminus a quo*. This judgment was clearly made on the evidence provided by Tortosa collection; but it is not supported by the evidence of two related collections discussed below. The Tortosa collection ends with a sequence of twelve decretals, which were not in the archetype, nine of which are otherwise unknown. Three relate to a crisis in relations between the Hungarian archbishops Andreas of Kalocsa and Lucas of Esztergom; they are addressed respectively to the suffragans and subjects of the two archbishops, to Lucas individually, and to the Hungarian king. Holtzmann conjectured that the letters were secured by Andreas at the time of the Lateran Council, at which he was the only Hungarian prelate present, the

---

56. London, British Library, Arundel 490, fols 210r–221r; analyzed by Holtzmann, ZRG Kan. Abt. 17 (1928) 548–555. Lisbon, Bibl. nacional, Alcob. 144 [314], fol. iv–39v; analyzed in Holtzmann-Cheney, *Collections* 8–25.

57. N. F. Palmer, *Zisterzienzer und ihre Bücher: die mittelalterliche Bibliotheksgeschichte von Kloster Eberbach im Rheingau* (Regensburg 1998) 72, 74–75, 246, 283–284, Plates 54–55, 169; cf. Rosy Schilling, 'The "Decretum Gratiani" formerly in the C.W. Dyson Perrins Collection', *Journal of the Archaeological Association*, 3d Ser. 26 (1963) 27–39, at 36.

letters being favorable to him in the conflict, and that in some way unique copies of the letters were brought to Spain.[58]

The Tortosa supplement also includes otherwise unknown decretals to Spanish recipients—two to Toledo, involving the church of Palencia; one to a certain R., concerning his desire to transfer to the Order of Calatrava, another to Spanish bishops concerning the Jews, and another to the bishops of Ávila and Salamanca, concerning a financial transaction between certain citizens of Lucca and the Master and Knights of St. James. There is clearly no doubt of the Spanish provenance of the finished Tortosa manuscript; but an entirely different picture emerges if the common stock of the Tortosa and Eberbach collections is examined. Its decretals are more frequently of English provenance than any other, the letters to Canterbury being significantly numerous, and grouped together. They are addressed to the archbishop of Canterbury, alone or with his suffragans, or to the suffragans, or to the monks and religious of Canterbury, and some of the inscriptions address the archbishop as apostolic legate. Moreover, there is an emphasis on the activities of Richard of Canterbury, Becket's successor, from the mid-1170s.

Any hesitation in accepting the English sources of the 'Tortosa' family stock is removed by consideration of the Alcobaça collection. Its contents present a striking reflection of the work of Richard of Canterbury, Roger of Worcester, and Bartholomew of Exeter. The decretals to Canterbury appear within two separated sequences (31–57 and 95–124), and are related to the Canterbury element already noticed in other collections. The Worcester decretals most strikingly appear in the single sequence 50–72, and it has been persuasively argued that access to Bishop Roger of Worcester's archives are the probable source.[59] The Exeter decretals appear most strikingly in a single block 73–85, and include two decretals otherwise unknown.[60] A remarkable feature of the collection is its preservation of the full form of the address for the individual letters, usually abbreviated or omitted in the collections, almost certainly recording their derivation from the originals. Still more remarkable, a close examination of the individual cases suggests that a sequence of Exeter decretals dates from the 1160s, during Becket's lifetime and when he was in exile, and reflects the work of Bishop Bartholomew in his diocese, whereas the Worcester decretals date from the 1170s, and reflect Roger's commissions

---

58. W. Holtzmann, 'Papst Alexander III. und Ungarn', *Ungarische Jahrbücher* 6 (1926) 387–426; C. Duggan, 'Decretal Letters to Hungary', *Folia Theologica* 3 (1992) 5–31.

59. Cheney, *Roger, Bishop of Worcester*, 203–207.

60. Duggan, 'Decretals to Exeter in Alcobacensis prima', in 'Decretals of Alexander III to England' *Miscellanea Rolando Bandinelli* (above, n. 5), 87–106.

as papal judge-delegate. The Exeter and Worcester decretals in *Alcobacensis prima* therefore record two quite distinct aspects of the judicial concerns of the English bishops. The Canterbury decretals draw on the wider transmission of Richard of Canterbury's decretals and other Canterbury material, from the mid-1170s. It cannot be supposed that the Alcobaça collection is not chiefly a derivative from English sources.[61]

The 'French' Group

The four collections of the 'French' group take their name from their present or past locations—Cambridge (*Cantabrigiensis*) is in the library of Trinity College, Cambridge; St. Victor I (*Victorina prima*) is in the Bibliothèque Nationale in Paris, but belonged to the canons regular of St. Victor; *Parisiensis prima* is also in the Bibliothèque Nationale, and Orval (*Aureavallensis*) is in the Luxembourg B.N., but belonged to the Cistercian house of Orval in Belgium.[62] The Cambridge and Paris I collections have been known in printed analyses since 1897, and Orval since 1927, but St. Victor I has become known in a summary analysis only since 1979.[63] The collections are all technically primitive, since they are not organized into books and titles on a subject-matter basis (except for a sequence of marriage decretals in Cambridge 75–100, most of which also appear as a single item as a list of inscriptions and incipits in St. Victor I, 100), and they do not apply the advanced systematic technique of decretal dissection. The individual items are numbered in sequence in the Orval manuscript (1–132), and their numbers are supplied in the printed analyses of the other collections (Cambridge 1–100; St. Victor I, 1–146; and Paris I, 1–185). The collections date from the closing years of Alexander III's pontificate († 1181), but the Orval collection is later in completion, since a letter of Lucius III to the archbishop of Toulouse is incorporated within it.[64] This letter is attributed elsewhere to Alexander III, and dated 1179–81, even in Holtzmann's *Regesta decretalium*, but the unique identification of Lucius in the Orval manuscript is conclusive. The manuscript also has the correct address that appears in some collections as Toledo.

61. Charles Duggan, 'English Decretals in Continental Primitive Collections, with Special Reference to the Primitive Collection of Alcobaça', *Collectanea Stephan Kuttner* (SG 14; Bologna 1967) 4.51–71, especially 63–71.

62. Cambridge, Trinity College, R.9.17, fol. 72r–107v; Paris, B.N. lat. 14938, fol. 226r–263r; Paris, B.N., lat. 1596, fol. 11–46; Luxembourg, Bibl. nat. 30, fol. 101r–117v.

63. *Cantabrigiensis*: Emil Friedberg, *Die Canones-Sammlungen zwischen Gratian und Bernhard von Pavia* (Leipzig 1897; reprinted Graz 1958) 5–21; Paris I: ibid., 45–63; *Aureavallensis*: Holtzmann, 'Beiträge zu den Dekretalensammlungen', 77–115; *Victorina prima*: Holtzmann-Cheney, *Collections* 26–34.

64. *Aureavallensis* 79: Lucius III Tolesano archiepiscopo. *Requisivit a nobis*: JL 14114, WH 887.

The provenance of the 'French' collections has been variously assessed. Van Hove (1945) judged that the Cambridge collection was made in England (1175–1179), that Paris I derived from it, and that Orval was assembled in Lorraine in the pontificate of Lucius III (1181–1185) or Urban III (1185–1187), depending partly on Paris I. In contrast, Stickler in 1950 called all four collections the 'Familia Gallica', and judged that all were made in France, an opinion confirmed by Holtzmann, who named these four 'the French group', and listed them in the order given here.[65] The evidence for assembly in France is persuasive, but equally so is the evidence of significant derivation from earlier English sources.[66]

The dual character is particularly well illustrated by the Cambridge Collection, whose large number of English decretals led Van Hove to consider it an English composition.[67] But the French provenance of the completed collection is demonstrated by its opening text. Under the heading 'Iste liber continet litteras romanas', the collection begins with Alexander III's encyclical letter on his election and the ensuing outbreak of the schism. The letter is known elsewhere, addressed to various recipients, but it is not otherwise found in canonical collections. The copy in the Cambridge Collection is addressed to Bishop Peter of Paris, the canons of the cathedral, and all the clergy of Paris, with the marginal rubric 'Littere Alexandri pape in tempore scismatis, misse clero parisiensi'.[68] The collection is written in two clearly distinct parts. The first part, 1–74 (fol. 72r–96v), includes an unbroken sequence of English decretals (21–33), and others inserted passim; the second part, 75–100 (fol. 98v–107v) comprises 26 decretals, all concerned with marriage questions, of which a striking number relate to Italian cases, addressed to Cassino, Termoli, Brescia, Anglona, Palermo, Trani, Bari, Pisa, Fondi, Salerno, and Bisceglie (twice). These letters are also found in St. Victor I, but in a different sequence, and more widely scattered. A primary English source for this component seems unlikely.[69]

Further evidence of the non-English provenance of the Cambridge codex is found in an independent sequence of letters (fol. 108r–129v) that

---

65. A. Van Hove, *Prolegomena ad Codicem Iuris Canonici* (2d ed. Malines-Rome 1945) 351; A. Stickler, *Historia Iuris Canonici Latini*, 1: *Historia Fontium* (Turin 1950) 223; Holtzmann, 'Über eine Ausgabe', 21–22.

66. See Duggan, *Decretal Collections* 128–130.

67. Van Hove, *Prolegomena* 351.

68. Peter Lombard, Master of the Sentences, elected bishop 1159, †21-22 August 1160.

69. Friedberg, *Canones-Sammlungen* 5–21; Duggan, *Decretal Collections* 128–130; idem, 'Italian Marriage Decretals in English Collections: with Special Reference to the Peterhouse Collection', *Cristianità ed Europa: Miscellane di Studi in Onore di Luigi Prosdocimi*, ed. Cesare Alzati (2 vols. Rome-Freiburg-Vienna 1994) 2.417–451, especially 417–418.

follows the canonical collection, beginning on a fresh folio recto. The letters deal very markedly with affairs of the French church. In 1885 Loewenfeld thought that the letters were a fragment of Alexander III's registers; Holtzmann rejected this view of the so-called 'Register fragment' in 1940, but conjectured that the collection could be a copy of letters excerpted from the registers. Pennington has emphasized the letters relating to Bishop Simon of Meaux and the clerk Herveus, judging that many of the letters would not have been enregistered, that all the letters probably date from the last four years of Alexander III's pontificate, and that they may derive from a collection of originals kept by Herveus himself.[70] Certainly the presence of these letters further supports the thesis of French provenance for the codex in which the decretal collection is preserved.

In much the same way, *Parisiensis prima* provides evidence of the combination of English and French canonical sources.[71] Indeed, the organization of the collection, according to recipients (Canterbury, York, London, Winchester, Exeter, Norwich, St. Albans, and Lisieux) confirms its English associations, although many of the inscriptions are incorrect.[72] For instance, items 99–106 are addressed to St. Albans, whereas the letters were in fact sent respectively to the abbot of St. Albans (99–100), Archbishop William of Sens (a single letter in six chapters, 101–105), and the bishop-elect of Asti.[73] The presence of rare English decretals within the closing sequence 165–185 is no less significant, however. Two are found only in this collection, and a third is found complete only in this collection and the Orval: no. 165 is addressed to the abbot and monks of Bardney in Lincolnshire, concerning complaints of the abuse of the abbey's hospitality by the wives of patrons of the abbey's churches; no. 177 is addressed to the dean of St. Martin's in London, concerning complaints by the clerk Hunfridus on his violent ejection from the church of St. Nicholas;[74] and a third

---

70. S. Loewenfeld, *Epistolae Pontificum Romanorum ineditae* (Leipzig 1885); Walter Holtzmann, 'Die Register Papst Alexander III. in den Händen der Kanonisten', QF 30 (1940) 13–87 at pp. 69–87; Kenneth Pennington, 'Epistolae Alexandrinae: A Collection of Pope Alexander III's Letters', *Miscellanea Rolando Bandinelli* 337–353.

71. Friedberg, *Canones-Sammlungen* 45–63. The collection opens with the canons of the 1179 Lateran Council, and the items run in a single sequence 1–185, but the number of decretals is less than this numeration suggests, since the component chapters of longer letters are counted as individual items: for example, 8–14 is the single letter *Fraternitatem*, to the archbishop of York.

72. The pattern of presentation was noticed by Juncker in the introduction to his analysis of the Italian collection *Berolinensis prima*: J. Juncker, 'Die Collectio Berolinensis', ZRG Kan. Abt. 13 (1924) 284–426.

73. Duggan, 'Italian Marriage Decretals in English Collections' 436–438 and 447, Appendix 5.

74. Friedberg, *Canones-Sammlungen* 61, 63.

decretal, found complete only in the Orval and Paris manuscripts, is addressed to the bishop of Worcester and the abbot of Evesham, concerned a prolonged marriage case involving the woman R.[75] The large proportion of English decretals which it contains, some otherwise unknown, together with their nature and subject-matter, their occasional rarity, and the curiously false attribution of some non-English letters to English, recipients all suggest the use of English materials.

At the same time, some forged texts have been detected. Two have recently been edited. One, purportedly of Alexander III to Bishop Gilbert Foliot, lamented the pope's frustrated hopes in the translation of Gilbert from Hereford to London; another to the archbishop of Bordeaux (within the Angevin territories) and his suffragans, on the avaricious oppressions of the clergy, alike by bishops, archdeacons, deans, and archpriests. The letter to Foliot is almost certainly a forgery, and that to the prelates of the Bordeaux province is very probably so. In these circumstances, a new analysis is essential.[76]

The Italian Family

The Italian primitive group comprises four decretal collections listed by Holtzmann in 1945: the Berlin, St. Florian, Bernkastel-Kues an der Mosel (Kues), and Douai collections, named after the modern location of their manuscripts.[77] To these was later added the San Ambrogio collection, in Milan.[78] Until recently, only the Berlin collection (*Berolinensis prima*) was known in printed analysis, through Juncker's exemplary study of the collection in 1924.[79] Among other features, he drew attention to the large number of English decretals in the collection, and to some of the topics dealt with in the letters—clerics, patronage, judicial process, marriage questions, and other themes. Other members of the Italian family were little known in analytical detail until the posthumous publication of Holtzmann's papers in 1979.[80]

The collection in the capitular library of San Ambrogio (*Ambrosiana*) re-

---

75. Ibid. 62 (1 Par. 176) = *Aureavallensis* 40.

76. C. Duggan, 'Improba pestis falsitatis: Forgeries and the Problem of Forgery in Twelfth-Century Decretal Collections (with Special References to English cases)', *Fälschungen im Mittelalter*, ed. H. Fuhrmann (MGH, Schriften 33; Hanover 1988) 2.328–330 nos. 3 and 4.

77. *Berolinensis prima*: Berlin, Deutsche Staatsbibl., Phillipps 1742 (cat. Rose, 96), fol. 287r–294v; St Florian, Stiftsbibl., III.5, fol. 173r–183r; Kues, now Bernkastel-Kues, Hospitalbibl., 229, fol. 67r–123v; Douai, Bibl. de la Ville, 590, fol. 1r–2v, 247r–248v (from Anchin).

78. Milan, Archivio capitolare di San Ambrogio S M.57, fol. 307v–320r.

79. Juncker, 'Die Collectio Berolinensis' cf. Holtzmann', *Traditio* 18 (1962) 453–454. The Duggan, *Decretal Collections* 130–132.

80. Holtzmann-Cheney, *Collections* 35–42, *Ambrosiana*; 43–63, *Florianensis*; 64–65, *Duacensis*; 66–74, *Cusana*.

flects very clearly the creative phase between Gratian's *Decretum* and the evolution of the new decretal collections. It comprises 62 texts of varied character (1–62), followed by the canons of the Third Lateran Council of 1179 (63–88). In Holtzmann's words, the collection 'illustrates the difficulty in defining a decretal collection as distinct from an appendix to Gratian.' It can be analyzed in four parts, the first (1–15) revealing features in common with the appendices to Gratian, and specifically with the Darmstadt and Harvard manuscripts.[81] The second part (16–53) includes letters of Alexander III and the canons of the Council of Tours (1163); the third part (54–62) comprises various items, including imperial constitutions and letters of earlier popes, and the canons of the Third Lateran Council (1179) compose the fourth and final part (63–88), perhaps an addition to an existing collection.

The St. Florian collection (*Florianensis*) is a large and finely presented collection of 172 items, its marginal gloss including references both to Gratian and to the Civil Law—the Digest, Code, and Authentica. The work was first transcribed with a serious misplacement in the order of its texts, but the error was noticed and the correct sequence, the rectus ordo, inserted.[82] The provenance of the collection has been much discussed. The large number of English decretals in the collection and the accuracy of English references are striking features of the collection, which includes one sequence of five decretals concerning a dispute over the church of Bungay in Suffolk, involving Earl Hugh of Norfolk and the chaplain Wimar.[83] Since there seems no doubt that the manuscript was transcribed in Italy, the presence of the Bungay decretals calls for comment. At one stage, Holtzmann conjectured that the collection's exemplar was once in England and was returned to Bologna with the English material; he later proposed that the letters were supplied by an English student to his teacher in Bologna: either way, the collector derived some of his material from an English source.[84]

In a similar context, Holtzmann spoke of 'the diffusion of a collection of this stock in England,' tabulating two short sequences in *Florianensis* respectively with the Berlin, Kues, and Fountains collections, and with the Berlin, Kues, Belvoir, and Claudian collections.[85] The correspondence between the collections is certainly very striking, but the transmission was almost certainly in the opposite direction, from England to Italy.[86]

---

81. Eight of its chapters were taken into the *Decretum* as paleae: see Holtzmann-Cheney, *Collections* 35, 37–38.
82. Holtzmann-Cheney, *Collections* 43–63.
83. Chodorow-Duggan, *Decretales ineditae* 81–86 no. 46.
84. Holtzmann-Cheney, *Collections* 45 and n. 8.
85. Holtzmann-Cheney, *Collections* 47.
86. Cf. analyses and discussions of *Wigorniensis altera* and *Belverensis*, above.

The Third Phase: The Systematic Collections

The systematic collections were the work of professional canonists, who were concerned above all with an organized and comprehensive presentation of their material for a range of judicial, juristic or academic purposes: as practical handbooks for canonists, for analysis and glossatorial commentary, and for teaching in the schools. The tradition includes seven distinct elements or lines of transmission: *Parisiensis secunda*, the Worcester Tradition (with seven collections), the *Appendix* group (of nine members), twelve collections or fragments of the 'Bamberg' group, four 'Frankfurt' manuscripts, three manuscripts of the 'Bruges' collection, and three Anglo-Norman collections. The designations 'Worcester' and 'Anglo-Norman' are accurate indications of provenance, but the names 'Paris II', 'Bamberg', 'Frankfurt', and 'Bruges' merely identify the present location either of the single manuscript (Paris) or of the first representative of the group to be discovered (Bamberg, Frankfurt, and Bruges).

Parisiensis secunda

The second 'Paris' collection, which has been variously assessed in the past,[87] appears as the first of the systematic collections, and its formal structure justifies that position in the printed lists. It was analyzed by Friedberg in 1897, in ninety-five short sections,[88] under such rubricated headings as *De consuetudine, De prioribus et posterioribus synodis, De novis statutis* (1–3); *De testibus, De purgatione canonica, De purgatione vulgari, De appellationibus* (29–

---

87. Paris, BN, MS lat. 1566, fol. 1–54v. Cf. Stickler, *Historia Iuris Canonici* 1, 223: 'Haec est prima collectio in titulos (95) divisa, sed ordo logicus valde est imperfectus'; A. Van Hove, *Prolegomena ad Codicem Iuris Canonici* (2d ed., Malines-Rome 1945) 352: 'ex 236 eius monumentis 180 sunt Gratiano anteriora, ita ut sit dicenda collectio canonum potius quam compilatio decretalium. Dividitur in titulos, ordine logico valde imperfecta'; Duggan, *Decretal Collections* 52: 'an extension of pre-Gratian traditions into the decretal era, intermingling ancient canons with more recent papal letters . . . the overall plan of composition was unsatisfactory'; Hanenburg, 'Decretals and Decretal Collections' 593: 'And the intermingling happens to be of ancient and recent conciliar canons with ancient and recent decretal letters . . . or in short, of ancient with new authorities . . . (p. 594) the compiler of Parisiensis II followed the *Decretum* closely in the arrangement of subject-matter. . . . (p. 599). Within the group of systematic collections, in the movement of replacing old law by new, Parisiensis II stands at the very beginning'; Landau, 'Entstehung' 126: 'Sie ist allerdings nur bedingt als Dekretalensammlungen zu bezeichnen, da von dem aufgenommenen Rechtsstoff mehr als 75% vorgratianischen Ursprungs sind. . . . Es bleibt höchstwahrscheinlich, das Bernhard diese Kanones-Dekretalensammlung als eines seiner Jugendwerk verfasste . . .'

88. In Holtzmann's numeration, the collection has 96 sections. Although Friedberg (*Canones-Sammlungen* 42) noted the marginal rubric 'De annuis pensionibus' between his numbers 63 and 64, he did not include it in his numeration of titles, and therefore there is a discrepancy of one between his numeration and Holtzmann's, from that point: inclusively from 64, Holtzmann's numbers = Friedberg's + 1.

32); *De foro rei sequendo, De clericis depositis, De participantibus excommunicatis* (44–46), etc. The material is presented in a clear and professional way, with a substantial marginal apparatus, including references to the *Decretum* and to Roman law, and to other relevant texts *supra* and *infra* within the collection itself, the latter device making it sometimes unnecessary to repeat a text relevant to more than one rubric. At the same time, however, the collection has something of the character of an extended appendix to Gratian. Not only does its arrangement of topics reflect Gratian's, but up to seventy-five percent of its material is pre-Gratian, and its new decretals are generally undissected.[89] It thus occupies a transitional position in the history of the formal canon law. Almost certainly an early work of Bernard of Pavia at Bologna, its dating limits of ca. 1177 to 1179 are fixed by its inclusion of the decretal *Quamvis simus*, to Bishop Richard of Winchester (21 July 1177), and its omission of the decrees of the Third Lateran Council (March 1179). Although the collection stands somewhat in isolation from the remainder of the systematic tradition, it is important evidence of canonical teaching in the school at Bologna in the late 1170s. But its pattern was soon to be abandoned by its author, Bernard of Pavia, in favor of compilations of the new, post-Gratian law (*ius novum*): the Leipzig (*Lipsiensis*) collection, post-1185, and, more importantly, *Compilatio prima*, 1189–1191.

The 'Worcester' (*Wigorniensis*) Group (deriving from Exeter-Worcester)

Formerly classified as primitive but now, more fittingly, as systematic, the 'Worcester' (*Wigorniensis*) group is of the highest interest for historians and canonists alike. It is among the more aptly named traditions, since there is no doubt that judges-delegate and canonists at Worcester played the decisive role in its evolution, though it is virtually certain that an earlier archetype was made at Exeter.[90] On the basis of the schematic organization of their contents, even in their earliest members, the collections belong to the systematic tradition as redefined above, despite the fact that their longer decretals, like those in Bernard of Pavia's *Parisiensis secunda*, were left undis-

---

89. To cite one example, 2 *Par.* 20.1a–e, under the title *De tempore ordinationis*, and 21.1, under *De filiis presbiterorum*, are simply the single decretal *Super eo quod quesitum*, to Bishop Robert of Hereford, which is distributed in six sections elsewhere in the systematic collection. The English inscriptions in *2 Par.* are sometimes corrupt. Hereford appearing as Lietene (Friedberg: Hetene) and G. Loncolniensi archidiacono as G. Inic. Archiepiscopo in the decretal immediately following; cf. Friedberg, *Canones-Sammlungen* 35.

90. An Exeter archetype probably existed in the early 1160s: see Charles Duggan, 'The Trinity Collection of Decretals and the Early Worcester Family', Traditio 17 (1961) 506–526 (especially 513–516 and 525–526, Appendix II); reprinted in my *Canon Law in Medieval England* VII, cf. 'Addenda et corrigenda' 4–5; idem, 'Decretals of Alexander III to England' 87–106, especially 89–98.

sected. The historical origins of the 'Worcester' tradition lie in the numerous papal commissions of Alexander III to bishops Bartholomew of Exeter (1161–1184) and Roger of Worcester (1164–1179), the latter a cousin of King Henry II and the only English bishop to share Becket's exile, the former the recipient of Alexander III's letter on the appropriate penances for those involved in Becket's murder. Together, they were, in Alexander's well-known phrase, the twin luminaries of the English Church. No less important was their friend and colleague from the Exeter diocese—Baldwin, archdeacon of Totnes, who retired to the Cistercian abbey of Ford ca. 1169, at the height of the Becket controversy, and was its abbot by 1175. He succeeded Roger at Worcester in 1180, accompanied by canonists from the Exeter diocese, and was archbishop of Canterbury from 1184, until his death at Acre in 1190. The work of these three prelates is clearly imprinted on the creative phase of the 'Worcester' tradition. Indeed, the Worcester collection itself, now in the British Library, was almost certainly completed in Baldwin's ecclesiastical household, in his first year at Worcester, or very shortly after (ca. 1181).

The First Generation of the 'Worcester' Group: The Worcester and Klosterneuburg Collections

Of the seven members of the 'Worcester' family discovered so far, two belong to the first and three to the second phase of the collection's evolution. The first generation comprises four collections or fragments: a fragment of six folios in the library of Trinity College, Cambridge (*Trinitatis*);[91] the Worcester collection, in the British Library (*Wigorniensis*); a fragment of two bi-folia, almost a palaeographical mirror reflection of *Wigorniensis* itself, in the Hereford cathedral library (the Hereford Fragment);[92] and a collection in the library of the Augustinian canons of Klosterneuburg (*Claustroneoburgensis*).[93] Even within this limited survival there is evidence of development within the archetype. A first recension was in existence by the end of 1181, when the core of *Wigorniensis* was derived from it;[94] but a further increment, including letters of Pope Lucius III, can be identified in the final sequence of the Klosterneuburg collection.[95]

91. Duggan, 'The Trinity Collection of Decretals'.
92. For the Hereford Fragment, see Charles Duggan, *Canon Law in Medieval England: The Becket Dispute and Decretal Collections* (London 1982), 'Addenda et corrigenda' 4, Study VII. It contains *Wigorniensis* 7.19–27 and 33–44.
93. Cambridge, Trinity College, R.14.9, fol. 82r–87v; London, B.L. Royal 10.A.II, fol. 5r–62v (*Wigorniensis*); Hereford, Cathedral Library, fragment of a decretal collection; Klosterneuburg, Stiftsbibl. 19, fol. 36r–87 (*Claustroneoburgensis*).
94. The latest datable item is *Recepimus litteras*, Alexander III to the bishop of Durham and the abbots of Bury St. Edmunds and St. Albans, 23 January 1181: WH 846, JL 14365.
95. *Claustroneoburgensis* 296–344; cf. nos. 302 (to the bishop of Worcester and the abbot of Evesham: WH 497; JL—) and 319 (to the bishop of Rapolla: WH 885; JL 15165).

The largest and best-presented of this early phase of development is *Wigorniensis* itself, which contains 274 decretals or parts of decretals (including nine duplicates) arranged as capitula and distributed through seven books as follows:

1. *De statu et iure coniugii sive contracti sive contrahendi* (49 chapters)
2. *De statu religiosorum et de eorundem privilegio* (37 chapters)
3. *De statu clericorum* (40 chapters)
4. *De statu et iure ecclesiarum* (50 chapters)
5 *De casibus, in quibus non est deferendum appellationibus* (13 chapters)
6. *De casibus, in quibus est deferendum appellationibus, etiam si causa sit appellatione remota commissa* (4 chapters)
7. *Ad informandum iudices in diversis casibus quandoque emergentibus* (81 chapters).[96]

The historical context of this collection, the functions of the recipients of the decretals, and the professional interests of the collectors are strikingly evident in the last three books, which deal with appeals and instructions for judges. These topics were not the primary interests of canonists in the schools, but they were of the utmost concern to practicing lawyers; and it is highly significant that, of the last eighteen decretals in *Wigorniensis*, at least twelve were addressed to, or refer by title to, one or more of the following: the bishop of Worcester, the bishop of Exeter, the abbot of Ford, and Prior Robert of Kenilworth, a familiar judicial colleague of the bishop of Worcester.[97]

Lohmann's analysis of *Wigorniensis* in 1933 revealed the complex relationship between the Worcester collection on the one hand, and the Klosterneuburg collection on the other. Detailed analysis showed that *Wigorniensis* derived its material from the archetype before Klosterneuburg and that it inserted additional letters at the end of each of its seven books. The Exeter-Worcester emphasis is evident in both the archetype and the supplements, notably at the ends of Books IV and VII, with a striking number of new decretals addressed to one or more of the recipients mentioned above (Exeter, Ford, Worcester, Kenilworth). The additional letters serve to underscore the Exeter-Worcester element in the archetype, and a close connection with the episcopal households of those two dioceses may be conjectured. A possible author of the Worcester collection may be suggested in the person of Master Simon Lovell. He was a member of

---

96. Lohmann, 'Die Collectio Wigorniensis' 39–43; Duggan, *Decretal Collections* 96–97.
97. *Wigorniensis* 7.64–81, not in the archetype; Duggan, *Decretal Collections* 49–57, 95–98 et passim, and Plate v.

Bartholomew's chapter at Exeter and archdeacon of Worcester from 1167, where he worked in turn with bishops Roger and Baldwin, the latter his former colleague in the Exeter diocese, as archdeacon of Totnes. A decretal of Alexander III, in 1161–1167, speaks of Simon reporting in person to him in a dispute involving the church of Veryan, in Cornwall (even its antique Cornish name Helerki is accurately preserved in the letter)—'Ex transmissa nobis relatione dilecti filii magistri Symonis Lupelli nobis est auribus intimatum quod A. sacerdote de Helerki de hac luce subtracto'.[98]

None of the decretals addressed to the bishop of Worcester in the archetype or its supplements in *Wigorniensis* were received by Baldwin as bishop of the diocese (though the letters addressed to the abbot of Ford were his), but letters that he received successively as bishop of Worcester and archbishop of Canterbury were inserted by later hands in the opening and closing folios. There is no doubt that the volume belonged to Baldwin himself or to a member of his circle.

The Klosterneuburg collection, analyzed by Schönsteiner in 1909, survives in a fine late-twelfth-century manuscript, where the collection follows, without interruption, a transcription of the decrees of the Third Lateran Council (1179). Although supplied with elegant red initials, the decretal collection is wholly lacking in rubrics, headings, and numeration, so that its underlying structure is obscured. Even the addresses of its individual letters have been omitted. It is in fact a fair copy of a derivative from the 'Worcester' archetype, taken at a stage later than *Wigorniensis* itself. On the one hand, it lacks the supplements peculiar to *Wigorniensis*; on the other, it has a supplement of its own (296–344), derived from the expanded archetype, which contained at least two letters of Lucius III.[99]

The Second Generation of the 'Worcester' Group

Two later lines of descent from the 'Worcester' group are recorded in three collections of the later twelfth century: the 'Cheltenham' collection, in an Egerton manuscript in the British Library, is so named from its earlier location in the Phillipps Library in Cheltenham; *Cottoniana* is among the Cotton manuscripts in the British Library, and *Petrihusensis* is found in seven quires distributed as end pieces in the binding of four different

---

98. Duggan, 'Decretals of Alexander III to England' 101 no. 77. For the suggestion that Master Silvester may have been involved in the compilation, see H.M.R.E. Mayr-Harting, 'Master Silvester and the Compilation of Early English Decretal Collections', SCH 2 (1965) 186–196.

99. F. Schönsteiner, 'Die Collectio Claustroneoburgensis', *Jahrbuch des Stiftes Klosterneuburg* 2 (1909) 1–154; cf. Lohmann, 'Die Collectio Wigorniensis' 45–48; Duggan, 'The Trinity Collection of Decretals' 509–510; W. Stelzer, *Gelehrtes Recht in Österreich. Von den Anfängen bis zum frühen 14. Jahrhundert*, MIÖG, Erg. Bd. 36 (Vienna 1982) 106, 194.

volumes of the library of Peterhouse, Cambridge.[100] The Cottonian and Peterhouse collections are now seriously mutilated or incomplete. The former was severely damaged by fire in the Cotton Library in 1731; and, although a part at least of every folio survives, many texts are now merely fragments or illegible. The dismantling of the Peterhouse collection (originally in the Dyngley Library) entailed the loss of the whole collection from 4.52. The collections are undoubtedly of English provenance, written by English scribes, probably in the same scriptorium.

The earliest of these three collections, the 'Cheltenham' collection, is also the most complex, since it combines substantial and clearly identifiable derivations from the 'Worcester' tradition with material from the 'Frankfurt' and 'Bamberg' collections, both made in France (ca. 1183–1185), respectively at Sens or Troyes and Tours. The collection itself was assembled in England, after 1188. It opens with the canons of the 1179 Lateran Council,[101] reproducing, with a single variation, the sequence found in the St. John's fragment of the *Appendix* discussed below. The canons are followed by eight letters of Innocent III, in a different hand, and then (fol. 18r–102r) the decretal collection arranged in 18 books.[102] Evidence for the probable date of completion of the work (excluding the Innocentian letters that follow the Third Lateran Council) is provided by the inclusion of material from Popes Lucius III (1181–1185), Urban III (1185–1187), and Clement III (1187–1191) towards the end of Book 18. The final decretal, Celestine III to the prior and chapter of Huntingdon, dated 25 July 1193, was entered by a different hand. The collection is well presented, with occasional marginal glossing.

The final surviving members of the 'Worcester' tradition, the closely related Cotton and Peterhouse collections, reflect the overall character of their earliest ancestors, being divided into a small number of books, without subdivision into titles, except for a single book in Peterhouse. Both open with the canons of the councils of Tours (1163) and of the Lateran (1179), followed by books of decretals. Despite mutilation by fire in the Cotton Library, increasingly severe towards the end of the codex, the Cotton manuscript retains at least a fragment of every folio. The first book of

---

100. London, B.L. Egerton 2819, fol. 11–102; London, B.L.Cotton Vitellius E.xiii, fol. 204–288; Cambridge, Peterhouse, MS 193, final quire; 114, first and final quires; 114, first and final quires; 193, first quire; 203, final quire; 180, first and final quires. For these collections, see Duggan, *Decretal Collections* 98–110, but note that, in the light of its advanced structure, the Worcester group should be classified as systematic.

101. Except that it lacks almost four canons through the loss of a folio.

102. Cf. Duggan, *Decretal Collections* 100–101. The list there should now be amended to include titles 2 (*De capellanis castrorum*) and 8 (*De matrimonio*). Holtzmann counted the conciliar decrees as Book 1 of the collection.

decretals deals with marriage questions (2.1–82), and the remaining books include the following topics: canonical judicial procedure (3.1–84), tithes and religious orders (4.1–90), simony and clerical status (5.1–73), churches and relevant matters (6.1–102), and prescription, spoliation, alienation, and sundry concluding items (7.1–63). The Peterhouse manuscripts run parallel with this arrangement, except that the book numbers assigned by Holtzmann vary by one, since he did not assign a book number to the conciliar canons in Peterhouse, though he had done so in *Cottoniana*. The surviving quires of the Peterhouse collection break off at Peterhouse 4.52 (equivalent to *Cottoniana* 5.36), and folios are missing between books 2 and 3.[103] Apart from some rearrangement in the sequence of decretals within the books, a major advance in technical organization is apparent in the second book, which is subdivided into titles according to subject-matter..

Conclusion

The first phase of the 'Worcester' tradition was clearly of the utmost importance in the technical evolution of canonical collections, providing the foundation for later systematic collections. It is clear that the *Appendix Concilii Lateranensis* (Lincoln, ex 1183), the 'Bamberg' collection (Tours, post-1185), the 'Bruges' collection (Reims, post-1187), and the English collection Tanner (1187–1191) derived much of their Alexandrine material from the 'Worcester' transmission. In this way, principally through the channel of the *Appendix* and 'Bamberg' collections, the 'Worcester' tradition significantly influenced the 'Leipzig' collection (Bologna, post 1185), and *Compilatio prima* itself (Bologna, 1189–1191), and so also ultimately, Raymond of Peñafort's official *Decretales* of 1234.[104]

But the 'Worcester' collections are also of the greatest value to historians in a wider context, not only in recording the increasingly pervasive role of English judges-delegate in specific cases, but also in preserving large numbers of decretals otherwise unknown. The newly discovered decretals in the first generation of the family were mostly of English provenance, frequently addressed to the bishops of Exeter or Worcester, or their judicial colleagues in those dioceses,[105] but the large number of otherwise unknown decretals in the Cottonian and Peterhouse collections is remarkable, not least for their wide geographical provenance. The collec-

---

103. In view of its many letters to English Cistercian houses, it is not surprising that M.R. James, *Descriptive Catalogue of the Manuscripts of Peterhouse* (Cambridge 1899) described one of the quires as part of a volume of Cistercian ordinances.

104. See esp. Landau, 'Entstehung' 125 (*stemma*), 127–128.

105. Printed in the analyses of the Worcester and Klosterneuburg Collections, respectively by Lohmann and Schönsteiner.

tors were certainly English, familiar with the Old English forms of English place names, and they incorporated many uniquely surviving English decretals; but, working in the mid-1190s, they included letters of Pope Alexander III († 1181) to Norwegian and Italian recipients,[106] which are unknown elsewhere. When the *Decretales ineditae saeculi xii* was published in 1982, a very large majority of its letters to all parts of Christendom, including one for Jerusalem, were found in either the Cotton or the Peterhouse collection or both.[107]

The *Appendix* Group (deriving from Lincoln-Oxford)

As explained above, this very influential group of collections takes its name from the title, *Appendix concilii Lateranensis*, given to the first printed edition, but it has no significance save as a description of the relative positions of the Lateran canons and the decretal collection in the now-lost manuscript used by its editor in the sixteenth century. Apart from that valuable witness to a lost source, the collection survives in a completed form in three manuscripts, respectively in Leipzig, Vienna, and Lincoln,[108] and in three fragments, where it is sometimes combined with other material.[109] The provenance of the collection has been much debated. Van Hove considered that the most probable place of origin was Italy, Stickler preferred England, and Kuttner-Rathbone showed that only Anglo-Norman schools of canonists used the *Appendix* in their commentaries.[110] Thereafter, Duggan, Landau, and Mary Cheney argued in support of its English provenance.[111] It is almost certainly of English authorship.

The most probable place of origin of the *Appendix* prototype was Lin-

---

106. Duggan, 'Italian Marriage Decretals'; idem, 'Decretal Letters to Hungary'.

107. Chodorow-Duggan, *Decretales ineditae*, passim.

108. Leipzig, Univ.-Bibl. 1242, fol. 73v–110v (from Altzelle); Vienna, Ö.N.B. 2172, fol. 2r–52v; Lincoln, Cathedral Chapter Library, 121, fol. 1r–61r; cf. Duggan, *Decretal Collections* 53–54, 135–139, 189–191; Holtzmann-Cheney, *Collections* 116–134.

109. Cambridge, St. John's College 148, fol. 61v–84v; Oxford, Oriel College 53, fol. 353r–354v (olim, 253r–254v) (*Orielensis*, formerly *Orielensis secunda*); Holtzmann-Cheney, *Collections* 127–131; Oxford, Oriel College 53, fol. 340–349 (olim, fol. 240–249) (which I call Bamberg O, on which see below; formerly called *Orielensis prima* in the literature).

110. Van Hove, *Prolegomena* 352; Stickler, *Historia* 224; Stephan Kuttner and Eleanor Rathbone, 'Anglo-Norman Canonists of the Twelfth Century', *Traditio* 7 (1949–1951) 283–284, reprinted in Kuttner's *Gratian and the Schools of Law*.

111. Duggan, *Decretal Collections* 135–139 et passim; Landau, 'Entstehung' 131; Cheney, *Roger of Worcester* 196. Paradoxically, Holtzmann, master scholar of the decretals, apparently never ceased to believe in an Italian origin for the collection, for in the papers published after his death he concluded 'the arguments hitherto advanced for an English origin of App. do not seem to me to be compelling.... I would suggest that one must look to Italy for the systematizer who first divided decretal-material by title': Holtzmann-Cheney, *Collections* 122–123.

coln, ex 1183, in the circle of Walter of Coutances,[112] an eminent royal administrator, who was successively archdeacon of Oxford and treasurer of Rouen, bishop of Lincoln (8 May 1183–March 1185), and archbishop of Rouen (summer 1184–1207); and an author may be sought in the person or circle of John of Coutances, Walter's nephew, archdeacon of Oxford from ca. 1184 and dean of Rouen not later than 1188.[113] While in that office he received Pope Celestine III's decretal *Prudentiam tuam* (13 July 1193) in response to a series of questions that he had sent to the pope. Significantly, the letter first appears in the supplement to the Lincoln manuscript of the *Appendix*, in which it is the first item.

Like the 'Worcester' stock, from which it developed, the *Appendix* is essentially a post-Gratian collection, recording and shaping new law (*ius novum*). It descended from the 'Worcester' tradition at a point preceding *Wigorniensis* itself, which has additional decretals unknown to the later collections. The 'Worcester' material was reorganized in numerous precisely focused titles instead of a few books of general scope, and it was subjected to the technique of decretal dissection, in which decretals dealing with a plurality of topics were dismembered and the individual segments distributed under the various titles according to their subject matter.

The printed edition (the vulgate *Appendix*) comprises 50 titles, of which the last is in large measure a derivation from the lost registers of Alexander III. Following the conciliar canons (title 1), three discernible strata identify successive recensions of the collection: titles 2–44 (which Holtzmann identified as the lost archetype of the family—the Ur-*Appendix*),[114] titles 45–48, and titles 49–50. In all probability a still earlier version, lacking some of the letters of Lucius III, Urban III, and Clement III, was transmitted to the 'Bamberg' collection (Tours), and thereby to the most famous line of transmission, to *Compilatio prima* and the *Decretales* of 1234. The Leipzig codex, from the Cistercian house of Altzelle, contains titles 2–47.15, following the 1179 canons.[115] Especially noteworthy are its marginal glosses,

112. For his English origins, see Giraldus Cambrensis, *Opera*, ed. J.S. Brewer, J.F. Dimock and G.F. Warner (8 vols, Rolls Series 21; London 1861–1891) 7.38. For his scholarly career, see Peter Landau, 'Walter von Coutances und die Anfänge der anglo-normannischen rechtswissenschaft', *"Panta rei": Studia dedicati a Manlio Bellomo*, ed. Orazio Condorelli, 5 vols. (Rome 2004) 3.183–204.

113. For Walter, *English Episcopal Acta*, 1: *Lincoln 1067–1185*, ed. David M. Smith (British Academy; London 1980) xxxviii–xxxix, 187–199, 210; *English Episcopal Acta*, 4: *Lincoln 1186–1205*, ed. David M. Smith (British Academy; London 1986) xxiii, xxx, xxxi, xl; for John of Coutances, ibid., 45, 50, 59, 95. The church of Rouen was administered by John during Walter's absence: *Gallia Christiana* 11 (1759) 116. He was elevated to the bishopric of Worcester in 1196.

114. Holtzmann, 'Die Register Papst Alexander III' 18–19.

115. Peter Landau, 'Studien zur Appendix und den Glossen in frühen systematischen Dekretalensammlungen', BMCL 9 (1979) 1–21.

which occasionally have the siglum Jo., identifying the English canonist John of Tynemouth, who was also cited in the glossed *Decretum* in Cambridge, Caius College, 676.[116] Equally, the Lincoln *Appendix*, which comprises titles 1–49 (with some variation in order), followed by the Lateran decrees (1179) and a supplement of twenty-three decretals which includes letters of Celestine III (1191–1198), is of unusual interest in the evidence it provides of active engagement with the material. Its copious marginalia include glosses in more than one hand, Roman law citations, and editorial emendations to the inscriptions and texts.

Three surviving fragments provide tantalizing evidence of the circulation of *Appendix* material and its combination with other sources. The fifteen pages (fol. 77v–84v) in Cambridge, St. John's College, MS 148, for example, prefaces a short derivation from the *Appendix*[117] with five widely distributed letters of Alexander III, Eugenius III, and Honorius II;[118] and the more substantial survivals in Oxford, Oriel College, MS 53, which belonged originally to the Cluniac priory of St. Andrew, Northampton, demonstrate a relationship with *Bambergensis*, discussed below, which was a rearrangement of the material in *Appendix*. In the fragment now named *Orielensis* (formerly *Orielensis secunda*), the plan of titles and rubrics corresponds with the *Appendix* titles 10, 11, and 13–18, and with 'Bamberg' titles 42, 34, 25, 7 + 44, 18, and 54. On this evidence, Holtzmann argued that *Orielensis* represents an intermediate stage between the *Appendix* and 'Bamberg' collections; further, his study of the *Orielensis* marginalia led him to argue that the glosses originated in Italy and even that the collection was of Italian provenance. Whatever may be said about the origins of *Orielensis* itself, there can be little doubt that the decretal contents derived from English sources. The second Oriel fragment, Bamberg *Orielensis*, corresponds with 'Bamberg' 33.21–56.3, and is especially notable for its appendix of 50 items (fols. 347va–349vb), which are related in some way with title 50 of the vulgate *Appendix*.[119]

---

116. Ibid., 19–21; Kuttner and Rathbone, 'Anglo-Norman Canonists' 317–327, 348; C. Duggan, 'The Reception of Canon Law in England in the Later Twelfth Century', *Proceedings Boston*, 371–377.

117. *Appendix*, 23.2, 23.1, 2.1–7 and 9.

118. C. Duggan, 'English canonists and the *Appendix Concilii Lateranensis*, with an analysis of the St. John's, Cambridge, MS 148', *Traditio* 18 (1962) 459–468; reprinted in *Canon Law in Medieval England*, no. 8; cf. 'Addenda et corrigenda' 5. The fragment is also of interest in a different context. It is sometimes claimed that no two collections present the canons of the 1179 Lateran Council in the same sequence, but the sequence of canons in the St. John's MS is identical with that preceding the 'Cheltenham' collection (discussed above); additionally the marginal comments for the Lateran canons 11 and 12 in the St. John's MS agree with those in the Lincoln *Appendix*.

119. See Holtzmann's collection in 'Die Register Papst Alexander III' 19–20.

It is clear from these survivals that the work of the Lincoln canonists was widely disseminated in Anglo-Norman and Angevin territories, and it was to be the principal link between the English and continental schools. Nowhere is this connection more clearly demonstrated than in the utilization of an *Appendix* collection by professional collectors in the cathedral school at Tours, where an English scholar, Master Philip of Calne, had taught canon law in the early 1160s,[120] and where Bartholomew de Vendôme, former dean of Saint-Maurice (the cathedral) (ca. 1155–1174) was archbishop from 1174 to 1206.[121] Soon after 1185, the Touraine masters reconstructed and expanded *Appendix* 1–44 to form the basis of the 'Bamberg' collection and its manifold descendants, which ultimately reached as far as the Gregorian Decretals. So rapid a transmission from Lincoln to Tours is readily explicable both by the interconnections between ecclesiastical centers in the Angevin Empire (the Lincoln-Rouen axis) and also by the translation of Walter of Coutances from Lincoln (where the base collection was made) to Rouen in 1185.

The 'Bamberg' (*Bambergensis*) Group (deriving from Tours)

The 'Bamberg' collection, now in the Staatsbibliothek in Bamberg, is a highly professional compilation, with an extensive gloss apparatus, arranged in fifty-five titles, followed by the canons of the Third Lateran Council (1179). Its derivation from the *Appendix* is evident, both in the verbal agreements of their titles and in parallel sequences of decretals within the titles, but they were rearranged in a more professional and systematic sequence, according to subject-matter, relating in Daudet's analysis to crimes, clerics, ecclesiastical property, procedure, and marriage, or in Landau's formulation, *crimen, clerus, iudicium, iudex, sponsalia*[122]—which is a remarkable anticipation of the formal structure later adopted by Bernard of Pavia for the five books of his *Compilatio prima: iudex, iudicium, clerus, connubium, crimen*. Evidence both of its sources and of the place of its reorganization is found in its significant addition of a new title (48) *De discordia Turonensis ecclesiae cum Dolensi*, on the primatial dispute between Tours and Dol, entered immediately after an expanded version of *Appendix* title 44, *De preeminentia Londoniensis et Eboracensis*.[123] The interest of the com-

---

120. Frank Barlow, *Thomas Becket* (London 1986) 79.
121. *Gallia Christiana* 14 (1856) 92–93.
122. P. Daudet, 'Bamberg (collection de)', DDC 2 (1937) 84–89, especially col. 87, and Landau, 'Entstehung' 133.
123. Bamberg B 47–48. The Bamberg MS inexplicably renders title 47 as 'De penitentia': an obvious mistake for 'De preeminentia.' The correct form of the title is found in related manuscripts of the Bamberg group: cf. Friedberg, *Canones-Sammlungen* 102; Duggan, *Decretal Collections* 137–138. On the long-standing dispute between Tours and Dol, see Raymonde

piler in this protracted local dispute is manifest here and supports the argument that the 'Bamberg' collection was made at Tours.

The wider 'Bamberg' group comprises twelve manuscripts or fragments, testifying to its wide dissemination.[124] Derivatives have been found in Amiens (Bamberg A, from the Premonstratensian abbey of St. Cornelius in Selincourt); in the Bibliothèque Nationale in Paris (Bamberg C, from the Benedictine abbey of St. Cornelius in Compiègne); in two manuscripts in the cathedral library in Tortosa (Bamberg D and a fragment, Bamberg T); in a collation of *Compilatio prima* with a lost 'Bamberg' manuscript from the Benedictine abbey of Marmoutiers (Bamberg M); and in a fragment from the Cluniac Priory of St. Andrew, Northampton (Bamberg O).[125] Even more importantly, copies of *Bambergensis* were soon transmitted to Bologna. The Bamberg manuscript of *Casselana* contains glosses citing Bolognese masters John of Faenza and Simon of Bisignano.[126] Bernard of Pavia compiled the 'Leipzig' collection (*Lipsiensis*) on the basis of a 'Bamberg' collection, which he expanded by inserting 223 pre-Gratian texts. When he came, ca. 1188–1191, to construct his highly important *Breviarium* (retrospectively named by the jurists, *Compilatio prima*, the first of the *Quinque compilationes antiquae*), his own 'Bamberg'-based 'Leipzig' collection formed one of his premier sources.[127] However, there is evidence that contradicts this

---

Foreville, *L'Église et la royauté en Angleterre sous Henri II Plantagenet (1154–1189)* (Paris 1943) 286–287 and n. 6.

124. Bamberg, Staatsbibl. can. 17 (P.i.ii.), fol. 1–47 (from cathedral library: Bamberg B); Amiens, bibl. de la Ville 377, fol. 83–132 (from Selincourt: Bamberg A); Paris, B.N. lat. 17971, fol. 153–183 (from St. Cornelius, Compiègne: Bamberg C); Tortosa, Bibl. del Cabildo 40, fol. 1–91 (Bamberg D); Tortosa, Bibl. del Cabildo 160, fol. 1–41 (Bamberg T); Oxford, Oriel College 53, fol. 340–349 (olim 240–249) (from priory of St. Andrew, Northampton: Bamberg O); Paris, B.N. lat. Baluse 77, fol. 324r–328v (collation of *Compilatio prima* with a lost manuscript of Bamberg from Marmoutiers 125: Bamberg M); Erlangen, Univ.-Bibl. 342, fol. 291–306 (Erlangensis), from St. Michael of Bamberg; Leipzig, Univ.-Bibl. 975, fol. 116–153 (*Lipsiensis*); Florence Fragment, Florence, Bibl. Laur., S. Croce, III sin.6, fol. 1v–2v (F); Kassel, Landesbibl. Jur. 15, fol. 1–26 [Kassel C]; Bamberg, Staatsbibl., Can. 18, fol. 25r–43v [Kassel B]; the Cracow Fragment, Kraków, 106: cf. A. Vetulani, 'Un fragment d'une collection systématique de décrétales antérieure à la "Compilatio Prima"', *Traditio* 16 (1960) 534–540. Walter Deeters, 'Die Bambergensisgruppe der Dekretalensammlungen des 12. Jahrhunderts' (Ph. D. Dissertation, Bonn 1956), especially 2–11.

125. The relationship between the manuscripts and their respective stages of derivation from the lines of transmission are made clear in the *stemma* deduced by Deeters, 'Die Bambergensisgruppe' 30. Bamberg A is a neatly written work, with moderate glossing intermittently; Bamberg C is incomplete, breaking off in *Qua fronte nos* (42.39); Bamberg D continues to 55.14, but Bamberg T preserves only the fragment 42.12–55.14. The final item in both Tortosa manuscripts is Alexander III's letter *Dilecti filii nostri*, to all prelates, concerning the Hospitallers, the original of which survives in Hospitaller archives (WH 354a, JL—, 1 Dec. 1166–1179).

126. Bamberg, Staatsbibl. Can. 18, fol. 25r–43v [Kassel B].

127. Landau, 'Entstehung' 133–137.

attribution of 'Leipzig' to Bernard. The 'Leipzig' collection contains a significant number of decretals otherwise unknown, many of them addressed to prelates in northeastern Italy (to the bishops, respectively, of Padua and of Castello, to the patriarch of Grado, to the abbot of San Apollinare in Classe, and others). Their presence is confirmation of the regional context of the manuscript, but since none was received into *Compilatio prima*, it is possible that the Leipzig manuscript is a later derivation from Bernard of Pavia's collection and was not compiled by Bernard.

At Tours, the anonymous compilers of the archetype of the 'Bamberg' group, the *Urbambergensis* in Deeters' nomenclature, made a decisive contribution to the professional development of the 'new law.' Through their work, the reorganized first recension of the English *Appendix* (titles 1–44) passed not only to Bolognese jurists but also to canonists working in England, Reims, and elsewhere.

The 'Frankfurt' *(Francofurtana)* Collection (deriving from Sens)

The 'Frankfurt' collection stands somewhat apart from the intricate pattern of transmission summarized so far, but has interconnections with it. This is a large compilation arranged in 63 titles, containing 713 chapters, almost half of which are pre-Gratian—a somewhat old-fashioned feature that it shares with works in the Italian academic tradition.[128] Its four surviving manuscripts, now respectively in Frankfurt, Paris (from Rouen), Troyes (from Clairvaux), and London (from St. Maximin in Trier),[129] testify to dissemination across a wide geographical region, embracing Champagne, Burgundy, and the Anglo-Norman territories; but it originated in Sens, or perhaps Troyes, ca. 1181–1183.[130] Its influence has been traced in the Norman and English schools, where it rivaled the *Appendix* as a textbook.[131] Evidence of its extensive use is found in the 'Cheltenham' collection of the 'Worcester' family (discussed above), the Rouen collection (*Ro-*

---

128. E.g. the Paris II *(Parisiensis II)* and 'Leipzig' *(Lipsiensis)* collections, discussed above at n. 88 and 127.

129. Frankfurt am Main, Staat-und-Univ.bibl., Barth. 60, fol. 2–85 [Frankfurt F]; Paris, B.N. lat. 3922A, fol. 173r–209r [Frankfurt R: from Rouen]; Troyes, Bibl. de la Ville, 961, fol. 1r–96v [Frankfurt T]; London, B.L. Egerton 2901, fol. 1r–97v [Frankfurt M: from St Maximin in Trier].

130. Peter Landau and Gisela Drossbach, *Die Collectio Francofurtana: Eine französische Decretalensammlung.* (MIC, Series B, 9; Vatican City 2007); Gisela Drossbach, 'Die Collectio Francofurtana und die fünf Bücher der Compilatio prima', *Iuris Historia: Liber amicorum Gero Dolezalek,* ed. V. Colli and E. Conte (Berkeley 2008) 145–159.

131. Landau, 'Entstehung' 137–143; idem, 'Studien zur Appendix und den Glossen in frühen systematischen Dekretalensammlungen', BMCL 9 (1979) 5–8. Cf. Charles Lefebvre, 'Francfort (Collection de)', DDC 5 (1953) 878–884.

tomagensis prima), post-1185 (discussed below), and in manuscripts of the *Appendix* itself. One of the most telling witnesses to its wider use is provided by the St. Maximin codex, which is manifestly a work of professional canonists, its texts being provided with a copious marginal apparatus and many additional inserts of decretals on slips of parchment. The inserts are in English script and frequently deal with English cases. The completed work is clearly English, perhaps of Lincoln provenance, post-1189. Moreover, it has about 260 glosses in common with the gloss apparatus of the *Appendix*.[132] Once again, the Lincoln-Rouen axis is revealed in the two-way exchange of canonical material: in this case, in the reception by English canonists of material originating in Sens and transmitted via Rouen to Lincoln. The rôle of the Rouen school, under the influence of the English Walter of Coutances (formerly of Lincoln), is again manifest.

The Rouen Supplement to Francofurtana: The Rouen Collection

The collection of canonical materials in Paris, B.N. lat. 3922A,[133] which was made at Rouen in the period ca. 1185 to 1210, is a remarkable testament to the work of Anglo-Norman canonists in the circle of the English Walter of Coutances. In addition to extracts and abbreviations from the principal canon and civil law texts, assorted papal letters, and two 'Ordines iudiciorum,'[134] the manuscript contains a copy of the 'Frankfurt' Collection itself,[135] a supplement to *Francofurtana* (the 'Rouen' Collection: *Rotomagensis prima*)[136] and further additions: a derivation from *Compilatio prima* (*Rotomagensis secunda*), with the insertion of additional papal letters (including some from Innocent III),[137] selections from the works of Rainer of Pomposa (ca. 1201) and Gilbertus Anglicus (1203),[138] decretals of Innocent III (*Rotomagensis tertia*), probably derived from the papal registers, whose latest date is 25 May 1207,[139] and an additional group of Innocentian

---

132. Duggan, *Decretal Collections* 195 and Plate VIII; Landau, 'Entsehung' 141.

133. Holtzmann-Cheney, *Collections* 135–207; cf. Pennington, 'Decretal Collections' 1190–1234 at n. 28.

134. Extracts and abbreviations from the *Decretum*, the Codex, Digest, Institutes, and Novellae of Justinian, the *Ordines 'Olim'* and *'Ulpianus de edendo'* and various papal letters occupy fol. 1–147: cf. Holtzmann-Cheney, *Collections* 135–138.

135. Fol. 173r–209r (Frankfurt Rot.).

136. Fol. 148r–167v, 245; analyzed in Holtzmann-Cheney, *Collections* 160–207; cf. Pennington, 'Decretal Collections' 1190–1234, at n. 46.

137. Fol. 211–227v, the so-called *Rotomagensis secunda*. See Holtzmann-Cheney, *Collections* 152–155.

138. Fol. 235ra–242rb: Holtzmann-Cheney, *Collections* 140–141, 159; fol. 228ra–234vb: Holtzmann-Cheney, *Collections* 139–140, 156–158.

139. Holtzmann-Cheney, *Collections* 136–137; cf. C.R. Cheney, *Traditio* 11 (1955) 149–162; Landau, 'Entsehung' 140.

letters, to 8 Aug. 1213.[140] *Rotomagensis prima* itself is a systematic collection in thirty-one titles, that mostly follow the pattern of the 'Frankfurt' collection with which it is bound up. The core of the 'Rouen Supplement' has nothing later than Lucius III, its date of completion therefore being post-1185, but the manuscript records with unusual clarity the further evolution of a collection in the hands of canonists, with the addition of decretals of Clement III, Celestine III, and Innocent III. The expansion of the basic collection was achieved, not by successive supplements appended to the original, but by the insertion of extra leaves, which in fact broke up the continuity of letters on previously facing folios; additional letters were also added in spaces in the existing margins, and at the top and bottom of existing folios. New texts were sometimes also written over erasures. The result is, in Holtzmann's words, a collection *in statu nascendi*.[141] The sources of the new material are complex but include letters taken from the papal registers and from other canonical sources.[142]

The Rouen provenance of the collection is confirmed not only by its survival in a Rouen manuscript, but by the evidence of the use of Rouen sources both in the core and in the later insertions. For example, in the seventeenth title, *De rescriptis*, Rouen recipients are named in core chapters 1, 2, 8, and 9, and in inserted chapters 15 and 16. And in one especially significant example, a decretal that Walter of Rouen had received as bishop of Lincoln is recorded three times as addressed to him as archbishop of Rouen, to which he had been translated on 17 Dec. 1184.[143] The compilation of so complex a manuscript is unlikely to have been the work of a single compiler, but Walter's entourage included two men with the interest and experience to organize such a project. His own nephew, John of Coutances, recipient of Celestine III's widely circulated decretal *Prudentiam tuam* (17 July 1193), was dean of the cathedral, and the distinguished canonist John of Cornwall was associated with them, which raises the probability that three of the key figures in the 'Rouen' canonical achievements, including Walter himself, were from the southwest of England.

---

140. Fol. 242ra–244rb; cf. Landau, 'Entstehung' 140; Stanley Chodorow, 'An Appendix to Rainier of Pomposa's Collection', BMCL 3 (1973) 55–61; Holtzmann-Cheney, *Collections* 141.
141. Holtzmann-Cheney, *Collections* 163; cf. ibid., Plates I and II.
142. E.g. 'Celestinus III Anconitano episcopo libro primo r(egistri)' (1.40); 'Idem Lincolniensi episcopo eodem libro' (1.43); 'Clemens III libro iii r(egistri) . . . Dat. Lat. xvi. kal. aprilis pont. n. anno iii.'(5.8).
143. Cf. 13.10, 17.2, and 20.11: a single letter, dismembered and distributed under the appropriate titles (JL 14965 + 14966).

The 'Bruges' Collection (compiled in Reims)

Through the same period, there was extensive canonical activity at Reims, where another Englishman, Master Ralph of Sarre (in Kent) was dean for the years 1176–1195/96. Evidence is provided by the so-called 'Bruges' collection, so named from the location of two manuscripts in the Bibliothèque de la Ville in Bruges. Friedberg analyzed the manuscripts and published the results in 1897.[144] The Reims provenance of the collection was clear from the large number of decretals, many not previously edited, to recipients in the province—the archbishop or his suffragans, members of the cathedral chapter, including its Dean Fulk, and heads of religious houses, notably the distinguished scholar Peter of Celle, abbot of St-Rémi of Reims.[145] The later discovery of a St-Rémi manuscript of the work in the Vatican Library[146] confirmed its provenance and disclosed an earlier version, which fixed the date of completion at post-1187.[147] Ludwig Falkenstein provided even more positive evidence when he identified the hand of the St-Rémi scribe Garnerius in the Vatican manuscript and in one of the two Bruges codices. Moreover, he emphasized the key role of Ralph of Sarre, one of 'St. Thomas's learned men' ('eruditi sancti Thome'), an associate both of John of Salisbury (who had acted as Archbishop Theobald of Canterbury's legal secretary in the 1150s) and of Gerard Pucelle (who had taught canon law at Cologne in the mid-1160s) and a friend of Master Fulk, who had preceded him as dean of Reims.[148]

The collection itself is a further telling example of the reception of English decretal materials in a continental center. The 'Bruges' compiler derived much of his material from an early member of the 'Worcester' group, which he significantly expanded, mainly with decretals received in the province of Reims.[149] But he also made a notable advance in the sys-

---

144. Bruges, Bibl. de la Ville 378, fol. 1–83 and Bruges, Bibl. de la Ville 379, fol. 1–83 (both from the Cistercian monastery of Dunes); Friedberg, *Canones-Sammlungen* 136–170.

145. Duggan, *Decretal Collections* 145.

146. Vatican, Ottob. lat. 3027, fol. 1–111; cf. Walther Holtzmann, 'Die vatikanische Handschrift der "Collectio Brugensis"', *Collectanea Vaticana in honorem Anselmi M. Cardinalis Albereda* (2 vols. ST 219–220; Rome 1962) 1.391–414.

147. The Vatican (St-Rémi) copy lacked Clement III's decretal, *Pervenit ad nos*, to the bishop of Sigüenza (WH 722, JL 16596, 3 July 1189), which proved to have been an addition in the Bruges manuscripts.

148. Ludwig Falkenstein, 'Zu Entstehungsort und Redaktor der Collectio Brugensis', *Proceedings San Diego* 117–162 (with plates), especially 140–144, 'Ralph of Sarre'; cf. also idem, 'Decretalia Remensia. Zu Datum und Inhalt einiger Dekretalen Alexanders III. für Empfänger in der Kirchenprovinz Reims', *Miscellanea Rolando Bandinelli* 153–216.

149. Its 'Worcester' ancestor cannot have been *Wigorniensis* itself, however, which has many decretals additional to the archetype.

tematic organization of its fifty-nine titles, though some of the long letters were left substantially intact.[150] By the end of the century, its influence can be traced in the Anglo-Norman St-Germain and Avranches I collections, both ca. 1198. The 'Bruges'–'St-Germain'–'Avranches' line is positively established by decretals that they uniquely preserve.[151]

The Anglo-Norman Group

Another aspect of the strong cross-channel links between the English and continental schools is revealed in the collections of the Anglo-Norman group. The three systematic collections Tanner, St-Germain (*Sangermanensis*) and Avranches I (*Abrincensis prima*) record a clear line of transmission from England to Normandy in the closing decade of the twelfth century.[152] Tanner (in the Oxford Bodleian Library) is a professionally organized work in seven books, subdivided into titles, with an independent appendix; *Sangermanensis* (from St-Germain-des-Prés in Paris) is arranged in ten books, similarly subdivided, and *Abrincensis prima* (at Avranches) has nine books in a corresponding pattern.[153] Their family lineage, through the period 1187–ca. 1198, is evident in both construction and contents and is confirmed in the textual transmission of individual decretals. It has long been recognized that the origins of Tanner are re-traceable jointly to the English 'Worcester' group and to the 'Bamberg' tradition, within the period 1187–1190. The 'St-Germain' collection, assembled in Normandy ca. 1198, was an intricate compilation of materials derived from Tanner, the 'Bruges' collection, and Bernard of Pavia's *Compilatio prima*, and the first 'Avranches' collection was derived from it shortly after. The Tanner–St-Germain–Avranches line has left no descendants and was apparently not used professionally in Normandy, where the canonists' textbook was the 'Frankfurt' collection *Francofurtana*, made at Sens ca. 1183. In contrast, Tanner is of intrinsic interest not only for its place in the history of the collections, but for its influential place in the Anglo-Norman schools. One exceptionally important product of the Oxford school, for example—the heavily glossed copy of the *Decretum* in Cambridge, Gonville and Caius College MS 676—not only reveals the opinions of renowned masters like John of Tynemouth, Simon of Sywell, and

---

150. For example, only the last segment of Alexander III's *Quamvis simus* was detached from the rest of the letter in *Brugensis* (13.5 + 34.12), whereas the letter appears in eight distributed chapters in the *Appendix* and Bamberg collections (App. 7.8, 8.6, 10.31, 7.9, 8.6, 7.10, 15,6, 39.2; Bamberg 33.8, 39.5, 42.31, 33.9, 39.5, 33.10, 44.4, 22.1).

151. E.g. WH 54, 141, 177, 942, 965.

152. Landau, 'Entstehung' 144–146, 'Die Sammlungen Tanner, Sangermanensis und Abrincensis'.

153. Oxford, Bodl., Tanner 8, fol. 93–212; Paris, B.N. lat. 12459, fol. 1–106v (*Sangermanensis*); Avranches, Bibl. de la Ville 149, fol. 79–109 (from Mont-Saint-Michel).

John of Cornwall but also provides evidence of an English canonist writing his glosses in the Caius manuscript with a close relative of the Tanner collection 'open beside him'.[154]

Short fragments of a decretal collection were discovered in 1938 in the Oslo State archives, used as binding material in one or more volumes. The manuscript was carefully written, with rubricated headings, marginal cross references, and decorated initials which exhibit Norwegian characteristics.[155] Although only eighteen decretals can be identified in the surviving folios, derivation from the 'Worcester' collection can be argued for most of fragment 1, where a sequence of seven decretals reflects the order of two separated sequences in the 'Worcester' collection, which appear also in the 'Worcester' derivative at Klosterneuburg.[156] The material in the second fragment has a distinctly different ancestry, however. Most of its material is found in collections of the Anglo-Norman group, and its inclusion of two decretals which are otherwise found only in *Tanner*, St-Germain, and Avranches I, suggests access to that tradition. The presence of a letter issued by Lucius III at Verona, fixes the *terminus a quo* for the collection at 1184–1185.[157]

The Last Collections

By the last decade of the twelfth century, the authority of decretal letters and the importance of decretal collections as repositories of current appellate case law were so well established that canon lawyers and canonical scholars were anxious to keep up to date with the latest decisions from the Roman curia. This desire produced two interrelated movements: the compilation of dossiers of recent letters and the exploitation of the papal registers themselves for authoritative texts.

---

154. Kuttner and Rathbone, 'Anglo-Norman Canonists' 340–342, Appendix A, 'On the use of Collectio Tanner and Related Texts in the English Schools'; cf. Duggan, 'The Reception of Canon Law in England' 377.

155. This is the opinion of Mr. Michael Gullick, who has recently examined the fragments. Oslo, Riksarkivet, latin fragment 152, consists of two separate bifolia. The first (1), fol. 1r–2v, formed the second or third leaves of a gathering; the second (2), fol. 1r–2v, formed the middle leaves of a gathering: Duggan, *Twelfth-Century Decretal Collections* 124 n. 2; Holtzmann, 'Über eine Ausgabe', 24; idem, 'La collection "Seguntina" et les décrétales de Clément III et de Célestin III,' *RHE* 50 (1955), 400–453, at 401 n. 2; idem and Eric Kemp, *Papal Decretals Relating to the Diocese of Lincoln in the Twelfth Century*, Lincoln Record Society 47 (1954) xiii; Charles Lefebvre, 'Fragment d'Oslo', *DDC* 6 (1957) 1180.

156. Oslo 3–5 + 6–9 = *Wig*. 2.9–11 and 2.20–23 = *Claustroneoburgensis* 96, 97, 99, and 109–113. It is likely, in fact, that Oslo originally contained the whole of *Wig*. 2.9–23 at this point, since the hiatus between Oslo 5 and Oslo 6 was created by the loss of one or more bifolia.

157. Oslo 13–14 = *Tann*. 4.6.2, 2.7.5 = *Sang*. 5.5.2, 2.7.8 = 1 *Abr*. 5.6.2, 2.5.5. For Lucius III's letter, *Ad aures nostras* (WH 62, JL 15198, dat. Verona), see Oslo 11 (frag. 2, fol. 1r).

Primitive Decretal Collections before *Compilatio secunda*

Just as the publication of Gratian's *Decretum* led to the practice of compiling supplements to his work—the so-called appendices to the *Decretum*—so also there was a comparable phase of primitive collections after Bernard of Pavia's *Compilatio prima* (1189–1191) and before Johannes Galensis' *Compilatio secunda* (1210–1215). Some were evidently devised as appendices to Bernard's work; others were independent collections of recent decretals, notably of Clement III (1188–1191), and Celestine III (1191–1198), and a few of Innocent III (1198–1216); explicit use of papal registers is evident in some, both in citation and sequence. The collections are named either by their place of origin (if known) or by their present location—Clairvaux (Prima and Secunda), Lambeth, St-Victor (Paris), Munich, Halle, Lucca, Berlin II, Reims, Tortosa, *Alcobaça secunda*, and Durham.

The First Clairvaux collection, *Claravallensis prima*, now at Troyes, previously called *Trecensis secunda*, is a relatively short collection of twenty-seven items, comprising decretals of Alexander III, Clement III, and Celestine III, and one of Innocent III. The decretals of Celestine predominate, but the collection ends with four decretals of Alexander III and includes a single letter of Innocent III. Despite its relative brevity, the collection contains letters of widely distributed provenance (including Trani, Ávila, Cologne, Sorento, Rouen, Nidaros, Canterbury, Albano, Sicily, Clermont, Bordeaux, and Genoa). Kuttner called it an appendix to *Compilatio prima*, which it immediately follows in the manuscript.[158] *Lambethana*, named for its location in Lambeth Palace library, comprises 42 chapters, including three additions in a different hand. The decretals range in time from Alexander III to Innocent III and are followed in the manuscript by a short formulary book. Holtzmann has shown its links with the Lucca and Munich collections and a short parallelism with a register extract found in the Halle and Munich collections, and also in the systematic *Rotomagensis prima* (discussed above).[159] *Victorina secunda* is a short collection of 19 items, mostly of Clement III and Celestine III. It has a close relationship with *Claravallensis prima*, from which the compiler took material.[160]

Monacensis, so named from its location in Munich, comprises 114 items, including decretals of all the popes from Alexander III to Innocent III, addressed to a wide variety of recipients. Collation reveals its relationships with the Halle, Lambeth, Lucca, and Berlin II collections, and also with

---

158. Troyes, bibl. de la Ville 944, fol. 89v–92v; Holtzmann-Cheney, *Collections* 214–216.
159. London, Lambeth Palace 105, fol. 214–218: Holtzmann-Cheney, *Collections* 217–218.
160. Paris, B.N. lat. 14610, fol. 175va–179rb; Holtzmann-Cheney, *Collections* 219–220.

the register-dependent collections discussed below (Cracow and Sigüenza).¹⁶¹ The collection *Hallensis* in the University Library in Halle comprises 90 items; it is noteworthy for its division of the individual decretals into chapters, with rubrics for some decretals and for some of their component chapters. The opening and later short sequences of two or three decretals suggest a relationship with *Monacensis*, and a later sequence of decretals of Innocent III reveals a closer and more extended relationship between the two collections.¹⁶² *Lucensis* is named from its location in the Biblioteca Capitolare Feliniana in Lucca and has been in print since Mansi's edition of 1762. The collection is notable for its numerous subject rubrics for individual decretals. Collation reveals a short correspondence between *Lucensis* and the Cracow and Munich collections; moreover, links with *Compilatio prima* are revealed by the correspondence between its subject rubrics and titles in *Compilatio prima* (although with abridgements), and its omission of items already found there.¹⁶³ *Berolinensis secunda*, now in the Staatsbibliothek in Berlin, is a fragment of thirteen folios. Holtzmann deduced from the script that the collection was of north Italian origin, and that the glosses are compatible with this attribution. Kuttner noted that a second layer of glosses came from Tancred's apparatus to *Compilatio secunda*. Its closest relationship is with *Monacensis*; it is related to a lesser extent with the Halle collection, and in a sequence of three items, with the Lucca collection. Holtzmann noted various mistakes in the decretal inscriptions and errors in the placing of inscriptions.¹⁶⁴

The incomplete Reims (*Remensis*) collection breaks off in mid-decretal. Three decretals of Alexander III appear among its early items, but otherwise the letters were sent by Clement III and Celestine III, and many were derived from the papal registers.¹⁶⁵ The Second Clairvaux collection (*Claravallensis secunda*), which follows *Claravallensis prima* in the manuscript now at Troyes, is a collection of 75 decretals of Alexander III, Lucius III, Clement III, Gregory VIII, Celestine III, and Innocent III.¹⁶⁶ Two noteworthy details are the inclusion of two decretals of Clement III to Ireland, otherwise

---

161. Munich, Staatsbibliothek, lat. 8302, fol. 94r–113r; Holtzmann-Cheney, *Collections* 221–232.

162. Halle, Universitätsbibliothek Ye 80, fol. 79–96; Holtzmann-Cheney, *Collections* 233–242.

163. Lucca, Biblioteca capitolare Feliniana 221, fol. 220r–229r; Holtzmann-Cheney, *Collections* 243–271.

164. Berlin, Staatsbibliothek fol. 306, fol. 1–13; Holtzmann-Cheney, *Collections* 272–278.

165. Reims, Bibliothèque de la Ville 692, fol. 32r–35v; Holtzmann-Cheney, *Collections* 279–283.

166. Troyes, Bibliothèque de la Ville 944, fol. 93r–100v; Holtzmann-Cheney, *Collections* 284–290.

unknown in decretal collections,[167] and two excerpts from a single letter to the archbishop of Nidaros (Trondheim: 37, 56).[168] The second Tortosa collection (*Dertusensis secunda*) is a work of 50 items, many furnished with rubrics. It has been attributed to the abbey of Ripoll.[169] The Second Alcobaça collection (*Alcobacensis secunda*) comprises 49 chapters, indifferently transcribed, and showing some evidence of local archival derivation. The majority of the letters are ascribed to Innocent III, and derivation from a systematic source has been suggested.[170]

The last post–*Compilatio prima* primitive collection, Durham II (*Dunelmensis secunda*), is the largest and most imposing of the whole group.[171] Its appendix character, and concentration on current and new law are evident from its position in the manuscript, where it follows transcriptions of *Compilatio prima* and the systematic collection of the Bolognese canonist Gilbertus Anglicus, and from its layout, which left ample space for the insertion of new material as it came to hand. Its opening sequence (1–67) was derived from a version of Rainer of Pomposa's compilation, its mid-section (68–138) from a relation of *Tanner* or *Sangermanensis* (discussed above); its concluding section contains twelve decretals of Innocent III and thirty-six items derived from post–*Compilatio prima* primitive collections, with an emphasis on letters issued by Clement III and Celestine III.

Extracts from the Papal Registers

The most familiar example of derivation from the papal registers is at the conclusion of the vulgate version of the *Appendix*, where the appended title 50 consists of a sequence of 68 items, mostly excerpted from the registers of Alexander III, but with six letters of Urban III (1185–1187) and one each from Clement III (1187–1191) and Innocent III (1198–1216) added at the end.[172] More extensive use of the registers is manifest towards the

---

167. *Cum in dandis*, to the archbishop of Dublin, 3 March 1190: WH 257, JL 16567; *Cum ad sedem*, to the archbishop of Cashel, 17 March 1190, WH 213, JL 16564; ed. in M. P. Sheehy, *Pontificia Hibernica* (Dublin 1962) 1. 63–64 no. 19, and 66–67, no. 21; the full texts appear together in the register derivative *Seguntina* 17 and 18. These are the only Irish decretals transmitted in the canonical collections.

168. *Cum non ab homine*, JL 17639a–d, and h.

169. Tortosa, Biblioteca del Cabildo 160, fol. 41v–48v; Holtzmann-Cheney, *Collections* 291–296.

170. Lisbon, Biblioteca nacional Alcob.173 [304], fol. 115r–126v; Holtzmann-Cheney, *Collections* 297–299.

171. Durham Cathedral Library C.III.3, fol. 123r–158ra; Holtzmann-Cheney, *Collections* 300–318.

172. Friedberg, *Canones-Sammlungen* 81–84; Holtzmann, 'Die Register Papst Alexander III' 21–69; cf. ibid., 19–21.

close of the century, and two collections in particular record their systematic use—the *Collectio Seguntina* at Sigüenza, identified by Fransen and analyzed by Holtzmann,[173] and *Cracoviensis*, identified and analyzed by Vetulani.[174]

The provenance of the Sigüenza collection is manifest. It opens with a sequence of decretals, mostly to Spanish recipients—Segovia, (Genoa), Pamplona, Zaragoza, Huesca, Zaragoza, etc.— and concludes with a sequence of five decretals, appended in a different hand, the first two of which are letters of Celestine III to the bishop of Sigüenza, dated 7 June 1197. The terminal limits of the main collection are early 1188 to mid-1194, except where two letters of Alexander III appear within the main sequence, and the whole collection ends with three more in the appendix. The individual letters are furnished with rubrics that briefly summarize their contents. Two adjacent letters in particular (107–108), illustrate the juristic interests of the compiler. Celestine III's letters *Prudentiam tuam* to John, dean of Rouen (17 July 1193) and *Bone memorie Alanus* to the prior and chapter of Huntingdon (25 July 1193) are provided with a series of rubrics that are all concerned with the judicial process.[175] This work is clearly a professional selection from the registers, mainly in sequence, but without the overall pattern of organization in the systematic collections. Nevertheless, among the numerous points of interest in the collection, it preserves ten decretals otherwise unknown, and, significantly for the professional study of the collections, reveals some correspondence with the important class of collections described as the primitive collections after *Compilatio prima*.[176] Use of the papal registers is also evident in the Cracow collection (*Cracoviensis*), which demonstrates the accumulation of the decretals, principally of Clement III and Celestine III, by masters in Bologna. Significantly, the collection follows a copy of Bernard of Pavia's *Compilatio prima*.

---

173. G. Fransen, RHE 49 (1954) 155–156 no. 8; W. Holtzmann, 'La "Collectio Seguntina" et les décrétales de Clément III et Célestin III', RHE 50 (1955) 400–453; cf. Duggan, 'English Decretals in Continental Primitive Collections' 57.

174. Kraków, Cathedral Chapter 89, 129–147: cf. A. Vetulani, 'Un manuscrit bolonais du chapitre cathédral de Cracovie', *Symbolae Raphaeli Taubenschlag Dedicatae* (Eos 48; Warsaw-Bratislava 1957)2.389–409, especially 401–402; 'L'Origine des collections primitives canoniques de décrétales à la fin du XIIe siècle', *Congrès de droit canonique médiévale, Louvain* (Louvain 1959) 64–72.

175. *Prudentiam tuam*, JL 17019; *Bone memorie Alanus*, JL 17055 + 16628 + 17675; cf. Holtzmann, 'Collectio Seguntina' 447–448.

176. E.g. Halle 3–4, 11–15, and 18–22 correspond with *Seguntina* 5–6, 111–115, and 27–31; cf. Holtzmann-Cheney, *Collections* 234.

Conclusion

The foregoing survey of decretal collections, from appendices to Gratian to the primitive collections composed after the appearance of *Compilatio prima*, has emphasized the technical aspects of the evolution of decretal law. The novelty of this highly creative phase in the history of canon law lay in its dependence both on actual appellate cases decided by papal judges-delegate throughout the various regions of the Latin Church and on the development of an academic study of the law and its procedures in the early schools, in Bologna, Lincoln/Oxford, Rouen, Tours, Padua, Montpellier, and elsewhere.[177] Without the widespread reception of Gratian's *Decretum* and the principles of papal judicial jurisdiction and appeals to the Roman curia from episcopal courts that it enshrined, so rapid a movement would have been inconceivable. Equally, without the crucial activity of Pope Alexander III, the pope under whom the major advances in the articulation of the theory of papal appellate jurisdiction were made, the creation of decretal law could not have been achieved. In the words of Walter Ullmann:

> The significance of his pontificate lies in the consistent translation of theory into reality ... his decretal legislation was precisely what the papacy needed most just at that time ... His decretals created living law, because they dealt with all the issues relevant to his contemporary Christian society. They were despatched to places as far apart as Durham and Salerno, Salamanca in Spain, Upsala and Linkoeping in Sweden, Braga in Portugal, Armagh in Ireland, Prague in Bohemia, Gran in Hungary and Cracow in Poland; while among frequent addressees were the kings of Denmark, England, France, Hungary, Portugal, Scotland, Sweden. Among the juristic topics with which his decretals dealt, were matrimonial matters, feudal, electoral, judicial, legatine, penal, disciplinary subjects, in addition to issues concerning collegiate ecclesiastical bodies, the rights of cathedral chapters and the disposal of goods during a vacancy, oaths, clerical duties, appointment of officials, details of tithes, rents and dues, prebends, immunities, extensive and restrictive interpretation of the law, constitutional problems, appellate jurisdiction, to mention just a few of the more important legislative acts that remained the law until Whitsun 1918, if not beyond. Through the Alexandrian legislation [or more accurately, appellate decisions] Gratian's theory became the universal law.[178]

---

177. Duggan, 'Papal Judges Delegate' 172–199.
178. Walter Ullmann, *A Short History of the Papacy in the Middle Ages* (London 1972) 199–200.

9

Decretal Collections 1190–1234

Kenneth Pennington

The flood tide of decretals that inspired the canonists to append small decretal collections to Gratian's *Decretum* or to organize them into independent works did not recede as the twelfth century edged toward the shores of the thirteenth. The papacy inexorably descended, in the words of R.W. Southern, 'into a vast ocean of litigation'.[1] Our hindsight gives us a perspective on these developments that was not apparent to jurists of the time. The bishop who addressed the Third Lateran Council and Pope Alexander III in 1179 used the metaphor of the papacy juxtaposed to the ocean quite differently from Southern's when the bishop addressed the opening assembly:[2]

---

1. Richard W. Southern, *Western Society and the Church in the Middle Ages* (The Pelican History of the Church 2; Harmondsworth 1970) 111.
2. Germain Morin, 'Le discours d'ouverture du concile générale de Latran et l'oeuvre littéraire de maître Rufin, évêque d'Assise', *Atti della Pontificia accademia romana di archeologia* (3d Series, Memorie 2; Rome 1923) 113–133 at 118: 'cui [Romanae ecclesiae] tantus praesidet pontifex, summus hic uidelicet patriarcha, qui nuper de oceano fluctuosae persecutionis uelut sol serenus egrediens . . . non solum praesentem ecclesiam, sed etiam uniuersum orbem spectatae claritatis fulgoribus illustrauit'. It was long thought that Rufinus had given this homily at the Council, but Roman Deutinger, 'The Decretist Rufinus—A well-known Person?' BMCL 23 (1999) 10–15, convincingly argues that he did not. See also Adele Simonetti, 'Rufino di Assisi e il cod. C.30 Sup. del Ambrosiana,' *Studi medievali* 31 (1990) 125–142.

> The great pontiff, namely the highest patriarch, presiding over <the Blessed Roman church>, who recently rose from the ocean of raging waves of persecution like a serene sun . . . illuminates not only the present church but the entire world with his worthy brilliance of shining splendor.

The bishop delivered his sermon in the church of St. John in the Lateran to more than three hundred bishops, a greater number of abbots, twenty-one cardinals, and laymen from all over Christendom. There was even a small group of Waldensians from Lyon. The twenty-seven conciliar canons dealt with a wide range of topics. Canons regulated the elections of bishops and stipulated the age necessary to be a bishop. The curia was definitively established as being the last court of appeal in ecclesiastical law. One of the council's canons, *Licet de evitanda,* determined the rules that should govern future papal elections. Alexander did not want a repeat of the schism that occurred after his election in 1159. Henceforth, for a papal election to be valid, two-thirds of the cardinals must have voted for the successful candidate. This rule has governed papal elections to the present day.[3]

The bishop who delivered the opening sermon knew that the papacy was shaking off the parochialism and schisms of the twelfth century. The church in Rome now offered the faithful good government and reliable justice. His metaphor of the pope as sun illuminating, warming, and comforting the world with his radiance encompassed much more than law, but he understood that ecclessiastical courts offered better justice than ever before and that the papal curia had become the court of last resort. That must have been an important part of his own image of the papacy's role in Christian society.

We can use numbers to support what the bishop knew from experience. Historians have counted roughly 10,583 papal letters from the early Church to 1159; in the period from 1159 to 1198, there are almost 7,000.[4] Many of these letters recorded various stages of legal disputes. The ma-

---

3. For his conciliar activity, see Robert Somerville, *Pope Alexander III and the Council of Tours* (Publications of the Center for Medieval and Renaissance Studies; Berkeley–Los Angeles 1977) and Raymonde Foreville, *Latran I, II, III et Latran IV* (Histoire des conciles œcuméniques 6; Paris 1965). See also my 'Pope Alexander III', *The Great Popes through History: An Encyclopedia,* ed. Frank J. Coppa (2 volumes Westport 2002) 1.113–122.

4. On the decretal collections and this definition in particular, see Gérard Fransen, *Les décrétales et les collections de décrétales* (Typologie des sources du moyen âge occidental 2; Turnhout 1972) 24–25, with excellent bibliography. In general see Detlev Jasper and Horst Fuhrmann, *Papal Letters in the Early Middle Ages* (History of Medieval Canon Law. Washington, D.C. 2001). On the general topic of this chapter see, Peter Landau, 'Die Entstehung der systematischen Dekretalensammlungen: In memoriam Josef Juncker' ZRG Kan. Abt. 66 (1979) 120–148, reprinted in *Kanones und Dekretalen* (Biblioteca eruditorum 2; Goldbach 1997) 227–255.

jority were what we today would call 'appellate decisions' of the papal curia. Much new law was contained in these decisions, and the jurists needed new tools with which to cope with the new rules that Rome made daily. If we might have any doubts how the bishop conceived the papacy, the end of his sermon is conclusive. He described the juridical role of the Roman church with graphic images:[5]

> I say that the Roman church did not usurp for itself the summit of such great privilege through statutes of law, synodal decrees, nor any human grant. Rather, the church was established by divine proclamation as the foundation of all churches, when Christ said to Peter: 'You are Peter and upon this rock I shall build my church', and 'Feed my sheep'. Truly this city of the Sun, this church is the head of the world, and is truly called and is one. It shall never be subject to another see. It distributes the keys and chairs of judgment to all other sees. It is the will and the power of the Roman church alone to call a general council and to establish new canons and abolish the old.

Forty years later Johannes Teutonicus would assert that the actual moment when Christ conferred supreme authority over the church on Peter is when He said to him: 'Feed my sheep' in John 21:17.[6] This sermon reflected a conviction of the late-twelfth-century jurists that the pope and the Roman church had an extraordinary role to play in a Christian society.

Ever since Gratian had made legal cases or 'case law' the central focus of his teaching, the canonists had responded to the challenge of the new law by collecting the court decisions reported in papal decretals. Unlike Gratian, who minimized the importance of new papal decretals in his *Decretum*, his successors placed the decretal at the center of their work in the schools and in the courts.[7] By the last decade of the twelfth century the canonists began to understand that a random collection of court cases was not very useful. Organizational principles were needed.

The first canonist to compile a thoroughly systematically organized

---

5. Morin, 'Discours' 119: 'Romana autem ecclesia per nulla iuris scita, per nulla statuta synodica, per nulla, inquam, humana beneficia culmen sibi tanti priuilegii usurpauit, sed solum de diuinae uocis sententia omnium ecclesiarum facta est fundamentum, dum ad beatum Petrum caeleste illud resultauit oraculum: "Tu es Petrus, et super hanc petram aedificabo ecclesiam meam", et iterum: "Pasce oues meas". Vere igitur haec ciuitas Solis, haec ecclesia caput orbis, uere una uocatur et est, quae nulli umquam alii sedi subicitur, per quam omnibus sedibus claues et tribunalia dispensatur, cuius solius arbitrium est et potestas concilium uniuersale colligere, canones nouos condere, et ueteres oblimare'.

6. Johannes Teutonicus to D.21 c.2 v. *Tu es Petrus*. Discussed by Brian Tierney, *Origins of Papal Infallibility 1150–1350: A Study on the Concepts of Infallibility, Sovereignty and Tradition in the Middle Ages* (Studies in the history of Christian thought 6; Leiden 1972) 31.

7. See Duggan's discussion of the pre-1190 'systematic' collections in the preceding chapter. Also Landau, 'Entstehung' 124–148.

collection was Bernard of Pavia. Sometime between 1189 and 1191 he compiled a collection of decretals that he arranged in five books and divided into titles. He called his new collection a *Breviarium extravangantium* (later canonists named it *Compilatio prima*). The term 'extravagantes' arose in the technical vocabulary of the canonists who wished to distinguish between those decretals in Gratian's *Decretum* and those which 'vagant extra Decretum' (circulated outside the Decretum).[8]

Bernard's *Breviarium* was not his first attempt to organize decretal legislation. About ten years earlier, he had compiled a decretal collection that modern scholars have named the *Collectio Parisiensis secunda*, after the manuscript in which it is preserved.[9] This early work of Bernard was not without merit and needs a new name to establish itself as an important milestone in the history of decretal collections.[10] I shall refer to it as Bernard's *Collection in 95 Titles*.

Friedberg was the last to study Bernard's collection carefully. Bernard cited the collection in his tract *De electione*, and many of the titles and chapters are incorporated into the *Breviarium*.[11] In the *Collection of 95 Titles* Bernard was just beginning to think through the organizing principles that he would use for a collection. In a very rough way, the general organization corresponds to the one that he invented for his *Breviarium*. Titles 1 to 22 contain many titles that he later placed in book 1 of his Breviarium; titles 23–50, book 2; titles 51–73, book 3; titles 74–83, book 4. However, these similarities are very inexact. The titles that treated criminal law that he eventually included in book 5 are scattered throughout the work. He had, evidently, not thought about canonical criminal law as a separate category as it was in Roman law. Bernard's organization in *Collection of 95 Titles* sometimes is frustratingly perplexing. His *Breviarium* is a much more systematic work. But one can begin to see the direction of his thinking about how a decretal collection should be constructed in the *Collection of 95 Titles*.

The collection was not well-received by the schools. Although Bernard

---

8. Fransen, *Décrétales et les collections* 19–25.

9. Dated 1177–1179 and preserved in Paris, B.N. lat. 1566, fol. 1r–54v. August Theiner, *Disquisitiones criticae in praecipuas canonum et decretalium collectiones* (Romae 1836) 117–120, first studied the collection and concluded that it had been excerpted from Bernard's *Breviarium*. He listed the rubrics on p. 119–120. J.M. Hanenberg, 'Decretals and Decretal Collections in the Second Half of the XIIth Century', TRG 34 (1966) 522–599 attributed the rubrics to Bernard, but not the texts. Peter Landau, 'Entstehung' 126 reaffirmed his authorship. I am not certain about attributing the *Collectio Lipsiensis* to Bernard; but see Charles Duggan's essay, Chapter 8 in this volume.

10. After Theiner, Emil Friedberg studied the collection and described it in *Die Canonessammlungen zwischen Gratian und Bernhard von Pavia* (Leipzig 1897) 21–45.

11. Friedberg, *Canones-sammlungen* 30–32.

cited it in his tract *De electione*, he seems to be the only canonist who ever referred to it.[12] Landau has pointed out that Bernard's first attempt to systematize the new papal decretal law (the 'ius novum') was of only regional importance. We have no evidence that the collection was ever used outside Bologna.[13]

Although Bernard's *Collection in 95 Titles* had not been a brilliant success, his *Breviarium* gained immediate acceptance in the schools. In his prologue to the collection, Bernard wrote that 'he had compiled "decretales extravagantes" from both new law and old law and organized them under titles'.[14] Bernard was modest. He revolutionized the study of the 'ius novum'. Earlier collections had been arranged according to titles, but none as systematically as Bernard's.[15] Roman law once again provided the canonists with a conceptual model. If we compare the titles of Bernard's collection in books one and two, after he has treated the types of law and ecclesiastical offices (1.1–1.25), with the organization of Justinian's Digest and Code, we can see that Bernard turned to Roman law for inspiration. The following list of titles from books one and two illustrates Bernard adoption of Justinian's titles and organization:

1.26 De pactis Dig. 2.14
1.27 De transactionibus Dig. 2.15
1.28 De postulando Dig. 3.1
1.29 De procuratoribus Dig. 3.3
1.30 De sindico Dig. 3.4–5
1.31 De hiis que vi metusve causa Dig. 4.2
1.32 De in integrum restitutione Dig. 4.1
1.33 De alienatione iudicii mutandi causa facti Dig. 4.7
1.34 De arbitris Dig. 4.8
2.1 De iudiciis Dig. 5.1
2.5 De ordine cognitionum Cod. 3.8, Cod. 7.19
2.6 De plus petitionibus Cod. 3.10
2.7 De feriis Cod. 3.12
2.12 De probationibus Dig. 22.3, Cod. 4.19
2.13 De testibus Dig. 22.5, Cod. 4.20
2.15 De fide instrumentorum Dig. 22.4, Cod. 4.21

12. Friedberg, *Canones-sammlungen* 31.
13. Landau, 'Entstehung' 126.
14. Bernard Papiensis, *Breviarium extravagantium*, ed. Emil Friedberg (Leipzig 1882) 1: 'ego B. Papiensis prepositus extrauagantia de ueteri nouoque iure sub titulis compilaui . . .'
15. See Charles Duggan's chapter 8 above.

With the structure of his collection Bernard underlined the interdependence of Roman and canon law in the late twelfth century and reminded students of canon law that Roman law was essential for their studies.

Bernard did not imitate the Digest by dividing his collection into a large number of books. He divided his compilation into five books, each with a general subject. Later canonists used the mnemonic verse

> Iudex, Iudicium, Clerus, Connubia, Crimen (Judge, Judgment, Clergy, Marriage, Crime)

to remember the contents of each book. Bernard's division into five books was used by almost every later collection. As Kuttner has pointed out, the Northern schools did not accept Bernard's compilation as quickly as Bologna did, and as we shall see, the Northern jurists tinkered with his and later collections.[16]

Bernard collected more than recent papal court decisions. When he wrote that he had compiled a collection of 'extrauagantes' he meant all materials that circulated independently of Gratian. He included many canons from ancient councils and synods, a large number of letters of Pope Gregory I, and many letters of pre-Gratian popes. The bulk of his collection, however, consisted of the decretals of Pope Alexander III (1159–1181). Alexander's court decisions had exercised an enormous influence on canon law, and the canonists had recognized his importance.[17] Bernard also included three texts of Pope Gregory VIII (1187) and three of Pope Clement III (1187–1191). These decretals, together with the fact that Bernard called himself the provost of Pavia—he held that post until 1191 when he became bishop of Faenza—establish the dates between which Bernard must have put the finishing touches on his collection.[18]

The jurists immediately began to teach Bernard's *Breviarium,* and they produced a number of commentaries on it.[19] In Northern Europe they also tinkered with his text by adding decretals to it. Their innovations were not new. Canonists had added material to established collections for centuries. The Pseudo-Isidorian Decretals, Burchard of Worm's and Ivo of Chartres' *Decretum,* The Collection in 74 Titles, and Gratian's *Decretum* had all undergone minor changes in their texts introduced by anonymous jurists. These collections were 'collectiones vivantes', and their texts re-

---

16. Kuttner, 'Bernardus Compostellanus' 284–286.
17. Friedberg, *Compilationes antiquae* vii–xxiii, tabulates the sources and composition of Bernard's *Breviarium.*
18. Gérard Fransen, 'Les diverses formes de la *Compilatio prima*', *Scrinium Lovaniense: Mélanges historiques Etienne van Cauwenbergh* (Louvain 1961) 235–253.
19. See my chapter 'The Decretalists 1190–1234'.

flected their use.[20] In Bologna by the end of the twelfth century, perhaps because the jurists' commentaries on the collections froze them in the form in which they were received, this practice of altering canonical texts seems to have diminished, if not completely disappeared. In Northern Europe, the practice continued until well into the thirteenth century.

Adam Vetulani began the modern exploration of Bernard's *Breviarium*.[21] In the nineteenth century, the editor of Bernard's *Summa decretalium* had conjectured that Bernard might not have included decretal letters of Clement III that were found in many manuscripts in his collection.[22] When he produced a register edition of the *Breviarium*, Friedberg rejected Laspeyres' conjecture.[23] Vetulani took up the question again by examining a manuscript in Krakow. Two of Pope Clement III's decretals were not in it, and Vetulani concluded, after having noted that Holtzmann had discovered the same two decretals missing from the Sigüenza manuscript, that all three of Clement's letters must have been missing from Bernard's original text.[24] Consequently, he proposed to fix the date of composition to 1187.

Vetulani had a genius for asking the right question about the textual problems of canonical sources.[25] His answers were not always fully satisfying, but the questions were brilliant. In this case, Gérard Fransen pointed out that Vetulani's conjecture had a fatal flaw: no manuscript of the *Breviarium* omitted the third letter of Clement.[26] Vetulani had, nevertheless, touched upon an important textual problem. Fransen set out to solve it and published the results of his study in two articles.[27] Fransen examined 92 manuscripts (as of 1965) out of more than 125 manuscripts of the *Breviarium*. He established a typology of three main groups. The first, to which he gave the Greek letter Σ, was the oldest and was made up of three manuscripts, Krakow, Grenoble, and Sigüenza. It originated in Italy and was probably Bernard's first attempt to revise his *Collection of 95 Titles*. Of the 912 chapters that Friedberg registered, these manuscripts omitted

20. See the remarks of Adam Vetulani, 'Deux intéressants manuscrits de la "Compilatio prima",' *Traditio* 12 (1956) 606.
21. Vetulani, 'Deux intéressants manuscrits' 605–611.
22. *Summa decretalium* (Regensburg 1860) xiv, n. 4.
23. *Quinque compilationes antiquae* vi.
24. Vetulani, 'Deux intéressants manuscrits' 610.
25. See the remarks of Stephan Kuttner, 'Research on Gratian: Acta and agenda', *Proceedings Cambridge* 17–18.
26. Fransen, 'Diverses formes' 236. See also Isaias da Rosa Pereira, 'Dois manuscritos alcobadenses da primeira Compilação', *Lumen* (1962) 9–23.
27. 'Diverses formes' and 'La tradition manuscrite de la "Compilatio prima",' *Proceedings Boston* 55–62. He never published the complete results of his study, which he outlined in the *Proceedings Boston*.

26. The second was a northern European version (φ). It shared 10 of the missing chapters with Σ, but included 21 to 24 additional chapters that Friedberg omitted from his edition. Fransen noted that none of the additional chapters could be dated later than 1193. This fact leads to the question, why did the Northern canonists stop adding chapters? But like most interesting questions, we cannot answer it. The last major version was the one that circulated in Bologna (Λ). This recension was probably made by Bernard ca. 1191. There are also manuscripts that represent a mixed version—Fransen calls them 'intermediate' versions—of the text that fall between two of these three types.

An example of the work of the Northern canonists on Bernard's *Breviarium* can be seen in a Parisian manuscript.[28] Kuttner discovered the manuscript and named it *Collectio Parisiensis IV*.[29] Holtzmann and Cheney studied the text and dubbed it *Rotomagensis*.[30] Cheney has shown that the canonist who owned this manuscript worked in Normandy, probably in Rouen. He used the *Breviarium* as his basic text, but added decretals of Clement III, Celestine III, and Innocent III, with a few letters of earlier popes, under their proper titles.[31] This Norman canonist completed his work sometime after 1203. Unlike the versions of the collection that Fransen has studied, this augmented *Breviarium* was a much more radical attempt to keep its contents up-to-date, and was, as we shall see, typical of Northern European canonical practice.

An important piece of evidence for the development of Bernard's *Breviarium* would be the glosses. If the canonists noted either that texts were missing or that they were added, one could draw important conclusions about the evolution of the text. Further, if the Italian or the Northern canonists glossed chapters that were lacking in one or more of the groups we could know which type circulated in a particular area. Little work has been done on this problem. Fransen has published glosses of canonists who noted that they would not or should not read a decretal that had been added to the φ group. Other apparatus comment on the decretals.[32] A complete study of which apparatus and jurists comment on which version of Bernard's *Breviarium* is an important next step for further research.

---

28. Paris, B.N. lat. 3922A, see Walther Holtzmann, *Studies in the Collections of Twelfth-Century Decretals*, ed. and revised by C.R. Cheney and Mary Cheney (MIC, Series B 3; Città del Vaticano 1979) 135–216. See also C.R. Cheney, 'Decretals of Innocent III in Paris, B.N. lat. 3922A', *Traditio* 11 (1955) 149–150.

29. *Repertorium* 313–314.

30. Holtzmann-Cheney, *Collections* 138–139.

31. Complete analysis in Holtzmann-Cheney, *Collections* 152–155.

32. Fransen, 'Diverses formes' 253 and 'Tradition manuscrit' 59.

Collections after *Compilatio prima*

The canonists still put together unsystematic collections after Bernard, but there were no more major systematic collections until the beginning of the thirteenth century.[33] There are probably two reasons for this hiatus. The pontificate of Pope Celestine III did not produce a great body of legal materials. He was the oldest man ever elected to the papacy and even contemporary canonists noted his shortcomings as a law-giver.[34] His successor, however, Pope Innocent III (1198–1216), made an immediate impact on the legal system by producing a large number of new, pathbreaking court decisions in the first five years of his pontificate. The canonists recognized the challenge that Innocent's curia posed and compiled a number of new collections of decretal law in the first decade of the thirteenth century.

The first canonist to seize the flag was Rainer of Pomposa. Not much is known about him, and his collection did not enjoy great success. He was a monk in the monastery of Pomposa and dedicated his collection to a certain Johannes, who was a papal chaplain. We do not know if he taught in the schools. Kuttner believes that he did not have a connection with Bologna because his rubrics do not use legal terminology.[35] The collection was known in Bologna. Albertus, Gilbertus, Alanus, and Bernardus Compostellanus used the collection.[36] The collection's use by Bolognese canonists could be interpreted as evidence that Rainer compiled the collection in an academic setting.

It is preserved in one complete manuscript and a fragment.[37] The great seventeenth-century scholar Etienne Baluze discovered and published it.[38] Rainier selected 123 decretals of Innocent III from the first four years of his pontificate (1198–1201), placing them under 41 titles.[39]

33. Holtzmann-Cheney, *Collections* lists collections compiled after Bernard's *Breviarium* containing letters of Clement III, Celestine III, and Innocent III.
34. Pennington, *Pope and Bishops* 11. For more positive views of Celestine's pontificate in general, see Volkert Pfaff, 'Der Vorgänger: Das Wirken Coelestins III. aus der Sicht von Innozenz III.' ZRG Kan. Abt. 60 (1974) 121–167; Collin Morris, *The Papal Monarchy: The Western Church from 1050 to 1250* (Oxford 1989) 202–204; also K. Baaken, 'Zur Wahl, Weihe und Krönung Papst Cölestins III.', DA 41 (1985) 203–211.
35. Stephan Kuttner, 'Rénier de Pompose ou Rainerius Pomposanus ou de Pomposa', DDC 7 (1960) 583–584. Frank Theisen, 'Die Dekretalensammlung des Rainerius von Pomposa und ihre Hintergründe', *Grundlagen des Rechts: Festschrift für Peter Landau zum 65. Geburtstag*, ed. Richard Helmholz, Paul Mikat, Jörg Müller, and Michael Stolleis (Rechts- und Staatswissenschaftliche Veröffentlichungen der Görres-Gesellschaft, NF 91; Paderborn 2000) 549–577.
36. Franz Gillmann, AKKR 105 (1925) 169, n. 3. Kuttner, 'Rénier' 584.
37. Reims, Bibl. mun. 692, fol. 1r–27r. Paris, B.N. lat. 3922A, see Theisen, 'Die Dekretalensammlung' 555.
38. *Epistolarum Innocentii III P.M. libri undecim* (Paris 1682) 1.543–606, reprinted in Migne, PL 216.1173–1272.
39. The last letter is Po. 1403, May–June 1203, Rain. 21.2.

Rainer's collection is significant in several respects. He was the first jurist to draw his decretals from the papal registers. In his prologue he stated that he took the letters from the first four volumes of the papal registers and, in some cases, 'cut up' (intercidere) decretals with cases containing various subjects and placed the parts under different titles.[40] Rainer departed from the model of Bernard of Pavia's *Breviarium* in several ways. He did not divide his collection into books as Bernard had done but placed the decretals in one book. The arrangement of titles of his collection differed significantly from the arrangements found in earlier decretal collections. Book 5 that treated criminal matters was particularly disorganized.

Rainer's collection was probably closer to Pope Innocent III's vision of law than to the practices and preoccupations of the schools. He eschewed Bernard of Pavia's organization. which reflected a juridical approach to the decretal collections. Instead of following models taken from Roman law, Rainer began his collection with a series of Innocent's decretals that dealt with papal power. The models for his emphasis on papal power were the eleventh- and early twelfth-century canonical collections.[41] They had been the first to give papal power primacy of place. His titles and organization may well reflect Innocent's political and ecclesiological agendas during the first years of his pontificate. Title two proclaimed that 'The priesthood is Greater than Secular Authority'. Title three affirmed the 'Primacy of the Apostolic See'. Title two contained a letter that Innocent wrote to King Phillip Augustus of France and another to the Byzantine emperor.[42] Innocent had instructed both rulers in his doctrine of papal authority and of the proper relationship between secular and ecclesiastical power. In title three Rainer included a decretal in which Innocent had tutored the Patriarch of Constantinople in the language and rules that governed papal primacy.[43] In the fifth title Rainer introduced a subject and a title that had never been part of any decretal collection: 'The translation of elected bishops after their confirmation may not be made without the assent of the Roman pontiff'. The translation of bishops was a key element in Innocent's ecclesiology, and Rainer must have known of Inno-

---

40. On the technical term 'intercisiones', see Pennington, 'French Recension' 60–61, n. 11. See remarks of Theisen, 'Die Dekretalensammlung' 553–554.

41. See my comments on Gregorian Collections in 'La legge nelle tradizioni Cristiane', *Il Cristianesimo Grande Atlante, 2: Ordinamenti, gerarchie, pratiche*, ed. Giuseppe Alberigo, Giuseppe Ruggieri, and Roberto Rusconi (3 vols. Torino 2006) 2.647–663. An English version can be found at http://faculty.cua.edu/pennington. Rainer's Prologue has been translated by Robert Somerville and Bruce C. Brasington, *Prefaces to Canon Law Books in Latin Christianity: Selected Translations, 500–1245* (New Haven–London 1998) 232–233.

42. *In Genesi legimus*, Po. 1055 and *Solite benignitatis affectu*, Po. 1278.

43. *Apostolice sedis primatus*, Po. 862.

cent's intent to establish this papal prerogative as a cornerstone of his authority over bishops.[44]

Although Rainer's collection had little influence, a number of Innocent's decretals on papal power and authority found a permanent place in the canonical tradition. The same Norman-French canonist who augmented Bernard's *Breviarium* for his library also abbreviated Rainer's collection and later added other letters of Innocent (and one of Alexander III) as an appendix to it. Holtzmann has proven that another English canonist who, like his colleague in Rouen, collected material to augment Bernard's *Breviarium*, incorporated large portions of Rainer's collection into his own.[45] This collection must have circulated fairly widely to have attracted the attention of these canonists who worked far from the Italian schools. Italian canonists used Rainer too. Gilbertus, Alanus, and Bernardus Compostellanus drew some of their material from Rainer's collection, as did the anonymous canonist who composed the *Collectio Palatina II*.[46]

Other materials in the Norman canonist's manuscript illustrate the plight of a provincial canonist. He knew of Bolognese collections, but continued to rely on the *Francofortana* as the collection that he made the foundation of his reference library for decretal law. He compiled a major decretal collection to supplement the *Francofortana* and referred to it as 'supplementum' in other parts of the manuscript.[47] Modern historians have called this collection *Rotomagensis prima*, although it is not clear whether this name accurately describes its historical importance.[48] The collection was a working copy. Cheney calls it a 'collection "in statu nascendi".'[49] Its crowded margins, splices of added parchment, and intricate notation are all signs of a working canonist who struggled with his texts. He had many sources from which he drew his material, some of which we cannot know. He borrowed from earlier collections and archival material from the recipients of decretals. Major sources were the collections

---

44. On Innocent's doctrine on translations, see Pennington, *Pope and Bishops* 15, 85–114. Also see a different interpretation in Sebastian Scholz, *Transmigration und Translation: Studien zum Bistumswechsel der Bischöfe von der Spätantike bis zum hohen Mittelalter* (Kölner Historische Abhandlungen 37; Köln-Weimar-Wien 1992). The dissertation of Mary Sommar, 'The Changing Role of the Bishop in Society: Episcopal Translation in the Middle Ages' (Ph.D. Dissertation, Syracuse University, 1998) may also be consulted.

45. Holtzmann-Cheney, *Collections* 301–302.

46. Kuttner, 'Rénier' 584 and 'Bernardus Compostellanus' 328.

47. Holtzmann-Cheney, *Collections* 143. On the *Francofortana* see Chapter 8, p. 282 above, 'Decretal Collections from Gratian's *Decretum* to the *Compilationes Antiquae*', by Charles Duggan.

48. Kuttner, *Repertorium* 297 (Parisiensis III). See Holtzmann-Cheney, *Collections* 160–207 for a complete anaylsis of it.

49. Holtzmann-Cheney, *Collections* 163 with plates to illustrate my next remarks.

of Rainer and Gilbertus (on whom see immediately below). Beginning with matrimony and ending with appeals, and arranging his collection in a completely different order from that which had become standard in Bologna, he divided the decretals into 31 titles.[50] To what purpose did he work? Did he teach or did he use this material in the courtroom? We cannot know.

Sometime during 1203 Gilbertus Anglicus published a major collection of decretals.[51] He followed the same pattern that Bernard of Pavia had established and divided his collection into five books, adopting most of Bernard's titles. He left out some of Bernard's titles, probably because he had no material for them, and added 13 titles of his own. Many of these titles were adopted by later compilers.

If there is some doubt whether Rainier worked in the schools, there is none about Gilbertus. His purpose was to collect those decretals of Alexander III and his successors that Bernard of Pavia had not included and to give an accounting of Innocent III's court decisions. Of the 258 chapters, Gilbertus chose 64 of Innocent's decretals. The remaining 194 chapters are selected from earlier materials. Shortly after he completed his collection, Gilbertus added an appendix containing 32 more of Innocent's decretals. The last decretal added to the main text dates March or April 1201, while the last text of the appendix dates June 1202. In some manuscripts the decretals in the appendix are placed under their proper titles.[52] Gilbertus also glossed his collection.[53]

Gilbertus' collection enjoyed some success. It circulated widely, was abbreviated, and, like other collections, especially North of the Alps, was augmented with decretals. We have already mentioned its use by the Norman canonist who worked in Rouen. He abbreviated the collection for his own use and mined decretals from it. Another abbreviation of the collection exists in a Fulda manuscript that Schulte thought was a first recension of the collection.[54] Two very similar, if not completely identical, exten-

50. Cheney in Holtzmann-Cheney, *Collections* 163–168, gives a thorough discussion of the canonist's sources.
51. Peter D. Clarke, 'The Collection of Gilbertus and the French Glosses in Brussels, Bibliothèque royale, MS 1407–09, and an Early Recension of Compilatio secunda', ZRG Kan. Abt. 117 (2000) 132–184.
52. London, British Library Harl. 3834 and Vercelli, Bibl. Capit. LXXXIX.
53. Rudolf von Heckel, 'Die Dekretalensammlungen des Gilbertus und Alanus nach den Weingartener Handschriften', ZRG Kan. Abt. 29 (1940) 180–225. Gilbertus' glosses are preserved in Salzburg, Stiftsbibl. St. Peter a.IX.18, fol. 118r–168r and Vercelli, Bibl. Capit. LXXXIX, fol. 1r–50r. On these manuscripts see Stephan Kuttner, 'The Collection of Alanus: A Concordance of its Two Recensions', *Rivista di storia del diritto italiano* 26 (1953) 37–38.
54. Heckel, 'Dekretalensammlungen' 116–117, 120–121. The manuscript is Fulda, Landesbibl. D.14, vol. 2r–31v.

sively augmented versions of the collection exist in two Northern manuscripts from Brussels and Uppsala.[55] The close correspondence between the two manuscripts demonstrates that the Northern schools must have had a body of common materials that they regularly added to Italian collections. Even the most striking difference between the Uppsala and Brussels texts, a letter of Innocent III to King Phillip of France that begins the collection in Uppsala but not Brussels, is also found at the beginning of another, non-augmented manuscript of Gilbertus' collection in London.[56] One can conclude from this evidence that there was a certain body of materials circulating with Gilbertus' collection in the North. Ten manuscripts of Gilbertus are extant, a goodly number for a collection that was superseded a few years after it was made.[57]

Gilbertus' collection did not satisfy the Bolognese jurists. No one glossed it. More importantly, Alanus Anglicus composed a new collection of decretals hard on the heels of Gilbertus. Alanus may have undertaken his collection, not because of any dissatisfaction with Gilbertus' collection, but because the flood of Innocent III's decretals continued unabated. For example, Gilbertus finished his collection just before *Pastoralis* began to circulate. *Pastoralis* was a major statement of decretal law that touched upon many different topics and was later included under many different titles of the decretal collections. The canonists immediately recognized its importance. They appended the decretal to Bernard's *Breviarium*,[58] to Gilbertus,[59] or to Rainier.[60] *Pastoralis* was also added to later collections and miscellaneous manuscripts.[61] Alanus incorporated the decretal into his collection and put its various parts under the appropriate titles. At this time Pope Innocent III's decretals became a significant part of decretal law. Alanus included many more of Innocent's decretals than Gilbertus had: 345 decretals in all, out of 484 for the entire collection.

55. Brussels, Bibl. Royal 1407–1409, fol. 93r–148v and Uppsala, Univ.-Bibl. C.551, fol. 1r–54v.

56. *Recepimus litteras*, Po. 1649, included in Innocent's special register on papal and imperial matters, RNI no. 64, edited by Friedrich Kempf, *Regestum Innocentii iii papae super negotio Romani imperii* (Miscellanea Historiae Pontificiae 12; Rome 1947) 177–183. Also in London, Lambeth Palace 105, fol. 220v–267v.

57. Holtzmann-Cheney, *Collections* xxvii–xxviii, conveniently lists the manuscripts.

58. Brussels, Bibl. royale 1407–1409, fol. 91r, Modena, Bibl. Esten. a.R.4.16 (lat. 968), fol. 77r–77v (with glosses of Silvester), and Vat. Pal. lat. 652, fol. 61v–62r.

59. Bamberg, Staatsbibl. can. 20, fol. 62v–63r, London, B.L. Harley 3834, fol. 201v, London, Lambeth Palace 105, fol. 269r–270v.

60. Reims, Bibl. mun. 692, fol. 28r–31r.

61. Cambridge, Caius College 150, fol. 151v, Ely, Diocesan Records (Cambridge University Library) Liber M, fol. 5r, London, B.L. Add. 24659, fol. 1r–2r, Valenciennes, Bibl. mun. 274, fol. 154v, Zwettl, Stiftsbibl. 162, fol. 213v (with glosses of Silvester).

Alanus followed the pattern established by Bernard of Pavia, but added a sixth book in which he treated sacramental topics, for which the final part of Gratian's *Decretum, De consecratione*, was an obvious model. Like Gilbertus, he must have added this section shortly after he completed his collection.[62] After having finished his collection, Alanus revised his work and produced a second recension.[63] Kuttner has shown that the school of Bologna accepted Alanus' collection in its second, not its first recension. And, Heckel's scepticism notwithstanding, the glosses that Alanus composed for the second recension prove conclusively that he was its author.[64]

The last attempt before Petrus Beneventanus' *Compilatio tertia* to bring order to Innocent III's court decisions and legislative decrees was Bernardus Compostellanus' *Collectio Romana*, compiled in 1208.[65] We have good information about the origins of Bernardus' collection from Tancred in his prologue to *Compilatio tertia*:[66]

> Finally master and archdeacon Bernardus Compostellanus, during a short stay at the Roman curia, compiled a collection of decretals from the registers of Pope Innocent III. Within a short time, the students at Bologna called this the Roman compilation. Some decretals were found in this collection that the Roman curia rejected, just as today (ca. 1220) several decretals of the Second Compilation are also rejected.

From Tancred we learn that Bernardus spent some time in Rome, where he worked on his decretal collection, and that the students of Bologna connected the compilation with his Roman stay and named the collection the 'Roman Compilation'. The curia was dissatisfied with his selection of decretals—some of the decretals were 'rejected'. Tancred explained that doubts about these decretals prompted Innocent III to send Petrus Beneventanus' collection of his decretals to the students at Bologna.[67]

---

62. Heckel, 'Gilbertus und Alanus' 147–157.

63. Kuttner was the first to discover this recension. He analyzed it in 'Collection of Alanus'. Holtzmann-Cheney, *Collections* xx, lists the known manuscripts and fragments. See also Kuttner, 'Decretal collections', *Traditio* 534–536.

64. Kuttner, 'Collection of Alanus' 51.

65. Kuttner, 'Bernardus Compostellanus' remains the definitive account of this collection. Heinrich Singer, 'Die Dekretalensammlung des Bernardus Compostellanus antiquus: Mit Benutzung der in Friedrich Maassens Nachlasse enthaltenen Vorarbeiten', SB Vienna, Phil.-Hist. Klasse 171 (Vienna 1914) has analyzed the collection.

66. Singer, *Bernardus Compostellanus* 3, n. 2: 'tandem magister Bernardus Compostellanus archidiaconus in Romana curia, in qua curia moram faciens aliquantum, de regestis domini Innocentii papae unam fecit decretalium compilationem, quam Bononiae studentes Romanam compilationem aliquanto tempore vocaverunt. Verum quia in ipsa compilatione quaedam reperiebantur decretales, quas Romana curia refutabat, sicut hodie quaedam sunt in secundis, quas curia ipsa non recipit'.

67. K. Pennington, 'The Making of a Decretal Collection: The Genesis of Compilatio tertia', *Proceedings Salamanca* 72–73.

Bernardus Compostellanus added more information about the problem of 'rejected decretals' in the epilogue to his collection:[68]

> You should reject some decretals of Innocent III that the schoolmen attribute to him. They are not contained in his registers and are not approved by him. I heard this from Innocent himself.

Bernardus then listed five decretals that circulated under Innocent's name in the schools but were not his.[69] Two important points can be made about this evidence. First, the canonists and the papacy were beginning to see that there was a close connection between the source of judicial authority within the church and the teaching and compilation of its law. The papacy had permitted the schools to exercise great freedom in their teaching, explicating, and compiling of canon law. Now the curia was beginning to examine the contents of these collections. Conversely, the jurists began to pay attention to the opinions of curial lawyers. The age of private collections was drawing to a close. Second, the curia and the pope understood that the papal registers provided a means through which decretals might be authenticated. This was not a new idea and may not have originated in the curia. For some time the canonists had indicated that a particular decretal was 'in registro' as a part of the inscriptions for decretals.[70]

Bernardus' collection contained only decretals of Innocent III. He chose 277 decretals from Gilbertus' and Alanus' collections and added 154 decretals that he may have taken from the papal registers. He also took some decretals from Rainier of Pomposa's collection.[71] Although he might have had access to the papal registers, he did not collate all the decretals he took from earlier collections with them. There is irrefutable evidence that sometimes he simply took decretals from other collections without examining them critically.[72] Bernardus' collection was not a spectacular suc-

---

68. Singer, *Bernardus Compostellanus* 114: 'In fine quiddam annectere affectionis ardor scolastice me cogit, ut quasdam decretales, quas sub nomine domini Innocentii III. habent scolastici, tanquam non suas respuatis. Neque enim in registris eius idem continetur, neque ab eo comprobantur, sicut ad os ab eo accepi'.

69. Christopher Cheney, 'Three decretal collections before Compilatio IV: Pragensis, Palatina I, and Abrincensis II', *Traditio* 15 (1959) 480–482, argues that Bernardus thought they were not forgeries but not attributed to the correct pope. Singer had held that they were not decretals.

70. Heckel, 'Gilbertus und Alanus' 157–158, has discussed Gilbertus' and Alanus' use of the notation 'in registro' in their collections. See also Uta-Renate Blumenthal, 'Papal registers in the twelfth century', *Proceedings Cambridge* 149–151, for the value that the curia placed on decretals found in papal registers.

71. Kuttner, 'Bernardus Compostellanus' 327–333. Kuttner corrects Singer on a number of points.

72. Pennington, 'Genesis of Compilatio tertia' 81–82.

cess. The manuscript tradition of his collection is confined to five manuscripts.[73]

The influence of Bernardus' collection also was limited because Petrus Benevantanus' *Compilatio tertia* replaced it circa two years later. Petrus undoubtedly used Bernardus' collection, but he treated the texts of the decretals much more conservatively than Bernardus had. Compostellanus wielded his editorial pencil with a vigor that bordered on rashness. He often cut decretals until the special facts of a case were obscured, if not erased. That practice severely limited the usefullness of the case law in the collection. His editorial policies may have, in part, accounted for the collection's short life.[74] In light of these facts it is surprising that his collection had a substantial impact north of the Alps. When the northern canonists revised *Compilatio tertia*, they replaced many of Petrus Beneventanus' editorial changes in the texts of Innocent's decretals with readings taken from the *Compilatio Romana*. They also took decretals from Bernardus' collection that Petrus had omitted and added them to the 'French recension' of *Compilatio tertia*.[75]

The state of decretal collections in the first decade of the thirteenth century can be seen from another perspective if we examine the contents of Italian manuscripts that were put together at that time. The canonists in Italy had the same problem that the Anglo-Norman canonist from Rouen had. They wanted a reliable corpus of texts that they could use in the classroom and cite in their glosses. There were no standard collections to which they could turn before ca. 1210. A glance at the contents of three manuscripts is instructive:

I. Vercelli, Bibl. capit. LXXXIX
   1. fol. 1r–50r: Collection of Gilbertus, with his apparatus.
   2. fol. 51r–136r: Collection of Alanus, with his apparatus.
   3. fol. 137r–220v: Decretals of *Compilatio tertia* not in Gilbertus or Alanus.
II. Salzburg, Stiftsbibl. St. Peter a.ix.18
   1. fol. 2r–117v: *Compilatio prima*, glosses by Richardus and Alanus.
   2. fol. 118r–168r: Collection of Gilbertus, with his apparatus.
   3. fol. 169r–243r: Collection of Alanus.

---

73. Kuttner, 'Bernardus Compostellanus' 328–329 and 'Retractationes' 21, where he notes a fragment in Douai, Bibl. mun. 598, fol. 1r–1v.
74. Pennington, 'Genesis of Compilatio tertia' 70.
75. K. Pennington, 'The French Recension of Compilatio tertia', BMCL 5 (1975) 53–71. See further discussion of the 'French Recension' of *Compilatio tertia* below.

4. fol. 244r–275v: Chapters from *Collectio Romana* not in Alanus and Gilbertus
III. Modena, Bibl. Estense a.R.4.16 (lat. 968)
  1. fol. 1r–76v: *Compilatio prima* with four layers of glosses.
  2. fol. 77r–v: *Pastoralis* (Po. 2350) with Silvester's glosses.
  3. fol. 78r–117v: *Collectio Estensis*, pre–Innocent III decretals taken from Gilbertus and Alanus.
  4. fol. 119r–235v: *Compilatio Romana*
  5. fol. 237r–255r: Decretals from *Compilatio tertia* not in the *Compilatio Romana*.
  6. fol. 255r–257r: Collection of decretals taken from *Compilatio secunda* to supplement *Collectio Estensis* (3.).

Two points can be made about the contents of these manuscripts. First, the canonists must have had difficulty keeping track of decretals outside *Compilatio prima*. Gilbertus and Alanus duplicated much material, but each collection contained decretals not in the other. Second, the supplementary collections that they concocted to fill lacunae undoubtedly compounded the problem of finding a particular text. The canonists who wished to cite these decretals in their works must have struggled with references to decretals. Bernardus' *Compilatio Romana* did nothing to alleviate these problems.

Whatever the shortcomings of Bernardus' *Collectio Romana*, Petrus Beneventanus compiled the first 'official' collection of canon law in late 1209 or early 1210. This collection, called *Compilatio tertia*, contained only decretals of Innocent III. Petrus followed the same pattern—five books were divided into titles—that was, by now, well established. Like Bernardus Compostellanus, he worked on his collection in the papal curia. Unlike any earlier collection, Innocent sent it to Bologna with a letter of approbation. Petrus had taught at Bologna before he became a papal chaplain ca. 1205. Later he bore the title of papal notary. Innocent appointed him to the cardinalate in 1212, and Honorius III elevated him to the cardinal-bishopric of Sabina in 1216.[76]

The doughty English litigant Thomas of Marlborough hired Petrus to 'learn the secrets of the curia' and described him as the best lawyer at the papal court.[77] Petrus established his place in legal history when he compiled a new collection of Innocent's decretals. The exact role of In-

---

76. Pennington, 'Genesis of Compilatio tertia' 67–68.
77. *Chronicon abbatiae de Evesham ad annum 1418*, ed. W.D. Macray (RS 29; London 1863) 153.

nocent III in the compilation and authentication of *Compilatio tertia* is not easy to determine. I have argued that we should not interpret Innocent's bull of promulgation, *Devotioni vestrae,* as it had been commonly read: that Innocent ordered Petrus to compile a new collection of his decretals. Rather, I think the evidence, though fragmentary, points to Petrus' having compiled the collection and having then presented it to Innocent III. Innocent approved his collection and sent it to Bologna with *Devotioni vestrae*. He was principally concerned to authenticate the decretals that it contained, wishing to solve the problems of authenticity that had plagued earlier compilations. Consequently, Innocent had not yet stepped into the role of Justinian. He did not 'order' Petrus to compile the collection, he simply authenticated a private collection—although he may have known that Petrus was working on the collection in the curia—and guaranteed that the decretals were genuine.[78]

Innocent vouched for the authenticity of the decretals in Petrus' collection by declaring that they could all be found in the papal registers.[79] We have seen that the canonists and then the curia had become preoccupied with the issue of authentication. Petrus had not, however, taken all the decretals in his collection from the registers. He took the majority from the collections of Gilbertus, Alanus, and Bernardus. He gathered other decretals from unknown sources that circulated in the schools and curia. He must have used the registers for the most recent decretals. Approximately forty-five decretals from Innocent's eleventh and twelfth pontifical years have no known source except the registers. In spite of Innocent's assurances, not all the decretals can be found in the registers.[80] The pope was, however, aware that some decretals had not been enregistered, and he ordered sixteen decretals that he and Petrus knew were not enregistered added to the eleventh year of his pontificate—the so-called 'canonical appendix'.[81]

The evidence of the decretals in this 'canonical appendix' to the papal registers proves that Petrus must have had access to the archives of the chancellery or to originals of the decretals.[82] The texts of the decretals

---

78. The evidence for this argument is given in Pennington, 'Genesis of Compilatio tertia' 67–79.

79. The text of *Devotioni vestrae* is printed by Friedberg, *Compilationes antiquae* 105. It is translated by Somerville and Brasington, *Prefaces to Canon Law Books* 233–234.

80. Pennington, 'Genesis of Compilatio tertia' 80.

81. Friedrich Kempf, *Die Register Innocenz III.: Eine paläographisch-diplomatische Untersuchung* (Miscellanea Historiae Pontificiae 9; Rome 1945) 95–102; two letters in the 'canonical appendix' had, in fact, been enregistered and must have been added in error.

82. I have given some evidence that the canonists knew some decretals in their original form as they had been sent from the curia, 'Genesis of Compilatio tertia' 80, n. 33.

in the canonical appendix were not taken from *Compilatio tertia* but from preliminary drafts of material with which Petrus must have worked. Although these decretals do have Petrus' editorial cuts in their lengths, they do not have, for the most part, the changes of wording that he introduced into their texts.[83] Second, Innocent or Petrus established a link between the papal registers, papal legislation, and the schools that would remain a fixture of canonical jurisprudence from this time on. Innocent understood that the Roman church had an interest in the teaching and dissemination of its court decisions and rescripts.

These editorial changes that Petrus and the earlier compilers made in the texts of the decretals are important pieces of evidence for determining the attitude of the canonists toward their texts. Petrus worked within the framework of earlier collections and usually took the form of the decretal as well as its wording from them. Although detailed work on Petrus' editorial methods has not been done, we can say that Petrus did compare the texts of the decretals in Alanus' and Bernardus Compostellanus' collections. He incorporated readings from both collections and added changes of his own.[84] The collections were more important sources than the registers.[85] For the history of canonical collections, the most important consequence is that the 'official' character of *Compilatio tertia* does not rest on Petrus' use of the papal registers—an impression that might be garnered from an uncritical reading of *Devotioni vestrae*—nor does that character reflect an attempt of Innocent III to seize control of the compilation of new canonical collections. Petrus' compilation was thoroughly in the tradition of the schools, and *Compilatio tertia* did not represent a break from earlier collections in methodology or sources.

Petrus' compilation was a resounding success. The Bolognese canonists embraced it immediately. After a period during which they had no clear idea which collections of decretals should be used in the classroom, they must have welcomed the stability that Petrus' papally authenticated collection represented. The collection stimulated the canonists to write a large number of apparatus for it, producing a remarkable body of works by ca. 1217.[86]

---

83. See my introduction to *Johannis Teutonici Apparatus glossarum in Compilationem tertiam* (MIC, Series A, 3; Città del Vaticano 1981) xxv.

84. Pennington, 'Genesis of Compilatio tertia' 79–89, examines Petrus' methodology.

85. I have given a small justification of this point in my examination of the decretal *Pastoralis*; see 'Genesis of Compilatio tertia' 90–92.

86. See my chapter on the Decretalists 1190–1234.

Decretal Collections after Compilatio tertia

The decretal manuscript of the Biblioteca Estense in Modena (the contents of which are outlined above) provides the best answer to the question why Johannes Galensis compiled *Compilatio secunda* on the heels of Petrus Beneventanus' *Compilatio tertia*. The collection dubbed the *Collectio Estensis* on fol. 78r–117v of the Modena manuscript was a compilation of decretals from Innocent III's immediate predecessors, culled primarily from the collections of Gilbertus and Alanus. Canonists must have found reference books like the Modena, Salzburg, and Vercelli manuscripts exasperating to use and to cite. Although Innocent III's decretals dominated canonical case law after 1210, his predecessors' decretals contained much of importance. The *Collectio Estensis* was an attempt to make the consultation of pre-Innocentian materials not in *Compilatio tertia* less difficult. Johannes Galensis responded to this problem of sources by compiling *Compilatio secunda*.

The name, *Compilatio secunda*, was given to the collection because its material mostly postdated the *Prima* and, except for a few decretals, predated the *Tertia*.[87] Johannes drew heavily from the decretals of Alexander III, Clement III, and Celestine III. He organized the collection into the same pattern of books and titles as the first two compilations.[88]

The scriptoria in Bologna and elsewhere soon began to produce manuscripts that combined the first three compilations in one book, and, within a very short time, the jurists almost completely ignored other collections in their writings and teaching. Florence, Biblioteca nazionale, Conventi soppressi ad ordinare, Vallombrosa 36 (325) is an early example of a manuscript that preserves the first efforts of the canonists to integrate the three collections into the work of the schools.[89] The glosses in the margins of *Compilatio tertia* refer to the first two collections as 'in primis' and 'in secundis'; references to itself are 'in ultimis'. In *Compilatio prima*, the glosses cite *Tertia* as 'in extr. Innoc. de rescript. et interpret. Cum adeo' or 'de rescript. Innoc. Ex tenore'. One might think that these references might predate the *Tertia*, but the same hand also refers to *Compilatio secunda* as

---

87. Kuttner, *Repertorium* 345, n. 1, noted that the seven decretals ascribed to Innocent III in *Secunda* are suspect.

88. Kuttner, *Repertorium* 345–354. No work has been done on the textual tradition of *Compilatio secunda*. We do not know if the canonists added decretals to the collection as they did for the *prima*, *tertia*, and *quinta*.

89. First discovered by Martin Bertram, 'Some additions to the "Repertorium der Kanonistik",' BMCL 4 (1974) 11. The manuscript also contains *Compilatio quarta* and the Fourth Lateran Constitutions, but these parts were clearly added later.

'in mediis'. Within a very short time, the canonists adopted a standard system of citation that they almost always uniformly used for the collections: 'extra. i.' or 'in lib. i.' for *Prima*, 'extra. ii.' and 'extra. iii.', 'in lib. ii.' and 'in lib. iii.' for *Secunda* and *Tertia*.

Innocent III's curia never slept, and the schools continued to be inundated with new decretals. Christopher Cheney has described the contents of three small collections of Innocent's decretals that constitute 'updates' of the *Compilatio tertia*. The collections are known by the names of the libraries in which they presently reside: *Pragensis, Palatina I*, and *Abrincensis II*.[90] These collections are all contained in manuscripts with other canonistic works. The decretals almost all date between the eleventh and sixteenth years of Innocent's pontificate. Another collection analyzed by Stephan Kuttner, the *Collectio Bambergensis secunda*, contains twenty decretals dating from December of 1210 to March of 1215.[91] They were appended to a manuscript that contained the *Decretum* of Burchard of Worms and the Fourth Lateran Constitutions, a combination that could have been put together only in the provinces.[92] Innocent's decretals were also gathered together as small appendices to earlier collections[93] or as individual items appended frequently to decretal collections or written into the margins.[94] These collections, appendices, and, perhaps, individual decretals circulating separately provided the canonists up-to-date decisions from Rome not yet included in the main collections.

The Northern canonists adapted the text of *Compilatio tertia* to their needs by inserting decretals into the text of the collection, not by compiling small collections of additional decretals. This 'French recension' of *Tertia* did not, for the most part add decretals later than 1210, the time that Petrus compiled his collection, but it did add a large number of Innocent's decretals under their respective titles.[95] Although the additional decretals are the most obvious features of this transmontane work, the redactor also reworked the texts of all the other decretals in *Tertia* and eliminated

---

90. Cheney, 'Three decretal collections before Compilatio quarta: Pragensis, Palatina I, and Abrincensis II', Traditio 15 (1959) 464–483. The portrait of Innocent III in Pragensis has attracted the attention of historians, see Gerhardt B. Ladner, 'Eine Prager Bildniszeichnung Innocenz' III. und die Collectio Pragensis', SG 11 (1967) 23–35 and Friedrich Kempf, 'Die Umschrift des Prages Miniaturbildnisses Innocenz' III.' *Storia e storiografia: Studi in onore di Eugenio Dupré Theseider* (Roma 1974) 661–667.

91. Kuttner, 'A collection of decretal letters of Innocent III in Bamberg', *Medievalia et Humanistica* New Series 1 (1970) 41–56, reprinted in *Medieval Councils, Decretals and Collections*.

92. Brief analysis by García y García, *Constitutiones Concilii quarti Lateranensis* 22.

93. E.g. the eleven decretals studied by Stanley Chodorow, 'An appendix to Rainer of Pomposa's collection', BMCL 3 (1973) 55–61.

94. '"Cum causam que": A decretal of Pope Innocent III', BMCL 7 (1977) 100–103.

95. Pennington, 'French Recension' 54–60.

many of Petrus Beneventanus' editorial changes. Surprisingly, the redactor followed the text of the *Collectio Romana*. Bernardus Compostellanus had adhered closely to the wording of the decretals in the registers. Petrus had made many changes or had adopted the changes introduced by Alanus and Gilbertus. The redactor eliminated those changes and restored the text as found in the *Collectio Romana* and the registers. He restored 'partes decisae' that Petrus had cut out of the originals.[96]

The French recension of *Compilatio tertia* is evidence that the canonists viewed Beneventanus' collection very differently from a modern lawyer's reception of a code. The redactor did not treat Innocent's collection as inviolable, and his handling of texts is far removed from modern ideas about legislative codes.

The Fourth Lateran Council of 1215 provided the canonists with a major body of new legislation that had to be incorporated into canon law. Innocent III promulgated seventy-one canons that touched upon all aspects of ecclesiastical life and discipline. The pope ordered the canons placed into the papal registers and probably sent copies of the canons to major bishoprics.[97] Johannes Teutonicus, Vincentius Hispanus, and Damasus Hungarus glossed the canons.[98] Johannes almost immediately incorporated the canons into a new decretal collection, *Compilatio quarta*.

Compilatio quarta had the most puzzling history of all the collections. A contemporary source recorded that Johannes had combined the canons of the Fourth Lateran with Innocent's decretals after *Compilatio tertia*. Johannes presented the new collection to Innocent III, but the pope refused to 'approve' (approbare) it.[99] We do not know why Innocent did not accept the collection. One might conjecture that Innocent wished that the conciliar canons be collected and circulated in a 'papal collection'. But he did nothing, and the Lateran canons circulated randomly. Whatever the reasons, canonists knew the story of Johannes' failure and treated the new collection with great caution. Johannes was the only canonist to gloss it, and Tancred left *Compilatio quarta* out of his history of canon law (ca. 1221). From the evidence of scattered glosses of several canonists that have

96. Ibid. 61–64. See also Steven Horwitz, 'Reshaping a decretal chapter: *Tua nobis* and the canonists', *Law, Church, and Society: Essays in Honor of Stephan Kuttner*, ed. Kenneth Pennington and Robert Somerville (Philadelphia 1977) 207–221.

97. The best recent discussions of the promulgation of the canons and their dissemination are García y García's introduction to his edition of the canons, *Constitutiones Concilii quarti Lateranensis* 3–38 and Duggin in chapter 10.

98. García has edited all three commentaries, *Constitutiones Concilii quarti Lateranensis*.

99. See Stephan Kuttner, 'Johannes Teutonicus, das vierte Laterankonzil und die Compilatio quarta', *Miscellanea Giovanni Mercati* (ST 125; Vatican City 1946) 608–634, reprinted in *Medieval Councils, Decretals and Collections*; Pennington, 'Genesis of Compilatio tertia' 76–77.

been preserved in a few manuscripts, we can assume that *Compilatio quarta* was taught in the schools in spite of Innocent's objections to the collection.[100] In any case, by the middle of the 1220s, *Compilatio quarta* was firmly established in the literature, and canonists cited it frequently in their works. The scriptoria in the schools soon added *Compilatio quarta* to the corpus of what came to be called the *Compilationes antiquae*. Many manuscripts preserve the first four compilations as a book.[101]

In contrast to Petrus Beneventanus, Johannes did not work on his collection in Rome and did not, therefore, have access to papal archives and registers as Petrus had. He probably drew his decretals from small collections of Innocent's letters, collections that have been lost or that were similar to *Pragensis*, *Palatina I*, and *Abrincensis II*. In the few cases in which we can trace the history of a particular decretal in earlier collections, we can see that Johannes' methods of handling and editing the texts were closer to those of Petrus than to those of Bernardus Compostellanus.[102]

The most interesting canonistic attempt to shape a decretal collection prior to Raymond of Peñafort's *Decretals of Greogry IX* was the *Collectio Salmanticensis*.[103] Between 1210 and 1212, the anonymous jurist who compiled the collection followed in large part the pattern of the *Compilationes antiquae*. He divided the collection into five books and combined decretals from the first three compilations, attempting for the first time to bring unity to the sprawling growth of decretal collections. He also cut out 'partes decisae' from the decretals, sometimes anticipating the same cuts made by Raymond of Peñafort in the *Gregoriana*. The collection was not a comprehensive compilation of decretal legislation, but rather an abbreviation of the first three *Compilationes antiquae*. The most striking statistic that reveals the compiler's purpose is that he chose only 301 chapters from ca. 1700 chapters of the first three compilations. Nevertheless, as García y García has noted, this collection marks the first time that a private jurist tried to unify the decretal collections, and his methodology anticipates Pope Gregory IX's mandate to Raymond.

Particularly significant papal decretals sometimes circulated independently of decretal collections. The first example, which I mentioned ear-

---

100. See Admont, Stiftsbibl. 22 and Cordoba, Bibl. del Cabildo 10.
101. Kuttner, *Repertorium* 372–381.
102. Horwitz, 'Reshaping a decretal chapter' 216, has traced the textual tradition of Innocent's decretal *Tua nobis* (4 Comp. 3.9.4) in which the pope treated the issue of lay possession of tithes.
103. Antonio García y García, 'Una coleccion de decretales en Salamanca', *Proceedings Boston* 71–92, reprinted in *Iglesia, sociedad y derecho* (Salamanca 1985) 171–191. The collection is contained in Salamanca, Biblioteca de la Universidad Civil, 2678, fol. 93r–154v.

lier, was the decretal-rescript *Pastoralis,* in which Pope Innocent III answered a series of questions from the bishop of Ely in 1204 (Po. 2350). It was immediately glossed and appended to decretal collections.[104] Pope Honorius III issued *Super speculam* on 22 November 1219 (Pressutti 2267); in it he forbade clerics in religious orders to leave their monasteries in order to study Roman law and medicine. He also ended the study of Roman law at the University of Paris.[105] Honorius sent *Super speculam* to recipients in all parts of Christendom. The canonists glossed it and appended it to decretal collections.[106] Both *Pastoralis* and *Super speculam* were incorporated into decretal collections, but the canonists signaled their importance by giving them an independent existence from the time of their promulgation. The jurists seem to have circulated these decretals privately; at least we have no evidence that the papacy encouraged the schoolmen to publicize important decretals and constitutions.

The last collection of papal decretals before the decretals of Pope Gregory IX *(Gregoriana)* was *Compilatio quinta.* Tancred, the archdeacon of Bologna and doctor of canon law in the law school, compiled the collection. Pope Honorius III ordered him to put together a collection of his decretals from the beginning of his pontificate (1217).[107] Tancred finished his task by 2 May 1226.[108] Like Bernardus Compostellanus and Petrus Beneventanus, Tancred worked in Rome and, like Bernardus, he drew Honorius' decretals directly from the papal registers. Leonard Boyle and Paulius Rabikauskas discovered marks of Tancred in the margins of Honorius' registers that noted decretals selected for inclusion into *Compilatio quinta.* The scribes must have been guided by these marks when they copied the decretals from the registers.[109] An unusual feature of the collection was the inclusion of a statute of Emperor Frederick II, *Hac edictali lege,* sections

---

104. The glosses of Silvester to *Pastoralis* can be found in Zwettl 162, fol. 213v and Modena, Bibl. Estense a.R.4.16, fol. 77r–77v

105. Stephan Kuttner, 'Papst Honorius III. und das Studium des Zivilrechts', *Festschrift für Martin Wolff,* ed. E. von Caemmerer et al. (Tübingen 1952) 79–101, reprinted with many additional notes in *Gratian and the Schools of Law.*

106. There are glosses in Lisbon, Bibl. nat. Alcob. 381, fol. 224r–224v and Florence, Laurenziana, Santa Croce V sin. 4, fol. 1r. Although there is a core of common material, the apparatus are slightly different in each manuscript. In Florence, some of the glosses are signed 'jo.', many are signed 'g.' or 'Guill.' There is no internal evidence in the glosses of 'jo.' that the glossator is Johannes Teutonicus.

107. Honorius' bull of promulgation is translated by Somerville and Brasington, *Prefaces to Canon Law Books* 234–235.

108. Leonard E. Boyle, 'The Compilatio quinta and the registers of Honorius III', BMCL 8 (1978) 9–19. See also Pennington, 'French Recension' 67–69.

109. Paulius Rabikauskas, '"Auditor litterarum contradictarum" et commissions de juges délégués sous le pontificat d'Honorius III', BEC 132 (1974) 213–244.

of which Tancred placed under nine titles. *Compilatio quinta* was the only post-Gratian decretal collection to contain secular legislation.

Although *Compilatio quinta* may have been the first collection that was ordered by the pope himself, it did not have great success. Only two canonists, Zoën Tencararius and Jacobus of Albenga, wrote apparatus for it; only seventeen manuscripts survive. Perhaps Raymond of Peñafort made the most critical commentary on the quality of Honorius' decretals when he eliminated almost 40 percent of them from the *Gregoriana*. Although Honorius commissioned and authenticated the collection, the canonists added decretals to the collection as the French canonists had altered *Compilatio tertia*. In their glosses they argued that *Compilatio quinta* did not preclude using other decretals that circulated outside the collection. They did not, in other words, treat a papally sanctioned official collection as one would treat a modern code.

With *Compilatio quinta* the papacy took control of its law. For the next century decretal collections were 'official' compilations, ordered by the papacy, and sent to the law schools. The age of the 'private' decretal collection had passed.[110] Shortly after he became pope, Gregory IX took the first step in this direction. He decided to bring unity to the somewhat chaotic state of decretal collections and summoned the Catalan Dominican Raymond of Peñafort to Rome in 1230. He asked him to compile a new codification that would replace all earlier collections of decretals with one volume. We do not know if Raymond worked alone or with other jurists in the curia. In his bull, *Rex pacificus*, with which Gregory promulgated the new collection in 1234, he called Raymond's work a *Compilatio,* but the canonists quickly adopted the name *Decretales Gregorii noni*, or later, *Gregoriana*. Along with Gratian's *Decretum*, it became the most important collection of papal decretals in the schools and in the courts of Europe during the thirteenth century.[111]

---

110. Giulio Silano, 'Of Sleep and Sleeplessness: The Papacy and the Law 1150–1300', *The Religious Roles of the Papacy: Ideals and Realities 1150–1300*, ed. Christopher Ryan (Papers in Mediaeval Studies 8; Toronto 1989) 343–361 at 357–360, argues that the canonists treated *Compilationes tertia et quinta* with more respect and as more 'official' than I have described in this chapter.

111. Somerville and Brasington, *Prefaces to Canon Law Books* 225–230 and Martin Bertram, 'Die Dekretalen Gregors IX. (1234): Kompilation oder Kodifikation?' *Magister Raimundus: Atti del Convegno per il IV centenario della Canonizzazione di San Raimondo de Penyafort (1601–2001)*, ed. C. Longo (Istituto Storico Domenicano; Rome 2002) 61–86.

10

Conciliar Law 1123–1215
The Legislation of the Four Lateran Councils

Anne J. Duggan

When a bishop declared at the beginning of Third Lateran Council in 1179 that only the Roman Church could issue decrees of universal character, he was proclaiming a principle which had inspired reforming popes since Leo IX. The resumption of regular Roman councils, usually held in the Lateran during Lent, had been a crucial element both in the progress of the 'Gregorian' reform movement and in the assertion of papal leadership of the church. At the same time, the schisms and crises of the papal-imperial controversy (ca. 1075–1122) forced the popes to travel extensively outside the papal states, holding councils and reiterating reforming decrees wherever they went. The 'Investiture' dispute thus brought the papacy into direct contact with trans-Alpine Europe. Popes and their legates presided at large councils, which reiterated the main messages of the reformers, condemned local abuses, and proclaimed papal primacy. The Church thus became accustomed to such plenary gatherings, which became increasingly more representative of the whole Latin Church—not merely of the Church in Rome, or the papal estates, or even Italy.

Of the three so-called 'general' councils held at the Lateran in the twelfth century, only the third, Alexander III's Lateran Council of 1179, can be regarded as fully ecumenical according to the standards of the time. During the thirteenth century, Alexander III's council and Innocent III's Lateran Council of 1215 were designated as Lateran I and Lateran II in the legislation of local councils in England and France,[1] and it was only in late medieval sources that the Lateran Councils of 1123 and 1139 came to be designated Lateran I and Lateran II, while those of 1179 and 1215 were duly re-numbered Lateran III and Lateran IV.[2] The Greek Church did not recognize the ecumenical status of any council later than the Second Council of Nicaea (786–787),[3] which came to be regarded as the seventh and last general council of the undivided Church,[4] and the dogmatic debates between Latin and Greek theologians at the Council of Ferrara-Florence-Rome in 1439 were based on the definitions of the seven ecumenical councils recognized by both sides.[5]

In fact, the so-called Lateran Councils I and II were indistinguishable in form and legislation from the many papal councils from the 1090s onwards, which were the most characteristic feature of the ecclesiastical reform movement of the period. Urban II's councils of Piacenza (1095),

---

1. C.R. Cheney, 'The Numbering of the Lateran Councils of 1179 and 1215', *Medieval Texts and Studies* (Oxford 1973) 206–207.
2. Cheney, 'The Numbering of the Lateran Councils' 203–208.
3. Cf. COD 131–156.
4. Although not immediately: see Vittorio Peri, 'L'ecumenicità di un concilio come processo storico nella vita della Chiesa', AHC 20 (1988) 216–244, especially 223–238. The subsequent Fourth Council of Constantinople (869–870) was accepted in the West but not in the East: cf. ibid., 157–159. The full list of eight general councils is given in Gratian, *Decretum*, D.16 c.8: 'Sancta octo universalia concilia, primum Nicenum ... octauum quoque Constantinopolitanum usque ad unum apicem immutilata seruare, et pari honore et ueneratione digna habere ... '. The Latins' request for the Greek text of the 'eighth council' to be read at Florence in October 1438, caused some consternation among the Greek delegates, and the decrees of the first seven alone were made the basis of doctrinal discussions. In defense of its own claim to be the seventh ecumenical council, Nicaea II listed three essential requirements for ecumenicity: presence, in person or by representatives, of the five patriarchs, with participation by the bishop of Rome and unanimity; doctrinal importance of the matters defined; recognition by the whole Church of the council's position in the series of ecumenical councils: cf. Peri, 'L'ecumenicità di un concilio' 220–222. For the Latin reception of decrees of this council, see Jean Gaudemet, 'Le deuxième concile de Nicée (787) dans les Collections canoniques occidentales', AHC 20(1988) 278–288.
5. I.e., Nicaea I (325), Constantinople I (381), Ephesus (431), Chalcedon (451), Constantinople II (553), III (680–681), and Nicaea II (787): Andreas de Santacroce, *Acta Latina concilii Florentini* (Concilium Florentinum documenta et scriptores 6; Rome 1955) 43–45; Silvestros Syropoulos, *Vera historia unionis non verae inter Graecos et Latinos: sive concilii Florentini* ed. and trans. R. Creyghton (Adrian Vlacq: Hagae-Comitis 1660) 169–171; *Les 'Mémoires' du grand ecclésiarque de l'Église de Constantinople Sylvestre Syropoulos sur le concile de Florence (1438–1439)*, ed. V. Laurent (Concilium Florentinum documenta et scriptores 9; Rome 1971) 330–335. Cf. C.-J. Hefele, *Histoire des conciles*, trans. H. Leclerq (11 vols. in 21; Paris 1907–1952) 7.2 pp. 976–977; J. Gill, *The Council of Florence* (Cambridge 1961) 147–151; Ivan N. Ostroumov, *The History of the Council of Florence* (largely based on Syropoulos), trans. B. Popoff (Boston 1971) 66–72.

Clermont (November 1095), Nîmes (July 1096),[6] Bari (October 1098), and Rome (April 1099),[7] Calixtus II's council at Toulouse (July 1119),[8] and Eugenius III's council of Reims (March 1148)[9] were all similar in character and legislation and not significantly different in authority, attendance, or reception.[10] It was only in retrospect that Lateran I and Lateran II were differentiated from the other papal councils of the period and associated with the more legally sophisticated and influential Lateran council of 1179. All three Lateran councils, however, belong to the same tradition and illustrate the increasingly effective exercise of legislative authority by the papacy. They continued and enlarged upon the reforming tradition of the papal synods of the late eleventh and early twelfth centuries regarding clerical discipline and freedom from lay authority, while consciously placing themselves in the venerable tradition of the early councils, sometimes citing the councils of Nicaea[11] and Chalcedon[12] by name. Calixtus II, especially, emphasized the antiquity of the sources for his legislation in 1123 by alluding to the 'canones apostolorum'[13] and by appealing to the au-

---

6. Mansi 20.801–920, 931–942. Mansi's texts must be used with some caution, however. For the decrees of Piacenza and Clermont, see. F. J. Gossman, *Pope Urban II and Canon Law* (Catholic University of America Canon Law Studies 403; Washington, D.C., 1960) 3–11; cf. Robert Somerville, 'The French Councils of Pope Urban II: Some Basic Considerations', AHC 2 (1970), 56–65 (reprinted in *Papacy, Councils and Canon Law in the 11th and 12th Centuries* [Aldershot 1990] no. 5), which shows that the so-called council of Limoges dated Dec. 1095 (Mansi 20.919–922) is a figment. For the complex textual traditions of the decrees of the council of Clermont, see idem, *The Councils of Urban II*, 1: *Decreta Claromontensia* (AHC, Supplementum 1; Amsterdam 1972).

7. Mansi 20.947–952, 961–970.

8. Mansi 21.225–234, where dated June. Calixtus' council held in difficult circumstances at Reims in October 1119 (Mansi 20.233–256), though widely reported, does not belong to the same category: cf. Robert Somerville, 'The Councils of Pope Calixtus II: Reims 1119', Proceedings Salamanca 35–50, reprinted in *Papacy, Councils and Canon Law* no. 12.

9. Mansi 21.711–736.

10. For the reception of Urban II's conciliar legislation, see Gossman, *Pope Urban II and Canon Law* especially 103–135.

11. Lat. I, c.7.

12. Lat. II, c.5.

13. Lat. I, c.8, 'secundum apostolorum canones'. This title was given to a sequence of fifty canons in the 'collectio canonum' made in Rome by the sixth-century Dionysius Exiguus († after 525) and transmitted to northern Europe in the *Dionysio-Hadriana*. They were derived from a fourth-century Greek compilation of 84 (or 85, depending on the system of numeration) so-called 'Apostolic Constitutions'. To his Latin translations of the first 49 (or 50), Dionysius Exiguus added the decrees of the councils of Nicaea (325), Antioch (341), Constantinople (381), and Chalcedon (451), and other early councils, as well as decretals of popes from Siricius († 399) to Anastasius II († 498): DDC, iv (1948) 1131–1152, especially 1113–1152. For the Latin text, see *Ecclesiae occidentalis monumenta iuris antiquissima*, ed. C.H. Turner (2 vols. Oxford 1898–1939) 1.1–32; M. Strewe, *Die Canonessammlung des Dionysius Exiguus in der ersten Redaktion* (Arbeiten der Kirchengeschichte 16; Berlin-Leipzig 1931) 1–10; cf. PL 67.139–148. For the Greek text, see H.T. Bruns, *Canones Apostolorum et conciliorum veterum selecti* (2 vols. in 1; Berlin 1839; reprinted Turin 1959) 1.1–8.

thority of the ancient fathers in such phrases as 'Sacrorum patrum exempla sequentes', 'sicut sanctis canonibus constitutum est', 'Sanctorum patrum canonibus consona sentientes', 'Sanctorum etiam patrum vestigiis inhaerentes', 'Paternarum traditionum exemplis commoniti', etc.[14] Both Innocent II and Alexander III referred to the authority of 'the canons' or 'the sacred canons'.[15]

Simultaneously however, the popes referred to the more recent tradition of papal legislation, naming the pseudo 'Pope Stephen'[16] as well as Gregory VII, Urban II, Paschal II, Innocent II, and Eugenius III,[17] and emphasizing their apostolic authority in such phrases as 'auctoritate sedis apostolicae ... probibemus', 'apostolica auctoritate praecipimus', 'auctoritate apostolica praecipimus', 'sancti Spiritus auctoritate confirmamus' (Calixtus II);[18] 'apostolica auctoritate decernimus ... apostolica auctoritate interdicimus', 'apostolica auctoritate prohibemus',[19] 'auctoritate Dei et beatorum Petri et Pauli ... interdicimus' (Innocent II);[20] 'commissa nobis auctoritate curemus', 'beatorum apostolorum Petri et Pauli auctoritate confisi' (Alexander III).[21] In all three councils, the language of the canons alternates between papal commands in the first person plural—'prohibemus', 'interdicimus', 'irritas esse iudicamus', 'statuimus', 'censemus', 'concedimus', 'statuimus', 'praecipimus', 'inhibemus', etc.[22] and impersonal decrees—'careat dignitate', 'deponatur', 'arceatur', 'careat', 'excommunicationi subiaceat', etc.;[23] and a growing sense of legislative authority is implied in the formulation of the decrees. Where Calixtus II issued short commands, Alexander III proclaimed basic principles, sometimes cited scriptural authority, and laid down carefully composed legal definitions. The twenty-two decrees of Lateran I occupy five pages of Alberigo's edition, the thirty canons of Lateran II fill seven, the twenty-seven canons of Lateran III comprise fifteen pages. Alexander's canons are thus, on average, more than twice as long as those of his predecessors, and reveal a greater sophistication in form and language, reflecting the

14. Lat. I, cc.1, 4, 12, 16, 20, 21.
15. Lat. II, c.26; Lat. III, cc.3, 13, 14, 15.
16. Lat. I, c.8, 'Praeterea iuxta beatissimi Stephani papae sanctionem': cf. Pseudo-Isidore, *Decretales pseudo-Isidorianae et Capitula Angilramni*, ed. Paul Hinschius (Leipzig 1863; reprinted Aalen 1963) 186.
17. Lat. I, c.19, Lat. II, c.7 (Gregory VII); Lat. II, c.7 (Urban II); Lat. I, c.10; Lat. II, c.7 (Paschal II); Lat. III, cc.2, 20 (Innocent II); Lat. III, c.20 (Eugenius III).
18. Lat. I, cc.1, 10, 12, 15. 19. Lat. II, cc.9, 10; cf. c.16.
20. Lat. II, c.18. 21. Lat. III, cc.11, 27.
22. Cf. Lat. I, cc.2, 5, 7, 9, 10; Lat. II, cc.1, 3, 4, 5, etc.; Lat. III, cc.1, 2, 3, 4, 6, 7, 9, 12, 13, 14, etc.
23. Lat. I, cc.1, 3, 4; Lat. II, cc.2–5, 9, 12–19; Lat. III, cc.3, 5–6, 8, 10–11, etc.

significant legal development which had taken place in the four decades following Lateran II and the publication of the last recension of Gratian's *Decretum* (ca. 1140–1144).[24]

All three councils were great ecclesiastical gatherings (each one in fact larger than its predecessor). Whereas Lateran I was attended by some two hundred bishops and abbots and Lateran II by more than one hundred bishops and an unrecorded number of abbots, Lateran III included about three hundred bishops and an unknown number of abbots and their attendants,[25] and some lay princes were present in person or by proxy. The councils afforded opportunities for individuals or groups to raise personal, local, or group issues. At the First Lateran, for example, the archbishop-elect of Bremen sought restoration of his metropolitan jurisdiction over the Scandinavian Church.[26] Conrad of Constance was canonized at Lateran I, and Sturmi of Fulda at Lateran II.[27] Bishops raised questions about the subordination of monasteries;[28] and the problems of heterodoxy and heresy were discussed at Lateran II ('Petrohusians', the followers of Peter of Bruys: c.2) and Lateran III (Cathars, etc., c.27). These councils reflect increasing ecclesiastical centralization under the authority of the papacy, but more significantly they suggest a growing centripetalism—a tendency to turn to the center for support and authority—paralleling the growth of the papacy's appellate jurisdiction. They also represent a growing commitment to legal and institutional unity and uniformity within the Latin Church.

The reform movement had emphasized the authority of ancient law, which in turn had spurred the creation of collections of law designed to serve the interests of the reformers. *The Collection in 74 Titles*, for example, was taken to Germany by papal legates, and there copied and circulated.[29]

---

24. Despite Anders Winroth's brilliant thesis that the first recension of Gratian was produced. c. 1139 and that the second recension—the much fuller, generally received 'vulgate' form—was produced later than 1140–1141, with a *terminus ad quem* of 1158 'at the very latest' (A. Winroth, *The Making of Gratian's* Decretum [Cambridge 2000] 142–144), the question of dating is far from settled.

25. Raymonde Foreville, 'Procédure et débats dans les conciles médiévaux du Latran (1123–1215)', *Rivista di Storia della Chiesa in Italia* 19 (1965) 21–37 (reprinted in *Gouvernement et vie de l'Église au Moyen-Âge* [London 1979] no. I) especially 24.

26. Foreville, 'Procédures et débats' 25.

27. Foreville, 'Procédure et débats' 26–27.

28. Raymonde Foreville, *Latran I, II, III et Latran IV* (Histoire des conciles oecuméniques 6; Éditions de l'Orante: Paris 1965) 56.

29. See John Gilchrist, *The Collection in 74 Titles. A Canon Law Manual of the Gregorian Reform* (Medieval Sources in Translation 22; Toronto 1980) 29; cf. idem 'The Reception of Pope Gregory VII into the Canon Law (1073–1141) Part II', ZRG Kan. Abt. 66 (1980) 192–229, at 204–205.

Councils, reform, and the revival of canon law and of papal and episcopal authority were closely interconnected, since an essential foundation of the reform movement was the re-assertion and re-definition of the disciplinary authority of the ecclesiastical hierarchy culminating in the papacy; and papal and legatine councils demonstrated the primacy of the popes. Even the protocol, which placed the pope on an elevated dais, surrounded by his curia and the cardinals, emphasized the pope's presidency.

Our knowledge of conciliar procedure is incomplete.[30] For neither Lateran I nor Lateran II is there a reliable contemporary report of the whole process, but it is likely that the procedure recorded for the papal council of Reims in 1119 was followed. After six formal sessions, the canons were dictated by John of Crema, written down by John, a monk of the Benedictine monastery of Saint-Ouen of Rouen, then formally promulgated through solemn recitation by the 'bibliothecarius' of the Roman Church, Cardinal Chrysogonus. The promulgation of the canons was followed by the excommunication of enemies in a dramatic ceremony in which 427 tapers were lit and extinguished. Finally, Pope Calixtus II issued indulgences and bestowed his blessing.[31] From the time of the Third Lateran Council, however, there survives an *Ordo Romanus* for the holding of councils, which prescribed the liturgical aspects of the occasion and three solemn sessions, culminating with the publication of the decrees in the manner of Reims 1119.[32]

From the surviving reports of various interested parties, it is clear that complex questions of jurisdiction and orthodoxy were not generally debated by the full council but assigned to special commissions of experts ('periti'). At Lateran I, for example, the dispute about Corsica was deputed to a commission of twelve archbishops and twelve bishops;[33] at Lateran III, the election of Bertold of Bremen was submitted to the adjudication of two cardinals, and two representatives of the Vaudois sect were examined by a commission presided over by a bishop.[34]

It is supposed that by the time of Lateran IV the papal chancery was sufficiently organized to make possible the rapid multiplication of texts

---

30. Foreville, 'Procédure et débats' 21–37.
31. Foreville, 'Procedure et débats' 23.
32. Cf. M. Andrieu, *Le pontifical romain au Moyen Age*, 1: *Le pontifical romain au XIIe siècle* (ST 86; Città del Vaticano 1938) 1.255–260; cf. Foreville, *Latran I, II, III et Latran IV* 195–199 (French translation).
33. Mansi 21.296–297 (*Annales Genuenses*, I); cf. Foreville, 'Procédure et débats' 30 (with French translation of the conciliar *Ordo*).
34. Arnold of Lübeck, *Chronica Slavorum* MGH Scriptores 21.132; Walter Map, *De nugis curialium* 1.31. Cf. Foreville, 'Procédure et débats' 31 (with French translation of W. Map).

of the decrees,[35] but there is no reliable information about the procedure adopted for the dissemination of the decrees of either Lateran IV or the first three Lateran councils. The evidence we have is conflicting. On the one hand, the survival of copies of Lateran decrees in local archives and chronicles implies that texts were taken away by the participants. Twelve canons from the 'alpha' recension of the decrees of Lateran I (omitting 11–12 and 15–17) were inserted into Symeon of Durham's *Historia regum*,[36] for example; Gerhoh of Reichersberg knew the legislation of Lateran II,[37] and four English chronicles recorded the full legislation of Lateran III.[38] On the other hand, the many discrepancies in the textual tradition of the legislation suggest that the participants may have constructed their own records. The confusion in the texts of Lateran I could be explained in this way. For Lateran II and III, the differences may be explained, at least in part, by the wider dissemination of the texts and the possibility that more than one archetype was made available for copying.

The First Lateran Council

The chief reason for the summons of the First Lateran Council of 1123 was the formal ratification of the settlement of the Investiture dispute, which had been reached at Worms in the preceding September (1122),[39] but many current issues were raised by interested parties—the claims of Bremen-Hamburg to metropolitan authority over Scandinavia; those of Ravenna to jurisdiction over Ferrara; the jurisdictional dispute between the bishops of Siena and Arezzo and between the monasteries of Saint-Macaire and Sainte-Croix in Bordeaux; the contest between Pisa and Genoa for ecclesiastical jurisdiction over the island of Corsica; and the canonization of Conrad of Constance.[40]

While these aspects of the council's business are well recorded in contemporary chronicles, the legislation has been less securely transmitted.

---

35. *Constitutiones Concilii quarti Lateranensis una cum Commentariis glossatorum*, ed. Antonio García y García (MIC Series A: Corpus Glossatorum 2; Vatican City 1981) 11.

36. *Symeonis monachi opera omnia*, ed. T. Arnold (2 vols. Rolls Series 75; London 1882–1885) 2.278–281.

37. See below, n. 39.

38. See below, n. 86.

39. According to Gerhoh of Reichersberg, who was present at the council, there was vocal opposition to the agreement that the German bishops should be elected in the king's presence and receive their 'regalia' 'per sceptrum': Gerhoh von Reichersberg, *Libellus de ordine donorum Sancti Spiritus*, ed. E. Sackur (MGH Scriptores 'Libelli de Lite' 3; Hannover 1897; reprinted Hannover 1956) 280.

40. Foreville, *Latran I, II, III et Latran IV* 51–53, 56. For a full discussion of the council, see ibid. 44–68.

Alberigo identified two recensions, 'alpha' and 'beta', the one with seventeen canons, the other with twenty-two,[41] and there are additional discrepancies and confusions. Various systems of enumeration occur in the learned literature; for simplicity, the number and order of the Alberigo edition have been followed here.[42] In its general canons, the council carried forward the 'Gregorian' attack on simony,[43] clerical marriage and concubinage,[44] and secular exploitation in all its forms. 'Following the example of the holy fathers',[45] the simoniacal acquisition of ecclesiastical office or promotion is prohibited, on pain of deposition (c.1); only those canonically elected may be consecrated as bishops, on pain of deposition (c.3); citing the authority of the Council of Nicaea (325), marriage or concubinage is forbidden to all clergy in the subdiaconate and above (cc.7, 21); and minimum grades are established for ecclesiastical office: only priests may be appointed provost, archpriest, or dean; only deacons may be appointed archdeacon (c.6).

Four canons deal with various forms of lay abuse of ecclesiastical persons or property: denouncing lay exploitation of the Church's goods as a form of sacrilege (c.8); forbidding lay fortification or control of churches (c.12, ad fin.) and lay acquisition of tithes, without episcopal permission (c.18); and threatening with anathema anyone who attacks or despoils

---

41. Alberigo, COD 188–189.

42. Alberigo, COD 190–94. For the Latin text and English translation, see *Decrees of the Ecumenical Councils*, ed. Norman P. Tanner, SJ (2 vols. Georgetown 1990) 1.190–194; for the Latin text and French translation, see Alberigo and Duval, *Les Conciles Oecuméniques* 2.1 pp. 416–425; cf. Foreville, *Latran I, II, III et Latran IV* 175–178. For an older English translation, but with a different order of canons, see H.J. Schroeder, *Disciplinary Decrees of the General Councils* (St. Louis–London 1937) 177–194.

43. Cardinal Humbert of Silva Candida († 1061) described simony as a form of heresy (following a tradition traceable to Pope Gregory I, 590–604), and went so far as to deny the validity of simoniacal orders or of sacraments conferred by simoniacs (*Adversus simoniacos libri III*, ed. F. Thaner: MGH 'Libelli de Lite' 1.118, 120–121, 189); Peter Damian († 1072), who considered simony a 'heresy' but not a transgression of faith (*Liber gratissimus*, ed. L. de Heinemann: MGH 'Libelli de Lite' 1.23), argued for the validity of the sacraments of wicked ministers, while condemning the viciousness of simony: (J. B. Oosterman, *Peter Damian's Doctrine on the Sacerdotal Office: A Canonical Study of the Validity of Orders and the Worthy Exercise of Ordained Ministry* (Catholic University of America Canon Law Studies 90; University Microfilms International, Michigan 1980) especially 12–13, 37–53, 204–205, 301–302. Cf. John Gilchrist, '"Simoniaca Haeresis" and the Problem of Orders from Leo IX to Gratian', *Proceedings Boston* 209–235.

44. Cf. Peter Damian's defense of clerical purity, discussed by Oosterman, *Peter Damian's Doctrine* 66–73. For general background, see Roger Gryson, *Les origines du célibat ecclésiastique du premier au septième siècle* (Gembloux 1970); Roman Cholij, *Clerical Celibacy in East and West* (Leominster 1988).

45. Perhaps an allusion to the second canon of Chalcedon (451), which had outlawed all forms of simony on pain of deposition for ordainer and ordained and anathema for any lay intermediary: cf. Alberigo, COD 87–88.

churches or monasteries, or injures their personnel, or attacks or robs those who come to churches and monasteries to pray (c.20).

At the same time, six canons sought to reverse the disintegration of episcopal authority which had occurred through the growth of private patronage and monastic exemption: the excommunicates of one bishop may not be received into communion by other bishops or abbots (c.2); the cure of souls or prebends may not be assigned by any lesser prelate without the approval of the bishop, since the sacred canons lay down that the cure of souls and the dispensing of ecclesiastical affairs should remain in the bishop's power (c.4); parish priests may be appointed only by bishops, and they may not receive tithes or churches from laymen without the bishop's permission (c.18); monks must be properly subject to their bishop: they may not celebrate public masses or visit, anoint, or hear the confessions of the sick,[46] and the priests who minister in their churches must be instituted by the bishop, to whom they are responsible for the cure of souls (c.16); neither monks nor abbots may lease churches or the property of bishops (c.19); and all alienation of ecclesiastical property is forbidden (c.22).[47] Most of the canons deal with strictly ecclesiastical affairs; but two concern matters of wider social importance. Consanguineous marriages are condemned and those who contract them are branded with infamy (c.9),[48] and the Truce of God is given general application (c.15).[49]

In addition to disciplinary questions affecting the whole church, the council dealt with matters of local or temporary import. The ordinations of Maurice Bourdin (anti-pope 'Gregory VIII') and the bishops consecrated by him were nullified (c.5); Pope Urban II's protection for crusaders was renewed, with penalties for those who had taken the Cross but failed to fulfil their vows (c.10); and five canons concerned malefactors in Rome and the papal states. Automatic excommunications were promulgated against laity who removed offerings from Roman churches (nam-

---

46. Cf. Giles Constable, *Monastic Tithes: From Their Origins to the Twelfth Century* (Cambridge Studies in Medieval Life and Thought 10; Cambridge 1964) 145–146.

47. Joseph F. Cleary, *Canonical Limitations on the Alienation of Church Property* (Catholic University of America Canon Law Studies 100; Washington, D.C. 1936) 23–42.

48. Francis X. Wahl, *The Matrimonial Impediments of Consanguinity and Affinity* (Catholic University of America Canon Law Studies 90; Washington, D.C. 1934) 9–19; For 'infamia', see n. 68, below.

49. This decree was a general application of a 'peace movement' which had its origins in late tenth-century France: see Jean-Pierre Poly, *La Provence et la société féodale, 879–1166* (1976) 191–204; cf. Hartmut Hoffmann, *Gottesfriede und Treuga Dei* (Schriften der MGH 20; Stuttgart 1964); H.E.J. Cowdrey, 'The Peace and the Truce of God in the Eleventh Century', *Past and Present* 46 (1970) 42–67; Thomas N. Bisson, 'The Organized Peace in Southern France and Catalonia, ca. 1140–ca. 1233', *American Historical Review* 82 (1977) 290–311; idem, 'Peace of God, Truce of God', DMA 9.473–475.

ing St. Peter's, St. John Lateran, S. Maria Rotunda, St. Nicholas of Bari, St. Giles: c.12 at the beginning), the makers and users of false coin (c.13), the brigands who attacked pilgrims to the holy places in Rome or merchants (c.14), anyone who attempted to hold the city of Benevento by military might (c.17); and, using the significant formulation, 'with the advice of our brethren and of the whole Curia and with the approval and agreement of the Prefect', Calixtus abrogated the 'wicked custom', whereby the property of deceased 'Porticani' was disposed of against their wishes and without the approval of their heirs (c.11).[50]

With these seven exceptions, the canons were all in the reform tradition. Indeed, another seven repeat, echo, or give greater prominence to earlier legislation (and an eighth refers to a decision of Pope Urban II).[51] The targets are simony, clerical concubinage, appointment of unsuitable ecclesiastics, and lay abuse of ecclesiastical persons, offices, or incomes, and the principal antidote is the restoration of ecclesiastical discipline through formal restatement of the law and reinforcement of episcopal responsibility and authority.

Within a very few years, the statutes of local councils in England, Normandy, France, and Spain began to echo the conciliar legislation. For most of these councils, little except their place and date has been recorded, not always accurately, but enough survives to demonstrate the wide dissemination of the Lateran's decrees.[52] Seven of its canons were echoed in Cardinal John of Crema's legatine legislation at Westminster in 1125;[53] five in William of Corbeil's, also at Westminster, in 1127;[54] two in Cardinal Alberic of Ostia's Westminster Council in 1138;[55] and five occur in Raymond of Toledo's council at Palencia in 1129.[56] But it is clear from even a brief comparison of the conciliar texts that the local legislators interwove gen-

---

50. Residents of the Leonine city, where St. Peter's was situated.

51. Cc.1–2, 6–9, and 21 all have precedents in recent councils: c.1 (cf. Toulouse 1119), c.9; c.2 (cf. Melfi 1089, c.15: Mansi 20.724), c.6 (cf. Toulouse 1119, c.2); c.7 (cf. Reims 1119, c.5); cc. 8, 21 (cf. Lateran 1110, cc.1–2: Mansi 21.8); c.9 (cf. Troia 1093, c.2: Mansi 20.789–790). For c.10, cf. Urban II's address at the Council of Clermont 1095 (Mansi 20.823).

52. Westminster (1125, 1127, 1129); Rouen (1128); Bourges, Chartres, Clermont, Beauvais, Vienne, Besançon (1125); Nantes (1127); Arras, Troyes (1128); Châlons-sur-Marne, Paris (1129); Barcelona (1126), Palencia (1129): Mansi 21.325–388; cf. Foreville, *Latran I, II, III et Latran IV* 69.

53. *Councils and Synods, with other Documents relating to the English Church* 1.1–2 ed. D. Whitelock, M. Brett, and C.N.L. Brooke (Oxford 1981) 1.2 pp. 738–741. Of the 17 canons, nos. 1, 4, 7, 9, 11, 13, and 16 reflect Lateran legislation: cf. Lateran I cc.1, 8 and 18, 6, 4, 2, 7, and 9.

54. Cf. *Councils and Synods* 1.2 pp. 743–749, cc.1, 2, 4, 5, 10 and *Lateran I* cc.8, 1, 6, 7, and 4. Brett and Brooke remark (p. 745), 'á propos' c.5, that 'it is noticeable that c.5 follows the wording of the Lateran council of 1123 more closely than that of Westminster [1125]'.

55. Cf. Ibid.1.2 pp. 768–779, cc.11 and 13 and *Lateran I* cc.20, 7 and 18.

56. Mansi 21.385–388, cc.5, 8, 9, 12, 16, 17; cf. *Lateran I* cc.7 and 21, 2, 9, 14 and 15, 18, 13.

eral with particular concerns, intermingled Lateran material with their own local sources, and adapted legislation to their own circumstances. The texts of the decrees were not regarded as inviolate: their prescriptions were summarized, abbreviated, and adapted to the structure of the local codes.

More importantly for the development of the learned law, fourteen of the twenty-two canons were received into Gratian's *Decretum*, in whole or in part, and thus found their way into the work which became the basis, not only for the academic study of canon law in Bologna and elsewhere, but also for the application of that same law throughout the ecclesiastical courts of Europe.[57] In this way, Lateran I made a permanent contribution to ecclesiastical law on simony, episcopal appointment, episcopal control over benefices, the requirements for ecclesiastical office, lay power in church affairs, consanguinity,[58] monastic competence, clerical immunity, clerical concubinage, and the alienation of church property. Omitted were three whose contents were covered by alternative texts[59] and five which could be deemed of local or temporary application.[60]

It is significant, however, that Gratian attributed none of these canons to a council. Except where he attributed four canons to Urban II (cc.18–20 and 22), his normal mode of citation is 'Item Calixtus papa'. The rulings are thus attributed to the pope and not to the council. Nevertheless, Gratian showed far more respect for the integrity of the individual texts. He sometimes merged two canons into one, but he did not significantly disturb the verbal integrity of his source.

Second Lateran Council (1139)

Just as the First Lateran Council was called to ratify the Concord of Worms and restore the authority of the papacy over a re-united Church, the Second Council of the Lateran was called to celebrate the ending of

---

57. Cc. 1, 3–4, 6, 8 (part), 9, 12, 14, 16b (attributed to Calixtus II), 18 (part), 19–20 (attributed to Urban II), 21 (attributed to Calixtus II), 22 (attributed to Urban II), were received into Gratian, *Decretum*: can. 1 = C.1 q.1 c.10; can. 3 = D.62 c.3; can. 4 = C.16 q.7 c.11; can. 6 = D.60 c.2; can. 8 (from 'Si quis [ergo]') = C.16 q.7 c.25; can. 9 = C.35 q.2–3 c.2; can. 12 = C.10 q.1 c.14; can. 14 = C.24 q.3 c.23; can. 16b = C.16 q.1 c.10; can. 18 (from *Decimas et ecclesias*) = C.16 q.7 c.39 (attributed to Urban II); can. 19 = C.16 q.4 c.1 (attributed to Urban II); can. 20 = C.24 q.3 c.24 (attributed to Urban II); can. 21 = D.27 c.8; can. 22 = C.12 q.2 c.37 (attributed to Urban II).

58. Until modified by Lateran IV (1215) c.50.

59. Canons 2, 7, 15. For can. 2, cf. C.11 q.3 c. 17; for can. 7, cf. D.28 c.2; for can. 15, cf. C.24 q.3 c.24, §1.

60. C.5, nullifying the ordinations of Maurice Bourdin; c.10, renewing Crusaders' privileges; c.11 on the *Porticani*; c.13 on false coining; and c.17 on Benevento.

the eight-year schism between Anacletus II and Innocent II.[61] This had been a 'Roman' schism, in that the dispute between the rival claimants to the papal office was principally a dispute between rival noble families within the city (Frangipani vs. Pierleoni), but it had occurred at a critical moment, since the papal leadership of the reform was imperilled by the existence of two opposing claimants to the chair of St Peter. Nevertheless, Innocent II had progressively secured the support of the Latin Church and, indeed, carried forward the reforms with councils at Clermont (1130), Reims (1131),[62] and Pisa (1135),[63] and in personal interviews with Louis VI of France, Henry I of England, and Lothar III of Germany. Attended by one hundred bishops, among whom was the Latin patriarch of Antioch, and an estimated four hundred abbots and lesser prelates, the council issued 30 decrees,[64] largely repeating the legislation of Innocent's own councils of Clermont, Reims, and Pisa,[65] together with that of earlier councils.[66] One decree merely repeats the prohibitions of Lateran I against consanguineous marriages (c.17). But although much of its legislation reiterated the principal themes of the reform, it did so with greater precision. Lateran I had prohibited the reception of excommunicates; Lateran II reinforced the prohibition by imposing the same sentence on those who knowingly communicate with excommunicates (c.3).[67] Three canons concern various forms of illicit traffic in sacred things, but whereas the First Lateran had issued a general condemnation of simony, whose essence is repeated in Lateran II (c.1: anyone receiving orders through simony is to be deposed), the Second Lateran details whole categories of of-

---

61. Foreville, *Latran I, II, III et Latran IV* 73–78; Alberigo, COD 195–196: cf. Tanner, *Decrees of the Ecumenical Councils* 1.195–196; Alberigo and Duval, *Les Conciles oecumeniques* 2.1 pp. 429–430.

62. Cf. Robert Somerville, 'The Canons of Reims (1131)', BMCL 5 (1975) 122–130, reprinted in *Papacy, Councils and Canon Law* no. 15.

63. Cf. Robert Somerville, 'The Council of Pisa, 1135: A Re-Examination of the Evidence for the Canons', *Speculum* 45 (1970) 98–114.

64. No formal record survives, but a scholarly consensus exists, based on Baronius, *Annales ecclesiasticae* 12 (1607) 277–280 and the Roman edition of 1612, *Concilia generalia ecclesiae catholicae* (4 vols. Rome 1608–1612) 4.21–23. For the decrees, see Alberigo COD 197–203. Cf. Tanner, *Decrees of the Ecumenical Councils* 1.197–203 (Latin and English); Alberigo and Duval, *Les Conciles oecumeniques* 2.1 pp. 432–445 (Latin and French); Foreville, *Latran I, II, III et Latran IV* 175–178 (French); Schroeder, *Disciplinary Decrees* 195–213 (English, with commentaries).

65. Cc.1–2, 4–7, 9–10, 12, 14–20 repeat or amplify decrees of the councils of Clermont 1130 and Reims 1131 (cf. Mansi 21.437–440, cc.1–5, 8–13; ibid., 453–462, cc.1–6, 10–17); cc.1–2, 15, and 30 echo or repeat canons of the Council of Pisa 1135 (cf. Mansi 21.487–492, cc.1, 12, 14, and 7).

66. Cc.3, 7, 10, 21–25 derive from the councils of the reforming popes: from Gregory VII, Rome (1078) c.10; from Urban II, Melfi (1089) cc.3, 21–22; from Calixtus II, Toulouse (1119) cc.3, 7, 23–25.

67. Elizabeth Vodola, *Excommunication in the Middle Ages* (Berkeley 1986) 27.

fice and spiritual ministry which are included in the prohibition, and adds infamy to the penalty of deprivation: anyone receiving ecclesiastical preferment of any kind (prebends, priories, deaneries, etc.) for payment is to be deposed and disgraced; any trafficking in sacred things (chrism, holy oil, consecration of altars, etc.) is to involve both buyer and seller in the penalties of 'infamia' (c.2);[68] no money can be taken for chrism, holy oil, or burial (c.24).

On the question of clerical morality and discipline, Lateran II is likewise more explicit: not only is marriage forbidden to clerics in the subdiaconate and above (c.6), but lay people are forbidden to hear the Masses of incontinent clergy (c.7), the inheritance of ecclesiastical office is forbidden (c.16), and sons of priests are not to serve churches, unless they have first lived in monasteries or houses of canons (c.21: *Presbyterorum filios*); and clerks must maintain the tonsure and wear appropriate ecclesiastical dress (c.4).[69] In repeating Lateran I's prescriptions about the appropriate sacerdotal grade for archdeacons and deans, Lateran II added that such offices were not to be conferred on unordained youths, and any refusing to receive the appropriate ordination were to be deprived of their offices (c.10, at the end). The misdeeds of religious or self-styled religious are similarly condemned in specific terms: following popes Gregory VII, Urban II, and Paschal II, professed nuns are forbidden to marry (c.8), monks and canons may not study secular law or medicine for money (c.9), men and women religious may not use the same choir (c.27), women who call themselves nuns but do not live according to the Rule of St. Benedict, St. Basil, or St. Augustine are condemned (c.26). On the other hand, the rights of religious to participate in episcopal elections is confirmed (c.28).

Equally, the attack on lay abuse of ecclesiastical institutions was continued: on the authority of Chalcedon (451, c.22), the seizure of the goods of deceased clerics was forbidden (c.5); lay persons may not have ecclesiastical tithes; lay owners of churches must restore them to the bishop's power, on pain of excommunication (c.10); ecclesiastical offices may not be received from laymen; laymen may not dispose of ecclesiastical goods (c.25); and false penitents, who feign repentance but do not give up the sin, are condemned (c.22).

Reflecting the continuing disorder and violence in many parts of Chris-

---

68. On this application of the Roman civilian penalty, see Vincent A. Tatarczuk, *Infamy of Law: A Historical Synopsis and Commentary* (Catholic University of America Canon Law Studies 357; Washington, D.C. 1954) 13–23, 27–32. Also Francesco Migliorino, *Fama e infamia: Problemi della società medievale nel pensiero giuridico nei secoli XII e XIII* (Catania 1985).

69. For a brief history, see Bernard J. Ganter, *Clerical Attire* (Catholic University of America Canon Law Studies 361; Washington, D.C. 1955) 4–18.

tendom, the Council reiterated with greater emphasis and precision Lateran I's embrace of the Peace movement, confirming the 'Truce of God'—cessation of military action during the sacred seasons of Christmas and Easter (from the beginning of Advent until the octave of the Epiphany [13 January] and from Quinquagesima Sunday until the Octave of Easter) and also every weekend throughout the rest of the year, from sunset on Wednesday until sunrise on Monday (c.12),[70] and proclaiming the general security of priests, clerks, monks, pilgrims, merchants, and rustics (c.11). But the extremely important decree *Si quis suadente* declared that anyone who laid hands on clerks or monks was automatically excommunicated for the sacrilege and could be absolved only by the Roman pontiff (c.15).[71] The condemnations of tournaments (c.14), of 'the murderous art of cross-bowmen and archers' (c.29), of arsonists, and those who lay waste the countryside (c.18), are part of the same commitment to peace and security. The ultimate sanction of denial of Christian burial is applied against those who die in tournaments or in the commission of arson;[72] and one year's service in Jerusalem or Spain is proposed as an appropriate penance for arson (c. 18). Bishops who relax the arson law are to be deprived of episcopal office for a year (c.19), and, in consultation with archbishops and bishops, kings and princes are permitted to act against such persons (c.20). In a similar and highly significant manner, the council condemned those (heretics) who impugn the sacraments and ordered them to be coerced by 'potestates exteras' (c.23). Also significant for the future was the strong condemnation of usury, which carried not only the penalty of 'infamia' but also denial of Christian burial for the unrepentant (c.13),[73] and the language used to nullify the ordinations of Pierleone (the anti-pope Anacletus II) 'and other schismatics and heretics' (c.30). It was as

---

70. Cf. Lat. I, c.15 and n. 49, above. There was a very similar formulation in the *Panoramia* (1095) attributed to Ivo of Chartres (PL 161.1343).

71. For a discussion of the implications of excommunication 'latae sententiae' in connection with this canon, see Vodola, *Excommunication* 28–31. See also Richard H. Helmholz, '"Si quis suadente" (C.17 q.4 c.29): Theory and practice', *Proceedings Cambridge* 426–438.

72. Cf. Charles A. Kerin, *The Privation of Christian Burial: An Historical Synopsis and Commentary* (Catholic University of America Canon Law Studies 136; Washington, D.C. 1941) 14–28. Christian burial was automatically denied to unreconciled excommunicates—this canon reinforced the general rule.

73. T.P. McLaughlin, 'The Teaching of the Canonists on Usury (XII, XIII, and XIV Centuries)', *Mediaeval Studies* 1 (1939) 81–147, 2 (1940) 1–22; Walter Taeuber, 'Geld und Kredit im Dekret Gratians und bei den Dekretisten', SG 2 (1954) 443–464; John T. Noonan, Jr., *The Scholastic Analysis of Usury* (Cambridge, Mass. 1957); John T. Gilchrist, *The Church and Economic Activity in the Middle Ages* (London 1969); Arwed Blomeyer, 'Aus der Konzilienpraxis zum kanonischen Zinsverbot', ZRG Kan. Abt. 66 (1980) 317–335; R.H. Helmholz, 'Usury in the Medieval English Church Courts', *Speculum* 61 (1986), 364–380; James A. Brundage, 'Usury', DMA 12.335–339. For 'infamia' and denial of Christian burial, see nn. 68 and 72.

a 'schismatic and a heretic' that Benedict XIII was deposed by the Council of Constance in 1417![74]

What is evident is the greater length and detail of these canons in comparison with those of the First Lateran Council, and the emphasis on consequences and penalties: those who do not enforce the law are to suffer; certain actions carry not only automatic excommunication but denial of Christian burial (participation in tournaments, usury, arson); and they embrace a wider social program: condemning usury, arson and devastation, tournaments, and the use of deadly weapons (bows and crossbows). In many ways, this was an extension of the Truce of God movement—attempting to protect certain categories of vulnerable noncombatants from violence at all times: clergy, travellers, and country-people.

Ordericus Vitalis considered the council of small value,[75] and Gerhoh von Reichersberg lamented the non-implementation in German lands of c.10 on the lay misuse of tithes and c.28 on episcopal elections,[76] but its canons influenced synodal legislation at Saintes in 1140,[77] and Eugenius III's council at Reims in 1148.[78] Eighteen of its thirty canons were received into Gratian's *Decretum*, in whole or in part,[79] and c.29 was received into the *Decretales* of 1234, where it is ascribed to Innocent III.[80] Lateran II thus contributed significantly to the development of the law on simony, clerical life

---

74. Alberigo, COD 437.

75. *Ecclesiasticae Historiae Libri tredecim: The ecclesiastical history of Orderic Vitalis*, ed. and trans. Marjorie Chibnall (6 vols. Oxford Medieval Texts; Oxford 1969–1980) Book 13, chapter 39, 6.529–531; cf. Cheney, 'The Numbering of the Lateran Councils' 204–205.

76. Gerhoh von Reichersberg, *Liber de nouitatibus huius temporis*, ed. E. Sackur (MGH Scriptores 'Libelli de Lite' 3; Hannover 1897; reprinted Hannover 1956) 290–291; *Dialogus de pontificatu sanctae Romanae ecclesiae*, ed. H. Boehmer (MGH Scriptores 'Libelli de Lite' 3; Hannover 1897; reprinted Hannover 1956) 3.534.

77. Dom Jean Leclercq, 'Les décrets de Bernard de Saintes', *Revue du Moyen Age latin* 2 (1946)167–170; Odette Pontal, *Les statuts synodaux français du XIIIᵉ siècle*, 1: *Les statuts de Paris et le synodal de l'Ouest (XIIIᵉ siècle)* (Collection de documents inédits sur l'histoire de France, Section de philologie et d'histoire jusqu'à 1610, in-8°, 9; Paris 1971) lv.

78. Mansi 21.711–736.

79. Whole: cc.2, 4–6, 8, 19–21, 26–28; part: cc.7, 10, 12, 15–16, 18, 22. Can. 2 = *Decretum* C.1 q.3 c.15; can 4 = C.21 q.4 c.5; can 5 = C.12 q.2 c.47; can 6 = D.28 c.2; can 7 (from 'Ut lex') = C.27 q.1 c.40; can 8 = last sentence of C.27 q.1 c.40; can. 10 ('Innouamus . . . honores' and 'Precipimus . . . sacerdotem') = D.60 c.3 and C.21 q.2 c.5; can. 12 (from 'Precipimus') = D.90 c.11; can. 15 ('Si quis suadente . . . suscipiat') = C.17 q.4 c.29; can. 16 (from 'auctoritate') = C.8 q.1 c.7; can. 18 ('Pessimam . . . interdicimus'. 'Si quis igitur . . . permaneat') = C.23 q.8 c.32; can. 19 = penultimate sentence of C.23 q.8 c.32; can 20 = last sentence of C.23 q.8 c.32; can. 21 = D.56 c.1 (ascribed to Urban II); can. 22 (from '[con]fratres') = D.5 'de poenitentia'; can. 26 = major part of C.18 q.2 c.25; can. 27 = last sentence of C.18 q.2 c.25; can. 28 = D.63 c.35. Gratian referred to c.28 in an earlier recension of his *Decretum*, the only Lateran II canon that he cited before he produced his vulgate edition.

80. Can. 29 = X 5.15.1. The ascription to Innocent III was probably a simple mistake, for *Compilatio prima* (5.9.1) correctly ascribed it to Innocent II (Cheney, 'The Numbering of the Lateran Councils' 205).

and behavior, violence to clerks (*Si quis suadente*: c.15), the non-hereditability of benefices (*Presbyterorum filios*: c.21),[81] arson and devastation, 'false religious', and the association of male and female religious in liturgical services. The legislation against tournaments and deadly weapons was largely ignored.[82]

Gratian's treatment of the canons of the second Lateran is similar to his treatment of those of the first. Only twice does he refer to a council as the source of the decrees (cc.18–20 and c.28), but even then he does not name the precise location. Canons 18–20 (combined in one citation) are identified as a general decree issued by Innocent II in the universal council ('Innocentius II in uniuersali concilio generaliter constituit'), and canon 28 is described as a decree of Pope Innocent issued in the general synod held in Rome ('in generali synodo Innocentii Papae Romae habita constitutum est')—as Cheney pointed out, they were 'seldom ascribed to a council and never to a Lateran council.'[83] Apart from his single mis-attribution to Urban II (c.21) the remainder of his citations are 'Innocentius papa' (cc.2, 7–8, 15) or 'Innocentius II' (cc.4–6, 10, 12, 22, 26–27) or 'Innocentius Papa II' (c.16). The legal compiler preferred the authority of the person who issued the ruling to the forum in which it was issued.

Third Lateran Council (1179)

Summoned in letters dated 21 September 1178, the Third Lateran Council assembled on 5 March and ended on 19 March 1179.[84] The *Acta* of the council, drawn up by William of Tyre, have not survived, nor has the official text of the canons been established, but contemporary chronicles contain ample accounts both of the proceedings and of the legislation.[85] No fewer than four English chronicles contain full texts of the canons,[86] and

---

81. Cf. Council of Rouen (1190), c.6: Dom G. Bessin, *Concilia Rothomagensis provinciae* (2 vols. in 1; Rouen; F. Vaultier, 1717) 1.95. For the application of this decree in England, see *Councils and Synods with Other Documents Relating to the History of the English Church*, 2.1: *A.D. 1205–1313*, ed. F.M. Powicke and C.R. Cheney (Oxford 1964) 98–99.

82. Philippe Contamine, *War in the Middle Ages*, trans. Michael Jones (Oxford 1984, reprinted Oxford 1987–1998) 72–73, 274–275.

83. Cf. Cheney, 'The Numbering of the Lateran Councils' 205.

84. Foreville, *Latran I, II, III et Latran IV* 134–158; Alberigo, COD 205–225. For a French translation of the canons, see Foreville, *Latran I, II, III and IV* 210–223. See also Hefele, *Histoire des conciles* 5.2 pp. 1086–1112; Schroeder, *Disciplinary Decrees* 214–235.

85. Alberigo, COD 210. In an unpublished Bonn dissertation, Walter Herold examined 36 sources for the canons and concluded that there were 34 different traditions. Stephan Kuttner published Herold's findings in a short note, 'Concerning the Canons of the Third Lateran Council', *Traditio* 13 (1957) 505–506. See also *Le troisième concile de Latran (1179): Sa place dans l'histoire*, ed. Jean Longère (Paris 1982).

86. *Gesta regis Henrici secundi Benedicti abbatis*, ed. W. Stubbs (2 vols. Rolls Series 49; Lon-

Ralph de Diceto, dean of St. Paul's in London, cited two canons from 'the many memorable decrees' issued by the council.[87]

Like its two predecessors, Lateran III met in the aftermath of schism and papal-imperial disputes. Since 1159 the papacy of Alexander III had been disturbed by an imperially supported schism of three successive anti-popes (Victor IV, 1159–1164; Paschal III, 1164–1168; Calixtus III, 1168–1178) and the Emperor Frederick I's attempts to impose imperial control on the North Italian cities. Alexander successfully negotiated the perils of the times. Despite the risks of the schism, he significantly advanced the legal and judicial role of the papacy, responding to appeals and issuing many hundreds of appellate decisions on cases brought to Rome from all the regions of the Latin Church outside German lands.[88] The Third Lateran was thus a demonstration of the restored unity of the Latin Church and a recognition of papal leadership within it; but it was also a culmination of the reform program pursued in papal and legatine councils for more than a century. The opening address reads like a panegyric to the eminent dignity of the Roman church, this 'city of the sun', 'the first and principal church ... over which presides this great pontiff and supreme patriarch', and proclaims its paramount legislative authority, 'Only the Roman Church has the power to summon a general council, to make new laws, and to abrogate old ones'.[89]

The twenty-seven decrees issued in the council concern four principal aspects of Church life: the election and appointment of clerics (cc.1, 3, 5, 8), clerical life and behavior (cc.11–16, 18), condemnation of abuses (cc.4, 6–7, 9–10, 17, 19), and sanctions against various social ills (cc.20, 23, 25) and illicit dealings with Jews, Saracens, heretics, and mercenaries (cc.22, 24–27).

---

don 1867) 1.222–238; *Chronica magistri Rogeri de Houedene*, ed. W. Stubbs (4 vols. Rolls Series 51; London 1868–1871) 2.173–189 (1869); *The Historical Works of Gervase of Canterbury*, ed. W. Stubbs (2 vols. Rolls Series 73; London 1879–1880) 1.278–292; William of Newburgh, *Historia rerum Anglicarum*, ed. R.G. Howlett, in *Chronicles of the Reigns of Stephen, Henry II, and Richard I* (4 vols. Rolls Series 82; London 1884–1889) 1–2 (1884–1885) 1. 206–223.

87. *Radulfi de Diceto decani Lundoniensis opera historica*, ed. W. Stubbs (2 vols. Rolls Series 68; London 1876) 1.430. Perhaps reflecting his own interests as dean of a major cathedral, he singled out the condemnations of illicit burials by Templars and Hospitallers (c.9) and the accumulation of benefices (c.13).

88. On decretals and decretal collections, see Chapter 8 in this volume, the article by Charles Duggan, with an extensive bibliography.

89. *Sermo habitus in lateranensi concilio, sub Alexandro papa III*, ed. G. Morin, 'Le discours d'ouverture du concile générale de Latran(1179) et l'oeuvre littéraire de maître Rufin, évêque d'Assise', *Atti della Pontificia accademia romana di archeologia* (3d Series, Memorie 2; Rome 1928) 116–120; for a French translation, see Foreville, *Latran I, II, III et Latran IV* 200–204, especially 202–203. It was long thought that Rufinus had given this homily at the Council, but Roman Deutinger, 'The Decretist Rufinus—A well-known Person?' BMCL 23 (1999) 10–15, has convincingly argued that he did not.

Election and Appointment

The four canons on ecclesiastical elections and appointments were to be of permanent importance. *Licet de vitanda* (c.1) laid down the principle that a two-thirds majority of the cardinals was required for a valid papal election, while accepting that the choice of the 'maior et sanior/ senior pars' should be accepted in other episcopal elections. *Licet de vitanda* has remained the basic electoral law of the papacy, with minor modifications, until the present day. *Cum in sacris* (c.3) established the basic requirements for admission to ecclesiastical office: 'aetatis maturitas et morum gravitas et scientia litterarum' (mature age, sound character, and literacy), and defined the age requirement as thirty for a bishop and twenty-five for any office involving pastoral responsibility (the cure of souls). In addition, bishops must be of legitimate birth, and all appointees must, within the canonical period, receive the appropriate clerical order for the office they have received—priesthood for deans and the diaconate for archdeacons. *Episcopus si aliquem* (c.5) required bishops who ordained priests or deacons 'sine certo titulo', without a specific benefice or sufficient private income, to maintain them at their own expense. And *Nulla ecclesiastica ministeria* (c.8) forbade the practice of promising benefices before the death of the incumbent; bishops (or chapters) must appoint new candidates within six months, or lose the right of appointment (creating the principle of devolution).[90]

Clerical Life

Five of the seven canons concerning clerical life and behavior reinforced the reforming regulations of the previous century: suspect women were to be removed from clerics' houses on pain of loss of benefice, clerical and lay homosexuality was condemned, clergy were forbidden to frequent nunneries (c.11), clergy might not engage in secular business (c.12), churches must be served by clerics who can reside in them (c.13); the accumulation of benefices (c.14, beginning), alienation of ecclesiastical property and venal appointment of rural deans were prohibited (c.15), but canons 16, 18, and 22 broke important new ground. *Cum in cunctis* (c.16) gave conciliar support to the principle of majority rule in ecclesiastical communities, so that decisions made by the 'maior et sanior pars' should not be obstructed by small cliques or bad local custom.[91] *Quoniam ecclesia Dei* (c.18)

---

90. Cf. G.J. Ebers, *Das Devolutionsrecht, vornehmlich nach katholischem Kirchenrecht* (Stuttgart 1906; reprinted Amsterdam 1965) 182–188.

91. Alberigo, COD reads 'seniori' for 'saniori' (p. 219, line 30), but 'sanior pars' has a long

ordered the assignment of a prebend in every cathedral church to maintain a master to teach clergy and poor scholars without payment, and the re-establishment of such arrangements wherever they had existed in collegiate or monastic churches in earlier times. The license to teach should be bestowed freely, and no suitable teacher should be denied.[92] And an important canon, *Cum dicat Apostolus* (c.23), allowed communities of lepers to have their own churches and priests, tithe free, as long as the rights of the parish church were not infringed.[93]

Abuses

Equally realistic was the approach to abuse. Instead of merely outlawing simony, three canons dealt with specific malpractice, regulating the rights of bishops, archdeacons, legates, and others to receive hospitality from their subjects, and imposing reasonable limits on the size of their trains (c.4),[94] forbidding fees for the induction of bishops, abbots, and other prelates, or for blessings, burials, or the conferment of the sacraments (c.7), forbidding monasteries to exact payment for entry into the religious life (c.10).[95] At the same time, *Cum et plantare* (c.9) condemned the abuses of privilege which undermined episcopal authority, by Templars, Hospitallers, and other privileged orders, and reiterated the rule that diocesan clergy could be nominated and removed only with the consent of the bishop.[96] The same concern for the appointment of suitable pastors is evident in *Quoniam in quibusdam* (c.17), which condemned abuse of churches by lay patrons, and in two wide-ranging decrees, *Quia in tantum* (c.14) and *Non minus* (c.19), further forms of lay abuse are condemned. Lay appointment of clergy, the imposition of secular taxes and imposts, lay possession of tithes, and the compulsion of clerks to appear before lay courts are all forbidden on pain of

---

tradition. Cf. Isaac S. Jacob, 'The Meaning of "Sanior Pars" in the Rule of St Benedict and Its Use in the Decretal Collection of Pope Gregory IX, with a Study of the Electoral Law as Found in the Decretum of Gratian' (Catholic University of America Canon Law Studies 437; reprinted University Microfilms International, Michigan 1964) 54–92.

92. Cf. Gaines Post, 'Alexander III, the "Licentia docendi" and the Rise of the Universities', *Anniversary Essays in Medieval History, by Students of C. H. Haskins* (Boston–New York 1929) 255–257.

93. Josef Avril, 'L'encadrement diocésain et l'organisation paroissiale', *Le troisième concile de Latran* 53–74.

94. The Council of Toledo (646) had limited bishops' retinues to 50 (Mansi 9.838). Cf. A. L. Slafkosky, *The Canonical Episcopal Visitation of the Diocese* (Catholic University of America Canon Law Studies 142; Washington, D.C. 1941), especially 24–28; Avril, 'L'encadrement diocésain' 55–57.

95. Cf. J.H. Lynch, *Simoniacal Entry into Religious Life from 1000 to 1260* (Columbus, Ohio 1976) 147–169.

96. For a discussion the Third Lateran's legislation on religious privilege, see Jean Becquet, 'Les religieux', *Le troisième concile de Latran* 45–51.

excommunication, while the transfer of tithes from one layman to another is forbidden on pain of denial of Christian burial (c.14); and the imposition of secular liabilities on churches is forbidden, on pain of excommunication (c.19). The abuse of power by ecclesiastical prelates is condemned in *Reprehensibilis valde* (c.6), which forbids excommunication or suspension without proper warning and orders due respect to be given to appellants, who must nevertheless prosecute their appeals or suffer financial penalties.

Sanctions

The fourth segment of the legislation, concerning broader questions of social and political life, opens with an almost verbatim recapitulation of four decrees which had already been promulgated in Lateran II,[97] forbidding jousts (c.20), confirming the Truce of God (c.21),[98] renewing ecclesiastical protection for priests, monks, clergy, lay brothers ('conversi'), pilgrims, merchants, and peasants (c.22), and a general condemnation of usury, punishable by excommunication and denial of Christian burial (c.25). The remaining three canons deal with relations with Jews, Saracens, and heretics. *Ita quorundam* (c.24) forbids the selling of arms or supplies to the Saracens, or Christian service in Saracen galleys, and condemns all acts of piracy or the maltreatment of victims of shipwreck; *Iudei sive Saraceni* (c.26) forbids Jews and Saracens to employ Christian servants. The very important last canon, *Sicut ait beatus Leo* (c.27), declared that all heretics (Cathars, Paterines, 'Publicans')[99] and their defenders and all who receive them are anathema. It forbade any support or aid to be given to them on pain of denial of Christian burial and dissolved all bonds of loyalty, homage and obedience owed to them. The canon also ordered secular powers to take punitive action against them and bestowed ecclesiastical protection on those who take such action under the bishop's direction to expel the heretics.[100] This canon was the precedent for the decree *Ad abolendam*, issued with the support of Emperor Frederick I at Verona in 1184, which established the principle of episcopal investigation of heretics. Lucius III declared all heretics anathema, commanded bishops to investigate and condemn them, and authorized the secular authorities to punish those who persisted in their heresy, both clerical (after degradation) and lay.[101] This latter decree, itself evidence of the threat to orthodox religion

---

97. Cc.20–22, 25 = Lat. II, cc.14, 12, 11, 13.
98. See n. 49, above for bibliography on the Truce of God.
99. See Henri Maisonneuve, *Études sur les origines de l'Inquisition* (2d ed. Paris 1960) 94–96, 102–163, et passim (Cathars); 151, n. 2, 155 (Paterines); 114–118 ('Publicani').
100. For the context and application, see Maisonneuve, *Origines de l'Inquisition* 126–135.
101. Mansi 22.476–478; cf. Maisonneuve, *Origines de l'Inquisition* 151–156.

posed by organized heresy, marks the first stage in the creation of the episcopal Inquisition. Canon 27 also condemned to equal execration mercenaries and their employers and supporters.

The Reception

The first two Lateran councils occurred in time to be received into Gratian's *Decretum* and thus become part of the learned law studied in the schools and applied in ecclesiastical courts throughout Christendom. The timing of the Third Lateran Council was equally fortunate. The intervening forty years had seen the creation of the decretal-based *ius novum* and the formation of a learned legal culture common to the whole Church. As early as the 1150s, new legal definitions from papal decretals were being inserted into copies of the *Decretum*; from the 1160s, collections of the new law, including the decrees of recent councils, were being assembled by judges-delegate and their circles in England.[102] Individual decrees of the Council of Reims (1148), for example, are found in six collections from the period;[103] the decrees of Alexander III's Council of Tours (1163) are found in seven English collections,[104] and the decrees of Richard of Canterbury's legatine council of Westminster (1175) were included in *Belverensis*.[105] The canons of Lateran III were immediately received into decretal collections and widely disseminated. Alberigo lists twenty-two collections which contain the whole text,[106] and he concluded that the decrees of this council were disseminated through the whole Latin Church and exerted a great influence on its courts and affairs.[107] Not surprisingly, all twenty-sev-

---

102. See Charles Duggan, chapter 8, above. Walther Holtzmann's opinion that the Third Lateran Council stimulated the making of decretal collections cannot be sustained in the light of this evidence.

103. *1 Dunelmensis, Fontanensis, 1 Rotomagensis, Florianensis, Cusana,* and *Oriel: Studies in the Collections of Twelfth-Century Decretals, from the papers of the late Walther Holtzmann* ed. and trans., C.R. Cheney and Mary G. Cheney (MIC Series B: Corpus Collectionorum 3; Vatican City 1979) 336, s.v. 'Remense'.

104. On *Belverensis* see Charles Duggan, *Twelfth-Century Decretal Collections and Their Importance in English History* (University of London Historical Studies 12; London 1963) 47, 71, n. 2, 155, 161, *Dunelmensis* (ibid., 79 and n. 1), Fountains (ibid., 80, n. 1), Bridlington (ibid., 90, 93), *Claudiana* (ibid., 91, n. 3), Cotton and Peterhouse (ibid., 104, n. 4). For the reception of individual canons, see Holtzmann-Cheney, *Collections* 336–337 s.v. 'Turonense'. Seven of its decrees reached the Gregorian *Decretales* (Cheney, 'The Numbering of the Lateran Councils' 208).

105. Duggan, *Twelfth-Century Decretal Collections* 47, 71, n. 2, 72, 73, 159–160. For the reception of individual canons, see Holtzmann-Cheney, *Collections* 337, s.v. 'Westmonasteriense' (1175).

106. Alberigo, COD 207–209; cf. Holtzmann-Cheney, *Collections* 335–336, s.v. 'Lateranum III'.

107. Alberigo, COD 209: 'Pro certo affirmare possumus huius concilii canones per totam latinam ecclesiam divulgatos esse atque in eius curis negotiisque maxime valuisse'; cf.

en canons were received into the *Liber extra*, the formal collection of law made by Raymond of Peñafort for Pope Gregory IX in 1234 and promulgated by him for use 'in iudiciis et in scholis.'[108]

At the same time, many of its decrees were echoed and amplified in diocesan and provincial councils throughout the West: at Rouen in 1190,[109] at Montpellier in 1195,[110] at Westminster in 1200,[111] and in the conciliar activities of reformers like Odo de Sully in Paris (†1209)[112] and Stephen Langton in Canterbury (1213 –1214),[113] as well as in the work of papal

---

Cheney, 'The Numbering of the Lateran Councils' 208: 'For canonists and administrators the memorable Roman council was that gathered at the Lateran in 1179 by Alexander III.' In addition to legal manuscripts, copies of the decrees are found, for example, in a manuscript containing sacred and profane texts in the library of the Augustinian house of Aureil in Limousin (Jean Becquet, 'La bibliothèque des chanoines réguliers d'Aureil en Limousin au XIIIe siècle', in *Vie canoniale en France aux Xe–XIIe siècles* [Aldershot 1985] 107–134, especially 122 no. 76: 'Decreta innouata in concilio Alexandri pape').

108. With the papal bull *Rex pacificus* (Friedberg, *Decretales* 2): 'Volentes igitur, ut hac tantum compilatione universi utantur in iudiciis et in scholis, districtius prohibemus, ne quis praesumat aliam facere absque auctoritate sedis apostolicae speciali'. For a translation of the bull see Robert Somerville and Bruce C. Brasington, *Prefaces to Canon Law Books in Latin Christianity: Selected Translations, 500–1245* (New Haven–London 1998). For the distribution of the canons, see Friedberg, *Decretales* xii, s.v. 'C. Later. III'.

109. Bessin, *Concilia Rothomagensis* 1.94–98: influence of Lateran III is found in: cc.9–10, forbidding clergy from undertaking secular business (cf. Lat. III, c.12); c.12, on visitations and procurations, opens, 'Sicut in Lateranensi Concilio cautum est' (cf. Lat. III, c.4;) c.13, on appeals (cf. Lat. III, c.6); c.14, forbidding excommunication without citation and judgment (cf. Lat. III, c.6). Cf. Raymonde Foreville, 'The Synod of the Province of Rouen in the Eleventh and Twelfth Centuries', *Church and Government in the Middle Ages*, ed. C.N.L. Brooke et al. (Cambridge 1976) 19–39, especially 38 (reprinted in *Gouvernement et vie de l'Église au Moyen-Âge* London 1979 no. 8); idem, 'La réception des conciles généraux dans l'église et la province de Rouen au XIIIe siècle', *Droit privé et institutions régionales: Études historiques offertes à Jean Yver* (Paris 1976) 243–253, especially 244 (reprinted in *Gouvernement et vie de l'Église* no. 9).

110. Mansi 22.939–950.

111. *Councils and Synods* 1.2 pp. 1060–7100; Mansi 22.713–722: c.5, restricting the trains of visiting prelates, 'Cum inter ea quae statuta sunt a modernis patribus Lateranense concilium' (cf. Lat. III, c.4); c.6, bishops to pay the stipend of any priest or deacon ordained without title, 'juxta tenorem Lateranensis concilii' (cf. Lat. III, c.5); c.7, excommunication to be proceeded by canonical process, 'Rursus Lateranensis concilii statuta sequentes' (cf. Lat. III, c.6); c.8, sacraments to be bestowed without charge, 'Sicut in Lateranensi concilio salubriter a sanctis patribus est provisum' (cf. Lat. III, cc.7, 18, 8); c. 10, forbidding clergy to keep concubines, 'Statuta etiam Lateranensis concilii reuerenter amplectentes' (cf. Lat. III, c.11); c.13, provision for lepers, 'concilii Lateranensis eciam institucione suffulti' (cf. Lat. III, c.23); c.14 (Mansi c.14, beginning), condemning abuse of privileges by Templars and Hospitallers, 'Lateranensis concilii tenore perpenso ... eiusdem auctoritate concilii' (cf. Lat. III, c.9); c.15 (Mansi c.14, at the end), condemning simoniacal entry into religious houses (cf. Lat. III, c.10).

112. See Pontal, *Les statuts synodaux* 52–97: c.55, on excommunication (cf. Lat. III, c.6), c.70, prohibiting lay possession of tithes (cf. Lat. III, c.15, at the end).

113. *Councils and Synods with Other Documents Relating to the History of the English Church*, 2, A.D. 1205–1313, ed. F.M. Powicke and C.R. Cheney (Oxford 1964) 1.2 pp. 57–96: influence of Lateran III is found in: c.101, *De eodem* [= *De regula religionis*], (cf. Lat. III, c.10); c.107, *De beneficio indigni privando*, includes the phrase, 'in concilio Lateranensi primo' (cf. Lat. III, c.14).

legates Robert de Courçon, Paris, 1213;[114] Rouen, February 1214;[115] Bordeaux, June 1214, and Peter of Benevento, Montpellier, January 1215.[116] Even more significantly, the council's legislation restricting ecclesiastical retinues and procurations (c.4), restricting vacancies to six months, after which the right of appointment would devolve on the next ecclesiastical superior (c.8), forbidding religious to receive tithes or churches from lay hands without the bishop's permission (c.9), forbidding plurality of 'beneficia curata' (c.13), ordering the appointment of schoolmasters (c.18), and forbidding the imposition of lay imposts and taxes on churches (c.19), was explicitly cited in five decrees of Lateran IV (1215),[117] and its influence can be detected in a further sixteen. The Fourth Lateran's decrees on heresy (c.3), clerical incontinence (c.14), bloodshed and tournaments (cc.18, 71), devolution in episcopal and monastic churches (cc.23, 29), election by scrutiny or compromise, accepting the 'maior vel sanior pars' principle (c.24),[118] the appointment of suitably qualified clergy (c.26), qualifications for ecclesiastical appointment (c.30), lay possession of tithes (c.32), appeals (c.35), clerical immunity from secular taxation (c.46), excommunications (c.47), monastic privileges (c.57), and various forms of simony (cc.63–64), all echo the prescriptions of Lateran III.[119]

Not only did the Third Lateran's legislation profoundly affect both the canon law and the provincial and diocesan legislation across Europe, its influence can be found in the moral and penitential literature of the time. Echoes of at least fourteen of its canons have been found in pastoral manuals composed in the late twelfth and early thirteenth centuries. Peter the Chanter, Alan of Lille, Robert of Flamborough, Peter of Poitiers, Thomas of Chobham, and Raymond of Peñafort include some of its provisions, Peter the Chanter, Alan, and Raymond citing the council or Alexander III by name.[120]

Although there is considerable continuity between the three Lateran councils, the Third Lateran significantly eclipsed its predecessors.[121] Its

114. Mansi 22.818–854.
115. Mansi 22.897–924.
116. Mansi 22.935–954; cf. Foreville, *Latran I, II, III et Latran IV* 241–243.
117. Lat. III, c.4 (cf. Lat. IV, c.33); c.8 (cf. Lat. IV, c.29), c.9 (cf. Lat. IV, c.61), c.13 (cf. Lat. IV, c.29); c.18 (cf. Lat. IV, c.11); c.19 (cf. Lat. IV, c.46).
118. Note the substitution of 'vel' for 'et': cf. Alberigo, COD 219, line 30.
119. Lat. IV, c.3 (cf. Lat. III, c.27), 14 (cf. Lat. III, c.11), cc.18, 71 (cf. Lat. III, c.20), c. 23 (cf. Lat. III, c.8), c.24 (cf. Lat. III, cc.1, 16), cc.26, 30 (cf. Lat. III, c.3), cc.32, 46 (cf. Lat. III, c. 14), cc.35, 47 (cf. Lat. III, c.6), c.57 (cf. Lat. III, c.9), c.63 (cf. Lat. III, c.7), c.64 (cf. Lat. III, c.10).
120. Jean Longère, 'L'Influence de Latran III sur quelques ouvrages de théologie morale', *Le troisième concile de Latran* 91–103.
121. Raymonde Foreville, 'La place de Latran III dans l'histoire conciliare du XIIe siècle', *Le Troisieme Concile de Latran* 11–17.

canons demonstrate a greater juristic maturity in language and construction, with greater precision both in the definition of misconduct and in the sanctions to be applied. Behind the legislation of Lateran III was the legal expertise built up through the pontificate of Alexander III, whose numerous decisions and responses to consultations from bishops and ecclesiastical judges across Europe had laid the basis of the decretal law which would ultimately form the largest single element of the Gregorian *Decretales* of 1234. The authority with which the council spoke, the clarity of its definitions, and the rapidity with which its legislation was disseminated throughout Latin Christendom assured its place both in the history of the Church and in the history of canon law.

The Fourth Lateran Council (1215)

Summoned by the bull *Vineam Domini Sabaoth* on 19 April 1213, the Fourth Lateran Council opened in Rome on 11 November 1215.[122] By all measures, it was the largest, most representative, and most influential council assembled under papal leadership before the end of the fourteenth century. It was attended by some four hundred bishops and eight hundred abbots, priors, and representatives of collegiate churches.[123] Each of the first three Lateran councils marked the end of a schism or the resolution of a dispute. The fourth, in contrast, marked the culmination of the career of Pope Innocent III (1198–1216), one of the most remarkable and successful popes of the Middle Ages, and represented his determination to provide effective mechanisms for reform. At the same time, it marked the culmination of the legislative and legal evolution that had been going on since Lateran I, combining derivations from the *ius antiquum* with more recent conciliar and decretal law. Its sources included twenty-four borrowings from Gratian's *Decretum*, eleven from *Compilatio prima*, three from *Compilatio secunda*, fourteen from *Compilatio tertia*, four from Lateran I, six from Lateran II, and at least twelve from Lateran III, as well as twenty-six from Innocent III's own decretals.[124] But just as Lateran III sur-

---

122. Innocent III, *Epistolae* 16.30 in PL 216.823–825; Foreville, *Latran I, II, III et Latran IV* 245–246, 327–329 (French translation); Alberto Mellone, 'Vineam Domini—10 April 1213: New Efforts and Traditional *Topoi*—Summoning Lateran IV', *Pope Innocent III and His World*, ed. John C. Moore (Aldershot 1999) 63–73, including a new edition of the letter, 72–73.

123. For the official list of cardinals, metropolitans, and bishops, see Foreville, *Latran I, II, III et Latran IV* 391–395; cf. J. Werner, 'Die Teilnehmerliste des Laterankonzils v. J. 1215', *Neues Archiv* 31 (1906) 577–593; Hefele, *Histoire des conciles* 5.2 pp. 1722–1733; cf. n. 129, below.

124. For a statistical analysis of the sources of Lateran IV, see Antonio García y García, 'La Biblia en el concilio 4 lateranense de 1215', AHC 18 (1986) 91–102, especially 96. He counts only 12 derivations from Lateran III, but six canons of the Third Lateran are cited explicitly: Lat. III, c.4 (cf. Lat. IV, c.33); c.8 (cf. Lat. IV, c.29), c.9 (cf. Lat. IV, c.61), c.13 (cf. Lat.

passed its two predecessors in the wider scope and greater legal maturity of its decrees, so did the scale of Lateran IV in its turn eclipse Lateran III. Conceived in the tradition of the ancient councils of the Church, principally Nicaea I (325) and Chalcedon (451), Lateran IV issued binding legislation whose prescriptions helped to shape the history of the later medieval church until the Council of Trent, and beyond.[125]

The period since the Third Lateran Council had been one of grave difficulty: the Latin Kingdom had been all but overwhelmed in 1187 (battle of Hattin); the Third Crusade had staved off disaster, but had not restored Christian control of the holy places in Jerusalem; the Fourth Crusade had diverted its attentions to Zara (modern Zadar, Croatia) and Constantinople; and the Catharist heresy had established itself in Toulouse and Northern Italy. Criticisms of ecclesiastical institutions abounded, and Innocent III recognized that a comprehensive program of reform was required to answer the challenges posed by critics, heterodox and orthodox alike.[126] The council was called, therefore, 'to extirpate vices and plant virtues, correct abuses and reform morals, suppress heresies and strengthen faith, pacify discords and strengthen peace, repress oppression and support liberty; to induce Christian princes and peoples to support the Holy Land with the financial aid of clerks and laymen; and many other questions, which would take too long to enumerate'—as the letters of summons expressed it.[127] Among these 'other questions', three major political problems engaged the pope's attention: the succession to the empire, the revolt against King John in England, and the settlement of the County of Toulouse after the Albigensian crusade. Formal decisions on all three problems were delivered during the final session of the council (30 No-

---

IV, c.29); c.18 (cf. Lat. IV, c.11); c.19 (cf. Lat. IV, c.46); and there are echoes of a further ten: Lat. III, c.1 (cf. Lat. IV, 24), c.3 (cf. Lat. IV, cc.26, 30), c.6 (cf. Lat. IV, cc.35, 47), c.7 (cf. Lat. IV, c.63), c.10 (cf. Lat. IV, c.64), c. 11 (cf. Lat. IV, c.14), c.14 (cf. Lat. IV, cc.32, 46), c.16 (cf. Lat. IV, c.24), c.20 (cf. Lat. IV, c.18, 71), c.27 (cf. Lat. IV, c.3); and the influence of Lat III, cc.8 and 9, cited in Lat. IV, c.29 and 81, is also evident in Lat. IV, cc.23 and 57.

125. '. . . generale concilium juxta priscam sanctorum patrum consuetudinem convocemus' (PL 216.824); cf. Foreville, *Latran I, II, III et Latran IV* 327 (French translation); cf. Gérard Fransen, 'L'Ecclésiologie des Conciles médiévaux', *Le Concile et les conciles*, ed. B. Bott et al. (Paris 1960) 125–141, at 127–128.

126. Hefele and Leclercq, *Histoire des conciles* 5.2 pp. 1233–1316; cf. Foreville, *Latran I, II, III et Latran IV* 227–244. See also Werner Maleczek, 'Laterankonzil, IV', LMA 5 (1990) 1742–1744.

127. '. . . in quo ad exstirpanda vitia et plantandas virtutes, corrigendos excessus, et reformandos mores, eliminandas haereses, et roborandam fidem, sopiendas discordias, et stabiliendam pacem, comprimendas oppressiones, et libertatem fovendam, inducendos principes et populos Christianos ad succursum et subsidium terrae sanctae tam a clericis quam a laicis impendendum, cum caeteris quae longum esset per singula numerare' (PL 216.824); cf. Foreville, *Latran I, II, III et Latran IV* 327–238 (French translation).

vember). The excommunication of the barons in revolt against King John of England was renewed; Count Raymond VI of Toulouse was deposed for collusion in heresy and Simon de Montfort was instituted as count in his stead; and Otto IV was finally deposed in favor of Frederick of Hohenstaufen, whose election as king of Germany and emperor-elect was formally confirmed.[128]

Important as these matters were in the general history of the West, Innocent's principal purpose remained reform. To this end, he ordered prudent persons in every province to conduct a general investigation into abuses which required apostolic correction, with written reports to be submitted to the council; and he enlarged the council membership to include the abbots and general chapters of Cîteaux and Premontré, the Grand Masters of the Temple and the Hospital, and representatives from cathedral and collegiate churches, kings, princes, and free cities. The Fourth Lateran Council was thus the largest and most representative of the medieval councils to that date. In addition to the Roman Province itself, no fewer than eighty ecclesiastical provinces were represented, including Latin prelates from Byzantium and the Holy Land.[129]

The scholarly consensus is that the constitutions were drafted by Innocent III himself.[130] The earliest manuscripts support this view, describing the canons as 'the constitutions or decrees of the lord pope Innocent III issued in the general Lateran Council';[131] and their latest editor, García y García, has commented on the close parallels between the phrasing of some of the constitutions and earlier writings or decisions of Innocent III.[132] Moreover, the pope's own authority is emphasized in the use of

---

128. Foreville, *Latran I, II, III et Latran IV* 258–272, 406.

129. There were 17 prelates from the patriarchate of Constantinople, four from Jerusalem, one from Antioch, and one Maronite, see Foreville, *Latran I, II, III et Latran IV* 391–392; cf. n. 123, above. On representation in councils and the Church during the thirteenth century, see Kenneth Pennington, 'Representation in Medieval Canon Law', *The Jurist* 64 (2004) 361–383.

130. Michele Maccarone, 'Il IV Concilio Lateranense', *Divinitas* 2 (1961) 270–298, especially 284; C.R. Cheney, 'A Letter of Innocent III and the Lateran Decree on Cistercian Tithe-Paying', *Cîteaux: Commentarii Cistercienses* 13 (1962) 146–151; *Constitutiones Concilii quarti Lateranensis una cum Commentariis glossatorum*, ed. Antonio García y García (MCI, Series A: Corpus Glossatorum 2; Vatican City 1981) 5–10; idem, 'Gobierno de la Iglésia universal en el concilio IV Lateranense', *Iglesia, sociedad y derecho* (2 vols. Bibliotheca Salmanticensis 89; Salamanca 1987) 2.123–141, especially 132–135 (reprinted from AHC 1 [1969], 50–68).

131. 'Constitutiones siue decreta domini Innocentii pape iii. in generali concilio Lateranensi edita', García y García, *Constitutiones* 6. Cf. idem, 'A New Eyewitness Account of the Fourth Lateran Council', *Iglesia, sociedad y derecho* 2.61–121, especially 67: 'deinde leguntur constitutiones domini pape. . .' (reprinted from *Traditio* 20 [1964] 115–178).

132. Antonio García y García has found 28 derivations from Innocent's own writings in the Council's decrees (26 from letters, 2 from *De altaris mysterio*): García y García, 'La Biblia en el concilio 4 lateranense' 96.

the first person plural—'Irrefragabili constitutione sancimus' (c.7), 'statuimus' (c.20), 'decreto presenti statuimus' (c.22), 'uolumus . . . interdicimus' (c.42), 'dolemus . . . uolentes' (c.44), sometimes combined with an expression of conciliar approval or authority—'sacra uniuersali synodo approbante sancimus' (c.5), 'sacri auctoritate concilii prohibemus' (c.43), 'Sacro approbante concilio prohibemus' (c.47). But if Innocent III largely devised the decrees, he did so in a context of wide consultation and promulgated them in a forum which represented the whole Church. The council had been in gestation from the beginning of his pontificate;[133] the questions raised reflected contemporary concerns;[134] and there was opportunity for individuals or groups to present their own views both before the council met and during the intervals between its three formal sessions.[135]

Legislation

At the final solemn session (30 November 1215), seventy-one constitutions covering a wide range of theological, legal, and disciplinary matters were promulgated by papal and conciliar authority.[136] Their contents can be analyzed under fifteen headings.

Faith and Heresy

The decrees began with a solemn profession of faith, *De fide catholica*, designed to define central tenets of Christian doctrine in the light of current debate among theological speculators like Joachim of Fiore[137] and Amaury de Bène,[138] as well as the questions raised by the Cathars and oth-

---

133. García y García, *Constitutiones* 8 cites a letter to the archbishop of Cologne, dated 20 Nov. 1202–13 Jan. 1203 (Potthast, 1767), which mentions the possibility of calling a general council to which the archbishop would be invited.

134. Indeed, parallels for many of the decrees can be found in local ecclesiastical legislation: London (Westminster) 1200, Paris 1209, Avignon 1209, Paris 1212, Montpellier 1214, Rouen 1214, etc. Cf. García y García, 'Gobierno de la Iglésia universal' 135–141.

135. Foreville, 'Procédure et débats' 25, 29–34; cf. García y García, *Constitutiones* 11; idem, 'Gobierno de la Iglésia universal', 125–126.

136. For the best edition of the constitutions, based on the 20 most reliable manuscripts, see García y García, *Constitutiones* 1–118, which corrects the vulgate edition: COD 230–271; cf. Tanner, *Decrees of the Ecumenical Councils* 1.230–271 (Latin and English); Alberigo and Duval, *Les Conciles oecumeniques* 2.1 pp. 494–577 (Latin and French); Foreville, *Latran I, II, III et Latran IV* 342–386 (French). For a summary translation of Innocent III's sermon delivered on 11 November 1215, see ibid., Appendix V, 333–338: from Richard of San Germano, *Chronica priora*, ed. A. Gaudenzi (Naples 1888) 90–93. See also Hefele and Leclercq, *Histoire des conciles* 5.2 pp. 1316–1398.

137. Paul Fournier, *Études sur Joachim de Flore et ses doctrines* (Paris 1909) 32–37; E. Buonaiuti, *Gioacchino da Fiore: I tempi, la vita, il messagio* (Rome 1931) 174–175; F. Roberti, *Gioacchino da Fiore* (Florence 1934) 81–131; Ioachimi abbatis *Liber contra Lombardum (Scuola di Gioacchino da Fiore)*, ed. C. Ottaviano (Rome 1934); E. Bertola, *La dottrina trinitaria in Pietro Lombardo* (Miscellanea Lombardiana; Novara 1957) 129–135.

138. G.C. Capelle, *Autour du décret de 1210, 3: Amaury de Bène: Étude sur son panthéisme form-*

er heretical groups.[139] The Trinity and the divine and human natures of Christ were defined in the language of the twelfth-century Parisian theologian Peter Lombard, whose *Quatuor libri sententiarum* had become the basic textbook of academic theology, but not without opposition.[140] The nature of Christ's presence in the Eucharist was similarly defined in scholastic terminology, which gave canonical approbation to the concept of transubstantiation (c.1).[141] These important theological definitions were followed by condemnations of Joachim (for his attack on the Trinitarian teaching of Peter Lombard) and Amaury de Bène (†1204), who had taught a version of pantheism, as well as unnamed heretics and their secular supporters (c.2). Canon 3 excommunicated and anathematized all heretics who challenged the doctrines just enumerated, and ordered those convicted to be handed over to the secular authorities for punishment; secular rulers are obliged to eradicate heresy from their territories on pain of excommunication; those who take up arms against heretics are to enjoy the privileges accorded to crusaders; and bishops who fail in their duty to oppose heresy and heretics are to be deposed (c.3).[142]

This decree did not establish a formal inquisition, but it provided the precedent upon which Gregory IX was to act in 1231–1233, when he renewed the sentences of excommunication and anathema against heretics and authorized systematic pursuit and punishment.[143] Canon 4 forbade, on pain of deposition, the Greek practice of purging altars on which Latins had celebrated and re-baptizing persons baptized by Latins. From there, it was a logical progression to proclaiming the hierarchical order of patriarchates: Rome, Constantinople, Alexandria, Antioch, and Jerusalem (c.5), which led into the important section on ecclesiastical order and discipline.

---

el (Bibliothèque thomiste 16, Section historique 14; Paris 1932); cf. Maisonneuve, *Origines de l'Inquisition* 166–168.

139. Maisonneuve, *Origines de l'Inquisition* commented on the similarity between the dogmatic definitions of c.1 and the professions of faith imposed on Durand de Huesca ('Poor Catholic') and Bernard Primus (Poor Lombard').

140. Jean Châtillon, 'Latran III et l'enseignement christologique de Pierre Lombard', *Le troisième concile de Latran (1179): Sa place dans l'histoire*, ed. Jean Longère (Paris 1982) 75–90; cf. Marcia L. Colish, *Peter Lombard* (Brill's Studies in Intellectual History 41; Leiden–New York 1994).

141. Michele Maccarone, *Studi su Innocenzo III* (Italia Sacra: Studi e documenti di storia ecclesiastica 17; Padua 1972) 390–396.

142. Citing and expanding Lucius III's decree *Ad abolendam*, issued at the Council of Verona in 1184 (Mansi, 22.476–478); cf. Maisonneuve, *Origines de l'Inquisition* 151–156.

143. Mansi, 23.73–75; cf. Maisonneuve, *Origines de l'Inquisition* 245–253. For a general survey of the Inquisition (with bibliography), see DMA 6.483–489 and H.A. Kelly, *Inquisitions and Other Trial Procedures in the Medieval West* (Aldershot 2001).

Order and Discipline

Following the lead of Lateran III, Innocent sought not merely to condemn malpractice and abuse, but to create mechanisms and structures which would continue the reform program beyond the time of the council. To this end, *Sicut olim* (c.6) ordered regular visitations to investigate clerical behavior, and annual provincial and diocesan synods to correct faults and reiterate the Council's own decrees; *Irrefragabili* (c.7) authorized bishops to correct their chapters, local custom notwithstanding; *Qualiter* (c.8) laid down rules for the prudent investigation of faults by prelates generally;[144] *Quoniam in plerisque* (c.9) authorized the appointment of special clergy to provide pastoral care for populations of different rites and languages; and in a very important decision, *In singulis regnis* (c.12) extended the Cistercian practice of General Chapters to all religious orders which did not already have them, but substituted triennial for annual gatherings, organized by province or region. The general chapters were to have a function similar to that of provincial and diocesan councils, with powers of visitation and correction.[145] The position of the much-debated *Ne nimia religionum* (c.13), which forbade the creation of new religious orders, suggests that the problem was regarded principally as a matter of ecclesiastical order, and the intention of the decree was to prevent the unregulated proliferation of local religious organizations.[146]

Preachers, Teachers, and Penitentiaries

A principal aim of the council was the regeneration of the spiritual vigor of the Church, which could not be brought about without investment in education and preaching. Again inspired by Lateran III (c.18),[147] *Quia nonnullis* ordered the appointment of masters to teach 'grammar', not only in cathedral churches but in all churches capable of supporting them, and the appointment of teachers of theology in all metropolitan churches

---

144. Lotte Kéry, 'Inquisitio—denunciatio—exceptio: Möglichkeiten der Verfahrenseinleitung im Dekretalenrecht', ZRG Kan. Abt. 87 (2001) 226–268 for a discussion of *Qualiter*.

145. Cf. U. Berlière, 'Innocent III et la réorganisation des monastères bénédictines', *Revue bénédictine* 22 (1920) 22–42, 145–159; Michele Maccarone, 'Riforma e sviluppo della vita religiosa con Innocenzo III', *Rivista di Storia della Chiesa in Italia* 16 (1962) 29–72, especially 31–41; idem, 'I capitoli istuiti dal IV concilio Lateranense', *Studi su Innocenzo III* 246–262.

146. For the context and implications of this decree, see Maccarone, 'Riforma e sviluppo della vita religiosa' 61–72; idem, 'La costitutione "Ne nimia religionum" del IV concilio Lateranense', *Studi su Innocenzo III* 307–337.

147. For its implementation in Germany, see Paul P. Pixton, 'Pope Innocent III and the German Schools: the impact of Canon 11 of the Fourth Lateran Council upon the cathedral and other schools 1216–1272', *Innocenzo III. Urbs et Orbis. Atti del Congresso Internazionale, Roma, 9–15 settembre 1998*, ed. Andrea Sommerlechner (2 vols. Rome 2003) 2.101–132, especially 115–132.

(c.11), while *Inter caetera* ordered the appointment of preachers and penitentiaries to assist in the discharge of the episcopal functions of preaching and penance (c.10).

Clerical Life

Much of the material in this section was a reinforcement of previous legislation—laying down penalties for incontinent clergy (c.14),[148] forbidding drunkenness and gluttony (c.15), ordering clergy to maintain the tonsure and avoid luxurious dress (c.16),[149] and ordering prelates to avoid unnecessary feasting and to attend services regularly and properly (17). But in renewing the ancient prohibition against ordained clergy participating in 'sentences of blood' or duels,[150] *Sententiam sanguinis* (c.18) extended its application to include all forms of involvement in the shedding of blood, judicial and non-judicial, forbidding clergy to act as scribes or recorders in courts where such sentences were issued, or to command companies of mercenaries or crossbowmen, or to engage in surgery; or even to bless ordeals of hot or cold water or hot iron.[151] This last was an extremely important decision which had immediate effect on those jurisdictions which still employed the ordeal as a method of proof in judicial process. The English royal council, for example, directed its judges to adopt other procedures on 26 January 1219, and the judicial ordeal ceased to be a feature of English Common Law.[152]

Religious Cult

This important segment partly echoes the work of contemporary reformers like Odo de Sully, bishop of Paris,[153] in ordering the proper maintenance of churches and oratories (c.19), the safe custody of chrism and the Eucharist (c.20),[154] and the regular attendance of priests at the sick-

148. Cf. Lat I, cc.7, 21; Lat. II, c.6; Lat. III, c.11. For general background, see Roger Gryson, *Les origines du célibat ecclésiastique du premier au septième siècle* (Gembloux 1970); Roman Choli, *Clerical Celibacy in East and West* (Leominster 1988); and Clarence Gallagher, *Church Law and Church Order in Rome and Byzantium: A Comparative Study* (Birmingham Byzantine and Ottoman Monigraphs, 8; Aldershot 2002) who compares celibacy in the Eastern and Western churches.

149. Cf. Lat. II, c.4: above, at n. 69.

150. Already in Gratian, *Decretum* C.23 q.8 c.30: 'Non debent agitare iudicium sanguinis qui sacramenta Domini tractent'; ibid., C.2 q.5 c.22: 'In novo testamento monomachia non recipitur.'

151. J.W. Baldwin, 'The Intellectual Preparation for the Canon of 1215 against the Ordeals', *Speculum* 36 (1961) 613–636. On the replacement of the ordeal with the *Ordo iudiciarius* in church courts see Kenneth Pennington, 'Due Process, Community, and the Prince in the Evolution of the Ordo iudiciarius', RIDC 9 (1998) 9–47

152. *Councils and Synods* 2.1 p. 49.   153. See below, n. 209.

154. Daniel R. Cahill, *The Custody of the Blessed Sacrament* (Catholic University of America Canon Law Studies 292; Washington, D.C. 1950) 8–12.

beds of the dying—expressed as a requirement that physicians urge the very sick to make provision for the health of their souls as well as their bodies (c.22), while the highly important *Omnis utriusque sexus* (c.21) commanded all Christians to confess their sins to their own priest and receive the Eucharist at least once a year, especially at Easter. The secrets of the confessional must not be revealed, on pain of suspension.[155]

Appointments and Elections

This section, too, can be regarded as reinforcement and clarification of existing legislation.[156] Cathedral and regular churches must not be vacant for more than three months, after which the right of appointment devolves on the next ecclesiastical superior (c.23);[157] elections should be made by scrutiny or by compromise (c.24);[158] elections made through secular abuse are null; those who accept them are debarred from any other ecclesiastical appointment; those who hold them are to be suspended for three years (c.25); those who confirm the appointments of unworthy candidates for ecclesiastical office are penalized by loss of rights and income (c.26); ordinands must be properly instructed (c.27); those who obtain permission to resign must be compelled to do so (c.28); renewing Lateran III's prescriptions, the accumulation of benefices with cure of souls is forbidden,[159] and appointments to benefices must be made within six[160] months, failing which the right devolves to the next superior (c.29);[161] prelates to appoint suitable persons, on pain of loss of right of appointment (c.30); sons of canons, especially bastards, not to be installed in the same churches as their fathers (c.31); patrons of parish churches to assign sufficient incomes to the priests in charge; and suitable income to be assigned to vicars (c.32); procurations not to be taken without visitation (c.33); and prelates must not burden their subjects with excessive demands (c.34).

---

155. Cf. Bertrand Kurtscheid, *A History of the Seal of Confession*, trans. F.A. Marks (Saint Louis 1927) 115–126; Paul Anciaux, *La Théologie du Sacrement de Pénitence au XIIe siècle* (Louvain 1949).

156. C.23 (cf. Lat. III, c.8); c.24 (cf. Lat. III, c.1); c.29 (cf. Lat. III, cc.8, 13–14); c.30 (cf. Lat. III, c.3); c.31 (cf. Lat. II, c.21); cc.33–34 (cf. Lat. III, c.4).

157. Ebers, *Devolutionsrecht* 182–188.

158. Anscar Parsons, *Canonical Elections* (Catholic University of America Canon Law Studies 118; Washington, D.C. 1939) 52–64.

159. For a discussion of the tacit obstruction to the full application of this and related canons, see J.W. Gray, 'Canon Law in England: Some Reflections on the Stubbs-Maitland Controversy', (SCH 3; Leiden 1966) 48–68, especially 54–60.

160. Note the important emendation of the generally received reading of 'three' months to 'six' months, bringing the canon into line with Lat. III, c.8: cf. García y García, *Constitutiones* 74, line 13.

161. Ebers, *Devolutionsrecht* 182–188.

Legal Procedure

The inclusion of so many long and complicated constitutions relating to different aspects of the operation of the system of canonical courts, is testimony to the legal revolution which had taken place since Gratian's *Decretum*. A Europe-wide system of canonical jurisdiction had come into being, and many questions of practice and procedure required authoritative definition. Constitutions 35–48 deal with technical aspects of the law. Defendants must not appeal without good cause before sentence is given; if they do, they are to be charged expenses (c.35); judges may revoke comminatory and interlocutory sentences[162] and proceed with the case (c.36); no one may be summoned more than two days' journey outside his own diocese without his express agreement; no one may impetrate papal letters without the approval of his superior (c.37);[163] a full written record of all proceedings must be kept in ecclesiastical courts (c.38); persons receiving property wrongly taken from another can be sued for restitution, the rigor of the civil law notwithstanding (c.39); if, because of the defendant's contumacy, a plaintiff is assigned possession of something, 'causa rei servandae', and is unable, through violence or trickery, to acquire or maintain possession of it within a year, he is, after a year, to be established as the true possessor, so that the defendant may not benefit from his own wrong-doing. Laymen may not be appointed arbiters in spiritual matters (c.40); prescriptions are valid only if made in good faith (c.41);[164] clergy may not invade secular jurisdiction in the name of ecclesiastical freedom (c.42); recusation of judges must be supported by evidence, which must be judged by an arbitrator; if proved, the judge may appoint another judge or send the case to a superior (c.48).[165]

Relations with the Secular Power

Lay princes had given up investiture with ring and crozier in the early twelfth century, but manifestations of the grossest forms of secular abuse of ecclesiastical persons and property still occurred in all parts of Christendom. In what can be called a codicil to the legislation of the twelfth

---

162. An interlocutory sentence was a judgment on a subsidiary issue which had arisen in the course of litigation.

163. Cf. R. von Heckel, 'Das Aufkommen der ständigen Prokuratoren an der päpstlichen Kurie im 13. Jahrhundert', *Miscellanea Francesco Ehrle: Scritti di storia e paleografia* 2 (ST 38; Rome 1924) 290–321 at 311–313.

164. Cf. N. Vilain, 'Prescription et bonne foi du Décret de Gratien (1140) à Jean d'André (†1348)', *Traditio* 16 (1958) 136–145.

165. Cf. Linda Fowler, 'Recusatio iudicis in civilian and canonist thought', *Post scripta: Essays on Medieval Law and the Emergence of the European State in Honor of Gaines Post*, ed. Joseph R. Strayer and Donald E. Queller (SG 15; Rome 1972) 719–785.

century, Lateran IV decreed that clerics should not take oaths of fealty to laymen without lawful cause (c.43); that lay princes should not usurp the rights of churches (c.44); that a patron who kills or mutilates a clerk shall be deprived of his office, and his heirs to the fourth generation will be deprived of entry to a college of clergy or prelature in a regular house, except by dispensation (c.45); that clerks must not be obliged to pay taxes on pain of excommunication (c.46).[166]

Excommunication

Here, too, Lateran IV repeated and extended the decrees of its predecessors: excommunication to be imposed only after warning in the presence of suitable witnesses and for manifest and reasonable cause (c.47); excommunications to be neither imposed nor lifted for payment (c.49).

Marriage

Among the difficulties associated with determining the validity of Christian marriage, the problems relating to consanguinity and clandestinity had caused great uncertainty in the twelfth century. The prohibition against inter-marriage between blood relations had been drawn so widely (up to the seventh degree of consanguinity) that it was difficult in practice to observe the canonical rules, especially in small rural communities and among the upper aristocracy. For this reason, in *Non debet reprehensibile* (c.50), Innocent III formally revoked earlier legislation,[167] and reduced the prohibited degrees of consanguinity and affinity to four (thus barring marriages between persons descended from the same great-great-grandparents).[168] At the same time, he re-issued the condemnation of clandestine marriages, declaring the children of such unions illegitimate, and ordered that intended marriages should be proclaimed in advance ('banns of

---

166. Cf. Lat. III, c.19; Raymonde Foreville, 'Répresentation et taxation du clergé au IVe concile du Latran (1215)', *Études présentés à la Commission internationale pour les Assemblées d'États XXXI* (XIIe Congrès international dessciences historiques; Paris-Louvain 1966) 57–74 (reprinted in *Gouvernement et vie de l'Église au Moyen-Âge* [London 1979]) no. 3.

167. Cf. Lat. I, c.9; Lat. II, c.17.

168. Francis X. Wahl, *The Matrimonial Impediments of Consanguinity and Affinity* (Catholic University of America Canon Law Studies 90; Washington, D.C. 1934) 18–19; Adhélmar Esmein, *Le mariage en droit canonique* (2 vols. 2d ed. Paris 1929) 1.371–393; R. H. Helmholz, *Marriage Litigation in Medieval England* (Cambridge Studies in English Legal History; London/New York 1974); cf. idem, in *DMA* 3.539–540. Innocent's action was not without precedent. In the 1160s, Alexander III had allowed such marriages on a remote Norwegian island (Greenland?), for example, and also in the Croatian province of Spalato (Split): *Decretales Ineditae Saeculi XII*, ed. Stanley Chodorow and Charles Duggan, MIC Series B 4 (Vatican City 1982) 149–151 no. 86, at 149; Charles Duggan, 'Decretal Letters to Hungary' 23–24 no. 10. Moreover, the reduction of the prohibition to four degrees was powerfully argued by Peter the Chanter in his *Verbum abbreviatum*: J.W. Baldwin, *Masters, Princes, and Merchants: The Social Views of Peter the Chanter and His Circle* (2 vols. Princeton 1970) 1.336–337.

marriage'), so that any lawful objections could be raised in advance of the ceremony (c.51).[169] The pope also declared that hearsay evidence was not admissible in matrimonial cases (c.52).

Tithes

Another matter of contention was the obligation of Christians to pay tithes to their parish church. The council condemned those who had their property cultivated by others (non-Christians) in order to avoid tithes (c.53); declared that tithe payments have priority over all other taxes and dues (c.54); ordered Cistercians and other privileged orders to pay tithes on all lands acquired by them in the future, whether cultivated by themselves or not (c.55);[170] and prohibited both secular and regular clergy from making any kind of agreement which would deprive the parish priest of his lawful tithe (c.56).

Religious Orders

The tensions between monasticism and episcopal authority were as old as monasticism itself. In a series of five constitutions (cc.57–61), Innocent III sought to mediate between the two, while recognizing the valid claims of each. *Ut privilegia* (c.57) gave precise instructions on the interpretation of the privilege of celebrating religious services during interdict, enjoyed by some orders; and the same privilege was extended to bishops in *Quod nunnulis* (c.58). *Quod quibusdam* (c.59) established that a religious may not pledge his faith or accept a loan without the knowledge of his abbot and the majority of the chapter; *Accendentibus* (c.60) forbade abbots to exercise rights which properly belonged to bishops, such as hearing matrimonial cases, imposing public penances, and granting letters of indulgence; and *In Lateraniensi* (c.61) reiterated earlier prohibitions against religious receiving tithes from laymen.[171]

Simony

Here, too, Lateran IV reflected earlier legislation:[172] no fees are to be exacted for the consecration of bishops, the blessing of abbots, or the or-

---

169. Thus making universal a practice that was already followed in some parts of the church: cf. James B. Roberts, *The Banns of Marriage* (Catholic University of America Canon Law Studies 64; Washington, D.C. 1931) 9–17. See also E. Diebold, 'L'application en France du canon 51 du IVe concile du Latran d'après les anciens statuts synodaux', *L'année canonique* 2 (1963) 187–195.

170. Cf. Cheney, 'A Letter of Innocent III and the Lateran Decree on Cistercian Tithe-Paying'; Giles Constable, *Monastic Tithes* 1–19, 303–309.

171. Cf. Lat. II, c.10; Lat. III, c.9.

172. Cc.63, 65–66 (cf. Lat. III, c.7); c.64 (cf. Lat. III, c.10). Cf. Lynch, *Simoniacal Entry* 179–195.

dination of clerics (c.63); monks and nuns may not require payment for entry into the religious life (c.64); bishops may not require gifts for instituting clergy or permitting entry to the religious life (c.65); clergy must confer the sacraments freely; may not charge burial fees, but can accept customary offerings (c.66). But concern with another form of trafficking in the sacred underlies the decree *Cum ex eo* (c.62), which sought to restrain both the exploitation of saints' relics and the excessive bestowal of indulgences. Old relics of saints might not be exhibited outside reliquaries or offered for sale; new relics could not be venerated without papal approval; *questors* for alms must have written authorization either from the Apostolic See or from a diocesan bishop, and may not depart from the text.[173] Moreover, episcopal indulgences may not exceed one year for attendance at the dedication of a church, and forty days for the anniversary.[174]

Regulations Relating to Jews and Moslems

The concern for the integrity of orthodox Christian belief and practice which was manifested in the opening canons of the council recurs in the closing constitution, which imposed restrictions on relations between Christians and non-Christians. Jews may not charge extortionate interest (c.67); Jews and Moslems must wear a distinct form of dress and not mock Christian ceremonies (c.68); Jews may not hold public office (c.69); Jewish converts to Christianity may not return to their former rites (c.70).[175]

The Crusade

The final action of the council (c.71) was to issue a call for a crusade, to take place in the following year (from June 1216), offering the benefits of the crusading indulgence to those who contributed to the endeavor, and the Church's protection to those who went in person, and imposing a three years' tax of one twentieth of ecclesiastical revenues on all clerics in the church, the pope and cardinals promising to pay a tenth.

---

173. For which the canon supplies the text of a form letter, *Quoniam ut ait Apostolus*, which could be used for the purpose.

174. For the interesting suggestion that the precise formulation of this canon owed much to existing English practice and the influence of Cardinal Robert Courson, see N. Vincent, 'Some Pardoners' Tales; The Earliest English Indulgences', *Transactions of the Royal Historical Society* 6th series 12 (2002) 23–58 at 55.

175. Kenneth R. Stow, 'Papal and Royal Attitudes Toward Jewish Lending in the Thirteenth century', *Association for Jewish Studies Review* 6 (1981) 161–184; John A. Watt, 'Jews and Christians in the Gregorian Decretals', *Christianity and Judaism*, ed. Diana Wood (SCH 29; Oxford 1992) 93–105. Cf. S. Grayzel, *The Church and the Jews in the XIIIth Century* (Philadelphia 1933); *Essential Papers on Judaism and Christianity in Conflict. From Late Antiquity to the Reformation*, ed. Jeremy Cohen (New York 1991) part 2.

The Reception

Almost a century of legal development had occurred since the First Lateran Council of 1123. During that time, the learned law had established itself in the schools and courts of Western Christendom and had been subjected to exhaustive academic scrutiny and debate. It followed that the decrees of the Fourth Lateran Council, intended to have immediate legal authority, were carefully drafted to provide unambiguous direction. Hence the decrees are very much longer than those of Lateran I and II, and mostly longer even than those of Lateran III. Moreover, a five-fold pattern, comparable with the five-fold structure adopted by Bernard of Pavia in the 'Leipzig' collection and *Compilatio prima* (iudex, iudicia, clerus, connubium, crimen), is broadly discernible in the ordering of the decrees,[176] and succinct rubrics were provided to facilitate incorporation into collections of law.[177]

Reception into the main stream of positive law was not long delayed. Almost immediately, the council's decrees were received into the 'ius novum', first into *Compilatio quarta* (compiled 1216; officially published 1216–17),[178] and then into the Gregorian *Decretales* of 1234.[179] In fact, its first two constitutions became the first two 'capitula' of the *Liber extra*.[180] Antonio García y García has demonstrated both the wide diffusion of the Lateran's legislation[181] and the speed with which it was incorporated into the scholarly legal tradition. Johannes Teutonicus, the leading professor of canon law at Bologna, composed an 'apparatus' on the decrees within months of the closure of the council;[182] his Portuguese colleague, Vincentius His-

---

176. One manuscript, Florence, Biblioteca Mediceo-Laurenziana, MS S. Croce III[sin.]6, fol. 254ra–261vb, arranges the canons in five parts, 'Prima pars novellarum', 'Secunda pars novellarum', etc., comprising cc.1–4, 5–22, 23–34, 35–49, 50–71, and the anonymous *Casus Parisienses* (possibly by Vincentius Hispanus) adopted a similar division (García y García, *Constitutiones* 17–18).

177. García y García, *Constitutiones* 119–172.

178. Johannes inserted all but c.42, *Sicut volumus*, relating to secular jurisdiction, and c.71, *Ad liberandam Terram sanctam* into his *Compilatio quarta*; Foreville, *Latran I, II, III et Latran IV* 312–313; Alberigo, COD 229; cf. Stephan Kuttner, 'Johannes Teutonicus, das vierte Laterankonzil und die Compilatio Quarta', *Miscellanea Giovanni Mercati* (ST 125; Vatican City 1946) 608–634; reprinted in *Medieval Councils, Decretals, and Collections of Canon Law* (London 1980) no. 10; cf. 'Retractationes', 9–11; García y García, *Constitutiones* 4.

179. All but c.42, *Sicut volumus*, relating to secular jurisdiction, c.49, on unjust excommunications, and part of c.71, *Ad liberandam Terram sanctam* were received into the *Liber extra* in 1234: Alberigo, COD 229, García y García, *Constitutiones* 4. For their distribution in the *Extra*, see Friedberg, *Decretales* xii, s.v. 'Conc. Later. IV'.

180. X 1.1.1–2, 'De summa Trinitate et fide catholica'.

181. Sixty-six manuscripts are still extant, and a further 14 have been lost: see García y García's chapter in this volume.

182. 'Johannis Teutonici apparatus in concilium Lateranense', ed. García y García, *Constitutiones* 173–270.

panus, composed another at about the same time or very slightly later,[183] and further glosses and commentaries were written by Damasus Hungarus (after 1216), and the anonymous authors of the *Casus Parisienses* and the *Casus Fuldenses* (both before 1220). Moreover, after their incorporation into *Compilatio quarta* and the *Liber extra*, they were minutely examined in the context of these formally promulgated compendia of canon law.[184] Although all the constitutions were glossed, the commentators were principally interested in the strictly legal aspects of the council's legislation. It is therefore not surprising that the most heavily glossed canons were those concerned with canonical process. The 'apparatus' of Johannes Teutonicus, for example, occupies eighty-four pages, of which just over thirty-four pages—more than a third of the whole—are devoted to the fourteen constitutions concerned with procedure (cc.35–48), and a similar disproportion is revealed in the works of his contemporaries. Vincentius Hispanus and Damasus Hungarus devoted about a quarter of their discussions to the procedural canons.[185]

But the Lateran decrees were not merely the province of academic lawyers. Copies of the decrees were carried away from Rome to the four quarters of the Latin world by the four hundred or so bishops and eight hundred abbots, priors, capitular representatives, and others. The contemporary records of the Latin Church bear testimony to their application to a greater or lesser extent throughout the thirteenth century, and beyond, in the different regions of the Latin Church.[186] Moreover, *Sicut olim* (c.6) greatly stimulated[187] the convocation of provincial and diocesan councils which promulgated local synodal statutes and reiterated decrees of the general council.[188] In stimulating the increasing regularity of diocesan

---

183. 'Vincentii Hispani apparatus in concilium quartum Lateranense', ed. García y García, *Constitutiones* 271–384. Despite the small number of surviving manuscripts, their geographical spread (Bamberg, Jumièges, Llanthony Secunda, Padua, Signy) suggests wide dissemination.

184. See García y García's chapter (11) below.

185. Cf. García y García, *Constitutiones* 187–270, of which pages 223–256 relate to cc.35–48 (Johannes); 287–384, of which pages 331–358 relate to cc.35–48 (Vincentius); 419–458, of which pages 437–447 relate to cc.35–48 (Damasus).

186. C.R. Cheney, *English Synodalia of the Thirteenth Century* (London 1941; reprinted Oxford 1998); M. Gibbs and J. Lang, *Bishops and Reform; 1215–1272*, with special reference to the Lateran Council of 1215 (London 1934) 94–179; cf. Foreville, *Latran I, II, III et Latran IV* 313–315.

187. Although it did not initiate them: see Cheney, *English Synodalia* 35–36; Pontal, *Les statuts synodaux* lxxi–lxxvii, 106; Paul B. Pixton, *The German Episcopacy and the Implementation of the Decrees of the Fourth Lateran Council, 1216–1245: Watchmen on the Tower* (Studies in the History of Christian Thought 64; Leiden 1995) 7–89; cf. Pontal, *Les statuts synodaux* 10–82.

188. Alberigo, COD 236 (cf. Tanner, *Decrees of the Ecumenical Councils* 236): 'canonicas regulas et maxime quae statuta sunt in hoc generali concilio relegentes'.

synods, the Fourth Lateran Council helped to create the medium for the dissemination of its own constitutions.

For England, the earliest evidence of the reception of Lateran decrees occurs in the extremely important set of statutes first issued by Bishop Richard Poore for the diocese of Salisbury in 1219 and then re-issued, with additions, in Durham 1228–1236.[189] The decrees are a mélange of recent ecclesiastical legislation, combining canons from the Third and Fourth Lateran Councils with chapters from Bishop Odo de Sully's synodal statutes for the diocese of Paris (before 1208) and Archbishop Stephen Langton's provincial statutes for Canterbury (1213–1214).[190] The Salisbury compilation was an immediate success. Derivatives, adaptations, and expansions were made in many dioceses in the succeeding century, as individual bishops sought in the wake of the Lateran Council to provide authoritative guidance for their administrators and clergy. Its influence can be traced especially in the statutes issued for the dioceses of Canterbury

---

189. *Councils and Synods* 2.1 p. 57, correcting Cheney, *English Synodalia* 50–51. Richard Poore had attended the Fourth Lateran Council, and he was a friend of Odo de Sully and a pupil of Stephen Langton: ibid., 52, 55–57.

190. *Councils and Synods* 2.1 pp. 57–96. Direct influence of Lateran IV is found in c.4, *De trinitate credenda* which ends, 'prout in capitulo concilii continetur' (cf. Lat. IV, c.1); c.8, *De fornicatione clericorum*, with the phrase 'in generali concilio statutum est' (cf. Lat. IV, c.14); c.1, *De superbia vitanda in verbo et gestu* combines parts of Lat. IV, c.16, Langton, cc.8 and 10, and Lat. III, c.14; c.13, *De potatione publica devitanda* (cf. Lat. IV, c.15); c.16, *De cupiditate clericorum vitanda* echoes in part Paris, vii. 4 (Mansi 22.679) and Lat. IV, c.66; c.17, *De consuetudine ecclesie laudabili et observanda*, with the phrase 'sicut in concilio statutum' (cf. Lat. IV, c.66); c.21, *Quod nichil exigatur pro baptismate* (cf. Paris, iii. 2–3 and Lat. IV, c.20); c.38, *Quotiens monendi sunt parochiani ad confitendum et ad communicandum* (cf. Lat. IV, c.21); c.51, *De premonitione excommunicationis*, opens 'Sacro approbante concilio' (cf. Lat. IV, c.47); c.55, *De sacramento redemptionis* (cf. Lat. IV, c.1); c.66, *De munditia vasorum et ornamentorum omnium* (cf. Lat. IV, c.19); 72, *De fraudulenta pensione non danda*, includes the phrase, 'sicut in concilio prohibitum est' (cf. Lat. IV, c.32); c.81, *De fornicatione et adulteriis*, includes the phrase, 'secundum statuta concilii' (cf. Lat. IV, c.7); c.85, *De clandestinis matrimoniis*, includes the phrase, 'secundum statuta concilii' (cf. Lat. IV, c.51); 90, *De gradibus matrimonii*, opens 'In generali concilio statutum est' (cf. Lat. IV, cc.50–51); 91, *De competenti termino contrahendi* (cf. Lat. IV, c.51); c.92, *De testimonio consanguinitatis in contractu* (cf. Lat. IV, c.52); c.98, *Ne medici suadeant egris aliquid quod sit in periculo anime*, ends 'Transgressor huius constitutionis penam in concilio statutam non (evadet)' (cf. Lat. IV, c.22); c.100, *De regula religionis* (cf. Lat. IV, c.13); 104, *De procuratione (visitationis)*, includes the phrases, 'sacri concilii vestigiis inherentes' and 'in Lateranssi concilio diffinita', 'secundum statuta concilii' (cf. Lat. IV, cc.33–34); 105, *De clericis episcopi suscipiendis*, includes the phrase, 'in concilio statutum est' (cf. Lat. IV, c.10); c.106, *De magistris scolarum* (cf. Lat. IV, c.11); c.107, *De beneficio indigni privando*, includes the phrase, 'nuper in generali concilio evidentius fuit expressum' (cf. Lat. IV, c.29); c.109, *Ne clerici optineant res laicales*, opens, 'Sacri concilii auctoritate interdicimus' (cf. Lat. IV, cc.43, 45); c.110, *De advocatis et feudatoriis*, opens, 'Sacri nichilominus concilii provisione diffinitum est' (cf. Lat. IV, c.45); c.111, *De stipendiis sacerdotum*, includes the phrase, 'auctoritate concilii precipimus' (cf. Lat. IV, cc.32). Papal mandates against hereditary succession in beneficis, received by the archbishop of York and the bishops of Lincoln, Worcester, London, Carlisle, Salisbury, Coventry, 1221–1235: *Councils and Synods* 2.1 pp. 98–99.

(1222 –1228), Durham (1228–1236), Durham peculiars in York (1241–1249), Salisbury (1238–1244), Exeter (1225–1237), London (1245–1259), and Chichester (1244–1253), and in an undated provincial council in Scotland.[191] Only slightly later, in a provincial council held in Osney Abbey (outside Oxford) in April 1222,[192] Archbishop Stephen Langton issued sixty statutes on sacramental life and ecclesiastical discipline, which echoed or summarized Lateran constitutions in fifteen cases, alluding to the council by name in seven.[193] Moreover, his final statute ordered observance of 'the council held at the Lateran by Pope Innocent III of holy memory', in respect of payment of tithe, and other provisions, and commanded the bishops to promulgate both the Lateran constitutions and his own, as appropriate in their diocesan synods.[194] The crucial importance of this council can be judged by its survival in about sixty manuscripts, only seven of which date from the thirteenth century, and from the inclusion of many of its constitutions in the great compendium of English ecclesiastical law composed by William Lyndwood in 1430.[195] Not long after Stephen Langton's council, the statutes (1222–1225) for an unidentified English diocese reveal important borrowings from Lateran IV,[196] and the synodal statutes promul-

---

191. *Councils and Synods* 2.1 pp. 165–167 (Canterbury) 201 (Durham) 435–445 (Durham peculiars in York) 364–387 (Salisbury) 227–237 (Exeter) 632–658 (London) 451–467 (Chichester); cf. Cheney, *English Synodalia* 62–89.

192. Ibid. 2.1 pp. 100–125. Sixty manuscript copies are known, testifying to the wide dissemination and enduring relevance of Stephen Langton's provincial code.

193. Ibid. 2.1 pp. 100–125. Direct influence of Lateran IV is found in: c.11 includes the phrase 'cum in generali concilio sit preceptum' (cf. Lat. IV, c.17); c.13, prohibiting clergy from involvement in sentences of blood, opens 'Auctoritate quoque generalis concilii' (cf. Lat. IV, c.18); c.14 orders that the appointment of vicars in prebendal churches and in churches belonging to religious houses should be made 'secundum formam generalis concilii' (cf. Lat. IV, cc.32, 61); c.24, on the appointment of confessors for the clergy (cf. Lat. IV, c.10); c.27, moderating the trains of archdeacons, refers to the number of packhorses 'statutum in concilio generali' (cf. Lat. IV, c.33); c.29. on the duties of an archdeacon, orders archdeacons to see that the Eucharist, chrism, and holy oil are securely locked 'iuxta formam generalis concilii' (cf. Lat. IV, c.20); c. 31 prohibits charging for burials, baptisms, marriages, or any other sacrament 'sicut in generali concilio expressius et diffusius est statutum' (cf. Lat. IV, c.66); c.33, on clerical dress (cf. Lat. IV, c.16); c.34, on clerical behavior (cf. Lat. IV, c.15); c.39, forbidding luxurious dress to nuns, religious women, monks, and canons regular (cf. Lat. IV, c.16); c.42, forbidding payment for entry into a religious house (cf. Lat. IV, c.64); c.43, forbidding the 'farming' of churches (cf. Lat. IV,c.32); c.46, on the Jews (cf. Lat. IV, c.67); c.47, ordering Jews to wear distinctive dress (cf. Lat. IV, c.68); c.33, on payment of tithe and observance of the Lateran constitutions (cf. Lat. IV, cc.53–55).

194. *Councils and Synods* 2.1 p. 125: 'Ut autem omnia fine bono concludantur, Lateranense concilium sub sancte recordationis papa Innocentio iii celebratum, in prestatione decimarum et aliis capitulis precipimus observari, et in synodis episcoporum constitutiones illius concilii una cum istis prout videbitur expedire volumus recitari.'

195. William Lyndwood (Guilelmus Lindwood), *Provinciale (seu Constitutiones Angliae)* (Oxford: H. Hall, 1679), cf. Tabula, ki[ra]; *Councils and Synods* 2.1 p. 101.

196. *Councils and Synods* 2.1 pp. 139–154, c.38, on the secure custody of holy oil and chrism

gated c. 1224 by Peter des Roches, bishop of Winchester, began with the declaration that 'The statutes of the Second[197] Lateran Council shall be observed by everyone in our diocese' (c.1).[198] The direct and indirect influence of Lateran legislation can be found in other English diocesan councils throughout the thirteenth century, as at Exeter (1225–1237), Worcester (1229, 1240), Lincoln (1239?), Norwich (1240–1243), Bath and Wells c. 1258), as well as in Cardinal Otto's legatine decrees issued at London in 1237.[199] That the Fourth Lateran Council became and remained general law for the English Church is confirmed by the conclusion to the preamble of the Bath and Wells statutes of 1258 which explicitly acknowledge the authority of the edicts of three councils, the Lateran, Oxford, and London: that is, Lateran IV, Stephen Langton's Oxford synod (1222), and Cardinal Otto's London council (1237).[200]

A comparable process is found in France. In the immediate aftermath of the council, a composite code, combining decrees of Lateran IV with the highly important sacramental and disciplinary decrees of Odo de Sully (†1208),[201] was issued at Tours (1215–1216)[202] and shortly afterwards (1220), Guillaume de Beaumont, bishop of Angers, promulgated a similar compendium of Odo's statutes and constitutions of the Fourth Lateran Council (which Guillaume attended).[203] In this case, the derivations from Lateran IV are usually identified as 'From the last Lateran Council', 'From the Lateran Council', etc., but some are not identified, and three chapters

---

(cf. Lat. IV, c.20); c.40, on publishing the banns of marriage, 'nuper in concilio super huiusmodi statutam' (cf. Lat. IV, c.51); cc.63–65, on clerical behavior (cf. Lat. IV, cc.14–16); c.77, on the appointment of vicars, 'cum in generali concilio nuper statutum esset' (cf. Lat. IV, c.61).

197. I.e. the Fourth: see Cheney, 'The Numbering of the Lateran Councils' 206–207.

198. *Councils and Synods* 2.1 pp. 125–137, at 126.

199. *Councils and Synods* 2.1 pp. 227–237 (Exeter), 169–181 (Worcester, 1229), 237–259 (Cardinal Otto), 294–325 (Worcester, 1240), 265–278 (Lincoln), 342–364 (Norwich), 586–626 (Bath and Wells); et passim.

200. *Councils and Synods* 2.1 p. 589, 'salvis in omnibus statutis conciliorum Lateranensis, Oxoniensis, et Londoniensis'.

201. For the attribution, see Pontal, *Les statuts synodaux français du XIII*[e] *siècle* 48–50; for the text, with French translation, see ibid., 52–97; cf. *Synodicon Ecclesiae Parisiensis* (Paris; F. Muguet, 1674) 3–21; Mansi 22.731–736 (shorter text), under the title 'statuta incerti loci'; cf. Foreville, *Latran I, II, III et Latran IV* 315. Cf. A. Artonne, 'Les statuts synodaux diocésains français du XIIIe s. au concile de Trente', *Revue d'histoire de l'Église de France* 36 (1950) 168–181. For the reception of Odo's statutes in England, see Cheney, *English Synodalia* 55–56; for their influence in Germany, see n. 209 below. For Portugal, see I. da Rosa Pereira, 'Les statutes synodaux d'Eudes de Sully en Portugal', *L'année canonique* 15 (1971) 459–480.

202. Text lost: cf. Pontal, *Les statuts synodaux* 106.

203. Odette Pontal, 'Les plus anciens statuts synodux d'Angers et leur expansion dans les diocèses de l'ouest de la France', *Revue d'Histoire de l'Église de France* 46 (1960) 54–67; Pontal, *Les statuts synodaux* 106, 138–239 (with French translation).

are wrongly attributed to the council.²⁰⁴ The Angers statutes became the archetype of a whole family of diocesan codes in Western France, copies of which were to be kept by every parish priest. They were adopted in Le Mans (1229), Tours (after 1229), Nantes (date unknown), Orléans (1231?), Bayeux (1300?), and Lisieux (date uncertain, but re-issued and updated in 1321) and influenced the compilations made in the thirteenth century in Autun (1286), Coutances (thirteenth cent.), Clermont-Ferrand (1268), Langres (thirteenth cent.), Lyon (after 1298), Nîmes (1252),²⁰⁵ Noyon (before 1285), Rouen (before 1235), Saintes (after 1255), and Sisteron (1241)— and indeed throughout the whole of France until the Council of Trent.²⁰⁶

204. Pontal, *Les statuts synodaux* 138–237, c.18, on priestly obligation to say the Office, 'Ex concilio lateranensi ultimo' (cf. Lat. IV, c.17); c.22, on the proper care of altar linen and vestments, with the phrase 'sicut continetur in concilio (lateranensi)' (cf. Lat. IV, c.19, end); c.23, *Ex concilio lateranensi de crismate* (cf. Lat. IV, cc.19 [end], 20); c.24, *Item de eodem*, forbidding the keeping of private possessions in churches, opens with the phrase 'In concilio firmiter inhibetur' (cf. Lat. IV, c.19); c.31, *Ex concilio lateranensi*, forbidding clergy to indulge in profane pursuits (cf. Lat. IV, c.16); c.32, on clerical dress (cf. Lat. IV, c.16); c.33, forbidding clergy to participate in sentences of blood, derived from the Council of Tours, 1216 (cf. Lat. IV, c.18); c.34, *Ex concilio lateranensi (et turonensi)*, forbidding clergy to take paid employment or to bless the elements in ordeals (cf. Lat. IV, c.18); c.37, *Ex concilio lateranensi*, on clerical behavior (cf. Lat. IV, c.14); c.38, excommunicating clergy who still retained 'suspect women' 'usque ad concilium lateranense ultimo celebratum' (cf. Lat. IV, c.14); c.39, *Ex concilio lateranensi*, on illegitimate children of priests and clerical and lay concubinage (falsely attributed to the council; derived from Odo de Sully, c.81); c.40, on reservation of relics, opens with the phrase 'Item in concilio est statutum' (cf. Lat. IV, c.62); c.41, *Ex concilio lateranensi*, on episcopal control of preachers and alms-collectors (false attribution; from Odo de Sully, c.68); c.64, allowing marriage from the fifth degree of consanguinity onwards (cf. Lat. IV, c.50); c.65 forbidding clandestine marriages (cf. Lat. IV, c.51); c.69, on clerical duties towards the sick, opens with the phrase 'Statutum est in concilio' (cf. Lat. IV, c.22); c.73, *In concilio lateranensi*, sacraments to be conferred freely (cf. Lat. IV, c.61); cc.75–76, on confession (cf. Lat. IV, c.21); c.80, *Ex concilio lateranensi*, on penance (possible allusion to Lat. IV, c.7).

205. Compiled by Pierre de Sampson and widely disseminated, it was adopted in Arles, Béziers, Uzès, and Lodève, and its influence can be traced in the work of Guillaume Durand (Mende) and Raymond de Calmont d'Olt (Rodez) and in synodal statutes in northern Spain and Italy. Manuscript copies survive in Italy, Spain, Switzerland, and Germany; see Odette Pontal, 'Quelques remarques sur l'oeuvre canonique de Pierre de Sampzon', AHC 8 (1976) 126–142, especially 127–132; cf. Mansi, 24.521–566 (wrongly attributed to Bishop Bertrand de Languisel and mis-dated 1284).

206. Pontal, 'Les plus anciens statuts' 57–59 and *Les statuts synodaux* 106–108, 136. According to Odette Pontal (p.136), 'pour toute la France du Moyen Age il [the synodal book of Angers] reste le synodal de base jusqu'au Concile de Trente.' For manuscript and bibliographical details, see A. Artonne, L. Guixard, Odette Pontal, *Répertoire des statuts synodaux des diocèses de l'ancienne France du xiiiᵉ à la fin du xviiiᵉ siècle* (Documents, Études et Répertoires publiés par l'Institut de Recherche et d'Histoire des Textes 8; 2d edition; Paris 1969) 80–81 (Autun), 115–116 (Bayeux), 205 (Clermont-Ferrand), 213–214 (Coutances), 257 (Langres), 297 (Le Mans), 279 (Lisieux), 287 (Lyon), 316–317 (Nantes), 337 (Noyon), 342–343 (Orléans), 378–379 (Rouen), 409 (Saintes), 421 (Sisteron), 453 (Tours); cf. Raymonde Foreville, 'Les statuts synodaux et le renouveau pastoral du XIIIᵉ siècle dans le Midi de la France', *Le Credo, la morale et l'Inquisition* (Cahiers de Fanjeaux 6; Toulouse 1971) 119–150 (reprinted in idem, *Gouvernement et vie de l'Église au Moyen-Âge* [London 1979] no. 15).

Meanwhile, a substantial derivation from Lateran IV was promulgated at Rouen in 1224, with the declaration, 'by the authority of the sacred general Lateran Council . . . we desire these especially to be observed, which are known to have been established in that council'.[207]

In two of the six provinces[208] of the German church the ground was prepared to some extent by reform-minded prelates before 1215. Odo de Sully's decrees influenced the synodal statutes of Archbishop Siegfried II of Mainz in 1209;[209] and statutes were issued for Toul, Liège, and Utrecht in 1192, 1203, and 1209, respectively, while decrees similar to the Utrecht code were promulgated in Cologne and Liège in 1209.[210] Twenty-one bishops and archbishops and perhaps forty or fifty other clerics constituted the 'German' contingent at the Lateran council,[211] and there is evidence of the immediate promulgation of its constitutions in the provinces of Salzburg (Archbishop Eberhard: 1216),[212] Trier (Dietrich II: 1216 and 1238),[213] and Mainz (Sieg-

207. Bessin, *Concilia Rothomagensis* 1.130–132: c.1 declares, 'auctoritate sacri Concilii Lateranensis . . . haec potissimum volumus observari quae in ipso Concilio constituta noscuntur'; cc.1–19 = Lat. IV, cc.6, 10, 7, 12, 13, 14, 15–16, 19–20, 21, 10, 27, 30, 31, 32, 47, 51, 53–54, 55, 59; cf. Raymonde Foreville, 'La réception des conciles généraux dans l'église et la province de Rouen au XIIIᵉ siècle', *Droit privé et institutions régionales: Études historiques offertes à Jean Yver* (Paris 1976) 245 (reprinted in *Gouvernement et vie de l'Église au Moyen-Âge* [London 1979] no. 9).

208. Bremen, Cologne, Magdeburg, Mainz, Salzburg, Trier.

209. Peter Johanek, 'Die Pariser Statuten des Bischofs Odo von Sully und die Anfänge der kirchlichen Statutengesetzgebung in Deutschland', *Proceedings Cambridge* 327–347, especially 345–347, for the Latin text; cf. Pixton, *The German Episcopacy* 149–151 (with English translation).

210. Pixton, *The German Episcopacy* 84–85. For the Utrecht statutes, see *Concilia Germaniae*, ed. J. F. Schannat and J. Hartzheim (11 vols. Cologne: Krakamp and Simonis, 1759–1775; reprinted Aalen 1970) 3 (1760) 488–490; cf. Anton Joseph Binterim, *Pragmatische Geschichte der deutschen National- Provincial- und vorzüglichsten Diöcesanconcilien vom vierten Jahrhundert bis auf das Concilium zu Trient* (7 vols. Mainz 1835–1848) 4 (1840) 458–465 (German translation).

211. For German attendance at the council, see Hermann Krabbo, 'Die Deutschen Bischöfe auf dem Laterankonzil 1215', QF 10 (1907) 275–300: 7 from the province of Mainz, 3 from Trier, 2 from Cologne, 4 from Salzburg, 2 from Bremen, 3 from Magdeburg, as well as the patriarch of Aquileia and the bishops of Trent, Basel, Cambrai, Riga, and Estonia; cf. Pixton, *The German Episcopacy* 190. For monastic and capitular representation, 'perhaps forty or fifty other clerics', see ibid., 190–193.

212. Pixton, *The German Episcopacy* 223–234: cc.8–9, on abuse by lay advocates (cf. Lat. IV, cc.44–45); c.11, compelling subdeacons and deacons who have married to return to the clerical state (cf. Lat. IV, c.14); c.14, on appointment of vicars (cf. Lat. IV, cc.30 and 61; confirmed by Pope Honorius III, Dec. 1217. Potthast 5635).

213. Pixton, *The German Episcopacy* 234, 240–241, 415–418. A council in 1216 is inferred; for the 1238 council see Mansi 23.477–486. 12 of its 45 decrees reflect Lateran legislation: 10–13, 15–16, 21, regulating clerical dress and tonsure (cf. Lat. IV, c.16); 14, forbidding clergy to frequent taverns, except on pilgrimages and journeys (cf. Lat. IV, c.16); c.17–18, forbidding clerical cohabitation with women (cf. Lat. IV, c.14); c.20, forbidding hawking and dicing (cf. Lat. IV, c.16); c.26, on sufficient income for vicars (cf. Lat. IV, c.32); c. 27, on the safe custody of the Eucharist ('corpus Domini'), holy oil and baptismal fonts (cf. Lat. IV, c.20); c.31, against heresy (cf. Lat. IV, c.3); two reflect that of the Third Lateran: c.9, forbidding clergy to engage in business (cf. Lat. III, c.12); c.34, against usury (cf. Lat. III, c.25; cf. Lat. IV, c.67).

fried II: 1218, 1233, 1239),[214] as well as reiteration at diocesan level in Constanz (1216), Hildesheim (1216), Metz (c.1219?), Chur (1219?), Halberstadt (1216–1220), Liège (1217), and Toul (1224).[215] For the provinces of Mainz, Salzburg, and Trier, therefore, echoes of Lateran IV reverberate through the synodal legislation of the first generation after 1216, and fairly wide knowledge of the its decrees can be established in monastic and cathedral churches.[216]

Evidence for the remaining three provinces is less secure, but early promulgation can be inferred for Cologne (Engelbert: 1220?)[217] and Magdeburg (Albrecht: 1220).[218] Later in the century, there is firmer evidence for the issue of reforming decrees covering clerical and monastic behavior in Cologne and Magdeburg in 1261.[219] Political difficulties impeded action at the provincial level in Bremen-Hamburg, however, but diocesan publication occurred in Merseburg (1216–1218), Prague (1216), and Naumburg (1217),[220] and the papal legate Gregory may have published reforming decrees in Ratzeburg, Schwerin, Lübeck, Olmütz, and Meissen in 1221–1222.[221] In 1225, another legate, Cardinal Conrad of Porto, presided at a legatine council at Mainz, which issued decrees for the whole German nation, and ended with a general mandate for the annual promulgation of the constitutions at provincial, episcopal, and other synods.[222] In due course they were incorporated into the Mainz synodal book in 1310.[223]

The story in Spain and Portugal is colored by the local preoccupations of the Spanish episcopate, impoverished by the 'reconquista', distracted by the jurisdictional dispute between Compostela and Toledo, and very much subject to royal control.[224] Although twenty-seven Spanish bishops and a considerable company of lesser ecclesiastics attended the council,[225] only

214. Pixton, *The German Episcopacy* 246–248, 418–419.
215. Ibid., 252–261, 334.
216. Ibid., 225–282, passim, 288–291.
217. Ibid., 282–261.
218. Ibid., 284–285.
219. Albert Hauck, *Kirchengeschichte Deutschlands* (5 vols. in 6, Leipzig 1896–1920; reprinted Berlin-Leipzig 1954) 5.1 p. 144. For Cologne, see Binterim, *Pragmatische Geschichte* 5 (1843) 162–178 (Conrad, '1260'); *Concilia Germaniae* 3.588–597 ('1260'); ibid., 596–615 (Werner, 1261); Mansi, 23.1012–1030 (Conrad, '1260'). For Magdeburg, see Binterim, 5.214–220.
220. Pixton, *The German Episcopacy* 259–260, 296–300.
221. Ibid., 291–296, 298–299, 300.
222. Mansi 23.1–8, c.14 (col. 7–8), 'districte praecipimus, ut archiepiscopi, episcopi, archidiaconi, & decani, in suo singuli concilio annis singulis celebrando eas publicari faciant servari'; cf. *Concilia Germaniae* 3.520–523; Binterim, 4.471 (German translation); cf. Pixton, *The German Episcopacy* 345–349.
223. Hauck, *Pragmatische Geschichte* 5.1 pp. 136–140; cf. Pixton, *The German Episcopacy* 348.
224. Peter Linehan, *The Spanish Church and the Papacy in the Thirteenth Century* (Cambridge 1971; Spanish translation published in Salamanca 1975) 4–19.
225. For the list, see Antonio García y García, 'El Concilio IV Lateranense (1215) y la Península Ibèrica', *Iglesia, sociedad y derecho* 2.187–208, at 190–192 (reprinted from *Revista española de teologia* 44 [1984] 355–375).

Bishop Gerald (Giraldo) of Segovia made an attempt, unsuccessful as it turned out, to apply some of the new constitutions in a synod in 1216.[226] Not until the legation of John of Abbeville, cardinal bishop of Sabina, was the full program of the Lateran reforms introduced into Iberia.[227] He visited the whole of the Spanish peninsula in 1228–1229, holding councils at Valladolid (1228), Salamanca (1229), Lérida (March, 1229), and elsewhere, the principal purpose of which was the emphatic promulgation of relevant Lateran decrees throughout the four ecclesiastical provinces of the Spanish peninsula.[228] Only those from Lérida have survived,[229] but it is likely that the legislation at Valladolid and Salamanca was similar in form and extent.[230] The very close dependence of the Lérida code on Lateran IV is evident from the arenga, which orders the general observance 'of the decrees of the holy general council, which have been for the most part neglected'.[231] Twenty-one of its thirty-seven statutes reflected Lateran legislation

226. Antonio García y García, 'Primeros reflejos del conc. 4 Lateranense en Castilla', *Iglesia, sociedad y derecho* 2.209–235 (reprinted from *Studio historico-ecclesiastica: Festgabe für Prof. Luchesius Spätling OFM*, ed. I. Vázquez Janeiro [Bibliotheca Pontificii Athenaei Antoniani 19; Rome 1977] 249–282). The clergy revolted, and Archbishop Rodrigo Jiménez de Rada of Toledo virtually nullified Bishop Gerald's statutes in 1220 (cf. ibid., 215). Reflections of the Lateran canons are found in 1.1, which refers to the 'statutum pape' on interdicts (cf. Lat. IV, cc.57–58); 1.3, clergy to serve in person or appoint perpetual vicars, 'serueutur statutum domini pape' (cf. Lat. IV, c.32); 1.11, episcopal elections, 'seruetur ius scriptum' (cf. Lat. IV, c.23); 2.3, archdeacon's procurations (cf. Lat. IV, c.33); 2.11, tithes (cf. Lat. IV, c.53); 2.17, forbidding communication with excommunicates, 'seruetur constitutio domini pape Innocentii' (cf. Lat. IV, c.3); 3.1–2, tonsure and clerical dress; 5–6, forbidding gaming and drinking in taverns (cf. Lat. IV, c.16); 3.10, forbidding clergy to hear confessions of non-parishioners (cf. Lat. IV, c.21); 3.13, § 3, archpriests' visitations: small entourage, may not take hunting dogs and hawks (cf. Lat. IV, cc.33, itself citing Lat. III, c.4); 3.16, forbidding Christians to eat or drink Jewish meat or wine (cf. Lat. IV, c.67–69); 3.17, forbidding clerical involvement in sentences of blood (cf. Lat. IV, c.18); 3.21 § 3, forbidding priests to participate in clandestine marriages (cf. Lat. IV, c.51). For a full discussion of synodal activity in Spain after 1215, see José Sánchez Herrero, 'Los concilios provinciales y los sinodos diocesanos españoles 1215–1550', *Quaderni Catanesi* 3 (1981) 113–177; 4 (1982), 111–197.

227. Although four of the eight the synodal statutes issued by Bernardo II of Santiago de Compostela in 1229 were based on Lateran constitutions, the choice of decrees was highly selective: *Synodicon Hispanum*, ed. Antonio García y García, et al. (Madrid, 1981–) 1.263–266, cc.2, 6–8 (cf. Lat. IV, cc.10, 32 (bis), 30).

228. Linehan, *The Spanish Church* 20–34; García y García, 'El Concilio IV Lateranense (1215) y la Península Ibèrica'.

229. Josep M. Pons Guri, 'Constitucions conciliars Tarraconensis (1229 a 1330)', *Analecta Sacra Tarraconensia* 47 (1974) 65–128, 48 (1975) 241–363, especially 47.75–92 (Latin); cf. J. Tejada y Ramiro, *Coleccíon de cánones y de todos los concilios de la Iglesia de España y de América* (6 vols. Madrid 1861) 3.329–342 (Latin and Spanish); Manuel Guallar Perez, *Los concilios Tarraconensis celebrados en Lérida (Siglos VI–XV)* (Lérida 1975) 107–147 (Spanish).

230. Linehan, *The Spanish Church* 28. For Valladolid, cf. *Thesaurus novus anecdotorum*, ed. Edmond Martène and Ursin Durand (5 vols. Paris 1717) 4.167–174 (a monastic parallel of the Valladolid legislation). On the reaction to John of Abbeville's legislation, see Linehan, *The Spanish Church* 35–53.

231. Pons Guri, 'Constitucions conciliaris Tarraconensis' 76: 'statuta sacri concilii gene-

and ten refer to the council in one way or another.[232] The whole program was reiterated ten years later by an energetic Catalan reformer, Pedro (Pere) de Albalat, archbishop of Tarragona. His first council (1239) concluded with a general promulgation of the statutes of the general council and of the papal legate;[233] and this was supplemented in 1241 by the promulgation at Barcelona of a *Summa* on the seven sacraments, which owed much to Odo de Sully's statutes.[234] More than a generation later, Rodrigo Gonzálvez at Compostela issued a series of decrees in the Lateran spirit (1289),[235] and the legal code published by Alfonso X of Castile received the Lateran legislation through the medium of the *Decretales Gregorii noni*.[236]

---

ralis que, pro magna parte, non sine gravi periculo, sunt neglecta, pleniori diligentia de cetero precipimus observari'.

232. Pons Guri, 'Constitucions conciliars Tarraconensis' 75–92 (the numeration in Tejada y Ramiro and Perez differs slightly), cc.1–2, on holding provincial and diocesan synods (cf. Lat. IV, c. 6); c. 3, on imposition of discipline, 'Constitutio de correctione subditorum edita firmius observetur' (cf. Lat. IV, c.8); c.4, on appointment of preachers and confessors, 'quia provide statutum est in concilio generali' (cf. Lat. IV, c.10); c. 5, on the appointment of masters to teach theology and 'grammar', opens 'Cum in generali concilio pia fuerit constitutione provisum' (Lat. IV, c.11; cf. Lat. III, c.18); c.7, against clerical incontinence (cf. Lat. IV, c.14); c.8, on clerical dress and behavior, forbidding involvement in sentences of blood (cf. Lat. IV, cc.15–18); c.9, on proper maintenance of altars, safe custody of holy oil, chrism, Eucharist, 'que . . . pie et provide statuta sunt' (cf. Lat. IV, c.20); c.10, on confession, 'districte servantes constitutionem concilii generalis' (cf. Lat. IV, c.21); c.11, against plurality 'post generale consilium (sic) . . . ante concilium . . . post concilium . . . ante concilium . . . secundum statuta generale concilii . . . iuxta statutum generale concilii' (cf. Lat. IV, c.29); c.12, on clerical ordination: none to be ordained without sufficient title, unworthy to be excluded, 'amodo districtius observari per penam super hoc in generali concilio constitutam' (cf. Lat. IV, cc.26, 30, 32; Lat. III, cc. 3, 5); c.13, on consanguineous and clandestine marriages (cf. Lat. IV, cc.50–51); c.14, Jews and Saracens to pay tithes (cf. Lat. IV, c.67); c.15, Jews to wear distinctive clothing (cf. Lat. IV, c.68); c.20, against charges for sacraments, opens 'Sicut in generali statutum est concilio' (cf. Lat. IV, c.66); c.21, forbidding payment for ordination (cf. Lat. IV, c.63); c.22, ordering general chapters, 'secundum formam generalis concilii' (cf. Lat. IV, c.12); cc.24–25, against improper dress for clerics and monks (cf. Lat. IV, c.16); c.30, if parishes not filled within the legal term, bishop may appoint (cf. Lat. IV, c.23); c.32, against infringement of rights of parish churches (cf. Lat. IV, c.56). Two canons refer back to Alexander III and the Third Lateran Council (1179): c.18, against abuse of lay patronage, 'sicut ex constitutionibus tam Lateranensis quam domini Alexandri noscitur institutum' (cf. Lat. III, c.14); c.35, forbidding the sale of military supplies to the Saracens, 'Constitutionem domini Alexandri ad memoriam reducentes' (cf. Lat. III, c.24).

233. Linehan, *The Spanish Church* 54–82; Pons Guri, 'Constitucions concilars Tarraconensis' 34–104, especially 104, c.12: 'dominus archiepiscopus precepit omnes constitutiones generalis concilii domini Innocentii papae et constitutiones domini Sabinensis Apostolicae Sedis legati [= John of Abbeville] et presentes constitutiones . . . per totam suam provinciam inviolabiliter observari'; cf. Tejada y Ramiro, *Coleccion de cánones* 1.349–361; 3 (1859), 29–32, especially 32. For his subsequent councils at Valencia (1240), Tarragona (1242, 1243, 1244, 1246, 1247, 1250), see Pons Guri, 'Constitucions concilars Tarraconensis' 104–128, 241–249.

234. Linehan, *The Spanish Church* 74–76; for the text, see idem, 'Pedro de Albalat, arzobispo de Tarragona y su "summa septem sacramentorum"' (Hispania Sacra 22; Barcelona-Madrid 1969) 16–30 (reprinted, *Spanish Church and Society 1150–1300* [London 1983]) no. 3.

235. *Synodicon Hispanum* 1.272–280.

236. J. Giménez y Martínez de Carvajal, 'San Raimundo de Peñafort y la Siete Partidas

For Hungary and Poland, the picture is much less clear. No fewer than three archbishops and eight bishops from Hungary and Dalmatia (then under Hungarian rule) attended the council,[237] but there is little evidence of reforming activity on their return. At least five Hungarian councils, provincial and legatine, have been recorded in some fashion for the period 1222 to 1276, with varying degrees of accuracy, but no legislation has survived.[238] A series of grave crises disrupted the normal exercise of ecclesiastical authority for much of the thirteenth century. The civil wars and political upheavals which followed the death of Béla III in 1196 disturbed the kingdom until 1235; but even worse was to follow. Hungary suffered terrible devastation, first in the Mongol invasion of 1241–1243 and then during the virtual anarchy under Ladislaus IV (1272–1290). Civil upheaval and unrestrained looting and destruction were scarcely conducive to ecclesiastical reform. The first evidence of the introduction of some of the Lateran decrees comes from the legatine council held in Buda in 1279 by the papal legate, Bishop Philip of Fermo.[239] In this very important legislation, which combined disciplinary decrees with liturgical and doctrinal instructions on the sacraments and basic Catholic belief,[240] direct dependence on the Lateran constitutions can be argued for the decrees against cleri-

---

de Alfonso X el Sabio', *Anthologica Annua* 3 (1955) 201–238 (cited by García y García, *Constitutiones* 4, n. 4).

237. The archbishop of Esztergom (Gran), and the bishops of Eger, Györ, Veszprém, Vác; the archbishop of Kolocsa and the bishops of Nagyvárad and Csanád; the archbishop of Spalato (Split) and the bishops of Hvar (Lésina) and Nona (Nin): Hefele and Leclercq, *Histoire des conciles* 5.2 p. 1731; cf. Foreville, *Latran I, II, III et Latran IV* 393.

238. Kalocsa (1122, before 1225); Esztergom (1252 [not 1256]); Buda (1263). The alleged council of Esztergom of 1276 is a figment. For these councils and supposed councils, see Lothar Waldmüller, *Die Synoden in Dalmatien, Kroatien und Ungarn: Von der Völkerwanderug bis zum Ende der Arpaden (1311)* (Paderborn 1987) 173–187, which corrects Gabriel Adriányi, 'Die ungarischen Synoden', AHC 8 (1976) 541–575, especially 544.

239. 'In castro Budensi, vesprimiensis Diocesis' (ed. Hube 72). Discussion of this council is complicated by the transmission of two versions of its decrees. The full text, set out in 128 *capitula*, derived from manuscripts in Warsaw and St. Petersburg, is available only in the now very rare *Antiquissimae consitutiones synodales provinciae gneznensis maxima ex parte nunc primum e codicibus manu scriptis typis mandatae*, ed. Romuald Hube (Petropoli: Cancellariae imperatoris,1856) 72–164, whereas the most widely available text, *Sacra concilia ecclesiae romano-catholicae in regno Hungariae celebrata ab anno Christi MXVI usque ad annum MDCCXXX-IV*, ed. C. Péterffy, S.J. (2 vols. Posony 1741–1742 and Vienna 1742) 1.106–126; Mansi, 24.269–308; Hefele and Leclercq, *Histoire des conciles* 6.1 pp. 247–257, breaks off at the beginning of c.75 (which it numbers 69), provides different rubrics and different numeration, and lacks cc.76–128 and the greater part of c.75. In the following analysis, the Budan decrees are cited according to Hube's edition, with the alternative numeration in square brackets. For the context, see Michael Szvorény, *Synopsis critico-historica decretorum synodalium pro ecclesia hungaro-catholica editorum* (Veszprém 1807) 32–45; Waldmüller, *Die Synoden in Dalmatien* 188–200; Adriányi, 'Die ungarischen Synoden' 545–546; cf. (with caution) Z.J. Kosztolnyik, 'Rome and the Church in Hungary in 1279: The Synod of Buda', AHC 22 (1990) 68–85, especially 76–81.

240. Hube, *Antiquissimae constitutiones synodales* cc.83, 88 (seven sacraments); cc.84–86

cal involvement in commerce, gaming, and hunting (c.9 [8]) and sentences of blood (c.10 [9]), and in the canon ordering the proper maintenance of chrism, holy oil, and the Eucharist (c.24 [21]). Moreover, a further four enactments referred specifically to 'the council', meaning the Fourth Lateran Council. The ordinance forbidding both the display of relics outside their shrines and the unlicensed recognition of new relics (c.28 [27]) invokes its authority ('In Concilio statutum est'); similarly, the decrees prohibiting the storage of private property in churches (c.43 [41]), instructing physicians to ensure the summons of priests to attend the dying (c.97 [-]), and prohibiting the imposition of fees for burials, weddings, and other sacraments (c.123 [-]), all cite the council ('In Concilio prohibetur', 'Statutum est in concilio'). Verbal dependence on the text of Lateran IV is evident in all seven cases.[241] For the rest of the code, however, the derivation is much less certain. The Budan decrees relating to clerical and monastic dress and discipline, as well as restrictions on Jews, reflect Lateran provisions, but without specific or significant verbal echoes, and the influence of other conciliar sources (Avignon 1209, Rouen 1231, Vienna 1267, and even the first council of Esztergom [now dated 1095?]) has been proposed.[242]

The political situation in Poland was scarcely better, as the disintegration of the kingdom into territorial principalities continued through the thirteenth century, exacerbated by the terror and destruction of the Mongol invasion; would-be reformers had a difficult task in the face of powerful secular interests.[243] The Polish contingent to the Lateran council

(Incarnation, Ascension, descent of the Holy Spirit); cc.89–96, 98 (baptism, confirmation, penance); cc.99–117 (Eucharist, care of altars, etc.) cc.118–120 (matrimony).

241. Ibid., c.9 [8], 'Clerici ... diligenter' (cf. Lat. IV, c.16, 'Clerici ... diligenter'); c.10 [9], 'Nullus clericus sententiam sanguinis ... intersit. Nec quisquam ... destinandas, nec illam partem chirugiae ... inducit' (cf. Lat. IV, c.18, 'Sententiam sanguinis ... intersit'; 'nec quisquam ... destinandas', 'nec illam chirurgiae artem ... impendat'); c.24 [21], 'Statuimus ut ... extendi', 'Si vero is ... puniatur' (cf. Lat. IV, c.20, 'Statuimus ut ... extendi', 'Si vero is ... ultioni'); c.28 [27], 'ut a modo ... approbatae' (cf. Lat. IV, c.62, 'ut a modo ... approbatae');

c.43 [41], 'ne supellectilia sacerdotis ... portentur' (cf. Lat. IV, c.19, 'ne huiusmodi supellectilia ... reportentur'); c.97 [-], 'districte injunctum medicis corporum...procedatur. Ceterum autem ... convertatur' (cf. Lat. IV, c.22, 'districte praecipimus medicis corporum...procedatur ... Ceterum ... convertatur'); and c.123 [-] is a verbal rearrangement of Lat. IV, c.66.

242. Waldmüller, *Die Synoden in Dalmatien* 194–195; Kosztolnyik, 'Rome and the Church in Hungary' 76–80. For texts of these councils, see Mansi, 22.783–794 (Avignon); Bessin, *Concilia Rothomagensis* 1.134–138; cf. Mansi, 23.213–222 (Rouen); Mansi, 23.1167–1178 (Vienna); Péterffy, *Sacra concilia* 1.53–62; Mansi, 21.97–112 (Esztergom I). For the date and legislation of Esztergom I, see Waldmüller, *Die Synoden in Dalmatien* 127–133.

243. Adam Vetulani, 'La pénétration du droit des Décrétales dans l'Église Polonaise au XIIIème siècle', *Acta Congressus Iuridici Internationalis VII saeculo a decretalibus Gregorii IX et XIV a codice Iustiniano promulgatis Romae 12–17 Novembris 1934* (5 vols. Rome 1935–1937) 3.385–405,

included the reformer Henry Kietlicz, archbishop of Gniezno, and four suffragans.[244] On his return, Archbishop Henry issued a general statute against incontinent clergy in 1218[245] and appointed two clerks to investigate clerical and episcopal misdemeanors;[246] Archbishop Pełka (Fulk, 1235–58) reiterated similar strictures in councils held in 1233, 1244 and 1257,[247] but the intervention of papal legates was required to introduce the Lateran decrees to any significant extent. Jacques Pantaléon, archdeacon of Liège (later Pope Urban IV) held a legatine council in Wrocław (for the province of Gniezno) in 1248. In addition to matters of local concern, many of the chapters echoed Lateran constitutions. The decree against lay abuse of ecclesiastical persons and property (c.11 [1]), and the regulations about tithe-payment (cc.15–17 [5–7]), are local applications of the general law; so, too, the injunction that parish priests should not bless the marriages of persons from another parish (23 [16]), and the prescriptions on the triple reading of the banns of marriage (c.24 [17]), the safe custody of baptismal water, Eucharist, and holy oil (c.27 [21]), and archdeacons' visitations (c.28 [22]).[248] Eighteen years later (1266–67), another legate, Cardinal Guido of S. Lorenzo in Lucina, visited Scandinavia and the provinces of Bremen, Magdeburg, Salzburg, and Gniezno, publishing decrees for each.[249] The Gniezno decrees on lay abuse (cc.2, 5), consanguin-

---

especially 389–394 (reprinted in *Institutions de l'Église et canonistes au Moyen Age: De Strasbourg à Cracovie*, ed. Wacław Uruszczak [Aldershot 1990] no. 2).

244. The bishops of Kraków, Wrocław, Włocławek, and Lebus: Hefele and Leclercq, *Histoire des conciles* 5.2 p. 1731; cf. Foreville, *Latran I, II, III et Latran IV* 393.

245. Hefele and Leclercq, *Histoire des conciles* 5.2 p. 1428.

246. *Concilia Poloniae*, ed. Jakub Sawicki, vi (Warsaw 1952) 8.

247. Ignacy Subera, *Synody Prowincjonalne Arcybiskupów Gnieźnieńskich* (Warsaw 1971) 41–45; cf. Hube, *Antiquissimae constitutiones synodales* 1–13; Vetulani, 'La pénétration' 395–396.

248. Hube, *Antiquissimae constitutiones synodales* 14–49 (based on early manuscripts in Warsaw and St. Petersburg), which combines two sequences of statutes in a single series numbered 1–31. Canons 1–10 are principally concerned with the cathedral of Gniezno; nos. 11–31 concern the province. Hefele and Leclerq (*Histoire des Conciles* 5.2 pp. 1707–1709, nos. 1–26) provides a summary of a later, variant and extended, version of the provincial decrees, based on Mortimer de Montbach, *Statuta synodalia dioecana sanctae ecclesiae Wratislaviensis* (Wrocław 1855) 307–310 (not available to me). In the following analysis, the legate's decrees are cited according to Hube's edition, with the alternative numeration in square brackets. C.11 [1] (cf. Lat. IV, cc.44–45), cc.15–17 [5–7] (cf. Lat. IV, cc.53–54), c.23 [16] (cf. Lat. IV, c.51), c.24 [17] (cf. Lat. IV, c.50), c.27 [21] (cf. Lat. IV, c.20), c.28 [22] (cf. Lat. IV, c.33). For the context, see Johann Heyne, *Dokumentierte Geschichte des Bistums und Hochstifts Breslau* (3 vols. Breslau 1860; reprinted Aalen 1969) 1.364–371; Vetulani, 'La pénétration' 397–398. For the importance of Jacques Pantaléon's legation for the development of legal institutions in the Polish and Hungarian churches, see Péter Erdő, 'Diritto canonico e cultura giuridica europea (con particulare riguardo ai "Paesi dell'Est"): I tribunali ecclesiastici medievali', *Il Diritto Ecclesiastico* 3 (1995) 687–705 at pp. 689–690.

249. Mansi, 23.1155–1162 (Bremen) 1161–1166 (Magdeburg) 1167–1178 (Vienna, for Salzburg); Hube, *Antiquissimae constitutiones synodales* 56–71 (Gniezno).

eous marriages (c.3), plurality (c.4), tithes (c.6), clerical litigation before lay judges (c.7), visitation and procurations (cc.8–9), annual councils (c.11), and association with Jews (cc.10, 12–14) reflect the legislation of the Fourth Lateran Council, but without citation or verbal dependence.[250] Of even greater importance, however, was the comprehensive code for Hungary and Poland, discussed above, published at Buda in 1279 by the papal legate Bishop Philip of Fermo. Together with the earlier directives of Jacques Pantaléon and Guido of S. Lorenzo, Philip's summary of current legislation formed the basis of the synodal statutes issued six years later (1285) by Archbishop Jacob Swinka of Gniezno and so passed into the law of the Polish church.[251]

Although the effective application of the decrees varied according to local conditions and customs, decrees of the Fourth Lateran Council passed into the general tradition of local synodal legislation throughout the West more than those of any other medieval council and influenced the compilation of manuals for priestly instruction.[252] The clear directives for confession, communion, and marriage, for the proper care of churches and sacred objects, and the rules for elections, the establishment of the majority principle in ecclesiastical corporations, the precise definition of contentious theological questions (the Trinity, the Eucharist, the natures of Christ), the reinforcement of episcopal authority, the clarification of judicial procedure, including the requirement that all ecclesiastical courts must keep a full written record of their proceedings, were all of permanent effect for the rest of the Middle Ages, and beyond.

---

250. Gniezno, cc.2, 5 (cf. Lat. IV, cc.43–45); c.3 (cf. Lat. IV, c.50); c.4 (cf. Lat. IV, c.29); c.6 (cf. Lat. IV, cc.53–56); c.7 (cf. Lat. IV, c.40); cc.8–9 (cf. Lat. IV, cc. 6, 33); c.11 (cf. Lat. IV, c.6); cc.10, 12–14 (cf. Lat. IV, cc.67–70). Cf. T. Silnicki, *Kardynał legat Gwido, jego synod wrocławski z r. 1267 I statuty tegoż synodu* (Lwów 1930); Adam Vetulani, 'The Jews in Medieval Poland', trans. M. Wajsblum *The Jewish Journal of Sociology* 4 (1962) 274–294 at 278, 285–289. Guido's ordinances were cited by Bishop Thomas of Wroclaw in 1279: Mansi, 24.327–330, 'iuxta tenorem Constitutionis (bonae memoriae) domini Guidonis Suaden. quondam in partibus Poloniae Apostolicae sedis Legati', (on clerical continence); 'iuxta tenorem Constitutionis domini Guidonis praefati', (on lay abuse); cf. Gniezno 1266 (ed. Hube) cc.2, 5–6; Vienna 1267 (for the province of Salzburg: Mansi, 23.1167–1178), cc.1–5, 7.

251. Hube, *Antiquissimae consitutiones synodales* 165–180 citing the decrees of the legates Philip and Guido against incontinent clergy (c.14). See above, at nn. 239–241 and 248–249; cf. Vetulani, 'La pénétration' 399–400; Subera, *Synody Prowincjonalne* 57–63.

252. L. Boyle, 'The Fourth Lateran Council and Manuals of Popular Instruction', *The Popular Literature of Medieval England* (Tennessee Studies in Literature 28; Knoxville 1985) 30–43.

II

The Fourth Lateran Council and the Canonists

A. García y García

The Fourth Lateran Council was celebrated in the Lateran Basilica, from the eleventh to the thirtieth of November 1215; the major fruits of this council were its 71 constitutions, which constitute the single most substantial collection of legislation put together by medieval popes for the reform of the Church and society of the time.[1] The Fourth Lateran Council, the most important of the five Lateran councils, is also more interesting to the historian of canon law than any of the other general councils of the Middle Ages. All of its constitutions passed into the *Compilatio quarta*, with the exception of c.42 and c.71, and into the *Liber extra*, except for c.42, c.49, and a large part of c.71. These constitutions were still being cited in the notes to 228 canons in the *Codex iuris canonici* of 1917, except for c.11, 22, 31, 43, 55, and 67–71, which dealt with issues no longer pertinent in 1917.[2]

It is very likely that preparations for these constitutions began from the time that Pope Innocent III summoned the Fourth Lateran Council, on

---

1. *Constitutiones Concilii quarti Lateranensis una cum Commentariis glossatorum*, ed. Antonio García y García (MIC, Series A: Corpus Glossatorum 2; Città del Vaticano 1981) 1–172, which contains a study and a critical edition.
2. Ibid. 494, which includes a table of equivalences.

the nineteenth of April 1213. In fact, these constitutions collected or recapitulated reform measures adopted by Innocent III throughout his papacy (1198–1216), as revealed by the fragments that are taken word for word from letters issued by this pope.[3] The idea of summoning the council began to gestate practically from the moment that Innocent ascended to the papal throne.[4]

The author of these constitutions was Innocent III himself, aided by his curia. Given the condition of the text as we know it, it is impossible to detect the hand of a particular canonist in the composition of the canons.

The major sources used by Innocent in these constitutions are the *Decretum* of Gratian and the first three Lateran councils of 1123, 1139, and 1179, as well as several provincial councils, such as the Council of Verona in 1184—an extensive passage of which is reproduced word for word in Fourth Lateran Council, c.3—and the Third Council of Toledo, c.69. The presence of councils from antiquity has also been observed among their sources: the First Council of Constantinople c.3 is reflected in c.5, and regulations from the First Council of Nicaea, c.5, Chalcedon, c.19, and the Second Council of Nicaea, c. 6 are repeated in the Fourth Lateran Council, c. 6. Norms taken from the First Council of Constantinople, c.6 and Chalcedon, c.21 are incorporated into the Fourth Lateran Council, c. 8.

The total number of constitutions from the Fourth Lateran Council has varied in the historiography, but the manuscript tradition raises the definitive number to 71 constitutions or chapters, with the unusual circumstance that c.71 had two recensions: the first circulated during the Council and the second was promulgated after it (December 14, 1215). The second recension of the canon is contained in the manuscripts and editions of the Fourth Lateran Council.[5]

The order in which the constitutions are arranged is not very systematic. It seems to adhere to the classic division of the five books that the canonists used for canonical collections by 1215—although this structure is very broadly constructed—a division introduced into canonical collections by Bernard of Pavia, by the following verse: iudex, iudicia, clerus, connubia, crimen. This division is made explicit in one of the manuscripts of the Fourth Lateran Council and in the *Casus Parisienses* as well.[6] In any case, the distribution of the constitutions within this five-part arrangement is far from perfect.

---

3. See the display of sources in García y García, *Constitutiones*.
4. Ibid. 169–186.
5. Ibid. 117–120, where the two versions are compared.
6. Florence, Biblioteca Mediceo-Laurenziana, S. Croce III$^{sin.}$6 fol. 254ra–61vb. See the description in García y García, *Constitutiones* 338ff.

The manuscript tradition of the Lateran constitutions consists of sixty-six manuscripts, and we know of fourteen others that are now either lost or in locations unknown to us.[7]

The constitutions were included in the papal register with a quasi-offical note ('Anno ab incarnatione Domini... ingens adfuit multitudo'), along with the list of participants in the Fourth Lateran Council.[8] Although it is generally true that codices of a work are not better simply because they are older, in the case of the Lateran constitutions, the best texts are certainly found among the oldest, doubtless because they are direct copies of the papal register—or because they are closer to the original contents of that register. In fact, the most recent edition (1981) is based on 20 codices selected according to these criteria.

The first printed edition of the Fourth Lateran Council (Cr^1) appeared in Cologne in 1539, prepared by Petrus Crabbe on the basis of a codex that is now lost. A second edition was published in Cologne in 1551 (Cr^2).

Both Surius in 1567 (Su) and Binius in 1606 (Bn^1) published copies of Crabbe's edition. The small variants that are recorded are simple 'lapsus calami'.

The Roman edition of 1612 (Er) basically follows that of Crabbe, introducing several variants based on Vatican codices, which were not the best of the surviving versions. Even so, this edition provides some improvement over the text of Crabbe—and was obviously better than those offered by the other editors we have just mentioned.

The text of the Roman edition was reproduced in the second edition of Binius in 1618 (Bn^2) and in the second royal Parisian version of the councils completed by Labbe-Cossart (Ep) in 1671, the main improvement of which was that it included the Greek text of the Fourth Lateran Council found in a Parisian codex of the fourteenth century. The latter had suffered various kinds of mutilation due to deterioration. The variants from a codex listed by D'Achery, which has not survived, were added to the Latin text. The text by Labbe-Cossart was reproduced by Hardouin in 1714 (Hr), by Nicolas Coleti in 1730 (Cl), and by Mansi in 1778 (Mi).

Claudio Leonardi's recent edition adopts the text of the Roman edition, and, in the apparatus of manuscript variants, includes all the variants that have appeared up to now in the different editions.[9] At times these are introduced into the text without any indication of their source. In a brief

---

7. Cf. García y García, *Constitutiones* 18–32 and 125–35.
8. J. Werner, 'Die Teilnehmerliste des Laterankonzils von Jahre 1215', *Neues Archiv der Gesellschaft für ältere Deutsche Geschichtskunde* 31 (1906) 575–593.
9. See COD 227–271.

but substantial introduction, Leonardi describes how modern scholarship has contributed to this subject, alluding to various new codices that have been taken into account in my 1981 edition and study.

The preparatory stages of the 1981 edition, which appeared in *Monumenta iuris canonici*, included a comparison of the variants in the 64 codices and the editions. The final, published version was edited on the basis of the 20 codices that were considered the best. The apparatus of manuscript variants also took into account the most difficult passages in Crabbe's 'editio princeps' and the Roman edition, as well as *Compilatio quarta* and the *Liber extra*.

No conciliar text of the Middle Ages made such an impact on the canonists as the Lateran constitutions of 1215. An indication of this is the quantity and quality of the commentaries that address these constitutions—both directly, as the commentaries on the conciliar version of the constitutions, and in an indirect way, once the texts were incorporated into the *Compilatio quarta* or into Gregory IX's *Liber extra*. We will consider the direct commentaries on the Lateran constitutions in greater detail below and will mention in passing those that dealt with them in an indirect form, written by canonists who discussed the *Compilatio quarta* and the *Decretals of Gregory IX*.

Johannes Teutonicus wrote an apparatus of glosses, the existence of which has been recognized since Schulte provided information about it.[10] Today, this apparatus is known in the following manuscripts:[11]

Budapest, Orságos Szénchényi Könyavtár (National Library), fol. 181r–182r (containing only a fragment of c. 1–5 and 71).

Bordeaux, Bibliothèque municipale, 400 fol. 238ra–247rb.

Florence, Biblioteca Medaceo-Laurenziana, Croce, IV$^{sin.}$2 fol. 254r–264v (basic text for the 1981 edition).

Graz, Universitätsbibliothek, 138 fol. 233r–246v.

Kassel, Landesbibliothek, Jur. 11 fol. 110r–123r.

The 1981 edition also took into account the indirect testimony of this apparatus contained in Johannes Teutonicus' apparatus to the *Compilatio quarta*, which, as I will explain below, reproduced a great deal of the commentary on the Fourth Lateran Council constitutions.[12]

---

10. Schulte, QL 1. 256.
11. Cf. García y García, *Constitutiones* 175–184 (a study) and 185–270 (the critical edition).
12. Edited in Antonio Agustín, *Antiquae Decretalium Collectiones comentariis et emendationi-*

As we have just suggested, there is a relationship of interdependence between Johannes Teutonicus' apparatus to the Fourth Lateran Council and his apparatus to the *Compilatio quarta*. Gillmann knew only the Kassel manuscript of apparatus to the constitutions of the Council and Johannes' apparatus to *Compilatio quarta*.[13] From this, Gillmann concluded that the apparatus to the constitutions was nothing more than an extract from Teutonicus' apparatus to the *Compilatio quarta*. With a fuller knowledge of the manuscript tradition of both apparatus, Stephan Kuttner maintained the chronological priority of the apparatus to the Fourth Lateran Council over the apparatus to the *Compilatio quarta*—in other words, the opposite of what Gillmann had affirmed.[14] The scholarly consensus that has emerged from the works completed for the 1981 edition has supported Kuttner's rather than Gillmann's thesis. Johannes Teutonicus used his apparatus to the Fourth Lateran Council in some chapters that became part of the *Compilatio quarta*, with certain changes. Aside from the many passages that are literally the same, there are, more importantly, glosses and passages that are absent from the apparatus to the Council. In spite of this, the apparatus to the *Compilatio quarta* constitutes indirect but useful evidence that was used in determining which text of the apparatus to the Fourth Lateran Council should be included in the 1981 edition. Antonio Agustín's sixteenth-century edition was not a critical one, as is revealed by the fact that there are numerous variants found in his edition and not in the manuscripts, but even so, it proved to be a source of useful references when it came to assembling the edition of commentaries on the Fourth Lateran Council.

Johannes Teutonicus' apparatus to the Fourth Lateran Council was composed very shortly after the Council's conclusion, on November 30, 1215. Teutonicus' apparatus to the *Compilatio quarta* was redacted at the same time that he was working on the constitutions and before the death of Pope Innocent III (July 16, 1216). It seems likely that Johannes Teutonicus' apparatus to the Fourth Lateran Council and that of Vincentius His-

---

bus illustratae, quibus acceserunt huic novae editioni Iacobi Cuiacii. . . et aliorum notae (Paris 1621) 797–843. On the first edition of Agustín's edition, printed at Lérida in 1576, see S. Kuttner, 'Antonio Agustín's Edition of the Compilationes antiquae', BMCL 7 (1977) 1–14.

13. F. Gillmann, 'Hat Johannes Teutonicus zu den Konstitutionen des 4. Laterankonzils (1215) als solchen einen apparat verfasst?' AKKR 127 (1937), 436–452, reprinted in H. Müller and R. Weigand, *Gesammelte Schriften zur klassischen Kanonistik von Franz Gillmann*, 3: *Schriften zu den Dekretalisten* (Forschungen zur Kirchenrechts-Wissenschaft 5.3; Würzburg 1993).

14. S. Kuttner, 'Johannes Teutonicus, das vierte Laterankonzil und die Compilatio quarta', *Miscellanea Giovanni Mercati* (Studi e Testi 125; Vatican City 1946) 5.608–634, reprinted in *Medieval Councils, Decretals and Collections of Canon Law* (London 1980).

panus were written at more or less the same time, although neither of these authors gives any sign of knowledge of the apparatus of the other.

Johannes Teutonicus' apparatus to the Fourth Lateran Council exercised a major influence on the Ordinary Gloss to the *Compilatio quarta* (which he wrote) and on Bernardus Parmensis' *Ordinary Gloss* of Gregory IX's *Liber extra*. When Bernardus Parmensis glossed the constitutions that Raymond of Peñafort had inserted into the *Liber extra*, he incorporated numerous passages from Teutonicus' glosses, more or less literally. Consequently, many of Teutonicus' glosses on the constitutions passed word for word into the *Ordinary Gloss* to Gregory IX's compilation

The basic text of the 1981 edition was taken from manuscript Florence, Biblioteca Mediceo-Laurenziana, Croce, IV$^{sin.}$2, which is more correct and closer to the original than the other manuscripts.

Vincentius Hispanus wrote a commentary on the *Constitutiones* shortly after the end of the Council.[15] The great sixteenth-century historian of canon law, Antonio Agustín, was the first to write about Vincentius' apparatus to the Fourth Lateran constitutions, although he does not seem to have known it directly, but learned of it from Vincentius' other works.[16] Gillmann studied it in the Bamberg manuscript and devoted a full study to it.[17] Stephan Kuttner discovered the other manuscripts, with the exception of the Charleville manuscript, which I found and which became the basic text of the 1981 edition.

The codices we know today are as follows:

Admont, Stiftsbibliothek, 22 fol. 245r–246r, which is the only fragment that partially contains cc. 69–71 of the second recension of this apparatus.

Bamberg, Staatsbibliothek, can. 20 (P.II.7) fol. 63v–70v.

Charleville, Bibliothèque municipale, 205 fol. 80v–99r (basic text).

Florence, Biblioteca Mediceo-Laurenziana, S. Croce IV$^{sin.}$2 fol. 238r–252v.

London, Lambeth Palace Library, 139 fol. 168–176.

Rouen, Bibliothèque municipale, 706 fol. 255r–268v.

---

15. Cf. García y García, *Constitutiones* 273–285 (study) and 286–384 (critical edition).
16. J. Ochoa, *Vincentius Hispanus, canonista bolonés del s. XIII* (Rome-Madrid 1960) 130 n.61.
17. Bamberg, Staatsbibliothek, Can. 20 (P. II. 7). Franz Gillmann, 'Der Kommentar des Vincentius Hispanus zu den Kanones des vierten Laterankonzils (1215)'. Mainz 1929. Erweiterter Sonderdruck (with an appendix) von: AKKR 109 (1929) 223–274, reprinted in H. Müller and R. Weigand, *Gesammelte Schriften zur klassischen Kanonistik von Franz Gillmann*, 3: *Schriften zu den Dekretalisten* (Forschungen zur Kirchenrechts-Wissenschaft 5.3; Würzburg 1993).

In the 1981 edition, the *Lectura* of Vincentius Hispanus to the *Liber extra* was also used as an indirect testimony of the text of this apparatus using a manuscript from the library of the University of Salamanca, 2186 fol. 1r–233v.

Vincentius Hispanus' apparatus to the Fourth Lateran constitutions survives in two recensions: the first, a very brief one contained in London, Lambeth Palace Library, 139, and the second in the remaining codices. The first recension contains fewer glosses, and these are also generally much shorter. The text and critical apparatus of the 1981 critical edition specify which parts belong to the first and which belong to the second recensions. Curiously, the Lambeth Palace manuscript not only contains a shorter recension of the apparatus but also abbreviates the Lateran constitutions. This could raise doubts about whether this first recension is an abridged version of the second, just as the text of the constitutions is abbreviated from a complete text. But this is not the case here, since the first recension of the apparatus omits fragments of constitutions that are not exactly the same as those omitted in the Lambeth Palace manuscript. Moreover, fragments of glosses have been redacted in different ways in these two recensions.

As far as this work's date of composition is concerned, we believe that it corresponds to the end of Vincentius Hispanus' stay in Bologna—more precisely, to the time between the closing of the Council (November 30, 1215), and Vincentius' departure for his homeland of Portugal, where he appears to be working in the second half of 1217.[18]

Although one scholar has affirmed that 'não ser absolutamente certa a compsição de este comentário em Bolonha'[19] ('it is not absolutely certain that he composed this commentary in Bologna'),[20] I believe that we can satisfactorily determine that the date of this apparatus corresponds to Vincentius' Italian period, for the following reasons: First, it is not logical to suppose that Vincentius set about writing an apparatus to the Council after the second half of 1217, when *Compilatio quarta* had already appeared, since at that point it would seem reasonable for him to compose an apparatus for the new compilation that included the constitutions but not the constitutions alone. Second, Damasus uses Vincentius' apparatus in

---

18. Cf. A. Domingues de Sousa Costa, *Mestre Silvestre e Mestre Vicente, juristas da contenda entre D. Alfonso II e suas irmãs* (Braga 1963).

19. Ibid. 496.

20. Cf. J. Ochoa, *Vincentius Hispanus* 41–43 and 132; he believes that Vincentius Hispanus left Italy in 1220 or a little thereafter. But Sousa Costa, *Mestre Sivestre e Mestre Vincente* 480–482, 483, and 494–498 demonstrates, with convincing arguments, that Vincentius appears to be working in Portugal during the second half of 1217.

its second recension, a fact that would be very difficult to explain if we assumed that Vincentius wrote it in Portugal. Moreover, Damasus' apparatus was written at the same time as Johannes Teutonicus', since they did not know each other's work. Third, the known documentation shows that Vincentius was completely dedicated to the task of governing the diocese of Lisbon. In such a situation, it does not seem likely that he would find the time necessary to devote himself to writing, as he will later on when he redacts his *Lectura* on the *Liber extra*. Finally, according to Gillmann, Vincentius' apparatus to the Council (referring to the second recension, since the first was not known to Gillmann) constitutes one of the sources for the *Ordinary Gloss* to the *Compilatio quarta*.[21] Today it is commonly agreed that Teutonicus glossed *Compilatio quarta* at the same time that he assembled the compilation.[22]

For all these reasons it seems likely that Vincentius Hispanus' apparatus to the Fourth Lateran Constitutions was redacted in Italy and not after the author's return to Portugal. It also seems certain that both recensions of the apparatus to the Fourth Lateran Constitutions by Vincentius Hispanus were redacted before *Compilatio quarta* appeared.

Vincentius' apparatus on the Constitutions shaped his own *Lectura* on the Decretals of Gregory IX, and later the commentaries of Johannes Andreae (*Novella*), and Hostiensis' *Lectura* on the Decretals of Gregory IX. The *Ordinary Gloss* on the *Liber extra* frequently includes glosses from this apparatus by Vincentius Hispanus as well. It is not yet clear whether these were taken directly or indirectly, that is, whether they came from Vincentius Hispanus' own apparatus to the Fourth Lateran Constitutions or from his later commentaries that incorporated passages from it.

Damasus Hungarus was the last canonist who wrote an apparatus of glosses on the Fourth Lateran Constitutions.[23] Stephan Kuttner guessed of its existence in 1934 when he discovered a passage in Damasus' *Summa titulorum* indicating that the jurist had written on the Constitutions. Damasus had referred to a constitution with the words 'ut ibi notaui', a piece of evidence that suggested an apparatus.[24] In 1937, Kuttner discovered an anonymous apparatus in, as it has turned out, the only codex which has survived, Biblioteca Mediceo-Laurenziana in Florence, S. Croce III$^{\text{sin.}}$6 fol. 86r–107v.[25]

21. F. Gillmann, 'Der Kommentar' 266–267.
22. Cf. for example A. M. Stickler, 'Johannes Teutonicus (Zemecke)', NCE 7.998; S. Kuttner, 'Johannes Teutonicus', *Neue deutsche Biographie* 10 (1974) 572.
23. Cf, García y García, *Constitutiones* 385–416 (study) and 417–458 (critical edition).
24. S. Kuttner, *Repertorium* 369–370; idem, 'Johannes Teutonicus' 618; idem, 'An Interim Checklist of Manuscripts (III)', *Traditio* 13 (1957) 157–158; cf. also *Traditio* 13 (1957) 468.
25. Cf. description in García y García, *Constitutiones* 388.

This apparatus begins with the words, 'Si persistant in contumacia'. In 1962, its authorship was attributed to Damasus Hungarus because of the interrelation between this apparatus and those that Damasus wrote to the first three *Compilationes antiquae*. They are found in Paris and Bamberg manuscripts.[26] In the entire apparatus there are only twenty-three glosses with corresponding sigla. Of these, sixteen bear the siglum of Vincentius Hispanus, and five carry that of Damasus.

The glosses attributed to Vincentius Hispanus are cited just as they are in his apparatus, except for one that is missing. But it is impossible to suppose that this apparatus could have been written by Vincentius Hispanus, because we already know his apparatus in two recensions. Indeed, we can tell that it was not Vincentius who introduced his glosses into this new apparatus, but someone else, because in one case Vincentius' gloss is refuted by the following words after it has been introduced: '. . . falsum dicit'. And in a second case, a gloss by Vincentius is followed by the words: 'Soluit magister Vincentius . . . Hec solutio non ualet'. Moreover, there are glosses attributed to Vincentius that then continue on after his siglum for several lines, indicating a hand distinct from that of Vincentius, completing or shaping his thought.

If we examine the apparatus to the Fourth Lateran Constitutions that begins, 'Si persistant in contumacia', we notice that its author frequently quoted his own commentaries to the first three *Compilationes antiquae*. These third person citations can be found to be first-person borrowings in Damasus' apparatus to these compilations. Some comments in this commentary are repeated in his *Quaestiones*.

If Damasus proves to be the author of first- and third-person citations referring to other works in the apparatus to the constitutions, his authorship of the apparatus 'Si persistant in contumacia' follows, not only of the five glosses that bear his siglum, but also of the many glosses that bear no siglum at all. Although this matter has nothing to do with the issue that concerns us here, these citations also reveal that Damasus wrote an apparatus to *Compilatio tertia*, despite the fact that this apparatus has not yet been located in any codex.

There is no explicit evidence in Damasus' apparatus to the Fourth Lateran Constitutions that would allow us to fix its date of composition. Through *Compilatio quarta*, which was finally accepted in Bologna ca. 1220, it is possible to establish a 'terminus ante quem'. The earliest possible date is obviously the end of the Fourth Lateran Council (November 30, 1215).

---

26. García y García, 'Observaciones'.

But we must still place Vincentius Hispanus' apparatus in its two recensions between the end of the Council and the composition of Damasus' apparatus to the Fourth Lateran Constitutions. Vincentius' 18 glosses in Damasus' apparatus, were taken from the second recension and not from the first. Much the same thing happens with the forty-odd glosses without sigla that also can be found in Vincentius' second recension, which Damasus inserted into his apparatus. These glosses do not generally appear in Vincentius Hispanus' first recension.[27]

My 1981 edition is based on the Florence manuscript. An anonymous canonist composed a 'casus' for the Constitutions that I will refer to as the *Casus Parisienses*.[28] Theiner published the prologue to what he called 'glosses' to the Fourth Lateran Council, which were found, according to him, in 331 in the Biblioteca Regia Parisiensis.[29] Stephan Kuttner encountered the same prologue in a Lisbon codex, Biblioteca Nacional, Alcob. 381 fol. 225r, down at the bottom of the page where the text of *Compilatio quarta* began.[30] I. da Rosa Pereira published this prologue, with the variants of the Parisian codex taken from Theiner.[31] Theiner's erroneous catalogue number was corrected by Martin Bertram, Paris, Bibliothèque nationale, lat. 3931, fol. 86va-88va. Nor is it right that it is a matter of 'glosses', as Theiner put it, except insofar as the work consists of several 'casus'. Theiner's edition is certainly imperfect, since there are 13 errors in very few lines. The author of this prologue divides the subject matter of the Lateran Constitutions into five parts, which, barring small differences, correspond to the divisions that appear in Florence, Laur. S. Croce III$^{sin.}$6. There is a striking resemblance between this prologue and Vincentius Hispanus' introduction to *Compilatio tertia*:[32]

> Quoniam non omnia gesta romanorum pontificum in corpore canonum poterant compaginari. . . . dominus sanctissimus papa Innocentius, pater eminentissime scientie et perspicacissimi ingenii, decretales epistolas . . .

He also called the Lateran constitutions 'novelle' or 'constitutiones'. All this suggests the possibility that the author of this prologue was Vincen-

---

27. For a more detailed look at this, see García y García, *Constitutiones* 389–416.
28. Cf. ibid., 459–463 (study) and 464–475 (critical edition).
29. A. Theiner, *Disquisitiones criticae in praecipuas canonum et decretalium collectiones seu Sylloges Gallandianae dissertationum de vetustis canonum collectionibus continuatio* (Romae 1836) 133 n. 12.
30. Kuttner, 'Johannes Teutonicus', 618 n. 6.
31. Isaias da Rosa Pereira, 'Dois manuscritos alcobadenses da primeira Compilação', *Lumen* (1962) 9–23 (the edition of the prologue is found on pp. 11–12).
32. Gl. s.v. *Innocentius*, principio ante 1.1. On Vincentius' prologue, see K. Pennington, *Popes, Canonists and Texts, 1150–1550* (Collected Studies 412; Aldershot 1993) VI 66.

tius Hispanus himself or a member of his school. It is well known that Vincentius wrote a 'casus' on *Compilatio tertia*. The uninhibited literary style typical of Vincentius also shines through in these 'casus', and it occurs in the allusion he makes to English, Polish, and Hungarian students in c.15: 'Reprehenduntur hic Anglici, Poloni et Hungari qui se inebriant et se ad garsel inuitant' (The English, Polish, and Hungarians are rebuked here; they are sots and treat themselves to garsel).[33] But there is no absolutely definitive proof that would allow us to attribute these 'casus' to Vincentius with certainty.

There are other 'casus' preserved in a Fulda manuscript that I will call the *Casus Fuldenses*.[34] Schulte first wrote about these 'casus', calling them 'Notabilien zur Compilatio 4.'[35] In an unpublished description by Seckel they are announced as 'Casus zu Compilatio 4', but Stephan Kuttner concluded that they must be several 'casus' to the Fourth Lateran Council.[36] They survive in the manuscript Fulda, Landesbibliothek, D.10 fol. 110rb–111rb. Like the rest of the literature dealing with the Lateran constitutions, these 'casus' appeared before 1220, the year in which *Compilatio quarta* was accepted in Bologna. My edition is based on a single codex, the text of which is very imperfect; fol. 111 appears torn in a diagonal direction, missing the fourth part of the first column and three quarters of the second, with the resulting loss of text. Neither the Latin nor the culture of the amanuensis rank very high.

The three commentators who glossed the Fourth Lateran Council Constitutions (Johannes Teutonicus, Vincentius Hispanus, and Damasus Hungarus) dedicated a special apparatus to the 'arbores consanguinitatis et affinitatis', emphasizing the doctrine of c.50 of the Council, which redefined the allowable degree of consanguinity and affinity for a valid marriage from the seventh to the fourth collateral degree. In a separate study, I have dealt with the extensive manuscript tradition and have provided a critical edition of these glosses.[37] Many later authors followed the example of these three canonists, including Johannes de Deo, Iohannes Egitaniensis, St. Raymond of Peñafort, Goffredus de Trano, and others.

Beginning with Johannes Teutonicus' apparatus for *Compilatio quarta* (received in Bologna ca. 1220) and continuing with the promulgation of

33. See García y García, *Constitutiones* 469.
34. Ibid., 467–481 (study) and 483–490 (critical edition).
35. J.F. von Schulte, 'Literaturgeschichte der Compilationes Antiquae, bseonders der drei ersten', SB Vienna 66 (1870) 55.
36. Kuttner, *Repertorium* 405–406.
37. A. García y García, 'Glosas de Juan Teutónico, Vincente Hispano y Dámaso Húngaro a los "arbores consanguinitatis et affinitatis",' ZRG Kan. Abt. 68 (1982) 153–185.

the *Liber extra* (1234), the jurists automatically considered the Lateran Constitutions included in these collections, which, as we have already seen, include almost all of the seventy-one constitutions. The importance of the canonists' commentaries on the Fourth Lateran Constitutions has been underestimated for two reasons: first, because these commentaries were to a great extent absorbed by later works, and second, because they were not discovered until a relatively recent date. The commentaries represent the canonists' strictly contemporaneous interpretation of the legal conciliar text of the Lateran constitutions.

12

The Internal Forum and the Literature of Penance and Confession

Joseph Goering

When Dante ascended to the Sphere of the Sun, he was directed by St. Thomas Aquinas to consider a circle of shining lights. One of the lights, St. Thomas tells him, is Gratian, 'who served the one and the other court so well that it gives pleasure in Paradise' ('che l'uno e l'altro foro / aiutò sì che piace paradiso', *Paradisio* 10.104–5).[1] The allusion to two 'courts' ('fora') would have puzzled Gratian, but to both Thomas and Dante it would have been a clear reference to the two broad arenas in which the Church's canon law was operative: the external forum of ecclesiastical courts and the internal forum of conscience and of penance.[2] This new

---

1. See A. Mostaza, 'Forum internum—forum externum (En torno a la naturaleza juridica del fuero interno)', *Revista Española de derecho canonico* 23 (1967) 253–331, at 258, n. 15; 24 (1968) 339–364.

2. Note that the term 'internal forum' is not a medieval usage; 'forum internum' was used in the post-Tridentine church to refer to what was called the 'forum poenitentiae' or 'poenitentiale', or the 'forum conscientiae' in the Middle Ages.

For a general orientation to the internal forum see: P. Capobianco, 'De ambitu fori interni in iure ante Codicem', *Apollinaris* 8 (1935) 591–605, 9 (1936) 364–374; K. Mörsdorf, 'Der Rechtscharakter der iurisdictio fori interni', *Münchener Theologische Zeitschrift* 8 (1957) 161–173; B. Fries, *Forum in der Rechtssprache* (Münchener Theologische Studien, Kanonistische Abteilung 17; Munich 1963); Mostaza, 'Forum internum - Forum externum'; W. Trusen, 'Fo-

metaphorical way of describing the Church's legal competence was invented in the decades immediately following the publication of Gratian's magisterial textbook (c. 1140). It refers to no precise jurisdictional boundaries but rather to two interrelated spheres of the Church's authority. The primary locus of the external forum is the ecclesiastical court; that of the internal forum is the court of penance ('forum poenitentiae' or 'forum poenitentiale').

In general, the external forum is concerned with public and manifest transgressions of the Church's law or of divine law, while the internal forum is the court of conscience ('forum conscientiae') where even secret crimes and sins are considered, along with manifest sins against God, neighbor, and self. The external forum is both mandatory and contentious: defendants are compelled to appear, and the truth of their case is sought through argument and counterargument. The court of penance is a voluntary forum which can only be entered of one's own free will, and where the penitent is simultaneously plaintiff and defendant. The external forum follows specific and carefully devised procedures under the supervision of experienced judges, lawyers, and trained personnel, while the penitential forum is more informal and less concerned with procedural details.[3] Nevertheless, both 'fora' administer the same canon law and they seek to attain the same goal doing so: to restrain vice and foster virtue in the Christian community.[4]

This chapter will describe the workings of the penitential forum during the two centuries after Gratian, and will sketch a history of the canonical literature that was written during those centuries to educate confessors and penitents. It may serve as a reminder that canon law was not just a system for lawyers, judges, and administrators, but was a body of jurisprudence that affected everyone, in the most intimate ways, in the confessional. If a widespread and deeply rooted juridical culture can be seen as one of the important legacies of the Middle Ages to our own times, then the cre-

---

rum internum und gelehrtes Recht im Spätmittelalter: Summae confessorum und Traktate als Wegbereiter der Rezeption', ZRG Kan. Abt. 57 (1971) 83–126.

3. Thomas Aquinas distinguishes the two fora in terms of their relative formality in his *Scriptum super Sententiis*: 'Ad secundum dicendum quod sacerdotes parochiales habent quidem jurisdictionem in subditos suos quantum ad forum conscientiae, sed non quantum ad forum judiciale; quia non possunt coram eis conveniri in causis contentiosis. Et ideo excommunicare non possunt, sed absolvere possunt in foro poenitentiali. *Et quamvis forum poenitentiale sit dignius, tamen in foro judiciali major solemnitas requiritur; quia in eo oportet quod non solum Deo, sed etam homini satisfiat*' 4.18.2.2.1 ad 2 (emphasis added).

4. See G. Le Bras, *Institutions ecclésiastiques de la chrétienté médiévale* (Histoire de l'église depuis les origines jusqu'à nos jours, 12.2; Paris 1959–1964) 1.109–112; G. Silano, 'Of Sleep and Sleeplessness: The Papacy and the Law, 1150–1300', *The Religious Roles of the Papacy: Ideals and Realities, 1150–1300*, ed. C. Ryan (Toronto 1989) 343–361.

ation of that culture owes a great deal to the close and regular contact of all Christians with the legal system and the science of jurisprudence as applied in the Church's internal forum of conscience and confession.

The Penitential Forum: "Courts" and Personnel

The Parish

During the centuries after Gratian's death the internal forum became a training ground for Christian consciences and a school where both clergy and laity would learn the Church's canon law. In a canon that may be seen as the fundamental charter of the Church's internal forum,[5] the Fourth Lateran Council of 1215 required that all adult Christians, both male and female, confess their sins to their own priest ('proprius sacerdos') at least once a year and strive to fulfill the penance enjoined.[6] This canon emphasized, first, the universality of the requirement of confession. Priests were required to make the sacrament available to "all the faithful of both sexes" ('Omnis utriusque sexus fidelis'). No one who had reached the age of reason ('anni discretionis') could be excluded, either because of sex or because of social status. Women as well as men, servants and slaves as well as bishops and popes, all were required to appear in the court of penance at least once a year and to confess faithfully ('confiteatur fideliter') to their own priest.[7]

In requiring confession to one's own priest the Council recognized that the simple priest of a parish exercised the same power to bind and loose sinners as was exercised by the Apostles and by the bishops who were their successors.[8] Throughout the twelfth century scholars had argued about

---

5. See M. Maccarrone, '"Cura animarum" e "parochialis sacerdos" nelle costituzioni del IV concilio lateranense (1215): Applicazioni in Italia nel sec. XIII', *Pievi e parrocchie in Italia nel basso Medioevo (Sec. XIII–XV): Atti del VI Convegno di Storia della Chiesa in Italia, Firenze, (21–25 Sett. 1981)* (Italia Sacra: Studi e Documenti di Storia Ecclesiastica, 35.2; Rome 1984) 1.81–195, especially 160–166; N. Beriou, 'Autour de Latran IV (1215): La naissance de la confession moderne et sa diffusion', *Pratiques de la confession: Des Pères du désert à Vatican II* (Paris 1983) 73–93; J. Avril, 'A propos du "proprius sacerdos": Quelques réflexions sur les pouvoirs du prêtre de paroisse', *Proceedings Salamanca* 471–486.

6. Fourth Lateran Council c.21 COD 245 = X 5.38.12: 'Omnis utriusque sexus fidelis, postquam ad annos discretionis pervenerit, omnia sua solus peccata confiteatur fideliter, saltem semel in anno proprio sacerdoti, et iniunctam sibi poenitentiam studeat pro viribus adimplere'.

7. Hostiensis discusses at length the various statuses of penitents, beginning with the pope ('Papa cui teneatur confiteri'), and delineates the characteristic sins of each group; *Summa aurea*, 'De poenitentiis et remissionibus' 15–44 (Venice 1574; reprinted Turin 1963) 1769–1794.

8. Hostiensis, *Summa aurea*, 'De poenit. et remiss'. 15, col. 1770: 'Unusquisque sacerdos catholicus tenet locum Dei viventis, et loco Dei potest absolvere poenitentem'.

the exercise, in the hands of simple priests, lower clergy, and the laity, of the "power of the keys" to loose and bind sinners in the sacrament of penance.[9] Attempts were made to limit the exercise of this power to bishops and highly trained priests. But the emerging consensus, expressed by the Lateran Council, was that the primary tribunal of the internal forum was to be found in the local community, and that the local priest charged with the care of souls ('cura animarum') was its primary minister and judge.[10]

According to canonical norms, the priest of a parish should be at least thirty years old, free of all impediments to the exercise of his office, and capable of performing correctly the divine services and sacramental rites of the Church.[11] At his ordination to the priesthood he received the sacerdotal powers, including the 'power of the keys'.[12] He was charged with residing in his parish and providing all the ecclesiastical services for his parishioners. He might have received some training for his vocation in the household ('familia') of a bishop or archpriest, or in a song or grammar school in the local community, and he would have learned the practical duties of his office during years of apprenticeship, as a cleric in minor orders or as a subdeacon or deacon, serving under a practicing priest. He may have had some advanced education in a monastic or cathedral school or even a university, but this was neither required nor expected of most ordinands.[13]

The priest of a parish had divided loyalties. Although he received his spiritual authority from the hands of the bishop, he was presented to his post by the patron of an ecclesiastical benefice who might be a layman, a cleric, or a lay or ecclesiastical corporation. If the patron's nominee to

9. The classic studies are: A. Teetaert, *La confession aux laïques dans l'Eglise latine depuis le VIIIe jusqu'au XIVe siècle* (Bruges-Paris 1926); P. Anciaux, *La théologie du sacrement de pénitence au XIIe siècle* (Louvain 1949); L. Hödl, *Die Geschichte der scholastischen Literatur und der Theologie der Schlüsselgewalt: Die scholastische Literatur und die Theologie der Schlüsselgewalt von ihren Anfängen bis zur Summa aurea des Wilhelm von Auxerre* (Beiträge zur Geschichte der Philosophie und Theologie des Mittelalters 38.4; Münster 1960). An excellent summary is found in J.W. Baldwin, *Masters, Princes and Merchants: The Social Views of Peter the Chanter and His Circle* (2 vols. Princeton 1970) 1.50–59.

10. Hostiensis, *Summa aurea*, 'De poenit. et remiss'. 14, col. 1766: 'Dic quod sacerdos parochialis ex quo sibi cura animarum commissa est ab aliquo episcopo sine alia licentia speciali potestatem habet audiendi confessiones parochianorum suorum, excommunicandi et absolvendi, exceptis prohibitis, quia in his consistit curam'.

11. Cf. 4 lat. c. 27, COD 248 = X 1.14.14

12. See Hödl, *Schlüsselgewalt* passim.

13. See L.E. Boyle, 'The Constitution 'Cum ex eo' of Boniface VIII: Education of Parochial Clergy', *Mediaeval Studies* 24 (1962) 263–302; idem, 'Aspects of Clerical Education in Fourteenth-Century England', *The Fourteenth Century* (Proceedings of the State University of New York Conferences in Medieval Studies; Binghamton N.Y. 1977) 19–32; both are reprinted in *Pastoral Care, Clerical Education and Canon Law, 1200–1400* (Variorum Reprints; London 1981); J. Goering, 'The Changing Face of the Village Parish: The Thirteenth Century', *Pathways to Medieval Peasants*, ed. J.A. Raftis (Toronto 1981) 323–333.

a benefice lacked the canonical or educational requisites for fulfilling the office of priest, he might nevertheless be installed as 'rector' or 'parson' ('persona') of the benefice, but he would be required to maintain a suitable priest in the parish to serve as his vicar. Such a vicar would provide pastoral care and ecclesiastical services in the parish perpetually, or until the rector was able to be ordained. Perpetual vicarages were established in many parishes, and in these the income of the benefice was divided on a permanent basis between the rector and the perpetual vicar, with the latter expected to exercise daily the care of souls in the parish.[14]

The parish priest was responsible to the patron who appointed him and to the local community which he served, but he also owed obedience to his bishop and to various officials charged with the supervision of pastoral care and ecclesiastical discipline in the diocese. As priest and confessor, he was expected to hear the confessions of his parishioners at least once a year, but he was also expected to confess his own sins regularly to a confessor appointed by the bishop and to have recourse to more skilled confessors if questions or problems should arise in hearing confessions and enjoining penances.

The authority of the priest in a parish was strengthened by the provision of the Fourth Lateran Council restricting the free choice of confessors and requiring parishioners to seek their own priest's permission if they wished to confess to someone else.[15] In special cases permission was readily granted. Pilgrims, travelers, students in the schools, and others who were absent from their home parishes for extended periods could seek out another priest to hear their confession, and arrangements for such confessions became common during the thirteenth century.[16] Excep-

---

14. See R.A.R. Hartridge, *A History of Vicarages in the Middle Ages* (Cambridge 1930).

15. Fourth Lateran Council, C.21, COD 245: 'Si quis autem alieno sacerdoti voluerit iusta de causa sua confiteri peccata, licentiam prius postulet et obtineat a proprio sacerdote, cum aliter ille ipsum non possit solvere vel ligare'.

The older practice urged penitents to seek out several confessors, or to choose the most qualified priest available. The classic authority was (Ps.) Augustine, *Decretum*, De pen. D.6 c.1: 'Qui vult confiteri peccata ut inveniat gratiam querat sacerdotem qui sciat ligare et solvere'. The practice of choosing one's own confessor continued, alongside the required annual confession to one's 'proper priest', throughout the Middle Ages, and was enshrined in one of the most popular medieval didactic poems, the *Peniteas cito, peccator*; see J. Goering, *William de Montibus (c. 1140–1213): The Schools and the Literature of Pastoral Care* (Studies and Texts, 108; Toronto, 1992), 121 (lines 27–29). For a discussion of the canonical literature on the choice of confessors see Ludwig Hödl, 'Die sacramentale Busse und ihre kirchliche Ordnung im beginnenden mittelalterlichen Streit um die Bussvollmacht der Ordenspriester', *Franziskanische Studien* 55 (1973) 330–374 at 332–340.

16. The canons of St. Victor and of Ste. Geneviève became confessors to the student population in Paris, and both major and minor penitentiaries in the papal curia heard confessions of pilgrims to Rome (see below).

tions were also granted within parish communities. Noble families might be permitted to retain a personal chaplain and confessor for their households. By the fourteenth century licenses were being granted regularly by bishops to allow lords and ladies to confess to their own priests and in their own chapels, rather than to their parish priest.[17] Hospitals, merchant and trade guilds, and confraternities also received permission to appoint chaplains and to confess to these rather than to their parish priest.[18] In such cases care was taken to protect the jurisdictional and financial rights of the parish priest while allowing some choice of confessors in the internal forum.

As members of the local community, the confessors were well acquainted with their people, with the sins that they might be expected to confess and the penances that they could sustain. The embarrassment and shame that might accompany confession to one's local priest was acknowledged, but the shame itself was seen as a therapeutic part of confession. Although local priests might lack formal education and legal training for the task of judging souls in the internal forum, they gradually came to see themselves, and to be seen by their people, as the proper priests and primary confessors in Christendom.

During the thirteenth century, the mendicant friars, who were highly trained and popular confessors, supplemented and often challenged the local priest's primacy in the internal forum.[19] The activities of the friar-confessors were closely regulated by bishops (and by the orders themselves) so as to preserve the basic principle that parishioners should confess to their own parish priest. Nevertheless tensions often ran high. Some parish priests were glad of the help they received from friars in hearing large numbers of confessions during the busiest days of the Lenten season, but many others resented the incursion of these outsiders and their tenden-

---

17. R.M. Haines prints a typical episcopal license granting a noble couple permission to choose their own confessor for two years in *Ecclesia anglicana: Studies in the English Church of the Later Middle Ages* (Toronto 1989) 51–52.

18. For confession in hospitals see the *Libellus pastoralis de cura et officio archidiaconi*, printed under the name of Raymond of Peñafort in the *Catalogue général des manuscrits des bibliothèques publiques des départements de France*, ed. F. Ravaisson (Paris 1849) 1.592–649, at 634–641. On guilds and confraternities see G.-G. Meersseman, *Ordo Fraternitatis: Confraternitate e pietà dei laici nel medioevo* (Italia sacra 24–26; Rome 1977).

19. See L.E. Boyle, 'Notes on the Education of the "Fratres communes" in the Dominican Order in the Thirteenth Century', *Xenia Medii Aevi Historiam Illustrantia oblata Thomae Kaeppeli O.P.* (Rome 1978) 249–267, reprinted in *Pastoral Care*; S.M. da Romallo, *Il ministero della confessione nei primordi dell'Ordine francescano in relazione ai diritti parrocchiali* (Milan 1949); Roberto Rusconi, 'I Francescani e la confessione nel secolo XIII', *Francescanesimo e vita religiosa dei laici nel '200* (Società internazionale di studi francescani, Atti dell'VIII Convegno Internazionale; Assisi 1981) 251–309.

cy to override the jurisdictional prerogatives of the parish. This competition among confessors fostered better education and training among both the secular and the regular clergy as each sought to meet the challenges presented by the other and the demands of an increasingly sophisticated populace. Competition was also welcome to penitents, who could choose the best confessor, on the one hand, or the most accommodating on the other.

A priest's competence in his penitential forum extended, theoretically, to the hearing of all confessions, the absolution of all sins, and the imposition of suitable penances. This extensive authority, accorded to him by virtue of his ordination, was one of the most striking implications of twelfth- and thirteenth-century penitential doctrine. In practice, however, the competence of the parish priest was somewhat circumscribed. The first limitation was one of common sense. Priests were urged to refer serious or difficult cases to their superiors for adjudication.[20] Such cases included those affecting persons of high social rank or those involving crimes and sins that were especially threatening to social stability and harmony in the parish. Often the priest might benefit from the intervention of a higher authority, and he was encouraged to avail himself of the opportunity. Other difficult cases arose from the growing sophistication of the canon law concerning marriage, usury, vows, oaths, and other matters. Parish priests received some instruction in the intricacies of the new canon law, but the aim of this teaching may have been as much to warn them of difficulties beyond their ken as to prepare them to deal with the problems themselves.

In addition to these voluntary constraints, several very specific limitations were placed on the parish priest's competence in the penitential forum. Public or solemn penance, imposed for notorious and serious sins, remained the preserve of the bishop.[21] The confession, absolution, and punishment of certain named sins, such as arson, murder, forgery, and other grave crimes, were reserved variously to the bishop or the pope.[22] The power of parish priests to absolve penitents from excommunication

---

20. *Libellus pastoralis de cura et officio archidiaconi* 610: 'Expediens est ut iniungat archidiaconus sacerdoti ut sciat poenitentias a sanctis determinatas . . . Injungat etiam ei quod, si circa haec vel alia difficilia aliquando dubitaverit, ad majorum consilium recurrat quam citius poterit'. See below for a more detailed discussion.

21. On solemn and public penance see Raymond of Peñafort, *De penitentia* 3.34.6, *S. Raimundus de Pennaforte Summa de paenitentia*, ed. X. Ochoa and A. Diez (Universa bibliotheca iuris 1.B; Rome 1976) 801. See R. Hill, 'Public Penance: Some Problems of a Thirteenth-Century Bishop', *History* 36 (1951) 213–226; M.C. Mansfield, *The Humiliation of Sinners: Public Penance in Thirteenth Century France* (Ithaca 1995).

22. See the discussion of reserved cases below.

was limited in certain cases, and sins that resulted in irregularity (a canonical hindrance to marriage, holy orders, and some legal actions) could be absolved only by higher authorities. In general, however, the parish priest enjoyed substantial competence in the penitential forum of his parish. His ability to advise and absolve parishioners was circumscribed only by his own political, social, and intellectual limitations, and by specific and named privileges of the bishop or the pope.

The competence of the priest extended to hearing confessions and imposing penances for acts such as theft, slander, and assault that might also be brought before various civil or criminal tribunals. The question arises whether a crime divulged in the confessional could be prosecuted subsequently in the external forum of the Church or the secular courts. The most effective hindrance to the movement of a case from the internal to the external forum was the 'seal of confession' that prohibited a priest, with the strictest sanctions, from revealing what he had heard in confession. The Fourth Lateran Council, in the same canon that prescribed annual confession, decreed that a priest who violated the secrecy of the confessional should not only be deposed from his office, but also be relegated to perpetual penance in a strict monastery.[23]

Furthermore, the goal of the Church's courts (and, to a large extent, of the secular courts as well) was the same as that of the confessional. They sought to lead sinners to confess their misdeeds, to be reconciled with God and with the community, and to make suitable amends to those who were injured. If these ends could be met freely, in the confessional, then no further adjudication was necessary. If a crime was manifest and public, however, or if it was to someone's advantage to prosecute the crime in a public forum, one gained no immunity through the confessional. Contrition, confession, and penance reconciled the sinner with God and with the Church, but provided no safeguard against punishment by temporal authorities. Moreover, the new juridical procedure of 'inquisitio', and the new emphasis on law as a means of active intervention in moral gover-

---

23. Fourth Lateran Council c.21, 245: 'Caveat autem omnino, ne verbo vel signo vel alio quovis modo prodat aliquatenus peccatorem, sed si prudentiori consilio indiguerit, illud absque ulla expressione personae caute requirat, quoniam qui peccatum in poenitentiali iudicio sibi detectum praesumpserit revelare, non solum a sacerdotali officio deponendum decernimus, verum etiam ad agendam perpetuam poenitentiam in arctum monasterium detrudendum'.

John of Kent (c. 1216), London, B.L. Royal 9.A.XIV, fol. 225va, has the priest give a penitent the following assurances: 'De me autem confidere potes quia novit Deus quod prius me permitterem decollari quam signo vel dicto te de confessione tua detegere, etsi patrem meum occideres, maxime cum sciam te mihi non mihi set ut Deo principaliter confiteri, Dei autem secretum nullus sane mentis presumat revelare'.

nance, gradually encouraged ecclesiastical authorities, from the pope to the local archdeacons and rural deans, to seek out sinners and to do for them in the external forum what they were unwilling to do for themselves in confession.[24]

Although the prosecution of criminal acts could not move easily from the internal to the external forum, movement in the opposite direction was possible and even salutary. The difficulties of proof and limitations of human discernment in the external courts could lead to judgments that were legally correct yet unsatisfying. In such cases judges might leave the principals to their 'consciences'. This implied more than a pious hope; it imposed on the recipient the very real obligation of examining his or her conscience in the internal court of penance, and of acting accordingly.

The Diocese

The bishop, head of the diocesan hierarchy, was the 'priest' of everyone in his diocese and had general oversight of the penitential forum.[25] He was the confessor of the diocesan clergy, the arbiter of difficult questions arising in the internal forum, and the person responsible for educating his subordinates concerning penitential discipline. He might exercise these duties personally, but he was frequently assisted by diocesan officials and 'coadiutores'.[26]

A confessor-general or 'penitentiarius' of the diocese was the bishop's vicar in all matters concerning penitential discipline. This official, much ignored in modern studies, played a crucial role in the internal forum. As the local expert in penitential law and theology, he heard confessions of the diocesan clergy, adjudicated cases reserved to the bishop from the local confessors, and supervised the imposition of public penances in the bishop's stead. Many of the manuals of penance and confession that proliferated during the thirteenth and subsequent centuries were composed by and for the diocesan penitentiary.[27]

---

24. See Silano, 'Of Sleep and Sleeplessness: The Papacy and the Law, 1150–1300', 343–361; R. Fraher, 'IV Lateran's Revolution in Criminal Procedure: The Birth of "Inquisitio", the End of Ordeals, and Innocent III's Vision of Ecclesiastical Politics', *Studia in honorem eminentissimi cardinalis Alphonsi M. Stickler* (Studia et textus historiae iuris canonici 7; Rome 1992) 97–111.

25. Hostiensis, *Summa aurea*, 'De poenit. et remiss.' 18, col. 1772: 'Ut tamen scias tres esse personas, quibus immediate subiecta est quaelibet anima, scilicet Papam, dioecesanum, et proprium sacerdotem'.

26. The administration of penance at the diocesan level still needs much study. For England see two essays by Haines, 'The Penitential System at Diocesan Level' and 'The Jurisdiction of the Subdean of Salisbury', *Ecclesia anglicana* 39–52, 53–66.

27. The most extensive discussion of the office of diocesan penitentiary is that of L. Thomassin in the eighteenth century. I have consulted the French edition of 1864: *Ancienne & nouvelle discipline de l'Eglise*, vol. 1, part x, ch. 10 ('Du théologal et du pénitencier') 379–391. See

Subordinate to the bishop and his penitentiary was a hierarchy of penitential authorities in the diocese. The Fourth Lateran Council encouraged bishops to appoint 'coadiutores et cooperatores' to assist them in preaching and 'in hearing confessions and enjoining penances'.[28] A canon of the Council of the Province of Canterbury, held at Oxford in 1222, illustrates one of the ways in which the Lateran injunction was implemented:

> Since souls are frequently endangered because of a shortage of confessors, or because rural deans and parsons are perhaps embarrassed to confess to their own bishop, we, wishing to remedy this malady, decree that certain prudent and discrete confessors should be established by the bishops in each archdeaconry, who can hear the confessions of the rural deans, priests and parsons. In cathedral churches where there are secular canons, let these canons confess to the bishop or to the dean or to other certain persons appointed for this purpose by the bishop and the dean and chapter.[29]

Another of the bishop's officials (and sometimes a powerful rival) was the archdeacon. As the name implies, an archdeacon was not necessarily a priest and thus could not hear confessions 'ex officio' nor serve as a priest and judge in the internal forum. This official represented the bishop in disciplinary and administrative matters affecting the local clergy. He heard cases and settled disputes in his own archidiaconal court and was an important figure in the Church's external forum. But archdeacons enjoyed substantial benefices and employed assistants to help in their disciplinary and pastoral work as the bishop's representative in the archdeaconry. Among these assistants one would expect to find experts in canon law and the procedure of the external forum as well as priests and clerics who were skilled in hearing confessions and exercising penitential discipline.[30]

---

also, Le Bras, *Institutions ecclésiastiques* 401; F. Broomfield, *Thomae de Chobham Summa Confessorum* (Analecta Mediaevalia Namurcensis 25; Louvain and Paris 1968) lvi–lviii, 213; *Robert of Flamborough Canon-Penitentiary of Saint-Victor at Paris Liber poenitentialis: A Critical Edition with Introduction and Notes* ed. J.J.F. Firth (Toronto 1971) 3–5; Haines, 'Penitential System' 39–51.

28. Fourth Lateran Council c.10, COD 239–40 = X 1.31.15

29. Council of Canterbury c.24, *Councils and Synods, with Other Documents Relating to the English Church, II: A.D. 1205–1213*, ed. F.M. Powicke and C.R. Cheney (2 vols. Oxford 1964) 1.113: 'Quoniam nonnumquam ob defectum confessorum vel quia decani rurales et persone forte erubescunt suo prelato confiteri, certum iminet periculum animarum, volentes huic morbo mederi statuimus ut certi confessores prudentes et discreti ab episcopo loci per archidiaconatus singulos statuantur, qui confessiones audiant decanorum ruralium, presbiterorum, et personarum. In cathedralibus autem ecclesiis ubi sunt canonici seculares, confiteantur ipsi canonici episcopo vel decano vel certis personis ad hoc per episcopum et decanum et capitulum constitutis.'

30. For a general discussion of the archdeacon, see Le Bras, *Institutions ecclésiastiques* 391–394. One of the most popular manuals of confession, Robert Grosseteste's *Templum Dei*, was probably written while Robert was serving in the household of Hugh Foliot, archdeacon of Shropshire and later bishop of Hereford from 1219 to 1234. See Robert Grosseteste, *Templum Dei Edited From MS. 27 of Emmanuel College, Cambridge*, ed. Joseph Goering and

The lowest level of penitential discipline in the diocese, just above that of the parish priest, was exercised by an official known variously as the archpriest or rural dean.[31] The archpriest, a common figure in Italy and much of the Mediterranean, was usually the head of a 'pieve' ('plebs') and of the several priests who lived together there and who traveled out to provide liturgical and pastoral services in the surrounding communities.[32] The archpriest was responsible for the education, training, and penitential discipline of the priests in his collegiate community.

In other areas, especially in France and England where parish priests lived usually in isolated churches rather than in a community, one priest would be appointed as the head or supervisor of a group of a dozen or so parish priests. These groupings were known as rural deaneries, and the priest in charge was commonly known as a 'rural dean' ('decanus ruralis'; not to be confused with the dean ['decanus'] of a cathedral chapter, a very high official, nor with the deacon ['diaconus'] who is a cleric not yet ordained to the priesthood). The rural dean was chosen from among the ranks of the parochial clergy or was appointed by the bishop or his delegate. All the priests of a rural deanery were expected to meet together regularly (often monthly) in a kind of chapter ('capitulum').[33] During these regular meetings they confessed their sins to the rural dean or to some appointed confessor, thus learning the new techniques of the confessional, and they received instruction in the Church's law and guidance in handling difficult cases in the internal forum.[34]

Frank A.C. Mantello (Toronto Medieval Latin Texts; Toronto 1984) 4–6; R.W. Southern, *Robert Grosseteste: The Growth of an English Mind in Medieval Europe* (Oxford 1986) 63–69.

For an excellent example of the archdeacon's pastoral activities, including his oversight of confessions and penitential discipline in his archdeaconry, see the *Libellus pastoralis de cura et officio archidiaconi*, especially the chapter 'Quomodo se habeat sacerdos circa confessiones et poenitentias', 609–611.

31. For a general discussion of the archpriest or rural dean see: Le Bras, *Institutions Ecclésiastiques* 428–434; Paul R. Hyams, 'Deans and Their Doings: The Norwich Inquiry of 1286', *Proceedings Berkeley* 619–646.

32. See *Pievi e parrocchie in Italia* (note 5 above); H.A. Kelly, *Canon Law and the Archpriest of Hita* (Medieval and Renaissance Texts and Studies 27; Binghamton NY 1984).

33. Even before the Fourth Lateran Council, Archbishop Stephen Langton provided that two confessors be established in each rural deanery of Canterbury diocese to hear the confessions of parish priests. The Statutes of Canterbury c.13, *Councils and Synods* 1.27 (1213–1214) provide: 'Quilibet autem sacerdos de consensu domini archiepiscopi suum habeat confessorem, et in quolibet capitulo [i.e. chapter of rural deans or archpriests] duo sint confessores quibus, a domino archiepiscopo constitutis, eiusdem capituli sacerdotes sua possint peccata confiteri. Si qua vero fuerint dubia que per eos expediri nequeant, vel si quis de sacerdotibus eis ob aliquam causam noluerit peccata sua confiteri, ad principales penitentiarios domini archiepiscopi recurrant. Si vero neutri eorum suum voluerit revelare peccatum, ad archiepiscopum veniat ut vel ei confiteatur vel sibi ab ipso alius assignetur cui velit et valet confiteri'.

34. See J. Goering and D.S. Taylor, 'The "Summulae" of Bishops Walter de Cantilupe (1240) and Peter Quinel (1287)', *Speculum* 67 (1992) 576–594.

The Papal Curia

The diocesan bishop's authority and activity in the penitential forum was echoed in the curia of the Roman pontiff. By the thirteenth century an office of papal penitentiary was established to hear confessions of curial members and of the numerous pilgrims and visitors to the court.[35] The papal penitentiary, like his diocesan counterparts, answered questions about difficult cases posed to him by penitents and diocesan penitentiaries, confirmed or adjusted the decisions of local confessors, and dealt with the cases reserved to the pope for absolution and disposition.[36] Popes regularly appointed penitentiaries to accompany the legations that they sent to various parts of christendom. Raymond of Peñafort, the most renowned penitential authority of the thirteenth century, served in such a capacity (as 'penitentiarius domini legati') in the service of a papal legate to Spain in 1228–1229.[37]

Procedure in the Internal Forum

The practices and procedures of the internal forum, as developed in the thirteenth century, informed and influenced judicial activity at every level of the Church, from the papal curia to the local ruridecanal court. These procedures, in turn, were influenced by the practices of the external courts and the teachings of the schools. Bishops, penitentiaries, and other skilled confessors kept abreast of procedural changes in the external courts and adapted these to the confessional. Raymond of Peñafort's influential *Summa de penitentia*, for example, incorporates large parts of his earlier 'ordo

---

35. The basic study is E. Göller, *Die päpstliche Pönitentiarie von ihrem Ursprung bis zu ihrer Umgestaltung unter Pius V* (2 vols. Rome 1907–11). See also C.H. Haskins, 'The Sources for the History of the Papal Penitentiary', *American Journal of Theology* 9 (1905) 421–450; M. Meyer, *Die Pönitentiarieformularsammlung des Walter Murner von Strassburg: Beitrag zur Geschichte und Diplomatik der päpstlichen Pönitentiarie im 14. Jahrhundert* (Freiburg 1979); F. Tamburini, 'La penitenzieria apostolica durante il papato Avignonese', *Aux origines de l'état moderne: Le fonctionnement administratif de la papauté d'Avignon* (Collection de L'École Française de Rome 138; Rome 1990) 251–268.

36. The range of penitentiary business can be seen in the surviving formularies: H.C. Lea, *A Formulary of the Papal Penitentiary in the Thirteenth Century* (Philadelphia 1892); Meyer, *Die Pönitentiarieformularsammlung*. For the surviving registers of the papal penitentiary see F. Tamburini, 'Il primo registro di suppliche dell'Archivio della Sacra Penitenzieria Apostolica (1410–1411)', *Rivista di Storia della Chiesa in Italia* 23 (1969) 384–427. See now Ludwig Schmugge, Patrick Hersperger, and Béatrice Wiggenhauser, *Die Supplikenregister der päpstlichen Pönitentiarie aus der Zeit Pius' II. (1458–1464)* (Bibliothek des Deutschen Historischen Instituts in Rom, 84; Tübingen 1996); Ludwig Schmugge, 'Cleansing on Consciences: Some Observations Regarding the Fifteenth-Century Registers of the Papal Penitentiary', *Viator* 29 (1998) 345–361.

37. See Ochoa and Diez, eds., *Summa de paenitentia* lxv–lxix.

iudiciarius' (*Summa de iure canonico*), and the surviving formularies of papal penitentiaries reveal their debt to the new procedural literature.[38] Nevertheless, procedures in the internal forum were less formal than in the external courts and they are not easily reconstructed by studying the procedure of papal and other 'external' courts. As is to be expected, the surviving documents from the diocesan and papal penitentiaries give a limited and somewhat distorted view of procedures in the penitential forum. These documents inform us about difficult cases and about special matters reserved for episcopal or papal attention, but the fundamental procedures in the penitential forum are those developed for the regular confession of sins and enjoining of penances in the humble parishes.

The procedures of the internal forum can best be studied at the most elementary level, that of a priest hearing a penitent's confession and assigning a penance. The evidence for such a study has become much more accessible in recent decades with the identification and study of numerous manuals and handbooks of penance, and it is on the basis of these texts that we can begin to outline the procedures and practices of the internal forum.

Admission into the Internal Forum

One mark of the growing importance of penance in the thirteenth century is the expansion of opportunities for entering the penitential forum. Regular confession preceding reception of the Eucharist one or more times a year was a common practice long before the thirteenth century.[39] As has been noted, the Fourth Lateran Council insisted on the minimal requirement of annual confession and communion; this 'Easter duty' remained an integral part of Catholic practice into the twentieth century. Preparation for the annual confession to the parish priest would begin on Ash Wednesday, at the beginning of the Lenten period of fasting, with traditional liturgical ceremonies and often with sermons on a theme such as: 'Penitentiam agite, appropinquabit enim regnum celorum' (Matt. 3,2).[40] The universality of the requirement, that 'Everyone . . . shall confess', seems to have

---

38. Ibid., *Summa de paenitentia* lxxxviii.

39. The requirement of annual confession was not an innovation of the Fourth Lateran Council: See P. Browe, 'Die Pflichtbeichte im Mittelalter', *Zeitschrift für katholische Theologie* 57 (1933) 335–383; P. Landau, 'Epikletisches und transzendentales Kirchenrecht bei Hans Dombois: Kritische Anmerkungen zu seiner Sicht der Kirchenrechtsgeschichte', ZRG Kan. Abt. 72 (1987) 131–154, at 146–150. But see the cautious comments of A. Murray, 'Confession as a Historical Source in the Thirteenth Century', in *The Writing of History in the Middle Ages: Essays Presented to Richard William Southern*, ed. R.H.C. Davis and J.M. Wallace-Hadrill (Oxford 1981), 275–322.

40. Alan of Lille, *Liber poenitentialis* 3. 50, ed. J. Longère (Analecta Mediaevalia Namurcen-

been taken seriously. Preachers sometimes note the obstacles experienced by some, especially the young, farm laborers, and the unfree, in attending the sacraments, thus implying an effort to accommodate them.[41]

The annual encounter of many Christians with their parish priest in the penitential forum may have been a fairly cursory event. Although attendance was mandatory, the mode of attendance and the actual confession of sins was voluntary, and must have varied greatly depending on the skill, learning and inclinations of both priest and penitent. Priests were sometimes warned about what to expect from their parishioners: 'The sinners of your parish will come to confession, I tell you, only during Lent, and not in the first or the second or the third week, but in the sixth week, or on Good Friday or Saturday or on Easter, drawn by the necessity of keeping a custom rather than by the compunction of true penance'.[42] The ignorance and incompetence of priests in hearing confessions was likewise legendary. We do well here to avoid exaggerated claims, either negative or positive, as to the quality of the procedures and the expertise of the participants in the local penitential fora. But the expectation that all Christians, clergy and laity alike, would appear in the internal forum of penance and confession at least once a year ensured a modicum of familiarity with the doctrines and practices of the Church's canon law even among people who would have had no direct experience of Church courts or of the external forum.

An annual Easter confession by all Christians marked the most obvious time for entering the internal forum, but many other opportunities existed besides. Confession to a priest 'in extremis', at the hour of one's death, was at least as widespread as Lenten confession, and probably has a longer history.[43] The importance of a final confession was so great that, at

---

sia 18; 2 vols. Louvain and Lille 1965) 2.158: 'Specialiter autem in initio quadragesimae, quod dicitur caput jejunii, parochianos convocet sacerdos, eisque specialiter de poenitentia proponat sermonem, eosque ad poenitentiam invitet'.

41. In the early morning of Easter Sunday, William de Montibus addressed a crowd of children, servants, and shepherds who had completed their Lenten penance, J. Goering, *William de Montibus (c. 1140–1213): The Schools and the Literature of Pastoral Care* (Studies and Texts 108; Toronto 1992) 559, cf. 19–20: 'Consuetudo est sancte ecclesie ut in hac die ueniant ad primam pueri, puelle, pastores, servientes qui pro seruitio dominorum suorum ad ecclesiam in aliis diebus uenire non possunt'.

42. From an anonymous sermon in Oxford, New College MS 94, fol. 12v–13r (before 1250): 'Nunc itaque, fratres, ueniunt ad uos peccatores parochianorum uestrorum immundi, fornicatores, adulteri, usurarii, auari, fures, rapaces, ebriosi, mendaces, periuri, proximum odio habentes . . . Veniunt inquam in quadragesima, et non in prima uel in secunda uel in tertia quadragesima septimana set in sexta uel die passionis Domini uel etiam in sabbato uel die paschali, necessitate conseruante consuetudinis magis quam compunctione uere penitentie ducti'.

43. The Fourth Lateran Council (c. 22: "Quod infirmi prius provideant animae quam corpori") required that a priest be called before a medical doctor to minister to the sick.

the point of death, one was permitted to confess even to a layperson or a heretic if no priest were available.[44] Prophylactic confessions also became very popular for those about to engage in some particularly dangerous activity (war, travel, childbirth, etc.). By seeking out a priest and confessing their sins, they forestalled the possibility of dying unshriven.

Many other occasions for confession were cultivated in the thirteenth and subsequent centuries. Confession and examination of conscience became a kind of spiritual exercise among both clergy and pious laity. 'Holy women' ('mulieres religiosae') in the Low Countries and elsewhere began to besiege priests with demands for frequent confession,[45] and confraternities of penitents and 'disciplinati' sprang up throughout Europe.[46] Many people were moved to penance and confession by popular preachers,[47] and the new mendicant orders (Dominicans and Franciscans) became training grounds for confessors and preachers almost as soon as they were founded.

Bishops, too, began to take an active role in fostering confessions among the laity in their dioceses. Bishop Robert Grosseteste (d. 1253) describes how, in introducing the new canonical procedure of 'inquisitio' into the visitation of the churches in the large English diocese of Lincoln, he also made provision for preaching and hearing confessions:

> After I was made bishop, I thought to myself how a bishop ought to be a pastor of souls . . . I began, therefore, to travel around my diocese, rural deanery by rural deanery, requiring the clergy of each deanery to come together at a certain time and place, and charging them to prepare their parishioners to assemble at the same time and place, along with the children ready for confirmation, to hear the Word of God and to confess. Usually, when all had come together, I preached to the clergy and a Friar Preacher or Minor preached to the

---

The Lenten sermon quoted above envisions many people calling on a confessor when in danger of death, Oxford, New College MS 94, fol. 13r.: 'Alii autem mandant uos in domos suas periculo mortis territi. Et quidem et isti et illi [those who confess tardily during Lent] toto anno in peccatis suis dormiunt nec salutis consilium querunt nisi, ut dictum est, uel consuetudine accipiente in pascha communionis uel necessitate mortis imminentes requirunt'.

44. The classic study is Teetaert, *La confession au laïques*.

45. This aspect of feminine piety, especially among the 'mulieres religiosae' of the early thirteenth century, remains little studied. See Elizabeth Makowski, *'A Pernicious Sort of Woman': Quasi Religious Women and Canon Lawyers in the Later Middle Ages* (Studies in Medieval and Early Modern Canon Law; Washington, D.C. 2005).

46. See G.-G. Meersseman, *Le Dossier de l'Ordre de la Pénitence au XIIIe siècle* (Fribourg 1971); idem, 'Disciplinati e penitenti nel duecento', *Il movimento dei Disciplinati nel settimo centenario dal suo inizio (Perugia-1260)* (Perugia 1962) 43–72.

47. For the connection of preaching and confession see R. Rusconi, 'De la prédication à la confession: transmission et contrôle de modèles de comportement au XIIIe siècle', *Faire croire: Modalités de la diffusion et de la réception des messages religieux du XIIe au XVe siècle* (Rome 1981) 67–85; Beriou, 'La naissance de la confession moderne'.

people. Thereafter, four friars heard confessions and enjoined penances. That day and the next, after the youngsters were confirmed, my clergy and I carried out the inquisitions, corrections, and reforms as these pertain to the office of the inquisition.[48]

In this example we see how closely linked were the internal forum of confession and the external forum of inquisition, correction, and reform.

Finally, we should note how the internal forum gradually became a place where one could seek advice from experienced confessors on matters of conscience and difficult moral questions. In one of the folktales collected by Italo Calvino, two friends have made a vow to each other that the first to marry would call on the other to be his groomsman, 'even if he should be at the ends of the earth'. When one of the friends dies and the other plans to marry, he has no idea what to do so he seeks the advice of his confessor. The priest admits that it is a ticklish situation, but advises the survivor: 'You must keep your promise. Call on him even if he is dead. Go to his grave and say what you're supposed to say. It will then be up to him whether to come to your wedding or not'.[49] Beneath the whimsical surface of this story lies evidence of the common and widespread expectation that even local parish priests would be able to give expert advice about questions of conscience and behavior. The priest in the story would have had little opportunity to study in detail the complicated canonical discussions concerning oaths, but he would have known the outlines of a correct response from having his own conscience formed by learned confessors in the confessional, and perhaps from reading in any of the myriad penitential manuals that circulated widely in the thirteenth and subsequent centuries.

Confession: Collecting the Evidence

Just as entry into the penitential forum was a voluntary activity, so too was the giving of testimony. No outside evidence was admissible in the

---

48. *Councils and Synods* 1.265: 'Ego post meam in episcopum creationem consideravi me episcopum esse et pastorem animarum ... Unde episcopatum meum cepi circuire per singulos decanatus rurales, faciens clerum cuiuscunque decanatus per ordinem certis die et loco convocari, et populum premuniri ut eisdem die et loco adessent cum parvulis confirmandis, ad audiendum verbum dei et confitendum. Congregatis autem clero et populo, egomet ut pluries proponebam verbum dei clero, et aliquis frater predicator aut minor populo. Et quatuor fratres consequenter audiebant confessiones et iniungebant penitentias. Et confirmatis pueris eodem die et sequente, continue ego cum clericis meis intendebamus inquisitionibus, correctionibus, et reformationibus secundum quod pertinet ad officium inquisitionis'. Grosseteste's visitation articles, stressing their canonical status ('canonice statuta sunt ... canonice punituros'), are printed ibid., 276–278.

49. 'One Night in Paradise', *Italian Folktales Selected and Retold by Italo Calvino*, G. Martin, trans. (New York 1980) 119.

internal forum; only the free, full, and truthful confession of the penitent was acceptable. The art of producing such a confession was one of the most important skills to be learned by priest and penitent in the later Middle Ages.

The procedure for hearing private confessions in the thirteenth century was an elaboration of the ancient liturgical practices of public penance (as seen especially in the liturgies for Ash Wednesday and in the *Ordines ad paenitentiam dandam*), and of the traditions of the early penitentials.[50] By the thirteenth century these traditional materials had been molded into a generally accepted set of procedures that would continue to govern the penitential practice for centuries.[51]

Private confessions generally took place in the church, but not in an enclosure such as the modern 'confessional'. The priest would sit in some open place and the penitent would stand with bowed head at a lower level or kneel. Neither was to look at the other, and the priest was to wear a cowl or hood that would discourage direct eye-contact.[52] The penitent

---

50. See C. Vogel, 'Les Rituels de la pénitence tarifée', *Liturgia opera divina e umana: Studi sulla riforma liturgica offerti à S. E. Mons. Annibale Bugnini in occasione del suo 70e compleanno*, ed. P. Jounel, R. Kaczynski, and G. Pasqualetti (Rome 1982) 419–427; R. Kottje, 'Busspraxis und Bussritus', *Segni e riti nella chiesa altomedievale occidentale* (Settimane di studio del Centro Italiano di Studi Sull'alto Medioevo, 33; 2 vols. Spoleto 1987) 1.369–395.

For the influence of the early medieval 'Ordines' on thirteenth-century practice see J. Goering and P.J. Payer, 'The "Summa penitentie Fratrum Predicatorum": A Thirteenth-Century Confessional Formulary', *Mediaeval Studies* 55 (1993) 1–50.

51. The description that follows is based on an early-thirteenth-century formulary known as the *Summa penitentie Fratrum Praedicatorum*, ed. Goering and Payer (see note above). Illustrative materials are drawn from other manuals and formularies of the late twelfth and early thirteenth centuries, including, in approximate chronological order, *Homo quidam* (c. 1155–1165), ed. Pierre Michaud-Quantin, 'Un manuel de confession archaïque dans le manuscrit Avranches 136', *Sacris erudiri* 17 (1966) 5–54; Alan of Lille, *Liber poenitentialis*; 'Ricardus', *De doctrina sacerdotibus* (=Ps. Praepositinus, *De penitentiis iniungendis*) Stuttgart, Würt. Landesbibliothek H.B. I 70, fol. 2r–19r; Robert of Flamborough, *Liber poenitentialis*; John of Kent, *Summa de penitentia*, London, British Library Royal 9.A.XIV, fol. 203v–232v; Thomas de Chobham, *Summa confessorum*; Robert Grosseteste, *Templum Dei*; Raymond of Peñafort, *Summa de penitentia*; 'Deux formulaires pour la confession du milieu du XIIIe siècle', ed. P. Michaud-Quantin, RTAM 31 (1964) 43–62; Master Serlo, *Summa de penitentia*, ed. J. Goering, *Mediaeval Studies* 38 (1976) 1–53; Hostiensis (Henricus de Segusio), 'De poenitentiis et remissionibus', *Summa aurea*; Peter Sampson, 'De sacramento poenitentiae', *Liber synodalis compositus per Magistrum Petrum de Sampsono ad instantiam Domini Raymundi Dei Gratia Nemausensis Episcopi*, ed. E. Martène and U. Durand, *Thesaurus novus anecdotorum* (Paris 1717) 4.1021–1070.

See also, L.K. Little, 'Les techniques de la confession et la confession comme technique', *Faire Croire* 88–99; R. Rusconi, 'Ordinate confiteri: La confessione dei peccati nelle "summae de casibus" et nei manuali per i confessori (metà XII - inizi XIV secolo)', *L'Aveu: Antiquité et Moyen-Âge* (Collection de l'École française de Rome 88; Rome 1986) 297–313.

52. *Summa penitentie Fratrum Praedicatorum* 27: 'Tunc etiam dicat ei sacerdos quod stet inclinatus ad terram . . . Sacerdos etiam audiens peccatorem caueat ne ipsum respiciat in facie et maxime ne respici possit et precipue si est mulier. . . Et prouideat si fieri potest ne sit

would begin by greeting the priest, and the priest would receive the penitent with a prayer or with words of encouragement.[53] If the penitent was unknown to him, the priest would inquire about the person's status (religious, clerical, lay), condition (beneficed, married, widowed, single) and office (merchant, mercenary, judge, prostitute, etc.)[54]

Next, the priest was urged to inquire into the faith of the penitent. Does he or she know the creed or the articles of faith, the 'Pater noster', the baptismal formula 'in nomine Patris et Filii et Spiritus sancti', in Latin or in the vernacular?[55] He should also ascertain that the person is truly repentant, willing to confess, and prepared to undertake whatever penance might be enjoined by the priest.

The penitent would then confess spontaneously the sins that came to mind, while the priest offered encouragement and direction. After this spontaneous confession the priest was to conduct his own interrogation, exploring areas that may have been touched on earlier or that seemed appropriate given the status and condition of the penitent.[56] The most common framework for this directed confession was the seven deadly sins (pride, envy, wrath, sloth, avarice, gluttony, and lust) or transgressions of the Ten Commandments, but many other paradigms were also recommended.[57] The emphasis in all the penitential treatises was on helping the

---

in loco nimis secreto et ut altius quam confitens sedeat, et caputium in capite teneat profunde'.

P. Sampson, *Liber Synodalis* 1028: 'Districte vero praecipimus, quod illi qui confessiones audient, in loco patenti audiant confitentes, non in occulto, & praecipue, si fuerint mulieres. Habeat autem sacerdos sollicitudinem diligentem, ne dum audit confessionem, in facie respiciat confitentem, praecipue mulierem; sed cappam indutam habeat, capucium in capite vestitum teneat, et inclinatum'.

53. John of Kent, *Summa de penitentia* (London, B.L. Royal 9.A.XIV, f. 225rb): 'Penitentium omnium fere consuetudo est suum confessorem primitus salutare, quibus sacerdos applaudens uultu, blandis uerbis, gaudenti animo respondeat: "Bene ueneris frater", uel ita dicens potius, "Deus det tibi gratiam reconciliandi te ei, et in amore eius de cetero uiuendi et uoluntatem suam per omnia faciendi".'

54. See Thomas de Chobham, 'De penitente suscipiendo: De officiis penitentium', *Summa confessorum* 290–309.

55. Sampson, *Liber synodalis* 1029: 'Debet eum primo interrogare presbyter utrum sciat "Pater noster", "Credo in Deum", "Ave Maria", et si non sciat, moneat eum ut addiscat'. cf. Chobham, 'De penitente suscipiendo' 289–290.

56. *Summa penitentie Fratrum Praedicatorum* 34: 'Nota tamen quod de omnibus istis circumstantiis debet ab omnibus querere nisi tacendum discretioni sacerdotis uisum fuerit. Verbi gratia, a pueris uel ualde simplicibus non est querendum, ut mihi uidetur, utrum est <fornicatio> in ecclesia, uel de modo. . .' See Hostiensis, *Summa aurea*, 'De poenit. et remiss.' 15–44, cols. 1769–1794, for an extended consideration of confession 'ad status', and compare the confession in Boccaccio's story of Ser Cepparello (*Decameron* 1.1).

57. See, for example, the two formularies edited by Michaud-Quantin: 'Deux formulaires', "Confessio debet",' 53: 'Et si peccator nesciat confiteri, tunc sacerdos ipsum adiuvet, currens per septem mortalia vel criminalia peccata, postea per quinque sensus, et tunc per cogitationes et voluntates.' Idem, 'Ad habendam', 60–62: 'Ad habendum salutiferae confes-

penitent to provide a full and detailed account of his or her sins. Such a confession might have been expected of a monk or an exceptionally devout person in an earlier period; by the thirteenth century it was being held up as a model for all Christians.

Two general categories of sins were recognized: venial and mortal. Venial sins were the small peccadillos of which everyone was guilty to some degree and which were forgiven in general confession, in recitations of the 'Pater noster' ('dimitte debita nostra . . .'.) or in reception of the Eucharist.[58] Mortal or 'deadly' sins could be forgiven only after explicit acts of contrition and confession, accompanied by promises of amendment, reparation, and penitential satisfaction.

The identification of 'mortal' or deadly sins was not a matter to be taken lightly. Raymond of Peñafort warns confessors against too quickly pronouncing a sin to be mortal, without clear canonical warrant.[59] He directs the inquiring reader first to the Decalogue (Ex. 20, Deut. 5), all transgressions of which are mortal sins, and also to the lists of sins in Romans 1 and Galatians 5, to 'Augustine's' discussion of mortal and venial sins in Dist. 25 d.p.c.3 of the *Decretum*, and to the individual titles of Raymond of Peñafort's own work ('supra in singulis tractatibus').[60] The reference to the preceding titles of his *Summa* reminds us that the entire canon law of the Church, and not just the titles 'De penitentia', contained the information a skilled confessor needed to diagnose sins and to make sound judgments in the internal forum.[61]

Nor was it enough for the confessor to identify a sin named in one of the authoritative sources. He must also lead the penitent to consider the

---

sionis ordinem, haec breviter conscripsi. Primo fiat de puerilibus, utpote de inobedientia patris et matris . . . Postea de septem mortalibus . . . Postea de septem sacramentis . . . Post de decem praeceptis decalogi . . . Postremo autem de quinque sensibus . . . Ad ultimum vero de omnibus membris et primo de capite'.

58. Alan of Lille, *Liber poenitentialis* 4.24, p. 178; cf. Gratian, De pen. D.3 c.20.

59. Raymond of Peñafort, 3.34.21, c. 817: 'Unum tamen consulo, quod non sis nimis promptus iudicare mortalia peccata, ubi tibi non constat per certam scripturam esse mortalia'.

60. Raymond of Peñafort, ibid. The canonist ('Ricardus') who wrote the 'De doctrina sacerdotibus' (c. 1200: formerly attributed to Praepositinus of Cremona and known as 'De penitentiis iniungendis') begins his chapter 'De generibus mortalium peccatorum' with the striking assertion: 'Revolutis sacre scripture libris, diutius excogitando inveniri possunt octoginta unum genera mortalium peccatorum', which he then duly lists: 'Commessatio, Ebrietas, Negligentia, Turpitudo' (Stuttgart, Würt. Landesbibl., MS HB I 70, fol. 4v; a critical edition of the 'De doctrina sacerdotibus' is in preparation). Cf. Chobham, *Summa confessorum* 14–31.

61. On the canonical sources of Raymond of Peñafort's *Summa de penitentia*, see J.P. Renard, *Trois sommes de pénitence de la première moitié du XIIIe siècle: La 'Summula Magistri Conradi': Les sommes 'Quia non pigris' et 'Decime dande sunt'* (2 vols. Louvain-la-Neuve 1989) 1.53–62.

'circumstances' of the sin.[62] If an adulterer should confess simply to 'fornication' or to 'a carnal fault' this is no true confession; the equivocation serves to disguise the graver sin of adultery. Likewise if a murderer fails to confess that the murder took place in a church, or that it was done by slow torture rather than quickly with a sharp knife, or that clergy were involved in the bloodshed, the sin takes on a different and more serious aspect.[63] Only after such a full and detailed confession would the priest be able to assess the extenuating and the exacerbating circumstances of the sin and of the sinner and come to a just, equitable and salubrious judgment in the internal forum.

Judgment

Absolution

Having heard all the evidence, the priest must arrive at a judgment concerning absolution of the sinner and satisfaction for the sins.[64] If the penitent is truly sorry for the sins committed, has confessed them fully, and is intent on avoiding them in the future, the priest should assure the penitent of God's forgiveness. Some informal indication that the sins are forgiven would be made immediately after the penitent's confession and before the negotiation of a suitable penance.[65] A formal, rit-

---

62. See Stephan Kuttner, *Kanonistische Schuldlehre von Gratian bis auf die Dekretalen Gregors IX.* (ST 64; Vatican City 1935) 22–30; J. Gründel, *Die Lehre von den Umständen der menschlichen Handlung im Mittelalter* (Beiträge zur Geschichte der Philosophie und Theologie des Mittelalters 39.5; Münster i. W. 1963).

63. Walter of Cantilupe (1240); printed in *Councils and Synods* 2.1069–1070: 'Debet igitur penitens quid fecerit non in genere sed quantum potest specificando confiteri. Quod si commisit adulterium non suffict dicere quod fornicatus est vel quia lapsu carnis peccavit, quia sic per generalitatem celaret peccatum suum . . . Quod si homicidium fecerit quis vel luxuriam in loco sancto, vel aliquod peccatum commiserit, gravius peccat quam si in loco non sancto . . . Deinde videndum est quibus auxiliis quid fiat. Ut si forte interfecerit quis hominem auxilio clericorum vel religiosorum, plus peccat quam si solus hoc fecerit vel etiam cum laycis . . . Considerandum est etiam quomodo perpetratum est peccatum, ut si forte quis hominem interfecerit minus peccat si cito et acuto gladio decapitet eum quam si diu torquendo et hebeti membra dilaniet, id est membratim dividat, dum adhuc vivat'. Cf. Goering and Taylor, 'The "Summulae"' 588.

64. Alan of Lille, *Liber poenitentialis* 3.47, p. 156: 'Caveat spiritualis judex, sicut non commisit crimen nequitiae, ita non careat munere scientiae; oportet ut sciat cognoscere, quidquid debet judicare: judicaria enim potestas hoc postulat, ut quod debet judicare, discernat. Diligens enim investigator, sapienter interroget a peccatore, quod forsitan ignoret, vel verecundia velit occultare'.

65. The *Summa penitentie Fratrum Praedicatorum* instructs priests to encourage a full confession by responding to the admission of a particular sin with words like: 'Dominus dimittat tibi' (line 45), and to follow the penitent's confession immediately with the words: 'Parcat tibi Deus. Dominus transtulit a te peccatum tuum, uerumtamen penam temporalem oportet te sustinere'. (lines 244–245). After assigning a penance, the priest is to conclude

ual absolution would be pronounced when the penitent was dismissed.⁶⁶

But the priest needed also to decide if the sins that had been confessed were within his power and jurisdiction.⁶⁷ Not only was he encouraged to send difficult cases on to his superior for adjudication, but also bishops and popes could reserve for themselves the absolution of certain grave sins and require that someone guilty of these be sent to the diocesan or papal penitentiary.⁶⁸ Lists and discussions of such 'reserved cases' proliferated in the thirteenth and subsequent centuries, as did memorial verses composed to help the simple priest to remember them.⁶⁹

---

with a general confession and absolution: 'In fine quoque generalis fiat confessio, et a sacerdote absolutio detur' (line 276).

66. The form of this absolution changes, during the course of the thirteenth century, from the deprecatory: 'May God forgive you' ('Deus absolvat te'), to the declarative: 'I absolve you' ('Ego te absolvo a peccatis tuis'). P.-M. Gy has argued that the new formula arose 'in the office of the papal penitentiary, or among the masters of Bologna, and that it connotes a development of the canonical aspect of the sacrament'. The declarative form is already presupposed in Innocent IV's commentary on the Decretals; see Gy, 'Les définitions de la confession après le quatrième concile du Latran', *L'aveu* 283–296 at 290 and n. 33.

67. 'Scire autem debent sacerdotes quod non habent potestatem absoluendi penitentes ab enormibus que sibi reseruant maiores prelati in synodis nisi in articulo necessitatis', John of Kent, London, B.L. Royal 9.A.XIV, fol. 231va–vb. Cf. Raymond of Peñafort, *Summa de penitentia* 3.34.18, pp. 814–5; Serlo, *Summa de penitentia* 9–11.

68. 'Et nota hic quatuor. Primo quod inferior debet absoluere absolute et sine condictione de pertinentibus ad se. Vnde non debet dicere "Absoluo te si ibis ad episcopum, alias non", sed debet absolute dicere "Absoluo te". Secundo quod de aliis debet penitentem remittere ad episcopum, dummodo ipse proponat eum adire. Tertio quod penitentia debet absolute de pertinentibus ad se penitentem absoluere. Quarto quod ex hiis sequitur quod sic remissus ad episcopum solum tenetur ei confiteri de casu propter quem remissus est, non de aliis', Herman of Saxony O.F.M., *Casus abstracti a iure* (A.D. 1337) c. 5, Assisi, Sacro Convento di S. Francesco 447, fol. 121v–127r, ed. E. Reiter, *Mediaeval Studies* 57 (1995) 1–39 at page 32.

69. *Summa penitentie Fratrum Praedicatorum*, lines 270–275, 40–41: 'Et nota quod quidam casus sunt seruandi episcopis, quidam domino pape. Vnde uersus:

Si facit incestum, defloret, aut homicida,
Sacrilegus, patrum percussor, uel sodomita,
Pontificem querat; papam si miserit ignem,
Clerici percussor fuerit quoque uel symonia'.

Another influential discussion was that of John of Kent, *Summa de penitentia*, London, Royal 9.A.XIV, fol. 231va–vb: 'Scire autem debent sacerdotes quod non habent potestatem absoluendi penitentes ab enormibus que sibi reseruant /231vb/ maiores prelati in synodis nisi in articulo necessitatis, cuiusmodi sunt publici feneratores, incendiarii, falsi testes, periurantes super sacrosancta propter lucrum uel dampnum aliorum, et specialiter in assisis ubi sequitur exheredacio et in causa matrimonii et cetera huiusmodi sortilegii, falsarii sigillorum et cartarum et huiusmodi, tonsores monete, impedientes testamentum racionabile, et qui incidunt in canonem late sentencie, specialissime si clericum percusserint, destinati sunt ad curiam romanam, proditores, heretici, symoniaci, et qui partum supponunt ad alicuius exheredacionem. Similiter qui partum opprimunt negligenter siue maliciose, per pociones et huiusmodi postquam conceptum animatum fuerit, raptores rerum ecclesiasticarum siue retentores omni casu nisi in mortis articulo et tunc sub condicione. Romam sunt destinandi qui in canonem late sentencie inciderunt et symoniam commiserunt, premissa per hos uersus possunt retineri:

While the enumeration of reserved sins varied from place to place, certain sins became the special object of ecclesiastical censure through the process of excommunication.[70] It was incumbent on the priest to discover whether the penitent had incurred excommunication, either by means of a formal sentence ('data sententia') or by committing a sin, such as striking a cleric, that carried with it an automatic sentence of excommunication ('lata sententia').[71] A parish priest could not lift the excommunication sanctioned or imposed by an equal or by a higher power, nor could he grant absolution to a person who was excommunicate.

Finally, it was the priest's duty to discover during the course of the confession any irregularities of life that would impede the proper performance of the penitent's duties and actions in society. For the laity this meant primarily irregularities in their marital status and for clerics irregularities in their holy orders. This aspect of the confessor's task called for a quite sophisticated appreciation of the Church's developing canon law. Robert of Flamborough was one of the first writers to make available to confessors the general outlines of the new canon law concerning marriage and holy orders. He devoted the bulk of his work (Books Two and Three) to an exposition of these difficult issues.[72] If irregularities were discovered in the confessional, it behooved the priest to give proper counsel to the penitent and to direct him or her to the pertinent ecclesiastical authorities for dispensation, reconciliation, or further judgment.[73]

    Deditus usure, faciens incendia, falsi
    Testes, sortilegi, falsarius atque monete
    Tonsor, legatum impediens, a canone uincti
    Proditor, ac heresim sectans, uendensque columbas,
    Supponens partumue necans, rerumque sacrarum
    Raptor, presbitero nequeunt a simplice solui'.

    See also, Chobham, *Summa confessorum* 212–218.

    70. For a general orientation see E. Vodola, *Excommunication in the Middle Ages* (Berkeley 1986); J. Zeliauskas, *De excommunicatione vitiata apud glossatores (1140–1350)* (Zürich-Rome 1967); F. Russo, 'Pénitence et excommunication: Étude historique sur les rapports entre la théologie et le droit canon dans le domaine pénitentiel du XIe au XIIIe siècle', *Recherches de science religieuse* 33 (1946) 257–279, 431–461.

    71. Robert Grosseteste includes in his *Templum Dei* schematic outlines under the rubrics: 'Casus quibus excommunicatur quis ipso iure' (16 cases), 'Solus papa absoluit uel aliquis eius auctoritate'(6 cases), 'Percussores clericorum ab alio quam a papa absoluendi sunt'(3 cases), 'Ab episcopo loci absoluendi' (5 cases), etc., cc. 7.3–12, pp. 39–43.

    72. *Liber poenitentialis* 1.4, p. 62: 'Ego in primis de difficilioribus me expedire consueui, de matrimonio scilicet cum laicis, de simonia et aliis quae circa clericos attenduntur cum clericis'. Robert Grosseteste reduces Flamborough's teachings to schematic form in his *Templum Dei*, cc. 12, 16, and 17, pp. 53–54, 57–62.

    73. John of Kent, London, B.L. Royal 9.A.XIV, fol. 226rb depicts the following conversation between a confessor and a penitent who has had intercourse with his wife's relatives, within the prohibited degrees: '*Sacerdos:* Non es in uero matrimonio. Non enim est uxor tua

Satisfaction

The last judgment to be made by the priest concerned the penance or satisfaction for sins. Because the penitential court is a voluntary forum, it is necessary that the penitent agree to undertake whatever penance the priest sees fit to enjoin. The priest might begin by saying: 'The ancient canons require seven years of penance for each mortal sin, but because you and I are in court ('in foro sumus') I will enjoin on you a penance which you are willing and able to sustain'.[74] The priest was taught to determine an appropriate penance using his own judgment ('ad arbitrium suum'), by considering the traditional penitential canons, the gravity of the sins, the circumstances of the sins and of the sinner, and the willingness and ability of the penitent to sustain the penance enjoined. The actual penances were a mixture of prayers, alms, fasts, and corporal disciplines: prayers were reparation for sins against God, restitution and giving of alms for sins against neighbors, and fasts and disciplines for sins against self.[75]

Much has been made in past scholarship of the supposed rigor and rigidity of the traditional penitential tariffs, and of the radical change that came into penitential practice with the introduction of 'arbitrary' or discretionary penances in the twelfth and thirteenth centuries.[76] If taken too

---

quam tu habes pro uxore. *Penitens*: Quid faciam? *Sacerdos*: Hanc oportet dimittere. Si possis predictum cubitum probare coram episcopo, celebratibur diuorcium et concedetur utrique alii coniugi. *Penitens*: Non possum, quia nemo scit nisi ego. *Sacerdos*: Habeas ergo hanc tanquam sororem uel cognatam, non tamquam uxorem, idest non cognoscas eam quia ita precepit Dominus Papa in Decretali. *Penitens*: Nec ego nec ipsa possumus continere ... Quid ergo faciam? *Sacerdos*: Finge uel fac peregrinacionem et uiuere alibi sine illa. *Penitens*: Si uendam que habeo potero in longinquis aliam ducere et in uero matrimonio uiuere et mori? *Sacerdos*: De hoc pete a tuo episcopo.'

74. *Summa penitentie Fratrum Praedicatorum*, lines 245–249, p. 39: 'Cuilibet peccato mortali debetur septennis penitentia secundum canones, tamen quia ego et tu in foro sumus iniungam tibi quod uolueris et potueris portare'. Cf. Alan of Lille, *Liber poenitentialis* 4.19, p. 173.

75. *Summa penitentie Fratrum Praedicatorum*, lines 250–56, p. 39: 'Et tunc ad arbitrium suum iniungat ei penitentiam, id est ieiunia et orationes et disciplinas et helemosinas et uotum pacis indifferenter, set, si potest fieri, pena respondeat culpe. Vnde sciendum est quod qui peccat mortaliter offendit uel Deum uel proximum uel seipsum. In Deum peccat quis per blasfemiam et per periurium et huiusmodi, et tunc debet satisfieri per orationes. In proximum peccat per uiolentiam et per iniuriam aliquam, et debet reddere rapinam uel usuram et huiusmodi, et debet satisfieri per helemosinas. In semetipsum peccatur per gulam et luxuriam, et debet satisfacere per ieiunia et per disciplinas et alias macerationes carnis.'

The mention of a 'peace bond' ('votum pacis') as a type of penitential satisfaction may reflect the importance of peace-making in the pastoral activity of the mendicant friars; see A. Thompson, 'The Revivalist as Peace-Maker', *Revival Preachers and Politics in Thirteenth-Century Italy: The Great Devotion of 1233* (Oxford 1992) 136–156.

76. The entire discussion of 'arbitrary' penances needs to be recast in terms of the larger developments in the juridical culture of the twelfth century; see now Laurent Mayali, 'The Concept of Discretionary Punishment in Medieval Jurisprudence', *Studia in honorem*

strictly, such an interpretation would lead to the erroneous view that the earlier confessors had no scope for judgment ('arbitrium') in the application of the penitential law. A strict reading would also lead us to expect that the traditional canons lost their power and importance during the thirteenth century, and were replaced entirely by the unfettered judgment of the individual confessors. Neither view is accurate.[77]

The thirteenth-century parish priest was expected to know the tariff-penances handed down by the ancient fathers.[78] Like the priests in earlier centuries, he learned how to temper these penances to fit the circumstances of sin and sinner. Insofar as there was a change in practice in the later Middle Ages, this can best be understood in the context of the changing juridical culture: The thirteenth-century priest was taught to supplement the traditional tariffs, and even to replace them, by using the new skills of the ecclesiastical judge and of the canonical consultant. Common to both earlier and later confessors was the expectation that they would apply the law, whether ancient or modern, with a view toward more than strict justice; like a wise judge, the confessor should love mercy and strive for equity; like a medical doctor, he should look after the health of the penitent's soul.[79]

Another aspect of penitential satisfaction that called for a knowledge of the latest teachings of the canonists was the restitution of ill-gotten gains.[80] Restitution, in the ancient law codes, was a rather simple proce-

---

eminentissimi cardinalis Alphonsi M. Stickler (Studia et textus historiae iuris canonici 7; Rome 1992) 299–315. A good discussion of the older views on the replacement of tariffs with arbitrary penances is P. Michaud-Quantin, 'A propos des premières Summae confessorum: Théologie et droit canonique', RTAM 26 (1959) 264–306.

77. See Joseph Goering, 'The *Summa* of Master Serlo and Thirteenth-Century Penitential Literature', *Mediaeval Studies* 40 (1978) 290–311, at 296–297; P.J. Payer, 'The Humanism of the Penitentials and the Continuity of the Penitential Tradition', *Mediaeval Studies* 46 (1984) 340–354, at 346–350.

78. The author of the treatise *Homo quidam* (1155–1165) 36, assumes that a 'penitential' is kept in the apse of the church, and he encourages the priest to study it frequently: 'Legat ergo sacerdos frequenter in abside ecclesiae poenitentiale romanum vel Theodori Cantuariensis vel Bedae vel Brocardi [= Burchard of Worms?] vel ex eis excerpta, quia, ut dicit Augustinus, poenitentiae non sunt legitimae, quae secundum canones non assignantur.'

Robert Grosseteste provides a list of traditional penitential canons along with instructions on how they should be 'tempered' for modern use in his 'De paenitentiis iniungendis', ed. J. Goering and F.A.C. Mantello, 'The Early Penitential Writings of Robert Grosseteste', RTAM 54 (1987) 52–112 at 93–110.

For the continued use of penitential canons see J. Longère, 'La pénitence selon le 'Repertorium', les Instructions et Constitutions, et le Pontifical de Guillaume Durand', *Guillaume Durand Évêque de Mende (v. 1230–1296): Canoniste, liturgiste et homme politique*, ed. P.-M. Gy (Paris 1992) 105–133.

79. On the antiquity of these images of physician and judge, and on their origins in Roman law see Silano, 'Papacy and the Law' 360–361.

80. See K. Weinzierl, *Die Restitutionslehre der Frühscholastik* (Munich 1936); cf. Hostiensis, *Summa aurea*, 'De poenit. et remiss.' 61–62, cols. 1844–1865.

dure requiring little sophisticated analysis on the part of the confessor; the penitent was advised to return stolen property and to perform a penance for the sin. With the growing complexity of the later medieval economy, the opportunities for new and more subtle types of illicit gain multiplied apace. If priests were to judge wisely in the internal forum they needed to understand some of the intricacies of the new profit-economy. It is generally acknowledged that the groundwork for the modern discipline of economics was laid by medieval canonists and theologians in their discussions of usury, simony, tithes, and just price. This scholastic analysis was undertaken not for its own sake, however, and not for its relevance to the church courts, but because it was necessary for preparing confessors and judges in the internal forum.[81]

As this discussion has suggested, the number and kinds of sins identified as 'mortal' or death-dealing increased dramatically during the thirteenth century, as did the ability of confessors to analyze sins and their circumstances. But the growing sophistication of moral and legal analysis, and the urgency with which sinners were taught to search their consciences for signs of subtle and previously unrecognized sins, resulted in a kind of penitential inflation. If penitents were to make a full examination of conscience and a complete confession of sins, they must also have confidence that the acts of satisfaction required of them could be sustained. The spectre of seven years of penance in recompense for each mortal sin would daunt one who was attempting a conscientious, detailed, and frequent confession of all sins of thought, word, and deed. If such confessions were to be required in the internal forum, provision must also be made to make the requirement supportable.[82] 'Arbitrary' penances, tempered according to the informed judgment of the priest, were one way to approach the problem. The confessor was often advised to counsel the penitent about what would be required by a strict interpretation of the ancient canons, and then to negotiate about what was a sustainable penance.[83] But the thirteenth century also saw the growth of other remedies and aids for the penitent.

---

81. See Baldwin, *Masters, Princes and Merchants* 1.261–311; Lester K. Little, 'Pride Goes before Avarice: Social Change and the Vices in Latin Christendom', *American Historical Review* 76 (1961) 16–49.

82. The problem was stated clearly by Alan of Lille, *Liber poenitentialis* 3.51, p. 158: 'Sciendum quod pro singulis peccatis non debet singillatim diversas injungere poenitentias; sic enim cuilibet poenitenti, infinitas injungeret poenitentias. Sed pro omnibus debet injungere unam, quam pro sui arbitrio inspecta quantitate et numero delictorum, debet diminuere vel augere'.

83. *Summa penitentie Fratrum Praedicatorum*, lines 245–247, p. 39: 'Cuilibet peccato mortali debetur septennis penitentia secundum canones, tamen quia ego et tu in foro sumus iniungam tibi quod uolueris et potueris portare'.

First among these was the expansion of penitential commutations, remissions and indulgences.[84] Commutations allowed the sinner to substitute one type of penance for another; building a bridge or repairing a church might replace years of penitential fasting, for example. The new penance was, in theory, equivalent to the one which it commuted.

A greater boon was granted by remissions and indulgences (known variously as 'relaxationes', 'remissiones', 'absolutiones', and 'indulgentiae'). These developed gradually during the twelfth and thirteenth centuries. They allowed a bishop to forgive as much of a penance as he saw fit without requiring an equal exchange of punishments. Indulgences came to play a crucial role in the spiritual and physical economy of the later Middle Ages. They provided opportunities for new kinds of social investment by the Church,[85] and stimulated new forms of piety and devotion among the faithful. By the end of the Middle Ages, indulgences were an integral part of penitential satisfaction in the internal forum.

A second powerful, if fearful, recourse for repentant sinners was found in purgatory. Although long present in the Christian world-view, purgatory became the subject of special attention in the twelfth and subsequent centuries.[86] As a place of purgation after death, it provided an opportunity for repentant and confessed sinners to complete the unfulfilled penances that were required of them in the internal forum. By the early thirteenth century confessors were being taught to warn penitents:

> Brother, it is necessary that you undergo punishment either in this life or in purgatory. But the pains of purgatory are incomparably worse than any suffered in this life. Your life is in your hands; choose therefore either to undergo sufficient canonical and authoritative penances here, or await purgation.[87]

---

84. The classic studies are H.C. Lea, *A History of Auricular Confession and Indulgences in the Latin Church* (3 vols. Philadelphia 1896); N. Paulus, *Geschichte des Ablasses im Mittelalter vom Ursprunge bis zur Mitte des 14. Jahrhunderts* (2 vols. Paderborn 1922–1923). The importance of confessors' manuals for the study of this topic has long been recognized; see J. Dietterle, 'Die Summae confessorum (sive de casibus conscientiae) von ihren Anfängen an bis zu Silvester Prierias, unter Berücksichtigung ihrer Bestimmungen über den Ablass', ZKG 24 (1903) 353–374, 520–548; 25 (1904) 248–272; 26 (1905) 59–81, 350–362; 27 (1906) 70–83, 166–188, 296–310, 431–442; 28 (1907) 401–431.

85. See Haines, 'The Indulgence as a Form of Social Insurance', *Ecclesia anglicana* 183–191.

86. Whatever the weaknesses of J. Le Goff's specific arguments, he deserves the credit for redirecting modern discussions of purgatory in a most helpful way; see his *La Naissance du Purgatoire* (Paris 1981), translated by A.H. Goldhammer, *The Birth of Purgatory* (Chicago 1984).

87. Flamborough, *Liber poenitentialis* 5.16, p. 277: 'Frater, oportet te vel in hac vita puniri vel in purgatorio. Incomparabiliter autem gravior est poena purgatorii quam aliqua in hac vita. Ecce anima tua in manibus tuis; elige ergo tibi vel in hac vita sufficienter secundum poenitentias canonicas vel authenticas puniri vel purgatorium exspectare'.

The canonists devoted a good deal of effort to delineating the correlations of penance and purgation, and the workings of the spiritual economy that centered around penance, purgation, and indulgences,[88] while new forms of prayers for the dead and 'purgatorial piety' sprang up as adjuncts to the business of the internal forum.[89]

Such, in general outline, was the procedure followed in the penitential courts of medieval Europe. It has been suggested here that penance was one of the chief ways that everyone came into contact, on a regular basis, with the workings of the canonical system and with the science of canonical jurisprudence. It remains to describe how penitential law was shaped by the schools and by the doctrines and the writings of professional canonists, and how it was taught to the priests and people on whom the workings of the internal forum ultimately depended.

Education for the Internal Forum

The most common way for laypersons and parish priests to learn the new penitential procedures and teachings of the internal forum must have been through social practice rather than by reading books or hearing lectures in the schools. In the twelfth and thirteenth centuries few priests, and even fewer laypersons, were alumni of the schools of law and theology where penitential doctrine was being developed. Although parish priests were expected to be literate, it is unlikely that many had the resources or the inclination to procure and to study the technical literature of penance and confession.[90] But every priest and every layperson, no matter what their educational attainment, was expected to confess regularly in the internal forum. We may presume that a simple parish priest would learn about the new doctrines and practices of confession when he confessed his own sins to a more learned priest, perhaps one who had been to the schools or had read or heard the teachings of the modern masters. The simple priest would, in turn, convey something of the new doctrines and practices to his own parishioners when he heard their confessions.

By its very nature such 'social learning' leaves no clear trace in the historical record. If we wish to recover what was being taught and learned

---

88. See P.V. Aimone, 'Il purgatorio nella decretistica', *Proceedings Munich* 997–1009.
89. See J. le Goff, 'Social Victory: Purgatory and the Cure of Souls', *The Birth of Purgatory* 289–333; R. Sweetman, 'Christine of St. Trond and Her Preaching Apostolate: Thomas of Cantimpré's Hagiographical Method Re-visited', *Vox Benedictina* 9 (1992) 67–97; idem, 'Visions of Purgatory and their Role in Thomas of Cantimpré's "Bonum universale de apibus",' *Ons geestelijk erf* 67 (1993) 20–33.
90. See above, note 15, on clerical education; Goering, *William de Montibus* 59–67.

in the parishes of Christendom, the best we can do is to study the schools where confessors received their training and the literature that was written to train them. Having done so, we will be able to speak more confidently about the ideas and materials that an individual priest or layperson would have been likely to encounter, even if we are unable to ascertain with certainty any single person's actual experience of the internal forum.

The Schools

Primary Schools

The first taste of school life and book learning for most people in Western Europe in the thirteenth and subsequent centuries was in the 'song' or grammar school. Here boys (and sometimes, girls) would learn the rudiments of reading and writing and be introduced to the liturgical life of the Church by learning its songs and chants by heart. Such schools, found in most parishes, were taught by the local priest, by other clerics, or by monks or canons in the vicinity.[91] Although the curricula of these schools encompassed no technical training in canon law, students encountered some elements of penitential doctrine and practice there. For example, by the end of the thirteenth century a short didactic poem on confession, entitled *Peniteas cito peccator* ('Do penance quickly, O sinner'), became a common set-text in the primary schools. This poem, originally composed for use in the cathedral school of Lincoln, was accompanied by a gloss that elucidated the legal and theological doctrine of penance. It became one of the most popular and widely quoted poems of the later Middle Ages.[92]

Diocesan and Cathedral Schools

Both the Third and the Fourth Lateran Councils (1179 and 1215) required that schools be established in every diocese to provide education free of charge to prospective clerics.[93] A few of these schools, and others that grew up alongside and in conjunction with them (e.g. the schools of Chartres, Orléans, Padua, Tours), are well known to modern scholars. But the vast range of scholastic activities in diocesan and cathedral schools is only beginning to be investigated.[94]

---

91. F.W. Oediger, *Über die Bildung der Geistlichen in späten Mittelalter* (Leiden 1953) remains a valuable survey.
92. Both the poem and its original gloss are printed by Goering, *William de Montibus* 107–138.
93. Lateran III c. 18 = X. 5.5.1; Lateran IV c. 11 = X. 5.5.4.
94. See the suggestive comments by A. Gouron, 'Une école ou des écoles? Sur les canonistes français (vers 1150–vers 1210)', *Proceedings Berkeley* 223–240; see also the essays in *Luoghi e metodi di insegnamento nell' Italia medioevale (secoli XII–XIV)*, ed. L. Gargan and O. Limone (Galatina 1989).

Often diocesan schools grew up around bishop's households or around communities of priests (i.e. collegiate churches or 'pievi') headed by a superior. Young clerics would first be taught in these households and schools, and then take up positions of pastoral care in the dependent parishes and churches.⁹⁵ The author of the *Summa ad iniungendam* (c. 1200) expresses the general expectation clearly in addressing his treatise to priests who had missed the opportunity of being raised in such a household:

> To the venerable priests N. and N., Richard, their devoted friend. . . . You have asked me to write briefly about how you should exercise your priestly office and especially how you should enjoin penances on your subjects. Desiring to fulfill your needs in so far as I am able, I have composed this treatise for you and for others *who have not been fed at the table of a paterfamilias and have not drunk deeply of the wine of his household*.⁹⁶

The course of study in these diocesan schools must have varied greatly from place to place, and most of the detailed historical evidence for local curricula and lectures is lost to us. Nevertheless, a significant number of the treatises, 'summae', and manuals on penance and confession that have survived were written by masters in these diocesan schools, and were presumably directed to students there. A careful study of this literature will help to illuminate the instruction that was offered to the students in these schools.

Schools of the Regular Canons and Mendicant Friars

For the history of penance and confession, the schools of the Regular Canons and of the mendicant orders are especially important. Perhaps the most famous school for confessors in the thirteenth century was in the Abbey of St. Victor in Paris. Robert of Flamborough, a canon and penitentiary of St. Victor, composed his influential *Liber poenitentialis* there between 1208 and 1213. Both before and after Robert's day the abbey was a center of penitential and confessional expertise serv-

---

95. The bishop's responsibility for educating parochial clergy is clearly expressed in the canon 27 of the Fourth Lateran Council, *De instructione ordinandorum*, COD 248: 'Cum sit ars artium regimen animarum, districte praecipimus, ut episcopi promovendos in sacerdotes diligenter instruant et informent vel per se ipsos vel per alios viros idoneos super divinis officiis et ecclesiasticis sacramentis, qualiter ea rite valeant celebrare'. The so-called 'seminary legislation' of the Council of Trent continues this tradition of episcopal schools as the primary locus of clerical formation (Session 23, 15 July 1563, c.18; COD 750–753).

96. Stuttgart, Württ. Landesbibl. HB I 70, fol. 2r: 'Venerabilibus sacerdotibus N. et N. Ricardus eorum devotissimus... Recolo vos a me postulasse quod brevem doctrinam vobis darem, qualiter in suscepto officio sacerdotali maxime erga subditos in penitentiis iniungendis administrare debeatis. Unde vestre caritati in quantum valeo satisfacere cupiens, quedam breviter ad vestram utilitatem et aliorum *qui in convivio patris familias non sunt refecti nec ab ubertate domus sue inebriati*, componere curavi'.

ing especially the large population of students in and around Paris.⁹⁷

A similar relationship between a community of regular priests specializing in confession and a nascent university may have existed in Oxford in the late twelfth and early thirteenth centuries. The prior of the Augustinian Abbey of Osney in Oxford, Clement, certainly acted as diocesan penitentiary and referred cases to the papal penitentiary between 1200 and 1203.⁹⁸ The same prior of Osney also corresponded with Senatus, the learned archpriest and penitentiary of Worcester diocese, concerning penitential practices, dispensations, and marriage questions.⁹⁹

From the thirteenth century onward, however, it was the schools of the mendicant friars that took the lead in training expert confessors. The point has been made recently that, 'although the original mission of the Dominican order was that of preaching, within four years of its foundation the order became an Order of Confessors as well as an Order of Preachers'.¹⁰⁰ The schools of the friars are best known today for their great scholastic theologians—Albert and Thomas, Bonaventure and Scotus, for example. But the practical training in the 'cura animarum' that was provided in these schools to thousands of lesser friars (the 'fratres communes'), and to other clerics who were permitted to attend, would seem to have had an even greater impact on the intellectual and social life of Europe. It is in the mendicant schools that we can see most clearly the development of a curriculum designed to train priests as ministers and judges in the internal forum.¹⁰¹

Universities

Of all the medieval schools, universities have been the most thoroughly and carefully studied. We can reconstruct with some certainty the con-

---

97. See C. Egger, 'De praxi paenitentiali Victorinorum', *Angelicum* 17 (1940) 156–179; J. Longère, 'Documents sur la confession à l'abbaye de Saint-Victor au 12e et au 13e siècles', *Petrus Pictaviensis <Summa de confessione> Compilatio praesens* (CCCM 51; Turnhout 1980) lxxv–lxxxvii; idem, 'La fonction pastorale de Saint-Victor à la fin du XIIe et au début du XIIIe siècle', *L'Abbaye Parisienne de Saint-Victor au Moyen Age* (Bibliotheca Victorina 1; Turnhout 1991) 291–313.

98. See C.R. Cheney, *Pope Innocent III and England* (Päpste und Papsttum 9; Stuttgart 1976) 66–67, 70–71.

99. See P. Delhaye, 'Deux textes de Senatus de Worcester sur la pénitence', RTAM 19 (1952) 203–224, at 205. Senatus describes himself as 'archipresbiterum ecclesie' [of Worcester] and as having 'penitentium curam et censuram confessionum', p. 204.

100. Boyle, 'Fratres Communes' 249.

101. See Boyle, 'Fratres communes'; L.E. Boyle, 'The *Summa confessorum* of John of Freiburg and the Popularization of the Moral Teaching of St. Thomas and Some of His Contemporaries', *St. Thomas Aquinas, 1274–1974: Commemorative Studies*, ed. A.A. Maurer (2 vols. Toronto 1974) 2.245–268 (reprinted in *Pastoral Care*); Rusconi, 'I Francescani e la confessione'.

tents of lectures, the textbooks and glosses, the disputed questions and other academic exercises, and the courses of study leading to degrees in civil law, canon law, and theology.[102] Much detailed work remains to be done, but the general outlines and content of a university education in the Middle Ages are becoming increasingly clear.

Students and masters congregated in university centers to discuss the latest and the most sophisticated analyses of intellectual questions. One is tempted, therefore, to think of university masters and students as pure scholars who would have little interest in practical questions concerning the care of souls and the internal forum, but the evidence suggests otherwise. Many of the most influential practical 'summae' and handbooks were written by university masters and their students. Raymond of Peñafort wrote his *Summa de penitentia* and *Summa de matrimonio* on the basis of his training at Bologna. Both Henry of Susa (Hostiensis) and Geoffrey of Trani taught at Bologna, and both composed extremely popular works (Hostiensis' *Summa aurea* and Geoffrey's *Summa super titulis decretalium*) for the use of pastors engaged in the care of souls.[103] We have every reason to believe that university masters and their students were deeply interested and involved in education for the 'cura animarum'.

Schools at the Papal Curia

The schools of theology, canon and civil law that flourished at the papal curia during the thirteenth century helped to train young clerics who were called from all parts of Europe to service in the households of the pope, the cardinals, and other curial officials.[104] These schools constituted a kind of curial academy where important questions could be discussed, theological and legal expertise could be solicited, and where an 'opinio curiae' could be formulated and expressed.[105]

---

102. The literature is too vast to summarize. The classic study is H. Rashdall, *Universities of Europe in the Middle Ages*, ed. F.M. Powicke and A.B. Emden (3 vols. Oxford 1936). For recent surveys see HUC, HUE, and HUO, as well as chapters 1 (Hoeflich and Grabher) and 4 (Brundage) in this volume.

103. For the pastoral intent of these works see their respective prologues: Hostiensis, *Summa aurea*; Gottofredo da Trani (Goffredus de Trani), *Summa super titulis Decretalium* (Lyon 1559; reprinted Aalen 1992). Both were widely known outside the law schools and quoted in the practical treatises and 'summae confessorum' of the thirteenth and subsequent centuries.

104. See H. Denifle, *Die Entstehung der Universitäten des Mittelalters bis 1400* (Berlin 1885) 301-310; R. Creytens, 'Le "Studium Romanae Curiae" et la maître du Sacré Palais', *Archivum Fratrum Praedicatorum* 12 (1942) 1-83; A. P. Bagliani, 'La fondazione dello "studium curiae": Una rilettura critica', *Luoghi e metodi di insegnamento nell'Italia medioevale (secoli XII–XIV)* 59-81.

105. Bagliani, 'Studium curiae' 80-81.

The schools of canon and civil law were 'private' schools that had grown up and been fostered in the shadow of the curia; only the lecturer in theology was supported by a pontifical stipend.[106] But even the curial 'theologian' was expected to be expert in matters pertaining to pastoral care, penance, and the internal forum. For example, the earliest theological master whose name is known to us, Bartholomew [of Breganza], O.P., was also papal penitentiary and chaplain under Innocent IV.[107] A thorough study of these curial schools and their masters, both legal and theological, would help to broaden our understanding of the education for pastoral care and for the internal forum that was available to those at the center of the ecclesiastical establishment.

This brief survey of the medieval schools suggests something of the institutional opportunities available to medieval clerics for learning about the 'cura animarum' and the internal forum. An even more abundant resource for such education was the burgeoning literature of pastoral care, and especially the *Summae de penitentia* and the manuals of confession that were produced in great profusion during the later Middle Ages.

The Literature of Penance and Confession

More than one hundred years ago Johann F. von Schulte divided the second volume of his magisterial *Geschichte der Quellen und Literatur des canonischen Rechts* into two parts. In the first he treated 'the pure jurists' (*die reiner Juristen*) and in the second part he discussed some fifty-seven authors 'who wrote for the internal forum' ('die Schriftsteller für das forum internum').[108] This second part of Schulte's history represents a pioneering effort to analyze the vast body of practical literature on penance and confession and to bring it within the purview of a scientific and scholarly study of the history of canon law.

As useful as was Schulte's division, it also helped to establish the view that there were two different types of medieval canonical writers, pure jurists on the one hand and practical authors on the other, and that the two groups had very little to do with each other. The reality was, of course, quite different. The boundaries between 'pure' law and practical application were constantly being blurred in the medieval schools. Just as the practice of penance in the internal forum was shaped and directed by the doctrines of the schools, so were the interests and teachings of the learned

---

106. Ibid. 67–74.
107. 'Bartholomaeum de ordine Praedicatorum, tunc capellanum et poenitentiarum suum, et regentem in curia nostra in theologica facultate', quoted in Bagliani, 'Studium Curiae' 64, n. 29.
108. Schulte, QL 408–456, 511–526.

masters shaped by the practical demands and the requirements of pastors and confessors engaged in the care of souls. It would be hard to find in the Middle Ages a 'pure' jurist, one whose writings were concerned with the Church's law only as a pure and scientific discipline. Nearly all canonistic writers were deeply (and often explicitly) concerned with practical goals and with the distinguishing characteristic of the canon law, its concern for the health of souls ('salus animarum').[109] Although the following survey discusses primarily those whom Schulte called 'writers for the internal forum', it is worth remembering that the practical literature of penance and confession formed an integral part of the larger juridical and canonical culture.

Much work has been done since 1877 on the literature of pastoral care and especially on the manuals and 'summae' written for the 'internal court' of penance, but the study of this literature remains in its infancy. We still have no adequate 'repertorium' of authors and of texts,[110] no comprehensive survey of manuscripts,[111] and not even a generally accepted taxonomy and terminology with which to carry out further research.[112] Nevertheless it is possible to sketch the broad outlines of developments and to discuss briefly a few texts that are representative of the vast literature produced in the two centuries following the publication of Gratian's *Decretum*.

From Gratian to Lateran III (1140–1179)

An anonymous author, writing probably in Normandy between the years 1155 and 1165, presumes that every church will possess a 'peniten-

---

109. Hostiensis, for example, argues in his *Summa aurea* that canon law, rather than theology or civil law, is the 'art of arts' and science of sciences that the Fourth Lateran Council had in mind when it proclaimed that the care of souls ('regimen animarum') was the highest discipline of study: 'Est igitur hec nostra scientia non pure theologica; siue ciuilis; sed vtrique participans nomen proprium sortita canonica vocatur; sicut ius emphyteoticum non est venditio nec locatio sed contractus per se vtrique participans, C. de iure emphy. l.i. et de hac legitur xxxi. di. Nicena, et hec nostra lex siue scientia vere potest scientiarum scientia nuncupari, infra de eta. et quali. Cum sit ars artium' (*Summa aurea*, Proemium).

110. The most important surveys are: Schulte, QL; Dietterle, 'Die Summae confessorum'; Teetaert, 'La confession aux laïques'; idem, 'Quelques "Summae de paenitentia" anonymes dans la Bibliothèque Nationale de Paris', *Miscellanea Giovanni Mercati* (6 vols. ST 121–126 Vatican City 1946) 2.311–343; P. Michaud-Quantin, *Sommes de casuistique et manuels de confession au moyen âge (XII–XVIe siècles)* (Louvain 1962).

111. See M.W. Bloomfield, B.-G. Guyot, D.R. Howard, and T.B. Kabealo, *Incipits of Latin Works on the Virtues and Vices, 1100–1500 A. D.* (Cambridge Mass. 1979). For Dominican writers see T. Kaeppeli, *Scriptores Ordinis Praedicatorum Medii Aevi* (4 vols. Rome 1970–1980), and for Franciscans, B. Roest, *Franciscan Literature of Religious Instruction before the Council of Trent* (Leiden 2004).

112. The most sophisticated attempt to classify the literature of penance and confession is L.E. Boyle's 'Summae confessorum', *Les Genres littéraires dans les sources théologiques et phi-*

tial', and that all priests should know its contents: 'The priest should read frequently, in the apse of the church, the Roman Penitential, or that of Theodore of Canterbury, or of Bede, or of Burchard, or excerpts from these'.[113] That the old penitentials, composed in the early Middle Ages, should still be recommended reading in the twelfth and subsequent centuries need occasion neither surprise nor scepticism. It is entirely plausible that some version of a 'penitential', excerpted and adapted by contemporary scribes and readers, should have been available in most parish churches, along with the liturgical and sacramental books that pertain to the priestly office.[114] These books may have born the names of such saintly and authoritative authors as Bede, Theodore, or Burchard, and even have retained some family resemblance to the traditional texts. But a cursory examination of the surviving manuscripts reveals that the copies being produced in the later Middle Ages are often quite different from those of the ninth, tenth, and eleventh centuries, and from the printed editions that represent these traditional penitentials to scholars today.[115] Only a detailed study of the many 'corrupt' (i.e. updated, augmented, excerpted,

---

losophiques médiévales: Définition, critique, et exploitation (Actes du Colloque international de Louvain-la-Neuve, 25–27 mai 1981; Louvain 1982) 227–237. It can be represented thus:

I. For Priests
   A Academic
      1. Summae confessorum
      2. Summae de casibus
   B Practical
      1. Summae confitendi
      2. Confessionalia (e.g. interrogations excommunications, penitential canons).
II. For Laity
   A. Preparation for confession
   B. Examination of conscience

See also his 'The Fourth Lateran Council and Manuals of Popular Theology', *The Popular Literature of Medieval England*, ed. T.J. Heffernan (Knoxville 1985) 30–43.

A simpler but less nuanced classification is proposed by C. Bergfield in his discussion of 'Beichtjurisprudenz', Coing, *Handbuch* 999–1015:

1. Comprehensive summae
   A. Organized systematically
   B. Organized alphabetically
2. Abbreviations and smaller systematic summae
3. Glosses and supplements
4. Treatises

113. *Homo quidam*, 36; see note 78 above.
114. See Gratian, *Decretum* D.38 c.4 and 5.
115. See, for example, the copies of the 'Corrector et Medicus', Book 19 of Burchard's *Decretum*, found in the fifteenth century codices in Bamberg, Staatsbibliothek Msc. Theol. 106 (Q.III.31) and 108 (Q.III.25), where the text of 'Burchard' provides only a bare framework into which are inserted excerpts from other authorities and from the teachings of the modern masters.

and rearranged) copies of the older penitentials will allow us to appreciate the way they continued to function as a basic resource in the internal forum of the later Middle Ages.

The period between 1140 and 1179 also witnessed the composition of some new penitentials. One of the most popular and best known of these is the *Penitentiale* of Bishop Bartholomew of Exeter, written between 1155 and 1170.[116] The bulk of the work consists in copies of authoritative penitential canons, drawn mostly from Burchard, Ivo of Chartres, and Gratian,[117] but Bartholomew also makes his own contributions to the growing literature and jurisprudence surrounding the penitential forum.[118]

Other types of treatises on confession were newly composed in this same period. One of the most interesting is the treatise *Homo quidam*, quoted above, probably written between 1155 and 1165, and published from an Avranches manuscript by Michaud-Quantin.[119] This treatise presumes in its readers a familiarity with the traditional penitentials, and discusses in detail many of the practical problems and questions that confront a priest in hearing confessions and assigning penances.

Michaud-Quantin describes the *Homo quidam* as 'archaic' because it ignores Gratian's *Decretum*. Gratian's work, indeed, marked a turning point in the history of penance as well as of canonical jurisprudence. His selections of penitential canons from Burchard, Ivo of Chartres, and from the older sources became normative for the rest of the Middle Ages. His quotations from the pseudo-Augustinian treatise *De vera et falsa penitentia*, helped give this revolutionary little work its authority and prestige.[120] But most of all Gratian provided scholars with a textbook that could help them to think systematically and to argue juridically about the important issues of Christian law and morality. For confessors and judges in the internal forum, the interest of Gratian's *Decretum* extended well beyond its treatises 'De penitentia' and 'De consecratione'; all the 'Distinctiones' and

---

116. A. Morey, *Bartholomew of Exeter, Bishop and Canonist: A Study in the Twelfth Century, with the Text of Bartholomew's Penitential from the Cotton MS Vitellius A. XII* (Cambridge 1937).

117. Such are the sources identified by Morey, *Bartholomew of Exeter* 173–174: but he cautions that he has sought to do no more than indicate 'the immediate sources of the Penitential, and that there is little doubt that further work would reveal far more than has been obtained'.

118. See Stephan Kuttner and Eleanor Rathbone, 'Anglo-Norman Canonists of the Twelfth Century: An Introductory Study', *Traditio* 7 (1949–51) 279–385 at 283, 295, 321, reprinted with additional material in *Gratian and the Schools of Law* (London 1983); J. Longère, 'Quelques "Summae de poenitentia" à la fin du XIIe siècle et au début du XIIIe siècle', *La piété populaire au moyen âge* (Paris 1977) 45–58.

119. *Homo quidam* 5–54.

120. *De vera et falsa penitentia* is printed in PL 40.1113–1130; its date (eleventh to twelfth century) and place of composition remain undetermined.

all the 'Causae' were relevant to the judge of souls. Dante's insight, quoted at the beginning of this chapter, was correct: practitioners in both the internal and the external fora of the Church learned their craft at Gratian's feet.

A final type of literature for the internal forum that began to flourish in the decades after 1140 is something that might be called the 'jurisconsult' for confessors. The most notable examples of these are papal responses to questions posed by confessors and penitentiaries concerning difficult cases. A few responses have survived in the canonical collections and in the papal registers; there must have been many more.[121] Other jurisperiti also offered professional opinions on matters of penance and confession. We have, for example, a series of six letters from the 1160s and 70s sent by the monk Senatus, archpriest and penitentiary of Worcester diocese in England, to various correspondents who had asked questions pertaining to the internal forum.[122]

From Lateran III to Lateran IV (1179–1215): The Interconciliar Period

Leonard E. Boyle has drawn attention to the period between the Third and Fourth Lateran Councils as a time of gestation for the practical literature of pastoral care that would flourish so widely in the thirteenth and subsequent centuries.[123] He draws particular attention to the 'new, independent literary genres such as "Quaestiones", "Distinctiones", "Summae", "Notabilia", and "Brocarda"', of the schools of canon law. These new literary forms, he argues, arose out of classroom situations, and, 'being didactic in origin and free of form', they were 'well suited to the popularization at a pastoral level' of scholastic teachings that touched on the practical care of souls.[124]

Research into the more practical examples of this new didactic literature emanating from the schools of law is only beginning. Giulio Silano has suggested that the *Distinctiones Decretorum* of the Bolognese-trained Richardus Anglicus, produced at Paris c. 1200, reflect something of the practical and popularizing interests of Parisian theological masters like Peter the Chanter. Richardus' *Distinctiones* represent a transformation of

---

121. See for example the letter of Clement III to the 'confessor of Salisbury' ('confessori Salesberiensi'), JL 16624. By the thirteenth century such questions were routinely handled by the office of the papal penitentiary.

122. These are mostly unpublished; see Mary Cheney, *Roger, Bishop of Worcester 1164–1179* (Oxford 1980) 58–61.

123. L.E. Boyle, 'The Inter-Conciliar Period 1179–1215 and the Beginnings of Pastoral Manuals', *Miscellanea Rolando Bandinelli Papa Alessandro III*, ed. F. Liotta (Accademia Senesi degli Intronati; Siena 1986) 45–56.

124. Boyle, 'The Inter-Conciliar Period' 55–56.

the more cumbersome and technical style of the Bolognese 'distinctiones' into a type of popular canonical literature, suitable for those studying for the 'cura animarum'.[125]

Another example of a text from the law schools that discusses practical questions concerning the care of souls is the *Notabilia super Decretum* found in Leiden, Rijksuniversiteit, MS Vulc. 48.[126] The work is divided into three parts, the first concerning clerics, the second concerning 'church business, both clerical and lay', and the third concerning the sacraments.[127] A number of contemporary masters are quoted, and the teachings of the canonists are applied to the unravelling of many practical questions. This text, and others like it, represent a rich and largely unexplored source for the history of canon law and its practical application.

Alongside these texts emanating from the law schools is a flourishing, if inchoate, practical literature from the schools of theology.[128] Peter Comestor and Peter the Chanter are the most famous of the teachers to apply their energies to solving practical questions. Martin Grabmann referred to them as representatives of a 'moral' and 'practical' school among the theologians[129] and characterized their work as an application of both law and theology to practical problems of the day.[130] Among their students, Cardinal Robert Courson was perhaps the most influential in continuing and developing the unique blend of canon law and theology that characterized the practical 'theology' of many Parisian masters in the late twelfth and early thirteenth century.[131]

---

125. G. Silano, 'The "Distinctiones Decretorum" of Ricardus Anglicus: An edition' (2 vols. Ph.D. Dissertation, University of Toronto 1981).
126. Fol. 9r–25v. A fragmentary version of this text, containing the prologue and a few lines of Part One, is found in a Munich manuscript; see Kuttner, *Repertorium* 182: 'Das Summenfragment "Inter cetera que ecclesiastice dignitati".' Another copy may be found in Munich, Staatsbiblio. lat. 16084.
A similar type of text is the *Notabilia de excommunicatione et penitentia*; see Kuttner, *Repertorium* 240–241.
127. 'In tres partes hoc opus distribuit. Prima enim gradibus et officiis clericorum deputatur. In secunda de ecclesiasticis negotiis, tam clericorum quam laicorum, puta de coniugiis disseretur. In ultima multiplex sacramentorum institutio et celebranda forma plenius edocetur', fol. 9ra.
128. On the growth of this literature see Goering, *William de Montibus* 29–42, 58–83.
129. M. Grabmann, *Die Geschichte der scholastischen Methode* (Freiburg im Breisgau 1909–1911; reprinted Darmstadt 1957) 2.476–501.
130. An excellent evocation of the interests and approaches of these writers is to be found in Baldwin, *Masters, Princes and Merchants*.
131. See V.L. Kennedy, 'Robert Courson on Penance', *Mediaeval Studies* 7 (1945) 291–366; idem, 'The Content of Courson's *Summa*', *Mediaeval Studies* 9 (1947) 81–107; N. Brieskorn, 'Die Kirche in der Gesellschaft des frühen 13. Jahrhunderts—Zwischen Kollaboration und Protest', *Ius et historia: Festgabe für Rudolf Weigand zu seinem 60. Geburtstag von seinen Schülern, Mitarbeitern und Freunden*, ed. N. Höhl (Würzburg 1989) 158–169.

Although the Parisian schools of law and theology were in the forefront of the effort to apply scholastic expertise to practical and pastoral questions during the interconciliar period, these schools never overshadowed the continuing production of penitential and confessional literature at the local diocesan level. New penitentials, manuals for confessors, 'summae', and treatises were composed for and by many individual bishops, diocesan penitentiaries, and masters and students in the cathedral schools. Alan of Lille dedicated his extensive and innovative *Liber poenitentialis* to Henry, archbishop of Bourges (1191–1199). In it he provided Henry with an up-to-date penitential, combining the traditional canons with the latest teachings of the schools of law and theology.[132] Peter of Roissy performed a similar service for the cathedral school at Chartres, where he was chancellor, in composing his *Manuale de mysteriis ecclesiae* (c. 1205), a vast 'summa' of pastoral law and theology.[133] William de Montibus, chancellor of Lincoln cathedral (c. 1185–1213), wrote a number of works on penance and confession. One of these, a brief verse-compilation entitled *Peniteas cito peccator*, circulated widely throughout Europe during the rest of the Middle Ages, and played an important role in shaping the way medieval people understood penance.[134]

Other diocesan officials contributed a similar variety of pastoral and penitential writings for diverse audiences during this period. Robert of St. Pair (de sancto Paterno), archdeacon and penitentiary of Rouen (c. 1200), wrote a brief *Liber penitentialis* for use in the archdiocese.[135] Gerald of Wales, who studied law at Paris in the 1170s, composed his *Gemma ecclesiastica* (c. 1197) to instruct the Welsh clergy concerning the sacraments and clerical morality.[136] Guy of Southwick composed a *Tractatus de virtute confessionis* for Bishop William of Hereford (1190–1198).[137]

The authors and recipients of many penitential texts written in this period remain unidentified, but the range and diversity of the literature is

---

132. See J. Longère, 'Théologie et pastorale de la pénitence chez Alain de Lille', *Cîteaux* 30 (1979) 125–188.

133. See V.L. Kennedy, 'The Handbook of Master Peter Chancellor of Chartres', *Mediaeval Studies* 5 (1943) 1–50.

134. The *Peniteas cito* is printed, along with William's gloss, in Goering, *William de Montibus* 107–138. William's other penitential writings include a *Speculum penitentis* 179–210, and *De penitentia religiosorum* 211–221.

135. Unpublished; see P. Michaud-Quantin, 'A propos des premières "Summae confessorum"', RTAM 26 (1959) 264–306 at 268–269.

136. Giraldus Cambrensis, *Gemma ecclesiastica*, ed. J.S. Brewer (Rolls Series 21.2 London 1862); translated by J.J. Hagen, *The Jewel of the Church* (Leiden 1979). The work is imbued with the fruits of Gerald's canonical studies; he presented a copy to Innocent III in 1199.

137. Printed by A. Wilmart, 'Un opuscule sur la confession composé par Guy de Southwick vers la fin du XIIe siècle', RTAM 7 (1935) 337–352.

noteworthy. For example, an unidentified 'R' addressed a penitential, in the style of Bartholomew of Exeter's compilation, to an equally unidentified 'Stephanus'. The penitential is divided into two parts: the first contains 26 numbered chapters and discusses penance in general, the second, with 87 chapters, is a collection of authoritative penitential canons.[138]

Another intriguing example of this not-quite-anonymous literature is the *Summa ad iniungendam penitentiam*, once attributed to Praepositinus of Cremona but now ascribed to an otherwise unknown 'Richardus' who was trained in canon law and composed his treatise (c. 1200) for two parish priests who felt the need for some formal instruction concerning pastoral care and especially the enjoining of penances.[139]

Monks also contributed. An anonymous Benedictine, writing during the reign of Frederick Barbarossa, composed a *Liber de penitentia* for his fellow monks which discussed many of the important questions of the day, and included a biting attack on monks who took part in Frederick's crusade journey of 1188.[140] Stephen, a Cistercian abbot of Stanlaw in England, is credited with the composition of a *Speculum confessionis*, written sometime before 1215.[141]

These examples are intended only to indicate the range of literature produced in the years before 1215 to educate clerics in the art of hearing confessions and assigning penances. This was a period of experimentation and exploration. The texts range from simple adaptations of the old penitentials to quite sophisticated applications of the teachings of the twelfth-century schools of law and theology to the church's penitential discipline.

Robert of Flamborough's *Liber penitentialis* (1208–1213) is an outstanding example of this latter type of treatise. His is the first penitential to make a full-scale application of the new canon law of the decretists and decretalists to questions of the internal forum.[142] Nothing is known of Robert's education and training before he became a canon (1205), and then penitentiary, of the Abbey of St. Victor in Paris. He probably studied in the Pa-

---

138. Unpublished; see Bloomfield, *Incipits*, nos. 1674 and 3457.

139. Unpublished; a critical edition is being prepared by J. Goering; see M. Boháček, 'Un manuscrit intéressant du "Compendium" de Werner von Schussenried', *Traditio* 18 (1962) 472–482; Stephan Kuttner, 'Summa ad iniungendam penitentiam', *Traditio* 19 (1963) 537–538.

140. Printed in PL 213. 863–904.

141. Unpublished; see Bloomfield, *Incipits*, no. 0184.

142. J.J.F. Firth's observation seems still to hold true: 'Insofar as can be determined at the present state of research, Flamborough was the first to make available to confessors in a short, readable, comprehensive work the new law of the decretists and of the decretals, organized in a practical way for solving cases of conscience', Firth, ed., *Liber poenitentialis* 17–18.

risian schools and is designated as 'magister' in some documents.[143] He may have studied canon law, and he certainly consulted the Parisian canonists carefully.[144] The story that Flamborough's penitential was approved or adopted by the Fourth Lateran Council is apocryphal,[145] but his new-style penitential may have been discussed and circulated at the Council, and it certainly helped give shape to the new literature for the internal forum that would flourish in the subsequent decades.

From the Fourth Lateran Council in 1215 to 1250

In the wake of the Fourth Lateran Council new manuals and 'summae' for confessors were produced in the same molds that had been cast in the interconciliar period. Peter of Poitiers and Jacques of St. Victor, both canons of St. Victor in Paris, continued the Victorine tradition of writing practical guides for confessors of their order.[146] John of Kent, a canonist of the 'Anglo-Norman school', composed a *Summa de penitentia* (c. 1216) based on Robert of Flamborough's *Liber penitentialis*. John clarifies Flamborough's arguments, bringing them in line with the latest teachings of the canonists, and devotes an entire book of his *Summa* to the kind of model-dialogues between priest and penitent that Flamborough had introduced here and there into his *Liber*.[147] New types of 'summae' and manuals were also developed in this period. One of the most popular, and most ambitious, was Thomas of Chobham's 'Summa' *Cum miserationes* ('Summa confessorum'). Thomas had studied at Paris at the turn of the twelfth and thirteenth centuries, and was subdean and penitentiary of Salisbury Cathedral when he composed his *Summa* (c. 1216).[148] Its unique blend of canon law, popular theology, and sensible advice to confessors made Thomas' one of the most widely copied and utilized penitential 'summae' of the later Middle Ages.[149]

St. Dominic and his friars became engaged in producing guides for

143. Firth, ed., *Liber poenitentialis* 1–8; Baldwin, *Masters, Princes and Merchants* 32.
144. *Liber poenitentialis*, 74: 'Sacerdos. Utique aliquis illorum qui hoc dicunt [i.e. quod votum simplex nullum dirimit matrimonium], legens Parisius in decretis, concessit mihi quod etiam cum sacerdote posset papa dispensare ut contraheret.'
145. S. Kuttner, 'Pierre de Roissy and Robert of Flamborough', *Traditio* 2 (1944) 492–499, at 496.
146. *Petrus Pictaviensis <Summa de confessione> Compilatio praesens*, ed. J. Longère, (CCCM 51; Turnhout 1980).
147. An edition is in preparation; see Goering, 'The *Summa de penitentia* of John of Kent', BMCL 18 (1988) 13–31.
148. Edited from three manuscripts by F. Broomfield, *Thomae de Chobham*. The most recent biography is in F. Morenzoni, ed. *Thomas de Chobham, Summa de arte praedicandi* (CCCM 82; Turnhout 1988) xxxi–xxxvi.
149. This substantial text survives in nearly 200 manuscript copies along with innumerable excerpted and abridged versions; it was printed twice before 1500.

confessors almost as soon as the Order of Preachers began to take shape. Among their earliest recruits were students and masters in the law schools. Three of these, Paul of Hungary, Raymond of Peñafort, and Hugh of St. Cher, serve to illustrate the lively interest amongst the early Dominicans in providing useful treatises to aid confessors. Paul of Hungary, a professor of law at Bologna, composed his *De confessione* c. 1221.[150] Paul divided his treatise into 26 titles treating the 'questions that arise concerning confession'.[151]

Raymond of Peñafort composed a much more substantial *Summa de penitentia* for the friars c. 1225. A Catalan by birth, Raymond of Peñafort studied and taught law at Bologna before returning to Barcelona, where he joined the Dominicans.[152] Raymond seems to have been influenced by the *Summa titulorum decretalium* of the canonist Ambrose (c. 1215),[153] and is the first writer to organize a penitential 'summa' into Books and Titles corresponding, in large part, to the divisions of the systematic decretal collections and 'Extravagantes'. Raymond's *Summa* was destined to enjoy unparalleled success in the succeeding decades, but in the 1220s his was only one among many such texts.

Quite a different type of text also flourished among the early Dominicans: the confessional 'formulary' or guide to hearing confessions. One of these, published by Michaud-Quantin, is associated with the writings of Hugh of St. Cher, a professor of law and a bachelor of theology at Paris when he entered the Dominican Order in 1225 or 1226. Hugh became one of the most influential Paris theologians, and then was made cardinal-priest of Santa Sabina in 1244.[154] Another such formulary, written to instruct the friars (and others) in the practical art of hearing confessions, is the *Summa penitentie fratrum predicatorum* (1220 x 1230) that circulated widely, and was even glossed as a school text in the mid-thirteenth century.[155]

---

150. Printed three times, but none is an adequate edition; see Michaud-Quantin, *Sommes de casuistique* 24–26, and the older literature cited there.

151. Prologue, printed in *Bibliotheca Casinensis seu Codicum manuscriptorum qui in tabulario Casinensi asservantur* (Monte Cassino 1880) 4.191: 'Quoniam circa confexiones pericula sunt animarum et difficultates quandoque emergunt, ideo ad honorem dei, beati nicolay et fratrum utilitatem ac confitentium salutem, tractatum brevem de confexione compilavi, sub certis titulis singula que circa confexionem requiruntur et incidunt concludentes ut facilius lector que velit valeat invenire'.

152. See Ochoa and Diez, eds., *Summa de paenitentia* lxiii–lxxxi; S. Kuttner, 'Zur Entstehungsgeschichte der Summa de casibus des hl. Raymund von Penyafort', ZRG Kan. Abt. 39 (1953) 419–434, reprinted in *Studies in the History of Medieval Canon Law* (London 1990) with 'Retractationes.'

153. Renard, *Trois sommes* 1.53–62, 453–455.

154. See Michaud-Quantin, 'Deux formulaires pour la confession' 48–57.

155. Goering and Payer, ed., *Summa penitentie*; for the glossed copy see pp. 48–49. Anoth-

From the 1220s onward, a steady stream of confessor's manuals and 'summae' of all shapes and sizes flowed throughout Europe. The literature written in England is known best to us, thanks to the pioneering investigations of Leonard E. Boyle.[156] A few examples suffice to indicate the general types of literature being produced. In the 1220s Robert Grosseteste wrote his *Templum Dei*, a schematic confessional guide for priests, based largely on the work of Robert Flamborough and John of Kent.[157] During the same decade he probably composed the works that have come down to us as the *De modo confitendi* and the *De penitentias iniungendi*.[158] In the 1230s an otherwise unknown 'Master Serlo' composed a short *Summa de penitentia* that integrated the old penitential teachings with the latest work of thirteenth-century canonists, including Tancred and Raymond of Peñafort.[159] The Cistercian bishop of Bangor, Cadwgan, composed a *Tractatus de modo confitendi*, probably during his episcopate (1230 x 1236).[160] Also during this period a group of reforming bishops in England published treatises on penance and confession designed to be circulated with their diocesan statutes and to be studied in the local convocations and chapters of clergy.[161] A fitting summation of this English tradition of pastoral and confessional writings is found in the anonymous *Speculum iuniorum* (c. 1250).[162] This substantial 'summa' is divided into two books, 'De malo' (including the 'evils' of crime, sin, and punishment) and 'De bono' (including the sacrament of penance). The author treats each topic, first, according to the teachings of the latest theological masters in the schools of Oxford and Paris. He then adduces evidence from English and conti-

---

er fine example is the *Confessionale* printed by A.C. Peltier among the works of Bonaventure, (Opera omnia 8; Paris 1866) 359–392.

156. 'A Study of the Works Attributed to William of Pagula with Special Reference to the *Oculus sacerdotis* and *Summa summarum*' (Oxford D.Phil. Dissertation 1956).

157. Robert Grosseteste, *Templum Dei*, ed. Goering and Mantello.

158. Published by Goering and Mantello, 'Early Penitential Writings of Robert Grosseteste' 52–112. Editions of Grosseteste's other penitential and confessional writings are in *Franciscan Studies* 30 (1970) 218–293, RB 96 (1986) 125–186, and *Viator* 18 (1987) 253–273.

159. Goering, 'The *Summa de penitentia* of Magister Serlo'; idem, 'The *Summa* of Master Serlo'.

160. Joseph Goering and Huw Pryce, "The *De modo confitendi* of Cadwgan, Bishop of Bangor, *Mediaeval Studies* 62 (2000) 1–27.

161. See Goering and Taylor, 'The "Summulae" of Bishops Walter de Cantilupe (1240) and Peter Quinel (1287)', 576–594. The treatises of Alexander of Stavensby (1224–1237) and Walter de Cantilupe (1240) are edited in *Councils and Synods* 1.220–226, 2.1050–1077 (under the name 'Peter Quinel').

162. See L.E. Boyle, 'Three English Pastoral Summae and a 'Magister Galienus",' *Collectanea Stephan Kuttner* (SG 11; Rome 1967) 135–144; J. Goering, 'The Popularization of Scholastic Ideas in Thirteenth Century England and an Anonymous *Speculum iuniorum*' (Ph.D. Dissertation, University of Toronto 1977). The attribution of this work to an otherwise unknown 'Master Galienus' is no longer maintained.

nental authors of pastoral manuals (Robert Grosseteste, Richard of Wetheringsett, Thomas of Chobham, William Peraldus, etc.), and he concludes his discussions with long, verbatim excerpts from Raymond of Peñafort's *Summa de penitentia* and *Summa de matrimonio* and from other canonists, especially Geoffrey of Trani.

Elsewhere in Europe a similar literary activity is evident. In Paris, William of Auvergne, Odo of Cheriton, and Robert of Sorbon wrote practical manuals and 'summae' for the internal forum.[163] Jean Pierre Renard has edited three anonymous 'summae de penitentia' which were produced in the German-speaking regions of Europe before 1250. They are comparable in style and organization, if not in scope, to Raymond of Peñafort's *Summa de penitentia*, and they include excerpts and borrowings from such works as Grosseteste's *Templum Dei*, and Thomas Chobham's *Summa confessorum*.[164] Peter of Albalat, archbishop of Tarragona (1238–1251) compiled a brief *Summa septem sacramentorum* for the use of his clergy.[165] The Bolognese canonist Peter Sampson composed a *Liber synodalis* (c. 1250) for the use of pastors and confessors in the diocese of Nîmes.[166] The Lyon Dominicans Cabertus Sabaudus and P. de Rosset, former students of law at Bologna, composed a similar treatise, the *Manuale curae pastoralis*, at the request of Henry of Susa (Hostiensis) while he was bishop of Sisteron (1243–1250).[167] The most ambitious penitential treatises from the pen of a secular cleric in this period were those composed by the famous Bolognese-trained canonist Johannes de Deo; he wrote both a *Liber pastoralis* and a very popular *Liber penitentiarius* (c. 1147).[168]

But Raymond of Peñafort dominated developments in the education of confessors and penitentiaries during the decades immediately follow-

163. William's and Robert's confessional tracts are printed among the works of William of Auvergne, *Opera omnia* (Paris 1674; reprinted Frankfurt a. M. 1963), Supplement, 2.238b–247a; see P. Glorieux, 'Le Tractatus novus de poenitentia de Guillaume d'Auvergne', *Miscellanea moralia in honorem eximii domini Arthur Janssen* (Bibliotheca ephemeridum theologicarum Lovaniensium 1.3; Louvain 1948) 551–565. F.N.M. Diekstra, The *Supplementum tractatus novi de poenitentia* of Guillaume d'Auvergne and Jacques de Vitry's lost treatise on confession, *RTAM* 61 (1994): 22–41; F.N.M. Diekstra, 'Robert de Sorbon's *Cum repetes (De modo audiendi confessiones et interrogandi)*', *Recherches de théologie et philosophie médiévales* 66 (1999), 79–153. Odo of Cheriton's *Summa de penitentia* (c. 1230) is extant in some 32 manuscript copies; see Bloomfield, *Incipits*, no. 3871.

164. Renard, *Trois sommes*, edits the *Summa magistri Conradi* (c. 1226), which had previously been attributed to Conrad of Höxter, O.P., an attribution challenged by Renard, and the Summa *Quia non pigris* (c. 1240), and the Summa *Decime dande sunt* (1230–1240).

165. Edited in P.H. Linehan, 'Pedro de Albalat, Arzobispo de Tarragona y su "Summa septem sacramentorum",' *Hispana sacra* 22 (1969) 9–30.

166. Cited above, n. 51.

167. Printed in Martène-Durand, *Thesaurus novus anecdotorum* 4 (Paris 1717) 1079–1098

168. Norbert Höhl, 'Johannes de Deo', LMA 4 (1990) 569.

ing the Fourth Lateran Council.[169] In 1234 Pope Gregory IX published the fruits of Raymond of Peñafort's editorial labors in his *Decretals* or *Liber extra*. Raymond immediately integrated this new canonical material into a second 'edition' of his own *Summa de penitentia*.[170] William of Rennes composed an 'apparatus' or gloss to Raymond's *Summa* (c. 1245), and both became standard texts in the Dominican schools for the duration of the thirteenth century. Raymond was famous in the order not just as an author but also as a 'teacher of penitentiaries' according to John of Freiburg, a lector in the Dominican schools at the end of the century.[171] After 1234 Raymond's *Summa* came to be known as the *Summa de casibus*, an indication of its usefulness in the schools as guide to discussing and resolving difficult cases in the penitential forum.[172] Dominican friars, and others who frequented the Order's schools to obtain training in practical theology and pastoral care, thus learned to apply the latest teachings of the canonists to knotty questions of the internal forum. They studied Raymond's text and its 'Apparatus' alongside the standard canonical glosses, and they supplemented these with such modern authorities as were to be found in Geoffrey of Trani's *Summa super titulis decretalium* (c. 1240), Hostiensis' *Summa aurea* (1253), and elsewhere in the canonical tradition. These schools set the standard by which education for the internal forum would be measured for centuries to come.

Penitential Literature from 1250 to 1300

The tradition of Dominican writings on penance and confession continued to flourish in the second half of the thirteenth century. Humbert of Romans, master general of the Order from 1254 to 1263, composed an important set of 'Instructiones' for the various offices in the Dominican Order. The chapter in his Instructions entitled 'De officio confessoris' also circulated independently as a separate treatise on confession.[173] Leonard

169. See A. Walz, 'S. Raymundi de Penyafort auctoritas in re paenitentiali', *Angelicum* 12 (1935) 346–396.
170. Kuttner, 'Zur Entstehungsgeschichte' 419–434; Ochoa and Diez, ed., *Summa de paenitentia* lxxvii–lxxxi.
171. John of Freiburg, *Summa confessorum* (Lyons 1518) v (emphasis added): 'Primo, tam de Textu quam de Apparatu seu glossa summe venerabilis patris fratris Raymundi quondam magistri ordinis nostri *qui penitentiarios dirigit*, registrum sive tabulam . . . ordinavi'.
172. See the discussion of the 'multiplex operis inscriptio' in Ochoa and Diez, eds., *Summa de paenitentia* lix–lxiii.
173. The 'De officio confessoris', chapter 46 of the *Instructiones*, is printed in Humbert de Romanis, *Opera: De vita regulari*, ed. J.J. Berthier (2 vols. Turin 1956) 2.360–69. For the independent circulation of this text see P. Michaud-Quantin, 'Textes pénitentiels languedociens au XIIIe siècle', *Le credo, la morale et l'inquisition* (Cahiers de Fanjeaux 6; Paris 1971) 151–172, at 152; Bloomfield, *Incipits*, nos. 2173, 2182. An edition of the 'De officio confessoris' is in preparation.

E. Boyle has drawn attention to an anonymous master's collection, made sometime between 1260 and 1280, for use in classroom teaching. The collection includes excerpts from the English Dominican provincial master Simon of Hinton's *Summa iuniorum* (c. 1250) and from Raymond of Peñafort's *Summa*, as well as a series of some 216 problems or 'casus' concerning the internal forum. Boyle describes the compiler's work thus:

> His method generally is to begin with Raymund's definition of a topic or with the heading, and then to retell one of Raymund's examples in the form of a casus, thus: 'De periurio. Aliquis captus ab hostibus propter metum qui potest cadere in virum constantem, iurat se daturum x. Queritur utrum obligatur ex tali iuramento? Et videtur multis auctoritatibus quod non. Tamen fere omnes doctores dicunt quod obligatur... Tamen Iohannes [Teutonicus] excipit iiii casus in quibus sic iurans non tenetur...'[174]

This Dominican tradition of literature for the internal forum reaches its peak, in the thirteenth century, in the writings of John of Freiburg.[175] John was lector in the Dominican priory at Freiburg-im-Breisgau, and continued to teach there even after he was elected prior of the house in 1290. His first contribution to the literature was a 'Registrum' or alphabetical index which guided the reader through the materials contained in Raymond of Peñafort's *Summa* and in William of Rennes' 'Apparatus'. Next he composed a *Libellus quaestionum casualium* that followed the order of Raymond's *Summa* but contained new material from the more recent canonical authorities. Finally, he wrote his own *Summa confessorum* (c. 1297–98), a text that first supplemented, and then supplanted, Raymond's *Summa* in the schools of the Order. John also composed a brief treatise for confessors, *De instructione confessorum*.[176]

The contributions of the Order of Preachers to the literature of penance and confession in this period has received more attention from modern scholars than those of the Minor Friars.[177] Perhaps the earliest Franciscan author to write an extensive work for the internal forum was Henry of Magdeburg, whose *Summa* (c. 1242) on the Decretals of Gregory IX was written 'so that priests could find their way to a knowledge of canon law'.[178] Henry's *Summa* played something of the same role in the Francis-

---

174. Boyle, 'Fratres communes' 262.
175. See Boyle, 'The *Summa confessorum* of John of Freiburg' 245–268.
176. See Kaeppeli, *Scriptores* 2. 433–443.
177. B. Kurtscheid, 'De studio iuris canonici in Ordine Fratrum Minorum saeculo XIII', *Antonianum* 2 (1927) 157–202, which concentrates on the Franciscan Province of Saxony, comprising most of modern-day Germany, and of Rusconi, 'I Francescani e la confessione' 253–309. See now, Bert Roest, *Franciscan Literature of Religious Instruction before the Council of Trent* (Leiden 2004) 314–355.
178. Henry of Magdeburg, *Summa*; quoted in Kurtscheid, 'De studio iuris canonici' 162:

can schools (at least in Germany) as Raymond's *Summa de penitentia* in the Dominican. Like Raymond's *Summa*, Henry's was soon accompanied by an 'Apparatus' of glosses (c. 1260), and a new recension appeared by the end of the thirteenth century.[179] An anonymous confrere supplemented Henry's *Summa* with a treatise entitled *Labia sacerdotis* which collected 'cases' and practical questions designed to teach the priest what he needs to know 'in order to fulfill his office and to counsel penitents'.[180] The author describes how this treatise, along with Henry's *Summa* and its 'Apparatus', will be 'useful to simple confessors, whether in hearing the confessions of others or in attending to their own consciences'.[181]

Another Franciscan who produced aids for the internal forum in this period was Clair of Florence, a canonist and papal penitentiary who was active between 1243 and 1261. His collections of practical questions and cases ('casus') seem to reflect the activity in the local schools of the Order.[182]

A Franciscan tradition of canonical and penitential writings continued to flourish from the middle of the thirteenth century, and the details of its growth and development await further study. But three works, composed at the end of the thirteenth century and in the first decades of the fourteenth, represent a remarkable culmination of this tradition within the Franciscan Order. One is the *Summa de penitentia* of John of Erfurt (1295, rev. ed. 1302). Organized into titles, like John of Freiburg's *Summa confessorum*, John of Erfurt's 'summa' draws on the canonists Hostiensis and William Duranti, and includes references to the *Liber Sextus* in its second edition.[183]

Even more ambitious, and more influential, was the *Summa de casibus conscientiae* or *Summa Astesana* (c. 1317) of Astesanus de Asti. Among the authorities that he brings to bear on solving cases of conscience, Astesanus enumerates all of the important canonists of the thirteenth century,

---

'Ut autem sacerdotibus pateat via ad scienciam iuris canonici, ideo frater Henricus Merseburg [sic] de ordine fratrum Minorum, quondam lector in Magdeburg, summulam iuris canonici quam habemus prae manibus communi utilitati deserviens compilavit'.

179. Kurtscheid, 'De studio iuris canonici' 162–168, 172–173.

180. Anonymous, *Labia sacerdotis*; quoted in Kurtscheid, 'De studio iuris canonici' 168: '"Labia sacerdotis custodiant scientiam". Huius scientiae necessitatem auctor describit quatenus triplicem scientiam in sacerdotibus requirit . . . ut officia proprii status adimplere et poenitentibus consulere sciant'.

181. Anonymous, *Labia sacerdotis*; quoted in Kurtscheid, 'De studio iuris canonici' 169: 'Qui simplicibus confessoribus utiles esse possent, sive in confessionibus audiendis aliorum, sive pro conscienciis propriis servandis'.

182. See Rusconi, 'I Francescani e la confessione' 296.

183. *Die Summa confessorum des Johannes von Erfurt*, ed. N. Brieskorn (3 vols. Frankfurt a.M. 1980).

as well as Johannes Andreae, the romanist Azo, and the famous Franciscan theologians Alexander of Hales and John Duns Scotus.[184]

The English Franciscan Peter Quesnel produced an equally comprehensive 'summa' in 1322, his *Directorium iuris in foro conscientiae et iudicali*. In order to make canonical teachings more easily accessible to judges in the internal and in the external forum, Peter divided his *Directorium* into four books, rather than following the more conventional order of the Decretal titles or distributing the materials under alphabetically ordered rubrics.[185] Like Astesanus, Peter names in his prologue all the important canonists and jurists of the thirteenth and early fourteenth centuries, and claims them as his authorities.

Education for the internal forum was never, of course, a monopoly of the mendicant orders, but their international system of schools certainly fostered the production, copying, and circulation of their didactic texts. The secular clergy also produced and commissioned the writing of 'summae' and manuals of confession, especially for local consumption. By the beginning of the fourteenth century, several of their number had achieved national and international recognition as authorities on the internal forum. William Duranti, papal official and bishop of Mende (1286–1296), and Berengar Fredoli, cardinal bishop of Tusculum (1309–1323) and papal penitentiary, wrote extremely influential works.[186] William of Pagula, an Oxford graduate 'utriusque iuris' who served as vicar of a parish and as penitentiary for a rural deanery and then for an archdeaconry, dominated the English scene for more than a century with his immensely popular *Oculus sacerdotis* as well as his *Speculum praelatorum* and his pastoral guide to canon law, the *Summa summarum*.[187]

---

184. Astesanus de Asti, *Summa de casibus conscientiae* (Rome 1728).

185. Peter Quesnel, *Directorium iuris in foro conscientiae et iudicali*; quoted in Rusconi, 'I Francescani e la confessione' 298: 'Istud autem opus in quatuor libri volui dividere ut qui pauper est et non possit se excusare quod non possit ad minus librum illum habere qui ad eius officium noscitur pertinere. Et ideo omitto scribere secundum ordinem Decretalium et secundum ordinem alphabeti ut totam unam materiam continuam valeam pertractare'.

186. On William Duranti see: *Guillaume Durand, Évêque de Mende (v. 1230–1296): Canoniste, liturgiste et homme politique* (Actes de la Table Ronde du C.N.R.S., Mende 24–27 mai 1990; Paris 1992), especially the contribution by J. Longère, 'La pénitence selon le *Repertorium*, les instructions et constitutions, et le Pontifical de Guillaume Durand' 105–133. On Berengarus Fredoli see A. Teetaert, 'La "Summa de paenitentia: Quoniam circa confessiones" du Cardinal Bérenger Frédol Senior', *Miscellanea moralia in honorem eximii domini Arthur Janssen* (2 vols. Louvain 1948) 2.567–600; P. Michaud-Quantin, 'La "Summula in foro poenitentiali" attribuée a Bérenger Frédol', *Collectanea Stephan Kuttner* (SG 11; Rome 1967) 147–167.

187. See the articles reprinted in Boyle, *Pastoral Care*, especially: 'The *Oculus sacerdotis* and Some Other Works of William of Pagula' and 'The "Summa summarum" and Some Other English Works of Canon Law.'

Penitential Literature of the Fourteenth and Fifteenth Centuries

During the fourteenth and fifteenth centuries the literature of the internal forum flourished as never before. New 'summae' and manuals for confessors continued to be written while old ones were copied and brought up to date. The literature produced during these centuries is too vast to summarize here, but brief notice might be made of three developments that proved especially popular.[188]

First was the refinement of the alphabetically organized 'summae'. Two Franciscan texts, Monaldus of Capodistria's *Summa iuris* or *Summa Monaldina* (1254 x 1274) and the *Tabula utriusque iuris* (before 1281) of John of Erfurt, are early examples of the type of alphabetical organization that would become standard in the later Middle Ages. John of Freiburg's concordance or *Tabula* (c. 1280) of Raymond of Peñafort's *Summa* and its 'Apparatus' also helped to establish the principles and practices of alphabetical organization, and the German adaptation of John's own *Summa confessorum* abandons entirely John's organization by titles and presents his doctrine under alphabetically arranged subject headings.[189] During the fourteenth and fifteenth centuries, some of the most popular and influential of the penitential 'summae' were organized alphabetically. These included the *Summa confessorum* (1338) of Bartholomaeus de Sancto Concordio of Pisa (better known as the *Summa Pisana casuum conscientiae* or *Pisanella*), the *Summa Angelica de casibus conscientiae* or *Angelica* (1486) of Angelus Carletus de Clavasio, and the *Summa summarum casuum conscientiae* or *Sylvestrina* (c. 1500) of Sylvester de Prierio.[190]

A second development that gathered momentum after 1300 was the production of confessional treatises and 'summae' in the various vernacular languages. Since the work of E.J. Arnould on the *Manuel des péchés* and of D.W. Robertson on *Handlyng Synne*, it has become widely recognized how large was the debt of much of English and Anglo-Norman religious literature to the Latin literature of penance and confession.[191] Recent re-

---

188. In addition to the general surveys noted above, n. 110, see Thomas N. Tentler, *Sin and Confession on the Eve of the Reformation* (Princeton 1977) 28–53. The vast and largely unexplored extent of the anonymous penitential literature from this period can be gauged by examining Bloomfield, *Incipits*. For a more specific geographical area, see indices 5 and 7 of Renard's *Trois sommes* 1.521–529, 530–532. Renard lists some 450 penitential and confessional texts that were copied into seventy-one codices, mostly from the Rhineland and Central Europe, that contain copies of the three short 'summae de penitentia' which he edits.

189. On these alphabetical 'summae', see C. Bergfeld, 'Katholische Moraltheologie und Naturrechtslehre: I. Beichtjurisprudenz', Coing, *Handbuch* 999–1015 at 1004–1008.

190. See Bergfeld, 'Beichtjurisprudenz'.

191. E.J. Arnould, *Le Manuel des péchés: Étude de littèrature religieuse Anglo-Normande (XIIIᵐᵉ*

search has begun to trace the same phenomenon in many of the vernacular languages of Europe from the thirteenth century onwards.[192]

A third type of literature that grew in importance during the final centuries of the Middle Ages was the treatise or 'monograph' on topics of special concern for the internal forum. Many of these treatises discussed questions related to the new mercantile and business activities of the time. Works such as Bernardino of Siena's *De contractibus et usuris*, John Gerson's *Libellus de contractibus*, William (Nicolaus) of Oresmes' *Tractatus de moneta seu de commutatione monetarum*, and John Nider's *Compendiosus tractatus de contractibus mercatorum*, illustrate the depth of thought and study that went into the analysis of contemporary economic practices as they relate to the internal forum of penance and confession.[193]

Conclusion

During the two centuries following the publication of Gratian's *Decretum* a new field of jurisprudence developed to meet the needs of those engaged in the hearing of confessions and the care of souls. This jurisprudence of the internal forum ('forum penitentiale', 'forum conscientiae') was shaped by, and helped to inform, the doctrines of the canonists and the practices in the Church's courts. As a result, penance and confession became one of the chief ways that everyone, lay and cleric alike, came into regular and close contact with the workings of the church's legal systems and with the science of canonical jurisprudence.

The importance of confession in the social and religious life of the later Middle Ages can scarcely be exaggerated. The Roman Catechism, produced in the wake of the Council of Trent, observed: 'Almost all devout Christians are convinced that everything holy and pious conserved in the Church at this time is to be attributed, in large part, to confession'.[194] The

---

siècle) (Paris 1940); D.W. Robertson, Jr., 'The Cultural Tradition of "Handlyng Synne",' *Speculum* 22 (1947) 162–185.

192. See, for example, M.D. Innocenti, 'Una "Confessione" del XIII secolo: Dal "De confessione" di Roberto di Sorbona (1201–1274) al volgarizzamento in antico milanese', *Cristianesimo nella storia* 5 (1984) 245–302; J.M.S. Rábanos, 'Derecho canónico y praxis pastoral en la España bajomedieval', *Proceedings Berkeley* 595–617; Die 'Rechtsumme' Bruder Bertholds: Eine deutsche abecedarische Bearbeitung der 'Summa confessorum' des Johannes von Freiburg (7 vols. Tübingen in progress).

193. See Bergfeld, 'Beichtjurisprudenz' 1011–1012; Winfried Trusen, 'Zur Bedeutung des geistlichen Forum internum und externum für die spätmittelalterliche Gesellschaft', ZRG Kan. Abt. 107 (1990) 254–285.

194. *Catechismus ex decreto Concilii Tridentini ad parochos* 2.5.36, 4th ed. (Rome 1907) 253; quoted in P.-M. Gy, 'Les bases de la pénitence moderne', *La Maison-Dieu* 117 (1974) 63–85, at 81: 'Ex eo facile intelligent, quod omnibus fere piis persuasum est, quidquid hoc tempore

same comment might be made, 'mutatis mutandis', about the creation and dissemination of a common juridical culture and a *ius commune* in Europe.[195] Although such a culture obviously owes its existence to a great many influences, the one ubiquitous experience of the Church's law that was common everywhere and to almost everyone, regardless of class, status, or gender, was that of the internal forum of penance and confession.

---

sanctitatis, pietatis et religionis in ecclesia, summo Dei beneficio, conservatum est, id magna ex parte confessionis tribuendum esse'.

195. See, for example, P.G. Grossi, 'Somme penitenziali, diritto canonico, diritto comune', *Annali della facoltà giuridica di Macerata* N.S. 1 (1966) 95–134; C. Bergfeld, 'Zur Jurisprudenz des "forum internum",' *Ius commune* 16 (1989) 133–147.

General Index

Accursius, 13–14, 95, 109
Ailmerus of Canterbury, 33
Aimeric, 126
Alan of Lille, 340, 416
Alanus Anglicus, 79–80, 84, 86, 95, 173, 202, 206, 219–21, 225–26, 301, 303, 305–12
Albericus, 76, 95, 174
Alberigo, Giuseppe, 325, 335n91, 338
Albertus, 220–21, 228, 301
Albertus de Mora, 76, 95, 126, 193–94, 199, 201
Aldricus, 95
Alexander of Hales, 425
Alexander III, Pope, 24, 44, 48, 70, 108, 115, 124–26, 131–35, 138, 177, 186, 191, 195, 197, 214, 218, 222, 250–51, 255–56, 258, 260–61, 263, 265–69, 272, 274, 277–79, 288–93, 298, 303–4, 312, 318, 321, 334, 338, 340–41, 350n168; Third Lateran Council canons, 334–38
Alger of Liège, 32, 34, 42
Altmann of St. Florian, 204–5
Ambroise de Cambrai, 103
Ambrose of Milan, 28, 35
Anastasius, Pope, 157
Angelus Carletus de Clavasio, 426
Anselm of Lucca, 3, 32, 34, 38–39, 44
Antoine de Mouchy, 50
Arnould, E. J., 426
Ascelinus, Magister, 200
Astesanus de Asti, 424–25
Augustine of Hippo, 28
Augustinus, Antonius, 52, 371–72
Azo, 13, 95, 223, 227–28, 237, 425

Baluze, Etienne, 301
Bartholomaeus Brixiensis, 83, 85n139, 86, 88–91, 94–95, 172, 234, 239
Bartholomaeus de Sancto Concordia of Pisa, 426
Bartholomew of Breganza, 410
Bartholomew of Exeter, 174–75, 264, 272, 274, 413, 417
Bartolomaeus Laurens, 248
Barton, John, 15, 18
Basil of Caesarea, 28
Bazianus, 61, 65, 75–76, 83, 89, 93, 141–42, 153–54, 201
Bellomo, Manlio, 18, 171, 242n169
Belloni, Annalisa, 76, 141, 165n209
Bede, 412
Benedict XV, Pope, 53
Benedict of Sawston, 208
Benedictus Levita, 30
Benencasa of Arezzo, 91, 95, 172–73
Benson, Robert, 135
Berardi, Carlo Sebastiano, 52
Berengar Fredoli, 425
Bernardino of Siena, 427
Bernard of Clairvaux, 120, 126–27
Bernard of Parma. *See* Bernardus Parmensis
Bernard of Pavia, 60, 62, 72n67, 74–75, 127, 194, 211–15, 218–22, 227, 241, 248, 251–52, 271, 280–82, 286, 288, 291, 296–306, 353, 368
Bernardus Balbi. *See* Bernardus of Pavia
Bernardus Compostellanus antiquus, 80–81, 86, 95, 207, 221–24, 226, 301, 303, 306–11, 314–16

Bernardus Papiensis. *See* Bernard of Pavia
Bernardus Parmensis, 144, 228, 372
Bertram, Martin, 146, 376
Bertrandus, 95
Bochenthaler, Stephan, 38
Böhmer, Justus Henning, 51–52
Boncompagnus, 23, 172, 242
Boyle, Leonard E., 245, 316, 414, 420, 423
Brant, Sebastian, 93–94
Brundage, James A., 2, 9, 11, 15, 18
Bulgarus, 12, 90, 95, 126, 132, 164, 170, 183, 196
Burchard of Worms, 7, 27, 33, 41, 47, 56, 163, 175, 191, 298, 313, 412, 413

Cabertus Sabaudus, 421
Cadwgan of Bangor, 420
Cairns, John, 19
Calixtus II, Pope, 320–21, 323; First Lateran Council canons, 325–28
Calvin, John, 52
Cardinalis, 62, 64, 67, 73, 80, 82, 95, 141, 178–80, 195, 199, 201
Carruthers, Mary, 16–17
Celestine II, Pope, 44, 48
Celestine III, Pope, 127, 215, 219, 249, 259–60, 278–79, 284, 288–91, 300, 312
Chappuis, Jean, 93–94
Cheney, Christopher R., 300, 303, 313, 333
Cheney, Mary, 277
Chodorow, Stanley, 25, 36n23
Clair of Florence, 424
Clement III, Pope, 127, 149, 199, 222, 250, 278, 284, 288–91, 298–300, 312
Clement V, Pope, 101, 113
Constantine, Emperor, 6
Crabbe, Petrus, 369–70
Cremascoli, Giuseppe, 146
Cresconius, 209
Cyprian, Magister, 78, 96

Daifer, Magister, 78, 189, 196
Damasus Hungarus, 87, 96, 166, 168, 228, 232, 314, 354, 373–77
Dante Alighieri, 119, 379, 414
Daudet, Pierre, 280
David of London, 78, 96, 189, 192
Deeters, Walter, 249
Dionysius Exiguus, 26, 33, 320n13
Donahue, Charles, 134
Duggan, Charles, 277
Dumoulin, Charles, 50, 52, 94

Eilbert of Bremen, 204
Engen, John van, 129
Ernst von Zwiefalten, Abbot, 39
Eugenius III, Pope, 48, 120, 124, 126, 249, 260, 279, 320–21, 332
Everard of Ypres, 166, 191

Falkenstein, Ludwig, 285
Ferrandus, 42
Fidantia Civitatensis/Fidantius, 78, 96
Firth, J. J. F., 417n142
Fraher, Richard M., 202
Fournier, Paul, 25
Fowler-Magerl, Linda, 180, 216
Fransen, Gérard, 25, 133n59, 165, 167, 169–70, 182–83, 189, 191, 291, 299–300
Frederick I (Barbarossa), Emperor, 48, 71, 125, 132, 138, 140, 170, 183, 250, 334, 337, 417
Frederick II, Emperor, 236, 242, 316
Friedberg, Emil, 25, 30–32, 51–52, 94n177, 270, 285, 296, 299–300
Fuhrmann, Horst, 34
Fulk, Master, 285

Gaius, 10
Gandulphus, 71, 73, 82–83, 96, 139, 189, 193–94, 197, 199, 201, 208
García y García, Antonio, 231–32, 235, 244, 315, 343, 353
Gautier de Coinci, 119
Gelasius I, Pope, 28
Geoffrey of Trani. *See* Goffredus de Trani
Gerald of Wales, 114, 175, 416
Gerard Pucelle, 96, 182–84, 196, 209, 285
Gerhoh von Reichersberg, 324, 332
Gilbert Foliot, Bishop of London, 257–58, 268
Gilbertus Anglicus, 221–22, 226, 283, 290, 301, 303–10, 312, 314
Gillmann, Franz, 37, 84, 148–49, 153, 181, 191, 208, 230, 371–72, 374
Giovanni Colonna, 23
Goffredus de Trani, 144, 377, 409, 421–22
Gouron, André, 73, 141, 164–65, 175, 179, 200, 242, 243n173
Grabmann, Martin, 177, 415
Gratian, 7–9, 11, 22–54, 96, 98–99, 110–11, 121–25, 127–31, 134–37, 140–42, 148, 150–51, 159, 161–62, 164, 172–73, 175–76, 180, 182, 185–87, 192, 196, 209, 212, 215, 218, 222, 227, 234–35, 240, 246, 253, 255, 260, 269, 271, 288, 292–93, 295, 298, 317, 328, 332–33, 338, 341, 349, 368, 379–81, 411, 413, 427

Gregory I, Pope, 28, 34–35, 298
Gregory VII, Pope, 7, 44, 260, 321, 330
Gregory VIII, Pope, 76, 149, 199, 222, 289, 298.
   See also Albertus de Mora
Gregory IX, Pope, 88–89, 143, 163, 240, 243, 245,
   247, 315–17, 339, 345, 370, 372, 422–23
Gregory XIII, Pope, 50–51
Gregory of Grisogono, 4, 32, 38
Guibert de Bornado, 60, 70, 139
Guido, Magister, 96
Guido de Guinis, 108–9
Guido of Baysio, 77, 88, 91, 93–96
Gullick, Michael, 287n155
Guy of Southwick, 416

Hadrian IV, Pope, 48, 179, 185
Hanenberg, Jacoba, 252
Hartwig of Bremen, Archbishop, 48
Haskins, Charles Homer, 1, 53
Heckel, Rudolf von, 306
Henry of Magdeburg, 423–24
Henry of Susa. See Hostiensis
Henry II, King of England, 137, 187
Holtzmann, Walther, 249, 251–53, 258, 260–63,
   265–68, 270n88, 276, 277n111, 278–79, 284,
   288–89, 291, 299–300, 303, 338n102
Honorius, Magister, 166, 192, 197–200, 217, 244
Honorius II, Pope 48, 279
Honorius III, Pope, 101–2, 108, 111, 209, 223,
   235–37, 239, 242–43, 309, 316–17
Hostiensis, Cardinal, 18, 96, 110n55, 144–45, 243,
   374, 409, 411n109, 421–22, 424
Hove, Alphonse van, 266, 277
Hugh of St. Cher, 419
Hugh of St. Victor, 43, 136, 196
Hugo, Magister, 12, 132, 199
Hugo of Sesso, 242
Hugolinus Presbyteri, 88–89, 96
Huguccio, 24, 64–67, 68n52, 77, 80, 81n123,
   82–84, 86, 89, 96, 122, 127, 136, 142–60, 173,
   179, 192, 202–4, 211, 215, 219–20
Humbert of Romans, 422

Innocent II, Pope, 28, 321, 329; Second Lateran
   Council canons, 330–33
Innocent III, Pope, 96, 111, 127, 143–45, 147–48,
   173, 203, 208, 211, 219, 225–26, 229–30, 232–34,
   260, 283–84, 288–90, 300–2, 304–16, 319, 332,
   341, 343–44, 346, 350n168, 351, 356, 367–68,
   371; Fourth Lateran Council canons, 344–52,
   381, 386, 388
Innocent IV, Pope, 89, 96, 101–2, 243, 399n66

Irnerius, 4–5, 7, 11–13, 96, 196
Isidore of Seville, 28, 33, 42, 162
Ivo of Chartres, 3–4, 26, 28, 31–32, 38–39, 42,
   174–75, 187, 298, 413

Jacobus, 12, 24, 96, 132
Jacobus Balduini, 109
Jacobus Colunbi, 14
Jacobus de Albenga, 87, 89, 96, 228, 236, 239, 317
Jacques of St. Victor, 418
Jerome, 28
Johannes Andreae, 96, 100, 144–45, 218, 223, 374
Johannes Bassianus, 13, 76, 90, 96, 140–41, 163,
   199, 207, 215–16, 219, 243n173
Johannes Calderinus, 96
Johannes de Deo, 142, 152, 377, 421
Johannes Egitaniensis, 377
Johannes Faventinus, 62n29, 63–65, 67, 69, 74,
   77, 78n106, 82, 96, 127, 136, 138–40, 192–93,
   195–97, 199, 201, 208–9, 211, 281
Johannes Galensis, 220, 226, 228–29, 234, 288,
   312
Johannes of Phintona, 94, 96
Johannes Teutonicus, 76–77, 81–91, 96, 111, 136,
   143, 148, 155, 168–69, 171–72, 210, 212, 222n65,
   223, 225, 228, 232–36, 238, 295, 314–15, 353–54,
   370–72, 374, 377
John Chrysostom, 28
John Duns Scotus, 425
John Gerson, 427
John Nider, 427
John of Cornwall, 284, 287
John of Erfurt, 424, 426
John of Faenza. See Johannes Faventinus
John of Freiburg, 422–23, 426
John of Kent, 201, 386n23, 399n69, 400n73,
   418, 420
John of Noyon, 203
John of Salisbury, 285
John of Tynemouth, 69, 96, 200, 244, 279, 287
John of Wales. See Johannes Galensis
John Paul II, Pope, 53
Julianus Pomerius, 35
Juncker, Josef, 61, 64, 75, 140, 268
Justinian, Emperor, 2–5, 8, 10, 19, 125–26, 213,
   297, 310

Kalb, Herbert, 136
Kunstmann, Friedrich, 214
Kuttner, Stephan, 29, 32–33, 39, 52, 70, 81–82,
   85–86, 88, 123, 127–28, 130, 135, 137, 140, 142,
   161–62, 166–67, 173, 182–83, 191–92, 205–6,

General Index

Kuttner, Stephan *(cont.)*
   208, 213n10, 214, 217–18, 221–24, 230, 240, 254–55, 277, 288–89, 298, 300, 313, 371–72, 374, 376–77

Laborans, Cardinal, 46, 124–25
Lancelotti, Giovanni Paolo, 51
Landau, Peter, 33–34, 37, 83, 252, 277, 282, 297
Larrainzar, Carlos, 39n33
Laspeyres, Ernst Adolph Theodor, 214, 218, 299
Laurentius Hispanus, 77, 79n108, 80–84, 86, 91, 96, 210, 219, 228–30, 233–34, 236, 238
Le Bras, Gabriel, 29
Le Conte, 50
Lefebvre, Charles, 215
Lenherr, Titus, 83
Leo I, Pope, 28
Leo IX, Pope, 48, 255, 318
Leonardi, Claudio, 369–70
Loewenfeld, Samuel, 267
Lohmann, Christian, 273
Lotharius of Cremona, 171
Lucius III, Pope, 125, 197, 222, 259, 261–62, 265–66, 272, 274, 278, 284, 287, 289, 337
Luig, Klaus, 19
Luther, Martin, 52

Maassen, Friedrich, 131–32, 141, 148
Maffei, Domenico, 101, 141
Maierù, Alfonso, 18
Marcoaldus of Padua, 228, 239, 242
Martino da Fano, 113
Martin of Braga, 26
Martin of Troppau, 23
Martinus, 12, 132, 170, 175, 196
Martinus Gosia, 96
Martinus of Zamora, 87, 96
Melanchthon, Philip, 52
Melendus, 76–77, 82–83, 96, 219, 224
Michaud-Quantin, Pierre, 413, 419
Monaldus of Capodistria, 426
Mörsdorf, Klaus, 37
Müller, Wolfgang P., 4, 142
Munier, Charles, 28, 35

Nicholas I, Pope, 28
Nicholas de Aquila, 201
Noonan, John T., 126n29, 129, 131–32
Nörr, Knut Wolfgang, 126, 230

Odo de Sully, 347, 355, 357, 359, 362
Odofredus, 23, 108, 110, 116
Odo of Cheriton, 421
Odo of Dover, 185, 188
Odo of Lucca, 28
Omnebene. *See* Omnibonus
Omnibonus, 46, 49, 124, 127
Ordericus Vitalis, 332
Origen, 28
Osbern of Gloucester, 147

P. de Rosset, 421
Paschal II, Pope, 28, 321, 330
Paucapalea, 40, 46–47, 57–58, 62, 69–71, 96, 122, 128–31, 135, 138, 176, 181
Paulus Hungarus, 162, 241, 419
Peitz, Wilhelm Maria, 33
Pelagius Gaitan, 87, 96, 223–24
Pennington, Kenneth, 39n33, 267
Pepo, 175
Peter Abelard, 42, 177
Peter Comestor, 415
Peter Lombard, 31, 44, 53, 136, 139, 175, 186, 266, 345
Peter of Albalat, 421
Peter of Blois. *See* Petrus Blesensis
Peter of Louviciennes, 188
Peter of Poitiers, 340, 417
Peter of Roissy, 416
Peter Quesnel, 425
Peter the Chanter, 340, 350n168, 414–15
Petrus, 60, 71
Petrus Beneventanus, 142, 226, 229, 306, 308–16
Petrus Blesensis, 71, 96, 119, 178, 189–90
Petrus Brito, 221
Petrus de Salinis, 94, 96
Petrus Hispanus, 65, 71, 75, 96, 218, 241
Petrus of Isernia, 242
Petrus Peverellus/Penerchus, 207
Philip of Calne, Master, 280
Phillip of Aquileia, 86, 97, 228, 239
Pillius, 97, 168, 239
Pithou, François, 51
Pithou, Pierre, 51
Placentinus, 13, 90, 97, 182, 207
Placidus of Nonantula, 32
Post, Gaines, 232
Praepositinus of Cremona, 417
Přerovský, Oldrich, 148
Princivallis of Milan, 97
Prosper of Aquitaine, 35
Pseudo-Isidore, 33–34, 45, 260

General Index 433

Rabikauskas, Paulius, 316
Raimundus de Arenis, 73, 141, 179. *See also* Cardinalis
Rainer of Pomposa, 283, 290, 301–5, 307
Ralph of Sarre, 285
Rambaud, Jacqueline, 47
Rashdall, Hastings, 111, 236, 243n173
Rathbone, Eleanor, 217, 277
Raymond of Peñafort, 87, 97, 228, 238, 240–41, 276, 315, 317, 339–40, 372, 377, 390, 397, 409, 419–24, 426
Renard, Jean Pierre, 421, 426n188
Riccobaldus of Ferrara, 145
Richard of Canterbury, 264–65
Richard of Wetheringsett, 421
Richardus Anglicus, 97, 162, 166, 172–73, 199–200, 202, 215–18, 220, 239, 241, 308, 414
Richardus de Mores. *See* Richardus Anglicus
Richter, Aemilius Ludwig, 51
Ridder-Symoens, Hilde de, 18
Robert Blund, 147
Robert Courson, 100, 110n54, 415
Robert Grosseteste, 388n30, 393, 400n71, 402n78, 420–21
Robert of Flamborough, 340, 400, 407, 417–18, 420
Robert of St. Pair, 416
Robert of Sorbon, 421
Robert of Torigny, 23–24
Robertson, D. W., 426
Roffredus Benventanus, 167–68, 170, 236, 242
Rogerius, 12, 183
Roger of Worcester, 264, 272, 274
Rolandus, Magister, 70–71, 97, 129, 131–35, 177–79, 181, 194, 196, 199, 201
Rolandus Bandinelli, 24, 131–32
Rosa Pereira, Isaias da, 376
Rufinus, 24, 35, 41, 45, 61–62, 64, 70–72, 82, 97, 124, 129, 131, 135–36, 138–40, 160, 175, 179–81, 183–87, 189, 193–95, 201, 209, 220, 293n2, 334n89

Salimbene of Parma, 145
Samson of Bury St. Edmunds, Abbot, 114
Sanz, Javier Ochoa, 230
Sarti, Mauro, 146
Sayers, Jane, 217
Schönsteiner, Ferdinand, 274
Schulte, Johann Friedrich von, 58, 78n106, 88, 93, 137, 141, 148, 176, 208, 304, 370, 377, 410–11
Seckel, Emil, 23
Senatus of Worcester, 414

Sicardus of Cremona, 97, 127, 140, 160, 166, 190–91, 197
Silano, Giulio, 162, 414
Silvester, 225–26, 309
Silvestre Godinho. *See* Silvester
Simon of Bisignano, 23, 64, 75, 97, 139–40, 190–92, 195–97, 200, 208, 220, 281
Simon of Hinton, 423
Simon of Southwell, 69, 97, 201
Simon of Sywell, 244, 287
Siricius, Pope, 6n25, 28
Sohm, Rudolph, 37, 53
Sousa Costa, A. Domingues de, 373n20
Southern, Richard W., 1, 293
Stelzer, Winfried, 186
Stephen Langton, 208, 355–57, 389n33
Stephen of Stanlaw, 417
Stephen of Tournai, 35, 41, 64, 72, 97, 103, 127, 136–40, 160, 174, 180–85
Stickler, Alfons M., 79, 81, 133n59, 139, 142, 148, 206, 213n10, 220, 224, 228, 266, 277
Sylvester de Prierio, 426

Tancred of Lombardy (Bologna), 88–89, 97, 216, 221, 223, 227–29, 232, 234, 237–39, 289, 306, 314, 316–17, 420
Thaner, Friedrich, 133, 135, 178
Theiner, Augustin, 376
Theodore of Canterbury, 412
Thomas Aquinas, 43, 379, 380n3
Thomas Becket, 137, 264, 272
Thomas of Chobham, 340, 418, 421
Thomas of Marlborough, 244, 309
Tierney, Brian, 202

Ullmann, Walter, 292
Urban II, Pope, 319, 321, 326–27, 330
Urban III, Pope, 138, 222, 262, 266, 278, 290

Vacarius, 15, 100, 200, 244
Vetulani, Adam, 25, 29–30, 39, 224, 291, 299
Vincentius Hispanus, 77, 87, 97, 228, 230–34, 236, 238, 314, 353–54, 371–77

Wahrmund, Ludwig, 180
Walter of Coutances, 283
Watson, Alan, 19
Weigand, Rudolf, 46–47, 123–24, 126n29, 128–36, 139–41, 212, 221, 223, 254
Weimar, Peter, 161
Will, Erich, 91
William de Montibus, 392n41, 416

William Duranti, 424–25
William Lyndwood, 356
William of Auvergne, 421
William of Drogheda, 245
William of Gascony. *See* Willielmus Vasco
William (Nicholas) of Oresmes, 427
William of Pagula, 425
William of Rennes, 422–23
William of Tyre, 333

William Peraldus, 421
Willielmus Vasco, 78, 87, 97, 141, 224–25
Winroth, Anders, 7, 25, 39, 129, 175n6, 322n24
Wolfger of Passau, 204
Wouw, Hans van de, 192

Zabarella, Cardinal, 100
Zeliauskas, Josephus, 83
Zoën Tencararius, 228, 236, 239, 317

Index of Citations

Pre-Gratian Canonical Collections
Ivo of Chartres
Collectio tripartita
  3.16.4: 27
Decretum
  9.53: 27

Decretum Gratiani
Prima pars
  D.1 pr.: 92
  D.1 c.1: 91–92
  D.1 c.2: 92
  D.1 c.4: 90
  D.1 c.12: 92
  D.2 c.6: 92
  D.3 c.3: 92
  D.3 c.20: 397n58
  D.4 c.3: 92
  D. 5 c.4: 62, 69
  D.8 d.a.c.1: 42
  D.11 c.1: 82
  D.11 c.4: 56, 82, 90, 92
  D.11 c.5: 56, 59
  D.12 pr.–c.6: 82
  D.13 c.2: 35n22
  D.15 c.3: 47
  D.17 c.1: 69
  D.18 c.11: 90
  D.19 c.6: 92
  D.20 d.a.c.1: 247n3
  D.20 c.1: 71
  D.21 c.2: 295n6
  D.23 c.1: 90, 92
  D.24 c.3: 90, 92
  D.25 c.1: 43
  D.25 d.p.c.3: 397
  D.26 c.3: 61
  D.27 c.2: 61
  D.27 c.8: 328n57
  D.28 c.2: 332n79
  D.28 c.13: 58
  D.29 c.1: 42
  D.30 c.17: 58
  D.31 c.1: 159
  D.38 cc.4–5: 412n114
  D.40 c.6: 157
  D.45 c.9: 35n22
  D.45 c.14: 35n22
  D.46 c.1: 35n22
  D.46 c.2: 35n22
  D.47 c.3: 35n22
  D.50 c.6: 90
  D.56 c.1: 332n79
  D.60 c.2: 328n57
  D.60 c.3: 332n79
  D.61 c.14: 47
  D.62 c.3: 328n57
  D.63 c.20: 43
  D.63 d.p.c.34: 42
  D.63 c.35: 332n79
  D.68 c.3: 41
  D.81 pr.: 35
  D.82 c.2: 77
  D.84 c.5: 57n7
  D.89 c.5: 32n14
  D.90 c.11: 332n79
  D.92 c.3: 57n7
  D.96 cc.13–14: 47

Secunda pars
  C.1 pr.: 58
  C.1 q.1 c.10: 328n57
  C.1 q.3 c.4: 80, 82
  C.1 q.3 cc.13–15: 82, 93
  C.1 q.3 c.15: 332n79
  C.1 q.7 d.p.c.6: 40
  C.1 q.12 c.7: 43
  C.2 q.1: 131
  C.2 q.1 c.2: 34
  C.2 q.1 c.12: 131
  C.2 q.2: 131
  C.2 q.5 c.22: 347n150
  C.2 q.6: 131
  C.2 q.6 c.28: 30n11, 40
  C.2 q.6 d.p.c.31: 24, 176
  C.2 q.7 c.10: 41
  C.3 q.1: 131
  C.3 q.5: 131
  C.3 q.6: 131
  C.3 q.7 c.2: 109n49
  C.3 q.7 c.7: 32n14
  C.3 q.9: 131
  C.3 q.9 c.7: 32n14
  C.6 q.1: 131
  C.6 q.1 d.p.c.11: 34n17
  C.7 q.1 d.p.c.42: 66n45
  C.8 q.1 c.7: 332n79
  C.9 q.3 c.17: 247n2
  C.10 q.1 c.14: 328n57
  C.11 q.3 d.p.c.24: 46
  C.12 q.2 c.21: 34n17
  C.12 q.2 c.37: 328n57
  C.12 q.2 c.47: 332n79
  C.12 q.2 c.65: 79

Secunda pars *(cont.)*
   C.13 q.2 d.p.c.7: 182
   C.15 q.3 d.a.c.1–c.2: 109n49
   C.15 q.3 cc.1–4: 30n11
   C.16 q.1 c.1: 32n14
   C.16 q.1 c.10: 328n57
   C.16 q.3 d.p.c.15: 90
   C.16 q.4 c.1: 328n57
   C.16 q.7 c.11: 328n57
   C.16 q.7 c.25: 328n57
   C.16 q.7 c.39: 328n57
   C.17 q.4 c.29: 332n79
   C.18 q.2 c.25: 332n79
   C.18 q.2 c.26: 79
   C.21 q.2 c.5: 332n79
   C.21 q.4 c.5: 332n79
   C.22 q.2 c.9: 62
   C.23 q.1 c.4: 149
   C.23 q.4 c.27: 89
   C.23 q.4 c.33: 149, 152
   C.23 q.8 c.30: 347n150
   C.23 q.8 c.32: 332n79
   C.24 q.3 c.23: 328n57
   C.24 q.3 c.24: 328n57
   C.25 q.1 d.p.c.16: 36, 44
   C.27 q.1 cc.11–14: 33
   C.27 q.1 c.19: 34n19
   C.27 q.1 c.40: 332n79
   C.27 q.1 c.41: 66n44
   C.27 q.2 c.8: 72
   C.27 q.2 c.11: 82
   C.28 q.1 c.16: 72
   C.33 q.3 *(De penitentia)*
     D.5 c.8: 332n79
     D.6 c.1: 383n15
   C.35 q.2–3 c.2: 328n57
   C.35 q.6 c.4: 27, 93
   C.35 q.6 c.8: 28, 32
Tertia pars *(De consecratione)*
   D.2 c.2: 68
   D.4 c.1: 82

Decretal Collections
Compilatio prima
   2.15.3: 126n29
Compilatio tertia
   1.1.1: 229
   3.33.7: 144n128
   4.14.1: 144n128
Compilatio quarta
   3.9.4: 315n102

Decretales Gregorii Noni (Liber extra)
   1.1.1–2: 353
   1.2.6: 229
   1.14.14: 382
   1.29.14.6: 92
   1.31.15: 388
   2.22.3: 126n29
   2.30.7: 92
   3.4.12: 111
   3.9.2: 90
   3.41.8: 144n128
   4.19.7: 144n128
   5.5.1: 115, 406n93
   5.5.4: 115, 406n93
   5.15.1: 332n80
   5.33.28: 101n16
   5.38.12: 381
   5.39.1–3: 256n32

Index of Manuscripts

Admont, Stiftsbibliothek
  7: 149n154, 152
  22: 225n86, 234n130, 235n135, 315n100, 372
  23: 39, 186
  35: 85
  43: 39, 186
  48: 59, 187
  55: 229n99
Alençon, Bibliothèque municipale
  134: 130n45, 131
Amiens, Bibliothèque de la Ville
  377: 281n124
Angers, Bibliothèque municipale
  189n84
Antwerp, Nyseum Plantin-Moretus
  M.13: 69, 194
Arras, Bibliothèque municipale
  27 (32): 195
  271 (1064): 78n102, 188n78, 189, 192n110, 195
  592 (500): 60, 68, 78
  599 (507): 195
  809 (472): 64
Aschaffenburg, Stiftsbibliothek
  26: 189
Autun, Bibliothèque municipale
  80a: 78
Avranches, Bibliothèque municipale
  149: 198
Avranches, Bibliothèque ville
  148: 85
  149: 286n153

Baltimore, Walters Art Gallery
  777: 49, 60-61, 63, 74, 133n60
Bamberg, Staatsbibliothek
  Can. 13: 67, 75, 84–87
  Can. 14: 61
  Can. 15: 59n19, 60, 68n52
  Can. 17: 249n11, 281n124
  Can. 18: 281n124
  Can. 19: 240n157
  Can. 20 (P.II.7): 372
  Can. 36: 181
  Can. 39: 183
  Can. 41: 151–52
  Can. 42: 206, 208n198
  Can. 45: 197n137
  Msc. Theol. 106: 412n115
  Msc. Theol. 108: 412n115
Barcelona, Archivio de la Corona de Aragón
  Ripoll 78: 39, 59
Beaune, Bibliothèque municipale
  5: 49, 224n77
Berlin, Deutsche Staatsbibliothek
  Hamilton 345: 31
  Phill. 1742: 61-62, 64, 75, 268n77
Berlin, Staatsbibliothek Stiftung Preussischer Kulturbesitz
  lat. fol. 2: 88
  lat. fol. 306: 289n164
  lat. fol. 462: 133n59, 178n21
  lat.q.193: 188n80
  Savigny 14: 133n59
Bernkastel-Kues. See Kues (-Bernkastel)
Biberach an der Riss, Spitalarchiv
  B 3515: 59-60, 62, 73, 254n21

437

Bologna, Biblioteca dell'Archiginnasio
A 48: 178
Bordeaux, Bibliothèque municipale
400: 370
Boulogne-sur-mer, Bibliothèque municipale
118: 90n163
Bratislava, Státny Archív
C.14: 67
Bremen, Universitätsbibliothek
a.142: 48, 56n6, 59, 70, 204
Brindisi, Biblioteca publicale arcives
A.I: 61n27, 73, 75, 85
Brugge (Bruges), Stadsbibliotheek (Bibliothèque de la ville)
366: 218n43, 231n111
378: 285n144
379: 285n144
Bruxelles (Brussels), Bibliothèque royale
1407–1409: 305n55, 305n58

Cambrai, Bibliothèque municipale
612: 152
646: 63, 67, 73
Cambridge, Corpus Christi College
10: 70, 194
Cambridge, Fitzwilliam Museum
Maclean 135: 194
Cambridge, Gonville and Caius College
6: 49, 90n163, 194
150: 305n61
676: 69, 200, 279, 286
Cambridge, Pembroke College
162: 49, 194
Cambridge, Peterhouse
193: 275n100
Cambridge, St. John's College
148: 277n109, 279
Cambridge, Sidney Sussex College
101: 64, 78, 194
Cambridge, Trinity College
R.9.17: 265n62
R.14.9: 272n93
Cambridge (Mass.), Harvard Law Library
64: 254n21
Chambéry, Bibliothèque ville
13: 59
Charleville, Bibliothèque municipale
205: 372
269: 80, 228n97
Cordoba, Biblioteca del Cabildo
10: 225n86, 235n135, 315n100

Darmstadt, Landesbibliothek
97: 59
542: 187n71
907: 133n59, 254n21
Douai, Bibliothèque municipale
586: 63, 73
590: 62, 73, 268n77
592: 207
640: 197n137
649: 202, 207, 218n39
Durham, Cathedral Library
C.I.7: 69, 193n112, 194
C.II.1: 69, 194, 201
C.III.1: 257n35
C.III.3: 290n171
C.IV.1: 64
V.III.3: 195

Ely, Diocesan Records (Cambridge University Library)
Liber M: 305n61
Erfurt, Stadtbibliothek
Amplon. quart. 117: 192
Erlangen, Universitätsbibliothek
342: 67, 79n108, 281n124
394: 231n110
Evreux, Bibliothèque municipale
106: 207

Firenze (Florence), Biblioteca Marucelliana
A.298: 60, 72
Firenze (Florence), Biblioteca Medicea Laurenziana
Edil. 96: 68, 90n163
Fesul. 126: 149n154, 152
Gadd. reliq. 2, 205n183
Plut. I sin. 4: 152
S. Croce I sin. 1: 90n163
S. Croce I sin. 4: 149n154
S. Croce III sin. 6: 281n124, 368n6, 374, 376
S. Croce IV sin. 1: 68
S. Croce IV sin. 2: 370, 372
S. Croce V sin. 4: 225n84, 235n134, 316n106
S. Croce (Plut.) V sin. 7: 33
Firenze (Florence), Biblioteca Nazionale Centrale
Conv. soppr. A. I. 402: 39
Conv. soppr. da ordinare, Vallombrosa 36 (325): 312
Frankfurt, Stadt- und Universitätbibliothek
Barth. 7 (1): 85n139
Barth. 60: 282n128

Index of Manuscripts 439

Fulda, Landesbibliothek
   D.14: 304n54
   D.22: 151–52

Gdańsk (Danzig), Biblioteka Gdánska Polskieg Akademii Nauk
   Mar. fol. 77: 194
Genève, Bibliothèque publique et universitaire
   lat. 60: 90n163
Gent (Gand, Ghent), Bibliothek der Rijksuniversiteit
   55: 59-60
   1429: 183
Gniezno (Gnesen), Biblioteka Kapitulna
   28: 60, 65, 68, 73–74, 77, 80, 86n141, 223n69
Göttingen, Universitätsbibliothek
   iur. 159: 184
Graz, Universitätsbibliothek
   69 (III 69): 90n163, 254n21
   71 (III 71): 68, 86
   80 (III 80): 67, 86
   106: 235n135
   138: 169n231, 370–71
   374: 225n85, 235n135
Grenoble, Bibliothèque municipale
   34 (475): 56, 59
   62 (482): 85–86, 224n77
   391: 165n209
   627: 133n59, 178
Grenoble, Bibliothèque ville
   11 (474): 59

Halle, Universitätsbibliothek
   Ye 80: 289n162
Hamburg, Staats- und Universitätsbibliothek
   cod. jur. 2231: 205n183
Heiligenkreuz, Stiftsbibliothek
   43: 59
   44: 56, 59, 64, 70–71, 134, 178, 254n21
Hereford, Cathedral Library
   P.VII.3: 67, 79

Innsbruck, Universitätsbibliothek
   90: 73, 141n112, 179, 254n21
Ivrea, Biblioteca Capitolare
   72 (C): 70, 86

Jena, Universitätsbibliothek
   El. fol. 56: 68

Kassel, Landesbibliothek
   Jur. 11: 370
   Jur. 15: 281n124
Klosterneuberg, Stiftsbibliothek
   19: 272n93
   87: 86
   101: 85n139
   656: 168–69
Köln (Cologne), Dombibliothek
   127: 49, 184
   128: 49
   129: 74
Köln (Cologne), Stadtarchiv
   W fol. 248: 124n14
Kraków (Cracow, Krakau, Cracovie), Biblioteka Jagiellońska
   106: 281n124
   356: 74, 90n163
   357: 61, 66n42, 68, 85n139
Kraków (Cracow, Krakau, Cracovie), Cathedral Chapter
   89: 291n174
Kremsmünster, Stiftsbibliothek
   364: 68
Kues (-Bernkastel) (Cues), Hospital (Cusanusstift)
   223: 68, 206
   229: 187n70, 268n77

Lambach, Stiftsbibliothek
   XVI: 56
Laon, Bibliothèque municipale
   371: 198, 205n185
   476: 75, 81
Leiden, Bibliotheek der Rijksuniversiteit
   Vulc. 48: 188, 415
Leipzig, Universitätsbibliothek
   695: 152
   975: 281n124
   983: 231n108
   984: 197n137
   986: 195
   1242: 277n108
   Haenel 17: 40, 60
   Haenel 18: 68
Leningrad, Publicnaja Biblioteka im. M. E. Saltykova-Shchedrina
   II mbr.10 (C.1): 205n183
Liège, Bibliothèque universitaire
   127 E: 205n183, 206, 208n198
Liège, Grand Seminaire
   6.N.15: 133n59

Lilienfeld, Stiftsbibliothek
  222: 67, 80
  223: 63, 65n39
Lincoln, Cathedral Chapter Library
  121: 277n108
  138: 49
Lisboa (Lisbon), Biblioteca Nacional
  Alcobaça 144: 263n56
  Alcobaça 173 (304): 290n170
  Alcobaça 381: 225n84, 235n134, 316n106, 376
London, British Library
  Additional 24658: 68
  Additional 24659: 305n61
  Additional 34391: 195, 200
  Arundel 490: 64, 72, 263n56
  Cotton Claudius A.iv: 261n49
  Cotton Vitellius E.xiii: 275n100
  Egerton 2819: 275n100
  Egerton 2901: 282n128
  Harley 3834: 304n52, 305n56, 305n59
  Royal 9.A.xiv: 386n23, 395n51, 399n69
  Royal 9.E.vii: 201n165
  Royal 10.A.ii: 272n93
  Royal 10.B.iv: 257n35
  Royal 10.C.iii: 218n39
  Royal 10.C.iv: 257
  Royal 11.B.ii: 133n59, 178n21, 257n35
  Royal 11.B.xiv: 200
  Royal 11.D.ii: 203
  Stowe 378: 65
London, Lambeth Palace Library
  105: 288n159, 305n56, 305n59
  139: 372–73
Lons-Le-Saunier, Archives départementales du Jura
  12 F.16: 149n154, 152
Lublin, Biblioteka Uniwersytecka Katolickiego
  1: 86
Lucca, Biblioteca capitolare Feliniana
  221: 289n163
Luxemburg, Bibliothèque municipale
  144: 151–52
Luxemburg, Bibliothèque nationale
  30: 265n62
  I.139: 59, 71, 206, 208n198

Madrid, Biblioteca Nacional
  251: 67, 77n99, 79n108, 219n52
  11962: 149n154, 152
  12790: 85n139
Madrid, Fundacio Lázaro Galdiano
  440: 59, 77n99, 78, 80

Mainz, Stadtbibliothek
  II.204: 48, 70
  477: 184
Malibu, California, J. Paul Getty Museum
  Ludwig XIV 2: 62, 73, 179
Marburg, Universitätsbibliothek
  33: 60, 63, 72, 74–75, 178
Melk, Stiftsbibliothek
  259: 81
  261: 68
  518: 231n110
Milano, Archivio Capitolare della Basilica di S. Ambrogio
  M. 57: 68
Modena, Biblioteca Estense
  a.R.4.16 (lat. 968): 223n73, 225n88, 226n91, 305n58, 309, 312, 316n104
Montecassino, Biblioteca Abbazia
  64: 56, 59
  66: 63, 66n42, 67, 73-74, 133n60
  68: 85n139
  396: 153
Moulins, Bibliothèque municipale
  22: 135n73
München (Munich), Bayerische Staatsbibliothek
  lat. 19: 370
  lat. 3879: 229n99
  lat. 4505: 59
  lat. 8302: 289n161
  lat. 10244: 68, 79
  lat. 13004: 49, 186
  lat. 14024: 60, 62, 78, 86–87
  lat. 16083: 198
  lat. 16084: 186, 187n72, 188, 415n126
  lat. 17161: 49
  lat. 17162: 136n83
  lat. 23551: 72
  lat. 27337: 68, 74n76, 199
  lat. 28161: 56n6
  lat. 28174: 68
  lat. 28175: 60, 63, 65, 66n42, 68n52, 73–74, 78, 80n116, 254n21

Napoli (Naples), Biblioteca Nazionale
  XII. A. 5: 60, 65, 66n42, 68, 74
  XII. A. 9: 69
New York, Pierpont Morgan Library
  446: 64, 72–73, 75, 78, 194
  903: 175

Olomouc, Statní Archiv
  C.O. 401: 86

Index of Manuscripts

Oslo, Riksarkivet
   lat. fragment 152: 287n155
Oxford, Bodleian Library
   Bodl. 357 (S.C. 2452): 251n15, 261n49
   Douce 218: 72, 178
   e Mus. 249: 257n35
   Laud Misc. 527 (S.C. 814): 257n35
   Lyell 41: 69
   Selden supr. 87: 218n39
   Tanner 8: 286n153
Oxford, New College
   94: 392n42, 393n43
   210: 69, 194
Oxford, Oriel College
   53: 196, 277n109, 279, 281n124
Oxford, University College
   117: 188n78, 190n92

Padova (Padua), Biblioteca Antoniana
   II.35: 235n135
Paris, Bibliothèque de l'Arsenal
   677: 68
Paris, Bibliothèque Mazarine
   1287: 68, 228n97
Paris, Bibliothèque Nationale
   lat. 1566: 270, 296n9
   lat. 1596: 265n62
   lat. 3884 I and II: 49
   lat. 3885: 80
   lat. 3888: 63, 65, 74, 80, 196
   lat. 3890: 59–60
   lat. 3891: 152
   lat. 3892: 149n154, 152
   lat. 3895: 60, 64, 71
   lat. 3903: 85, 87
   lat. 3905 B: 65n39, 69, 193
   lat. 3922A: 282n128, 283, 300n28
   lat. 3931: 376
   lat. 3932: 225n81
   lat. 3934: 198
   lat. 11714: 231n108
   lat. 12459: 286n153
   lat. 14316: 64, 71
   lat. 14317: 63, 74
   lat. 14591: 197n137
   lat. 14605: 60, 70
   lat. 14610: 288n160
   lat. 14938: 265n62
   lat. 14997: 183
   lat. 15001: 177, 255n24
   lat. 15393: 68, 228n97
   lat. 15396: 151, 153
   lat. 15397: 151–53

lat. 15994: 191
lat. 16538: 181
lat. 16540: 181
lat. 17971: 281n124
lat. Baluse 77, 281n124
nouv. acq. lat. 1576: 205–6
nouv. acq. lat. 1761: 39
nouv. acq. lat. 2443: 169n231
Paris, Bibliothèque Sainte-Geneviève
   341: 63
   342: 68, 202
Perugia, Biblioteca Comunale
   C.M. 4: 65, 66n42, 81
Pommersfelden, Bibliothek Schönborn
(Schlossbibliothek)
   41 (2918): 190
   142: 71, 75, 80n116, 86n141, 90n163, 133n60, 254n21
Poznań (Posen), Archiwum Archidiecesjalne
   28: 224n76
Praha (Prague), Knihovna Metropolitní Kapituly (Bibliothek des Metropolitankapitels)
   I.19: 67
Praha (Prague), Národní Museum
   XVII. A. 12: 62, 77n100

Reims, Bibliothèque municipale
   676: 67, 79
   689: 191n98
   692: 289n165, 305n60
Roma (Rome), Biblioteca Angelica
   1270: 68, 75
Rouen, Bibliothèque municipale
   E 21 (707): 90n163, 133n60
   706: 372
   749: 149n154, 152

St. Florian, Stiftsbibliothek
   III. 5: 60, 64, 70, 72, 134, 178, 205, 268n77
   XI.605: 205
   XI.720: 205
St. Gallen, Stiftsbibliothek
   673: 39n33
St. Mihiel, Bibliothèque municipale
   5: 86
St.-Omer, Bibliothèque municipale
   454: 59–60, 80n116
St. Petersburg, Public Library
   fol. II vel. 10: 151–52
Salamanca, Biblioteca de la Universidad Civil
   1930: 152
   2186: 373
   2491: 205n183

Index of Manuscripts

Salzburg, Stiftsbibliothek
   St. Peters a.ix.18: 220n55, 226n91, 304n53,
      308, 312
   St. Peters a.xii.9: 65
Seo de Urgel, Biblioteca Capitular
   8: 219n52
   2019: 235n136
Stuttgart, Hauptstaatsarchiv
   VI.62: 133n59
   VI.63: 133n59
Stuttgart, Württembergische Landesbibliothek
   HB I.70: 395n51, 407n96
   hist. fol. 419: 191

Tarazona, Biblioteca de la Catedral
   10: 86
   97 (9): 152
   151 (3): 149n154, 151–52, 219n52
Toledo, Biblioteca del Cabildo
   4.5: 62n30, 69
Tortosa, Biblioteca Capitular
   40: 281n124
   144: 262n55
   160: 281n124, 290n169
   240: 49, 59
Tours, Bibliothèque municipale
   559: 87
Trier, Bischöfsliche Seminarbibliothek
   6:61.8: 72
   8: 64, 66, 68n52, 73–75
Trier, Stadtbibliothek
   906: 62n29, 65, 66n42, 69, 75
   907: 59–60, 85, 87n150, 193n112
   922: 218n39
Troyes, Bibliothèque municipale
   103: 64, 254n21, 255n28
   385: 218n46
   944: 288n158, 289n166
   961: 282n128

Uppsala, Universitet-Bibliotek
   C.551: 305n55

Valenciennes, Bibliothèque municipale
   193: 182
   274: 305n61
Vaticano, Città del, Biblioteca Apostolica Vaticana
   Borgh. 261: 240n157
   Borgh. 272: 152, 205n183
   Chigi. E.VIII.206: 59, 68n52

Ottob. lat. 3027: 285n146
Pal. lat. 228: 187
Pal. lat. 622: 68
Pal. lat. 625: 68
Pal. lat. 652: 305n58
Pal. lat. 658: 79n108, 81
Reg. lat. 1039: 124n14
Reg. lat. 1061: 199
Ross. 595: 67
Vat. lat. 1339: 115n83
Vat. lat. 1347: 115n83
Vat. lat. 1367: 80, 84, 86–87, 223n73
Vat. lat. 2280: 149n154, 152
Vat. lat. 2494: 60–61, 68n52
Vat. lat. 2495: 73–75, 78
Vat. lat. 3529: 56, 59, 70, 179
Vendôme, Bibliothèque municipale
   89: 231n108
Venezia (Venice), Biblioteca Nazionale Marciana
   IV. 117: 86
Vercelli, Archivio capitolare
   XXV (118): 49, 63, 71-72, 74, 76
   LXXXIX: 220n57, 226n91, 304nn52–53, 308, 312
Verdun, Bibliothèque municipale
   35: 183
Verona, Biblioteca capitolare
   CLXXXIV (164): 49, 73
   CXCIV: 149n154, 151–52

Wien (Vienna), Nationalbibliothek
   2070: 79
   2082: 85n139
   2125: 183
   2163: 198, 223n66
   2172: 277n108
   2221: 204
Wolfenbüttel, Herzog-August-Bibliothek (Landesbibliothek)
   Helmst. 33: 68
Worcester, Cathedral Library
   Q.70: 133n59
Würzburg, Universitätsbibliothek
   M.p.th. f.3: 55
   M.p.th. f.146: 55

Zürich, Zentralbibliothek
   C.97.II: 133n59
Zwettl, Stiftsbibliothek
   31: 64, 75
   162: 197n137, 223n66, 225n88, 305n61, 316n104